SYSTEMIC FRAGILITY
IN THE GLOBAL ECONOMY

SYSTEMIC FRAGILITY
IN THE GLOBAL ECONOMY

BY

JACK RASMUS

CLARITY PRESS, INC.

© 2016 Jack Rasmus

ISBN: 978-0-9860769-4-7
EBOOK ISBN: 978-0-9860769-3-0

In-house editor: Diana G. Collier
Cover: R. Jordan P. Santos

Library of Congress Cataloging-in-Publication Data

Clarity Press, Inc.
2625 Piedmont Rd. NE, Ste. 56
Atlanta, GA. 30324 , USA
http://www.claritypress.com

TABLE OF CONTENTS

PART II: THE DEAD CAT'S 9 LIVES: KEY TRENDS OF SYSTEMIC FRAGILITY

To Ingrid
Best friend and companion for life and forever
for her patience and understanding

INTRODUCTION

Half way through the second decade of the 21st century, evidence is growing that the global economy is becoming increasingly fragile. Not just in fact, but in potential as well. And not just in the financial sector but in the non-financial sector—i.e. in the 'real' economy.

The notion that the global crash of 2008-09 is over, and that the conditions that led to that severe bout of financial instability and epic contraction of the real economy are somehow behind us, is simply incorrect. The global economic crisis that erupted in 2008-09 is not over; it is merely morphing into new forms and shifting in terms of its primary locus. Initially centered in the USA-UK economies, it shifted to the weak links in the advanced economies between 2010-2014—the Eurozone and Japan. Beginning in 2014, it shifted again, a third time, to China and emerging markets where it has continued to deepen and evolve.

It is true that the main sources of instability today are not located in the real estate sector—the subprime mortgage market—or the credit and derivatives markets that were deeply integrated with that market. Nor is the real economy in a rapid economic contraction. The problem in the real economy is the drift toward economic stagnation, with global trade and real investment slowing, deflation emerging, and more economies slipping in and out of recession—from Japan to Brazil, to Russia, to South Asia and Europe's periphery, even to Canada and beyond. On the financial side, it's the continued rise of excess liquidity and debt—corporate, government, and household—that is fueling new financial bubbles—in stocks in China, corporate junk bonds, leveraged loans, and exchange traded funds in the US, government bonds in Europe, in currency exchange and financial derivatives everywhere.

Financial instability events and crashes, and the real economic devastation that is typically wrought in their wake, do not necessarily occur in repeat fashion like some video rerun. The particulars and details are always different from one crisis to another. At times it's real estate and property markets (USA 1980s, Japan 1990s, global 2007). Other times, stock markets (tech bust of 2000, China 2015). Or currency markets (Asian Meltdown 1997-98) or government bonds (Europe 2012). But the fundamentals are almost always the same.

What, then, are those fundamentals? How do they originate and develop, then interact and feed back on each other, creating the fragility in the global economic system that makes that system highly predisposed to the eruption of financial crises and subsequent contraction? What are the fundamentals that ensure, when some precipitating event occurs, that the financial instability and real contraction that follows occurs faster, descends deeper, and has a longer duration than some other more 'normal' financial event or recession? What are the transmission mechanisms that enable the feedbacks, intensify the instability, and exacerbate the crisis? And how do the fundamentals negate and limit the effectiveness of fiscal-monetary counter measures attempting to restore financial stability and real recovery? Indeed, what is meant by 'systemic fragility', why is it important, and why do most economists not address or consider it in their forecasts and analyses?

Fundamental Trends & Determinants

The book will argue there are 9 key fundamental trends underlying the growing fragility in the global economy:

- the decades-long massive infusion of liquidity by central banks worldwide, especially the US central bank, the Federal Reserve, along with the increasing availability of 'inside credit' from the private banking system;

- the corresponding increase in private sector debt as investors leverage that massive liquidity injection and credit for purposes of investment;

- the relative redirection of total investment from real investment to more profitable financial asset investment;

- a resultant slowing of investment into the real economy, as a shift to financial securities investment diverts and distorts normal investment flows;

- growing volatility in financial asset prices as excess liquidity, debt, and the shift to financial asset investing produces asset bubbles, asset inflation, and then deflation;

- a long run drift from inflation to disinflation of goods and services prices, and subsequently to deflation, as real investment flows are disrupted and real growth slows;

- a basic change in the structure of financial markets as new global financial institutions and new financial markets and securities are created, and an emerging new global finance capital elite arises, to accommodate the rising liquidity, debt, and shift to financial asset investment;

- parallel basic changes in labor markets resulting in stagnation and decline of wage incomes and rising household debt;

- growing ineffectiveness of fiscal and monetary policies as debt and incomes from financial assets rise, incomes from wages and salaries stagnate and household debt rises, and debt on government balance sheets increases while government income (taxes) slows—which together reduce the elasticities of response of investment and consumption to interest rates and multiplier effects from government fiscal policies.

Key Variables and Forms of Fragility

A main theme that emerges is that the preceding nine fundamental trends evolve and develop dynamically over time. Those nine trends also mutually determine each other, in the process contributing to a general condition of fragility in the economy. Systemic Fragility is therefore a dynamic condition that is first and foremost the consequence of the interaction of the above 9 key real factors or trends. In turn, those nine forces act upon three key variables to produce Systemic Fragility: debt, income required to service debt, and the 'terms and conditions of debt' (T&C).[1]

Debt, income and T&C dynamically interact to raise fragility within the three main economic sectors—business financial, household consumption, and government balance sheet. However, systemic fragility is dynamic not only **within** a given form—i.e. financial, consumption, and government—but also **between** them. Not only may the level of fragility grow as real trends raise the magnitudes of debt, income and T&C within a sector or form, but the interactions between the three variables within a sector may exacerbate the level of fragility as well. Moreover, the feedback effects between the financial, consumption, and government balance sheet forms of fragility can further exacerbate the intensity of fragility on a systemic level.

Fragility is therefore not a linear process, proceeding from one level to the next higher as debt or income rise and/or fall, respectively, as some have described it. It is a very dynamic process, with multiple feedback effects within and between its primary sectors or forms. Systemic fragility is not a simple adding up of levels of fragility that develop within financial, household, and government sectors of the economy. How fragility between those sectors mutually determine each other and raise fragility at a systemic level is equally important.

This focus on dynamic interactions requires identifying and explaining the 'transmission mechanisms' within and between the three fragility forms. Some of the more important 'transmission mechanisms' include the price systems associated with both financial assets and real goods, government policy shifts and changes, as well as the psychological expectations of various agents—in particular the investor-finance capital elite, households as consumers, and government policy makers at central banks, legislatures, and executive agencies. Emphasis is placed on the price systems as especially important transmission mechanisms for the development of fragility.

The dynamic interactions—i.e. the feedback effects and the enabling transmission mechanisms—intensify the overall fragility effect. Moreover, the intensity due to interactions or 'feedback effects' varies with the phase and condition of the business cycle.

Fragility is therefore more than just the sum of its three parts. It is a dynamic process and that process has a historical trajectory based on real conditions as well as subjective, psychological expectations of real actor-agents. Because fragility is the product of internal trends and variables, it develops and grows endogenously, as economists say.

Another important characteristic is that rising systemic fragility renders the global economy more prone to eruptions of financial instability, on the one hand, and further contributes to accelerated contractions of the real economy in the wake of the instability events when they occur. That acceleration leads to a deeper and therefore often longer duration of real contractions.

Two important corollary themes follow from the general analysis of Systemic Fragility in this book. Both challenge prevailing economic orthodoxy. Both reject the notion that the global capitalist economy, in national or global form, tends to be long run stable and returns to equilibrium due to market forces and/or government policy intervention when unstable.

The first challenged orthodox assumption is that the capitalist price system will work its supply and demand 'magic' at the level of markets to restore equilibrium and stability. Contrary to contemporary economic analysis, the analysis of Systemic Fragility that follows maintains that the price system is not a force for stabilization. Rather, in the 21st century it has increasingly become a force for destabilizing the system. That is particularly true of the role played by financial asset prices. Not all price systems are the same. There is no 'one price system' that fits all, where supply and demand together work to moderate instability, which is a major tenet of mainstream economic analysis. There are instead several price systems. More volatile financial asset prices behave differently and appear increasingly to drive the prices of goods (products), factors (wage or labor) and even money (interest rates) in the 21st century as financial asset investing becomes increasingly dominant within global capitalism and real asset investment in turn declines.

A second challenged orthodox assumption is that government fiscal-monetary policies can stabilize the system when such policy action is used to complement pure market forces and the one-price system. However, as the analysis of Systemic Fragility will argue, this is increasingly less the case as fragility builds within the global system. Systemic fragility blunts and reduces fiscal-monetary policies aimed at generating a recovery by negating in part the effects of elasticities of monetary policy and interest rate changes and multiplier effects on government spending and tax policies. Weaker and unsustainable recoveries are the result of the growing ineffectiveness of fiscal-monetary policies in attempts to stabilize the system, whether financially or in real terms. The failure of such policies is manifested in economic growth 'relapses' (sharp slowing or negative growth for single quarters) or short and shallow repeated descents into recessions. Those subpar recoveries may also, under certain conditions, descend into bona fide economic depressions.

Instability in the Real Economy

As chapters 1 and 2 that follow will address in more detail, the real side of the global economy is slowing. That slowdown was temporarily masked by the brief surge in China and emerging market economies' (EMEs) growth that occurred between 2010-13 for specific, but temporary, reasons. Initial signs that regional growth in China-EMEs was beginning to dissipate emerged in late 2013. Since then the forces underpinning that growth have weakened further, and now in 2015 growth is slowing in that region more rapidly.

The real goods producing economy is likely already in a global recession. Industrial production is falling, durable goods and factory output is slowing or declining in many countries. Investment in real assets is down sharply, incomes associated with production are stagnating or declining, productivity is almost stagnant, and a general drift toward disinflation and deflation has been underway for some time.

Perhaps the best indicators of this real slowdown is the collapse of world commodity and oil prices. Key industrial commodity prices for iron ore, copper and other key metals have collapsed by more than half, and crude oil by two-thirds from levels just a few years ago. Non-metal commodity prices have fared little better. Country economies highly dependent on such production and export—Brazil, Russia, Venezuela, Nigeria, South Africa, and even Australia and Canada—are nearly all in recession, or quickly approaching it. China's economy is undoubtedly growing at no more than 5% annually, much less than the officially reported 7%, and well below the 10%-12% of just a few years ago. And as China slows, so too do various South Asian economies, highly integrated and dependent upon China's economic performance.

Europe has been oscillating at an historical, sub-par rate of growth between -1% to 1%, after having experienced a double-dip recession in 2011-13, and an historic weak recovery in some of its strongest economies thereafter—including France, Italy and even Germany. Today those same economies continue to struggle to fully recover. Meanwhile Europe's periphery languishes in continued recession, not just the southern but now the northern, Scandinavian and Baltic regions as well.

At the same time, in the world's fourth largest geographic unit, Japan lapses in and out of recessions—four since the 2008-09 crash—despite having introduced a multi-trillion dollar quantitative easing central bank monetary injection since 2013. That injection produced a brief stock market surge but no substantial effect on its real economy or growth, which is slipping into recession yet again.

The much-hyped 'healthy recovery' of the US economy is, moreover, mostly media and politician spin. The US economy has experienced four 'relapses' in its real growth since 2010, where growth collapses for a quarter or turns negative. To the extent that real growth has occurred it has been in the shale-oil patch and associated transport and industrial production activity. That has been coming rapidly to an end, however, as global oil prices in 2015 have collapsed a second time, and may fall to as low as $30 a barrel by some estimates. US real unemployment is still around 12%, masked by gains in low pay, part time and temp jobs in the service sector. US exports and manufacturing are slowing, as the dollar rises from long term interest rate upward drift, and soon may rise further due to short term rate increases by central bank action expected in late 2015. Construction remains stagnant at levels well below 2006-07's previous peak, as only high-end income households can afford housing purchases. Household consumption remains mostly debt-financed as median incomes decline and wage growth seven years after the 2008 crash still fails to appear. Meanwhile, government agencies redefine what constitutes US GDP and growth as a means of boosting growth figures.

After the weakest recovery in more than a half century itself disappears, growing desperation with the slowing real economy has led government policy makers to try to obtain for their corporations a slightly higher share of the slowing world trade and production pie. In Europe and Japan, the response has been to de facto devalue their currencies by means of QE and massive money injections in order to lower production costs and stimulate exports. An accompanying hope is that the currency devaluation will also stimulate stock and bond investments that might in turn raise domestic real investment. But neither has succeeded in either economy. So Europe has already begun, and Japan plans, to press for more cost reduction through 'labor market reforms' that reduce wage costs—the alternative option.

Dueling QEs and de facto currency devaluations have only set off currency wars. European and Japanese efforts to in effect 'export' their slow growth have only resulted in China, Asia, and EMEs also devaluing their currencies to boost their exports, setting in motion a 'race to the bottom'—with Europe and Japan almost certain to introduce yet more rounds of QE in 2016 in response.

Unlike in 2010-12 there is no China-EME growth surge mitigating the failed recoveries in Europe, the US, and Japan. Now the former are leading the global real economic slowdown. And there is no evidence the advanced economies of the US, Europe and Japan will assume the bolstering role previously played by China-EME in turn. In fact, as the China-EME slowdown accelerates, Europe and Japan will be further affected. And US manufacturing and industrial production will slow further as well, as long term interest rates and the value of the US dollar continue to drift upward regardless of what the Federal Reserve does with short term rates in 2015 and beyond.

Financial Instability in the Global Economy

No less evident is a growing financial instability in the global economy at mid-year 2015. At the top of that list are the events unfolding in China's equity markets, and behind that, continuing instability in financing for local government infrastructure, residential and commercial housing, in asset management financial products, and in the financing of old line industrial companies, many of which are now technically bankrupt.

A classic bubble in China's major stock markets began in 2014, resulting in a 120% increase in stock values in just one year. Implementing government policies intended to redirect excess liquidity and financial speculation away from out of control shadow bank financing in local government infrastructure and housing, China in effect redirected excess liquidity and capital into its equity markets. The strategy also sought to find a way to stimulate real investment from private sources by means of engineering an escalation in financial equity assets. It was hoped the wealth effect from equities inflation would also stimulate private consumption. The increased reliance on private investment and consumption would in turn reduce the need for the Chinese government to generate economic growth by means of the prior strategy: increased government direct investment, with massive central bank and foreign capital money inflows in support, and manufacturing exports growth as well. That prior strategy had run its course by 2012-13 and China began to shift to the new private sector driven strategy. But Chinese central bank money injection, foreign money inflows, and redirection of money capital from China's bubbles in real estate to China's equity markets did not produce real economy investment any more than money injection via QEs did in Europe, Japan or the US-UK. Instead, it set off a financial bubble in China stocks.

The Chinese stock bubble then began to unwind in June 2015 with a loss of more than $4 trillion, the consequences of which are still unfolding in global financial markets. One such consequence has been the intensification of competitive devaluations and a ratcheting up of currency wars in the $5.7 trillion global currency exchange markets. Already festering with the introduction of $1.7 trillion and $1.3 trillion in dueling QEs by Japan in 2014 and the Eurozone in 2015, currency wars have clearly accelerated further with yet unclear consequences for both financial and real instability in the global economy. With its stock markets unwinding, China subsequently returned in part to an export-driven strategy to boost its already rapidly slowing real economy. That has taken the form of initially a 2%-4% decline in its currency, the Renminbi-Yuan. Currencies quickly responded in Asia and beyond to the Chinese stock decline, currency devaluation, and the likelihood of more of the same as China's real economy slows.

Chinese events have accelerated the already sharp declines in currency exchange rates, with the Euro and Japanese Yen already down by 30% since 2014, and now major Asian currencies rapidly declining as well from Indonesia to Thailand to Singapore, Taiwan, and even Australia and South Korea.

The obvious spillover and contagion underway by late summer 2015 has been increasing volatility and contraction in stock market prices globally. Collapsing currencies and stock markets mean accelerating capital flight from EMEs and even China. To try to slow the outflow, EMEs raise their domestic interest rates, which slows their domestic real economies further, producing more stock price collapse. Growing financial instability in stock and currency markets will begin to feed off of each other at some point, a condition which the global economy may have already entered.

Financial instability may be reflected in escalating financial asset price bubbles, or the unwinding and collapse of those bubbles. The collapse of world oil and commodity prices that has been underway since 2013-14, and now appears to be accelerating once again in summer 2015, is another strong indicator of growing financial instability in the global economy.

Continuing economic stagnation in Europe, Japan, and to a lesser extent in the US economies has resulted in world commodity and oil price weakness. China's real economic retreat since 2014 has exacerbated that weakness. And in crude oil markets, the intensifying competition between capitalist energy producers in the US shale-oil fields and the Saudi-Gulf led producers has driven the oil price decline still further. Collapsing in 2014 from $120 a barrel to $50 in early 2015, crude prices have again begun to descend further and could go as low as $30 a barrel according to some estimates. The collapse of world oil prices—a financial asset as well as a natural resource—will have further negative effects on financial markets no doubt, especially when combined with general commodity price deflation that continues without relief.

Thus at the top of the list of financial instability today are fragile and collapsing equity markets, extreme volatility in currency markets, and the continued collapse of global commodity prices and oil.

But other financial assets are also in bubble 'range' in 2015, as a result of the massive excess liquidity injected into the world economy since 2008 and the resulting escalation of debt, especially on the corporate and banking side of total debt.

Record low central bank engineered rates since 2008, virtually zero for bank borrowers, has injected at minimum $15 trillion into the global economy. That's in addition to the nearly $10 trillion in central bank QE injections. Moreover, both forms of liquidity creation are still continuing. Liquidity has generated record financial asset prices—from stocks, corporate bonds, and sovereign bonds to derivatives, and other forms of financial assets—as well as exchange rate speculation.

Bubbles in corporate bonds are also at a peak, though not yet as obvious a problem as stock prices, commodity prices, or currency exchange rates. But they will be. At high risk are corporate junk bonds, which may yet be impacted by collapsing oil prices and corporate defaults in the US shale-oil sector spilling over to other corporations. Less unstable, but no less a 'bubble', are corporate investment grade bonds. Global issuance averaged less than $1.5 trillion a year in the half decade leading up to the 2008 crash. In the past five years since 2010, that annual average issuance is more than $2.5 trillion—i.e. more than $5 trillion additional issued compared to historical averages.

Government bonds have entered unknown territory as well, especially in Europe, where they increasingly sell at negative rates. That is, buyers pay governments interest to buy their sovereign bonds, instead of vice-versa, in order to find a temporary safe haven for their excess liquidity. The bond world is turned on its head, with yet unknown consequences for future financial instability, witness the bond 'flash crash' of a few years ago, the causes of which are still unknown. There is a growing problem of disappearing liquidity in the bond trader market, as banks exit and more risk-taking shadow banks assume their role, amid warnings of the possibility of an even faster collapse of bond prices due to lack of liquidity in the bond trading sector. It is unlikely that a new financial instability event will involve subprime mortgages. A classic stock market crash may prove the precipitating event. Or perhaps a bond market crash. Should the latter happen in the much larger bond sectors of the global economy, it will make a subprime mortgage or even stock market crash appear mild in comparison.

Behind the more obvious stock, bond, commodity, oil, and currency instability—all of which are now rising as of late 2015, there are numerous smaller but perhaps even potentially more unstable financial asset markets globally.

There are leveraged loans and debt markets now helping to fuel a record mergers and acquisition boom. There are exchange traded funds (ETFs) in which retail investors are over-exposed as they desperately search for 'yield' (higher returns) on increasingly risky investments. There are localized real estate bubbles in London, the US, Scandinavia, Paris, and Australia as wealthy investors flee with their capital from China and emerging markets to invest in preferred high-end properties in the advanced economies. There are bank-to-bank 'repo' markets in the US where liquidity appears insufficient and shadow bankers are allowed to play a larger role. And then there are the various unknown conditions in global derivatives trading, where much of the pure 'betting' and speculating on financial securities remains still very opaque seven years after the 2008 crash when derivatives played a strategic role in the rapid spread of financial contagion from the subprime bust.

In short, there are any number of growing sources of financial instability in the global economy today. And nearly all appear to be in a continuing drift toward more fragility and instability, not less.

In the book that follows, fragility is viewed as a key condition that leads to financial instability and may itself even precipitate a financial instability event—banking crashes, stock market collapses, credit crises, widespread liquidity and even solvency crises across sectors or major institutions, plunging currency exchange rates, money capital flight, a collapse of financial asset values, and/or defaults and bankruptcies—to name the most obvious. Depending on the scope and severity of the financial instability events, the real economic downturn that follows a financial crisis-precipitated contraction is qualitatively and quantitatively different from what might be called a 'normal' recession. Some economists have called this a 'great recession'. Having taken issue with that term, this writer has referred to it as an 'epic' recession—i.e. a kind of muted depression. Whichever the term chosen, it appears a drift toward another more serious instability event is underway in the global economy. Fragility is growing system-wide, and fragility leads to, and indeed may precipitate, financial instability on a scale sufficient to generate another contraction in the real economy. And while fragility leads to financial instability, which may precipitate and then exacerbate a subsequent contraction in the real economy, the latter contraction in turn tends to exacerbate systemic fragility as well. A self-sustaining negative cycle of financial and real instability can occur. And policy makers today are far less prepared or able to deal with it than previously.

Outline of the Book

Following a brief overview addressing the consistently over-optimistic forecasts of global growth by business and international economic bodies in chapters 1-2, recent key global developments are highlighted in chapters 3-6 that reveal the global economy in 2015 is experiencing greater potential for financial instability than ever since 2007-08.

Chapters 3-6 provide selected cases reflecting today's growing instability in global oil and commodity markets; the steadily intensifying commodity price deflation; Emerging Market Economies' collapsing currencies, capital flight, growing local financial market instability, rising import inflation, and declining export income necessary to finance dangerously accelerating external debt; the growing desperation of policy makers and central bankers in Europe and Japan to jump start their economies, as they introduce 'dueling QEs' and 'internal devaluations' designed to reduce labor costs in an effort to drive down their currencies in order to capture a larger share of exports amidst a slowing of total world trade; and the growing financial asset bubbles in China which policy makers there have been unable to contain or reduce. Whether China, Europe-Japan, Emerging Markets, or Global Oil-Commodities—all reflect financial instabilities in the global economy at a time when a growing number of real economies continue to weaken as well. These developments and events serve, one might argue, as the 'canaries in the global financial coal mine'.

In Part Two of the book, chapters 7 through 15, the discussion moves from selected case narratives highlighting the most obvious contemporary evidence of global instability—in emerging markets, Europe and Japan, and China—to a deeper level discussion focusing on 9 key variables behind the next financial crisis now developing endogenously within the global financial system today. Here discussion focuses on the real, material conditions and forces that underlie the appearances of the crisis.

Part Two provides a transition to the all-important need for theory to understand where the global economy has been, is now, and, most important, where it may be going in the coming years. Without the projections enabled by theory, only empirical narratives remain. Without coming to grips with the most important information of the past, descriptions of the present can provide no accurate forecast of the future. Unfortunately, this is the state of much of contemporary economic analysis today.

So what are the limitations of contemporary economic analysis on the subjects of financial instability, investment, and the relationships between financial cycles and real cycles? That is the subject of Part Three and chapters 16-18 of this book. Chapter 16 critiques in detail the two major wings of contemporary mainstream economic analysts—what this writer has termed 'Hybrid Keynesians' and 'Retro-Classicalists'. It is argued that neither wing sufficiently understands the relationships between financial asset investment, real asset investment, and what this book views as the accelerating 'speculative investment shift' that is the consequence of those new relationships. Nor does either sufficiently understand how debt and incomes have grown increasingly mutually interdependent in a negative way, instead of functioning individually as positive sources of economic growth. Both misunderstand how financial asset prices destabilize the system. And both have an overly optimistic assessment of the role of traditional policies—the one monetary and the other fiscal. Their largely shared conceptual apparatus thus serves as an obstacle to understanding the new characteristics of the 21st century capitalist economy.

Chapter 17 challenges the dominant wing of Marxist economic analysis today that argues that the falling rate of profit from production of real goods (by what Marxists define as productive labor) is the key (and virtually only) driver of the slowing of the global economy and in turn is responsible for the shift to financialization of the economy. This book will argue that this is a kind of 'mechanical' application of Marxism that ignores and misunderstands the exchange side of the circuit of capital that Marx himself never fully developed. The falling rate of profit (FROP) approach represents a 'glass half filled' theory. It views all instability as determined by the production of real goods by only productive labor—i.e. those workers who produce real goods and related support services. Causation between the real and financial sides of the economy is viewed as a 'one way street' only, from production to financial, instead of a more likely mutual interaction between the two sectors. What the falling rate of profit theorists fundamentally fail to understand, it will be argued, is that it is investment that drives the economy—not a particular form of financing, i.e. profits—that drive investment.

Like the two wings of mainstream economists, the FROP wing of Marxist economic analysis thus lacks an adequate conceptual apparatus for properly understanding the relationships between financial asset and real asset investing in the 21st century global economy. In important ways, none of the three wings accurately reflect the richer views and ideas of those economists with whom they are associated. The 'Hybrid' Keynesians distort Keynes; the 'Retro-Classicalists' also misrepresent Keynes and others in their effort to restore classical economic analysis of the 18th-19th century; and the 'Mechanical Marxists' fail to understand Marx's own method and to recognize where Marx was going in his final thoughts on banking, finance, and new forms of exploitation only beginning to emerge in late 19th century capitalism.

Chapter 18 addresses the major contributions by the economist, Hyman Minsky, whose work is most associated with the idea of what he called financial fragility. Writing mostly in the 1980s and 1990s, Minsky broke new ground in a number of ways on the subject of how financial cycles and real cycles mutually impact. His key contributions are noted. However, much was left unsaid by Minsky, who did not get to see the 21st century's full manifestation of his initial observations. While noting his contributions, this chapter describes in detail the limits of his theory as of the mid-1990s, suggesting where it might have had to go in order to more fully explain how fragility in general is a major determinant of both financial and real instability of the global economy in the 21st century.

Part Four of this book provides this writer's own analysis and theory of where the global economic crisis has been, and where it may be headed. That analysis is subsumed under the conceptual notion of 'Systemic Fragility' that has been referenced and raised in part in the preceding chapters, and which is summarized in more detail in this final chapter 19, 'A Theory of Systemic Fragility'. Accompanying this summary chapter is an addendum, consisting of equations that represent the main arguments of chapter 19.

The concluding chapter's preliminary statement of a theory of Systemic Fragility is envisioned as an effort to begin to develop a new conceptual framework for the analysis of financial and real cycle interactions that represent the dominant characteristics of the capitalist global economy in the 21st century. It is viewed as merely a first step.

1

FORECASTING REAL & FINANCIAL INSTABILITY

The Chronic Problem of Over-Optimistic Official Forecasts

Economics used to be called the 'dismal science'. But no more. If one were to review the predictions of mainstream professional economists today—both in and out of academia—a bright future for the global economy appears on the horizon.   Conservative by nature and unwilling to risk disapprobation by their professional colleagues, academic economists play it safe and consistently avoid factoring into their forecasts the major shifts in conditions and policy that tend to play a greater relative role in the trajectory of the global economy during times of instability. And times have been anything but stable in recent decades.

Professionals that work directly in business and government face further pressure to forecast conservatively and to remain safely within a bubble of the most recently available data. To boldly project the future based not only on immediate data, but on longer term trends, political events, or what are sometimes call 'black swan' events, is strongly discouraged by their employers—both private and government alike. A departure too far from the consensus of peers may result in an analyst being singled out in complaints by clients or investors. Unpleasant negative forecasts affect customers' bottom lines and are highly unwelcomed. So playing it safe is even more the rule for private sector forecasters. It's better to be conservative. Better to err on the optimistic side than the pessimistic. That way one's employment is more assured in the longer run.

So what we get from the 'polyannas' of the economic forecasting trade are consistently over-optimistic forecasts about the future trajectory of the global economy. Like modern day Candides—contemporary reproductions of French philosopher Voltaire's 18th century novel—they depict the present and future as 'the best of all possible worlds'—famous last words raised even as the French revolution was about to turn society upside down. The present (economy) is the best possible we can get and the future will be better still.

The reasons given for their perennial rosy forecasts have all been heard before, in fact for the past six years, namely: inflation is low, long term interest rates are low, central banks will ensure short term rates stay relatively low, if raised the hike will take place slowly in small increments that won't disrupt the economy, central bank monetary policy is accommodative, bank lending is picking up, households and businesses have repaired their balance sheets (i.e. reduced debt), personal incomes are rising, jobs are being created again, and, now the latest positive to this list—falling oil prices will boost consumer incomes and thus household spending.

Typical of the optimistic commentary of the past six years was the dean of the British press commentators, Martin Wolf, who concluded this past year, "Another year of quite decent global growth is, in brief, far and away the most likely outcome in 2015."[1] His USA counterpart, *New York Times* hybrid-Keynesian (aka liberal), Paul Krugman, added, "the economy is doing much better... adding 6.7 million jobs since Obama took office... So I'm fairly optimistic about 2015, and probably beyond..."[2] The British economic historian, Harvard professor and ideologist with close ties to the USA business elite, Niall Ferguson, added in one of his *Wall Street Journal* editorials, "The U.S., its economic recovery firmly established, despite learned talk of secular stagnation, is looking Dauntless."[3] Economists entrenched in the business and banking sector appear even more optimistic than their academic brethren. Peter Oppenheimer, chief strategist for the global investment bank, Goldman Sachs, proclaimed, "Just at the time when people have given up projecting a growth pick-up, this could be the year when it does surprise on the upside."[4]

However, the surprises were not the kind Oppenheimer supposed. The US GDP relapsed, turning negative again in the first quarter 2015 for the fourth time in as many years, and has yet to regain any momentum. Japan slipped into yet another recession at mid-year. Europe continued to stagnate despite its trillion dollar QE launch in February. By late summer it became increasingly clear that China's economy was slowing more rapidly than official reports were claiming—not at the official 7% of annual GDP rate but as low as 4%-5% according to a growing number of independent sources. Emerging market economies (EMEs) were descending into recession, one after the other, as global commodity prices continued to deflate, China's demand slowed, and their currencies plummeted, as capital flowed back to the US in expectation of higher interest rates and returns, and as the global currency war intensified. Hardest hit of the EMEs were the oil producers—Russia, Nigeria, Venezuela, Mexico, Indonesia, and others—as the global price of crude oil began to decline, after briefly stabilizing at $65 a barrel earlier in the year, from a 2014 high of $120, now falling again below $40 by summer's end.

In other words, this is not the kind of forecast predicted by the Wolfs, Fergusons, Krugmans, and Oppenheimers at the start of 2015. But this hasn't been the first time they, and their profession's consensus view, had missed by wide margins the actual trajectory and facts. Nor likely will it be the last.

Consequently, among the vast majority of mainstream economists today—including from the research arms of the most notable global institutions like the IMF, World Bank, BIS, OECD, US Federal Reserve, Bank of Japan, etc.—the view is the same today as nearly a year ago: the global economy is recovering and will continue to do so. But is it? And will it?

2014: Transition Year for the Global Economy

Official forecasts for the global economy for 2014 missed their mark due to a number of 'surprises' that either were not anticipated or not given sufficient weight or consideration. Major problems in the global economy, developing below the radar in 2013, began to emerge more clearly in 2014. The 'surprise' 2014 events included:

- decline in global commodity prices, including the first stage of the collapse of world crude oil prices from $120 to $50 a barrel;

- collapse of the US GDP at the beginning of the year—the third such since 2011;

- China's real economy slowing;

- failure of Japan's $1.7 trillion QE to stop deflation or generate recovery in its real economy;

- emerging deflation and continuing stagnation in the Eurozone, raising the inevitability of a Eurozone QE in 2015;

- the beginning of a drift upward in US long term interest rates;

- slowing world trade volume, and rising instability in emerging markets as their currencies weakened, exports slowed, and capital flight back to the advanced economies began.

Europe

In 2014, economies in Europe's eastern and northern peripheries began to show signs of slowing, thus joining the southern tier of Spain-Portugal-Italy-Greece. More countries' economies slipped into recession, barely grew, or continued to stagnate at depression levels of output. Cracks began to appear not only in Europe's severely weakened 'southern tier' economies but in Scandinavia and select eastern European economies as well. This occurred, moreover, just as one of Europe's core economies, France, also began to stagnate and struggled to avoid deflation.

Exports from Euro economies to global markets in 2014 were slowing. Euro manufacturing began contracting. Unemployment remained unchanged at 11% levels throughout the Eurozone and the jobs that were created were overwhelmingly part time, temporary, and thus low paid. Euro banks continued to not lend and consumer spending remained sluggish except for Germany and a few other countries. The UK, which enjoyed a short recovery in 2013-14 based on a property boom driven by capital inflows from emerging market investors and China, began once again to slow. The Eurozone southern periphery barely changed—up a little for Spain and down some for Italy. The Ukraine crisis and Russia's reciprocal sanctions promised to slow the central and eastern European economies further. Scandinavian economies like Finland and Sweden stagnated or slipped into recession. The prospect of deflation throughout Europe became a reality, as general prices for goods and services fell to 0.2% by year end.

Further dampening effects on consumption and therefore growth occurred as a result of the continuation of fiscal austerity policies plus the introduction of additional new austerity policies in the form of 'structural' and 'labor market' reforms. Sanctions on trade with Russia, and Russia's counter-sanctions, reduced exports and production to a degree not anticipated in the forecasts. The impact of Japan's major QE program introduced in 2013, which took full effect in 2014, was also underestimated. Japan's currency exchange rate fell significantly against the Euro as a result of its $650 billion a year QE program, which permitted it to garner some of Europe's share of exports to China and Asia. Eurozone banks continued to go slow on bank lending to non-financial businesses, contrary to forecast assumptions that predicted bank lending into the real economy to rise. The collapse of world oil prices after mid-2014, affecting the UK and Norway economies, was virtually unanticipated. The extent of EME economies' slowing EME demand for Euro exports was seriously underestimated.

The picture in 2014 in Europe was therefore hardly robust, and certainly did not justify the optimistic forecasts for the region for 2015. But none of these foregoing events and conditions were apparently considered by the 'polyannas' of prediction who proclaimed at year end 2014 that the Euro region would add significantly to global economic growth in 2015!

Japan

The same forecasters also failed to see the deep contraction in Japan's economy that began in the summer of 2014 and then, once its latest recession set in, they failed to integrate it into their predictions for Japan for 2015. Despite having fallen into recession again 2014—the fourth since the 2008-09 global crash—Japan instead was predicted to have an accelerating recovery in late 2014. That prediction was based on Prime Minister Shinzo Abe's much-hyped '3 Arrows' program being fully implemented in 2014, which then stalled and did not occur. In addition to a massive $1.7 trillion QE program benefitting bankers and investors, what did occur was a sales tax hike for consumers. While the QE and sales tax hikes were implemented, the '3rd arrow' was not. It consisted of proposals for a token $29 billion infrastructure investment plus calls for Japanese corporations to voluntarily raise wages—which they promptly rejected. Instead of consumption rising and the economy recovering, wage incomes continued to decline, having fallen every year since 2008, as sales taxes rose. But none of this was anticipated in the overly optimistic predictions for Japan's contribution to global economic recovery in 2015.

Again, official global forecasts were based on the most promising assumptions, and shifts from policy changes or failures were typically not factored in. Nor were the likely negative developments associated with a faster decline of EMEs than predicted.

China

To check its own growing tendency toward slower growth, in 2014 China introduced yet another round of fiscal and monetary stimulus—its third in as many years—to keep its economy growing at prior levels. Forecasts assumed that if and when China's economy slowed, it would respond successfully to keep its growth rate well above the 7% annual rate.

While its GDP growth rate was still more than 7% in 2014, that rate had been slowing from double digit levels ever since 2012. That 7% growth for 2014 was made possible by China introducing three consecutive 'mini' fiscal stimulus programs, accompanied by continuing central bank money injections and offshore money flowing in to China's local government infrastructure markets. The official view further assumed China's manufacturing and exports could be maintained at prior levels, regardless of the state of the global economy, slowing world trade, or oil and commodities markets collapse. Forecasters assumed that China had performed so well right through the 2008-10 global collapse, and with its $4 trillion of currency reserves, it could counter whatever negative forces might arise to successfully maintain its 7% or higher growth rate. A kind of policy invincibility was assumed for China's economic leadership: that it had bucked the global trends thus far, and would continue to do so.

China was typically viewed in official global forecasts as contributing significantly to global growth in 2014, and that it would continue to do so, based on its policy of injecting more fiscal stimulus whenever the economy showed initial signs of lagging, plus the impression China would successfully make the turn from exports to internal growth without much difficulty.

Throughout 2014 China continued to struggle with major structural problems, which forecasters repeatedly failed to adequately consider: the battle with financially destabilizing global shadow banks causing financial bubbles and undermining China's local government debt and property markets; the struggle to phase out old inefficient industrial enterprises before widespread corporate defaults occur; and the need to transition from government direct investment projects and exports driven growth to more consumer spending and private business investment. Hardly any of these major challenges were even remotely achieved in 2014. Forecasters' assumptions were incorrect.

Global Oil Deflation

Global oil prices had been deflating throughout 2013-14. The deflation accelerated in June 2014 as Saudi Arabia and its OPEC supporters increased supplies in an attempt to drive US shale gas and oil competitors out of the global market. US shale producers cut costs but not output in response. Other global oil producing economies—Russia, Venezuela, Nigeria and others— also continued to produce more in order to ensure continued revenue levels as the price of oil fell. China demand decline and Euro-Japan slow growth lowered prices further.

Collapsing oil prices spilled over to other commodities and financial asset prices. Oil company stocks fell and with it the once high levels of energy company investments in real assets. Capital spending globally slowed. Falling crude oil and oil commodity futures financial assets began translating by year end 2014 into asset as well as real goods deflation.

Based on the decline in oil prices, forecasters predicted that the lower cost of oil and gasoline at the retail level would lead to more disposable income for consumers and consumption spending that would boost GDP. But that didn't happen. The lower oil prices had little effect on consumers' spending, who either saved the income, used it to pay down household debt or redirected it to rising rents, food, and other costs.

Yet another error made by forecasters was the prediction that the 2014 fall in oil prices would stabilize in 2015 and therefore have only a temporary effect on GDP. They then based their forecasts for 2015 on this erroneous assumption. Once again, the effects were underestimated and therefore growth overestimated in turn.

EMEs

Emerging market economies began an economic tailspin in 2014. The solid growth for most EMEs from 2010-2013 began to reverse in 2013 as the US central bank announced it was sharply reducing its four year long, $4 trillion dollar QE program. Money immediately began to flow out of emerging markets, in what was called at the time the 'taper (QE) tantrum'. The US Fed announcement set in motion outflows of capital back to the US and other advanced economies, slowing investment into the EMEs, causing a decline in EME currency exchange rates, and rising domestic inflation due to higher import prices. To slow the exodus of money capital, many EMEs began to raise domestic interest rates. All these developments together served to begin to slow EME economies in 2014. Falling oil and commodity prices, slowing China demand, and declining yen and Euro currencies from QE policies also took a toll on EME growth. A negative economic 'perfect storm' began to brew over emerging market economies. It would intensify in 2015.

Those EMEs whose commodity mix included crude oil exports were particularly hard hit—Russia, Venezuela, Nigeria and others, which quickly entered recession territory in 2014. EME financial markets thereafter slowed sharply reflecting the recessions and money capital flight. One after another EME economies slipped into recession in 2014. Many more would follow in 2015. But don't tell all that to polyanna forecasters who still forecast 3%-6% growth rates for EMEs in 2015.

USA

In the first quarter of 2014, the USA economy contracted in GDP terms for the third time since 2011. It was a clear forewarning for 2015 that would go unheeded. The contraction occurred again, a fourth time, in early 2015.

A robust recovery in the summer of 2014 led forecasters to assume it would continue. The often heard argument in late 2014 was that the USA economy is 'exceptional' and not impacted by other global trends. The US economic horses will pull the dead-weight global economic wagon forward into sustained recovery in 2015. But the optimists failed to recognize that the 4% GDP growth rates of 2014's second half were due to the confluence of a series of special, one-time factors that boosted the US recovery temporarily. They would not repeat in 2015; forecasters assumed that they would.

Much of 2014 US growth was generated by the shale oil & gas boom, concentrating investment in drilling rigs, equipment, and related transport, in certain states only. That shale boom began to reverse in the second half of 2014, however, as the global oil glut and price crash began to take effect. But the oil price collapse temporarily lowered US import prices, which raised the contribution of net exports to US GDP. US growth in late 2014 was also temporarily stimulated by more spending on health care services in the second half of 2014, as the Obama health care program starting taking effect. That too was a one-time sign-up event that would add consumption to US GDP in late 2014, but nothing further in 2015. In addition, government military spending surged in the second half of 2014, as the federal government released more funds for military equipment purchases, as it typically does just before national elections take place in November. All these 'one-off' contributions to US

GDP numbers were temporary or one time contributions to US growth in 2014. They would dissipate by 2015.

A beneath the surface look at the USA 2014 second half 4% economic growth surge would have suggested that most of the forces behind that surge were not sustainable. Which they weren't. Forecasters assumed, however, that the positive contributing factors to US GDP and growth were more or less permanent and would carry into 2015. The further assumption was that the negative factors were not permanent, but temporary, and would not carry over to 2015. But they did.

The Prediction Dilemma Posed by SWANS—Gray and Black

The term, 'gray swan', is derived from the idea expressed by Nassim Nicholas Taleb in his 2007 book, *Black Swan*. A black swan refers to a virtually unpredictable and unforeseen event that disrupts the economy in a major way. Black swans occur in nature but their appearance is unpredictable. Similarly for economic events. At least so goes the theory. An example of a black swan might be the collapse of the Lehman Brothers investment bank in 2008 that set off the banking crash of 2008. A 'gray swan' is an adaptation of the idea that suggests similar unforeseen and unpredictable economic events may occur, but without as much negative impact.

Gray swans can also be more numerous than black swans, and their collective impact—even in the case of just a few occurring simultaneously—can easily undermine a previously overly optimistic forecast. In times of fundamental fragility and instability in the system, as is occurring today, gray swans also tend to appear more frequently. But forecasters have no way to anticipate or to integrate them into their predictions.

At the top of the list of gray swan events that occurred in 2014 is the global oil glut and price collapse, driven by Saudi and gulf emirates deciding to boost oil production with the intent of driving US shale gas and oil upstarts out of business. That swan landed in June 2014, flying in from nowhere, totally unanticipated. It quickly began having a negative impact on the shale oil & gas, alternative energy, and related industries in the US economy.

Since global oil is not only a commodity, but also a financial asset, the oil price deflation set in motion in mid-2014 clearly had 'feedback' effects as well on global commodity price deflation and other financial markets.

Gray swans can also change color—to black. The oil glut effect on falling commodity prices can spill over to other financial asset markets and prices. Defaults among corporate junk bonds in the US shale gas patch clearly have that potential. Gray swan oil deflation accelerating the decline in general commodity prices can further destabilize EME economies—both financial and real.

Other political goals of Saudi, and likely US, governments may have been involved in the Saudi vs. US shale economic war that erupted mid-2014. The eruption of a crisis in the Ukraine and the subsequent imposition of sanctions on Russia, reciprocated by Russia on Europe, is another swan event. The necessity of bailing out the collapsing Ukraine economy put additional economic pressure on the European economy, and may have raised risks for some Euro banks' eventual solvency as well. So gray swans may emerge due to political events as well.

One or more global stock markets experiencing a major correction of 20% or more could also set off a gray swan event. The USA Dow-Jones stock market is over-extended. Every time a correction is about to occur, either the US central bank pumps more liquidity into investors' pockets with another QE program, sending stocks higher, or trillions of dollars of investor cash on the sidelines rushes back in to check the stock level adjustment once again. Meanwhile, financial fragility continues to build, promising a more radical correction and bigger drop in stock prices at some later date. That bigger correction might qualify as a 'gray swan' event. Yet another possible 'gray swan' might be the eruption of a currency war, leading to an event similar to the 1997 'Asian Meltdown'.

As noted, gray and even black swans may occur in political form as well. A Greek exit from the Eurozone would almost certainly result in a rapid demand by Portugal, Spain, and Italy for debt restructuring, and even debt expunging, or they too would leave the Euro currency union. That would almost certainly lead to a quicker and deeper European recession. An open war between NATO and Russia in Ukraine would easily do the same. So would a series of populist parties assuming power in Europe, a more direct confrontation between China and Japan over the oil-rich offshore islands between them, or even a breakout of the Ebola plague from western Africa into Europe or the USA. Any of the above could prove a 'gray' swan event, with potential major impacts on the global economy.

None of these economic or political risk factors are typically considered, however, in forecasts of the global economy. Some sort of improved adjustment for such risk factors should be included in forecasts, especially as in today's unstable global economy where major disruptions now appear increasingly frequently, as in 2014 when the global economy was caught off-guard by the unanticipated severe oil and commodity price deflation. Surely a black, or at minimum a gray, swan-like event.

Over-optimistic official forecasts for the global economy for 2014 were carried forward once again into 2015. Even though it was clear that the deflation in global commodities and oil was likely to accelerate, that Japan and Europe were not responding to QE or monetary stimulus, and that emerging markets were likely to experience increasing stress—official forecasts by global economic institutions like the IMF and World Bank, as well as central banks and government statistics agencies, continued to suggest the economy in 2015 would experience only mild and temporary downward adjustments.

IMF's Global Economic Forecasts

The October 2014 report of the International Monetary Fund concluded that the global economy would grow faster in 2014 compared with the preceding year, and that it would grow at a still faster rate in 2015 than 2014. It forecast growth to accelerate a full half of a percentage point, from 3.3% in 2014 to 3.8% in 2015. 2016 would do even better, rising to 4.1%.[5] Embedded in that highly optimistic projection, the EMEs would grow at a rapid 5.0% rate in 2015, and China would grow in both 2014 and 2015 well above a 7% annual rate in both years.

A year later, on all counts the predictions appear to be wrong. Even in its subsequent April 2015 adjustments to its 2014 forecasts, while the IMF reduced its forecast of just six months prior, it still predicted a 3.5% rate of global growth for 2015 and 3.8% for 2016. Such revisions are likely still overestimations.

Key emerging markets like Brazil, South Africa and oil producers like Russia and Nigeria, are all deep in recession, though the IMF forecast projected positive growth in all instances. Even the IMF's April 2015 'revisions' clearly miss the mark for emerging markets in Latin America, for the South Asia trading partners of China, and for the oil producing economies like Russia, Nigeria, Indonesia and even Canada. IMF forecasts for Japan have also been repeatedly wrong, overestimating to the upside. It has missed Japan's recessions that occurred in 2011, 2014, and its latest emerging contraction in mid-2015—just as it totally missed Europe's 2011-12 double dip recession.

A major problem with both IMF forecasts, October 2014 and April 2015, is that the IMF doesn't adequately account for the effects of the collapse in world oil prices that began in June 2014 and then began declining even further in a second phase later in 2015. Another problem is that other events of the summer 2014, and after, were also not anticipated or fully factored in.

This failure to anticipate, followed by a token adjustment which is indicated as temporary, layered over by a prediction that robust growth will soon follow in 2016, occurred again in the IMF's latest, October 2015 Outlook report, in which it reduced its global growth forecast from a previous 3.3% annual rate to 3.1%.[6]

This token and temporary adjustment was made despite:

- the continuing effects of the Greek crisis in Europe, and the obvious failure of the Eurozone QE to boost the real economy, and growing stagnation in France and Scandinavia;

- Japan's slipping into its fourth recession in 2014, recovering briefly for just a few months, and then sliding into another -1.6% downturn in 2015;

- the faster decline in world commodity prices than initially estimated, which is slowing growth even more than projected in emerging markets in Latin America, Russia and Asia;

- China's real economy slowing now at a more rapid pace, the collapse of its stock market bubble, and the shift from its prior policy of a stable currency to allowing it to devaluate.

All these developments, emerging early summer 2015, justify only a 0.2% downward adjustment in global growth, according to the latest IMF July 2015 forecast.

Oil deflation's second 2015 drop, China's slowdown and stock bubble unwinding, key emerging markets recessions, the resumption in 2015 of an even more intense global currency war—these are all at least 'gray' swan events that were missed or consistently not given sufficient weight in IMF forecasts, including its most recent.

The limits of the IMF data and forecasts for 2014 and 2015 are perhaps most evident in its super-optimistic estimate of the growth of world trade, both in advanced and emerging market economies. The volume of world trade was projected to rise rapidly in 2014 and again in 2015. How that will be accomplished is a mystery, however, given the collapse in China's exports, the freefall in oil and nearly all other commodity prices in 2014-15, the failure of Japan and Eurozone QEs and currency devaluations to appreciably increase their net exports, the disinflation in goods and services worldwide, and the growing number of slowing economies and emerging market recessions.

Whether measured in container ship loads, the 'Baltic dry index', or The World Trade Monitor, global trade has been slowing since 2012, has fallen in four of the first five months in 2015 and has risen only 1.5% over the past year. The slowing of global trade appears correlated with the slowing of global real investment, since trade volumes are heavily weighted with capital intensive goods. And in general, forecasters have no explanation why global real investment, and the associated world trade in capital goods, is slowing.[7]

The response to the obvious convergence of seriously negative forces is the same it has been the entire last decade: make a token adjustment, say it's temporary, and predict a return soon to the robust growth path.

Since the 2008 global crash, the IMF has come under growing criticism from various independent sources for its repeatedly over-optimistic forecasts. This growing critique prompted the Fund to admit in early 2014 that its forecasts "have tended to be consistently over optimistic at times of country-specific, regional and global recessions … the data show they [IMF forecasters] may need to take better account of the international repercussions of developments in the Chinese, German, and US economies." [8] Apologies notwithstanding, it continued to overestimate thereafter. In its October 2014 Report, it responded yet again to mounting criticisms, admitting that, even though it had "pared down" its over-optimistic predictions, "global growth still surprised on the downside relative to each success World Economic Outlook forecast." It noted it had particularly missed negative trends in emerging market growth, especially the BRICS, but also Japan, Asian, and even Europe. Consequently, "there has been a general tendency toward repeated over-prediction of growth".[9] The apparent reasons for the missed forecasts, it noted, were due to its over-prediction of real Investment growth. However, while admitting error, it offered no further explanation why this real investment growth was consistently less than it had forecast.

IMF forecasts are relied upon consistently, and repeated by mainstream economists and the business media. The findings and data are often incorporated into academic and government institutions' reports, not just on the global picture but data selected out as relevant to the host country's economy. Just as in the next chapter it will be shown that GDP as an indicator consistently provides an overestimation of the state of the global economy, so too do international economic bodies like the IMF consistently overestimate. The result is the global economy appears more stable and more recovered than it in fact may actually be. The IMF is not alone in the consistent, general over-optimistic global economic forecasts.

World Bank 2015 Forecasts

The World Bank, the IMF's sister global capitalist institution, released this past January its initial bi-annual forecast for the global economy for 2015 and beyond.[10] And like the IMF, it too continued to overestimate global recovery in 2015.

In its January 2015 semi-annual Report, the World Bank continued to predict the global economy will grow faster in 2015 than it had in 2014. In July 2014 it had estimated the global economy would grow in 2015 at 2.6%. It then raised that 2015 forecast in January 2015 to 3.0%. In its latest June 2015 update, however, it recognized the global economy in 2015 was not growing anywhere near to 3% but was experiencing what it called a 'soft patch'—i.e. a temporary condition. It therefore made a token, nominal adjustment in June 2015, predicting it would expand at 2.8%.[11] Just the opposite appears likely to be the case, however, with 2015 global growth almost certainly to come in much less than the 3%, highly likely less than the 2.8%, and perhaps even below the actual 2.4% for 2014.

Despite all this, the World Bank's latest June 2015 Report maintains that its forecasts for a return to robust growth in 2016 and 2017 will remain unchanged. China will continue growing at around 7%, according to the World Bank, for the next two and a half years, through 2017. India will grow at nearly 8% through 2017.[12] Despite the sharp economic slowdown occurring among emerging economies in late 2015, their growth is expected to accelerate from 2015 to yet higher levels in 2016-17.[13] These are all absurd assumptions given the facts increasingly evident as of mid-2015.

So we have the same pattern as the IMF: initial over-optimistic and overestimate growth projection, subsequent adjustment and correction for the error, followed by a continued overestimate of global economic growth. Like the IMF, the World Bank consistently lags behind the global economic curve, playing catch up with adjustments that still over-shoot the reality.

The January 2015 World Bank Report predicted that both the Eurozone and Japan will somehow grow robustly in 2015. Japan's economy, however, contracted -1.6% in the second quarter 2015. Europe continued to stagnate at 2014 growth rates, even as the German economy slowed and France totally stalled in mid-2015. The World Bank predicted emerging economies like Brazil would grow modestly, even when collapsing commodities prices and demand already pushed it and other Latin American economies into recession. Emerging markets growth is projected to accelerate in 2015, to 4.8%, and again in 2016 even further. China was predicted to continue to grow in excess of 7.0%, although by mid-year that scenario is all but impossible, while the USA economy would accelerate to an average 3.2% annual growth rate in 2015, even though it collapsed to virtually zero growth in the first quarter of 2015 and appears to be 'recovering' at an annual rate of only 1.5% in the first half of 2015. Despite raising the estimate for USA growth in 2015, the Bank's chief economist, Kaushik Basu, admitted USA growth at 3.2% "is really not enough" to pull the rest of the global economy out of a slowdown.[14] Predictions of continued robust growth in China and India— and its overestimation of growth in Europe, Japan and Latin America— appear to be the basis for its higher 2015 growth forecast in 2015 for the global economy.

Notwithstanding the World Bank Report's optimism to the upside for 2015, it covered its bets for 2015 in January by noting four major downside risks: the "persistently weak global trade"..."the possibility of financial market volatility" due to rising interest rates in major economies (e.g. the USA), "low oil prices in oil-producing countries", and "the risk of a prolonged period of stagnation or deflation in the Euro Area or Japan". But while covering its back by acknowledging the serious and growing downside risks, the World Bank Report—like the IMF—has chosen to give little or no weight to those risks actually occurring. That was true in its January 2015 Report, and continues to be so in its subsequent June 2015 update.

For example, in its June 2015 update, while acknowledging that emerging economies may indeed be slowing, it nonetheless predicted that "recovery in high income (i.e. AEs) countries is expected to gain momentum". Apparently it has ignored Japan's -1.6% second quarter GDP renewed collapse and the likely further impact on its recovering from that country's plummeting exports to China and beyond. The US is forecast to "expand at a robust pace" and the forecast for China's economy has not changed from its January Report, according to the World Bank. But a 2% growth for the US is hardly 'robust', and the already slowing manufacturing, industrial production, and exports sectors for the US may easily result in a less than 2% US growth in the second half of 2015. And this is before any possible Federal Reserve interest rate hike. As for China, it appears the World Bank has largely missed the obvious accelerating slowdown in China's real economy. But any forecast for China economy that hasn't changed in the past nine months—as is apparently the case with the World Bank's—is a priori worthless.

So why have both the IMF and World Bank had a history since the 2008 global crash of overestimating growth and recovery, requiring them repeatedly to correct those overly optimistic forecasts?

The reasons why these two global institutions tasked with providing data and predictions for the global economy regularly err to the positive side are in part political and part cultural. Member countries don't like to hear negative estimates of their economies, which lead to poor government bond ratings that raise borrowing costs that in turn impact budgets and fiscal programs. In this regard, governments act much like private economic forecasting companies and academics: Forecast too negatively and clients will complain you're impacting their business. Or, in the case of academic economists, the implicit message is 'continue to forecast bad news for our industry and company and contributions to your college or business school will be reduced'. Then there's the cultural factor. Among economists in all sectors—academic, business or government—there is less reputation at risk if one misses a forecast by under-estimating than by overestimation. So official sources like the IMF and World Bank—like private forecasters— prefer to continue to err to the upside, only noting the downside factors as possibilities, and repeatedly adjusting their forecasts (and apologizing) when the latter continually occur.

OECD Forecasts

The research arm of 34 of the more 'advanced economies', the Organization for Economic Cooperation and Development, OECD, in its latest bi-annual projections in June 2015, forecast the global economy to grow by 3.1% in 2015. This was a notable downward adjustment from its previous 3.7%, but still well above the IMF and World Bank adjusted forecasts. Moreover, like the IMF and World Bank, the OECD predicted global economy's slower growth in 2015 would give way to a renewed robust 3.8% growth in 2016. This near 4% growth was based on the highly dubious assumptions that China would continue to grow 6.8% in 2016, that current US GDP growth rates would accelerate nearly by half, and that falling world oil prices and QE policies in Japan and Europe would finally begin to have a net positive impact on their real economies which to date has not been the case. Not least, the 3.8% growth was further based on the assumption that world real investment, now growing barely above 2%, would somehow double to 4% in 2016—the fastest rate since 2008.[15] Thus the OECD pattern of overestimation, followed by token adjusting, and a general de-emphasizing of the major developments underway pointing to a further, and perhaps even faster, slowing of global growth, reproduces the IMF and World Bank views.

Global Central Bank Forecasts

This bias toward overestimating growth by major global economic institutions like the IMF, World Bank, and OECD is often replicated on a national level by central banks and government statistical agencies as well. An inspection of economic growth forecasts by the Bank of Japan, the European Central Bank, and the US Federal Reserve show the same history of forecast error.

There's no need to review them all. However, by way of example, the US Federal Reserve's annual year end 'center tendency' projections of US GDP growth since 2011 have also consistently overestimated US economic growth now for the past five years.

Here's what the Fed's own data shows for the US economy:

Year	Fed 'Center' GDP Projection	Actual GDP
2011	3.0-3.6%	1.6%
2012	2.5-2.9%	2.2%
2013	2.3-3.0%	1.5%
2014	2.8-3.2%	2.4%
2015	2.6-3.0%	1.5% (1st half)

Source: Federal Reserve Board, Wall St. Journal, August 22-23, 2015, p. A8.

A similar scenario of overestimated forecasts since the 2008 crash exists for other major Advanced Economies' central banks and other major statistical agencies, Statistics Bureau of Japan, France's INSEE, Statistics Canada, the US Commerce Dept., and so on.

The Inability to Forecast Financial Instability

If global institutions, governments and private forecasters have been consistently missing the trend and trajectory of the global real economy, their predicting of the financial economy has been magnitudes even poorer. That is in large part due to the fact they have no models for understanding financial cycles whatsoever, let alone how financial cycles impact the real economy and cycles, and vice-versa. On the financial side, it is mostly intuitive guess work about 'commodity super cycles', 'yield curves', or the 'VIX', a S&P 500 stock volatility indicator. If events of the 2008 crash, and even before, are any indicator of the impact of financial instability on the real economy, one would think at least a partially reliable indicator—i.e. a 'Financial Cycle GDP' or something like it—would have been developed.

Mainstream economists are trained in using and building models of the economy based on 'real variables' that are quantifiable—i.e. production, wages, real investment, prices, export volumes, M2 and other money variables. Their models, and GDP statistics per se, specifically exclude financial variables. This is a bias that goes back to the original development of National Income Accounting (GDP) to the 1920s and 1930s. It was the real economy that required recovery. So real data was necessary. Economic exigencies of World War II enhanced the need to understand how the real economy was performing, in order to assess how to mobilize real production for war time while trying to maintain economic stability for the rest of the civil economy.

To some extent, the dominant new economic analysis paradigm deployed during wartime—Keynesian analysis—focused predominantly on real variables as well. That dominant approach and its bias on real indicators continued well into the post-war period. Financial variables may have contributed significantly to the great recession happening, but the real economy was the focus for recovering. Keynes himself, of course, was not opposed to understanding financial variables, but his seminal work, the General Theory, gave little attention to them.[16] For decades thereafter mainstream economic analysis, and the data it employed, was heavily biased toward real variables to the exclusion of financial variables. GDP statistics specifically exclude reference to financial assets and volatility.

Beginning in the 1970s and 1980s, and accelerating thereafter, financial variables have become increasingly important in determining how the real economy itself performs. The stability of the global real economy and real economic growth have become far more dependent on financial stability than ever before. However, the models and economic analyses have not 'caught up' with this reality.

The closest thing to forecasting financial instability are embedded chapters or passages and commentary in the reports on the global economy by the IMF-World Bank, independent research consultancies like McKinsey Associates and others, and central banks. The bank of central banks, the Bank of International Settlements (BIS), perhaps comes closest with its periodic reports on global debt trends. But what all these partial commentaries lack is a concise and reliable forecasting and predicting of global financial instability trends and a measurement of financial instability akin to GDP for the real economy—as poor as GDP as an indicator may be. Even more important, what is missing is some kind of quantitative indicator for how a missing 'Financial GDP' impacts 'Real GDP' and vice-versa.

The consequence of all this is that economists, mainstream and government, almost always miss predicting the next financial crash and major instability event. They never see it coming, because they don't know what proper data to watch, or even have the data. If they had, they still have no theory or model of financial cycles and instability on which to base their conclusions. One therefore cannot critique the failures of institutions and the economics profession for poor financial cycle forecasting, since the forecasting itself is virtually non-existent except for 'guestimations' based on limited data on 'super cycles', 'yield curves' and the like. It is left to a few prescient, iconoclast individual economists who periodically raise warnings of an imminent financial crisis, and who then are almost always ignored.

Given that financial forces and variables are playing an increasingly important role in determining the growth and stability of the global capitalist economy in the 21st century, this leads to a consistent failure to predict the trends and trajectory of that real economy as well. What the consistent over-optimistic forecasts reflect is a bias toward assuming the robust recovery in China and EMEs in 2010-2012 would not collapse or even slow appreciably; and that the chronic recessions, stagnation, and relapses in Japan, Europe and US would not continue. But they did. The result was a 'Dead Cat Bounce' recovery which appears by 2015 may have little left in the way of bounce.

Endnotes

1   Martin Wolf, 'An Economist's Advice to Astrologers', *Financial Times*, January 7, 2015, p. 7.

2   Paul Krugman, 'The Obama Recovery', *New York Times*, December 29, 2014, p. A17. For this writer's definition of a 'Hybrid-Keynesian', and its mirror-image counterpart in the mainstream economics profession, 'Retro-Classicalists', see chapter 5 that follows, which provides an in-depth critique of what's wrong with the mainstream economics profession's analysis and forecasting ability with regard to the global economy since 2008.

3   Niall Ferguson, 'The Divergent World of 2015', *Wall Street Journal*, January 3, 2015, p. 9.

4   See Ralph Atkins, 'What Could Possibly Go Wrong', *Financial Times*, January 3, 2015, p. 11.

5   All the following data are from the International Monetary Fund, *World Economic Outlook*, October 2014, Table 1.1, p. 2.

6   International Monetary Fund, *World Economic Outlook*, October 2015, p. xv.

7   For example, the OECD research arm, representing 34 of the world's largest economies, expects investment to expand by a mere 2.3% in 2015. However, typically it predicts it will accelerate to 4% in 2016. So the trend of the past decade somehow will be reversed, but no explanation why so is offered.

8   Hans Gensberg and Andrew Martinez, 'On the Accuracy and Efficiency of IMF Forecasts', Independent Evaluation Office of IMF, February 12, 2014, p. 1.

9   IMF, *World Economic Outlook*, October 2014, p. 39-40.

10   *Global Economic Prospects*, World Bank, January 2015.

11   *Global Economic Prospects*, World Bank, June 2015, p. 3.

12   The World Bank has apparently accepted India's highly questionable upward revision of its GDP by 2% which it accomplished merely by redefining its GDP—a controversial trend growing among emerging markets as they slow.

13   For an interview with World Bank President, Jim Yong Kim, see 'The Outlook for Emerging Countries', *Wall St. Journal,* June 22, 2015, p. R5.

14   Ian Talley, 'World Bank Lowers Global Outlook', *Wall St. Journal,* January 14, 2015, p. 11

15   For summaries of the OECD report, David Jolly, 'OECD Sees Slow Recovery Worldwide', *New York Times*, June 4, 2015, p. B7, and Ferdinando Giugliano, 'OECD Slashes Global Growth Forecast', *Financial Times*, June 4, 2015, p. 2.

16   Chapter 16 covers this in more detail.

2

THE 'DEAD-CAT BOUNCE' RECOVERY

Mythology says cats have nine lives. Sometimes markets collapse and then quickly recover a small part of the decline, only to retreat further and deeper once again. They are described as having had a 'dead cat' bounce—i.e. a false recovery that leads quickly to a return to the previous trend--the economic cat having 'flopped over' again, this time for longer or even permanently.

That's a scenario similar to what happened in the great depression of the 1930s. The initial collapse of the US stock market in October 1929 was followed by an initial quick recovery in the markets. It appeared in 1929-30 as if the economic consequences associated with the stock market crash would produce only a recession. 1929-1930 was relatively severe as recessions go, but not extraordinary, affecting mostly manufacturing and construction activity and not yet the general US economy. But the 1929 stock crash eventually led to a regional banking crisis in 1930, and then to a series of widespread banking crashes, each more severe than the preceding—at least three banking crashes, to be precise, in 1931, 1932, and 1933. The cat bounced several times, each time more dead than the previous.[1]

Dead Cats and Epic Recessions

Sometimes the cat bounces, jumps up, does not flop, but instead proceeds on wobbly legs, in a half-walk, half-falling fashion. Something like a zombie-cat, shuffling along, dragging its feet. That describes the cat's post-crash recovery following the 1907-09 US financial crash and recession. For the next five years the cat stumbled in and out of recession twice more, between 1909 and 1914. Brief, unsustained recoveries from the 1907-09 financial crash and contraction lasting six to 18 months were followed by repeated short, shallow descents into recession or shorter economic relapses. What resulted was a 'stop-go' recovery post-1909. Recessions and relapses were followed by equally unimpressive, truncated recoveries of similar dimension.[2]

Something very similar to 1907-1909 and the subsequent sub-normal recovery period to 1914 occurred in the US economy with the 2007-09 crash and the subsequent, 2010-15, 'stop-go' period during which US growth was about half that of normal post-recession recovery periods. On only brief occasions did the US economy actually grow normally following the official end of the 2009 recession. On no fewer than four occasions during the 2010-15 period the US economy 'relapsed' to zero or less for single quarters, recovering briefly thereafter. As this writer predicted in late 2009, the US recovery in particular would follow a trajectory much like that of 1908-14. According to the prediction, "The most likely scenario (post-2009) is, given the still serious problems remaining in both the financial system and the real economy, the economy for the next one to two years will show a pattern of unsustainable growth and recovery; recoveries that are short and shallow, and perhaps even followed by renewed declines, also short and shallow".[3]

In the case of the US, the 'short and shallow' followed by renewed declines assumed the form of single quarter contractions or zero-near zero growth rates. But were it not for the official redefining of the meaning of GDP during the period in order to boost GDP estimates, a bona fide recession, albeit mild, for two consecutive quarters in the US either during the winters of 2011-12 or 2012-13, might have been recognized for what, up to the redefinition, it was.

For other major regions of the global economy—Japan and Europe—the short, single quarter relapses in the US went deeper and lasted longer. They experienced bona fide recessions in 2011-12. For Japan, it was even a case of 'triple' or even 'quadruple' dip recessions, occurring both before and after 2011-12. Europe experienced at least one major Euro-wide recession in 2011-13, with continuing depressions in its southern periphery economies from Spain to Greece for most of the five year period after 2009. Thus during 2009-2014, as predicted, the world economy experienced—at least in the advanced economies of Japan, Europe, and the US—brief, unsustained recoveries followed by equally short, shallow recessions or single quarter relapses.[4]

And in fact, when the advanced economies of US, Japan, Europe are considered together, the global economy had clearly slipped into a double dip in the advanced economies circa 2011-12.[5] This double dip in most of the global economy was generally overlooked by the offsetting rapid growth at the time in China and the emerging markets. The rocks in the global stream were just below the water level, but they were there.

I called this scenario of a stop-go, subnormal economic recovery in the advanced economies from 2010-2014 a Type I 'Epic Recession'. An epic recession is quite different from normal recessions. Mainstream economists typically only distinguish normal recessions, which are precipitated by either supply or demand policy shocks. Such externally caused contractions are typically brief in duration and relatively shallow. That enabled traditional fiscal and monetary policies to address and counter them somewhat successfully. But an 'epic' recession is a different economic animal. It is not precipitated by external shocks but rather by internal, endogenous financial instability events. Its enabling causes—like its precipitating causes— are also different from normal recessions. And in fundamental terms, epic recessions are also different since they are associated with conditions of systemic fragility. The same conditions that cause the financial instability that precipitates the real contractions also make the real economy more susceptible and sensitive to the financial instability when it does erupt. Thus, real contractions that follow an epic recession are typically deeper, descend faster, and therefore take longer to fully recover from. The different internal conditions also render traditional fiscal-monetary policies—so successful in correcting normal recessions—significantly less so in the case of epic recessions.[6]

The term 'epic recession' was used alternatively to 'great recession' in order to distinguish it quantitatively and qualitatively from normal recessions, something the advocates of 'great recession' have not done. The 'epic' definition also challenged the notion that a recession ends when the economy simply stops contracting further—that is, at the nadir point—which is how the official ending of recessions is defined. However, that represents only a 'half cycle'. A true recession, an 'epic' recession, should be defined and measured by a full cycle; that is, by the period and processes involved over the full span of time from the beginning of the contraction to the period at which all that was lost during the contraction was again restored. By this 'full cycle' definition of an epic recession, the US economy did not fully recover until around late 2013, and the European and Japanese recessions still have not since their economies in 2015 are still producing at levels below that which prevailed in 2007. Only China and the emerging market economies truly 'recovered' from 2008-09, but as subsequent chapters will show, that recovery has not lasted either. Starting in 2014 they have been descending, one by one, and now more collectively, into recessions once again.

Epic recession was a term also introduced to distinguish what has been happening since 2009 from the more popular term created by economists in early 2009, 'great recession'. This writer took issue with that latter terminology, since it remained essentially undefined and unexplained in quantitative-qualitative details from prior recessions that obviously were not 'great'. For mainstream economists since 2009, the recent narrowly defined 2007-09 recession was 'great' simply because somehow it was 'worse than' preceding normal recessions while 'not as bad as' the great depression of the 1930s. This was unacceptable. One cannot explain the different phenomena—the normal recessions, the 2007-09 recession, and bona fide depressions—merely with 'analysis by adjectives'.

Nor can one hope to explain what had happened in 2007-09 without a consideration of financial instability forces that had clearly been involved. Mainstream economic analysis largely fails to integrate the role of financial forces in the crash and subsequent 'epic/great' recession, except as to argue it was due to financial deregulation and subprime mortgage excesses (i.e. on the liberal-left) or that it was due to 'asymmetrical information' or 'moral hazard' (on the right). The former explanation reduced the explanation to government policy or 'bad guy rogue lenders'; the latter to 'interferences with individual decision making or else moral failures of individuals'. In either case, the argument was the markets were not at fault. It was not the inherent nature of capitalist enterprise or finance that was responsible, 'endogenously' or otherwise, for the 2007-09 crisis. Failures of the system that were more fundamental than government or individual behavior levels were not responsible for the crisis, according to mainstream economics. It was either policy or bad behavior of a minority. However, financial and other endogenous causes did underlie the 2007-09 crash, as well as the subsequent sub-normal recovery of 2010-15.

One of the several qualitative characteristics of an epic recession is that it is experienced more or less globally. That was clearly the case during 2007-2009. The global economy thereafter diverged—with the emerging markets growing robustly in 2010 and after, just as the advanced economies either relapsed or experienced repeated bouts of stagnation and recession. But that divergence may now be coming to an end as of mid-2015. The convergence is growing once again. The AEs are still not growing any more robustly than they had since 2010. And China and emerging markets are growing far more slowly or declining in growth terms. And with Europe and Japan either stagnating or in recession, there is no way that the slow, subnormal, 'stop-go' growth in the US economy can substitute for the formerly fast growing Chinese and emerging markets. The 'de-coupling' of China and emerging markets from the AEs, which was talked about in 2010, is ended; re-coupling is now underway, as the global slowdown also drifts toward a more generalized, shared condition of stagnant growth or worse.

That is what is fundamentally different circa 2015 compared to 2009. A definite new phase or stage of the post-2009 continuing 'epic' recession is now emerging in the global economy. The only open question is which financial asset markets and financial instability event will precipitate the next major contraction, and will it be more serious than that of 2007-08?

In short, in 2015 the dead cat may have again bounced, but it is now flopping over on its back once more.

Another characteristic of the dead cat recovery since 2009 is that the potential for financial instability has not been significantly reduced. That instability is based fundamentally on the growth of excess debt—private sector debt and especially private business debt—that fuels financial speculation. The debt in turn is a direct consequence of excessive liquidity generation into the global economy. As subsequent chapters will discuss in detail, both excess liquidity and excessive debt directed to financial asset speculation are far larger in 2015 than they were in 2007-08. So too are financial asset bubbles, any one of which may burst at any time—it's only a question of which and when—sending the real global economy into an even faster descent than it is now undergoing.

Some financial asset bubbles have already broken and are collapsing in asset price deflation—global crude oil futures, China and other equity markets, Euro sovereign bonds, and currencies of a growing number of countries in emerging markets. Other bubbles are perched precariously on a financial cliff edge—like corporate junk bonds, exchange traded bond funds, leveraged buyout loans, and others.

The dead cat bounce recovery is also associated with the declining effectiveness of traditional fiscal-monetary policies. Central banks globally have assumed the role of 'animal rescue officers', to use a metaphor. They have been running around the countryside trying to resuscitate and revive dead cats wherever they can find them, feeding them the oxygen of free money and liquidity. That has driven down world inter-bank interest rates to zero or even below (negative rates). But the central bank oxygen bottles are almost empty. In the event of another major crisis—dead cat flop—they have no more interest rate reduction left with which to try to revive the poor cat. If they can't, the rigor mortis of depression may well set in.

Economists and policy makers are also at a loss to understand or explain how and why during the 2010-15 epic recession, 'stop-go' growth period—now about to experience more 'stop' than 'go'—that real investment is chronically slowing even faster than growth and that the drift everywhere globally is toward deflation in goods and even services. They scratch their heads and say it must be some kind of 'secular stagnation' going on. In fact, there is a kind of 'secular stagnation debate' that has been occurring in recent years.   But how and why the global economy is stagnating secularly, and especially how that may be related somehow to financial forces, is poorly explained by the debaters. Given the conceptual framework they work with, they continue to phrase the issue in narrow terms of 'supply' or 'demand' of real variables, keeping within their economics training comfort zone.   They therefore cannot adequately embrace the new anomalies and realities of the 21st century global economy that their theories and models fail to address—most notably financial forces and variables.[7]

Five Realities of the Post Crash 'Bounce'

The post-crash 2010-2015 period is characterized by the following dominant developments:

- A rapid slowing of the China economy starting in 2012, now accelerating in 2015, following a short real economic boom (the bounce) of 2009-12;

- A freefall of emerging market economies in 2014-15 following their commodities boom 'bounce' of 2010-12, as commodities demand and prices after 2012 deflate rapidly, money capital inflows from advanced economies reverse, and their currencies collapse;

- Japan's economy continuing to slip in and out of recessions, as massive money QE injections fail to generate real investment and growth;

- Europe economic growth chronically stagnating, growing in the 1% average range after a double dip in 2011-13, and also, like Japan, unable to generate sustainable real investment and growth;

- The US economy stuck in a stop-go recovery punctuated by periodic 'relapses' to zero or less quarterly GDP growth, unable to accelerate beyond an average 1.5% to 2% annual growth—about half of historically normal.

What the historical economic record after 2009 shows is that key sectors of the global economy—like Japan and Europe—have never really recovered from the 2008-09 global crash. The 29 country Euro Area has experienced at least a double dip recession, and the 19 country Eurozone almost a third recession since 2009. The situation of Japan is even less debatable. By 2014 it had officially experienced no less than its fourth official recession since 2009 and now appears to be entering a fifth as of late 2015.

The following graphs illustrate the repeated recession and stagnation scenarios for Japan and Europe that have been the dominant characteristics of these regions of the global economy for the past half decade. Chapter 4 analyzes the causes and trajectories of Japan and Europe in more detail.

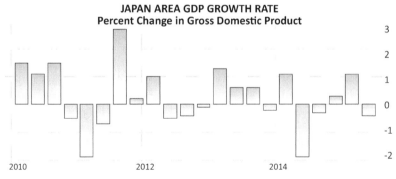

JAPAN AREA GDP GROWTH RATE
Percent Change in Gross Domestic Product

SOURCE: TRADINGECONOMICS.COM CABINET OFFICE JAPAN

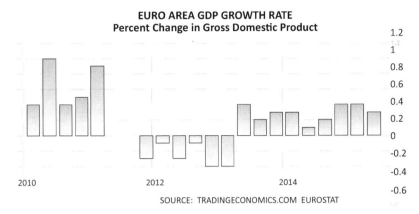

EURO AREA GDP GROWTH RATE
Percent Change in Gross Domestic Product

SOURCE: TRADINGECONOMICS.COM EUROSTAT

Economies that did initially recover during 2010-12—like China and other commodity-dependent emerging market economies—began to slow notably in terms of growth rates again after 2012. Chapters 3 (emerging markets) and 6 (China) will describe in further detail the real and financial forces behind both the boom (2010-12) and the subsequent slowing of China and the corresponding collapse of key emerging market economies—like Brazil, Russia, Turkey, Indonesia and others—that began to emerge 2014-15.

For the moment, the following graph shows China's dramatic shift to a slower growth pattern that commenced in 2012. The quarterly figures reflect, moreover, China's likely overestimation of its GDP numbers. For example, the most recent data continue to show China's official 7% growth rate projections. But a growing list of reliable independent research sources, including the global banks closely associated with China's trade and investment, HSBC and Standard Charter, both located in Hong Kong, are estimating that China is more likely growing in the 5%-6% range, and perhaps even lower.

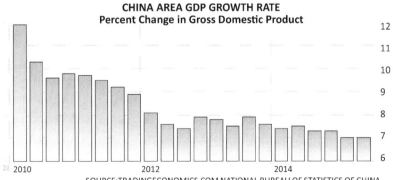

CHINA AREA GDP GROWTH RATE
Percent Change in Gross Domestic Product

SOURCE:TRADINGECONOMICS.COM NATIONAL BUREAU OF STATISTICS OF CHINA

Brazil and Russia are two of the biggest economies hit hard by the global crash in commodities and oil prices that began in mid-2014, and then subsequently accelerated again a year later. They are perhaps an extreme example of the growing economic crisis in emerging markets, but they nevertheless reflect a general trend occurring throughout the EMEs after the 'bounce' period of 2010-2012. Nowhere perhaps is it more evident that the brief global 'recovery' of those years is over and the new normal is contraction—the question is: just how fast and how far.

Brazil is indicative of a number of other Latin American economies, including Venezuela, Chile, Peru, Argentina (and even to a lesser extent Mexico where the trend is less pronounced due to its export integration with the US economy). All are heavy commodity producing economies that benefited from massive money inflows from the US, Europe and Japan during the bounce period of 2010-12 as well as from constant growing demand for their commodities from China at the same time. As both sources—China and AE money capital—began to evaporate after 2013 their growth rates followed. In 2015, given the upward drift of long term interest rates in the AEs (US and UK) and prospects of their central banks raising rates still further, combined with the growing global currency war initiated by Japan and Europe, thereafter joined by China, EME currencies' collapse began to accelerate even faster—generating more capital flight, import inflation, and thus slowing real economic growth still further.

Brazil's growth trajectory reflects the fate of the various commodity exporting EMEs similar to it. Russia's reveals the similar fate of highly dependent oil producing economies, from Nigeria to Indonesia to North Africa and even Canada-Mexico. All are slowing rapidly and many are already deep in recession territory.

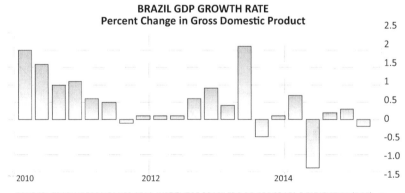

BRAZIL GDP GROWTH RATE
Percent Change in Gross Domestic Product

SOURCE: TRADINGECONOMICS.COM INSTITUTOE BRASILERO DE GEOGRAFA E ESTATISTICA (BGE)

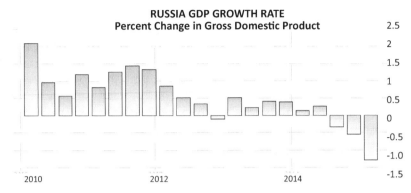

RUSSIA GDP GROWTH RATE
Percent Change in Gross Domestic Product

SOURCE: TRADINGECONOMICS.COM FEDERAL STATE STATISTICS SERVICE

Everywhere in the business press the number one question raised throughout 2015 has been whether the US economy can pick up the slack of a faster decline in growth beginning to occur in the rest of the global economy. The question reframed becomes: can the US decouple from the trajectory of the global economy and prevent its further decline? In other words, can it play the brief role that China and EMEs did in 2010-12 in the immediate aftermath of the 2008-09 crash and contraction? If it can, does that mean another 'bounce' for the once dead cat? Even if maybe not as 'high'? If not, i.e. if the US cannot decouple and grow faster, what will that mean for the global economy? Will the almost dead cat simply roll over again in 2016 and beyond?

The view that the USA economy is about to take off on a sustained growth path that will lift the rest of the global economy has been the unofficial economic mantra of the US government, business press, and much of the academic economics establishment now for the past four years. Each time the economy grows at around 4% for a single quarter or so, the same shout is raised—the US economy has turned the corner and is taking off! And each time it 'relapses' back to zero or less growth.

The most recent version of this 'economic spin' was floated in the second half of 2014, based on the 5% GDP growth rate in the July-September 2014 period in the USA. However, as this writer explained at the time, special circumstances—both short and long term—were responsible for the 5%. It was an aberration. The US economy, it was predicted, would fade again in 2015—as it had done on three prior occasions in 2011, 2012, and early 2014.

As I pointed out there were temporary, short term factors involved with the 5% growth rate that could not be sustained. These included: government spending surges just prior to national elections, business inventory and capital spending just prior to Xmas holiday shopping in expectation of sustained consumer spending that doesn't materialize, temporary boosts in net exports, etc. Moreover, there were longer term conditions as well that allow the USA economy to perform at a level slightly higher than other economies, even when a global slowdown is underway.

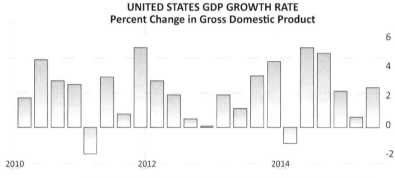

UNITED STATES GDP GROWTH RATE
Percent Change in Gross Domestic Product

SOURCE: TRADINGECONOMICS.COM U.S. BUREAU OF ECONOMIC ANALYSIS

These include special characteristics of the USA economy—like its massive military spending that it can boost on short notice, its control of the international reserve and trading currency (the dollar), the special influence of its central bank (the Federal Reserve) on other central banks, USA dominance in global capital markets, and its effective control of various international economic institutions.

Elsewhere in the global economy the end of the 'bounce' may have taken the form of bona fide double and triple dip recessions—as in the cases of Europe and Japan—and even more volatility in emerging markets. But due to the US economy's long term advantages—i.e. of an international economic system it set up post-1945 to ensure those advantages—the 'bounce' translates for the US instead into a slower growth rate, half of its historical normal at around 1.5%-2%, instead of recessions or extended economic stagnation periods. [8]

Thus special factors allowed the USA to maintain a relatively higher growth rate in general over the longer term as well, compared to other major AE economies, and weather the extreme economic storms that periodically afflict emerging market economies. Often this higher relative US growth rate is achieved at least in part at the expense of other economies. In other words, just as the USA is capable of 'exporting' its inflation, it is also capable of 'importing' other economies economic growth. That is, because the US dollar is the premier trading and reserve currency, by raising interest rates and the value of the dollar US policy makers can slow inflation in the US. That rise in rates causes foreign capital to flow back to the US, and the higher dollar results in import inflation in the other countries as well. The money capital flows to the US, conversely, result in less investment in the other countries, thus slowing their growth, while encouraging investment in the US and US growth.

Perhaps the latest prime example of the 'importing' is the USA-engineered shale oil and gas boom of recent years. As just one example of how the global oil glut created by the USA shale boom works indirectly to 'import' growth from elsewhere: falling global oil prices are linked to the rise of the US dollar. That rise draws back to the US economy massive capital flows from EMEs globally, which stimulate the US economy. The capital outflows, in turn, slow the EMEs; the latter raise their domestic interest rates, which slows their economies, and cut government spending to reduce deficits which slow EMEs still further. And that's just one 'transmission mechanism' by which the USA can, and does, import growth from elsewhere to itself.

Another interesting oil-related characteristic of the post-bounce period is that the OPEC economies, led by Saudi Arabia and the Emirates, feel they are politically and economically powerful enough to challenge the US shift to oil and shale gas. It is this challenge by the Saudis that accelerated the crash of global oil prices that began in 2014. A clear test of economic wills between US producers and the Saudis is thus clearly underway, with significant negative consequences for the global economy.

In short, it is virtually impossible that the US economy will grow sufficiently in 2015 and beyond to play the role China did in creating a 'bounce' from 2010-2012. If China could not continue the bounce beyond 2010-12, when it was growing at a 10% plus annual rate, there's little reason to believe the USA will prove any different even at a 4%-5% growth rate. And there is no way the USA economy will grow at that 4% rate—or even at 3% annually for that matter. And certainly its current 2% and less rate will never suffice to generate another 'bounce'.

Take away the short 'bounce' of 2010-12 in just the China-EME sectors of the global economy and what remains is a kind of broad based, five year long global stagnation that has not been experienced since the Great Depression of the 1930s. The similarity has led some economists to argue that the global economy, the AEs at least, have been experiencing a kind of muted, 21st century form of Depression since 2009. Although economists have never agreed upon what actually constitutes a depression, quantitatively or qualitatively, the point that the global economy is experiencing a new kind of muted depression in the 21st century has some initial validity.

Secular Stagnation—A New Normal?

A watered-down form of this muted depression thesis is the current, running discussion in the global business press on what is called the 'secular stagnation debate'. Initiated by mainstream liberal economist, Larry Summers, in 2014, the secular stagnation debate crowd argue, in brief, that changes in the nature of the 21st century labor force are responsible for both demand and supply failures in the economy that are holding back growth. Not only is more income growth and thus Demand needed, but also Supply Side structural changes in the work force are needed to raise worker productivity and therefore growth.[9]

But secular stagnation economists are nonetheless at a loss to explain how and why during the 2010-15 period real investment is chronically slowing faster than growth and the drift everywhere globally is toward deflation in goods and even services. How and why the global economy is stagnating secularly, and especially how that may be related somehow to financial forces, is poorly explained by the debaters. Given the conceptual framework they work with, they continue to phrase the issue in narrow terms of 'supply' or 'demand' of real variables, keeping within their economics training comfort zone.   They therefore cannot adequately embrace the new anomalies and realities of the 21st century global economy that their theories and models fail to address—most notably financial forces and variables.

Whether one calls it 'muted depression' or 'secular stagnation', those now raising these terms reflect a greater awareness, at least in some quarters, that the global economy is indeed in a long term slowing trend.

Industrial Production and Trade Recessions Are Already Here

Among the best indicators perhaps that the 'bounce' is over and that the general trajectory of the global economy is now clearly downward is what is already happening with global industrial production and with global trade. It may reasonably be argued the world economy is already experiencing a recession in both industrial production and trade.

Global trade initially boomed after 2008-09 from its contraction of more than 12%. That trade boom was concentrated mostly in the Chinese and emerging markets regions of the global economy. Trade between AE economies nearly fell to nearly zero in 2012, as Europe and Japan entered recessions and the US economy slowed. But even in China and the EMEs the trade surge proved more of a 'bounce' than a sustained expansion.

World trade grew annually for the two decades before 2008 at a rate on average twice that of GDP. Continuing that longer term trend, in 2007 World Trade grew at 6% while global GDP rose by 3.5%. However, after collapsing in 2008-09 along with GDP, world trade during the 'bounce' period surged to 13.8% in 2010, more than three times the growth of GDP. It remained twice the rate level of GDP in 2011, slowed to the same growth rate of 2% in 2012, after which world trade volumes 'crossed', for the first time in decades growing less than GDP in 2013 at only 2.2%. Trade then turned negative in the first quarter of 2014 and recovered only to 0.7% in the first quarter of 2015—but this anemic recovery in early 2015 occurred before the further contraction of commodities and oil and the collapsing of currencies that commenced after mid-2015.[10] If global recession were therefore measured in terms of world trade volumes, the global economy may well have entered recession in the second half of 2015, or at least come very close.

Industrial production is composed of three elements: manufacturing, mining and utilities energy generation. Mining everywhere is slowing or in contraction. In China, which represents a fourth of world manufacturing output, the sector has been contracting every month since late 2014. China's industrial production has been falling even longer, as has electricity generation. The US represents roughly another fourth of global manufacturing. While it has been growing modestly, that growth is slowing toward a no-net increase level. Rising interest rates and the US dollar will blunt demand for US exports, and thus manufacturing, which comprise most of exports, even further. Manufacturing in Europe remains stagnant, and will almost certainly drop in many major EMEs in 2015-16. World manufacturing and industrial production are therefore also very close to recession.

Redefining GDP to Overestimate Global Growth

What's in a number? This and preceding chapter 1 have referred to the convention of indicating global economic growth by use of the statistic called Gross Domestic Product, or GDP. Even when challenging the estimates, as in Chapter 1, the reference was still GDP. But what if GDP itself grossly overestimates economic growth? And that overestimation is getting worse, as governments have been increasingly manipulating the data and definition of GDP in order to entice out still higher estimates of growth?

The reliability of GDP as a measure of growth and global recovery has recently become even more debatable as country after country—not just the USA, but Europe and emerging markets—has in recent years redefined the meaning of its GDP in order to boost its level and rates.

In the USA this was done in 2013 by deciding to include what were once business expenses and not includable in GDP as now investment and included in GDP. The US changes were made retroactive as well, with the greatest weight adjustments given to the most recent years since the 2008 crash. Today they add no less than $500 billion a year in terms of GDP growth.

Nor has GDP growth statistics manipulation been confined to the US. In Europe a number of countries have changed their GDP definitions, or are about to, in order to include illegal drug dealing and prostitution as legitimate services to include in GDP, even though it is virtually impossible to accurately estimate the prices and volumes of such due to data unavailability. But no matter. What can't be gathered accurately, can be 'made up' based on some new statistical assumption or methodology.

That same trend to redefine one's way to GDP growth is underway globally, witness Nigeria's recently redefining its GDP by record amounts in order to make itself the largest economy in Africa. As real growth and recovery becomes increasingly difficult, there's always growth by statistical manipulation.

Even more egregious has been the case of India. After having indicated a growth of 4.7% for the 2013-14 fiscal year, in February 2015 India redefined its GDP and revised it upward to 6.9% for the year. That's a statistical gain of 2.2%. Manufacturing, trade, finance—all were revised upward sharply. The revisions were described by economists elsewhere as "less than credible" and merely a shifting of the goalposts, as other India data showed a continuing weakness in business and consumer activity.

Manipulation of GDP data and stats may be becoming more overt as economies slow, as the preceding examples illustrate, but manipulation has always been a factor. For example, there's the problem of adjusting GDP by inflation in order to get the reported 'real GDP' numbers that the

IMF, World Bank, and other media pundits refer to. Countries estimate their inflation rates differently. But global economic recovery is thereafter estimated by 'rolling up' the various different cross-national inflation rates into what is called 'Purchasing Power Parity' (PPP) estimates. PPP adjustments in turn are wrought with questionable assumptions, are more 'art' than 'science', and are therefore highly unreliable.

Then there's the broader question of whether even GDP itself is the best indicator of economic growth. Apparently the economists tasked with declaring the start and end of a recession don't think so. GDP is only one of several indicators that the US National Bureau of Economic Research (NBER) economists consider in declaring a recession's start and finish. Instead of GDP, they refer to industrial production, retail sales, employment, net exports and other indicators to decide whether the US economy is in recession or not. Other countries don't necessarily do it the same. So comparing GDPs and recovery across country borders is even more an 'art', given the different ways countries define GDP, gather data accurately or not, and make adjustments to price inflation in order to get to 'real GDP' numbers. How accurate, therefore, then can estimates of aggregate global GDP be?

The question of what's happening with global growth becomes even more debatable when one digs still further behind the false façade of GDP levels and GDP rates and asks: how about jobs growth? Can there be recovery without job creation? Take Japan, where unemployment and job growth have changed little since 2008-09, remaining at around 3.5%, right through the subsequent three additional recessions that have followed. Or the Eurozone, where 55%-70% of all the jobs created since 2008-09 have been part time and temp jobs. How about the USA, where 6 million jobs have allegedly been created since 2009, but just as many workers have left the labor force. Six million in the front door, and 6 million out the back door. The three advanced economies of the USA, Europe and Japan constitute nearly $40 trillion in annual economic growth, or roughly two-thirds of the global economy. Can no jobs in Japan, half time jobs in Europe, and a churning of jobs from full time to half time work in the USA represent growth?

GDP as a measure of growth, whether in levels or rates, tells us nothing about whom that growth has benefited. That is at least as important as measuring 'what' (goods and services) have been produced in greater volume. For example, in the USA, stock, bonds, and other financial markets have more than doubled from recession lows, with

US stock markets 180% above 2008 and corporate profits nearly double levels from the prior boom period peak of 2006-07. The wealthiest 1% households now reportedly have secured for themselves no less than 95% of all the net annual total income growth since 2009, according to University of California, Berkeley economists' studies. [11] Meanwhile, median family real wages and incomes for the remaining households in the USA have declined every year for the past five years, continuing a trend that actually started around 2000 at the current century. Can it be said then that the US economy has grown if capital incomes have accrued 95% of all the gains in national income? Growth for whom?

Europe and Japan present a similar scenario. There too, wage incomes have not recovered while capital incomes have continued to grow. Even in China and the emerging market economies like Brazil and others, the scenario regarding incomes growth is the same. Wouldn't therefore National Income, not GDP, be a better measure of global economic growth?

Whether one chooses to employ GDP data, or incomes data, or jobs or trade or industrial production, or whatever data, it is debatable at best that the global economy is growing as much as GDP numbers referred to above indicate. They represent significant overestimations even when unchallenged. In other words, the dead cat bounce of 2010-12 was not as high as indicated. And the cat's fading condition today, in 2015, is likely even worse than indicated.

What all the foregoing means is that estimates and forecasts of global economic growth are highly debatable and in most cases significantly overestimated. And if incomes and distribution are used as the benchmark concept, then there's been and continues to be virtually no growth for the vast majority of economies and sectors.

Global economic recovery has thus been dubious at best. And is likely to become more so in the near future, however estimated.

One More Bounce?

Part Two, and Chapters 7-15 that immediately follow, look at the bouncing cat's 9 lives, in the form of the most important current nine macro trends in progress in the global economy today. Each of the nine trends reflects a decline in economic vitality in the global economy today. Together the trends point to a growing condition of 'systemic fragility' in the global economy—a kind of brittle aging of long run secular trends and more intensive short run cycles, both real and financial. A kind of economic atherosclerosis.

Maybe the cat doctor can perform some kind of transplant for today's economic cat, that will enable the aging feline to get up and run around in circles a while longer—like he did with the economic organ transplant of the 1970s-80s called neoliberalism; or with the even earlier post-1945 USA Bretton-Woods/imperial transplant. Both operations lasted about 30 years before the cat flopped and rolled over again. Can he be revived a third time, for another decade or two? Or for another short term bounce at least? Or has today's dying cat perhaps bounced his last, and it's time to bury him, and go and find a new animal?

Endnotes

1   See chapter 6 of this writer's *'Epic Recession: Prelude to Global Depression'*, Pluto books, May 2010.
2   Chapter 5, *Epic Recession: Prelude to Global Depression*, 2010.
3   Jack Rasmus, *Epic Recession: Prelude to Global Depression*, 2010, p. 244.
4   Chapter 7, *Epic Recession: Prelude to Global Depression*, 2010.
5   This was covered up, obfuscated, to some degree by the robust recovery of China and other emerging markets between 2009-2012, many the larger of which were enjoying strong growth in the 8%-12% GDP range. That range is now likely 5% for China to as low as -3% to -5% for economies like Brazil, Russia, and others in between that are either stagnating or contracting.
6   See this writer's 2012 publication, *'Obama's Economy: Recovery for the Few'*, Pluto Press, 2012, for a specific focus on US fiscal-monetary policy and the writer's prediction the Obama policies of 2009-11 would fail to generate a sustained US economic recovery but would result instead in a 'stop-go' recovery similar in a number of ways to 1908-1914. The two periods, 1908-14 and 2009-12 shared the common policy failure of 'bailing out the banks' monetary measures, but little or no fiscal stimulus follow-up to 'bail out' the rest of the economy.
7   For a brief review of the issues in the 'secular stagnation' debates, readers are referred to some of its main proponents, like former Treasury Secretary, Larry Summers (a demand sider in the debate) and academic economist, Robert Gordon (a supply sider).
8   The 1.8%-2.0% GDP average is the range reported officially before the USA altered its definition of GDP in the summer of 2013. That redefinition added 0.2%-0.3% to US GDP estimates, around $500 billion a year, as a result of including R&D, business expenses, and other intangibles now as part of business investment—a questionable change that essentially boosted US GDP, going forward and retroactively, by means of what this writer has called 'economic growth by statistical manipulation'.
9   Larry Summers, 'Bold Reform is the Only Answer to Secular Stagnation', *Financial Times*, September 8, 2014, p. 9. Summers typically argues that the secular stagnation is due to demand side forces, whereas others, like economist Robert Gordon, point to supply side factors.

10   All data from the World Trade Organization, *World Trade Reports*, from 2007 through 2015.

11   See the extensive work of UC Berkeley economics professor, Emmanual Saez, and his ELSA database on global income inequality trends.

3

THE EMERGING MARKETS' PERFECT STORM

An economic perfect storm is now developing offshore. Its winds of economic destruction are gaining momentum. Where it first makes landfall is unknown for now, but its 'eye' is clearly located in the emerging markets sector of the global economy.

Earlier the source of growth that propped up the global economy from 2010-13—preventing an otherwise likely descent into global depression in the wake of the 2008-09 economic crash—the Emerging Market Economies (EMEs) are today the focal point of a continuing global crisis that has not ended, but whose eye has only shifted from the AEs to the EMEs. Both the slowing global economy and the forces building toward yet another global financial crisis are concentrated in the EME sector.

What an accelerating decline of the EME sector, representing 52% of global GDP, means for the rest of the world economy is ominous. Continuing weak growth in the advanced economies (AEs) today does not appear capable of offsetting the EME's current slowdown and decline. That is a fundamental difference from 2010-2013, when EME growth largely offset stagnation and weak growth in the AEs over that period. In net terms, therefore, the global economy is far weaker today in terms of real growth prospects, and is growing simultaneously more unstable financially as well.

The EMEs are being economically pounded today from multiple directions:

- the slowing of the Chinese economy and China demand for EME commodity exports;

- weak demand for EME commodity and manufactured exports by Europe and Japan;

- the drift toward higher interest rates in the US and UK;

- the escalation of currency wars provoked by QE policies of Japan and Europe and China's currency devaluation response of August 2015;

- the additional impact of collapsing world crude oil prices for those EMEs whose economic growth and stability is dependent on crude oil production and exports;

- China's stock market bubble and implosion of 2015.

These are problems *external* to the EMEs themselves, largely beyond their control, although impacting them severely nonetheless. But external forces that cause EME economic instability in turn exacerbate additional *'internal'* problems that result in further EME economic contraction and fragility. Moreover, internal and external factors interact and feedback on each other, causing still further instability in both real and financial sectors.

The additional internal factors exacerbating EME economic instability include:

- the collapse of EME currencies;

- escalating capital flight from EMEs back to the traditional advanced economies (AEs) of US, Europe, and Japan;

- rising consumer goods inflation;

- EME policy responses to currency decline, capital flight, and inflation;

- collapsing EME equity (stock) markets;

- a growing threat to EME bond markets issued in dollar denominated debt.

This combination of external and internal problems does not bode well for EME future real growth and financial stability—nor in turn for the global growth or world financial instability in stocks, bonds, and foreign exchange markets.

As for the EME real economy, according to the European mega-bank, UBS, EMEs together grew at only a 3.5% annual rate in the first three months of 2015. But that includes China as an EME, with an official growth rate of 7%. If China is excluded, the 2015 growth rate of all EMEs is only a few tenths of a percent above zero. And if China's real GDP rate is at 5% or less, as many sources now maintain, it's probably no more than zero. In other words, EMEs as a group—half of the world economy—have virtually stalled. Moreover, that data only represents conditions as of March 2015. Events which may occur in the near future—such as China's further economic slowdown, rising US interest rates, and a deeper plunge in global oil and commodity prices—will almost certainly further depress EME economic conditions as a group to recessionary levels.

As for EME financial instability indicators, EME stock prices have fallen more than 30% from their 2011 highs, not counting China's summer 2015 stock market contraction of more than 40% from June through September 2015.[1] In the even more important bond markets, more than half of the acceleration in global debt since 2007 has occurred in private sector debt in general, of which the EMEs in turn have been responsible for more than half, according to a recent McKinsey Consultants study. Much of escalating EME private debt is of 'junk' quality, especially in regions like Latin America and Southeast Asia. That means the debt must be paid back in US dollars, which makes EMEs dependent upon selling more exports in the a global economy where trade is slowing everywhere. Either that, or more must be borrowed at ever higher interest rates to finance the debt. And should income from exports decline further, EME corporate defaults can be expected to rise rapidly. Defaults on government debt are also likely to rise among EMEs, especially where government borrowing has grown in US dollar denominated debt—as is the case in many African EMEs.

EMEs are therefore growing significantly more 'fragile', with both governments borrowing in dollars and private sector corporations loading up on dollar denominated junk bond debt. Odds in favor of a subsequent EME bond bust are a growing possibility, following in the wake of the EME stock declines already underway across the sector. The prospect of a double-edged financial instability event—involving both stock and bond markets—would have serious repercussions and contagion effects for the global financial economy at large.

What's An EME?

Before proceeding in terms of further detail concerning the deteriorating condition of EMEs, some conceptual clarifications may be useful. First, what is an EME?

The International Monetary Fund (IMF) identifies EMEs as the 152 emerging and developing economies. The MSCI Stock Index, in contrast, identifies 51 economies, with 28 of the 51 comprising the very small in GDP terms 'frontier' economies and the remaining 23 as larger EMEs. Various other definitions list economies in between in terms of GDP, asset wealth, and other factors.

Economies like Brazil, Indonesia, India, Mexico, Turkey, Argentina, South Africa, and others certainly qualify as EMEs. But it is questionable whether China belongs in that category, as the second largest economy (and largest in PPP inflation adjusted terms). Whether economies like South Korea are EMEs is also questionable. Chile is considered an EME, and is 'larger' in a number of economic ways than Portugal, which is not regarded as an EME. Australia is not regarded as an EME, but exhibits many of the characteristics of one, with its dependence on commodity exports, its ties to China, and its recent currency swings like other EMEs. And where do Russia, Saudi Arabia, smaller Eastern Europe economies, and Singapore fit in the various classifications of EMEs?

The oil producers, like Nigeria, Venezuela, Iran, North African and other middle eastern economies, and again Mexico and Indonesia comprise a special subset of EMEs. A second tier of commodity producing EMEs usually includes economies with strategic materials or services, like Chile-Peru (copper), Singapore (finance). A third tier of EMEs are sometimes referred to as 'frontier' economies. The so-called BRICS (Brazil, Russia, India, China, South Africa) are often considered the more important economies within the EMEs, although states like Mexico, Turkey, Indonesia and a few other EMEs are important as well. Still other ways EMEs are classified at times are as 'commodity producing' EMEs, or as 'manufacturing' EMEs, although a number of larger EMEs share characteristics of both commodity and manufacturing producing.

However one may choose to classify the group, the essential point is that the above spectrum of EMEs constitutes a major bloc in the global economy. Along with China, their growth after 2009 and until 2012-13 kept the global economy from collapsing into depression, at least temporarily. That growth, both real and financial, enabled advanced economy (AE) banks, shadow banks, and investors to recapitalize and realize a new level of corporate profits and AE corporate stock price appreciation. But that was yesterday, which began to end in 2012-13, and at mid-year 2015 has begun to rapidly draw to a close. The temporary surge of the EMEs and China in the immediate post-2009 period has ended convincingly as of late 2015. That phase of development of the global economy and economic crisis is over.

A transition has begun. EMEs are under extreme economic pressure from falling demand for their commodities, oil and semi-finished goods, from accelerating capital flight as US and UK raise rates, from growing currency instability in the wake of Japan-Europe QEs and then China's currency devaluation, from slowing global trade and slowdown in exports, and from sliding stock markets and growing fragility in their financial markets in general. A wildcard adding additional potential economic stress and disruption is the growing political instability in various EMEs—in particular at the moment in Brazil, Malaysia, Turkey, South Africa, Venezuela, and soon elsewhere.

External Forces Destabilizing EMEs

The China Factor

The Chinese economic slowdown, accelerating in late 2015, produced a collapse in *China's demand for commodities and oil* that much of the EME growth of 2010-12 was based upon.[2] That declining commodities demand has had a double negative effect on EME economies: first, it has slowed commodities production and exports from the EMEs to China, and consequently EME economic growth; second, the decline in demand for EME commodities has caused a collapse of commodities prices, i.e. commodities deflation, which in turn has lowered revenues and profits in the EMEs and further dampened production.

With Chinese growth closer to 5% GDP (and some estimate as low as 4.1%) instead of its official 7%, China's demand for EME commodities has plunged. Formerly absorbing approximately half the global demand for copper, aluminum, and other metals, nearly half of iron and steel, and roughly a third of food commodities, and 12% of world oil—a decline in Chinese demand has had a major impact on EME exports and production.

China's slowdown is reflected in the Bloomberg Commodity Index (BCOM) of 22 key items which has fallen by late summer 2015 by 40% since 2012, to its lowest point since 1999. As commodities output has fallen, world commodity prices have deflated in the 25%-50% range, and even more for crude oil which has fallen from a $120/barrel high to $40 in a little over a year, from 2014-2015. The greatly lower volume plus the deflating price for commodities translates into a slowing of domestic production of the same and thus of EME growth rates in general.

The slowdown in EME exports is not just a function of China demand, of course. Stagnation in the European economy since 2010 and repeated recessions in Japan have also slowed demand for EME commodities and manufactured goods. And as the EMEs have begun to slow as a group after 2013, demand for commodities EMEs might mutually have sold to each other has slowed as well, adding further to the downward spiral of slowing commodities demand, commodities price deflation, lower EME exports, and ultimately slower EME growth.

According to the independent corporate research house, Capital Economics, in the year between June 2014 and June 2015, EME imports growth slowed by 13.2%. However, EME export growth is slowing even faster. In just the March through May 2015 period, exports growth slowed by 14.3%. In Latin America alone, after having peaked in 2011 at $550 billion, exports from those economies fell to $480 billion in 2014 and are projected to decline to as little as $400 billion in 2015. According to World Trade Organization data, after rising 20% from 2011 through 2013, developing countries (EMEs) combined exports peaked in the first quarter of 2014 and began slowing thereafter.[3] The EMEs most heavily impacted have been Brazil, South Africa, various South Asian economies since 2014 and EME oil producers as well, beginning the second half of 2014.

The AE Interest Rate Factor

Simultaneous with the decline in Chinese demand for commodities, a policy shift began around 2013 in the advanced economies (AEs)—the US and UK initially. The shift involved a *retreat from their 2009-2013 policies of QE and zero interest rates*. The US and UK QEs were wound down by late 2013. Both US and UK then announced intentions to start raising short term interest rates from their near-zero levels. Just the announcement of their intention to raise short term rates sent long term interest rates drifting upward.

Just the announcement of a *rise in US-UK interest rates* has had a negative impact on EMEs; the actual rise in short term rates, when it comes, will impact them even more. The process is roughly as follows: rising rates in the core AE economies (US-UK) attract money capital back to the AEs from the EMEs, after having flowed in massive volumes from the AEs to the EMEs in the previous 2010-13 period. The money capital (i.e. *capital flight)* flows back seeking the higher returns from rising rates in the US-UK, given the expectation of slowing growth in the EMEs from China commodities demand decline simultaneously. Thus the two forces—slowing commodities growth in EMEs and rising interest rates in the AEs—combine to have a doubly negative effect on EME capital available domestically for growth.

When the US Federal Reserve announced in 2013 that it was going to 'taper down' and then discontinue its quantitative easing, QE, program this was interpreted by financial markets in the EMEs that the excess liquidity created by the QEs would no longer flow into EME markets and economies as much as before. EME markets reacted, in what was called the 'taper tantrum', contracting sharply, and capital flight from EMEs back to the AEs—the US and UK in particular—rose. The Federal Reserve quickly backed off in July 2013, and EME markets temporarily stabilized.

Once QE3 was discontinued in late 2013 by the US, the focus of concern by EMEs shifted to the growing possibility of US and UK central banks' raising short term interest rates. The US Federal Reserve signaled its rate rise plan in January 2014 and the EME panic returned. Once again the US Federal Reserve backed off from an immediate hike in US rates.

But the prospects of eventual rising rates were already taking a toll on the EMEs. EME capital flight was already happening by 2014, in anticipation of the eventual rise in US-UK rates. EME capital flight then received another 'shot in the arm' in June 2014, as global oil prices began to collapse. By the second half of 2014 capital flight was in full swing. And in 2015, further shocks from China's growth slowdown, stock market implosion, and currency devaluation would accelerate it even faster.

Global Currency Wars

Japan began implementing its first massive QE money injection program in April 2013. That drove down Japan's currency, the Yen. Japan's QE action led to the currency wars ratcheting up just as the slowdown in global commodity markets was about to begin and as the US Federal Reserve signaled its intention to raise interest rates—both events increasing downward pressure on EME currencies. Japan's QE especially depressed its currency in relation to China's Yuan, which rose by 20% in relation to the Japanese yen.

To compete with Japan for global exports to China, which rose with Japan's de facto devaluation from QE, many EMEs lowered their currency values. Japan then accelerated its QE program in late 2014. This came just after global oil prices began to slide rapidly the previous summer. Japan's QE, the Fed's talking up US rates, and the oil deflation resulted in the beginning of the sharp decline in EME currencies in the second half of 2014 and the associated escalation of net capital outflows and capital flight from QEs.

Currency wars escalated further in early 2015, as the Eurozone introduced its version of an 18 month, $1.1 trillion dollar QE program starting March 2015. Its currency then declined, putting more pressure on already falling EME currency exchange rates to do the same. China initially allowed its currency to appreciate in relation to the Euro by around 20%, as it had in relation to the Yen. Those decisions cost China a significant loss of global export share and global trade.

However, following China's stock market crash that began June 12, 2015, China reversed its policy and responded to the QE-induced Yen and Euro currency devaluations. In August 2015 China entered the currency wars by devaluing the yuan by approximately 4%. That was to be only the start.

The QE devaluations by Japan and the Eurozone together escalated the global currency war, as slowing global trade volume has led more AEs to attempt to capture a larger share of the slowing global trade pie by devaluing indirectly by QE policies. The currency war, plus rising US interest rates, and then China's response together required EMES to increase downward pressure on their currencies in an attempt to adjust to the currency initiatives by the AEs. Failure to do so would mean a further decline in EME share of world exports and thus of economic growth at home. But doing so also meant falling exchange rates would add further impetus to already net capital outflows and capital flight, which it did. EMEs thus found themselves circa mid-2015 caught in a vise—of AE/China driven devaluations and rising US-UK rate prospects—and at a time when demand for their commodities globally were in freefall. The most seriously impacted EMEs, would be those whose commodity exports mix was composed, half or more, of crude oil.

Global Oil Deflation

In early 2014 the collapse of global crude oil prices began, yet another major development exacerbating capital outflow. Since collapsing oil prices are typically associated with a rising US dollar, they have a similar effect as rising US interest rates. Both drive up the US dollar and consequently lower EME currency values.

So what's behind the collapse in global crude oil prices in the first place? The start to that answer lies in the Saudi and US economies. As the global economy has continued to slow since 2013, not only has it provoked a currency war but also an energy production war. While the currency war was set in motion by Japan and Europe's 'dueling QEs', the energy war was precipitated by the Saudis and emirate OPEC partners as a response to the challenge of US shale oil and gas producers.

From 2008 to 2014 global oil production rose by 80% to 9 billion barrels a day. That supply increase was driven in large part by the boom in China and EME real economies that characterized the second phase, 2010-13, of the global economic crisis. China's 2009-10 fiscal stimulus, nearly 15% of its GDP, and its accelerating demand for EME commodities that accompanied it, plus the liquidity inflows to China and the EMEs from the advanced economies that enabled the financing of it all—explain much of the 80% global oil supply surge from 2008 to 2014. So when the demand origins of that supply surge began to weaken after 2013 in China and the EMEs, the natural result was an excess of supply and the beginning of oil price decline around mid-2014.

However weakening oil demand is only part of the picture. Simultaneous with the demand decline by 2014 was an augmentation of supply. North American oil production expanded sharply in 2014—as a consequence of the shale gas/oil boom by then in full swing in the US as well as Canadian tar sands production growth. That further weakened oil prices significantly. So did Libya's quadrupling of its oil output in 2014. And all that was further exacerbated by many independent EME oil producers, whose oil production was more or less nationalized, expanding their output despite the falling price, in order to maintain foreign currency reserves and revenues desperately needed by their governments to keep their budget deficits manageable.[4] Toward the end of 2014, crude oil prices had fallen from $115 a barrel to $70 a barrel.[5]

In retrospect, it appears the Saudis in 2014 tried to eliminate their new shale oil competitors by increasing their oil output, convinced that if the price per barrel of oil could be reduced to $80, that would be uneconomical for US shale producers, forcing them to leave the market. This would return control to global market oil prices to the Saudis and their friends. But this view proved to be dramatically wrong. US shale producers, whose production is based on new lower cost fracking technologies, were able to reduce costs and remain profitable even at $40 a barrel, according to a Citigroup analysis at the time, by shutting unprofitable wells and expanding output in those which were profitable; their cost cutting made it even more profitable to continue producing at previous output levels. US 2014 oil production rose to its highest level in 30 years. And by November 2014 the global price of crude had fallen by 40%.

It was about to fall much further. Global oil deflation crossed a threshold of sorts with the November 28, 2014 OPEC meeting in Vienna, Austria, at which Saudi Arabia drove a decision by OPEC not to reduce production of crude oil, but to maintain OPEC production at 30 million barrels a day, and thus let the price of oil to continue to drop. Many of OPEC's non Saudi-Emirate members were clamoring for a cut in production to raise the price of oil. So too were many of the non-OPEC players, like Russia. But the Saudis resisted. The question immediately arises, why would OPEC and the Saudis so decide? Purely business logic would argue OPEC should have voted to cut oil production to support the global price of oil. But they didn't.

Possible explanations include: First, with $750 billion in foreign currency reserves, Saudis could hold out earning oil revenues at lower levels for some time. Smaller producers like Venezuela, Nigeria and others could not. Second, the stakes were high for the Saudis. They were quickly losing control of global oil prices to the new US driven technology and output surge. OPEC and the Saudis knew that global shale production of oil and gas posed a relatively near term existential threat to their dominance. But there was even more to the story. Saudi Arabia and its neocon friends in the USA were targeting both Iran and Russia with their new policy of driving down the price of oil. The impact of oil deflation was already severely affecting the Russian and Iranian economies. The Saudi policy of promoting global oil price deflation found much favor with certain political interests in the USA, who wanted at the time to generate a deeper disruption of Russian and Iranian economies to forward their global political objectives.

An immediate impact of the Saudi November 28, 2014 decision was a further fall in global oil prices. Thereafter, the currencies of the other EME oil producers began to decline faster than before. EME and Euro stock markets also contracted. Saudi currency and stock markets were not affected, since they pegged their currency to the US dollar. Further currency decline would also generate more capital flight from the EMEs. To recall, it was the second half of 2014 through the first quarter of 2015 when EME capital flight began to accelerate rapidly, amounting to nearly $1 trillion in outflows over the nine month period. That magnitude of capital outflow, thereafter unavailable for domestic investment in the EMEs, contributed to slowing domestic EME investment and growth that also began to contract in 2014.

In the first quarter of 2015 the US economy's GDP came to another standstill, which reduced global oil demand further and deflated global oil prices still more. The Eurozone also stalled, prompting the introduction of its QE program. The dollar and Euro weakened, and currencies of many EMEs followed, especially the oil commodity producers like Venezuela, Nigeria, Russia and others. In the spring of 2015 the US Congress then began debating lifting the ban on US oil and gas exports, threatening a further surge of gas and oil supply on global markets. That prospect suggested further downward pressure on oil prices.

Nine months of consecutive negative data out of China by spring 2015 suggested strongly that the Chinese economy was slowing faster than the repeated assurances given by China officials that it would remain at a 7% GDP growth level. Then in mid-June the Chinese stock markets began to implode. That too helped deflate global oil prices. Global oil futures, a financial asset, are influenced by—and influence in turn—other financial assets. The connection between oil futures as a financial asset and equity assets is the global professional investors who speculate in both. When one asset class declines too rapidly it has a negative impact often on other asset classes, as investors retreat from markets in general and wait to see what happens.

In August 2015 oil prices recovered some of their $75 a barrel losses of the preceding year, rising from $38 a barrel lows back to the mid $50s on rumors that the Saudis and friends might agree to some kind of production cut. That sent oil prices scaling upward overnight by 20% and more. They retreated when the rumors proved incorrect. That kind of 20% price swing overnight shows how little oil prices are the result of supply and demand forces, and the extent to which they are determined by professional financial speculators driving the oil commodity futures market. Then August data for China and EMEs showed their real economies were slowing even faster than official reports. And Iran announced it would pump more oil at whatever price. Oil prices fell again. And so did EME currencies, stock markets, and the outflow of capital back to AEs.

What the past eighteen months clearly reveals is that the global oil deflation, already emerging due to a slowing global economy by 2014, accelerated as a result of the competition between US shale oil and gas producers and Saudi-Emirate producers attempting to re-assert their effective monopoly control over the price of world oil. As the Saudis and the North American shale gas producers battle it out over who would dominate the global oil industry, the EMEs continue to pay the greater price.

Both directly and indirectly, global oil deflation has functioned as an accelerator to the growing economic instabilities in the EMEs since 2014. Declining currencies, commodities exports and prices, along with capital flight and currency wars, etc.— are all intensified by the global oil deflation.

Who 'Broke' the EME Growth Model?

Like the slowing China commodities demand, AE interest rates, and global currency wars, the global bust in oil prices reflects forces largely out of the EMEs' control. These are external developments imposed on them over which they have little influence. How they respond to these developments of course is a matter of some choice. However, as the following discussion of 'internal forces' (i.e. EME responses) shows, the range of choices available is not all that good. For example, while an EME might choose to stem capital flight by raising its own domestic interest rates, that only slows its real economy even further. Or if the EME responds by trying to expand its exports by reducing their cost of production, that might mean less consumer spending and less domestic growth that in turn encourages further capital flight. Reducing government spending to offset rising import goods inflation has the same effect. And so on.

What all this suggests is that much of the causation for the EMEs' growing economic problems originates in policies in the AEs and China— just as previously, from 2010-2013, much of the expansion of the EMEs also emanated from those same 'external' sources. It's not that the 'model' of growth used by EMEs is 'broken', a favorite theme recently in the US-European business press.[6] It is that the AEs 'exported' their growth to the EMEs during 2010-2013 through their monetary policy, and now are 're-importing' that growth back by reversing that monetary policy. The current economic weakness of the EMEs might therefore be labeled: 'Made in the AEs'.

A recent article by Kynge and Wheatley concludes: "The dynamic economic models that allowed developing nations to haul the world back to growth after the 2008-09 financial crisis are breaking down—and threatening to drag the world back towards recession".[7] But was the model created by the EMEs, or imposed on them by the AEs back in 2010? And is that model now being 'broken' as a result of EME decisions made 2010-2013, or is in the process of breakdown due to decisions once again being made in the AEs and, to an extent, by the Saudis?

The interesting and even more fundamental question is why did the AEs focus on the EMEs as their source of initial recovery from the 2008-09 crash instead of their own economies? And why now, in 2014-2015, have AE policymakers decided to reverse that policy? The AEs, in particular the US and UK, made the conscious policy decision in 2009 to generate recovery first by bailing out their banks and financial institutions by means of massive liquidity injections. That injection, and the financial asset investment and speculation that produced financial profits restored banks' balance sheets. AE policy makers also decided early to accelerate recovery for non-financial multinational corporations by incentives to expand investment and returns in emerging markets, including China, because the returns there promised to be quicker and larger compared to investment in their own AEs. This dual strategy worked for both finance capital and non-finance multinational corporations, both of which recovered quickly and realized record profits. But it left the AEs own economies stagnating for the next five years, as other forms of real investment languished. The AE policy shift that began in 2013 thus in effect represents a refocus on their own economies, by bringing money capital back to try to stimulate domestic investment as they (US and UK) discontinue QEs and raise interest rates, in a desperate attempt to get AE GDP rates back up. But that means at the expense of the EMEs in this phase of the post-2008 crash and continuing slowing global economy.

The preceding four major 'external' forces that are now having an increasing negative effect on the EMEs are the result of conscious policy decisions made by the AEs, China, and in the case of the oil deflation, by Saudi Arabia and its petro allies. Of course, deeper conditions have forced all three to make these policy decisions: the AEs have not been able to get their economies back on a reasonable growth path since 2010; China has not been able to make the transition to private investment and consumption driven growth; and the Saudis and friends have decided to try to drive the US shale oil producers out of business to protect their long run strategic control of oil production and oil prices. Nevertheless, the consequences for the EMEs of these conditions and policy shifts in the AEs, China, and the Saudi-Emirate economies have been serious. And the consequences have been growing worse by the day. If the next depression is said to be 'made in the emerging markets', it will have been the AE-Chinese-Saudi decisions that ultimately made it.

Internal Forces Causing EME Instability

Notwithstanding who is ultimately responsible for the rapid deterioration of EMEs today, it is important to note that the various external causes of that deterioration have set in motion additional internal forces that further exacerbate the EME decline and that, in part, are also the consequence of policy choices made by the EMEs themselves.

In attempting to confront the economic dislocations caused by the external forces, EMEs have had to choose between a number of highly unattractive trade-offs: raising domestic interest rates to slow capital flight; spending their minimal foreign currency reserves to keep their currency from falling; cutting government spending to try to reduce inflation from rising imports; lowering their currency exchange rate in order to compete on exports with AE countries doing the same; and so on. All these choices, however, result in short term and temporary solutions to the external caused forces. The choices almost always lead to a further deterioration of EMEs' real economy and deepening financial instability.

EME Capital Flight
Capital outflow has multiple negative effects on an economy. First, it means less money available for real investment that would otherwise boost the country's GDP, create jobs, and produce incomes for workers for consumption. Capital flight also discourages foreign investors from sending their money capital 'in' as well. So as capital flows out, often capital inflow simultaneously slows or declines. Both produce a double negative effect on money capital available for domestic investment in the EME. More outflow plus slowing inflow also means less purchases of EME stock by investors as they take their money and run. Falling equity values discourage money in-flow still further. A downward spiral thus ensues between capital flight, less investment, a slowing economy, and slowing or declining stock prices.

The scope and magnitude of the capital flight is revealed by recent trends in the EMEs. Net capital inflows for the EMEs were mostly positive prior to the 2008-09 crash, starting at $200 billion in 2002 and rising thereafter. During the 2008-09 crisis, however, there were EME outflows of $545 billion. Starting in late 2009, as the EMEs boomed and benefited from the redirection of the massive liquidity injections by the AE central banks and the concurrent China commodity demand surge, net capital inflows to the EMEs rose rapidly once again. Roughly $2.2 trillion in capital flowed into the EMEs from June 2009 to June 2014.

But that inflow all began to reverse, slowly at first but then at a faster rate, beginning with the 'taper tantrum' of 2013 when the Federal Reserve signaled its intention to raise interest rates. EME capital outflow began, but it was temporary, as the Federal Reserve soon backed off in response to the EMEs' 'tantrum'. Capital flight resumed again in January 2014 when the Federal Reserve signaled once more its intent to raise US rates. EMEs panicked but net inflows returned as the Fed back-pedaled a second time. But it was to be the last time for the Fed to do so.

By mid-2014, EME net outflows and capital flight resumed with a vengeance, as Chinese growth slowed faster, oil deflation set in, QE currency wars intensified, US interest long term rates starting drifting upward in expectation of Fed policy, and EME real economies and currencies began to slow rapidly. The corner had been turned so far as EME capital outflow was concerned after mid-year 2014.

For example, from July 2014 through March 2015, the 19 largest EMEs experienced net capital flight of no less than $992 billion, or almost $1 trillion in just nine months. And that was only the largest 19. The $992 billion, the most recent available data, represents an outflow of more than twice that occurring during a similar nine month period from July 2008 through March 2009, when a $545 billion net outflow occurred. So the capital flight crisis for the EMEs is twice as serious as during the 2008-09 crash. Not only does the $992 billion represent only the 19 largest EMEs, but the nearly $1 trillion pre-dates the China stock market collapse that began in June 2015 and China's shift to a devaluation of its currency policy the following August. Therefore, the third and fourth quarters of 2015 will likely show that EME capital flight will exceed the preceding nine months' $992 billion. A trillion more in capital flight could easily occur in just the second half of 2015.[8] That will mean the five years of accumulated $2.2 trillion inflow will be reversed in just 18 months. That magnitude and rate of capital flight and outflow suggests, in and by itself, a massive economic contraction may be soon forthcoming in the EMEs in 2016 and beyond.

EME Currency Collapse

Currency decline is directly associated with capital flight. The greater the rate of flight, the greater the rate of decline, or collapse. That's because capital flight requires investors in the country to convert the country's currency into the currency of another country to which they intend to send the money capital. That involves selling the EME's currency, which increases its supply and therefore lowers the price of that currency, i.e. its exchange rate. And when many investors are selling an EME currency, it also means a drop in demand for the currency that further depresses its price.

There have been three phases of EME currency decline since 2013. The first during the 2013 'taper tantrum'. The second commenced mid-2014 with the collapse of global oil prices and the growing awareness China's was slowing. The third phase began the summer of 2015, as China's stock markets collapsed and it subsequently devalued its currency, the yuan. The stock market crash in China quickly set off a wave of similar stock contractions throughout the EMEs. Investors sought to pull their money out and send it to the AEs, as both a haven and in anticipation of better returns. More EME money capital was converted to dollars, pounds, euros and yen, sending those currencies' values higher (and thus pushing EME currencies still lower).

As an indication of the magnitude of the impact of capital flight and currency conversion on EME currencies, the J.P. Morgan EME Currency Index fell by 30% from its peak in 2011 by July 2015, virtually all of that in the past year, 2014-2015. An equivalent index for Latin America compiled by Bloomberg and J.P. Morgan revealed a more than 40% decline in currency values for that region's EMEs during the same period.

In just the first eight months of 2015, January-August, some of the largest EME currencies have fallen by more than 20%, including those of Brazil, South Africa, Turkey, Columbia, Malaysia, while others like South Africa, Mexico, Thailand, Indonesia and others dropped by more than 10%.

In yet another vicious cycle, the collapse of currency exchange rates for EMEs causes an even greater momentum in capital flight. No investors, foreign or domestic, want to hold currencies that are falling rapidly in value and expected to decline further. They take their losses, take their money capital out of the country, convert to currencies that are rising (US dollar, UK pound, and even the Euro or yen) and speculate that price appreciation will provide handsome capital gains in the new currencies. Currency decline thus has the added negative effect of provoking a vicious cycle of capital flight-currency decline-capital flight.

One would think that declining currency values would stimulate export sales. But only in a static world. In a dynamic world of ever-changing forces and economic indicators, declining currencies for different EMEs that are occurring in tandem mean a race to the bottom for all. No country gets a competitive export advantage by currency devaluation for long, before it is 'leap frogged' by another doing the same, negating that advantage.

In addition, the advantages to economic growth from expanding exports might also be easily offset by declining real investment due to accelerating capital flight, rising domestic interest rates implemented by governments in desperate efforts to try to stem the capital outflow, falling stock market prices associated with the net capital outflows, and slowing domestic consumption for various reasons. The latter developments typically overwhelm the very temporary relative advantages to exports gained from declining currency exchange rates—as has happened, and continues to happen, in the case of the EMEs post-2013.

Domestic Inflation

Currency decline has the added negative effect of directly impacting domestic consumption by contributing to import inflation. When a currency declines, the cost of imported goods goes up. And if imports make up a significant proportion of the EMEs' total goods consumed, then EME domestic inflation rises. Many EMEs in fact import heavily from the AEs, for both consumer goods and semi-finished goods that they then re-manufacture for consumption or re-export for sale. If consumer inflation is significant, it means less real consumption and therefore slower EME growth; and if producer goods import inflation is significant, it means rising costs of production, less production and again, less EME growth.

Capital flight due to currency decline also contributes to inflation, albeit in a manner different from import inflation due to currency decline. Import inflation affects consumption, whereas capital flight works through investment. More capital outflow translates into less investment, which means less productivity gains, higher production costs and cost inflation. In short, currency decline, capital flight, and EME inflation all exacerbate each other, and combine to have significant negative effects on EME real growth. It starts with currency decline, which accelerates capital flight and reduces investment and also contributes to inflation which slows real consumption as well.

The decline in China that reduced global commodities demand, the deflation in commodities that followed, the subsequent currency decline and capital flight, and the eventual imports-goods inflation together reduced consumption, real investment and economic growth. These elements all began to converge in the EMEs by mid-2014. After mid-2014 additional developments exacerbated these negative trends further—including the global oil deflation, growing prospects of US interest rate increases, intensifying currency wars, and the unwinding of Chinese and EME stock markets.

The multiple challenges faced by EMEs from these developments, intensified and expanded in the second half of 2014 and after, forcing the EMEs into a general no-win scenario. They have responded variously. Brazil, South Africa and a few other EMEs have raised their domestic interest rates to slow capital flight and attract foreign capital to continue to invest, although that choice has slowed their domestic economies more. Another option, using their foreign currency reserves on hand, accumulated during the 2010-2013 boom, to now buy their currencies in open markets to offset their decline, works only to the extent they accumulated foreign reserves during the 2010-13 period. Many EMEs did not. And those who had accumulated have been depleting them fast. Similarly unpromising, they can try to reduce their currency's value by various means, in order to compete for the shrinking pie of global exports. That means participating in the intensifying global currency war 'race to the bottom', in a fight they cannot win against the likes of China, US, Japan and others with massive reserves war chests. What the oil producing EMEs have done in response to the growing contradictions with which they are confronted is to just lower the price of their crude in order to keep generating a flow of income upon which their government and economy is dependent. Others face the prospect of simply trying to borrow from AE banks, at ever higher and more undesirable terms and rates, in order to refinance their growing real debt.

While the EMEs enjoyed a robust recovery from 2010 to 2013, thereby avoiding the stagnation, slow growth, and recessions experienced by the AEs during the period, now the roles after 2013 were being reversed. AE policies began creating massive money capital outflows from the EMEs, slowing their growth sharply, causing financial instability, and leaving EMEs with a set of choices in response that promised more of the same. The case example of Brazil that follows reflects many of the *'Hobson's choices'* among which the EMEs have been forced to choose, as well as the negative consequences they pose for EME economic growth and financial instability.

Brazil: Canary in the EME Coal Mine?

No country reflects the condition and fate of EMEs better than Brazil. It's a major exporter of both commodity and manufactured goods. It's also recently become a player in the oil production ranks of EMEs. Its biggest trading partner is China, to which it sells commodities of all types—soybeans, iron ore, beef, oil and more. Its exports to China grew fivefold from 2002 to 2014. It is part of the five nation 'BRICS' group with significant south-south trading with South Africa, India, Russia, as well as China. It also trades in significant volume with Europe, as well as the US. It is an agricultural powerhouse, a resource and commodity producer of major global weight, and it receives large sums of money capital inflows from AEs.

In 2010, as the EMEs boomed, Brazil's growth in GDP terms expanded at a 7.6% annual rate. It had a trade surplus of exports over imports of $20 billion. China may have been the source of much of Brazil's demand, but US and EU central banks' massive liquidity injections financed the investment and expansion of production that made possible Brazil's increased output that it sold to China and other economies. It was China demand but US credit and Brazil debt-financed expansion as well—as is the case of virtually all the major EMEs. That then began to shift around 2013-14, as both Chinese demand began to slow and US-UK money inflows declined and began to reverse. By 2014 Brazil's GDP had already declined to a mere 0.1%, compared to the average of 4% for the preceding four years.

In 2015 Brazil entered a recession, with GDP falling -0.7% in the first quarter and -1.9% in the second. The second half of 2015 will undoubtedly prove much worse, resulting in what the Brazilian press is already calling 'the worst recession since the Great Depression of the 1930s'.

Capital flight has been continuing through the first seven months of 2015, averaging $5-$6 billion a month in outflow from the country. In the second half of 2014 it was even higher. The slowing of the capital outflow has been the result of Brazil sharply raising its domestic interest rates—one of the few EMEs so far having taken that drastic action—in order to attract capital or prevent its fleeing. Brazilian domestic interest rates have risen to 14.25%, among the highest of the EMEs. That choice to give priority to attracting foreign investment has come at a major price, however, thrusting Brazil's economy quickly into a deep recession. The choice did not stop the capital outflow, just slowed it. But it did bring Brazil's economy to a virtual halt. The outcome is a clear warning to EMEs that solutions that target soliciting foreign money capital are likely to prove disastrous. The forces pulling money capital out of the EMEs are just too large in the current situation. The liquidity is going to flow back to the AEs and there's no stopping it. Raising rates, as Brazil has, will only deliver a solution that's worse than the problem.

Nor did that choice to raise rates to try to slow capital outflow stop the decline in Brazil's currency, the Real, which has fallen 37% in the past year. A currency decline of that dimension should, in theory, stimulate a country's exports. But it hasn't, for the various reasons previously noted: in current conditions a currency decline's positive effects on export growth is more than offset by other negative effects associated with currency volatility and capital flight.

What the Real's freefall of 37% has done, however, is to sharply raise import goods inflation and the general inflation rate. Brazil's inflation remained more or less steady in the 6%-6.5% range for much of 2013 and even fell to 5.9% in January 2015, but it has accelerated in 2015 to 9.6% at last estimate.

With nearly 10% inflation thus far in 2015 and with unemployment almost doubling, from a January 4.4% to 8.3% at latest estimate for July, Brazil has become mired in a swamp of stagflation—i.e. rising unemployment and rising inflation. Brazil's central bank estimated in September 2015 that the country's economy would shrink -2.7% for the year, the deepest decline in 25 years. With more than 500,000 workers laid off in just the first half of 2015, it is not surprising that social and political unrest has been rising fast in Brazil.[9]

The near future may be even more unstable. Like many EMEs, Brazil during the boom period borrowed the liquidity offered by the AEs bankers and investors (made available by AE central banks to their bankers at virtually zero interest) to finance the expansion. That's both government and private sector borrowing and thus debt. Brazil's government debt as a percent of GDP surged in just 18 months from 53% to 63%. The deteriorating government debt situation resulted in Standard & Poor's lowering Brazil government debt to 'junk' status.

More important, private sector debt is now 70% of GDP, up from 30% in 2003. Much of that debt is 'junk bond' or 'high yield' debt borrowed at high interest rates and dollar denominated—i.e. borrowed from US investors and their shadow and commercial banks and therefore payable back in dollars—to be obtained from export sales to US customers, which are slowing. An idea of the poor quality of this debt is indicated by the fact that monthly interest payments for Brazilian private sector companies is already estimated to absorb 31% of their income.

With falling income from exports, with money capital fleeing the country and becoming inaccessible, and with ever higher interest necessary to refinance the debt when it comes due—Brazil's private sector is extremely 'financially fragile'.[10] How fragile may soon be determined. Reportedly Brazil's nonfinancial corporations have $50 billion in bonds that need to be refinanced just next year, 2016. And with export and income declining, foreign capital increasingly unavailable, and interest rates as 14.25%, one wonders how Brazil will get that $50 billion refinanced. If the private sector cannot roll over those debts successfully, then far worse is yet to come in 2016 as companies default on their private sector debt.

Brazil's monetary policy response has been to raise interest rates, which has slowed its economy sharply. Brazil's fiscal policy response has been no less counter-productive than its monetary policy. Its fiscal response has been to cut government spending and budgets by $25 billion—i.e. to institute an austerity policy, which again will only slow its real economy even further.

The lessons of Brazil are the lessons of the EMEs in general, as they face a deepening crisis, a crisis that originated not in the EMEs but first in the AEs and then in China. But policies which attempt to stop the capital flight train that has already left the station and won't be coming back will fail. So too will competing for exports in a race to the bottom with the AEs. Japan and Europe are intent on driving down their currencies in order to obtain a slightly higher share of the shrinking global trade pie. The EMEs do not have the currency reserves or other resources to outlast them in a tit-for-tat currency war. Instead of trying to rely on somehow reversing AE money capital flows or on exports to AE markets as the way to recovery and growth, EMEs will have to try to find a way to mutually expand their economic relationships and forge new institutions among and between themselves as a 'new model' of EME growth. They did not 'break the old EME model'; it was broken for them. And they cannot restore it since the AEs have decided to abandon it.

EME Financial Fragility & Instability

Instability in financial asset markets matters. It is not just a consequence of conditions and events in the real, non-financial sector of the economy. Anyone who doubts that should recall that it was the collapse of shadow banks, derivatives, and housing finance practices that not only precipitated the crash of 2008-09, but also played a big role in causing the more rapid and deeper real economy contraction that followed. Financial asset markets have also played a major role in the stop-go, sub-normal recovery of the AEs since 2009. Financial assets and markets will play no less a role in the next crash and greater contraction that is forthcoming.

Other examples prior to 2008-09 provide further evidence of the importance of financial forces in real economic contractions. The dot.com tech bust of 2001 and the recession that followed were the result of financial asset speculation. The 1997-98 'Asian Meltdown' crisis was fundamentally about currency speculation. Japan's crash in 1990-91, prior recessions in the US in 1990, the US stock market crash of 1987, junk bonds and housing crises in the 1980s, the northern Europe banking crisis of the early 1990s—all had a major element of financial instability associated with them. So finance matters.

Declining equity markets are a signal of problems in the real economy, of course. They are also a source that can exacerbate those problems. For example, China's stock bubble implosion of 2015 is contributing to the further slowing of real investment in China and to the major capital flight now exiting that economy. The capital flight will in turn cause more instability in global currency markets and accelerate financial asset prices in property and other asset markets in the UK, US, Australia and so forth. The China equity market collapse has had, and will continue to have, depressing effects on stock markets elsewhere in the world. The major stock index for emerging markets, the MSCI Index, has declined more than 30% from its highs. Stock markets of major economies like Brazil, Indonesia, and others have all fallen by 20% and more in just the first seven months of 2015. Financial asset deflation is occurring not only in oil commodity futures, but in global equity prices as well.

Falling stock values also mean that corporations may be denied an important source of income—i.e. equity finance—with which to make payments on corporate debt. One of the major characteristics throughout the EMEs is that many of EME corporations have borrowed heavily during the boom and now must continue to make payments on what is now to a large extent 'junk' or high yield debt, and high yield debt also borrowed in dollars, from their various sources of income. But raising money capital by means of stock issuing or stock selling is extremely difficult when stock prices are plummeting.

As its currency exchange rate falls for an EME, it means whatever income a company has available now 'pays less' of the debt—effectively, the company's real debt has risen. Rising real debt is therefore an indicator of growing financial fragility as well—there is declining income with which to pay the debt. Falling currency may also make it more difficult for a company to refinance its debt, or force it to do so at an even more expense interest rates. That too reflects growing financial fragility.

Still another financial market is the oil futures market, especially for those EMEs who are dependent on oil production and sales. Oil is not just a product. It is a financial asset as well. And when the price of that financial asset collapses, the income of the oil producer EME also collapses in many cases. Expectations of future oil prices determine current oil prices, regardless of actual supply and demand in the present. So the more prices fall the more professional speculators may drive the deflation further. Creating a global oil commodities trading market has had the result of introducing more financial instability into the global market for oil. Income from oil production may thus be impacted significantly and negatively by financial asset price movements.

Finally, the EMEs are clearly highly unstable with regard to bond markets—both sovereign or government bonds as well as corporate bonds. And in many EMEs much of the corporate debt (and some government debt as in Africa) is denominated in dollars and therefore must be repaid in dollars. As the aforementioned McKinsey Consultant study shows, one half of all the increase in global debt since 2007 has occurred in EMEs and the lion's share of that has been in private corporate debt. From 2010 to mid-2015 more than $2 trillion in EME bonds have been issued in dollars, with another $4 trillion plus issued in local EME currencies. Asian Bond debt is 113% of Asian economies' combined GDP, a record high, according to the J.P. Morgan EMBI+ bond index. As more EMEs attempt to address their crisis by raising domestic interest rates, as Brazil and now South Africa have done, that will drive bond prices down dramatically. A general bond price collapse will make stock market declines pale in comparison as to the consequences for global economic stability. And if corporations in the EMEs can't refinance their mountain of debt at rates they can pay given their declining sources of income, then a wave of corporate defaults will rock the EME and global economy.

As the economic problems for the EMEs multiply in coming months, the financial market problems will become more serious, not just for EMEs but for AE banks and investors in the wake of their debt defaults. And when financial markets 'crack', they typically lead to a new level of economic crisis in the real economy in turn. Most recently, Oxford Economics research has predicted the EMEs aggregate GDP growth rate will fall to its lowest level since the 2008-09 crisis. Other sources warn the situation is beginning to look more like 1997, when a major financial crisis involving EME currencies erupted. It is quite possible 2016 may witness that kind of real and financial sector negative interaction once again.

Endnotes

1   Based on the decline of the 'MSCI Stock Index', the major index for EME stocks, from 2011 to mid-2015.

2   For an assessment of China's real economy's slowdown and growing financial instability, see chapter 6.

3   WTO Press Release 722, September 23, 2014

4   Russia, Venezuela, Nigeria, Iran, Angola, and others all depend on oil revenues for more than half of their annual budgets and for critical imports of food and consumer goods.

5   Textbook supply and demand theory explaining how prices are determined was thus turned on its head. Declining demand and falling oil prices did not result in a corresponding decrease in supply and a return of prices to equilibrium.

6   See for example the extended article by James Kynge and Jonathan Wheatley, in the global British business periodical, *Financial Times*, 'Fixing a Broken Model', September 1, 2015, p. 8

7   Kynge and Wheatley, *Financial Times,* September 1, 2015, p. 8.

8   See J. Kynge and J. Wheatley, 'The Great Unraveling', *Financial Times*, April 2, 2015, p. 5, and J. Kynge and Roger Blitz, 'Emerging Markets Rocked by $1tn Capital Flight', *Financial Times*, August 19, 2015 p. 1.

9   Social unrest is similarly rising in other EMEs with conditions deteriorating similarly to Brazil's—in particular Malaysia, Turkey, Nigeria and Indonesia.

10   As the term 'financial fragility' is used here, it refers to a condition where the income flow of a company is increasingly insufficient to cover interest and principal payments on the debt. The debt may also rise and contribute to fragility, and the terms and conditions of its payment (rates, term, etc.) may be restrictive making payment on the debt difficult, apart from the level of debt and flow of income.

4

JAPAN'S PERPETUAL RECESSION

'Perpetual Recession' is the phrase that perhaps best characterizes Japan for the past two decades. The general conditions afflicting the global economy in the 21st century were experienced first by Japan well before the end of the 20th. So were the solutions, monetary and fiscal, that have failed to generate a sustained global recovery in the 21st, employed as well without success in Japan earlier. The consequence has been a more or less perpetual recession now for more than two decades. Japan's economy has been in and out of recession seven times since 1993, with an eighth now emerging in 2015. In between recessions, Japan's economy has been characterized by slow growth, stagnation, and extended periods of deflation.

The three recessions that occurred during the decade 1993-2002 were interrupted by recoveries that averaged barely 1% GDP growth during the decade. After growing robustly throughout the 1980s without experiencing any recession whatsoever, a major financial bubble crashed in the early 1990s. A 'stop-go' recovery followed that was more 'stop' than 'go'. Japan's response to the financial crash of the early 1990s was to bail out the banks with liquidity injections by the central bank, the Bank of Japan (BoJ). For the rest of the non-financial economy, the response was austerity fiscal policies to compensate for the budget deficits caused by the repeated recessions and subsequent short and shallow recoveries.[1]

A fourth recession in Japan followed the global tech bubble bust and recession of 2001. In the 2002-2008 recovery period that followed, while the rest of the global economy recovered Japan was barely able to generate an average 0.5% annual GDP growth. Thereafter, from 2008 on, Japan experienced no fewer than four additional recessions: a four quarter contraction 2008-09, another three quarter decline in 2011, followed by another shallower three quarter in 2012, and then a brief, but deeper, two quarter contraction mid-year 2014. Most recently, in the second quarter 2015 Japan's GDP has retreated once again. That will make it Japan's fifth recession in seven years since 2008 and its eighth in a little more than two decades.

Japan represents what this writer has called an 'epic' recession. Epic recessions are defined by short, shallow contractions followed by brief and unsustainable recoveries—i.e. a 'stop-go' scenario that may last for years. The short, shallow recoveries help to ensure that repeated contractions will follow—like continuing shock waves after the major earthquake, the initial financial crash. Each subsequent shock in turn makes the economy more fragile and unstable. Epic recessions are also precipitated by financial bubbles and crashes—not policy or demand and supply 'shocks' associated with 'normal' recessions. Japan's economy clearly belongs in the former category. Before Japan descended into a decades-long period of weak, brief recoveries and repeated recessions, Japan experienced a major financial bubble in 1985-1990 that crashed immediately thereafter, followed by a series of rolling banking crises throughout the decade. So to understand Japan's economy today and its decades-long stagnation, eight recessions, and chronic lack of real investment and goods deflation, it is necessary to go back to the origins of the financial crisis in the 1980s.

Japan's 'Made in the USA' Bubble and Crash

On the eve of Japan's 1990-1991 financial crash, in 1989 the value of real estate in Japan was $24 trillion—i.e. four times that of the value of real estate in the entire US although Japan had less than half the US population and only 60% of US GDP. Japan real estate values accounted for 50% of all the value of land in the world (while representing only 3% of total area)

Nor was Japan's financial bubble limited to real estate. Japan's Nikkei 225 stock market in 1989 had a price-earnings ratio of 80, compared to 15 in the US. Its shares were priced at 60 times earnings. The total valuation on the Tokyo Exchange was 590 trillion Yen and it accounted for

42% of the value of all global stock markets combined. Eight of the world's ten most valuable corporations were in Japan in 1989 (only two are in the top 100 today). Japan's financial bubble was a classic real estate bubble combined with a stock market bubble—a double bubble waiting for the first opportunity to implode.

So how did Japan become so financially fragile? It had been known prior to the bubble as 'Japan Inc.', a new dynamo of efficient manufacturing and exporting of quality and highly competitive real goods throughout the 1970s and into the 1980s. Shifting course, Japan embarked on a massive financial asset buying spree in the latter half of the decade. But why did it begin shifting at that time from its prior successful model of competing for world exports in manufactured goods? Why did it shift from a manufacturing and exports driven growth model to a financial investment and financial speculation model?[2]

A key turning point occurred in 1985. It was then that the US economic policymakers—employing a 'carrot and stick' approach— began to force Japan in earnest to shift from its manufacturing-exports economic model,[3] based on highly competitive manufacturing and exports to begin focusing more on financial markets and financial investing.[4]

Starting around 1985, the US insisted that Japan further stimulate its domestic economy, which was already growing robustly, or that further restrictions on Japan imports to the US would be imposed. The idea was to get Japan to generate excess inflation that would make its exports in turn less competitive with US companies. The 'carrot' was the US offer to open the US market to Japanese investors to buy US real estate and other assets. But in return, the US demanded that Japan further stimulate its already robust economy with a view to generating an inflation that would make its exports less competitive. The new arrangements on trade and financial flows between the US and Japan were worked out in what was called the 'Plaza Accords' of 1985. As part of the Plaza agreement, Japan agreed to increase its domestic spending, raise inflation, and allow its currency, the Yen, to appreciate in value, thus making its exports more expensive in the US

For the decade 1985-95 the US dollar declined in value relative to the Yen, which doubled in value by the early 1990s. This was called the 'Endaka', or high yen crisis in Japan. Japan's financial bubble involved not only real estate and stocks but also currency asset appreciation.

Since Japan's 1980s economic growth was based on production for exports, the higher yen caused a collapse of exports, manufacturing, and Japanese economic growth. Japan's growth rate quickly slowed, from more than 5% in 1985 to less than 3% in 1986. In response, Japan's central bank began pumping even more money into the economy to lower interest rates to offset the economic slide. Interest rates fell to a postwar low by 1987. The lower rates stimulated business and investor borrowing and debt, but much of it flowed either into financial investing in property, stocks, currency speculation, and other financial asset markets, or to finance Japanese investments offshore. By 1987, Japan's stock markets were valued more than those of the US. At the same time, Japanese investing offshore elsewhere in Asia rose six-fold from 1985 to 1989.

When the US stock market crashed in October 1987 as a consequence of excess financial speculation in junk bonds and real estate, the US pressured Japan to stimulate its economy even further, which Japan gladly did. After all, the 1985-87 shift to financial assets was producing significant financial capital gains. As a result of another global meeting engineered by the US in 1987 in France, leading to agreements called the 'Louvre' Accords, Japan lowered its interest rates still further. That liquidity injection fed Japan's rising debt boom, further feeding financial instability. Japan's real economy thus became seriously overstimulated by1989 and overloaded with debt.

By 1990 Japan's policies had produced one of the largest domestic financial asset bubbles in history. As the Nomura Research Institute in Japan noted at the time: "permanent low interest rates was responsible for the bullish sentiment that caused asset prices to surge ... thereby creating the bubble".

Japan had transitioned to a financial investment driven economy from a highly competitive manufacturing, export driven economy. Japan was more than willing to make the shift, of course. No political or military pressure from the US was necessary. For Japan's business and financial elite it meant even greater and quicker financial profits.

After five years of record low interest rates, central bank liquidity injections, and record credit-debt extension fueling financial markets and foreign money flows, by the close of 1989 Japan's overheated, financial investment driven economy reached a crisis. To cool off the economy, the Bank of Japan started raising interest rates in May 1989, peaking a year later at 8%. That was the signal for investors to 'take their money and run', cashing in the historic financial asset profits realized from 1985 through 1989—at least those investors able to get out early. Most got caught in a classic financial asset deflation, unable to sell in the rout that followed.

Japan's Rolling Banking Crisis

Japan's financial markets started crashing in early 1990. Its main stock market, the Topix, collapsed more than 60% in 1991-1992, drifting still lower to 72% off 1990 highs by 2003. Real estate prices quickly joined the equities asset deflation in 1991, collapsing 81% over the subsequent decade. A brief, partial recovery by both categories of financial assets from 2004-2007 would give way to another collapse in 2008-09 to -72% and -81% for stocks and real estate, respectively. Financial asset deflation was thus a major characteristic of Japan's economy for more than two decades starting in 1991. Deflation in goods and services has taken place as well. The linkage between the two forms of deflation has been a chronic weakness in real fixed capital formation by Japanese business. After rising by more than 100% during the decade of the 1980s, capital formation began crumbling after 1990. By 2009, it was 30% below levels of 1990.[5]

The slowdown of Japan's real (non-financial) economy accelerated in 1992, and Japan entered a deep recession in 1993-1995. In response, the Bank of Japan (BoJ) reduced interest rates in eight steps, to a low 0.5% by 1995 to try to stop the decline. However, lowering rates by traditional monetary means had little effect on real recovery—as is always the case in post-financial crash contractions. A low cost of investing means little when financial assets are deflating or even stagnating and opportunities for profit making are lacking, since financial investing is less a function of cost of capital than it is of expectations of rates of return. Neither investors nor businesses want to borrow and expand so long as prices are deflating. Lower interest rates fail therefore to generate rising prices in those conditions.

By 1995, as recession deepened and financial asset values collapsed, a growing number of small banks and housing finance companies consequently began to fail. Japan policy makers and the BoJ attempted to bail out the banking system by injecting 685 billion Yen into the system. But that still did not halt the financial crisis or address the growing volume of bank held non-performing loans on bank balance sheets that held back bank lending.

Five years of a recession and slow growth economy resulted in rising government deficits, as government tax revenues collapsed. Japanese government policy makers then made a second classic policy error: in addition to relying primarily on lowering interest rates and pumping more liquidity into the banking system, in expectation of increasing bank lending that would not happen, Japan raised taxes in order to try to recover some of the lost tax revenue contributing to the deficits. That only made the real economy's recovery weaker, as all fiscal austerity policies tend to do in epic recession conditions.

A second recession followed in 1997 and more banks began to fail, including some of the larger this time. A second financial crisis was emerging. Asian economies were also crashing at the time, 1997-98, which reduced Japan's exports.[6] As exports and manufacturing fell, Japan introduced significant fiscal austerity measures. Sales taxes were raised from 3% to 5%, households' social security taxes were also raised, and income taxes increased. Meanwhile, news leaked that Japanese banks were sitting on more than $1 trillion dollars in bad assets and non-performing loans that they had been hiding for seven years after the 1990 original crash. The BoJ quickly injected another $1.8 trillion Yen into the new round of failing banks. Some were even nationalized, in an attempt to remove the mountain of debt on balance sheets in the expectation that would encourage banks now to lend. It didn't. Interest rates were then further reduced to 0.25%. Yet all the monetary measures and central bank liquidity still did not stabilize the banking system or generate bank lending to domestic businesses. The economy sank into another deep recession over the next 18 months. The tax hikes were in part reversed by 1999, but they had already done their damage.

Deflation spilled over from asset prices to consumer goods prices by 1998 for the first time. More banks began to fail. More liquidity was subsequently injected into fifteen failing banks in 1999. Several failing large banks were also forced by the government to merger. In 1999 the BoJ introduced its ZIRP (zero interest rate policy) to stimulate the recovery. Still no real effect. It attempted to raise rates minimally, ending ZIRP, in 2000, but as soon as it did the economy sank again. Rates were lowered once more, to 0.15%. A temporary consumption voucher program to households with children and elderly assisted some but was soon discontinued. Government deficits and debt rose further at decade's end, primarily due to declining tax revenues from years of chronic low growth and repeated recessions.

Japan's economy stumbled through 2000 and into 2001. A global collapse of tech industry stocks occurred in 2001, sending Japan's stock market lower again by 50%. More Yen were injected into the banks by the Bank of Japan and rates were now reduced from 0.25% to zero as

Japan re-introduced its zero interest rate program (ZIRP) that was briefly suspended in 2000-01. At the same time, the BoJ launched its first 'quantitative easing' QE program as well, buying 1.2 trillion Yen a month of government bonds, which it thereafter expanded by buying another 2 trillion Yen worth of stocks held by banks. Stock purchases by the BoJ were raised to 3 trillion Yen in 2003. Deflation continued nonetheless through 2005.

Various Japanese governments after 2000 experimented with moderate forms of austerity in a desperate effort to raise revenues and cut government costs to slow rising government deficit and debt. Nevertheless, Japan's debt to GDP ratio rose from approximately 125% to 175% from 2000 to 2006.

Over the longer term, slow and no growth and repeated business tax cuts effectively reduced government tax revenues by more than 18% by 2005, compared to 1990 levels. Japan's GDP grew only 13% over the 15 year period from 1990 to 2005, confirming the view that slow growth and associated tax revenue shortfalls are almost always the major cause of deficits and debt and not excessive government spending. Japan's 15 year total GDP growth of only 13% represents a mere 0.8% annual average— and that's 13% overall before the next deep crash of 2008-09 and the four recessions that were to follow over the coming decade, 2005-2015.

Lessons of 1990-2005 Ignored

The purpose of the preceding brief survey of Japan's economic history is not to just provide a historical narrative. It is to show how the same errors of policy in response to the financial crash, bank failures, and stagnant real economy were repeated—not only in Japan throughout the 15 year period, but in 2008-09 again, and once again after 2009 by the US and rest of the advanced economies.

What the history of Japan's 'lost long decade' shows is that monetary policy typically fails in the wake of a financial crash-precipitated recession. Even extreme versions of central bank liquidity injections—i.e. ZIRP and QE—have no more effect than conventional central bank bond buying measures. Reducing interest rates even to zero, in the hope of stimulating real investment and preventing deflation, whether financial asset or goods deflation, have little intended effect.

Japan's experience decades ago (and continuing today) shows that central banks can pump trillions into the private banking system but the money will just sit there, bottled up—or will flow offshore to finance multinational corporations' global investment plans, and/or will be diverted into financial asset investing. Whatever lending to domestic businesses that does occur is largely directed to rolling over old loans and debt, which, like offshore financing and financial asset speculation, also adds nothing to real growth.

ZIRP and QE were continued by Japan despite their obvious unsuccessful track record.[7] The two 'extraordinary' monetary measures would be resurrected again by the US and UK in 2009, promoted by policy makers and the media as if they were something radically new, to show the worried public that US and UK central banks were acting boldly and pre-emptively. But ZIRP and QE had already been tried—in Japan 1990-2005—and utterly failed. US Hybrid Keynesians, like Paul Krugman and Ben Bernanke, nonetheless championed QE and ZIRP, providing convoluted economic arguments why they would succeed and defending them repeatedly after 2009 even when they did not.[8]

There are interesting parallels between Japan's real estate-stocks-currency bubble, financial crash, the global recession that followed, and Japan's failed monetary and fiscal policies, on the one hand, and the subsequent similar events of 2008-2014 in the US and Europe. What is even more eerie, however, is the similarity between Japan 1990-2005 and the even more recent real estate-stock bubble and crash now occurring in China in 2014-15.

Not so surprising or interesting perhaps is that Japan itself since 2013, has again begun repeating the errors of 1990-2005—i.e. resorting to QE and ZIRP monetary policies while raising taxes and resorting to fiscal austerity.

Japan's Five Recessions

To fully appreciate the preceding paragraph's main point, it is necessary to briefly review what has happened to Japan's economy from 2008 through mid-2015.

Like the entire global economy, Japan contracted sharply during the 2008-09 global recession, falling four consecutive quarters, including an extraordinary -15% quarterly drop in early 2009. It temporarily benefited from the global commodities boom of 2010, but then promptly fell into recession again in 2011. A surge in GDP in the post-Fukushima period, as extraordinary government spending followed that nuclear meltdown and Tsunami crisis, soon dissipated. Japan slipped into recession again in 2012—a period during which the entire global economy barely averted another global recession, as Europe experienced a double dip recession and nearly another financial crisis and the US economy stagnated at that year's end. Expectations of recovery fueled another brief period of positive growth in 2013, but that was soon cut short by a 4th recession in 2014 precipitated by austerity measures as the government raised sales taxes.

The following graphic shows Japan's real economic performance in the period since 2000, during which five bona fide recessions have occurred. Its response to the 2001 tech bust-driven recession was notably a greater failure than that of other economies, lasting four quarters during which its economy contracted. [9] Japan would experience recession four more times thereafter. Not shown on the graph is the likely recent emergence of a fifth recession, commencing the second quarter of 2015, as Japan's GDP contracted again by -1.6%. Japan's latest 2015 contraction reflects a rapid slowing of China and Asian EMEs to which Japan is highly exposed through its export trade.

Japan's economy since 2000
Change in quarterly GDP figures (annualised)

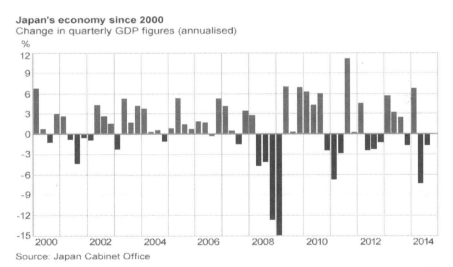

Source: Japan Cabinet Office

Japan's policy response to the 2008-09 financial crash and deep contraction differed from China's and the US-UK's. Unlike China's massive 15% of GDP fiscal stimulus in 2008-09, Japan did little to boost government spending or to cut taxes to stimulate its economy. Nor did it initially embark upon another central bank liquidity injection. It introduced no new QEs.[10] Nor could it do much in terms of a ZIRP, a zero interest rate program, since it already had a near zero rate policy in effect, given its 0.1% BoJ loan rate offered to banks.

Japan in 2008 invoked neither fiscal stimulus nor monetary stimulus. It was between a policy 'rock and a hard place' as they say. Nearly two decades of slow to negative growth had already ballooned its budget deficit and government debt. Its government debt to GDP ratio was already 167% by 2008. Its conservative state bureaucracy and pro-business Liberal Democratic Party, that together dominated and determined economic policy, were more inclined toward balancing budgets than embarking on a China-like massive deficit spending and government direct investment approach. Boosting housing and construction to get a quick recovery evoked still fresh memories of Japan's speculative real estate boom and bust of 1985-1998 and the banking instability consequences that followed throughout the 1990s. It wasn't about to spend more, like the Chinese would in 2009, and exacerbate an already fragile budget-debt situation.

Nor like the US and UK was it going to introduce another QE. Its central bank's (BoJ) balance sheet had already more than doubled over the preceding decade due to QEs and other bond buying activities, from a debt load of 52 thousand billion Yen in 1998 to more than 125 thousand billion Yen by 2008—or in dollar terms from about $430 billion to more than a $1 trillion, when measured in 2015's Yen-Dollar currency exchange rate of 120 Yen to the dollar. And insofar as interest rate policy was concerned, Japan had already shot off its ammunition by lowering interest rates to virtually zero by 2008.

So in the immediate aftermath of the 2008-09 Japan initially did little to respond to the global 2008-09 crash and the recession that immediately followed. That initial policy immobilization would doom Japan's economy over the next five years, 2008-2012, to the weakest performance among all the advanced economies. Over the next five years, it would experience three recessions. Its economy would be contracting or completely stagnant during more of the 20 quarters than it would be growing.

Japan's Response to Recession, 2008-2012

From the start of 2007 through 2010—a period of four full years—consumer spending in Japan remained stagnant at around 295 thousand billion Yen ($2.4 trillion).[11] Business gross fixed capital spending fared even worse. Over the same period it fell from roughly 117 thousand billion ($975 billion) in 2007 to 97 thousand billion in 2008 ($816 billion)— a decline of 16% where it then remained stuck for several years, through mid-2011. To offset the consumption and fixed investment collapse, government spending picked up some after 2008 but not enough to offset the business spending reductions. Over 2008 through 2010, spending rose from an average of 93500 Yen in 2008 to only 96000 in 2010, or about $25 billion more.

Business fixed capital spending had become a chronic problem for Japan going back as far as 1990. After growing by a significant 100% between 1980 and 1990, it declined throughout the 1990s. By 2008 it had declined cumulatively from 1990 by 7.7%. It fell another 8% in 2009. Not until the Fukushima crisis in early 2011 did it begin to rise a little, only to level off again throughout 2012 and into early 2013.

A major reason for Japan's poor fixed capital formation has been the lack of bank lending. By the end of 2011, four years since the 2008 crash, total bank loans were still at the same level as at the start of 2008. The weak bank lending was not for lack of liquidity provided by the BoJ over the period, however. Central bank rates to private banks were lowered from 0.1% to zero by the end of 2010. Interbank lending rates were a record low of 0.25%. And the M2 money supply, as a measure of central bank provided liquidity, rose by 8% from 2008 through 2010. So where did the money go, if consumption was stagnant and business capital spending falling? It certainly didn't flow into enabling an expansion of industrial production, which fell by 40% in 2008-09, recovered only briefly in 2010 and then recorded negative growth every month from 2011 through most of 2013 (except for a brief period of a few months in early 2012). The same mostly declining trajectory applied to manufacturing.

And with Japan's economy having fallen into a 'double dip' recession once again in 2010-2011 after the already sharp contraction of 2008-09, it was not surprising that deflation in goods and services—a chronic problem from the 1990s—become more entrenched after 2008 as well. Japan's GDP Deflator index fell by roughly 10% from early 2008 through 2013.

The same goods deflation problem did not characterize financial asset prices, however. Japan's Nikkei 225 stock index peaked at approximately 14,000 before 2008. During the crash of 2008-09 it fell to 8,000, but then rose quickly again to 11,000—a gain of 38% from 2009 lows. This recovery indicates that much of the BoJ's liquidity injection after 2008 flowed into equities investment. Part likely also went to offshore foreign direct investment by Japanese multinational firms. Part went to non-financial companies to refinance old debt or else hoarded on private banks' balance sheets. The rest remained hoarded on balance sheets. What also remained was an apparent anomaly of 10% deflation in goods and services prices amidst an inflation in stock financial asset prices of 38%.

The immediate recovery of financial asset prices following the 2008-09 crash was occurring worldwide, however, not just in Japan. The experience was even more significant in the US and UK economies, although less so in the Eurozone. The reflation of financial asset prices reflects the common policy across the AEs at the time of massive central bank liquidity injections in response to the 2008-09 crash. And everywhere among the AEs the recovery in financial asset prices was having little effect on real investment and goods deflation.

At the close of 2010, both Japan and Europe begin to diverge in their real economies from the US and UK economic trajectories. The US and UK, starting in 2009, had introduced even more massive liquidity injection programs than Japan (or Europe) in the form of their own QE direct bond buying-money printing programs. The US would introduce a second QE2 version in late 2010. It would escalate that in October 2012 with a further QE3, this time 'open ended' in terms of bond buying; that is, with no limit in potential amount of money printing and no time limit to end the buying. Simultaneously the UK's Bank of England was injecting more than $650.

In contrast, Japan was reluctant to engage in another QE, having previously done so with little effect.[12] Japan had pioneered the QE idea, introducing a very limited program in 2001 that lasted until 2006 when it was suspended. Japan is thus the 'Home of QE'. The 2001-06 experience with QE proved disappointing. Although the Bank of Japan increased the money base by 18% as a result of QE bond buying after 2001, real economic growth was disappointing. QE was discredited by 2006. From that point, Japan relied on reducing interest rates to 0.25%.

Japan's Ministry of Finance was never completely convinced that QE bond buying would generate much real growth. After the 2008 crash, however, the Bank of Japan and the Ministry found themselves caught in political battles over policy between Japan's two dominant parties—the Democratic Party (DP) and the Liberal Democratic Party (LDP), the latter having ruled Japan for nearly all the period from

1990 to 2008. The debate over returning to QE raged as the 2008-09 crash and recession occurred. QE was re-introduced in 2010, albeit in a very minimal form, limiting bond buying to short term government bonds of 3 years or less and putting a cap on the amount that might be purchased.

Japan nonetheless slipped into double dip recessions in 2011. As it entered its double dip in 2010-2011, Japan's stock markets began to contract once again. A very brief and shallow recovery of Japan's economy in the second half of 2011—due largely to post-Fukushima spending—quickly collapsed and Japan entered its third post-2008 recession in 2012. From the start of 2011 through 2012 its stock markets therefore contracted again from 11,000 in early 2011 to 9,000 at the close of 2012. [13]

By mid-2012 Japan's industrial production and manufacturing had been falling consecutively for 13 and 11 months, respectively. Capital investment was not growing. Central bank and external debt was rising. Lending by banks was flat, despite zero rates available from the BoJ and interbank rates of 0.20%. Both goods and financial asset deflation was the general rule. Wages were falling, while government debt as a percent of GDP had risen to 200%. The LDP's prime ministerial candidate, Shinzo Abe, appeared to easily win the national elections scheduled for November 2012.

Abe's campaign called for a massive money stimulus. The BoJ should, at minimum, double Japan's bond buying. An inflation target goal for the program should be 3%, not the current 1%. The QE program, moreover, should be 'open ended'—i.e. with "unlimited easing". Interest rates should be lowered to zero, or even 'negative'. Abe's aggressive shift on QE and monetary stimulus was no doubt influenced at the time by the chairs of the US Federal Reserve (Fed), Ben Bernanke, and of the European Central Bank (ECB), Mario Draghi. Draghi just months previous had announced the ECB would do "whatever it takes" to get the Eurozone's stock prices and economy back on track, as the Eurozone had also fallen into its own double dip recession. And Bernanke, in October, had just announced the US's own expanded QE3—now also 'open ended' with no time limit, at $80 billion in bond buying every month in what amounted to a 'QE to infinity' program. Both the US dollar and Euro declined in relation to the Japanese Yen as a result, threatening thereby to slow Japanese exports and its economic growth, already in recession territory, even further. Currency wars by 'dueling QEs' among the AEs thus dates from the second half of 2012.

Shirakawa's Warning

The governor of the BoJ at the time was Masaaki Shirakawa. Of the old school, suspicious of the potential of QE to boost real investment, Shirakawa had gone along with demands of the political parties to reintroduce some kind of QE back in 2010. But the compromise reached was a limited QE—buying bonds that were short term only and with a low cap on how much based on Japan's GDP. That would keep the BoJ's cost down, since short term bonds carried low rates. Throughout 2012, as Japan's third recession continued, pressure mounted for Shirakawa to increase the bond buying. The BoJ's asset purchasing limit was therefore raised five times, to 101 trillion Yen ($841 billion) by the end of 2012. But the BoJ's compromise trick was that the additional buying was scheduled not to occur until 2014. So there would be no immediate impact so far as the QE advocates, Abe and the LDP, were concerned.

Shirakawa represented the wing of monetary policy in Japan that believed that liquidity injections would not stimulate the real economy. That view believed the problem was on the supply side of Japan's economy. What was needed, instead of more QE, was structural reforms to improve Japan competitiveness in export markets, raising worker productivity, incentives to invest in production, and so on.

The Shirakawa formula of more QE but only later was rejected by Abe and the LDP, which won a landslide election victory in November 2012. At the BoJ's January 2013 meeting, Shirakawa agreed to Abe's targeting of a 2% inflation goal and buying another 10 trillion Yen, bringing the Japanese QE total to an equivalent $1.2 trillion. But the BoJ held firm to limiting purchases to short term, 3 year, government only bonds. The short term, government bonds only policy in 2013 contrasted with the US QE3 program, which was not limited to government bonds, was scheduled to buy another $1 trillion in bonds in 2013 alone, and was 'open ended with more to come thereafter in potentially unlimited amounts.

From that point, Shirakawa was on the way out as his term of BoJ governor was to end in April 2013. Abe would replace him in March 2013 with his candidate, Hiruhiko Kuroda, who had been a sharp critic of Shirakawa and had called for a massive increase in BoJ bond buying. Shirakawa, in departing from the post in March 2013, at the end of Japan's fiscal year, exited with a warning that still echoes for unabashed advocates of central bank bond buying, QE, programs as the solution to generating real economic recovery and ending deflation. As he noted in his departing speech, "past figures in Japan as well as Europe and the US show that the link between money base and prices has been broken". Monetary policy in general, and QE in particular, can only buy time. Only restructuring with fiscal stimulus can lead to longer term recovery.

'Abenomics' 1.0: Back to the Future

On April 4, 2013 the new prime minister, Abe, and his new BoJ central bank governor, Kuroda, launched the most aggressive QE and ZIRP program on the planet to date—more aggressive than even that of the US, given the size of Japan's GDP and economy at the time.

Japan's QE included a 2% target for inflation to be achieved within no more than two years and a 70% increase in bond buying monthly, up from 3.8T yen per month to 7.5T yen. The bond buying would include longer than three year securities. And would be 'open ended'. The goal was to double Japan's monetary base, from a dollar equivalent of $730 billion a year to $1.46 trillion. More might be purchased, it was noted. Kuroda called it QQE, or QE squared as the media termed it. QE was both 'quantitative' and 'qualitative', the latter referring to potential purchases of not just government bonds but other financial assets such as REITs (real estate investment trust securities), ETF (exchange traded fund) stock securities, corporate 'Junk' (high interest rate) bonds, and commercial paper. The idea—and theory—behind the massive, unlimited, and other financial securities forms of QE buying was that QE would raise 'inflationary expectations'. Investors and consumer households would now believe, because the program was so massive, that inflation was now bound to happen. They would rush to invest and spend in anticipation of it happening. And inflation would consequently occur.

Japan's QE—like all QEs—was based on an 'if you build it they will come' theoretical foundation. It was a desperate concoction that ignored the extreme complexities of investing and consuming psychology that in many ways does not follow traditional assumptions about psychological behavior on the part of fragile households and businesses burdened with excessive debt and facing stagnant income streams with which to pay for that debt in the future.

Japan's QQE program faced a number of potential problems typically associated with QE: first it would drive down the Yen and perhaps stimulate exports, but the reduction in the exchange rate for the Yen would also raise import inflation and discourage domestic household consumption and domestic based investment. Second it would certainly result in asset bubbles in stocks and real estate. Third it could exacerbate currency wars, resulting in other countries devaluing by QE money injections; that would offset any gains initially from QE encouraging exports. Fourth, the reduced interest rates at which to borrow Yen in Japan would increase demand by EMEs and offshore investors to buy Yen and use it to speculate in other currencies. Thus, the expanded money supply from Japan bond buying would flow offshore. It would encourage capital flight, in other words. It could also destabilize Japan's $10 trillion bond market, the second largest in the world, by reducing available liquidity. Bond prices would actually therefore rise, not fall, in the aftermath of introducing QQE.

Notwithstanding these potential problems, the immediate effect of QQE was a bubble-like surge in Japan's stock market values. The Nikkei 225 rose by 80% from November 2012 to May 2013 after Abe's election and in anticipation of the promised massive liquidity that would be available for stock purchases. Cash began to pile up in corporate balance sheets from the speculative stock-related capital gains, as corporations invested in financial assets more than in the real assets. Some real asset investment and growth did occur in 2013, in expectation of more exports. However, by year end corporations had accumulated cash equal to one half of Japan's GDP, having continued to invest "less than their cash flow now in physical assets", according to Kuroda.[14] Japanese companies' cash piles, rising ever since 2008, amounted to approximately $1.75 trillion by the end of 2012. Corporate cash accelerated even faster after the introduction of QQE in April 2013, to a large extent a consequence of capital gains from stock and other financial asset investments, profits from exports from a falling Yen exchange rate, and continued wage compression. Corporate cash reserves would rise still further, to $2.65 trillion by June 2013.[15]

Abe promised as part of his 'Abenomics' program that wages would rise to fund consumption. But the reality after April 2013 was a continued decline in real wages from a previous zero growth level at the start of 2013, to a steady decline in real wages of -2% in 2013, and on to another drop of -3% in 2014. Part of the general wage decline was due not just to lower nominal wages. It was also due to the shifting of full time to part time work. Abe made it easier for companies to dismiss permanent workers and hire part time and temp workers, who are paid less. By the end of 2014 no fewer than 38% of Japan's labor force of about 33 million were part time-temp workers, having risen by more than 2 million during Abe's first two years in office.[16] Nominal wage increases were also lagging during the period, as Abe's plan to lift wages was purely voluntary, calling on Japanese business in April 2013 to raise base wages by a paltry 1%. Of course, they refused to commit any of their growing cash hoard to higher wages for the rest of 2013 and 2014. Abe's answer at the end of 2014 was to propose a series of corporate tax cuts, to encourage cash bloated companies to raise wages to stimulate demand.

The business tax cuts would, of course, add to Japan's ballooning government debt. So Abenomics 1.0 also called for raising the consumption tax, from current 5% in two steps to 8% in April 2014 and another 2% in April 2015. Corporate tax cuts, consumption tax hikes, and token government spending represented 'Abenomics' so-called 'second arrow', accompanying the first arrow of massive BoJ monetary expansion. A third 'arrow', as it was called, was proposed to address structural reforms.

The tax and spending provisions, and to some extent the restructuring third arrow, represent Japan's version of 'austerity' fiscal policy. Spending would at first be slightly expansionary, to accompany the massive money injections by the BoJ, but then would be taken back after the economy presumably started growing.[17] So Japan's austerity program was characterized by token spending and business tax cuts upfront, followed by retraction of that spending and loss of revenue from the business tax cuts in the form of a series of consumption taxes to follow in April 2014 and 2015.

One difficulty faced by Abenomics 1.0 is that it was launched into the global headwinds growing in mid-2013 with the beginning of the slowdown in both China and the EMEs. Over the preceding decade, Japan's exports had grown increasingly dependent on demand from both China and from Southeast Asian economies. And Japan's private banks after April 2013 accelerated their lending ever faster to offshore markets in Asia. While not made public at home in Japan, the promotion of offshore lending and investment was always an unannounced priority of Abenomics as well—i.e. a silent 'fourth arrow', as Abe pledged for Japan to invest $110 billion offshore in the next several years. But now China and EMEs were beginning to slow. After a short 9 month recovery in 2013, Japan's economy began to slow once again by the end of that year. Then came Abe's second arrow—the sales tax hike from 5% to 8%--in April 2014.

In anticipation of the sales hike, consumers had 'moved up'

their purchases so when the tax cut came, the impact on consumption—comprising more than half of Japan's GDP—was especially severe. Abenomics grew exports, making corporations more profits, but it also raised inflation from imports, reducing consumers' real income and consumption. Churn to part time/temp jobs reduced workers' earnings further, and Japanese corporations balked at voluntarily raising wages. In short, consumption collapsed after April 2014 and Japan fell into its fourth recession since 2008 in the second quarter 2014. Like all AE recovery strategies after 2008, QEs boosted capital incomes, profits, and the wealthiest households' incomes but did little for jobs and wage incomes needed to sustain an economic recovery. They created waves of income for banks, businesses, and investors but those waves crashed on the rocky shore of stagnant and declining wage incomes, and then ebbed further with the slowing of demand for Japanese exports by China and EMEs.

Abenomics 2.0: Doubling Down on Policy That Doesn't Work

This 2014 collapse back into recession was followed by a further escalation of bond buying by the BoJ in the fall of 2014. This time the BoJ would purchase stock funds as well as bonds, as the BoJ's holdings of Exchanged Traded Stock (ETF) funds thereafter were projected to double from 3.5 trillion Yen to 7 trillion by 2016. Japan's stock market surged 5% on the announcement.[18] The government's pension funds also began buying stocks in large volumes. But the drift toward deflation continued nonetheless, wages still fell, corporate cash hoards rose further, and consumption—comprising more than half of Japan's GDP—sagged as the Yen's fall accelerated and caused rising import inflation that reduced real incomes still further. QQE was reducing consumption more than it was stimulating investment from exports. Doubts at year end 2014 were beginning to rise about unlimited QQE and Abenomics 1.0 in general.

Abenomics 2.0 is predicated on the absurd assumption that when something doesn't work, do more of it. In the face of failure, step up the effort that has failed. This is true in general concerning most forms of monetarist economic theory. Monetarists believe that more money (or less) is the solution to all problems economic. If the economy isn't growing and deflation is emerging, pump in more liquidity; if it's growing too fast and creating inflation, just retract it. Monetarists are never proven wrong because their defense is always 'you didn't try it long enough'. Of course, what's 'long enough' is never defined.

Abe and Kuroda made the mistake in 2013, however, of saying how long was enough. They declared in launching QQE in April 2013 that the goal was a 2% inflation target. Bond buying would go on as long as necessary until the 2% was achieved. By as late as July 2014, Kuroda was still insisting that 2% was within reach and, in fact, Japan was on track. But by year's end he adjusted, saying the real obtainable rate was now 1%. His consistent reference to 2% and even 1% was making Abe nervous, according to reports. It was becoming the benchmark and proof of whether Abenomics was failing or not—and by the inflation target measure it clearly was. The collapse of world oil prices starting mid-2014 added to the general deflationary trend. China and EMEs continued to slow as well. And as import inflation and no wage growth was slashing consumption spending, corporations were either hoarding cash or sending it offshore. The 2% target seemed to be moving further away, instead of nearer.

The escalation of BoJ bond buying in the second half of 2014, Abe's announced suspension of the second consumption tax hike set for April 2015, and the LDP's landslide win in Japan's Parliament giving it a majority together provided a temporary boost to consumer and business sentiment. Investment and consumption recovered slightly at year end 2014 as Japan emerged once again from recession. Japan's economy in early 2015 was experiencing yet another 'short, shallow recovery'. But the 2.4% initial GDP growth estimate for the first quarter of 2015 was largely composed of business inventory buildup. Minus inventories, real growth was only 0.4%. Not surprisingly, by spring 2015 the economy contracted once more, a fifth time, by -1.2% for the quarter. Consumer spending, business investment, and exports all declined. Only business inventories continued to add to GDP, suggesting the third quarter was likely to register a further negative GDP rate as excess business inventory buildup of the first half of 2015 would almost certainly contract in the second half. A decline in GDP in the third quarter 2015 would make it Japan's fifth recession since 2008.

Despite the renewed slowdown, corporate profits continued to surge to record levels in 2015, to 29.4T Yen ($240 billion), and more than double that when Abe took office in 2012. Dividend payments and stock buybacks by companies reached record levels as well. And by the end of May 2015, stock prices on the Tokyo exchanges, at 591T Yen in total value, exceeded the 590T Yen level at the peak of Japan's stock bubble in December 1989. Capital incomes, in other words, continued to do quite well despite the repeated recessions and weak temporary recoveries.

As Japan re-entered recession again in the spring of 2015, the BoJ and Kuroda at first signaled no change in its accelerated $660 billion a year bond buying program. As Kuroda in mid-July said, "I have no expectation of ongoing weakness in growth".[19] But even the IMF, with its conservative forecasts, publicly differed with Japan in a warning that Japan's GDP would register less than 1% for all of 2015 at best estimate. The IMF noted that slower wage growth was a problem, as was Japan's 250% of GDP government debt load, the highest in the world. Moreover, all the bond buying by the BoJ to date was also absorbing available bond supply, causing a potential problem of bond liquidity in the future should bond prices start falling rapidly. IMF further noted that the BoJ and Japan's estimates of growth were grossly over-optimistic and based on unrealistic assumptions.

By August, Abe indicated a new $20 billion fiscal stimulus might soon be needed, as household spending contracted -3.1% and exports -16.5%. Talk increased that the BoJ would further escalate its buying—this time more stocks plus other securities—after its October 2015 meeting. At the same time as suggesting a fiscal stimulus, however, Abe recommitted to his plan to go through with raising the sales tax to 10% in 2017—thus continuing austerity policies—even as surveys showed the likely tax hike was already depressing consumption and slowing the economy in 2015.

Growing Fragility in the Japanese Economy

After a quarter century since the 1990-1991 financial crash, and after no less than eight recessions, decades-long chronic deflation, slowing real investment, record government debt levels, falling wage incomes, and continued policy failures, Japan's economy remains one of the most fragile in the world. It is a classic case of 'epic' recession and economic fragility. The real economy suffers from low real investment at home, declining wage incomes and therefore stultified consumer demand. Government efforts to 'plug the gap' with decades of business tax and spending cuts has raised debt as a percent of GDP to 250% without having an appreciable sustained real economic effect. With stagnating and falling real wage incomes, it cannot get consumption going. With Japanese corporations redirecting record profits to offshore investing, to financial asset markets, or just hoarding the cash piles, real investment and jobs creation other than part time-temp work chronically lags. Japan's export driven growth model is also floundering, as Chinese and Asian EME demand decelerates. So investment, consumption, and exports are all failing. This has left desperate efforts at unlimited QE and liquidity expansion by Japan's central bank as the Japanese government's main alternative, while its fiscal policy vacillates between token stimulus and forms of mini-austerity measures. The fragility in the real economy is evident in that monetary stimulus generates ever diminishing real growth, while it promotes and enables ever greater financial asset investing. Not only are the normal transmission mechanisms between money injection and real growth broken, but the responsiveness of the real economy to money supply boosting and money multipliers have also broken down. In parallel, the fragility on the fiscal side is growing as well, evident in the fact that government tax cuts and spending injections also produce less and less real growth as fiscal multipliers have deteriorated.

With the private sector unable to achieve sufficient economic momentum to push the economy to a sustainable growth rate, the government has attempted to fill the gap. But in the process it too has become increasingly fragile, as it adds a mountain of sovereign debt to its balance sheet. The mountain of government debt is itself an indicator of excessive debt in the private sector and slowing income growth for households in that sector. The government has raised its debt in an effort to reduce debt and fragility in the private sector—but without real results in the process.

The only segment of the economy that has benefited has been wealthy investor households, financial institutions, and large non-financial corporations. That too is a consequence of government policies that have added to the record government debt levels. One can only imagine what the Japan economy will look like should another 2008-09 crash take place.

Financial fragility, not just government balance sheet or household fragility, is also rising in Japan. China's stock market plunge in 2015 and its loss thus far of about 50% of its total valuation (more than $5 trillion), plus China's real economic slowdown, has been translating into contagion for Japan's stock markets. The only thing preventing a China-like collapse of Japan's stocks is the repeated doses of liquidity Japan's BoJ has been pumping into its economy since 2010, and especially since 2012, in an increasingly desperate effort to keep stock prices up. Financial fragility today is not just evident in Japan's equity markets. The $10 trillion bond market is becoming more fragile as well. The BoJ (and now pension funds) buying of highly volatile and risky exchange traded stock funds is but one example. Periodic problems with bond liquidity availability in the event of a bond sell-off are growing as well.

So potential and actual economic instability in Japan's real economy, as well as potential instability in Japan's stock and bond markets, are rising. What happens to the global economy may prove as determinative of Japan's efforts to end its 'perpetual recession' as any policy within Japan itself. In particular, global events in China, financial asset markets worldwide, and competitive QEs in Europe and EME devaluations and recessions.

Endnotes

1   A response that would be very much replicated by other advanced economies after the 2008 crash.

2   A similar question may be asked of China, commencing in the second half of 2014 and continuing today. China's recent shift has similarities to Japan's in the late 1980s. While neither Japan nor China totally abandoned their manufacturing-exports growth strategy by shifting to financial assets, the relative shift was clear in both cases. Japan's real estate-stock bubble collapsed in 1990-91, as has China's in 2015.

3   Not totally different from US insistence in recent years that China change its growth model from investment in real goods and exports, to more private sector driven internal investment while opening up its economy more to AE finance corporations.

4   US goods exports were highly uncompetitive throughout the first half of the 1980s decade, not only because US production was less efficient but due to Reagan administration economic policies. Reagan policies beginning in 1981 had the US central bank raising short term US interest rates to record levels of 18%-24%. That rise sucked in foreign capital to the US economy, in the process raising the value of the US dollar significantly. That of course made US corporations highly uncompetitive virtually overnight. US rates thereafter remained relatively high until the late 1980s. To offset US corporations' lack of competitiveness due to the high dollar, instead of action to lower the dollar's value, the US policy was to get the Japanese to raise the Yen's value.

5   The above statistics are from tradingeconomics.com, measured in thousands of billions (trillions) of Yen values.

6   The 1997-98 financial crisis throughout Asia is sometimes known as the 'Asian Meltdown'. It was a consequence of excess debt and borrowing from western banks by the countries involved and a financial crash involving currencies as the financial asset class.

7   Japan would resurrect QE once again in 2013 with much hoopla but no different effect. Then it repeated the mistake of 1997 by raising sales taxes again in 2014, throwing the economy into yet another recession.

8   Some justification arguments were: ZIRP will work if accompanied by an explicit inflation target; real interest rates can be pushed below zero if the public's inflation expectations rise; QE and printing money will signal the central bank's

firm commitment to creating inflation which will raise inflationary expectations; QE will lead to currency depreciation that will stimulate aggregate demand; QE purchases will expand the money base by buying up non-performing loans and show further commitment to inflation and raise expectations of inflation further; etc.

9   The US contraction, where the dot.com tech bust originated, in contrast lasted only one quarter, cut short by the events of 9-11 and the US government's significant boosting of defense spending immediately in its wake.

10   As a result of its prior QE and liquidity policies, the BoJ balance sheet, reflecting past bond buying efforts, had already risen from 52,000 billion Yen in 1998 to 125,000 by 2008. (A Yen in September 2015 is approximately 120 to the US dollar, so the BoJ's balance sheet of past bond buying in 2008 amounted to about $1.04 trillion in today's exchange rate).

11   Based on an assumed 2015 Yen to dollar exchange rate of 120.

12   And as the next chapter will show, Europe's central bank, for other reasons than Japan's central bank, would lag on liquidity injection as well. Thus, both Japan and Europe equity and financial markets would 'recover' less rapidly than the US and UK's.

13   In contrast, US and UK stock markets continued to surge and gather momentum during this period.

14   Kuroda interview in *Financial Times*, December 13, 2013, p.1.

15   And that did not include banks and shadow banks. See Eleanor Warnock and Toko Sekiguchi, 'Japan's Abe Vows to Push for Higher Wages', *Wall St. Journal*, December 16, 2014, p. 4.

16   This trend post-2008 to hire more part time and temp while reducing full time workers was not limited to Japan. It characterizes all the AEs. The much vaunted 'job growth', from the US to Japan to Europe has been largely 'job churn', as two workers replaced one full time or were hired in lieu of a full time, thus making it appear as if job creation were growing. It explains a large part of why job gains have not been accompanied by wage gains in the process.

17   This plan was also not unlike the Obama-US version of austerity: an initial $800 billion spending program in early 2009, followed by another $855 billion business tax cut in late 2010, and thereafter followed by $1 trillion of spending cuts in August 2011 and another $500 billion in spending cuts in January 2013. The US spending was also heavily defense oriented with subsidies to states. The tax cutting was heavily business oriented, and business tax cuts were made permanent in January 2013 for the next ten years, at a cost of $4 trillion through 2022.

18   The BoJ's decision in November followed a government decision to have the Government Pension Investment Fund to also start buying more stock, shifting 138 trillion Yen from bonds to stocks. The GPIF also noted a shift to purchasing more international bonds and stocks.

19   *Financial Times*, July 16, 2015, p. 22.

5

EUROPE'S CHRONIC STAGNATION

If the defining characteristic of Japan's economy since 2008 has been perpetual recession, then Europe's has been chronic stagnation. Europe, and in particular its 17-country core Eurozone group, has been fluctuating between+1% and -1% growth for most of the post-2008 period, whereas Japan has been fluctuating at a still lower level of growth or in recession.

Neither the Eurozone nor Japan has yet recovered the level of economic output they had in 2007-08.[1] That's more than $20 trillion in combined global GDP that is still mired in 'epic' recession conditions—i.e. a kind of muted depression—seven years after the 2008 crash. Add to that $20 trillion the growing number of EMEs that have slipped into recession by 2015—and major independents like South Korea, Australia, Canada and others sliding toward zero growth or worse—it is likely that more than half the global economy in 3rd quarter 2015 is either stagnant or declining.

Much of that half continues, however, to bet that by focusing on stimulating its exports, and growing its share of slowing total global trade, that it can somehow extricate itself from stagnation and decline. That bet is a high risk gamble that will likely not pay off, as the recent history of the Eurozone economy itself since 2010 clearly shows.

The Limits of Exports-Driven Recovery

Since 2009 Europe in general, and the Eurozone in particular, has focused increasingly on exports-driven growth as the primary strategy of recovery from the 2008-09 global crash. So too have Japan and the EMEs. And until 2013, so had China as well.[2] But exports-driven growth, especially since 2009, means one country's export gain is often another's loss. The global economy in the longer run consequently slows, as more and more countries retreat from domestic real investment and focus on exports as their primary growth strategy, driving down export and import prices and lowering the value of total trade.[3]

While mainstream economists argue otherwise, based on their archaic theories founded on erroneous assumptions, the historical record since 2010 clearly refutes their argument that more trade, and free trade, always means more economic growth.

As recent data in late 2015 from the World Trade Organization shows, for nearly a quarter century, from 1983 to 2005, the growth of world trade averaged 6% a year. Since 2010 it has averaged only half that at 3%, which includes a boost from a significant but brief surge in trade in 2010-2011 that quickly abated. World trade in 2015 is projected to grow by a mere 1%, but may actually grow less since, for the first time since 2009, global trade actually contracted in the first half of 2015.

Thus, as more countries have tried to focus on expanding exports after 2008-09 as the means by which to grow their lagging domestic economies, the growth of total world trade has progressively slowed. Despite the dramatic slowdown in world trade since 2011, the competition for a shrinking world trade pie continues to intensify as more countries—including most notably those in the Eurozone—turn increasingly to export-driven growth as their primary strategy for recovery.

Not only the period since 2011, but also the decade of the 1930s, contradict the accepted view of mainstream economists that more trade always leads to more growth. In both periods, intensifying export competition resulted in slower global growth. Global trade slowed sharply as a result of competitive devaluations by countries during the 1930s global depression decade, enacted as governments lowered their currency exchange rates by fiat—i.e. legal declaration. Today it is devaluations by central bank liquidity injections that depress currency values and 'internal devaluations'. And now emerging as well, internal devaluations are implemented by what is called 'labor market restructuring', occurring in the form of draconian cuts in wages and benefits to provide an export cost advantage. In the Eurozone today, both forms of devaluation—by central bank liquidity injections and labor cost cutting—are being implemented.

In the 21st century much of global capitalism has been shifting to financial asset investing at the expense of real asset investment. But it has also been reorienting a good part of what real investment remains after the financial shift, to growing exports and trade instead of real investment targeting the domestic market. As a consequence of both shifts—to financial asset as well as export-oriented investment—real investment in the form of infrastructure development, industrial production, new industries development, etc., that might have been directed toward the domestic economy, has slowed.

Unlike financial asset investment, real investment redirected to export production does provide some real growth and income creation. However, export-driven investment and growth is sporadic, volatile, and tends to be short lived. Since more and more economies are playing the 'beggar my neighbor' export card, an export advantage of one country quickly tends to dissipate, as other countries respond with similar export-oriented policies. The net result over time is intensifying competition that leads to more volatile, unsustainable, and unreliable growth for those that lose out in the 'exports first' competition.

Increasing dependence on trade and exports creates imbalances between the different sectors of the global economy that tend to slow the growth of trade over time: China and EMEs grow their exports, and thus their domestic economies, at the expense of Europe and Japan (2010-2012); Japan responds with QE and other monetary measures to drive down its currency to try to gain a temporary export advantage (2013-14); Europe then injects liquidity via QE and other measures in response in pursuit of the same (2015); China eventually responds with measures to lower its currency (2015-16); Europe and Japan follow with still more QE programs (2016?). And so the export 'tit for tat' game goes.

The outcome is currency wars as each sector of the global economy targeting exports for domestic growth attempts to gain a temporary advantage at the expense of the other. Long term, however, currency wars end up reducing world trade, as inter-capitalist competition and fighting over a slowing global export economic pie intensifies.

Select individual economies may benefit from an exports-driven growth strategy, but only in the short run. There may even be net benefits globally, but again only in the short run. Over time, intensifying exports competition leads to destabilizing devaluations by QE and other central bank measures; to more resort by countries to internal devaluations cutting wages, benefits, and disposable incomes that reduce domestic consumption and growth; and to more imbalances in global money flows that contribute to more financial instability as well—all of which slow global growth in the longer run.

Whichever the means—liquidity injections or labor cost cutting—the results are the same. Whether in the 1930s or today or in Europe or elsewhere, those who benefit do so at the expense of the losers, whose collective loss typically exceeds those who gain—for a total net loss to the global economy.

Nowhere has this consequence of an exports-driven growth strategy been more evident at a regional level than in the Eurozone. For more than a decade now, Germany and other northern European economies have benefited—at the expense of growing indebtedness and slowing growth in many of the Eurozone's peripheral economies (Spain, Portugal, Greece, Ireland, and even Italy).

Stripped of the ability to lower their currency as a result of having joined the Euro, having given up their central bank independence by joining the

German-dominated European Central Bank (ECB), and unable to reduce unit labor costs to match Germany and other northern European economies, the Eurozone periphery economies were forced to rely on German-Northern Europe bankers' and governments' money capital in-flows as the primary strategy by which they hoped to recover from the 2008-09 crisis. That strategy has proven a dismal failure.

German Origins of Eurozone Instability

The chronic stagnation that has characterized the Eurozone over the past decade begins in Germany—in Frankfurt, the seat of the German-dominated European Central Bank (ECB), and in Berlin where Germany's finance ministry also dominates Eurozone fiscal policy through a coalition with its allied northern and eastern Europe foreign ministers whose economies are dependent on German trade and financial relations.[4]

With a de facto majority, Germany and its allies dominate the ECB, whose governing body is composed of the head central bankers of the 19 Eurozone countries.[5] A German-led coalition of finance ministers also functions as a bloc within the European Commission (EC), which determines much of the Eurozone policies on fiscal measures, austerity, and government debt bailouts.

The ECB and EC constitute two of the three key pan-European institutions that make up the so-called 'Troika' in Europe which together determine much of the Eurozone's neoliberal policies. The third Troika member, the International Monetary Fund (IMF), located in Washington DC, operates on a more US-Europe consensus. It is less directly influenced by Germany and its allies than the ECB and EC. The IMF may occasionally critique the EC-ECB policy choices, including at times the pace and magnitude of Eurozone austerity fiscal measures. But the IMF tends to eventually fall in line with the ECB and EC where matters directly impacting European economic issues are involved.

The exports first policy and the chronic stagnation in the Eurozone economy begins in 1999 with the creation of the Euro. The Euro enabled Germany to become the dominant force with regard to exports and trade within the Eurozone, especially in relation to the southern and eastern periphery regions. German exports dominance within the Eurozone in turn has created severe trade and capital flow imbalances[6] within the Eurozone—imbalances that have played a key role in the excessive debt accumulation in the Euro periphery after 2009.

While the Euro laid the groundwork for a major increase in trade throughout the Eurozone, the question was who was going to benefit most? That is, which economy would get the lion's share of the increased internal European goods trade flow?

The country that would gain the most from the anticipated escalating internal trade within the Eurozone would be the country able to lower its production costs the most.   The alternative option of lowering costs to get an exports advantage by devaluing one's currency was no longer available to countries that had adopted the Euro as common currency. The country that would dominate intra-Eurozone exports trade would be the country most successful in lowering its unit labor costs—i.e. the one which reduced wages, benefits, and squeezed more productivity out of labor the most.   After joining the Euro in 2002, Germany quickly sought to position itself as the most successful low cost exports producer within the Eurozone and the EU in general.

As the Eurozone began to emerge from the 2001-02 tech recession, the Germany economy was considered the laggard of the Eurozone and was referred to as the 'sick man' of Europe.   In 2005 its unemployment rate was 11.3%. It thereafter enacted extensive labor market reforms and cut corporate taxes from a rate of 45% of profits to a low of 15%. The labor market reforms included reductions of wages, restructuring of collective bargaining, cuts to welfare, raising the pension age and encouraging and enabling new employment in the form of part time work. By 2014, more than half of all German jobs created after 2009 were part time jobs.[7] Together, the spending program cuts, the labor market reforms dramatically reducing labor costs, and the deep cuts to corporate taxes resulted in a classic demonstration of currency 'internal devaluation' by deep corporate cost reduction. By 2005, Germany was in a position to reap the lion's share of intra-Eurozone exports and trade.

The adoption of the Euro meant that other European countries, especially the periphery, could no longer offset Germany's internal devaluation cost-cutting with reductions in their currency exchange rates. That was neutralized effectively by the Euro. The Euro was also valued high at the time, so that periphery countries that borrowed from German and northern banks in Euros could buy large volumes of German exports. Conversely, it meant they would also incur large amounts of debt to German and northern European banks.

German exports to other Eurozone economies surged, as German banks loaned funds to periphery banks, periphery companies, and to periphery governments in turn. Much of the lending by both German-Northern Europe banks and periphery banks as well went into the housing and commercial property markets in Spain, Ireland, and elsewhere, where prices were rising rapidly and reached bubble levels by 2007-08. The boom spilled over to other industries and sectors of the periphery economies, as is typical in a housing and real estate construction and financial asset boom. Ever rising prices in real estate, properties, and in general in turn encouraged still more lending, as collateral values for real estate and properties rose. More lending, more debt, more market price escalation followed in an upward spiral, as financial asset prices continued to rise.

German non-financial businesses benefited from the increased sales of their exports to the periphery. German banks benefited from financing the export trade. Banks especially benefited from the rising flow of money capital now coming back in the form of interest payments as debt accumulated in the periphery, and as periphery businesses, investors, and wealthy recycled their share of profits from the speculative boom and growth back into the northern banks for safety and future re-investment as well.

This successful strategy convinced German bankers and leaders that if Germany could pull itself out of a deep recession and crisis in 2003-05 by means of austerity and exports, then so could other Euro economies do the same, later after 2010. Germany enacted austerity and it appeared to work. Why couldn't Greece, Portugal, Spain, Ireland and others then do the same? What this view conveniently ignored, however, is that the German recovery post 2005 occurred in the context of a solidly growing European and world economy after 2003— not a collapsing and stagnating economy after 2009. The success of their own exports plus austerity policies before 2009 convinced German financial and economic elites, and their politicians, that a focus on exports combined with fiscal austerity worked; it was therefore not necessary to establish a Eurozone-wide banking union to centralize monetary policy. National central banks were sufficient to carry out monetary policy as a supplement to the focus on exports and fiscal austerity.

This view pushing an austerity fiscal policy, a central bank with limited powers, and an exports oriented growth strategy would have profound effect on future Euro recovery when Germany became the dominant player after 2010. It would mean Germany would recovery first and most, while other Eurozone economies would struggle and thus call for more banking union and less fiscal austerity.

When the global crisis of 2008-09 hit, like the US and UK, Europe too had created a kind of real estate bubble. But the property crash in Europe was not as widespread as in the US. It was regional, located largely in the periphery and even there mostly in Ireland, Spain, and to a lesser extent Portugal. Nor did the financial real estate bubble involve shadow banks and derivatives as extensively as in the US. The Eurozone's banking system was still largely dominated by commercial banks and other local, traditional forms of banking. The economic contraction that followed events of 2008-09 was serious, but not as much so as in the US and even UK.

Despite its less severe downturn in 2008-09, Germany in 2009 forced the invoking of an obscure rule that had been introduced earlier in the decade at the time of the creation of the Euro: that rule called for a kind of budget balancing—achieved by means of fiscal austerity—in the event of a crisis. The rule in question called for a ceiling on government budgets and spending, according to which deficits could not exceed 3% of annual GDP. A related rule required that government debt could not exceed 60% of GDP. The deficit-debt ceiling rule was activated by the EC and Eurozone governments in 2010.[8]

By the next full fiscal year, 2011, the full impact of the rule—which in effect required perpetual austerity—began hitting economies hard. At the same time, Germany and its allies in the ECB pushed for the central bank to raise interest rates.

The rate rises that followed in 2011, combined with the austerity policies now taking effect in 2011, exacerbated an already weakened Eurozone economy that had barely just begun recovering from the 2008-09 crash.

The new emphasis on policies of austerity and ECB rate increases also coincided with and exacerbated the debt crises that emerged in 2010 in the weakest of the Eurozone periphery economies—Ireland and Greece. The rate hikes caused bond rates in the Ireland, Greece, and elsewhere in the periphery to rise still further in 2011. The austerity cuts made it increasingly difficult to service the debt, as tax revenue income fell sharply. Government balance sheet fragility in the periphery deteriorated as a consequence of both rising debt and declining tax revenue needed to service the debt, due to austerity.

The Eurozone economies declined further, especially in the periphery, thus requiring still more austerity to meet the 3% budget deficit rule that Germany insisted Eurozone economies adhere to. Fiscal austerity, rate increases, and deteriorating sovereign debt began to negatively feedback upon each other, leading to a still further decline in GDP, again especially in the periphery economies. The weakest of the periphery economies, Greece and Ireland, required still more bailout, which meant debt added to prior debt in order to continue to make payments to Northern Europe lenders on previously incurred debt.

Greece received a 73 billion Euro bailout in May and in November Ireland received an 85 billion Euro bailout. In exchange, they were required to implement even more draconian austerity measures. 'After all, if Germany did it, why can't they' was the rationale heard in northern Europe banking and political circles at the time.

This perverse combination of sovereign debt crises in the periphery; a banking system that was still not recapitalized (i.e. still technically insolvent) with bank lending declining; rising interest rates engineered by the Eurozone central bank; and ever deepening and severe austerity policies—together drove the Eurozone into a severe 'double dip' recession beginning in late 2011.

After growing at a Eurozone wide 3% annual GDP rate in the second half of 2010, nearly all the Eurozone economies began to slow noticeably in early 2011. And not just in the periphery. Growth in the northern European economies stagnated by the summer of 2011 as the periphery economies fell deeper into recession by the third quarter. By the final months of 2011 virtually all Eurozone economies, including Germany, were contracting. The Eurozone's double dip recession was underway; it would last another 18 months, through early 2013. The decline was even more severe in some ways than that experienced during the first recession associated with the global crash of 2008-09.

Eurozone's Double Dip Recession: 2011-2013

After having contracted roughly -10% during the 2008-09 crash, the Eurozone recovered slowly in 2010. Despite a very short and weak recovery from the 2008-09 contraction, the Eurozone central bank, the ECB, raised interest rates sharply in two quick steps, from 1% to 1.5%, in early July 2011, even as the Eurozone growth rate had slipped to only 0.2% when the rate hikes were implemented. It was a classic example of central bank rate hikes implemented prematurely—in an economy still overly sensitive to rate hikes due to excess household and business debt overhang from the preceding boom period and asset prices still not fully recovered yet from the 2008-09 crash.

Both the debt overhang and the asset price weakness served to exacerbate the negative effects of the ECB interest rate hikes on the real economy.[9] The ECB rate hikes were also implemented as Euro bank lending to non-bank businesses was still declining, thus further exacerbating the effect. Raising rates only made banks even more reluctant to lend. The negative effect of the rate hikes on the real economy was almost immediately and significantly felt throughout the region.

At the time the ECB rate hikes were justified by the ECB, and in particular German ministers and Germany's central bank chair, as necessary in order to check escalating inflation. But the inflation spike of 2010-11 was not due to domestic conditions. It was due to speculation in oil and rising demand for oil and commodities driven by the surge in China and EME economies in 2010-11. The inflation was therefore external, supply driven and temporary. Raising domestic rates within the Eurozone to reduce demand in the region would therefore not dampen inflation, given these external global forces. Nevertheless, an ideological preoccupation with preventing goods inflation, in Germany in particular, prevailed and was cited to justify the premature rate hikes. The decision revealed the dominant influence of German and allied central bankers within the governing council of the ECB. This decision to raise rates in 2011, given prevailing conditions, would prove disastrous.

Rising interest rates were not the only factor that drove the Eurozone economy into its double dip recession in 2011. The rate rises coincided with the advent of more severe austerity policies enacted in 2010, now beginning to have their full force and effect. Italy, France, Netherlands, Spain as well as Ireland and Greece all introduced spending cuts ranging from $17 to $24 billion for the year, in addition to raising sales (value added or VAT) taxes, property taxes, and some income taxes. Outside the Eurozone proper, European Union (EU) countries also introduced austerity programs. The UK's austerity budget passed in 2010 called for a 20% budget cut. More than $130 billion was cut from the budget for 2011 and after. The UK's VAT was raised from 17.5% to 20%, which was typical.

As the Euro economies slowed, so too slowed their tax revenue intake, raising their deficit levels well beyond the 3% of GDP rule. Consequently, even more spending cuts and sales tax hikes were called for in 2012. Spain cut another $80 billion, Italy another $7 billion. Greece tens of billions more, as it required a second bailout. France introduced what it called a neutral budget plan, cutting business taxes and reducing spending elsewhere.

Surging global oil prices in 2011-12 took a further toll on the Eurozone economy, further depressing real investment that was already falling due to the freeze up in bank lending, the higher ECB rates, and financial asset deflation. It is estimated that Europe's oil import costs rose from $280 billion in 2010 to $402 billion in 2011, in effect taking $122 billion out of the economy that might have been otherwise invested or consumed.

As nearly all Euro economies slowed or contracted, so did exports and imports, making their contribution to the general slowdown. Eurozone-wide unemployment rose quickly, from 9.8% to 12.2%. In the southern periphery economies, the jobless rate was more than double, as in Spain and Greece unemployment rose to 27%. Rising unemployment and austerity, combined with high debt loads, in turn translated into declines in household consumption as well. All the main elements of economic growth—government spending, household consumption, exports, and business investment—were thus slowing or in decline by mid-2012.

Real investment measured in terms of gross fixed capital formation sharply declined in the 2008-09 crash and then continued to progressively fall during the short recovery that followed and throughout 2011. The focus on exports and external growth, on austerity fiscal solutions, and on raising interest rates led to a chronic decline in real investment. This was true not only of the Eurozone but the entire 27-country European Union. According to a study by McKinsey Associates business consultancy, investment between 2007 and 2011 fell by more than 350 billion euros, or nearly $500 billion—a decline equivalent to 20 times the contraction in private consumption.

In the periphery, falling investment amid rising real debt levels led quickly to collapsing government bond prices, intensified by the professional investor-speculators betting on the fall and thus accelerating it. While external commodity-driven inflation in goods was occurring, financial asset price deflation was also becoming a serious concern. Stock and bond prices were accelerating, as the Euro currency also fell from $1.45 to $1.35. Real estate and property price deflation was particularly severe in Spain and Ireland. Financial instability was thus occurring in parallel to the real economy's contraction then underway. Badly timed central bank rate increases, counterproductive austerity policies, intensifying sovereign debt crises, and collapsing financial assets all combined to exacerbate the downturn. Given that the private banking system was still fragile, banks loaned even less than before. Bank lending in early 2012 fell at its fastest rate since 2009: whereas bank lending in early 2008 grew at a 12% annual rate, by June 2012 it had essentially stalled, now growing a mere 0.3% annual rate.

The Eurozone economy thus stagnated through the summer of 2011. And by the fourth quarter virtually all the economies were in recession. That decline would continue until the spring of 2013, for a total of six consecutive quarters—i.e. longer and with a greater total negative impact perhaps than the shorter 2008-09 crash and recession. Equally important, by the summer of 2012 it was clear that the real contraction was no longer concentrated in the periphery economies only; it now had clearly begun to spill over and deepen in the northern European 'core' economies as well.

ECB Opens the Money Spigot ... Just a Little

After the ECB raised interest rates in April 2011 and again a second time in July, it was forced to reverse its policy and quickly lower interest rates in November and December, from 1.5% back down to 1%. But the move had virtually no effect on the slide to recession by then well underway. Meanwhile, the sovereign debt crisis was worsening fast and bank insolvency was still widespread.

Government debt to GDP ratios rose further in 2011. The debt levels in the periphery economies—Ireland, Portugal, Greece and others—were now well over 100%. Spain's ratio was approaching the century mark, and Italy's rose to 123% debt to GDP. Private bank debt was even higher, averaging more than 127% of GDP across the Eurozone. By 2012, Spanish, Greek, and even French, Belgian, and Italian banks were growing increasingly insolvent. A banking crisis throughout the Eurozone, not just a government debt crisis in the periphery, thus loomed large on the horizon. $200 billion was needed just for refinancing old bank loans coming due in early 2012 alone. And total long term corporate and government bond refinancing needs for all of 2012 amounted to no less than $1.29 trillion.

What was emerging was a financial crisis situation potentially greater than even that confronted in 2008-09. Moreover, the financial instability was overlaid on a rapidly declining real economy as well. The possibility of one crisis exacerbating the other, sending the region into a downward spiral of real and financial asset deflation, was therefore high.

Given this situation, Eurozone finance ministers and the ECB decided not only to lower interest rates rapidly at year end, but to introduce extraordinary emergency programs to bailout both governments and banks as well. The great Euro liquidity injection was about to begin.

Unlike the US and UK, the liquidity injections did not take the form of ZIRP and QEs, at least initially. True ZIRP and QE would have to wait until 2015. The prevailing Eurozone view at the time was that austerity was sufficient to refloat the economy. Monetary policy would merely buy some time for austerity to start having an effect. Monetary policy was still limited to the ECB reducing interest rates, as the Eurozone economy fell deeper into recession in early 2012.

Two government debt bailout programs were introduced under the aegis of the European Commission in 2010 and early 2011. However, although potentially large they were limited in their application to only the most severe sovereign debt cases. The first program, introduced at the time of the eruption of the first Greek government debt crisis in early 2010 to provide bailout for Greek banks and government, was called the European Financial Stability Facility (EFSF). It earmarked 780 billion Euros specifically for government bailouts, just about $1.1 trillion in exchange rates at the time. Greece would acquire 164 billion euros from it in May 2010 (and a second bailout of 165 billion euros in March 2012). Ireland was given 68 billion later in November 2011. Portugal would receive about $29 billion in April 2011 and Spain much later $123 billion. A second, smaller program run by the European Commission directly was called the European Financial Stabilization Mechanism, or EFSM. Introduced in January 2011, it amounted to 60 billion euros in loan guarantees to bailout financing that might be raised from private sources.

But these were select, targeted government bailout funds and not meant to directly bail out private banks or flood the general economy with liquidity—as the US and UK quantitative easing (QE) programs in 2009 were designed to do. Moreover, the total funding of the two Eurozone government bailout programs were mostly commitments on paper. Only roughly half of the approximately $1.2 trillion in bailout funding provided by the EFSF and EFSM was eventually disbursed to Greece, Ireland and other periphery economies.

In the EFSF and EFSM government bailouts, the respective governments were supposed to pass on the bailout funds to their banking systems as well as use them to refinance their own debt. But typically more went to government than to the private banks, which continued to experience very unstable and fragile conditions. The bureaucratic EFSF and EFSM were thus failures in terms of private sector bank bailouts. Not surprisingly, bank lending continued to contract throughout 2011-2012. Many Eurozone banks remained technically insolvent, with available capital far less than necessary should a classic run on the banks emerge. However, the arrangements did conform to the German preference for rigid 'rules' governing bailout fund distributions.

Yet another bailout program was introduced in 2012 as the banking and debt crises intensified and the real economy's slide into double dip accelerated. It was an emergency program called the 'Long Term Refinancing Operation' or LTRO. Unlike the prior two government bailout programs, the EFSF and EFSM, it directly targeted banks. The LTRO allocated initially 489 billion euros to 523 banks facing the need to rollover 200 billion euro loans beginning January 2012, just months away. Another 530 billion euros in funding was added to the 489 billion quickly in February 2012 when it had become clear the earlier amount was insufficient to head off a banking crisis. The combined two issues equaled 1,012 billion euros, or about $1.3 trillion at the time. That raised the total bailout funding—for governments and banks—now potentially available to more than $2.3 trillion.

As the Eurozone economy slid faster into recession in the first half of 2012, a new institution was created to centrally administer the various funds (EFSF, EFSM, LTRO), called the European Stability Mechanism, or ESM. Introduced in June 2012, like the LTRO it was also given authority and funding for bank bailouts, providing another 500 billion euros ($600 billion roughly).

All were introduced in a period of just over six months, from December 2011 to June 2012, with total bailout funds now amounting in dollar terms to approximately $3.15 trillion. While undoubtedly a large sum, once again much was still on paper and represented targeted bailouts of select governments or banks in the most severe trouble. Germany and its allies in the ECB and European Commission (EC) reluctantly agreed to the programs but required various bureaucratic approvals, as well as subsequent approval votes of their respective Parliaments, before the programs might actually disburse funds. In other words, just as Germany was the obstacle on the fiscal front, insisting on rigid rules and implementation of extreme austerity measures in exchange for bailout funds, so too it continued to function as an obstacle to massive direct QE liquidity injections.

All the preceding emergency bailout programs were technically in place by June 2012, at least on paper, as the real economy and debt crisis deteriorated further. The new chair of the ECB, Mario Draghi, had assumed office in November 2011. No time was wasted by Eurozone elites to demand he do still more to stimulate the economy by monetary measures. Fiscal policy was politically frozen as an option. The only tool left was monetary policy action by the ECB. As the Eurozone fell deeper into recession by mid-year, Draghi stole a page from the US central bank playbook that US chairman, Ben Bernanke, had introduced earlier in the decade when Bernanke declared that in the event of a major crisis, if necessary, he would 'drop money from a helicopter'. Draghi therefore stated boldly and publicly that the ECB would 'do whatever it takes' to ensure banks and the economy were provided with all the necessary liquidity. Central bank massive liquidity injection, along the lines of the US and UK, was coming. Exactly when and how was still unclear. Nevertheless, Eurozone stock and bond markets surged on the Draghi announcement of July 2012.

To substantiate his determination to do "whatever it takes", a subsequent fifth bailout program was announced soon after in September 2012. It was called the OMT or 'Outright Monetary Transactions' program. Much like the US third version of QE that was about to be announced in October 2012, the OMT was defined as an 'open-ended money injection' program. That is, it would provide an unspecified amount of bailout as needed and therefore potentially unlimited funding.

OMT meant that the ESM, authorized to spend 500 billion euros, with the remaining funding from the EFSF and ESFM and the LTRO all under its umbrella as well, could now purchase bonds from countries which were not already in a bailout program. Government bond purchases could occur pro-actively, even before a formal bailout program was introduced. The OMT had the added feature of the option to purchase a broader range of securities, not just sovereign bonds, in doing 'whatever it takes'. Yet the purchases still had to get approvals of the bureaucracies and legislatures that were still dominated by the German bankers and their allies. Germany and friends kept their finger on the distribution purse strings. Unlike the US and UK central banks, the ECB still could not unilaterally make purchases that it wanted or targeted simply on its own authority.

The ECB, in other words, was (and still is) not really a true central bank. It is the executive disbursement agency for the governing council composed of the 25 Euro central banks, still dominated by a German and allied northern and east European central bankers majority.

As the bureaucratic maneuvering with regard to monetary policy within the ECB, EC, and other agencies continued throughout early 2012, financial and real economic instability worsened in the Eurozone. The private banking system remained fragile, and banks continued to refuse to make loans, especially to small and medium enterprises in the Eurozone. While the ECB was now permitted to 'turn on the money spigot', given the highly bureaucratic management structure of the bailout funds and the German-imposed set of rules that required layers of approval before funds might be disbursed, very little actual general liquidity had yet to flow. That would only occur with a QE program.

But Germany and allies were adamantly opposed to a banking union, as well as to other central bank powers like Eurozone-wide banking supervision authority for the ECB, a true Eurozone-wide deposit insurance program, and a Eurozone bond which were all prerequisites for the introduction of a true QE program like that introduced by the US and UK to date. Germany did not want a true centralized central banking system—a bona fide banking union like the US Federal Reserve or Bank of England—any more than it wanted a more unified fiscal union in the Eurozone. It had little to gain and potentially much to lose from both.

Germany was doing quite well in most of 2012 and therefore had little interest in giving up or diluting any power it was exercising through its influence in the ECB, EC and elsewhere. In the first half of 2012, moreover, Germany was still growing modestly, even as the rest of the Eurozone was now deep into its double dip recession. That would change, however, when the German economy also began to decline sharply at the end of 2012 due to a significant drop in its exports. Toward the close of 2012, the value of total German exports fell from the low 90 billion euros range at the start of the year to 80 billion at the end of 2012. The German economy was now joining the general Eurozone recession.

That narrow, parochial and nationalist position meant that the Eurozone—with the second largest combined GDP after the US at the time—would remain the weak link in the global economic system, perpetually responding to crises real and financial, but never really able to generate a self-sustained economic recovery above 1% or for very long. Its long term fate was therefore to stagnate at best, which it would continue to do.

Germany's Export Pivot to Asia

But didn't Eurozone stagnation mean that exports to the rest of Europe would decline for Germany? Yes, it did. But after 2010 Germany was already orienting more toward exports to China and the EMEs, which were now booming. During the 1990s Germany was not particularly export driven. After 2010 it would become one of the most exports-dependent. Exports would constitute 20% of its GDP by 2015, about the same as its domestic gross capital investment contribution to its GDP. Its leading export products were autos, machinery and equipment, and chemicals—i.e. just the items that China and other EMEs were interested in as imports. But this was making it increasingly dependent on global economic conditions outside Europe. If the phrase 'as Germany goes, so goes the Eurozone' is correct, then overlaid was the phrase 'as the global economy goes, so goes Germany'.

What Germany's economic pivot to China and Asia meant is that the Eurozone periphery economies, which had provided such a lucrative destination for German exports up to 2011, were now increasingly on their own so far as German and northern money lending to them to finance expansion and purchases of exports were concerned.   With the recessions of 2008-09 and 2011-13 those money flows going to the periphery to buy German exports and develop periphery infrastructure, housing, and commercial property were drying up as Germany turned 'east' in its export strategy. That left the periphery with massive debts from the previous money flows from northern Europe bankers that benefited Germany and northern Europe. In a kind of 'economic strip-mining', to use a metaphor, the periphery economies were left to clean up the mess on their own. Alternatively, they could continue to borrow money from German and northern banks, global investors, and German and northern Eurozone governments—but now primarily not to finance import purchases or internal development but rather to continue making payments on the previously incurred debt—i.e. increasing their debt in order to pay old debt and ending up paying even more interest on total debt than before.

Money capital to pay for money capital, but not money capital to grow periphery EU economies. That was the new 'German arrangement', as

Germany pivoted to push export growth to Asia. Thus the Euro banks, especially in the periphery, were still not bailed out and remained financially fragile. Simultaneously governments fell further into ever more debt as their tax revenue source of income declined, requiring greater government debt bailout.   And with austerity now ravaging their economies as well, rising unemployment and wage compression meant growing household consumption fragility as well. It was a classic case of growing government balance sheet fragility, adding to bank financial and household consumption fragility. The entire Eurozone system was thus becoming 'systemically fragile'.

Eurozone's 2nd Short, Shallow Recovery: 2013-2014

The Eurozone recovered from its double dip recession in the spring of 2013—but only barely. Eurozone growth averaged a mere 0.2% per quarter throughout 2013, driven largely by Germany's economy which accounts for about a third of the total Eurozone. The Eurozone would continue to grow at a similar tepid 0.2% average GDP rate through the following nine months of 2014.

Indicative of the weak recovery was the consistent decline in the rate of inflation in goods and services, which steadily fell within a year from more than 2% annual rate to 0.8% at the end of 2013. Disinflation—i.e. a slowing rate of inflation—would continue through 2014, crossing into deflation—i.e. negative prices—at the end of 2014. Wage growth would fall even faster than goods and services prices, from 2.8% at the start of 2013 to 1% at year-end 2014. Retail sales continued to contract throughout 2013, as did manufacturing and industrial production. Services spending remained flat during 2013.

The point of all this data is to show that the Eurozone's weak 0.2% recovery in 2013 was not due to internal growth factors—whether consumer or business spending. It was due primarily to exports, and in particular German and northern European exports. Germany's growth exceeded the Eurozone region, accelerating in early 2013 due to expanding trade with Asia and, to a lesser extent, due to rising exports to the US as the value of the US dollar rose. Remove Germany and exports in general from the Eurozone growth numbers, and the Eurozone's 2011-2013 double dip recession continued another six to nine months throughout 2013, rather than officially ending in April 2013.

The weak Eurozone recovery of late 2013-2014 was of course also attributable to the continuation of fiscal austerity measures, as well as ineffective central bank interest rate policies that did little or nothing to stimulating the real economy.

In a March 2013 meeting of finance ministers in Brussels, the pro-austerity argument was reaffirmed, even as France and Spain were given two additional years to reach the 3% budget deficit rule and other region economies were also given more leeway. However, in exchange for the 'stretching out' of austerity, as it was called, German and Dutch ministers demanded more structural reforms by those given the extensions.

It was about this time as well that the need for labor market structural reforms was resurrected aggressively by Germany and others. Labor market 'reforms' meant reducing wage and benefit costs to lower the price of exports in order to stimulate domestic economies by export demand. This is sometimes referred to as 'internal devaluation'.

Such reforms were an echo of policies introduced in Germany in 2005, and again in 2010, as German politicians and business leaders shifted to driving down labor costs to give German businesses an export advantage with competitors. Labor cost restructuring was a key element of austerity and exports-driven strategy and should always be viewed in that light. Twice within five years, in 2005 and 2010, Germany reduced pensions, cut unemployment benefits, allowed more hiring of part time workers, as well as weakened unions' collective bargaining. Now it wanted the rest of the region to do the same—but this time, however, in the context of their undergoing two recessions in just four years.

Spain was the first to follow Germany in adopting the 'labor market restructuring' approach and by the end of 2013 had cut real wages by 15%. Its exports coincidentally rose by the same 15%. Workers were thus subsidizing— in effect 'financing'—Spain's recovery. Labor market restructuring was but the latest form of austerity. Old forms of austerity were continuing elsewhere in the Eurozone. Netherlands introduced a new 8 billion euro spending reduction program. France announced it would soon sell its major stake in many private French companies, as well as consider later raising pension retirement ages and reducing unemployment and family benefits as well. Labor market restructuring was thus coming to France. Italy too was planning for it. And in Greece, the second bailout deal called for 25,000 public worker layoffs and additional wage cuts of 25% before the ESM and ECB would agree to release more bailout money. 'Old' austerity was still much alive, while new forms were being developed and introduced as well.

But austerity did nothing to resolve the problem of still growing sovereign debt. Austerity policies purport to cut spending to restore deficits and reduce debt—thereby somehow encouraging investors to invest. But if that is the main justification for austerity, it continued to accomplish the opposite in 2013-2014; it continued to create more deficits and more debt. Nor did the more than $3 trillion in available bailout funds reduce government debt levels. By mid-2013 the debt levels of all the major Eurozone governments had continued to rise. All were approaching, or were already well over, the 100% of Debt to GDP ratio economists generally agree is a threshold making a future instability event highly likely.

If austerity policies failed to reduce debt or lead to real economic growth, then so had central bank monetary policies during 2013-2014. Despite the ECB having cut interest rates to 0.5% in May 2013 and then 0.25% in November 2013, lending by traditional banks had not improved, especially for small and medium businesses. The ECB's latest initiative, the 'OMT' program, didn't help. In the Eurozone, small and medium businesses depend almost totally on traditional bank loans, not bonds, so ECB government bond buying through the OMT or other bailout funds didn't help. Nor did ECB programs targeting specific bank bailouts. Bailing out banks didn't mean they would turn around and start lending. That was an erroneous key assumption that was by now clearly disproven not only by the Eurozone experience but by bank bailouts in the US, Japan, UK and elsewhere. Banks can be bailed out, but won't necessarily lend.

The linkage between low interest rates, bank bailouts, and money injections as monetary means to generate real investment and general economic recovery , was clearly now broken in the post-2008 crisis world. Large multinational corporations in the Eurozone could tap into what are called global capital markets following the example of US shadow banks offering their corporate junk bonds to global investors or US Money Market Funds providing capital. But small-medium businesses could not. Thus, as the ECB lowered rates and managed its trillion euro bailout funds, Eurozone private bank credit growth declined every month. Bank lending was actually negative every consecutive month throughout 2013 and through the first nine months of 2014 as well, as banks consistently complained they still had too many non-performing loans (NPLs) on their balance sheets—i.e. were too fragile to loan.

No longer in official double dip recession, during 2013-2014 movement in the Eurozone economy became more 'crab-like'—i.e. moving sideways, and slowly. Only Germany was doing somewhat better than the region, by focusing increasingly on exports targeting China and Asia. By 2013, 25% of all Europe's exports were to China and Asia, most of which originated in Germany. This China-Asia export shift effectively impoverished the rest of the Eurozone economies, especially the periphery economies that were now saddled by debt, both public and private, and unable to obtain capital with which to grow their real economies out of recession and stagnation (or depression in the case of Greece, Spain, and Portugal).

On the other hand, while the Eurozone real economy languished, the Euro stock markets and their professional investors were doing quite well during 2013. Already the Euro equity markets had risen by 40%. Corporate cash was piling up on balance sheets, approaching $1 trillion, and dividend payouts to investors continued to rise even faster than in the US.

But the limits of Germany's export growth strategy were soon to reappear. By 2014 the IMF estimated that more than half of Germany's (and Spain's) growth of exports came from sales outside Europe. Should the value of the Euro rise relative to other major competitors, then the 2013 export boomlet could quickly dissipate, and with it the moderate German growth that enabled the Eurozone to raise its economic head briefly above recession with its meager 0.2% growth.

In 2014 three developments began to occur with just that consequence: Japan's 2013 introduction of its own massive QE program that significantly reduced the value of its currency, the Yen, by more than 20% to the Euro began to take effect and impact German-Euro exports to China and elsewhere. Like Germany, the Japan focus was also on exports to China and Asia. In late 2014 Japan further escalated its QE program, raising the competitive pressure further on the Eurozone. Second, throughout 2014 the US continued to keep the dollar low by not raising interest rates. That ensured further competition for China-Asia export markets. Third, the global oil glut erupted in mid-2014 and commodities sold by EMEs collapsed in price and volume. That drove down the currencies of emerging market economies. The Euro consequently rose rapidly against the dollar, the Yen, and emerging market currencies, reaching a two year high of $1.38.

With austerity continuing to depress domestic economies in the Eurozone, with central bank monetary policies and 0.25% rates failing to generate Eurozone bank lending, with government debt levels still rising throughout the region, and with unemployment remaining well above 11% with more than 19 million out of work—there was little internal Eurozone source for growth.

And now at year end 2014 it appeared the strategy of dependence on exports for growth by Germany-Eurozone was about to collapse as well. Japan, EMEs, and even US currencies were falling in 2014, thus offsetting Germany-Eurozone export competitiveness. It was also becoming clear that by mid-2014 the major source of German-Eurozone exports—i.e. China—was beginning to slow significantly as well. German exports declined once again at year end-2014, thus raising the specter that the major source of the Eurozone's poor growth performance of 2014 would fade once again, throwing the region into yet another triple dip recession in 2015.

Eurozone's QE Money Firehose: 2015

If 2012 witnessed the creation of the bailout funds that didn't work, and if 2013-14 witnessed the introduction of a ZIRP (0.25%) interest rate policy that didn't work, then in 2015 the ECB and the Eurozone shot its last monetary policy bullet in the form of a Eurozone version of a massive QE liquidity injection program.[10]

The Eurozone's dominant economic event of 2015 was the introduction of a European version of quantitative easing, or 'QE'. In December 2014 the ECB all but announced it intended to go forward with a QE program. Almost immediately the Euro currency began to fall against the dollar, having risen initially in 2013 by 12% and 40% from its historic pre-crisis lows.

The ECB crossed this 'monetary policy Rubicon' in late 2014. Conditions strongly suggested the $13.2 trillion Eurozone region was potentially about to slip into another recession in 2015—as Euro/German exports began experiencing increasing pressure from the accelerating slowdown in China, Asia and the EMEs and the US economy showed signs of slower growth as well.

Continuing fragility in Euro banks was another growing problem. That concern had just prompted the ECB to conduct a 'stress test' to allay public concerns about banking system stability—always the purpose of such tests that always produce positive results regardless of the real condition of banks. The French and Italian economies were also showing severe weakness at year end 2014. Greek and other peripheral countries' debt conditions were worsening. Unemployment was still 1.8%.

For the first time in five years core deflation in goods and services turned negative across the Eurozone in general, declining -0.2%. The red warning flags went up. Something more must be done. But nothing more would be done with regard to fiscal policy, with austerity policies effectively locked in. And lowering interest rates was no longer an option. Rates were already virtually zero. Worse, should deflation continue, real interest rates would actually rise, above zero, and slow the economy. The task to do 'whatever it takes' was turned over to the ECB and its chairman, Mario Draghi, who signaled in December 2014 that QE was coming.

In response to the ECB's imminent decision, not only did the Euro currency start to plummet, from a high of $1.38 to the dollar to what in the next few months would be a low of $1.07, but conversely, Eurozone stocks accelerated by 25% in anticipation of QE.

In January 2015 the ECB announced a 60 billion euro a month liquidity injection QE program, indicating it would continue purchasing bonds at that rate for at least the next 18 months through September 2016. That amounted to a money injection of about $1.2 trillion.[11]

The justification and 'selling' of the program was that it would boost financial asset prices—stocks, bonds, etc.—that would in turn boost business confidence and eventually lead to real investment in goods and production as well. This is always the traditional argument for QE. The first part is of course true. QE and money injection does boost financial markets. It also initially reduces currency exchange rates. The 'free money' quickly goes into financial assets, providing a quick return on investment. But the free money does not go into real asset investment in an equivalent way. Cheap money reduces the cost of investment, but that doesn't necessarily mean a competitive rate of return on real investment compared to investment in financial assets, which is the real determinant, not the cost of money.[12]

German opposition to the QE program was not sufficient to stop it. In Germany, the slowing of exports on the horizon given events in China and the EMEs, and the new more aggressive escalation of QE by the Japanese in late 2014, caused a split in the German-northern and east European allies bloc within the ECB and among the 19 Eurozone finance ministers. Some saw QE as necessary to lower Euro exchange rates to restore German-Eurozone exports. They of course were right. As noted, the Euro did decline significantly even in anticipation of the QE announcement. After a low point of $1.07 to the dollar, for the rest of 2015 the Euro once again drifted up, by late summer 2015 back to $1.15 where it was when QE was announced in January. In the interim, however, German exports did accelerate in 2015, from a previous low of 85 billion Euros at the end of 2014 to a new high of 110 billion. However, other German elements opposed QE since it represented more centralized authority to the ECB and less to the national central banks. QE also represented a further step toward a bona fide banking union, opposed as well by Germany.

In the longer run, the contra-QE argument that would prove most convincing was that QE would ultimately prove ineffective at best at stimulating real growth for the Eurozone over the longer run.

First, critics of the program noted that 80% of the lending in Europe was provided by bank loans to private businesses and households—not by bonds.[13] The fact that almost all the ECB bailout addressed bond buying meant it would have little effect on bank lending and real investment by non-bank businesses. QE bond buying was about protecting and subsidizing the assets of investors and governments, and would not lead to more bank lending, real investment, or general economic recovery.[14] Secondly, the Eurozone banking system was fragmented along national lines and national banking systems. How much QE bond buying would occur within each national economy? How would proportionality in bond buying be assured? A third critique that followed this last point is there was no single Eurozone-wide bond to buy, only the bonds of each of the 25 countries. Did that mean Eurozone countries would now be responsible for the bonds of those Eurozone countries that default? Would their taxpayers have to foot the bill? This had always been Germany's concern and why it opposed the creation of a true Eurozone bond all along, as well as why it insisted in having final say in any bailout program.

Yet another critique was that the bank bailout program, the LTRO, had not proved particularly successful thus far with regard to stabilizing the private banking system. Despite having bought 528 billion euros to date, the private banking system in the region was still not sufficiently capitalized and thus unstable and refused to make loans. Another point was that how could a QE program significantly influence the economy by reducing bond interest rates, when interest rates on government bonds were already approaching zero?[15]

In another often heard criticism, the concern was that introducing a QE would take the pressure off the economies that needed to undertake the kind of fiscal and labor market restructuring that Germany had successfully introduced earlier in order to become more efficient. Germany wanted the rest of Europe to become like itself—that meant the kind of restructuring that it had undertaken to become more export driven. QE would delay this restructuring. Finally, some critics had noted whether there were even enough bonds or private securities available in some of the national economies for the ECB to purchase.

Notwithstanding all these serious criticisms, the ECB proceeded in January 2015 to introduce its Eurozone version of QE. It announced it would buy bonds and non-bond securities now, up to a total of 60 billion Euros every month, or $68 billion, for the next 18 months starting in March 2015 through September 2016. The mix of bond vs. non-bond securities was set at 50 billion vs. 10 billion euros respectively. In a significant change to prior policy and programs, the buying would be 'open ended', much like the US QE3 program. That is, it would continue potentially beyond the 18 months and $1.1 trillion total for as long and as much as necessary until a 2% Eurozone-wide inflation rate was achieved. In what were important concessions to Germany, 80% of losses on bonds of other countries would have to be covered by those countries' own central banks, not the ECB, and bond buying would be proportional to each country's contribution to Eurozone-wide GDP.

With the $1.2 trillion QE program, the Eurozone now had allocated total liquidity injection in the amount of $4.3 trillion. That was 'open ended' and subject to further general liquidity injection in subsequent QE2 and after programs. Having already reduced interest rates to 0.05% as well, the Eurozone now also had clearly introduced a ZIRP program.

The justification for the now massive liquidity injection was that QE and ZIRP provided the confidence necessary for banks to loan and businesses subsequently to invest in real assets. It was the monetary policy analog to the justification for austerity fiscal policy—i.e. it would restore business confidence which, once returned, would lead to real investment, jobs, wage income recovery, consumption and eventual GDP recovery. Business confidence restoration was thus the key 'transmission mechanism' to both austerity and liquidity overkill. But in neither case, however, did the transmission work. The 'mechanisms' were in fact a fantasy, and ideological construct of policymakers intent on simply ensuring that the assets of corporations, bankers and investors would be protected, while they hoped somehow the economy would eventually recover.

'Triple Dip' Recession on the Horizon?

By the summer of 2015 it had become abundantly clear that the global economy was rapidly slowing—led by China's accelerating slowdown, emerging markets' deepening recessions as global commodity deflation intensified, the collapse of Chinese stock markets, and the ratcheting up of global currency wars.

The Eurozone's Germany-driven exports first strategy was unraveling.

The $327 billion liquidity injection by the ECB from March through August 2015 had raised the Eurozone growth rate by a statistically insignificant 0.2%. The drift toward deflation in Eurozone goods and services continued, with inflation projections for all of 2015 down to only 0.1%. Greece's debt crisis erupted a third time, resulting in still 86 billion more euro debt imposed on the country along with more austerity, ensuring further debt and austerity to come. US-dictated sanctions on Russia contributed to the slowing of German and select east European economies. The initial advantage the Eurozone QE achieved in reducing the Euro and stimulating exports had dissipated in less than six months, as other economies—including China—devalued their currencies in turn and as the US decided not to raise interest rates and held back dollar revaluation. After an initial 16% decline of the Euro to the dollar in the months leading up to the Eurozone QE, by September 2015 the Euro's value remained at the $1.2-$1.14 range that it held the preceding February before QE was introduced. As fast as the ECB was able to reduce the Euro's exchange rate, other countries reduced theirs—in a currency war 'race to the bottom'.

Nor was the outlook promising for the Eurozone resurrecting its exports-first strategy, given that Asian economies and China were slowing; that Japan was planning to introduce still more QE to offset the Eurozone and China's August 2015 devaluations; and that the US decided in September to hold its interest rates steady thus preventing the dollar from rising further.

Euro government debt to GDP continued to rise to 93%. EU banks were desperately trying to deleverage their balance sheets still bloated with non-performing loans now equivalent to three times Eurozone GDP levels. With bank lending still moribund, Euro non-bank companies began turning increasingly toward raising junk bond debt in capital markets, which escalated 73% in the first half of 2015. Private corporate debt was thus being piled on to government debt.

By third quarter 2015, financial markets globally were becoming more unstable as well. After initial gains of 25% with the QE announcement, German (DAX), French (CACS) and other Euro stock markets gave up their gains by late summer 2015. US stocks were following China's down. Still more Euro government bonds slipped into negative interest rate territory. And currency markets were weakening. Non-Eurozone European economies—Switzerland, Denmark, Sweden and others—decoupled their currencies from the Euro to discourage speculators and were also discussing more QEs. The Swiss franc and other currencies immediately began to appreciate, cutting into exports and driving their economies toward stagnation and recession.

At its September 3, 2015 meeting the ECB decided to signal more QE was likely coming. It cited the increasing concern with China's slowing economy and thus slowing demand for imports (from Europe and elsewhere) as well as the effects of China's continuing stock market freefall. No doubt it also waited to see what the US central bank would do concerning rates in 2015 and whether

Japan would leap into another round of QE before year end. ECB chairman, Mario Draghi, indicated it was 'willing and able to act' further to increase the 'size, composition, and duration' of its QE program if and when necessary. But apparently not before the US and/or Japan made the next move. Meanwhile, however, political pressures continued to build within the Eurozone as more no-Euro countries within the European Union moved to reduce their rates and inject more liquidity.

On the other hand, while having initially conceded on the first QE, Germany and allies were not yet in agreement to accelerate it with another expanded, QE2. Nor would they support a lifting of austerity rules governing national budgets and debt. Germany's influential finance minister, Wolfgang Schaubel, reaffirmed that rules had to be followed with regard to government budget limits. Governments needed instead to restructure their debts and banks needed to build capital buffers—even if that meant less bank lending—before any new QE initiatives were possible. And in an especially interesting proposal, they proposed that any decisions about fiscal or bailout rules enforcement should be taken out of the European Commission and given to a new "independent fiscal board", much like the ECB's governing council, which could veto national government budget plans.

As the third quarter 2015 closed, debate within the Eurozone also turned increasingly—not to whether finally to introduce programs to generate internal investment, jobs and growth, as might be expected— but to whether to expand QE still further; or alternatively, to focus more aggressively still on 'internal devaluation' to reduce business costs and push to implement more 'labor market reforms'.

If QE was failing to generate exports, then more wage and benefits reduction was viewed as the answer to export competitiveness in a stagnant global trade environment. With unemployment levels still well above 11% throughout the Eurozone, however, more wage compression was destined only to reduce consumption and growth further. Nevertheless, severe wage compression was imposed on Greece in its humiliating third bailout of August 2015, Spain intensified its policy of subsidizing exports with wage cuts, and the new liberal Renzi government in Italy moved closer to passing comprehensive labor market reforms as well. In France, a new finance minister from business circles was placed in office and President Hollande announced a new initiative to expedite labor market reforms. Throughout Europe, new limits on workers' right to strike and bargain were introduced or proposed.

Labor market reforms and restructuring would serve several purposes: first, it was another means by which to carry out wage compression to reduce export costs; as a form of 'internal' devaluation it reduced the need for further devaluation via another QE; and, not least, it served as a form of austerity policy as well.

Lessons the Eurozone Has Yet to Learn

By 2015, the lessons of the Eurozone's experience since 2009 were still largely unheeded by Germany, northern Europe bankers, bureaucrats in the Troika pan-European economic institutions, and ruling political parties in key European countries.

1.   A strategy focusing on export driven growth is at the mercy of other economies doing the same. All economies can adopt the same strategy, which tends to negate the other. All gains are wiped away in an exports-first 'race to the bottom'. An export-first growth strategy only works when the global economy as a whole is growing and trade expanding. And that was no longer the case. By 2013 and certainly by 2014 economies were slowing rapidly, including China's, and with that so too slowed global trade and general demand for exports.

2.   Bureaucracy- and central bank-managed banking bailouts don't necessarily lead to bank lending and real investment. Nor do $3.1 trillion bank bailout slush funds necessarily solve the problem of widespread technical bank insolvency. Private bank non-performing loans (NPLs) must be pro-actively removed from bank balance sheets. Furthermore banks must be required to lend in exchange for bailouts and the composition of that lending must reflect where loans are most needed—and not to financial asset speculation.

3.   History shows austerity fiscal policies don't reduce sovereign deficits or debt, and therefore provide no incentive to capital-returning and real investment. In fact, austerity is a disincentive and in net terms discourages capital committing to growth projects.[16] Government direct public investment, including the direct hiring of the excess unemployed, must constitute the core of fiscal policy. Government spending must focus on job creating investment projects and not on subsidies that dissipate in the short term.

4.   Lowering interest rates to zero does not necessarily lead to more bank lending either. A new anomaly in the post-2008 crash global economy is that reducing interest rates has little effect of stimulating real investment; and conversely, raising rates has an immediate and significant effect on discouraging real investment and slowing economic growth. Both are the consequence of growing systemic fragility in the economy. Contrary to mainstream economic theory, reducing the cost of investment—whether from lower interest rates, business tax cuts, free money or whatever—does not lead to investment given conditions of financial fragility and 'epic' recession—i.e. in the context of short shallow recoveries following repeated similar recessions and relapses in real growth.

What is required for investment to return is expectations of sustained profitability. But profitability is itself relative. Real asset investment, even if profitable, will not recover significantly if profits from financial asset investment are consistently greater than from real asset investment. Low interest rates thus encourage relatively more profitable financial asset investment and speculation. With each announcement of a new bailout program and each reduction of interest rates by the Eurozone central bank, financial asset markets surged while real investment continued to stagnate or fall. In other words, the link between interest rates and cost of investment on the one hand, and real asset investment on the other, has been broken and new stronger links between money, rates, and financial assets are replacing the former.

Nonetheless, still not having absorbed these lessons, it appears the Eurozone will 'stay the course' into 2016 and beyond. It will almost certainly embark upon yet another monetary quantitative easing or QE solution, most likely sooner than later. It will continue to fall behind the curve as both government and private debt continues to grow, as the ability to finance that debt grows more difficult. It will simultaneously continue to rearrange the deck chairs on its Titanic fiscal austerity programs, thereby imposing still more austerity as it evolves new forms of labor market restructuring and a more centralized bureaucratic pan-European organization. And it will continue to pursue some kind of exports-driven strategy to try to obtain for itself a growing share of an already shrinking global exports and global trade economic pie.

Endnotes

1   Excluding Germany, which has recovered to pre-recession output levels.
2   Until 2013 China too was largely an export-driven growth economy, although massive infrastructure investment also characterized its growth strategy through 2012. As its exports plus infrastructure strategy began to produce declining returns after four years, China attempted to shift to a more 'internal' growth-driven strategy. It has experienced problems in doing so, however, in part due to the financial instability that has afflicted China as speculative money capital inflows followed its goods exports outflows to the rest of the world economy.
3   This of course is contrary to prevailing economic theory in which trade, and free trade in particular, is a kind of a 'holy grail', never to be doubted or challenged: more trade means more growth and free trade means more trade and thus growth. But the reality is that free trade and more trade leads to net slower global real growth over time, given the diversion of real investment to more volatile investment targeting exports instead of less volatile real investment in the domestic economy. Economic theory does not account, however, for longer term negative effects from a greater relative focus on export driven growth.
4   These include Netherlands, Austria, Slovakia, the Baltics, and other non-Euro ministers within the European Union in Scandinavia, Hungary, and Poland depending on the issue.
5   Six additional countries not in the Eurozone formally also participate on the governing council of 25.
6   Imbalances in exports are referred to as 'current account' imbalances. They are associated, however, with corresponding 'capital account', or money flow, imbalances in turn. The money flows lead to debt and financial instability in the periphery, as Germany gains in real economic terms that enable it to maintain

financial stability. Thus Germany exports not only goods but financial instability to its periphery export neighbors as well.

7 In economies like Italy and Spain part time labor constituted up to 70% of all new hires. Part time and temporary employment—sometimes called 'contingent' labor—has been a primary means of reducing total wages since such employment is paid typically half to two-thirds of equivalent full time wages and often with fewer benefits. It also allows employers significant cost savings by allowing them 'flexibility' to hire and fire on short notice.

8 Germany also simultaneously deepened its own 'labor market restructuring' in 2010 to cut labor costs still further.

9 Just as debt and asset deflation tend to minimize the potential positive impacts of interest rate cuts on economic recovery.

10 'Work' in this context means getting banks to lend to non-bank enterprises and in turn having non-banks invest in expanding domestic production that creates jobs and raises wage incomes and consumption.

11 With the $1.2 trillion QE program, the Eurozone thus established a potential liquidity injection of $4.3 trillion, if one includes the preceding targeted government and bank bailout programs—the EFSF, EFSM, ESM, LTRO, and OMT—with their remaining $3.1 trillion funds.

12 It is interesting to note that his view that boosting stock and bond markets will lead to more business confidence and thus more real investment was the very same view that had been used in China to justify the Chinese government introducing various measures to encourage stock buying after mid-2014. Those measures and buying would lead to a financial bubble in stocks that would burst a year later in June 2015—more on which in the next chapter.

13 By contrast, in the US 20% of lending is through bank loans and 80% through what are called 'capital markets' (corporate bonds, commercial paper, leveraged loans, securitized loans, venture capital and the like provided through shadow banks of various kinds and not traditional commercial banks). In other words, the structure of Eurozone finance did not make QE as effective as in US and UK in bank bailout or for general liquidity injection.

14 Which is generally true with regard to all QE programs. Protecting the wealth of investors is then justified by such programs as leading to a renewal of business confidence that therefore, through that medium or 'transmission mechanism', it is leading to real investment recovery in turn. However, the 'mechanism' has no empirical verification.

15 Germany's 10 year government bond was already below 0.5%. It and others would eventually turn negative.

16 From the standpoint of mainstream economic theory, three 'holy grails' are imbedded in the above policies and represent economic ideology rather than economic science: monetary policies of low rates don't stimulate real investment; austerity policies don't convince investors to commit new capital; and export and free trade doesn't 'lift all boats' for all parties trading—just for some and even for them only temporarily.

6

CHINA: BUBBLES, BUBBLES, DEBT AND TROUBLES

As preceding chapters have documented, the weakest links in the global economy today—the emerging market economies (EMEs)—are locked in an economic tailspin, hammered by slowing global demand for their commodities, commodity and financial asset deflation, falling currency values, capital flight, slowing real investment, rising debt and import inflation, and general economic stagnation or recession. The EME downward spiral that initially began to emerge in 2013 is now accelerating two years later. At the same time the second and fourth largest regional economies in the world—Japan and Europe—have still to this day never really recovered from the 2008-09 global crash to pre-crash levels. Both Europe and Japan have continued to hover between repeated recessions and stagnant growth, at best. The US economy since 2009 has done only slightly better, growing at half the normal post-recession rate and collapsing on four different single quarters since 2011 to near-zero or negative GDP growth rates, in what is best described as a sub-normal 'stop-go' economic trajectory.

Until recently, China has been exception to this general scenario characterizing the advanced economies (US, Europe, Japan). For much of a brief period from 2009 through 2012 China's economy boomed, growing at double digit GDP rates. However, beginning in 2013—and concurrent with the slowing of global trade, the collapse of world oil prices and accelerating global currency wars—China's rapid real growth has slowed significantly, a slowdown that is gaining momentum in 2015.

China's share of world exports has been under attack since 2013 by Japan's, and then Europe's, de facto currency devaluations resulting from their quantitative easing (QE) programs. Those QE programs have driven the Euro down by 23%, and the Yen by an even larger 30% against China's currency, the Yuan-Renminbi, since 2013. Those policies, along with the general slowdown in world trade, have slowed China's exports, a centerpiece of its economic growth. The exports slowdown in turn has caused China's manufacturing sector to contract consistently since 2014. By pegging its currency to the US dollar in June 2010, China's exchange rate has risen by 10% to 30% against many of its Asian competitors since 2013, as the Yuan has risen in tandem with the rising US dollar.

The slowing in China's exports and manufacturing sector has been accompanied since 2013 by a slowing in what was another major growth source in China during 2009-2012—infrastructure investment in industrial and commercial projects and residential real estate.

China's Successful Fiscal Recovery Strategy: 2009-2012

Much of China's infrastructure boom of 2009-2012 was the consequence of government direct investment, which rose to more than 45% of China's total GDP. Local infrastructure and industrial expansion projects contributed to the boom as well. These were financed in large part by local and regional governments' proceeds from local land sales and 'hot' money inflows from offshore shadow bankers and speculators. As millions of rural Chinese moved from the countryside to the cities to provide the labor force for the industrial, manufacturing, and infrastructure expansion, residential housing also boomed after 2009, financed from many of the same sources.

So China recovered rapidly after the 2008-09 global crash, while the advanced economies remained stagnant, slipped in and out of recessions, or struggled with a 'stop-go' trajectory.

That different recovery trajectory for China was due to China's different policy choices. Unlike the advanced economies (AEs)—the US, UK, Europe and Japan—China's immediate response to the global financial and economic crash of 2007-09 was not to rely almost exclusively on monetary policies—i.e. central bank liquidity injections—in order to bail out the banks and hope thereby to generate economic growth. Unlike the AEs, China's financial institutions at the time were mostly nationalized government banks and were not plagued by collapsing financial asset prices caused by over-lending to speculators and shadow bankers, as was the case for the AEs. At least not in 2008-09. Moreover, there were no shadow banks to speak of in China in 2009 to drag down the traditional banking system. That would change dramatically over the next half decade, but was not yet a factor in 2009.

So for the moment, in 2009, China's recovery policy focused on fiscal measures, at the heart of which was a massive direct government spending program aimed at rapidly expanding real asset investment and projects in industrial, commercial, infrastructure, housing and manufacturing. China's banking system basically provided the money supply to fund the real investment boom. It had no great financial asset losses on their balance sheets that would discourage lending, as in the AEs. Moreover, since China had nationalized public banks, the banks would lend when the government told them to do so, and to whomever the government said they should—on infrastructure, buildings, manufacturing and industrial expansion, housing, equipment, etc.

AE's Failed Monetary Recovery Strategy: 2009-2015

China's fiscal direct government real investment spending for recovery approach contrasted sharply with the AEs, where the strategy for recovery has without exception focused since 2009 primarily on monetary policies by AE central banks. AEs have implemented a 'bail out the banks first' strategy, in the hope banks would then lend to stimulate real asset investment. That would lead, according to monetary theory, to real job creation and wage income growth to keep the growth momentum going. It would then raise real goods prices as well as stock prices, to further fuel and stimulate consumption, to drive private investment further, and so on.

But the AE money injection by central banks to bail out the private banks first strategy proved a total failure. The banks would not lend to small and medium businesses for real investment expansion. Lending targeted multinational corporations who invested abroad or shadow banks that in turn redirected the money flows to financial asset speculation. Stock and other financial asset prices would inflate but do little for the real economy. Lack of real investment in the AEs kept job creation slow and in low paying service industries. Wage incomes did not grow, and therefore neither did real investment. Real goods prices slowly disinflated and drifted toward deflation, thus discouraging real investment and consumption still further. Employers attacked wages and benefits of workers unable to defend themselves due to the massive unemployment and slow recovery. Profits from cost reduction, not sales revenue, became the new norm.

Near zero interest rates for banks, shadow banks, and speculators had an additional perverse effect: corporations issued record new corporate bond debt. That debt, profits from cost cutting, and the historic tax cuts benefitting businesses and investors that accompanied the monetary policies, added still more income to businesses. But instead of being directed to real investment, their excess net income was redistributed to investors as record stock buyback and dividend payouts, redirected to financial asset markets where prices were booming, or remained hoarded on business balance sheets. All these coinciding factors resulted in AEs recovering at a tepid pace (US) or else stagnating long term and repeatedly slipping in and out of recessions (Japan, Europe) after 2009. The AE strategy of 'monetary policies first'—i.e. as recovery policies primarily targeting bankers, investors and multinational corporations first—was thus a failure. This contrasted sharply with China's 'fiscal policy first' approach—i.e. a massive government direct investment and manufacturing for exports strategy—which proved quite successful in generating recovery, at least initially for the 2009-2012 period.

But the two main sectors responsible for China's double digit growth between 2009-2012, i.e. manufacturing & exports and direct government investment, have both cooled significantly since 2013.

They worked amazingly well for several years, 2009-2012, pulling up the emerging markets along with China as China's demand for their commodities and semi-finished goods surged, and mitigating the effects of the 2007-09 crash on the immediate post-2009 global economy. There is little doubt that China's policies and growth post 2009 played the key role in preventing an even weaker global recovery than occurred from 2009-2012. Without China's fiscal-direct investment strategy, it is quite likely the entire global economy would have experienced another global contraction circa 2011-12. Instead it stumbled along, with Europe-Japan in and out of recessions, the US growing at sub-historical post-recession levels, while China and emerging markets in tandem recovered.

Yet even China's successful 2009-2012 manufacturing + exports + government direct investment strategy began to slowly unravel in 2013, also impacting the emerging markets it had pulled along with it in 2009-2012. And that unraveling has gained steam in 2015.

The question is: why did China's real economic growth start to slow after 2012? What has that growth slowdown had to do with China's shift in policies after 2012? With the massive liquidity and debt generated in China post-2009? And with the shadow bankers and AE finance capital inflows and the financial asset bubbles these created after 2012— including the most recent China stock bubble unwind?

China's Liquidity Explosion

Concurrent with its massive fiscal stimulus of 2009, estimated at around 15% of its GDP at the time, China opened the floodgates to money injection into its economy. At first that liquidity came from its central bank, the PBOC, and other government banks to finance industry and infrastructure expansion. To an extent this was necessary. If the record fiscal stimulus focusing on direct investment, expansion of its manufacturing and industrial production base, and buildup of supporting infrastructure was to happen successfully, a significant increase in its monetary supply was necessary. Without a corresponding monetary increase, the stimulus would not result in the double digit real GDP growth that it did. But this liquidity injection from official banking sources was in excess of what was necessary to finance real asset investment in manufacturing, mining, structures, and supporting infrastructure.

China's M2 money supply had increased by about 15 trillion Yuan, from 25 to 40 trillion, during its prior boom period, 2000 to 2008. Starting in 2009, from a M2 level of about 40 trillion, however, it doubled to approximately 80 trillion by 2012. In 2013 the money floodgates would open still further, with M2 rising to 135 trillion by mid-year 2015—a gain of 55 trillion in just a little over two years!

In dollar terms, at the 2010-mid-2015 exchange rate of the Yuan fixed at 6.2 to the dollar, liquidity as M2 tripled, from roughly $6.5 trillion in 2009 to $19.5 trillion. That acceleration has continued, with M2 rising another $2.5 trillion in just the last nine months from October 2014 through July 2015. In other words, liquidity was growing twice as fast as the growth in China's real GDP.

Even when defined narrowly as M2 money supply, this magnitude of liquidity injection was excessive. Perhaps the injection between 2010 and 2012—from $6.5 to $13 trillion—was necessary to ensure the growth of real production and GDP. But the further acceleration of money into the system that began in late 2012-2013 would only spill over increasingly to finance more financial asset investment instead of real asset investment in infrastructure, manufacturing, and industrial production. Furthermore, around 2012, in addition to the official excessive M2 liquidity, overall liquidity was boosted still further by foreign money capital inflows that China not only welcomed but facilitated. Foreign direct investment by AE based banks and multinational corporations provided part of this. But another source was the rise and expansion of shadow banks and speculators, both global offshore as well as domestic Chinese shadow banks.

Prior to 2009 there were virtually no shadow banks in China. As a result of a series of reforms opening up China's financial system after 2010 to global finance capital, by 2014 shadow banks would provide 30% of all the accumulated debt in China from all sources—governments, corporations, banks. With the rise of shadow banks, 'inside credit' would add still further to the 'money credit' forms of liquidity, supplementing further the official M2 and money capital inflow forms of liquidity.

Perhaps the most important point to be made about China's liquidity explosion is that, as liquidity has surged from various sources— official and shadow—it has not gone into real asset investment at a similar rate. As liquidity accelerated from $6.5 trillion to $22 trillion—more than doubling as a percent of China's GDP—China real asset investing has continued to slow as a percent of GDP. As latest data for August 2015 now show, according to Thomson Reuters Datastream Research, China's fixed asset investment as a percent of GDP has declined from 22% at the end of 2011 to only 11% at mid-year 2015. Industrial production has similarly fallen by half.

So the next big question is: where has the massive liquidity explosion since 2009, accelerating after 2012, gone if not to real asset investment? That amount of liquidity was created for some purpose. It was not created to sit around on bank balance sheets. The answer is: it went into financial asset investing instead of real asset investments, or else was sent offshore for other purposes. But in the case of China, it was mostly the former during the period in question.

A central theme of this book is that the massive, excess liquidity being generated globally in recent decades is getting redirected largely toward financial asset investment and speculation. It is loaned out by banks and shadow banks to other financial institutions and financial investors, often for the purpose of speculation in financial instruments of various kinds, both traditional (equities, bonds, foreign exchange, etc.) as well as newly created (futures, options, derivatives of all kinds, etc.). That massive liquidity surge is then leveraged as debt increasingly in financial asset markets. The greater profitability it produces in financial investing in turn redirects investment capital out of real asset investing, which then slows. That slowing leads to goods deflation, as financial asset investing leads to financial asset inflation.

It appears that China has now capitulated to this global trend.

The Inevitable Debt Crisis

The primary indicator of excess liquidity and financial asset investment and speculation is debt. Debt—i.e. credit extended by lenders—is the mediating element between liquidity and financial asset investing. Excess liquidity is necessary for the availability of excess credit to be loaned out as debt. The leveraging of debt is an indicator of financial asset over-investment and financial speculation that eventually leads to financial asset bubbles, instability events, and periodic asset bubble crashes. And when those crashes are of sufficient scope and magnitude, an economy-wide—or even global—financial crisis results.

In parallel with China's exploding liquidity, its total debt has also nearly quadrupled from 2007 to mid-2015. According to a recent 2015 study by McKinsey &Company, the global business research and consulting firm, China's total debt rose from $7.4 trillion in 2007 to $28.4 trillion through mid-2014.[1] That total represents 282% of China's GDP at mid-year 2014, among the highest in the world

The problem with China's debt, however, is not just its magnitude, nor even its rate of increase. Both are impressive enough. The even greater problem is its composition— the proportion of the debt that is private business associated debt. China national government debt is not particularly severe as countries go. But that of private businesses is, and especially older basic industrial companies including the many that are government enterprises.

By far the largest part of the $28.2 trillion in outstanding debt in China, as of mid-2014, was held by non-financial businesses. At 125% of China's $9.4 trillion 2014 GDP, that's about $11.9 trillion. Add another $6.2 trillion for financial institutions' debt. That's more than $18 of the $28 trillion, roughly two-thirds of its total debt as business-financial, of which, corporate debt is roughly $16 trillion in 2015.

Local government debt is another problem of major dimensions in China, and should be viewed in part as wrapped up with private sector business debt.   Over 10,000 local government entities in China set up 'off balance sheet' property investment vehicles called LGFVs (local government financing vehicles). Borrowing heavily from shadow banks, they then over-invested in local property markets. LGFV debt was approximately 18% of China GDP in 2008, or $634 billion. According to a Chinese government survey done at the end of 2013, it rose to about $3 trillion for that year. Projections are it will rise further, to 45% of China GDP in 2015, or $4.6 trillion.

Another approximate $3.8 trillion represents household debt in China as of 2014, according to the McKinsey study, about half of which is household mortgage debt. That $3.8 trillion rose from $1.9 trillion in 2010. But the amount today may be actually higher, since the $3.8 trillion McKinsey estimate predates the bubble in Chinese stock markets that began growing rapidly after the 2014 data by the McKinsey study. As the stock bubble grew, 'margin debt' lending by brokers to *retail* stock market investors, i.e. households who constitute 85% of China's stock buyers, rose by as much as another $.85 trillion in just one year, from July 2014 to June 2015, according to some estimates.

Extrapolating from the mid-2014 figures, China's total debt therefore likely will exceed $30 trillion in 2015—just about three times China's nominal annual GDP. About $26.5 trillion is private sector debt of various kinds and related off balance sheet local government, LGFV, real estate debt. The rest is general government debt of about $4 trillion. That private sector + LGFV debt represents a $20 trillion increase in private sector debt alone since the 2008 crash—an unprecedented, historic rise in debt in only five years or so.

That debt would not have been possible without the massive liquidity injection by banks, foreign money capital in-flows, shadow bank source funding, and forms of 'inside credit' like margin debt, most of the latter of which is reportedly provided by shadow banks as well. And debt has consequences, especially when of that magnitude and composition. It becomes particularly important when the real economy is slowing or declining and when deflation is a factor, both in financial securities prices as well as in real goods and services prices.

China's Shadow Banks

Shadow banks as a major source of credit and debt in China are a phenomenon of the post-2009 period. A study by JP Morgan Bank in 2012 estimated that the shadow banking sector in China grew from only several hundred billions of dollars in total assets under management in 2008, to more than $6 trillion by the end of 2012.[2] By 2013 the total had risen to more than $8 trillion, according to the research arm of Japan's Nomura Securities company. Shadow bank total assets rose another 14 percent and $1 trillion in 2014—to more than $9 trillion. A study by McKinsey research in 2014 determined shadow banks accounted for no less than 30% of China's total debt issued in 2013.[3]

At the center of shadow bank instability has been the so-called 'Investment Trusts'.   According to McKinsey Research, Investment Trusts today account for between $1.6-$2.0 trillion (of the roughly $9 trillion) of all shadow bank assets in China. Trusts' assets grew five-fold between 2010 and 2013. Approximately 26 percent of the Trusts provided credit (and therefore generate debt) to local governments for infrastructure spending, another 29 percent to industrial and commercial enterprises, another 20 percent to real estate and financial institutions, and other 11 percent to investors in stock and bond markets. Local government debt in particular has risen by more than 70 percent in China since 2010. In other words, shadow bank credit has gone mostly to those sectors of China's economy where debt has accelerated fastest and produced financial bubbles.

That rapid growth in shadow banking was the direct consequence of China leadership deciding to open China's economic doors to foreign money capital big time around 2010. Whereas in the US and UK, and later Japan and Europe, the main engines of liquidity creation in the wake of the 2008-09 global crash were zero interest rates and quantitative easing, in China the liquidity injection was no less impressive in terms of magnitudes but it took place on the one hand through more traditional central bank measures—traditional bond buying, lowering of reserve requirements, etc.—to which was added the money inflows from the advanced economies on the other.

As later chapters will elaborate, the advanced economies (AEs) starting in 2008 pumped liquidity amounting to around $25-$30 trillion into their economies in the form of central bank engineered zero interest rates and QE. A significant part of this AE liquidity injection flowed out of the advanced economies and into emerging markets after 2009, including China. So China's massive liquidity was similar in content but different in source and intent from that of the US, UK, Europe and Japan which relied heavily on zero rates and QE. But shadow banks in both cases—the AEs and China—play significant roles in transmitting that massive liquidity into investors and financial markets in the form of leveraged debt. A difference was which markets. In the AEs, the liquidity and debt was directed into stock and bond markets and derivatives of various kinds.

In China's case, it initially flowed into local government financed housing, land speculation, and commercial and industrial real estate. Some also went into what are called 'wealth management products', or WMPs. And some into 'trust' loans that provided refinancing funding for state owned enterprises (SOEs) that were unable to qualify for better rates from traditional bank loans. Only beginning in 2014 did the liquidity-debt flow into China's equity markets. So just as shadow banks played a key role in destabilizing the financial systems in the AEs up to 2008-09, their destabilizing effect was delayed in the case of China to 2010 and beyond. And there is no way that a $9 trillion money injection in just four years could fail to destabilize and create financial asset bubbles. An important question is what role did these bubbles—in local infrastructure and housing, in WMPs, in propping up failing SOEs, and then in equity markets—play in contributing to China's concurrent real economy slowdown? Was it merely coincidental that the slowing of China's real economy began in earnest, circa 2012-13, as its financial asset bubbles began to grow and multiply?

The main financial vehicles closely associated with China shadow bank lending include 'trust accounts' offered by Trust institutions that invest on behalf of high end investors, both in China and abroad. Another is the 'wealth management products', the WMPs, which are financial assets of various kinds sold to mid- to high-end investors—many of whom got rich initially from the local land, real estate, and local government infrastructure bubble and moved on, taking profits, and reinvesting in the WMPs. Another is 'entrusted loans', in which financing is provided for companies to lend to each other, including many state owned enterprises, or SOEs. Many of the old-line industrial companies have loaded up on 'entrusted loans' in particular, which amount to China's version of AE 'junk bond' corporate financing.

Shadow banks can be defined either by the financial instruments or markets, as per above, or In terms of their institutional forms. Shadow banks in China include traditional forms like hedge funds and private equity firms. Reportedly there were 4000 Chinese hedge funds and private equity firms launched in the first half of 2015 alone, no doubt spawned by the then-escalating bubble in China's stock markets. But China's shadow banking system includes many new forms of shadow banking that have recently arisen in the AEs, like peer-to-peer lending companies, finance companies, etc., as well as forms relatively more prevalent in China, like microcredit companies. However, 'Trust' companies are a particularly important form of shadow bank in China.

Trusts in China have served as the conduit for loans to local governments that in turn fed the real estate bubble. They also function as intermediaries between companies and wealthy investors to raise funds for many non-financial companies in desperate need of credit to remain in operation. Trusts are therefore a kind of 'junk bond' agent for corporations unable to obtain credit on normal banking terms but willing to pay a higher interest rate for credit in order to buy time to remain in business. And they also serve as aggregators of retail investors' money capital directing their investments into stocks and other derivative financial instruments.

China's Triple Bubble Machine

Thus far China has faced three financial bubbles since 2013 which are in various stages of collapse and therefore financial asset deflation. The first is the local government property and infrastructure bubble. The second, the corporate junk bond and refinancing bubble involving older industrial companies and SOEs. In both cases, China's central government has been intervening to prevent a rapid collapse of the bubbles and financial assets, trying to slow them down, prevent contagion, and extend the period of unwinding. The third bubble, in its two major stock markets, Shanghai and Schenzhen, began to form in late summer 2014. In a year's time, the stock markets surged 120%, clearly a bubble, and then began collapsing in June 2015. Since June 2015 the central government has been desperately intervening on an unprecedented scale to prevent the stock collapse from gaining momentum, just as it has been since 2013 to contain the deflating of the previous housing-local infrastructure bubbles that continue to be a problem.

The first bubble, in local real estate property, was driven by local governments, their off balance sheet financing vehicles, the 10,000 or so LGFV funds, and shadow bank financing (domestic and foreign) providing the liquidity and debt that fueled financial speculation in real estate from 2011 to 2014. Real estate prices rose to record levels in 2013. That bubble finally began to deflate in 2013-14. The collapse of the over-investing in housing and local infrastructure meant that a major stimulus to China's real economy was thus removed after 2013, or at least significantly reduced. It has been estimated that housing constitutes 10% of China's GDP. So its collapse and retreat has taken away a major underpinning to China's real economy. In other words, the collapse of financial asset prices, and their subsequent deflation, has direct effects on a real economy's GDP.

The effect of the housing bubble as it expanded also impacted the real economy. China's central government intervened several times to slow the housing bubble before 2014 but without much effect. Each time it intervened by raising interest rates it simultaneously slowed the real economy as well as the real estate sector. As this happened, China then lowered rates again and introduced fiscal mini-stimulus packages to get the real economy back on track. This in turn restarted the real estate bubble. This see-saw policy to try to tame the shadow banks and keep the economy growing at the same time was attempted several times before 2014. Thereafter, China adopted a more targeted approach to attacking its shadow banks, speculators, and their local government official allies feeding the bubble in local real estate and infrastructure. By 2014 real estate prices began to moderate. However, the speculators and the profits they made from the real estate bubble then moved on—to investing and speculating in the new financial asset opportunity associated with the WMPs, the 'asset management fund' securities.

The WMPs fueled the continuing bubble in what other economists in the past have called 'ponzi' finance, providing high interest loans from 'trust accounts' managed by Trusts and other shadow banks to enterprises becoming increasingly fragile. A parallel development in the boom in 'high yield' (junk) bonds was occurring simultaneously in the US and AEs. But as China's real economy has continued to slow, fragile enterprises are increasingly unable to repay even these high cost WMP (junk) loans. On several occasions since 2014, the Chinese central government has had to bail them out and absorb the losses. As China's real economy slows more rapidly in 2015-16, it is questionable whether the central government can continue to bail out ever-wider potential debt payment defaults by these enterprises. Should it not do so, the market value of the WMPs will also deflate rapidly, just as housing has.

China's third clear financial bubble has been the acceleration in its stock markets. China's stock bubble of 2014-15 and its current collapse has several roots. First, it is the outcome of a conscious shift in policy by China made in 2014, to redirect the massive liquidity and debt that had been destabilizing its internal financial system—i.e. in housing, local government investment, real estate, and desperation financing of failing enterprises—into the stock markets. In 2013 a major policy 'turn' was decided by China's leadership, of which the encouragement by the central government of the stock bubble was one element.

That major policy turn was to move toward encouraging more private investment and private consumption as major drivers of the economy, and to therefore shift away from the prior heavy reliance on direct central government investment and export sales, as was the previous case. That direct investment plus exports growth strategy had begun to lose momentum by 2013. Future growth based on exports was about to become more difficult, as both Japan and Europe had entered double dip recessions and US growth showed no signs of accelerating. Japan introduced its QE program, designed to drive down its currency exchange rate and make it more competitive in export markets. Europe introduced its own liquidity version, a kind of 'pre-QE' called Long Term Refinancing Option (LTRO), with the same objective in mind. The US signaled it would raise interest rates which meant emerging markets would be severely economically impacted at some point and thus reduce their demand for China's exports as well. Global trade showed signs of initially slowing.

An export-driven strategy was therefore less reliable, China apparently decided. At the same time, it was also growing clear there were limits to the Chinese government's direct investment stimulus to growth. Unoccupied commercial and residential projects proliferated, including almost vacant new cities. China apparently therefore decided at an important Communist Party conference in 2013 to 'restructure' by shifting to more private sector driven growth. That is, to encouraging more private business investment and private consumption. Boosting the stock market was therefore viewed as the solution to enable the transition to more private investment and consumption.

Stimulating the rise of stock prices was also considered to have a double beneficial effect. It would divert money capital out of the over-heated local housing and real estate-infrastructure market—which it did. Higher stock prices would in theory also provide an important funding source for SOEs and other non-financial enterprises in trouble. If their stock price rose, it would reduce their need to borrow more debt at higher rates with more stringent terms of repayment. Debt would be exchanged for equity, reducing their financial fragility. Higher stock prices also meant, in theory at least, that enterprises in general would realize higher capital gain income, from which they could and would invest in expansion. Real asset investment would result, providing jobs and income for more workers and thus more private consumption. Rising stock prices would also have a positive 'wealth effect' on high end retail investors in the market, and also promote more private consumption. Higher stock prices would assist in the strategic shift to more private sector investment and consumption as the key drivers of economic growth.

It appeared a stock market boom was therefore the answer to several strategic challenges: first, the stock boom enabled plans to restructure toward more private investment and consumption; second, it addressed the need to tame the shadow banks and the bubbles they were creating by redirecting money flows into stocks; third, the new investment and consumption would get the China economy back on a faster GDP growth path—a path that was clearly slowing as the slowdown in global trade promised to negate an export driven growth strategy.

So China's government undertook a series of measures in 2014 to rapidly expand stock values. However, the timing was inopportune. Emerging markets were already under growing pressure and slowing. Their income from commodities exports was declining. The domestic real economies of Japan and Europe economies were not recovering as planned and their demand for Chinese exports was not rising sufficiently. Then, in June 2014, the collapse of global oil prices commenced. To boost the markets, China's central bank, the Peoples Bank of China (PBOC) began lowering interest rates in late 2014, in the first of what would be five consecutive cuts. It further injected liquidity into the markets by lowering reserve requirements of banks to get them to lend even more. In mid-November 2014 it introduced several changes to open the economy and markets further to foreign money capital. And, as a clear signal as to where the additional liquidity should flow, it introduced measures to encourage even more aggressive buying of stocks on margin. A flood of 'retail' investors came into the market in early 2015 as a result. Soon, the margin buying by retail investors, especially, was getting out of hand. Measures were introduced to slow the trend, to no avail.

After rising 120% in a year, the dam broke in China's two major equity markets in June 2015. Stock prices crashed by 32% in just two weeks on the Shanghai exchange and by 40% on the Schenzen. Just as it had intervened to help create the stock boom, China policy makers quickly intervened again, this time to try to quell the collapse. Various measures were introduced to prevent selling of stocks, including suspension of trading at one point of nearly three-fourths of all the listed companies on the exchanges. Short selling of stocks was banned. Major shareholders (more than 5% of total shares) were banned from selling. Other measures were initiated to get buyers back into the market to buy stocks. SOEs were required to buy their stock, even if it meant raising more debt. State investment funds were ordered to buy. The PBOC provided more liquidity to brokerages to buy stock. And in another 180 degree turnaround, margin buying terms were again loosened and encouraged. In other words, there was a return to massive liquidity injections to try to resolve the problem that excess liquidity had helped create in the first place. That additional liquidity would translate into yet more financial debt earmarked for financial asset investment and speculation. The long run problem—too much liquidity and therefore too much leveraged debt feeding financial markets—became the short run solution. But the solution would again add to the long run problem.

China's strategic policy shift in 2013—away from direct government investment, manufacturing and export driven growth, and monetary policy in service to that real investment and exports approach—amounts in retrospect to a strategy for recovery not unlike that failed approach adopted by the advanced economies from the beginning of the crash of 2008-09, a strategy that relied primarily on monetary measures that accelerated liquidity in the system. Fiscal policy was token at best (or negative in Europe and Japan), assuming forms of austerity. AE central banks believed that massive money injections would flow into real asset investment as banks resumed lending to non-financial enterprises. Liquidity would result in rising prices that would restore business confidence and lead to real investment. Real investment would bring back jobs, and therefore income and consumption. Wealth effects from rising financial asset values would add further to consumption. More consumption would stimulate more real investment in turn, creating a kind of 'virtuous cycle'. But nothing like that happened. The liquidity flowed in large part instead into financial asset investing and financial markets, boosting stocks and bonds but little else.

China differed from the AEs in the initial period of 2008-10. Fiscal policy came first, and monetary policy and liquidity was primarily accommodative. But that began to reverse as a result of a series of measures, first in 2010 and then in 2013. The liquidity and debt explosions in China thus came later, well after the AEs, and in different forms. The eventual financial asset bubbles occurred in different markets as well.

But China's experience, especially after 2013, shows the same problems with AE recovery strategies that focus on liquidity injection that ultimately lead to excessive debt leveraging that tends to flow into financial asset markets. They lead to financial asset bubbles, to the need for still more liquidity to prop up the financial asset deflation that inevitably occurs when bubbles unwind and prior debt cannot be repaid. Excess liquidity leads to debt leads to more liquidity and yet more debt. It is a vicious circle leading to financial fragility and instability. A vortex. A whirlpool that sucks up money capital that might otherwise have gone into real investment, to create jobs, real incomes, consumption and finally more real investment and economic growth, but instead goes into the black hole of financial asset speculation, to disappear forever at some point as financial asset deflation sets in and drags the real economy with it.

China's Real Economic Slowdown: 2013-2015

The experience of China since 2009 shows that real investment and financial asset investment are causally related in important ways— contrary to mainstream economic theory that tends to view them as determined by their own more or less independent set of forces.

As financial bubbles grew in China over the period in question, accelerating in intensity, number and form, China's real economy has continued to slow in terms of its GDP growth rates. From double digit annual growth rates in the immediate post-2008 period, China's latest growth is officially 7%. However, almost no independent sources believe that figure is accurate. The most optimistic alternative sources estimate its latest growth at 6.2%, and others range in the 4.5% to 5.5% range. At the very low end, some suggest growth is occurring at a mere 3.1% annual rate.

Whatever the GDP estimate, which are unreliable for many reasons, other key indicators in China strongly suggest the real economy is growing much slower than official forecasts for 2015. China's industrial production hit a 15 month low in July 2015, growth rates falling by half in the last eighteen months. A more accurate indicator of overall economic growth compared to GDP, electricity consumption, has declined from a 10% annual growth rate to 0% by mid-year 2015. Railway freight traffic, new home construction, and imports have all turned negative since mid-2014, a year ago. Auto sales have fallen nearly -7% for the past year. The manufacturing sector in China has consistently contracted over the past year month by month. Latest available data for August 2015 indicate China's important manufacturing sector continued to contract, the worst month since early 2009 and now at its lowest point in the last 78 months. And not just consumption and manufacturing are flashing 'red'. When measured in terms of gross fixed capital formation, critically important real asset investment in China is slowing rapidly. In 2009 its annual rate of growth was 25%. That fell to 10% in 2013 and only 6.6% in 2014. 2015 figures will no doubt record less.

In short, various indicators of China's real economy show it is not only slowing, but is doing so rapidly. For reasons explained in prior chapters, GDP as the key indicator of growth tends to overstate that growth, and is becoming increasingly inaccurate as governments redefine and manipulate the GDP statistic to bolster growth figures.

China Global Contagion Effects

If China's shift to relying more on monetary policies creating excess liquidity, debt, and financial bubbles has had a negative effect on China's real domestic growth, then China's slowing real growth is clearly having a negative effect in turn on the global economy.

China's declining demand for commodity imports is exacerbating an emerging markets slowdown also in progress and accelerating. Slowing Chinese demand for commodities and semi-finished goods is having a significant impact on imports from Latin American countries like Peru, Chile, Venezuela and Brazil. While not an emerging market, Australia provides natural resources in large volumes to China, and its economy is slowing as China slows as well. Many Asian and South Asian economies that are tightly integrated with China are slowing in tandem with China. China's slowing economy is also having an impact on its demand for imports from Europe and Japan, thus offsetting those countries recent QE policies attempting to devalue their currencies to boost their exports and stagnating or declining growth rates. Despite massive QE money injections and currency exchange rate declines for the Yen and Euro, their exports to China have not risen appreciably.

China's slowing has resulted in a shift in its own currency strategy that is further impacting other Asian economies. In a major policy shift in August 2015, China began to allow its currency to slowly drift lower, in what will no doubt be a long term trend. That is adding more impetus to Asian currency declines and the emerging global currency war reignited by Japan and Europe in recent months. As Asian emerging markets' currencies plummet in reaction to China's, further economic instabilities are growing in their own economies.

China's slowdown has also exacerbated the global oil price deflation trend. As China's demand for oil declines, oil producing economies compete more intensely by lowering prices in order to encourage sales and revenues elsewhere from other buyers. Also on the financial side, China's current stock market collapse is clearly spilling over to other equity markets worldwide. The collapse will almost certainly mean less real investment, and therefore less consumption, in China, further reducing China's demand for imports and thus other economies. And if China's market collapse spills over to other AEs, then a similar negative effect on investment and consumption in those other economies will almost certainly occur as well. Declining stock prices create a negative 'wealth effect' on consumers who reduce spending in turn; equity deflation also discourages real investment as non-financial companies move to the economic sidelines and conserve cash.

Only in those emerging market economies where their currencies are collapsing is inflation on the rise. But that is only because their falling currency exchange rates make import prices rise. Elsewhere in the AEs, and wherever currency exchange rates change moderately, goods deflation has become a real problem. Like the AEs, China's currency has been one of the most stable for more than a decade. Because its currency, like those of the major AEs, remains more or less stable there is little import inflation occurring in China. Not so for goods deflation, however.

The slowing of real investment in China is steadily translating into deflation for real goods and services as well. China's producer prices have fallen for 40 consecutive months, by nearly -6% in the past year. Import prices are down by -10% year to date. And its consumer price index has declined from a 2% annual rate a year ago to a mere 0.18% most recently. In other words, with declining real investment comes real goods deflation. Conversely, with rising financial asset investment, comes financial asset inflation. The parallels are not accidental.

Goods deflation is a strong indicator of the failure of monetary policies relying heavily on liquidity injections as the primary recovery tool. Conversely, the same monetary tools generate excessive financial asset inflation. Could it be therefore that the one (financial asset inflation) is related causally to the other (goods deflation)? Or, to say the same, could it be that the determinants of both forms of investment—financial asset and real asset investment—might therefore somehow be causally related?

The overall impact on the global economy of a China, responsible for 15% of the world's GDP, that is slowing in real terms, and simultaneously struggling to contain financial asset bubbles that are multiplying in number and growing in magnitude, cannot be underestimated.

China & Global Systemic Fragility

The trends and relationships in China—between excess liquidity and accelerating debt, real vs. financial investment, real investment and goods deflation, financial asset speculation and financial price bubbles, etc.—is not unlike what is happening globally in Europe, Japan, and even the US. Financial bubbles and asset inflation have been growing, as real investment and economies have been trending down long term and drifting steadily toward deflation. As liquidity, debt and financial asset investing rises, creating financial asset inflation and bubbles, real investment slows or declines, depressing earned income growth by households in turn and resulting in further real investment slowing. The eventual outcome is deflation in goods and services prices, while financial asset bubbles continue to grow.

Occurring unevenly and at different paces, these trends are happening across the global economy today. In no place or economy is the example of these processes clearer than in China today—i.e. slowing real growth v. frothing financial bubbles, financial investing and speculation v. real investment, financial asset inflation v. the drift toward goods deflation. Among all the major economies of the world, the trends and processes are at their most developed stage in China. China is the instability canary in the global economic coalmine—both real and financial. China's economy today is a clear indication that something has fundamentally changed in the global capitalist economy in the 21st century—something not very well understood yet by mainstream economists, and even less so by central bankers and government policy makers.

To begin understanding what has been happening in China— as well as the EMEs, Japan, Europe, and globally in general—on more than an empirical or narrative level, it is important to consider events and developments from a more theoretical perspective. That requires addressing the key nine variables central to a theoretical perspective, which is undertaken in Part Two that follows. That requires as well the development of a new conceptual framework that will enable the exploration of fundamental questions such as: how are financial asset and real asset investing related? How does each determine the other? Which relationship and causal determination is perhaps stronger in today's world of 21st century global capitalism? What are the implications for Systemic Fragility and instability for the global economy in the months and years immediately ahead? In Part Two, the nine key variables fundamental to Systemic Fragility in the global economy are examined. Part Three then considers why contemporary economic analyses have failed to understand the key relationships between these 9 variables that lead to Systemic Fragility. The final Part Four provides this writer's explanation and theory for how the variables produce Systemic Fragility in the global economy today, and how that is leading to more instability and an eventual crisis potentially worse than that experienced recently in 2008-09.

Endnotes

1   McKinsey Global Institute, 'Debt and (Not Much) Deleveraging', Executive Summary, February 2015, p. 3,10.

2   *Financial Times*, June 16, 2014, p. 5. See also Jack Rasmus, 'China and Its Shadow Bankers', *Counterpunch*, January 9, 2015.

3   Tom Mitchell, 'China's Shadow Banking Loans Leap', *Financial Times*, January 15, 2014.

7

SLOWING
REAL INVESTMENT

Investment can take different forms. It can mean investing in financial assets—i.e. stocks, bonds, real estate properties, foreign currencies, derivatives of all kinds, and other forms of financial securities. That is sometimes called 'financial asset investment' and will be addressed separately in more detail in chapters that follow. Real investment as referenced in this chapter and book means investment in physical assets that create producer and consumer goods and services. Our reference is to real investment in its 'gross' form—i.e. before adjustments for legal factors like depreciation write-offs that represent tax and accounting distortions of the change in real investment.

Real investment may also refer to government investment as well as private investment in goods and services. Adding public to private real investment as part of our understanding of the term is important when addressing an economy like China's, for example, where government investment is extremely high and where government actually owns a large proportion of the manufacturing facilities and businesses. Even in the USA, estimates are that government real investment annually is around $300 billion or so—a not insignificant sum. Big differences between countries can distort the real investment estimate and global trend. But for now, public investment too is excluded, and our focus is on private sector business investment.

'Gross private domestic investment' is the term given in the USA to real investment. It includes investment in equipment, commercial buildings, residential housing, and, recently, IP or intellectual property (software, R&D spending, arts & entertainment creations, changes in value of trademarks, logos, etc.). As noted in chapter one, the USA redefined its definition of GDP in 2013 to include new categories of business investment as a way to boost its GDP numbers. Those changes show up in the IP contribution to Gross Private

Domestic Investment. However, it is questionable whether much of the value of the latter IP should be considered real investment. This writer does not think it should. So here, IP category contributions to real investment are excluded.

Another problem with the US government's 'Gross Private Domestic Investment' as an indicator of real investment is that it includes residential housing investment, which tends to be highly volatile, especially in recent years. Its contribution to real investment in the USA, and other select economies with their own housing bubbles, was artificially high in the 2003-06 period and artificially low in the 2007-10 period. To get a more stable estimate of the real investment trend it is therefore also useful to exclude residential housing investment from the real investment trend.

Finally, gross private domestic investment, as defined in USA GDP accounting, is not necessarily how other countries define the term—though European and emerging economies have also been redefining their GDP in order to boost their GDP numbers in recent years, but in ways different from the USA, as indicated in Chapter 1.

Given these various problems and issues of definition and cross-country comparisons associated with 'gross private domestic investment', the best alternative proxy indicator for global real investment is global CAPEX data. Global CAPEX, or capital expenditures, refers to business investment in new business equipment and in business structures (factories, offices, etc.) as well as upgrades to that equipment and structures. The data referenced hereafter is therefore derived from Standard & Poor's annual Reports on Global CAPEX. This data is based on a large representative sample of the biggest 2000 corporations worldwide that are the largest CAPEX investors, and presumed representative of the broader trend.

Real Investment vs. Financial Investment

The relationship between real asset investment and financial asset investment is critical for understanding why real investment has been in decline since 2000, as well as why the global economy is drifting toward deflation, why income inequality is growing, and so forth.

Distinguishing between real and financial asset investment is also the first requisite for understanding how physical asset and financial asset investment determine each other. The distinction and the understanding how the two forms of investment mutually affect each other is further essential, in turn, for understanding the idea of 'systemic fragility'. The relationships between real and financial asset investment is therefore a major element of analysis. Those relationships will be addressed more fundamentally and in more detail in the chapters that follow, and especially in the concluding chapter on theory. For the remainder of this chapter, the focus is the global decline in real asset investment.

Real asset investment is clearly undergoing a long term slowdown. That slowing is secular. That is, it is not just a result of the business cycle crash of 2008-09. It has been going on for decades in the AEs and in recent years appears to have become a similar development and trend in the EMEs, and also includes China.

This long term slowdown, accelerating in the 21st century, is of major significance. Without real asset investment growth, normal job growth slows. Without normal job growth, income growth slows. Additional slowing, stagnating and declining real wage growth and therefore further income stagnation follows. Income growth issues lead to consumption demand issues, which in turn feed back on investment. The combined result is both household consumption and business investment slow, and GDP and economic growth with it in the end. Since income is a key variable associated with fragility, as it slows or declines, fragility has a tendency to rise. Another related effect is the rise in fragility that occurs as households and businesses acquire more debt in order to make up for declining cash flow and disposable income. Real investment growth is thus critical for both maintaining income growth and restraining debt, both for businesses and households.

The key questions become: what are the various causes for the long term slowing of real asset investment? What are some of the consequences of slowing real investment for the global economy? Is slowing real investment responsible for the increasingly obvious problem of insufficient consumption demand? Conversely, can government spending to boost consumption demand lead in turn to an increase in business real investment? Will incentives to cut business costs (taxes, interest rates, etc.) automatically lead to an increase in business real investment? Or will business simply hoard the cost cuts and still not invest?

Slowing Real Asset Investment

Standard & Poor's Global CAPEX report for 2014 showed unequivocally that real investment since 2000 has been slowing dramatically. After a historically weak average recovery in the first half of the last decade, real investment turned negative again during 2008-10 for the three years, having fallen by more than 10% in 2009 alone. After a short, weak recovery in 2011-12, real investment turned negative again in 2013, falling 1.0% worldwide. In its mid-year 2014 report, S&P forecast another 0.5% decline for 2015.[1] That proved an underestimation.

For 2014, every region of the global economy eventually registered negative growth in CAPEX except the US, which was still enjoying a capital spending surge focused on the gas & oil patch. That US exception soon collapsed, however, in 2015. Eight months later, in August 2015, the S&P's latest survey therefore projects a third consecutive year of negative total global investment in 2015, with a further decline by 1.0%

The crash of crude oil prices by more than 50% in the second half of 2014, followed by a second downturn in oil prices in the second half of 2015, could easily result in a decline in global CAPEX in 2015 beyond the 1% contraction projected by S&P. Reflecting this possibility, the S&P therefore forecast another 4.0% contraction in real investment for 2016, amounting to a fourth consecutive year of contraction.[2]

Considering the two biggest economies—US and China—at the beginning of 2015 economists at JP Morgan noted US real investment had declined sharply in the 4th quarter 2014 and they therefore were reducing their USA CAPEX growth estimates for 2015 to zero. For China, the Standard & Poor's research forecast CAPEX growth for 2014 at only 1%, down from 4% growth in 2013. That would contract further in 2015. Both estimates for the US and China may prove too optimistic, however, by the time 2015 comes to a close.

For Standard & Poor's researchers—as for most of the economics community—this decline constituted a 'conundrum'. As the 2015 Report noted, "the puzzle why CAPEX growth is not stronger remains, as our (2000) survey companies have $4.4 trillion in cash and equivalents on their balance sheets." [3]

Putting this in terms of billions of real dollars, real investment (including the energy sector) at mid-year 2014 was no larger than it was in 2006—i.e. both years were at around $2.8 trillion globally. Moreover, the collapse of energy sector investment in the last half of 2014 makes that $2.8 trillion estimate low in terms of the likely further decline. If energy is excluded, all other industries' total global real investment has actually declined every year since 2006.[4]

In terms of rate of CAPEX growth, it is not improbable that the global economy could experience a real investment contraction of major proportions again in 2015-16. And in terms of total real dollars, real investment levels could fall back to those of a decade ago.

If this scenario does arise, has the global economy entered, or is it soon to enter, another global economic contraction of similar dimensions to 2008-09? If real investment trends are any indicator of broader global GDP growth and correlated with GDP, then 2015-16 could surprise dramatically to the downside in terms of both global real asset investment and global economic growth.

The significant takeaway from the S&P reports and data is that global CAPEX real investment came to a virtual halt around 2008-09 and has never recovered—with the exception of the energy boom in oil and then shale, which are now ended and indeed are collapsing. So there has never been a recovery of real investment at all since the 2008 crash, apart from the brief oil boom which is now also in freefall.

If investment is the essence of capitalist production, and the foundational basis for continued economic growth, then the data suggest the global capitalist economy came to a virtual halt about a decade ago and has not really recovered since—except for a brief energy boomlet that has now also clearly ended and is collapsing as well!   It is therefore not surprising that both Europe and Japan have been 'in and out' of recessions for the past six years, that the USA has been experiencing not much better than a 'stop-go' recovery, that emerging markets everywhere are tumbling into recessions, and that even China is struggling with increasing difficulty to maintain its target of a 7% GDP growth rate.

Causes of Slowing Real Investment

While some Marxist economists erroneously think that real investment is primarily financed from profits, making falling profits the reason for falling investment (and vice-versa), mainstream economists see additional economic variables as driving (or failing to drive) real investment, not just profits. In fact, the notion of profits or some kind of retained corporate earnings as the primary determinant of investment is a simplistic 19th century view. In today's context, even viewing bank loans as a source of investment finance is inadequate, especially in advanced financialized economies like the USA and UK, where 'capital (money) markets' (equity markets, debt markets, etc.) and shadow banks have become a larger relative source of finance for real investment.

When analyzing investment mainstream economists typically consider capacity utilization as a determinant of investment. If most of the available production facilities are being used, businesses are more likely to invest to expand that capacity. The same for aging capital stock.

Causes of failure to invest include expected low net returns on new investment, rising costs of investment, or just general economic, and even political, uncertainty. Some analysts take a longer view and suggest that the shift to services and intangibles as a proportion of the economy is because these sectors require less real investment in order to produce a profit compared to more traditional goods-producing industries.

All these factors may have some influence on the decision to invest in real factories, equipment, structures, etc., and thus negatively impact real asset investment trends. But they have always been around. Today's post 2000 extremely weak global real investment requires a deeper analysis of what is slowing it worldwide despite record levels and margins for profits. Thus, mainstream economists, like Marxists, cannot adequately explain the slowing global real investment. For them it's a 'conundrum'.

Other possible explanations for slowing global real investment are explored in more detail in chapters 11 and 12 that follow, 'The Shift to Financial Asset Investment' and 'Structural Change in Financial Markets', respectively. For the present, a possible list of some alternative, not yet sufficiently considered, causes of real investment slowdown include:

- Record cash hoarding by non-financial global corporations

- Massive stock buyback and dividend payouts to shareholders

- A drift toward deflation in goods and services

- Expectations of excessive future debt servicing requirements

- Banks hoarding reserves and reluctance to lend

- Success in growing profit margins without real investment

- A shift to speculative investing opportunities

The book will return in chapters 11-12, to explore these more recent forces behind the slowing real investment trend; and in the concluding theoretical chapter 19 as well to explain how and to what extent these forces are related to the three forms of fragility (financial, consumption, and government balance sheet) and how they contribute to systemic fragility.

Endnotes

1   Standard & Poor's, *Global Corporate Capital Expenditures Survey*, June 30, 2013; and July 10, 2014.
2   Standard & Poor's, *Global Corporate CAPEX Survey Overview*, August 3, 2015.
3   Standard & Poor's, *Global Corporate CAPEX Survey Overview*, August 2015.
4   These others include utilities, consumer staple goods, consumer discretionary goods, information tech, telecom services, industrial, and materials. The big four—industrials, utilities, materials and energy--represent 80% of total real investment spending worldwide.

8

DRIFT TOWARD DEFLATION

Deflation is generally defined as a decline or fall in prices. It is sometimes confused with disinflation. Disinflation is when the *rate of increase* in inflation is slowing. And of course inflation is when prices are rising. But what prices?

It is important to distinguish which prices are actually deflating. Prices for goods and services, sometimes called consumer prices? Producer (business to business) goods and services? Prices for financial assets—like stocks, bonds, currencies, derivatives or other financial securities? So there are at least two distinct kinds of prices and deflation that are of special interest for purposes of analysis—i.e. for goods and services (consumer and producer) and for financial assets.[1]

The distinction between goods and services deflation and financial asset deflation is particularly important. For one thing, as will be explained in more detail in subsequent chapters, the two different price systems don't necessarily 'behave' the same. Second, how the two price systems interact and mutually determine each other is of critical importance for analysis of economic instability and for systemic fragility that leads to instability in particular.

Most economists believe that both types of price systems—goods and financial assets—are driven by supply and demand forces in the same way. But this is not necessarily true. And because they believe supply and demand forces work through prices to stabilize financial assets as well as goods and services, they typically misunderstand the destabilizing role financial asset prices have on the financial system and, in turn, the real economy. They thus almost never accurately predict financial crises. Much more on this in subsequent chapters.

Deflation Effects on Investment, Consumption, and Financial Assets

Inflation may stimulate consumer spending and even business investment. Disinflation may or may not have a negative, slowing effect on investment and/or consumption. But deflation can, and often does, have a negative impact on both business investment and consumer spending: it may freeze up consumer spending, especially on housing and other big ticket items. Or lead businesses to put on hold, or even reduce, investment plans.

Deflation can set off a process and chain of events that accelerates economic slowdowns.

Suspending investing may be even more pronounced in the case of financial asset investing. Less sophisticated household consumers may jump in and buy as prices fall earlier in the process of decline. Businesses may not be able to wait for prices to 'bottom out' before deciding to invest. But professional investors in financial assets will wait, once financial asset prices begin to decline, until they think the 'bottom' is reasonably close before re-entering and investing again in financial asset markets. That is one (of several) reasons why financial asset prices tend to behave more volatilely compared to goods and services prices.

Deflationary expectations by consumers and businesses also pose a particular dilemma. If inflation accelerates due to 'inflationary expectations' (such as occurred in the USA in the early 1980s), those expectations can be countered by government central banks dramatically raising interest rates and precipitating a recession. The recession shakes out inflationary expectations, and prices then abate. But it doesn't work that way for deflationary expectations. Lowering interest rates does not necessarily check deflation and deflationary expectations. That's because interest rates cannot be lowered to less than zero to counter deflationary expectations, while they can be raised without limit if necessary to check inflationary expectations.

From Global Disinflation to Deflation

A review of the global economy in 2015 shows a decided drift toward goods and services deflation in a number of key regions and economies. The scenario for financial asset prices appears more mixed. Some regions and markets appear to be churning and struggling, having peaked. While still others—like oil, commodities of all kinds, real estate property prices in select regions, equity markets, corporate junk bonds, and some foreign exchange currencies in emerging markets—all appear to have turned negative and are rapidly deflating.

Europe

Of the major regions of the global economy, the 18-economy Eurozone clearly crossed into goods deflation territory in late 2014. It has been in and out of deflation ever since. The Eurozone had been on a sharp disinflation trajectory since early 2012, when inflation peaked at around a modest 2.5%. By early 2014 it had slowed to 0.4%, and by year end 2014 entered deflation territory with -0.2%—the first time outright deflation occurred in the Eurozone since records were first kept for the region in 1997.[2] Sixteen of the eighteen Eurozone economies experienced deflation in consumer goods prices in December 2014.

While the return to goods deflation in the Eurozone was heavily determined by collapsing global oil prices, nevertheless 'core' (minus energy prices) inflation for the entire year of 2014 was only 0.8%--well below the official Eurozone Central Bank's target of 2.0%. Oil commodity prices cannot explain the region's deflation alone. Much is due to its continued real economic stagnation and lack of consumer spending and business real investment stagnation.

Even key European economies outside the Eurozone currency union— like the UK, Sweden, Switzerland and others— experienced rapid disinflation and then deflation at year-end 2014. The United Kingdom's rate hit a 14 year low of 0.5% in December 2014, while Sweden's had fallen to approximately zero. The UK entered deflation territory in April 2015, the first such in 55 years.

The region's drift deeper into deflation accelerated in early 2015, and was probably a major reason for the Eurozone Central Bank (ECB) decision in late January to introduce its first official 'Quantitative Easing' (QE) $1.2 trillion monetary injection program that commenced in March. Eurozone goods prices deflated -0.6% in January and another -0.3% in February and fell again, a fourth consecutive month, in April. Beyond the Eurozone, in the broader European Union prices either stagnated or declined in the same period.

After six months of ECB money injections of more than $400 billion, from March through September 2015, the Eurozone slid back into goods deflation again in September. That included the German economy as well, where prices deflated at -0.2% that month. Instead of acknowledging that QE and money injections don't necessarily generate goods price increases, the ECB and Euro economic policy makers renewed their debate over the need to sharply increase the QE injections, perhaps from $1.2 to $2.4 trillion, and even before the end of 2015 should events in Japan, China, and the US justify.

Nor was the drift toward deflation in the Eurozone an issue in just the goods markets. Financial asset markets, especially Euro stocks, currencies, and bond markets, also experienced deflation throughout 2014 and continuing into 2015.

The Eurozone's QE program was also supposed to restore stock markets and other financial assets. Here too, however, it also failed to prevent deflation in financial asset prices. The Eurozone's foreign exchange currency, the Euro, a financial asset, declined by almost 20% as a result of QE. Northsea oil commodity prices for Euro oil producers like Norway and the UK also continued to decline. Meanwhile, Eurozone government bond prices barely rose, despite government bond interest rates in country after country turning negative across the region throughout the year.[3]

Thus the drift toward deflation continues slowly but steadily in Europe, the product of stagnating and falling real investment, weak jobs and household income growth and consequent weak consumer spending, austerity fiscal policies by governments, and failed monetary policies by central banks to stimulate investment or generate a sustained recovery in stocks and other assets.

Japan

The other major deflationary pole in the global economy is Japan, which has been in and out of deflation (mostly in) for the past quarter century since its financial crash in the early 1990s. Except for two very brief spikes in inflation in 1997 and 2007, when inflation rose a modest 2.0%-2.5%, Japan has experienced goods and services deflation or stagnation consistently from 1996 to 2015.

It experienced a short period of modest goods inflation recovery following its massive 2013 QE monetary injections. However, the brief goods inflation of 2013-14 did not occur because QE stimulated real investment and consumer demand. Much of the inflation recovery was due to escalating import prices as Japan's QE reduced the value of its currency, the Yen, by 20% and more against the US dollar, Euro, and other currencies, which raised the general price level. The price level was also artificially boosted by a general sales tax hike early in 2014 which added to the price level. Japan's 2014 recession, the third since 2009, reversed inflation once again, as tightening austerity policies since 2014 led to slowing (disinflation) prices again by 2015. Goods inflation slowed to a 0.2% annual rate by early 2015. Falling consumption and exports in 2015 precipitated its fifth recession in seven years, with the result that goods prices descended into deflation territory once again by August 2015 to a -0.1% rate for core inflation.

Financial asset and securities prices initially surged in the wake of the introduction of QE in April 2013. Japan's stock market price index rose rapidly by more than 70% following QE until eventually leveling off, revealing once again that money injections by central banks do produce inflation—just not goods and services inflation but financial asset inflation. However, just as in Europe, Japan's stocks did not rise for long but quickly dissipated as the economy slide into recession in 2015 again, raising calls for still more QE (as in Europe). Stock prices fell sharply after August 2015, in tandem with China's stock market crash. Deflating financial assets continued beyond equity markets in Japan as well. Government bond prices fell, as did Japan's currency, the Yen, as QE continued unabated.

China

The story of goods deflation in China is not yet consumer prices, but producer prices that have been deflating for some time. Consumer prices fell sharply in China, from a 6% annual rate in 2012, falling steadily and settling in to a 1%-1.5% range for 2015. Producer prices similarly plummeted in 2012, leveled off, but then began to deflate further again over the past year, 2014-2015. The contraction in producer prices has been consistent every month since the start of 2015. The contraction reflects the sharp slowdown in China's manufacturing and industrial production sector since mid-2014. As that general economic slowdown continues, prospects are high that the deflation in producers goods will continue as well.

On the financial side, the story is China's stock market collapse that began in June 2015 that has continued, contracting by 40% and wiping out $5 trillion in asset values so far. Certain financial asset derivative securities have continued to decline notably, as has real estate property prices in its housing and commercial local property market that had previously attained bubble dimensions. The Yuan, the currency, has also begun to decline after a first technical devaluation in August 2015, after having been pegged to the dollar for years.

Emerging Markets

The main story for EMEs is commodity deflation—which represents both goods as well as financial assets. Oil is both a commodity and a financial asset as it trades in the form of futures contracts among global financial speculators. The same applies to a lesser degree to other forms of industrial commodities that trade similarly. In both sense, commodities deflation is one of the more significant forms deflation has assumed in recent years, especially since 2014. There is no 'disinflation' here; it is bona fide, and deep, deflation.

Oil has fallen from $120 a barrel to the mid-$40 a barrel range. Some estimates are it will fall further through 2016, potentially as low as $20. That's a deflationary price collapse or more than 80%. That is deflation associated with depression conditions. Many other industrial, and even non-industrial commodities are falling in the 30%-40% range, also arguably in the range associated with classical depression conditions.

Since many emerging market economies are highly dependent on oil and commodity production and exports, their economies have contracted sharply in real terms as a consequence of collapsing oil and commodity physical export volumes and prices. Goods deflation in general has been the outcome. Labor prices, wage deflation, has subsequently followed the real recessions and goods deflation, showing once again how deflation in one 'price system' eventually spills over to the next.

Tightly integrated with the commodity goods + general goods + wage deflation is financial asset deflation. Not just the deflation in commodity futures securities but stock prices throughout the emerging markets as well. Deflation and its consequences results in capital flight from emerging markets, which exacerbates the price declines in all the above price systems, real and financial.

With much of the borrowing by domestic corporations in the emerging markets undertaken in dollars (Latin America especially), corporate bond prices also deflate as it becomes apparent corporations in the EMEs are unable to generate sufficient dollars from exports, now declining, in order to make payments in dollars to banks and shadow banks from which they previously borrowed and incurred excessive debt.

Yet another financial asset that is experiencing deflation is the currencies of the emerging market economies. Many have been in virtual freefall since the onset of commodities price collapse and the upward drift of the US and UK long term interest rates since 2014. Currency collapse encourages still more capital flight from the EMEs, exacerbating all the above from yet another direction. Efforts by EMEs to raise their domestic rates to halt capital outflow and raise the value of their currencies have only resulted a further economic slowdown in their domestic economies that feeds upon all the deflationary trends still further.

The scenario for EMEs is therefore deflation spreading and deepening on all fronts—real and financial. The ultimate consequence will be growing corporate and thereafter sovereign defaults, as income sources for financing past debt dry up and bankers and investors in US, UK and other advanced economies refuse to 'roll over' and refinance the debt.

USA

Everywhere in the business press the number one question raised at the start of 2015 is, given that the rest of the world economy is slowing or in recession, can the apparent continuing economic growth in the USA prevent a further collapse of the global economy? That question is problematic under the most robust US growth conditions. It is impossible should US real investment and growth continue to slow, resulting in goods price deflation or even continuing disinflation.

Like much of the global economy, the scenario for the US is also a drift toward deflation in goods prices, albeit at a much slower pace than in Europe, Japan, and certainly emerging markets. But the drift—in the form of 'disinflation' thus far—is nonetheless evident. And signs are beginning to emerge of financial asset prices beginning to reverse and deflate as well, especially the main stock indices, or being on the verge of doing so as they 'churn and froth' at the top, as they say.

USA real goods & services prices in the closing two months of 2014 declined -0.3% and -0.4% for November-December, respectively. This was the largest monthly decline in six years in the USA. Optimists argue that decline is due largely to the fall in global crude oil prices and therefore gasoline, energy and food prices in the USA, or what is called 'headline' consumer inflation. But when the crude oil-gasoline and other volatile items are excluded from consumer prices in the USA—what is called 'core' inflation—USA consumer goods & services prices still fell to 0.1% in November and to 0% in December. For the entire year, 2014, USA headline consumer price inflation was only 0.8%, well below the US central bank's target of 2%.

Buttressing the disinflation trend in the USA, business-to-business (producers price) inflation showed an actual deflationary, not just disinflation, trend in the closing two months of 2014: declining by -0.2% and -0.3%.

While goods prices recovered somewhat in the first half of 2015, after mid-year they began to disinflate and fell by 0.1% in August. Meanwhile, producer price gains slowed every month throughout 2015, suggesting further downward pressure on consumer prices to come and a continuation of the disinflation and drift toward deflation in goods.

Financial asset prices in 2015 have also begun to show a growing tendency to decline. US stocks peaked in 2015, with the most well known, 'Dow Jones' average falling from a record high of 18,200 to just under 16,000. Not a 'bear market' yet, but definitely a major correction underway that could easily accelerate. Various other financial asset markets have begun to show signs of increasingly instability, including corporate high yield (junk) bonds associated with the oil and gas sector, leveraged loans, and other speculative securities the prices of which have escalated in recent years to unsustainable levels and are likely to reverse soon and perhaps do so dramatically in terms of rate of decline.

While deflation is least pronounced in the US economy, disinflation is clearly underway in both goods and financial asset markets. It would not take much of a crisis erupting in the rest of the global economy to have US growth slow significantly and goods prices shift from disinflation to stagnation or worse, followed by greater downward volatility and deflation in financial asset prices.

Good vs. Bad Deflation Debate

As the global economy steadily drifts toward deflation today, a debate has arisen between whether there is 'good deflation' and 'bad deflation'. This debate sometimes confuses disinflation with deflation. Disinflation—i.e. slowing but still rising prices—may stimulate consumer spending and business investment. But deflation more often has the opposite effect. True deflation almost always has a negative effect on consumption and virtually always does on investment.

A typical variant of the theme of 'good' deflation is that falling prices due to major improvements in productivity are an example of 'good deflation'. Productivity means companies reduce their unit labor costs and thus retain more income for themselves. There are several faulty assumptions with this argument, however.

First, productivity typically results from new technology improvements. That means the cost savings are often associated with new equipment which is accompanied by worker layoffs. That reduces wages and incomes. Economic growth may rise due to the greater output, but wage incomes don't. A greater imbalance occurs between output (supply) and the ability to purchase it (demand)—a problem which is itself of growing proportions and importance today. So the assumption that productivity will reduce prices means it reduces labor prices (wages). A second assumption, that businesses experiencing greater productivity will share it with consumers by lowering prices, is also not necessarily true or borne out by the data. The business may simply hoard the additional income, distribute it to shareholders in stock buybacks and dividends, use it to purchase competitors offshore to hid the income from tax collectors, or all the above—which is what happens more than sharing the productivity gains with consumers by lowering prices—i.e. good deflation. As for productivity sharing, not only are the gains from productivity not shared with consumers in the form of lower prices, but productivity has not been generally shared for decades with workers of the companies in general. One may thus argue that productivity does not result in goods price declines, but does result in labor price (wage) decline.

An application today of the 'good deflation' vs. 'bad deflation' debate is the spin given of late by media and some mainstream economists to the recent collapse of world crude oil prices. The collapse of crude oil is argued as representing 'good deflation'. That is, its net effects will be positive for consumption and therefore economic growth. Consumers' savings from lower oil prices will be spent on other goods and services. The problem with this view is that it assumes a one-to-one shift of spending, from oil and gasoline to other products and services. It thus ignores the more likely possibility of consumers using the extra income from lower oil prices to pay down past debt or to save, as they worry about the future of the economy. Some of the oil (gasoline) price reduction is also spent on imports, which produce no net benefit for the growth of the economy in question and in fact net negative for GDP growth. And in oil producing economies, the net effects are clearly negative, as the collapse in oil prices means sharp declines in real investment and therefore jobs and incomes, and in turn consumption, for a broad spectrum of the economy.

The 'oil deflation is good deflation' assertion furthermore ignores the related deflationary effects on both goods and financial assets prices that occur as prices for global oil deflates. For oil is not just a commodity but also a financial asset; and as it collapses its contagion spreads to other financial assets. The good deflation vs. the bad deflation is thus mostly a fantasy, and one of the many propositions that permeate mainstream economic analysis today that qualify as more ideology than science.

Oil, Commodities, and Financial Asset Deflation

It is irrefutable that a major trend in oil and commodities deflation has been well underway in the global economy since 2014 and shows little sign thus far of abating. In 2014 alone, oil commodity prices deflated by more than 50%. A brief, partial recovery in 2015 restored the price decline to about 40%. But in the second half of 2015 oil prices began another further fall, to the low $40 range, equivalent to a roughly two thirds drop from previous peaks. More importantly, the consensus is that oil prices will continue to deflate well into 2016, given slowing global demand and continuing excess supply.

Crude oil futures prices are a kind of financial asset that is traded on global exchanges. As a financial security, deflation has been the case just as have prices for the physical commodity itself.

The global oil glut is often explained as a case of excess supply or declining demand. But supply and demand explanations are not the fundamental causes. These concepts are only 'intermediary' explanations and are often employed to obscure the real causes that drive the supply and demand changes. In the case of global oil, these fundamental forces are in part political and part economic, although the politics and economics are inseparable. In 2014 the Saudi-Emirates alliance in the Middle East decided to drive down the price of global oil in order to bankrupt and destroy their emerging competition in the US among the fracking shale oil and gas companies; this is one fundamental force behind the collapse of global oil prices. Technology enabled the rise of competition from US shale producers, which challenged Saudi and friends' ability to dominate world oil price. The Saudis thus created an excess supply added to the extra supply brought to world markets by US shale producers. So the real cause of the excess supply, and thus falling global oil prices, is the intensification of competition between regional global capitalist forces. To say simply 'supply' is thus to obfuscate the real causes behind the supply.

But the demand element, and forces behind it, have also been a major contributory factor in the oil price collapse. Those more fundamental demand side forces include the slowdown in the China economy, and the causes behind that development in turn. Technology also qualifies as a fundamental force playing a role on the demand side driving down oil prices. Alternative energy like solar and other forms is reducing the demand for oil. It is not so much the actual impact of alternative energy in the immediate period, but the generally accepted prospect by global oil producers that it will soon have a major impact. Politics plays a role here as well, as climate change is becoming an accepted fact within voting electorates.

In short, to understand the dynamics of the current global oil glut and deflation, it is necessary to view it from a broader perspective, one that accounts for inter-capitalist competition in various forms, changing technology, and politics within and between capitalist states. It is not a simple question of supply and demand. That is the mere appearance of the causation of the oil deflation. The essence lies in capitalist technology change, shifting relationships of economic power between the regions, financial structure and policy changes, and political forces as well.

Other commodity price deflation—for copper, iron ore, aluminum, other industrial metals, etc.—is also driven by many of the same forces underlying the global oil deflation: The current slowing of the Chinese economy and therefore demand for industrial commodities, but also the prior overproduction of these commodities that grew in the wake of the China-EME development boom of 2010-2012. The overproduction could not have been possible, however, without the financialization of the global economy that was also occurring, nor without the massive injection of money capital by central banks in the US-UK-EU-Japan that took place as well from 2009 on that debt-financed the expansion. Financialization thus preceded overproduction. And now that overproduction is 'feeding back' on the financial side, resulting in financial asset price deflation.

A specific US example of this general process of oil commodity output boom and subsequent financial asset bust has occurred in the case of the expansion of the shale oil-gas fracking industry in the US after 2009. The shale boom could not have happened without US banks and shadow banks providing a mountain of corporate junk bond financing to the drillers and shale producers, amounting to hundreds of billions of dollars of new credit in the last few years. So finance enabled the shale overproduction, which resulted in the oversupply of the oil in the US and globally, which then provoked the Saudi response and further global oil over-supply, at a time when global demand was also weakening. What appears as over-production is thus more fundamentally the consequence of finance capital expansion.

A short list of different commodities shows, according to the Bloomberg Commodities Index covering 22 major commodity classes, that commodities deflation as of August 2015 had declined to its lowest level since 1999, contracting by 40% in just the past three years.[4] The key commodities of copper and iron, have fallen 25% and 45%, respectively. And the rout is accelerating. The S&P GSCI Total Return Index of 24 commodities fell 14% just in July 2015, to levels of 2008.[5]

Commodities deflation has a contagion effect on other financial assets and securities. For example, as commodities prices fall, that decline has the effect of causing the currencies of the countries dependent on commodity exports to fall as well—i.e. further deflate. Commodities deflation also drags down stock market prices in those economies' stock exchanges. Thereafter, commodities deflation eventually spills over to non-commodity goods prices in turn. The feedback on financial assets then occurs in reverse as well, and stock and bond prices weaken still further. A downward deflationary spiral occurs, with goods, and financial asset price deflation each depressing the other.

At some point the downward deflation spiral leads to a rise in defaults. Defaults lead to bankruptcy, which lead to asset firesales and in turn an acceleration of financial asset deflation and its spread. There is thus a dynamic process of debt-deflation-default that sets in, with defaults feeding back on deflation, exacerbating it further, and real debt rising as well. The tip of the iceberg of this process is evident in the case of the huge global commodities trading company, Glencore, that investors and markets just became aware in September 2015 was on the verge of technical bankruptcy.[6] Having taken on massive debt in its expansion phase before 2014, falling commodities prices and export volumes are resulting in a classic example of collapsing income revenue as its real debt rises. Glencore's stock price thus collapsed 30% in a single day recently. And there are many 'Glencores' out there in the global economy whose CEOs and managers are attempting to cover up their severe debt financing problems.[7]

Another example of how defaults result from the debt-deflation dynamic and in turn feed back on it is the imminent crisis brewing in the junk bond market in the US associated with the shale producers approaching bankruptcy. A spillover in junk bond defaults from shale to the rest of the junk bond market is a likely consequence as well. And how a general junk bond crisis affects other financial markets in the US, and globally, is anyone's guess.

What global oil and commodities deflation reveals is that it is both real physical product (goods) deflation and simultaneously financial asset deflation. And that financial asset deflation is capable of precipitating and exacerbating a vicious downward spiral of negative interaction between goods and financial asset deflation. Not least, that interaction is capable of spilling over to the rest of the economy as well.

Deflation is a dangerous condition, and oil-commodities deflation a particularly dangerous game, because deflation is not easily countered by monetary policies—currently the favored policy tool of the global political and finance capital elite. Inflationary expectations may be countered by monetary policies raising interest rates sufficiently high to provoke a serious recession, as occurred for example in the US in 1980-82 period under Reagan. But the opposite response, i.e. to reverse deflationary expectations, is not responsive to monetary policy responses.

QE and Deflation

As US bond guru, Bill Gross, admitted publicly in late 2014, "prices go up, but not the right prices"… "Four trillion dollars in the U.S., two trillion US dollar equivalents in Japan, and a trillion U.S. dollars coming from the ECB's Mario Draghi in the Eurozone. The trillions seem to seep through the sandy loam of investment and innovation straight into the cement mixer of the marketplace."[8] Gross's views reflect a more accurate view of QE than is typical of his academic economist colleagues. Gross's views echoed that of Stephen King, group chief economist at the global giant bank, HSBC, who also acknowledged that "It is already abundantly obvious that unconventional policies", (meaning central banks' QE experiments), have had a bigger impact on financial asset values than on the real economy."[9]

QE programs of course result in stimulating financial asset inflation. But what about deflation? Does QE contribute to deflation, whether in goods or financial assets? The answer is 'yes' to the latter and, in the longer run, yes as well to the effect on goods deflation.

The former effect seems contrary to central banks' claims that QE will return the economy to a 2% annual general goods inflation rate. But nowhere has this happened in fact after seven years of such experiments. The logic argued is that QE and money injection will raise stock and bond prices, generate capital gains for businesses and investors, who will then invest it in real assets. But, as noted previously, the latter does not happen. It doesn't get redirected to real asset investment for reasons explained. The exceptional profits from financial asset inflation may in fact divert potential investment away from real assets and into financial asset investment and speculation. So, in effect, QE may actually reduce real investment—with a further consequent decline in employment, income, and consumption which then reduces demand for real goods that leads to goods deflation. So indirectly, QE, it may be argued, contributes to goods deflation not goods inflation. The correlation between QE and declining prices at least suggests this is true. And no evidence or correlation suggests the opposite, that QE will raise the general price level to 2%.

QE programs of course have the obvious immediate effect of boosting financial asset prices, especially stocks and real estate. But the boost is typically excessive, leading to stock and other price bubbles. Those bubbles then burst and rapid deflation of financial asset prices follow. So, in the longer run, QE and money injection programs lead to financial asset deflation as well.

Austerity and Goods Deflation

Austerity fiscal policy involves reducing government spending, raising taxes, and/or selling off government public assets and infrastructure to private buyers. Austerity reduces both government demand for goods and services as well as consumer or household demand. Less demand generally can mean a decline in goods and services prices if the austerity is significant and widespread.

Austerity policies may also directly impact household income and spending, not just through the medium of government spending or taxation. For example, policies that provide legal changes that allow businesses to reduce wage incomes more easily, as in the case of what is called 'labor market restructuring' or labor market reforms. These are designed to improve business incomes at the expense of household incomes for wage earners.

Reducing business wage costs and thus adding to business disposable income is proposed as a means by which to increase business real investment. But the argument that cost reduction leads to investment has little evidence of support. In contrast, reducing wage incomes for median income households does have a negative effect on consumption, and therefore on prices of goods and services.

Goods deflation is fundamentally about declining demand for goods; and austerity is fundamentally about wage income compression that leads to slowing demand for goods. It is not coincidental that where austerity programs have been most severe—as in Europe and Japan—goods deflation has also been the strongest trend.

Unlike QE, austerity fiscal policies have little direct effect on financial asset prices, whether inflation or deflation.

Deflation and Systemic Fragility

Like investment, deflation is a key variable contributing to systemic fragility. Just as slowing real investment reflects a shift to financial asset investing and the growth of business leverage and debt, deflation results in a decline in income growth necessary to make payments on that previously incurred excessive debt accumulation.

Goods deflation impacts business income negatively in two ways: price declines mean less revenue income, and conditions that require the price reductions almost always reflect slower volume of sales of those goods as well. Less available income lead to taking on more debt in order to externally finance day to day operations costs. Thus deflation drives business income down while increasing business debt load. This combination of slowing income amidst rising debt equates to rising business financial fragility.

A parallel situation occurs with consumer households as goods prices deflate. Deflating goods prices are generally associated with a stagnating economy or recession. That means layoffs and wage compression (i.e. labor price disinflation) or even outright wage deflation are typically accompanying the goods deflation. Stagnating or falling household wage incomes mean less income to pay household debt accumulated in a prior post-recession recovery phase.[10] If that recovery phase was weak, as it was between 2009-2014, household debt accumulation was likely significant. Thus, declining wage income occurs while real household debt rises as deflation takes place. Like businesses, households may then add more debt to offset their income decline and enable continued debt payments. The combination of falling household income amidst rising real debt payment obligations thus reflects growing household or consumption fragility.

And a similar process occurs among governments. Business goods deflation and household wage deflation spills over to government price deflation. Government 'prices' are taxes. Tax cuts—i.e. price declines—occur as governments add more debt from deficit spending as well.

By these processes, goods deflation spills over from business to households to governments, in a form of contagion effect. The deflation forces in each of the three also feedback on each other.

Imposed upon this general goods deflation process, moreover, is deflation in financial asset prices. Deflating financial asset values create massive losses on business balance sheets. That leads business to set in motion the reduction in real investment and the goods price cuts and wage reductions in order to free up income needed to continue to make payments on debt that accumulated. In other words, collapsing financial asset prices precipitate the processes of contagion and feedback effects just described in many cases. And where financial asset deflation may not precipitate, it certainly accelerates and exacerbates the processes.

Endnotes

1   There are other 'price systems' of importance as well. There are prices for 'factor inputs'—i.e. labor, land, and resources. The price for labor is especially important, called typically the 'wage'. Prices for money are also important, another word for what is generally called 'interest rates'. How goods and financial asset prices interact with wages and interest rates is important. However, for purposes of our analysis, we are most concerned with financial asset prices and how they interact with goods and services prices, since these appear more critical for the determination of instability.

2   Eurostat data reference

3   Interest rates, as the price for money, turning negative—i.e. deflating—was a new phenomenon, but one which also represents another form of deflation occurring. It is an example how deflating financial asset prices can spillover to other price systems—not only for goods but for money prices (interest rates).

4   'Commodities Reel Across the Board on Demand Growth Fears', *Financial Times*, August 24, 2015, p. 3.

5   Tatyana Shumsky, 'Commodities Slide Deeper Into a Rut', *Wall St. Journal,* August 1, 2015, p. B5.

6   Neil Hume, James Wilson, and David Sheppard, 'Glencore Scrambles to Halt Downward Spiral', Financial Times, October 3, 2015, p. 12.

7   Gavin Jackson, 'Rout Tests Miners with High Debt Loads', Financial Times, July 25, 2015, p. 12.

8   Jennifer Ablan, Reuters News, 'Deflation is a growing possibility: Bill Gross', Fidelity.Com News, November 3, 2014.

9   Andy Bruce, 'Deflation Ogre', Reuters News, Fidelity.Com News, January 19, 2014

10   The long run stagnation or decline in wage incomes over the last several decades has led to secular household debt accumulation to offset the wage stagnation, even as inflation occurs. When deflation sets in, cyclical conditions accelerate the household debt accumulation, exacerbating the debt condition further.

9

MONEY, CREDIT & EXPLODING LIQUIDITY

How then have money credit and non-money forms of credit expanded almost exponentially in the last half century? And how have those expansions contributed to financial fragility, consumption fragility, government balance sheet fragility—and ultimately to systemic fragility?

Liquidity refers to money and near-money forms of financial securities. Money is typically considered currency, coins, and financial securities like Certificates of Deposit and savings accounts that are convertible to currency in a very short period.

Some would include as money, perhaps, precious metals like gold and silver. But it is debatable whether gold and other metals constitute money in the 21st century, in which no gold standard or even quasi-gold standard exists and gold is generally not accepted as money for ordinary transactions. Gold, silver and other past forms of money are therefore today best considered forms of financial assets, both in their physical sense as well as in the sense of futures trading of financial securities based on gold, silver, etc. as commodities. Others would argue that virtual money like 'bitcoins' and other similar substitutes that are now appearing also constitute money. But while bitcoins are used as exchange in a limited sense, they are more properly understood as another form of financial asset, in this case a virtual electronic form of asset.

A basic characteristic of money is that it serves as a 'medium of exchange'—that is for ordinary transactions buying goods and services. But money functions as something more. It has what economists call the characteristic of providing a 'store of value' for its holder. And it is its store of value characteristic that makes money such a volatile and potentially destabilizing element in the economy. Store of value is what enables investment—a special case of an exchange transaction. For example, when a buyer purchases a good from a seller, an exchange takes place. Money is given to the seller in exchange for the good to the buyer. But in the case of investment, money is given to the buyer of the money itself, with a promise to return it plus an additional amount sometime in the future. In other words, the exchange does not complete for both parties in the present period, say time t, as does a goods transaction. With investment, exchange is completed sometime in the future, time t + 1, when the money is returned. During the interim, the value of the exchange can change. The value of the money sold may change form but may also change quantity. The value of the exchange thus may rise or fall. That introduces potential volatility in the value of the money sold to the buyer, i.e. invested .

Investment is thus a strange animal. It introduces time delay and volatility to the exchange of money relationship between buyer and seller of money when investment takes place. And as the volume of money that enters the economy for purposes of investment grows, the potential for volatility rises.

The buyers of money—i.e. bankers and investors—prefer volatility to the upside—which raises the price of money (aka inflation) and results in capital gains when they eventually resell it. Furthermore, the quicker they can 'turn around' a sale, the more that can be made. So investors like investments that they can jump into and out of in the short term—i.e. they prefer liquid markets in which they can both buy and sell on short notice. The shorter the investment transaction cycle the more of such transactions can be made. The shorter the term of the investment, and the more liquid the character of the market, the safer the investment. Short term investing also means costs are lower compared to longer term investing—hence once again the returns are better on average.

To sum up: professional investors—individuals and their institutions that invests on behalf of those individuals—prefer to invest in volatile financial securities in in highly liquid markets in which they can jump in and out (buy and sell) on very short notice (sometimes even minutes or seconds with 'fast trading' systems for stocks, hedging trades, etc.). And the faster they can move the safer the investment, the lower the cost, and the still greater the potential return and capital gain. Investing in financial securities and assets is therefore preferable, in their view, to investing long term in a mom and pop business that won't pay back for years or decades and may go under in the interim.

And as the ranks of professional financial investors—aka the new finance capital elite—grows worldwide, as their income and investable wealth increases, as the institutions (e.g. shadow banks) that invest on their behave proliferate, and as the financial instruments and liquid markets in which to invest multiply and expand—so too does the volume of financial asset investing. Liquidity is their 'life force'. And, as will be explained shortly, 'debt' that flows from the availability of liquidity is their sustenance.

Now, there is a downside to this. The relatively short term nature of financial asset investing means the volatility and gains may not be great in the very short term. The way financial asset investors address that downside to short term investing is to invest very large sums of money in the very short term trades. On the other hand, professional investors always prefer to use other people's money instead of their own. They prefer to hoard their own assets and wealth, or commit just the minimal necessary amount to make an investment. They prefer to borrow. But for that to occur—as their ranks, their liquid markets, their securities expand— very large volumes of money are required to enable the debt creation.

That is, vast sums of liquidity need to be available. Or, alternatively, a complement to liquidity in money forms needs to be invented. In the former case of liquidity in money form, this is where the role of central banks comes in— especially the US central bank, the Federal Reserve. In the latter case of alternative 'complement to liquidity as money', this is where technology and the creation of what is called 'Inside Credit' comes in.

Both central banks' policies and technology are therefore the two driving forces behind the massive increase in liquidity—as money and as inside credit—that has occurred in the global monetary system since the end of World War II. And as we'll see, that explosion of liquidity leads directly to the accumulation of excess debt in the private sector—the business sector in particular but also households—that is fundamental to the development of financial and consumption fragility and the more frequent financial instability events that accompany systemic fragility.

Liquidity as Central Bank Money

The explosion in central bank provided money forms of liquidity— defined as currency and near-money—has experienced several milestones since 1945. The first was the creation of the Bretton Woods international monetary system in 1944. Another important milestone event contributing to the liquidity explosion include the breakdown of that Bretton Woods system, with the Smithsonian Agreements in 1971-73. That breakdown led to what is called the 'managed float' monetary system, where central banks are allowed to pump liquidity into the global economy in order to maintain some exchange rate stability for their national currency, to stimulate economies when recessions occur, and bail out financial institutions when losses and crashes occur. A third necessary milestone for the liquidity explosion to unfold was the elimination of controls on global money and capital flows in the 1980s, led by the USA. Following that, the digital revolution in technology and the creation of the internet in the 1990s. Simultaneously after 1980, the rise of financial engineering and financial creations like derivatives, securitization, and super-leveraging—created in order to accommodate the massive liquidity growth. Then, in the USA, the Greenspan 'put', between 1986-2006, and the 'Bernanke put' of 2006-14 that followed. And, simultaneous with the US central bank policies unleashing liquidity into the system, the parallel rise in volume of other currencies used for financial asset investment globally as well, like the British pound, the Euro, Yen and, now emerging as well, the China Yuan.

The Bretton Woods international monetary system set up in 1944 put the US dollar as the primary substitute for gold as the global reserve and trading currency. The british pound was relegated to a secondary role, and it and all other currencies were 'pegged' to the US dollar and the dollar pegged to $35 an ounce. That retained the fiction of gold as still relevant even though the gold standard totally collapsed in the 1920s. With the dollar now reigning supreme the USA central bank, the Federal Reserve, was now free to pump liquidity into the global economy without restraint. It 'retired' US government war debt, which meant liquidity provided to banks in exchange for US bonds held by private investors. The banks in turn then loaned extensively to US multinational corporations that, for the next 15 years, went on a foreign direct investment binge globally, buying up war-depressed prime industrial assets in Europe and Japan. The US government also provided billions in direct loans to the UK, Europe and Japan in the immediate post-war period. The Marshall Plan—which were payments by the US government to US companies and thus a kind of government subsidy to US corporations—added to the liquidity. As the USA expanded its military bases worldwide, that meant more dollars spent into the global economy. The Cold War after 1948 disseminated still more dollars worldwide. Meanwhile, US corporations continued investing and expanding worldwide, sending more dollars into the global economy. By the late 1950s markets for dollars were available in Europe and worldwide.

The flooding of dollars worldwide had negative consequences. It eventually undermined US balance of payments accounts, as US exports as a share of total exports declined as Europe and Japan began to compete effectively with the US. US corporations' foreign investment continued, while net exports declined, leading to the balance of payments problems in the 1960s. That meant the dollar declined in value in fact, even though it was still pegged to gold at $35 per oz. Europeans and other countries began to dump their huge accumulation of dollars and demand gold in exchange from the USA. That led in turn to the collapse of the Bretton Woods system in 1971-73, as the USA under Nixon simply refused to honor the $35 an oz exchange. The resolution was called the Smithsonian Agreement in 1973.

That small bit of history is provided because the collapse of the dollar-gold standard, i.e. Bretton Woods system, meant that henceforth the USA and other central banks would inject money into their economies to keep their currencies within a 'range' to other currencies, especially the dollar. This was called the 'managed float' system, except time would show it was not managed much at all! Especially by the USA central bank.

From 1973 to the present the US Federal Reserve repeatedly pumped liquidity for a growing list of reasons into the US, and therefore the global, economy since dollars still flowed out of the US economy for all the reasons noted above.

The recession of 1973-75, the most serious to date since 1945, led to Federal Reserve (Fed) liquidity injections to lower interest rates to stimulate the real economy. The re-emergence of financial instability in 1966, 1970, and 1973 meant more liquidity injections to bail out financial institutions and markets, though still limited to individual institutions and select markets.

The rise of OPEC and the 'Petrodollar' market added to the already established, and still growing, 'Eurodollar' market. Oil prices shocks in 1973 and 1979 drove up the price of oil, as the US economy became more dependent on imported oil, thus increasing the flow of dollars out of the US to pay for the larger quantities of higher priced oil. Another deep recession in 1981-82 led to another Fed monetary injection.

The next major milestone in the liquidity explosion came in the 1980s, in the form of the US ending remaining controls on international capital flows. Other economies followed suit and did the same. The US then deregulated broad financial segments of its domestic economy as well, in particular housing finance and junk bonds. That led to the financial crises of the 1980s in these markets, in response to which the Fed injected more money to bail out exposed financial institutions. That occurred during 1986-1990, as Alan Greenspan, appointed in 1986, assumed the role of the new Fed chairman. That began the period known as the 'Greenspan Put', from 1986-2006, during which the Fed provided unbounded liquidity to USA financial institutions whenever their investments and assets appeared to lose value: there was the Tequila Crisis in Mexico, when US banks were about to experience losses; the Long Term Capital Management hedge fund crisis in the early 1990s, the Asian Meltdown crisis of 1997-98, when currency losses threatened bank balance sheets, the dot.com technology stocks boom and bust, and the artificial housing boom that began in 1997. The recession of 2001, precipitated by the tech bust a year earlier, required liquidity to help ensure recovery—especially important after 9-11 and the fear that political events would interrupt recovery from the 2001 recession. By 2002, however, the sluggish US recovery appeared to slow. US growth and disinflation appeared as real threats. How to quickly stimulate growth again, was the challenge. Housing stimulus is often the fastest way. But the US housing cycle, begun in 1997, had largely run its course by 2003. The answer was for the Fed to artificially push it still higher by lowering interest rates to 1%, and by deregulating banks still further to allow them to engage in securitized subprime mortgage lending. That gave the housing sector another unsustainable short term boost. The US economy recovered in 2003-04, in time for the Iraq war, George W. Bush's 2004 re-election, and Alan Greenspan's reappointment by him for another term. But the artificial boost to the Housing sector would lead to another financial crisis, this time linked to other credit markets. It would require an even greater Fed injection of liquidity to bail out the financial institutions. That would be called by the name of Greenspan's successor, appointed Fed chairman in 2006, Ben Bernanke—and the 'Bernanke Put'.

In the interim from the mid-1990s to mid-2000s a technology revolution occurred that in effect accelerated the injection of central bank money into the global system. In addition, a new additional global currency would be added, the Euro, created in 1999.

The technology revolution was the advent of digital technology that created the internet in the 1990s and thereby enabled the almost instantaneous transmission of money across global markets. This allowed the liquidity created by the Fed and other central banks to circulate many times faster than before. The 'stock' of money created by the central banks was thus multiplied several-fold as the flow of money, i.e. its rate of circulation, increased due to technological innovations like the digital internet. The supply of money (liquidity) can be understood as a stock, an existing volume. But if it circulates faster, then the supply of money is also a function of its 'velocity'. The more money turns over, the more supply of it there is. If one considers the role of technology and the internet on accelerating financial investment turnovers, it is arguable that liquidity has also grown with the advent of the internet and its impact on financial transactions.

The latest and perhaps most massive increase in money liquidity in the global system has been the consequence of the USA and other advanced economies' experimenting with Quantitative Easing (QE) policies since 2009. By virtually printing money and buying financial assets held by the new finance capital elite, the USA central bank since 2009 pumped around $4 trillion into markets, the Bank of England another $650 billion, the Bank of Japan $1.7 trillion (and more coming) and the European Central Bank about $1.4 trillion indirectly (in the form of its LRTO and OMT programs) plus another $1.3 trillion in its 2015 QE just announced. That's about $9 trillion to date in just five years or so.

The question is where is all this money liquidity going? It can't be going into real asset investment, which is slowing, as noted above. So where is all this excess liquidity flowing? One could argue: into financial assets and financial asset speculative investing—as the proliferation of financial asset markets, financial instruments, financial institutions serving those markets and selling those instruments (e.g. shadow banks and deep shadow banks), and the escalating financial asset inflation globally together serve as evidence.

But money liquidity driving financial assets is not the total story. The steady increase in liquidity in the global system was accompanied by an additional milestone development that also has accelerated liquidity growth. That additional development is the growth and spread of financial engineering, as it is sometimes called, that has created financial innovations like 'securitization', has expanded 'leveraging' (the ratio of borrowed money to one's own capital invested) immensely, and has created the derivatives revolution that today is worth hundreds of trillions of dollars in investment totals worldwide in the form of 'swaps' and other forms of financial assets based upon (i.e. derived from) other financial assets. Financial engineering leads to the second major form of liquidity explosion in recent decades called 'Inside Credit'.

Liquidity as Inside Credit

With regard to investing (whether real or financial), money may serve as credit but credit need not assume the form of money.

The explosion of money liquidity by the actions of central banks, especially the US Fed, since 1944 for the various reasons noted above—i.e. Bretton Woods, post-1973 managed float, global capital flows deregulation, rise of euro and petro dollar markets, Greenspan and Bernanke 'puts', more frequent and deeper recessions requiring monetary stimulus, more frequent and widespread financial bailouts, technology changes, financial engineering, etc.—all result in continued liquidity injections adding up to a massive long term injection. But all that was still liquidity in the form of central bank money. There are additional, de facto liquidity injections provided by the expansion of inside credit that have also come about for purposes of financial asset investment.

Inside money (as opposed to outside money provided by central banks) occurs when financial institutions—commercial but mostly shadow banks— permit an investor to borrow more credit based on the value of the collateral of already purchased financial assets. If an investor's financial investments in derivatives or other securities rises in price and therefore value, the investor is allowed to purchase even more 'on credit'. It's much like buying stocks on margin for any retail investor. But here the purchase on credit is for more esoteric financial instruments. Typically, the investor puts up a small amount in his own cash—perhaps 5% and 'borrows' the remaining 95%, which is provided based on the collateral value of already made investments.

This kind of 'inside credit' is almost totally limited to financial asset and securities investments. One is not allowed, for example, to buy a new car based on the value of the principal paid to date on one's previous car loan. That is a goods transaction, not a financial transaction.

It is a misunderstanding to think that central banks 'create' money. They provide incentives to private banks to create money. In the final analysis, private banks create money. And they can do it by loaning out money that central banks deposit in them, the private banks, which then extend credit to those taking out a loan, for example, from the bank. But banks, and especially shadow banks, do not need 'money' from central banks to extend credit. In the era of extreme financial securities engineering, they have developed other ways to extend credit without money backing it up to customers-investors. Financial engineering, of course, is for the benefit of financial investors—i.e. the new finance capital elite in particular. Nonetheless, inside credit represents a form of liquidity that is injected into the global economy, into financial asset markets in particular

The extension of credit—whether in central bank money form or in forms of inside credit—result in the expansion of debt. For every credit there is a debt, in other words. So we have a logical progression: from massive liquidity explosion to credit expansion to debt accumulation. And as the next section indicates, debt accumulation may occur to finance real investment or to finance investment in financial securities. There is no instability problem so long as borrowers who financed real investment are able to pay the principal and interest on what was borrowed as it comes due. That requires earning an income flow on the real investment to pay the principal and interest. And there's no problem for financial asset investment so long as the prices of those financial assets continue to rise. But once the financial asset price inflation slows or reverses, and financial asset deflation occurs, then the 'income' with which to pay for the original financial investment disappears. And that's a potential instability problem and a road to default on either principal or interest or both.

In other words, there's an important causal relationship between debt accumulation, deflation, and default, or what this writer has called the debt-deflation-default nexus which is a transmission mechanism to producing greater financial fragility.

10

RISING
LEVELS OF
GLOBAL DEBT

The number one consequence of the explosion in liquidity has been the escalation of credit and therefore debt at all levels—household, corporate, and government. Contrary to the often heard claim, the increase in debt levels globally have not reversed or even moderated since the official end of the great recession in mid-2009. They have increased, and rapidly in some sectors and regions of the global economy. If debt is a major determinant of fragility, and therefore instability, then this increase in system-wide debt has been creating a corresponding growth in systemic fragility and with it the potential for instability.

Like the uneven growth and recovery since 2009 in the global economy, the increase in global debt has been uneven and shifting from region to region, even though the total debt has been rising inexorably.

Prior to the crisis erupting in 2007, the debt increase was concentrated heavily in the advanced economies (AEs), especially the US, UK, and Europe. Much of that occurred in housing and consumer credit, but also in bank and other corporate debt.[1]

In the subsequent phase, from 2010 to 2013, the focus shifted as debt escalated faster now in China and the emerging markets, as much of the liquidity injections and credit flowed from the AEs to China and the EMEs during this period. During the same period, as the China-EME shift occurred, there was only token debt deleveraging in the meantime in AE households. Corporate AE debt, however, now also began to rise rapidly in the AEs as well in this second phase, as global corporate new bond (debt) issuance alone averaged more than $1 trillion a year for the next five consecutive years. An equally massive corporate debt acceleration occurred in China and the EMEs. AE government debt also continued to rise after 2010 as AE, US and

UK governments cut taxes and bailed out their banking and corporate sectors. In Europe, this government debt escalation was particularly concentrated in governments in the Euro periphery area.

The following data from the Bank of International Settlements shows these critical sectoral trends and concentrations associated with rising global debt during the second phase, from 2009 through 2013:

Table 10.1
Global Debt Change 2008 through 2013[2]($trillions)

	End 2007	End 2013	Change 2007-13
(TOTAL DEBT)			
Advanced Economies	$135	$150	$15
Emerging Economies	$70	$95	$25
(NON-FINANCIAL CORPORATE)			
Advanced Economies	$47	$48	$1
Emerging Economies	$30	$47	$17
(GOVERNMENT)			
Advanced Economies	$37	$55	$18
Emerging Economies	$20	$22	$2
(HOUSEHOLDS)			
Advanced Economies	$50	$48	-$2
Emerging Economies	$21	$25	$4

What the data reveal is that corporate debt actually accelerated globally after the 2008-09 recession. Nor has the recovery since 2009 abated or reduced the private (corporate based) debt surge. It has gotten worse, much worse. Meanwhile, the data suggests the household sector has not significantly reduced debt overhang, except perhaps for the wealthiest households.[3] Finally, while household debt has leveled off, government debt has continued to rise nonetheless, especially in the AEs. The shift after 2009 has therefore been only relative, from the household sector and banks to the non-financial corporate sector especially and with government debt continuing to rise still higher. The most significant and worrisome sectoral trends 2010-2013 have been the still escalating rise in non-financial corporate debt, especially in the EMEs, and the continued growth of AE government debt. As the BIS report's summary noted, "globally, the total debt of private nonfinancial sectors has risen 30% since the crisis". Moreover, banks have only recovered unevenly, while "private debt keeps growing".[4] And overall, for both government and all private, total debt has risen by approximately $40 trillion since the crisis.

The Continuing Rise in Global Debt

Non-financial corporate debt has continued to accelerate in 2014-2015. In the US alone, more than $2 trillion in new issuance of corporate bond debt has taken place. That includes $879 billion in the nine months of 2015, so the total is likely to come closer to $2.5 trillion by year end. And that does not include other forms of corporate debt, such as commercial and industrial loans, commercial paper, and so forth. While traditionally less a share of total credit in Europe and Asia, corporate bond debt is rising rapidly in those regions as well. A new trend has also been US corporations issuing bonds in Euro debt, a rapidly rising trend. Then there's the EMEs and China, where corporate debt issued in US dollars is a major element of such total debt—a fact that will no doubt result in extreme instability for non-financial corporations in the regions once US interest rates begin to rise.

The problem potential from debt refinancing is not limited to the EMEs. China also faces a major challenge. And US corporations must somehow find the means to refinance $4 trillion in debt that is scheduled to mature and need refinancing between 2015 and 2019. Should US rates rise, the possibility of not securing refinancing is significant. And it's not just that the interest rates to refinance will prove costly, but that many non-financial corporations will be unable to obtain new credit at any rate of interest.

It has been estimated that US corporations' aggregate debt burden is today 2.62 times earnings—the highest since 2002. The potential for rising debt defaults is therefore not insignificant in the remainder of the decade, in the US, EMEs and globally.

For purposes of fragility analysis, defaults translate into financial asset deflation as asset firesales typically are a prelude to a default, and as default leads to restructuring under bankruptcy provisions by the courts. The processes precipitated by financial asset deflation described in the preceding chapter 9 become increasingly real.

What's also crucially different about the 2010-2015 global debt period, when compared to the pre-2008 debt escalation, is that it has been occurring as income sources for servicing that debt are declining or under serious stress in a number of corporations and a large proportion of consumer households, as well as for various geographical regions that avoided income-debt servicing difficulties, as in the EMEs and China. It appears only the largest corporations and the wealthiest 10%-20% of households who have benefited from stocks and bond capital gains have accrued excess income, or have been able to deleverage previous debt. Households, state and local government units, non-corporate businesses, and smaller-medium corporations dependent on high cost, lower quality debt are today in a weaker income position by far compared to pre-2008 and thus far less able to service larger debt levels in the event of another crisis.

The Myth of US Debt Deleveraging

Given the obvious data on continuing rising debt, it is therefore something of a myth—indeed a purposeful misrepresentation—perpetrated by politicians and the media—that since 2009 the global economy in general, and the USA in particular, has been able to 'work off' the excessive debt accumulated prior to the 2008-09 economic crash. And if debt levels are an important factor in rising fragility then as debt levels have continued to rise so too has systemic fragility, all things equal.

In the USA, the argument is typically made that the financial system is improving, given that debt deleveraging (i.e. debt retirement) is occurring for households and businesses alike since 2009. But a closer look shows this has not occurred for most households, whether in the US or elsewhere, and is certainly not occurring for most non-financial businesses or government units.

While economists and the media contend that a 20% deleveraging of debt by consumers has occurred in the USA since 2009,[5] two-thirds of that 20% is not 'healthy' deleveraging, where consumers use income to pay down debt, but rather due to banks and creditors writing off loans due to consumer defaults. So true US household deleveraging—where household reallocate income to pay down debt—is about 7% at best, and most of that is likely concentrated among the wealthiest households with incomes sufficiently high enough that they mostly save instead of consume. That leaves 80%-90% of US consumer households still burdened by a significant debt overhang more than five years after the official end of the 2008-09 crash.

Another problem with the 20% deleveraging figure is that it omits a number of other important categories that make up household debt in the USA today, like higher education loans, payday loans that afflict the lower income groups of the working class, unpaid medical bill debts, and the like.

Even disregarding these uncounted categories of debt, net total household debt deleveraging in the USA is undoubtedly not even 7% as suggested.

Consumer deleveraging is associated with three factors that reveal how debt fragile consumers still remain:

1) Mortgage debt has declined because banks and lenders simply wrote off many of the loans in default. The defaults occurred because from 2003-2006, home buyers were lured into what were called 'liar loans' they couldn't afford. Almost $4 trillion of such subprime mortgages were issued. Teaser mortgage rates were offered: 1% and no money

down. But when rates started rising, subprime mortgage homeowners defaulted, unable to pay the principal or interest on the loans. More than 14 million USA homeowners were thus 'foreclosed' by their banks. Much of it was slowly written off by the banks over time. In fact, mortgage debt in the US has declined from $9.5 trillion in 2007 to approximately $8 trillion today. That debt was therefore reduced, showing up as deleveraging for households. But again, the idea that consumers 'paid off' that debt, i.e. deleveraged by income servicing of debt, is not accurate. It was written off in large part by the banks as bad debt.

2) A similar 'write off' occurred in the US with credit card debt. As millions lost their jobs or had their hours of work or wages cut, they simply stopped paying, and defaulted on their credit cards. Banks and credit card companies got stuck with the debt. As in the case of mortgage debt, the issuers of the credit cards had to write a good part of it off.

3) Only the wealthiest 10% of households have therefore been able to significantly deleverage their debt. Those households experienced a growth of income after 2009. US academic studies show that no less than 95% of all the net additional income gains from 2009 through 2013 accrued to the wealthiest 1% US households.[6]While that income growth occurred mostly for the top 1% households, it did enable a couple million households in the USA (out of 124 million) to reduce their debt. The rich and very rich may have repaired ("deleveraged") their balance sheets, but the important consideration here is that the overwhelming remaining majority of households have not.

If one were to look at how various household groups did in terms of deleveraging, it would undoubtedly show that the wealthiest households did deleverage, but as one went down the annual income scale it would show less and less deleveraging. Certainly as one approached the median household income level, very little deleveraging would appear, and even less for households below the median.

Indeed, debt for many households rose substantially after 2009—as millions of students took on college loan debt after 2009. Total student debt in the USA is now more than $1.3 trillion, having risen hundreds of billions since 2009. More than 40 million people, students and former students, owe student loans averaging $33,000. And more than one in five have already defaulted on the loans.

Not just student debt, but credit card debt has begun to rise again as card companies have again begun to throw card applications at households at rates close to the pre-2008 period. Mortgage debt is rising—mostly higher priced homes. And auto companies are selling cars primarily by offering virtually free financing. So many are buying cars again, but on 'subprime auto' debt terms, with payments typically stretched out for 6 and more years in order to allow buyers to afford the higher car prices. So debt continues to rise again for consumer households in the USA. The pattern is not that much different in other advanced economies. Household debt has risen in Europe, and there's the $4 trillion increase in EME household debt, according to the Bank of International Settlements report previously noted.

Nor has corporate or non-corporate business debt been deleveraged. Corporate deleveraging may occur in the form of a refinancing of pre-existing debt at a lower rate, by the sale by banks of non-performing loans, or by business consolidations that expunge the debt in part.

Once again, using the USA example, the largest source of business debt is corporate bonds, which come in two basic varieties: investment grade and junk bonds (issued by companies with poor growth prospects and which therefore have to pay a high bond interest rate to buyers). A conservative estimate by the US Federal Reserve is that US corporate debt will have risen from $6 trillion in 2007 to $12 trillion as of end of 2015. A more aggressive private estimate is that the total US corporate bond market exceeded $10 trillion at the end of 2014, rising by $2.275 trillion in 2014 alone, according to the business research firm, Dealogic. That's more than a 20% increase in the last year alone. And that doesn't even count other forms of corporate and non-corporate business debt in the USA since 2009, like the commercial paper market for shorter term corporate debt, now more than $1 trillion, or the corporate loan market worth more than $2.7 trillion. Or loans for commercial property, private equity leveraged loans which have risen more than 70% in recent years, and so on.

Even mainstream economists acknowledge there has been a bubble in corporate bond issuance since 2009, especially in what's called 'high yield' corporate, or junk, bonds. Trillions of dollars in these have been issued in the USA alone in recent years, especially the last three, and that debt represents a continued leveraging trend, not de-leveraging.

If household debt in the US has, at best, leveled off and if US corporate debt is accelerating—hardly evidence of deleveraging, are government units (federal, state, local) successfully deleveraging in recent years?

Mainstream economists also like to obfuscate the problem of rising debt levels by using a debt ratio: debt as a percentage of GDP to indicate government deleveraging. But this is misleading. If nominal GDP rises in relation to debt it makes it appear as if the rising debt problem is being improved. But nonetheless, debt levels are still rising. Their counter is that rising GDP means that servicing (paying) of the debt is easier, thus reducing the instability potential of debt. But GDP does not 'pay for' debt servicing. Government Income pays for it. And that means income as government tax revenue or income savings from government spending reduction. And not some aggregate concept like GDP and

National Income, but actual household disposable income. So, debt to GDP is not a very useful or accurate concept to employ when trying to estimate the effect on fragility from rising debt.[7]

Accelerating private sector debt is not just a problem in the USA, it is a problem elsewhere as well in the global economy. Non-financial corporate debt in emerging markets has been a particular problem since 2007.   This EME corporate debt is also potentially especially volatile, since much of it is denominated in US dollars. That means if the dollar rises in value in relation to EME currencies, which it has been doing in 2014, then EMEs will have very significant difficulty servicing this mountain of debt that has been accumulated. Major default risks in the EMEs, but including state owned enterprises (SOEs) within China as well, are very possible.

When considering bank loans, trust loans, and other forms of debt, total debt in China has risen from 130% of GDP in 2008 to more than 240% of GDP today—and that's a GDP that is more than $10 trillion. China is a financial volcano waiting to erupt.

Debt and Fragility

As subsequent chapters will explain in more detail, debt is a critical element determining fragility. Rising debt levels raise fragility within the system and thus consequently raise the tendency toward financial instability.

When occurring in a context of slowing or declining income availability, necessary to pay for previously incurred debt, the outcome from a combination of rising debt amidst declining income can lead to a still further intensification of fragility and consequent instability.

The following chapters 11 through 13 thus take a closer look at how income flows, and the three price systems (for goods, financial assets, and wages) associated with those flows, additionally contribute toward a rise in systemic fragility as well.

Endnotes

1   For global debt and trends during the pre-2008 crash period, see McKinsey Global Institute, '*Debt and Deleveraging: The Global Credit Bubble and its Economic Consequences*', January 2010. Before continuing, for purposes of working definition, the debt referred to here includes household or consumer debt, corporate debt, and sovereign (government) debt. Household debt includes mortgage debt, credit card debt, installment debt, auto debt, and other special kinds of debt like student loan debt, medical debt, payday loans and other types of personal loans. Corporate debt includes corporate (investment grade and junk) bonds, commercial paper, corporate loans, commercial property loans, commercial & industrial loans, various forms of securitized loans like lever-

aged buyouts, and other loans. Government debt includes federal or national debt (loans and bonds), state or regional government bonds & loans, municipal (city)bonds, special local government bonds (e.g. school districts), government sponsored enterprises (GSEs) like Fannie Mae/Freddie Mac in the USA that hold mortgage debt, and debt on the balance sheets of central banks. That represents a definition of 'total' government debt, addressed in more detail in chapter 15. For now, government debt is referred to as federal or national government debt, in the form of sovereign bonds and loans.

2   Data is from the Bank of International Settlements, '84th Annual Report', Basel, Switzerland, June 2014, roughly estimated and rounded. See also the '*16th Geneva Report on the World Economy*', International Center for Money and Banking, Geneva, September 2014. More detailed examination of these global trends by country is addressed in chapter 14 to follow, and, in particulars, in the preceding Chapters 3-6.

3   See analysis below

4   BIS 84th Report, p. 9, 10.

5   The 20% deleveraging so often cited, by the way, is only roughly half of the average of 38% deleveraging that has occurred in the US in the wake of previous economic contractions. So deleveraging is only half 'normal' thus far after five years of recovery.

6   See Chapter 13 for details of these studies by professor Emmanual Saez of University of California at Berkeley.

7   A third source of government income is borrowed income, as governments sell bonds to investors and use the 'income' for general spending. But such income is really a form of additional debt and does not 'deleverage' or reduce total debt. The one exception to this is if the new borrowing and debt is secured at a lower rate of interest and used to retired older debt with a higher rate of interest. In such cases, a kind of government debt deleveraging does occur. Some argue that governments' motivation to keep zero interest rates going for seven years is to offset government debt by issuing bonds with lower interest rates. Some governments, in Europe, now require buyers of their government debt to pay the government for the privilege of buying the bonds, thus offering negative rates. As of late 2015, apparently no less than $1.7 trillion of bonds are now offered at negative rates.

11

THE SHIFT TO FINANCIAL ASSET INVESTMENT

A key question is whether the shift to financial asset investment is the consequence of slowing real asset investment (i.e. equipment, structures, etc.) or whether the shift to financial asset investing is itself the driver of the slowdown in real investment. While a correlation clearly exists between the two forms of investment—real asset investment slowing and financial asset investment growing—the important question is, which drives the other? Furthermore, is causality in the relationship mutual? And if so, how?[1]

The slowing of real investment in recent decades has major consequences for the real economy—for the creation of decent paying jobs, household income stagnation and decline, weak recovery of household consumption, and therefore below historical average economic growth rates. The jobs-income-consumption decline may be temporarily offset by more credit availability to households to maintain consumption. But rising credit means more household debt in the present period, which means more household real income must be diverted to make interest payments in the future. In other words, in the short term, household debt may offset real income decline and help maintain consumption, but in the longer run it reduces household disposable income and slows consumption. And in the longer run, both the added debt and lower disposable real income add to household consumption fragility.

But slowing real investment is also associated with rising financial debt and therefore fragility in the business sector as well.

Origins of the Financial Asset Investment Shift

There are several fundamental forces behind the shift to financial asset investing. They include:

- Faster rate of increase in financial asset prices, and therefore profits, relative to real goods prices and goods profits over the course of a normal business cycle;

- Acceleration of the rate of increase of financial asset prices relative to goods prices in recent decades, beyond that occurring in a normal business cycle, due to the explosion of liquidity, credit, and the rise in leveraged debt to finance financial assets;

- Lower cost of production, and therefore higher profit, of financial securities compared to production of real goods—producing greater profits for the former compared to the latter;

- The absence of supply constraints to slow financial asset inflation over the cycle, in contrast to supply constraints in the case of goods prices;

- Less risk and uncertainty for financial asset investment due to the highly liquid nature of financial markets, providing rapid ease of entry and exit from markets in which financial assets are sold;

- New global institutional and agent structures that implement the investment in financial securities in highly liquid markets;

- Far lower incidence of taxation on financial securities compared to real goods.

These forces collectively enable financial asset prices to rise—and they do—much faster than goods prices over even a normal business cycle, thus providing potential greater excess profits from price-driven capital gains compared to goods prices and profits. The excess liquidity, credit, and debt leverage of recent decades accelerates prices and profits still further as well. Other characteristics—apart from price—associated specifically with financial assets, securities, and financial markets add to the greater relative profitability. The gap between prices, and therefore profits, that emerges between the two forms of investment is therefore accelerating in today's world of global financialization.

The greater relative profitability between financial and real asset investing draws money capital increasingly into financial asset investment, and over time does so at the expense of capital available for real asset investing. Greater financial asset profitability thus 'crowds out' real asset investment. Or, a more accurate metaphor perhaps might be, 'sucks money capital out' of real investment that otherwise might have been committed to real asset investment.

Enabling Causes of the Shift

At the most fundamental level, the shift from investing in real assets to financial asset investing occurs because the structure of the global economy today incentivizes financial asset investment more than real asset investment. Financial markets are more liquid and offer a greater potential return. Investors can move their capital in and out of more liquid financial markets more quickly—thus avoiding losses and taking quick advantage of capital gains.

Financial markets are more prone to price escalation due to the tendency toward excess demand in relation to supply: more demand results in higher prices and therefore more opportunities to sell for quick capital gains. Investors can invest and disinvest more quickly. Financial asset and securities markets are fundamentally price-driven markets, not markets where goods must be sold in large volume in order to realize profits or where price increases are constrained by supply forces over the course of a business cycle.

Because markets for financial securities are highly liquid, long run risk and uncertainty is less compared to real asset investment. That too makes financial asset investing potentially more profitable. As investors are always trying to reduce risk, uncertainty, and the potential for loss, reducing the time period during which an investment rests in an asset is one way to do so. Reducing the time period involved in investing in physical goods or assets is less viable than reducing the time period when investing in financial securities and assets.

The creation or production of financial securities eliminates the need for raw materials, almost all labor, and semi-finished good inputs—all of which have a cost. Physical goods have a 'cost of goods' associated with their production. But financial securities typically have little, if any, cost of production that may reduce profitability or raise risks and uncertainty that may be involved in obtaining and ensuring availability of inputs for production. Supply costs as well as supply constraints are thus minimized for financial assets. Prices of financial asset securities are determined instead in large part by demand for those assets, not by supply. The greater role of demand, and the minimal role of supply, may make financial asset prices more volatile. However, being largely demand driven, financial assets are also therefore potentially more profitable—especially in the short run and so long as prices continue to rise. Conversely, that same volatility may result in greater losses. But that only means financial asset prices may fall as rapidly as they rose, and in some cases even faster. Profits may be made from deflating financial assets as well as from their rising prices—a condition not shared by goods price deflation.

Another important enabler for the financial investment shift is the creation of an institutional structure that directs the excess liquidity, credit and debt increasingly toward financial asset investment. That institutional structure is composed of financial institutions called 'shadow banks'.[2] A closely related structure which has newly arisen is the global finance capital elite, consisting of 'inside agents' who manage shadow banking operations and investing, as well as their client investors who function as 'outside agents'. Agents may assume both roles; hedge fund managers, for example, manage the investing while also providing their own capital for investment. Without this institutional structure of shadow banks and agents, the excess liquidity, credit and debt would not be redirected in as great a volume to financial asset markets. In many cases, the structure creates not just the markets but also the financial 'engineering' and the financial securities that are invested.

Financial asset profits tend to be greater since financial profits are taxed as capital gains, often at a much lower rate than profits from sale of goods or services. That also raises their relative profitability compared to real goods. There are virtually no 'financial securities' taxes of any consequence in any economy today. Because financial securities are moveable globally in an instant, their profits can also be diverted instantaneously in order to avoid taxation. Tax avoidance and fraud is thus immensely easier. Capital gains from financial investing may also be realized from deflating financial asset prices, just as from rising prices. Real investment and goods profits cannot similarly be realized from falling goods prices.

In other words, financial asset investing is simply more profitable than real asset investing in most cases—due to greater upside volatility of prices, less relative risk and uncertainty due to easier and faster access and exit from markets that are highly liquid, lower cost of production involving financial assets, less mitigation of price escalation due to supply constraints over the cycle, and more favorable taxation.

While the preceding market characteristics of financial asset inflation serve as the key enabling forces for the greater relatively profitability of financial asset investing, it is the introduction of excess liquidity, credit and debt leveraging that is further accelerating the tendency of financial asset prices and profitability to outstrip real asset investment and goods prices. That accelerated tendency then feeds an abnormal shift from real to financial asset investing that is characteristic and increasingly dominant in the 21st century.

Expanding Price-Profit Gaps

The enabling causes above are reflected in a new characteristic process defining capitalist business cycles that develops over the course of the cycle 'boom' phase in recent decades: a growing gap between the two price systems— financial asset and real goods. That price gap in turn creates a corresponding gap in relative profits as well between financial assets and goods.

That process works something like this: as money capital is increasingly diverted to financial investment over the course of a business cycle, it stimulates the demand for financial securities which leads to a rise in financial asset prices.

And as financial asset inflation occurs, the continual growth in liquidity (as noted in the preceding chapter) permits investors to leverage still more financial asset investing with more and more debt—in turn, leading to still more financial asset demand and more financial asset inflation. Liquidity, excess credit, and debt leveraging thus feeds and accelerates the growth of financial asset investing— driven by, and in turn driving, further financial asset inflation. The upward spiral in financial asset investing and inflation continues, until financial bubble dimensions are reached and the process abruptly breaks.

A widening gap between financial asset inflation and goods price inflation thus emerges, well beyond that which normally occurs in the course of a business cycle between real goods and financial assets. The growing relative price gap means a similar gap in relative profits from goods investment and production compared to investing in financial securities. This widening price-profit gap leads to a further shift to financial assets, from less profitable real investment to increasingly profitable (price and capital gains driven) financial asset investing. In this scenario, clearly financial asset investing initially drives the processes and keeps them going and expanding.

All the foregoing basic determinants of the shift to financial asset investing have been put in place over the past three to four decades: the explosion in liquidity, the debt and leveraging practices, the proliferation of financial instruments, the highly liquid markets, the institutional network of financial brokers called shadow banks, the finance capital elite of agents who focus primarily on financial asset investing, and the digital technology (internet, digital storage, fast processing of trades, etc.) that supports the globalized financial investing markets.

How Big Is the Shift?

What is the evidence for a shift to financial asset investing? There are basically three ways to estimate, all three of which are related and approach the question from different perspectives.

1. Identify the shift to financial securities that have the characteristics of short term, price driven, capital gains-oriented investment. For example, one might identify stock-equity investment growth that is less than one year, i.e. short term capital gain-oriented, as 'speculative'. So might equity (stock) investing that is associated with short selling, options trading that occurs in 'dark pools', computerized 'fast-trading', hedge fund arbitraging, overnight foreign exchange currency trading, corporate high yield or junk bond investments that are associated with high risk companies or industries, as leveraged loans used for corporate acquisitions by private equity firms, and corporate debt borrowed from banks called 'repurchase agreements' (repos)—to name just a few of the more obvious 'speculative' sources and practices.

2. Identify the financial institutions that are the main sources of such investing, and their magnitude—the 'shadow banks' and the global shadow banking system, which predominantly moves money capital around globally to exploit short term price change opportunities for profitable capital gains among the many, proliferating, and highly liquid global financial asset markets today.[3]

It is important to note that the shadow banks, despite their rapid growth, are not the only institutional source of financial assets, or even speculative financial assets. The traditional, commercial (regulated) banks and financial institutions engage in financial and speculative financial investing indirectly, by providing funding for the shadow banks in not insignificant sums. So the two main forms of financial institutions—shadow and traditional—are integrated in many ways, and the lines between them increasingly blur. In fact, the regulated, commercial banking system also participates directly in financial and speculative financial investing, even though those practices have been circumscribed somewhat (not much) by efforts of government banking regulators and governments in the USA, Europe, and to a lesser extent globally, as well as by central banks responsible for commercial banks' regulation and supervision.

However, the trend is clear: the direct speculative financial investing activity of commercial banks is being reduced in the longer term—for reasons that include government regulation of the commercial banks but also economic and market forces. What are called 'capital markets' are clearly eclipsing the role of traditional bank lending to non-financial business. Conversely, the financial-speculative activities of shadow banks are clearly rising and expanding as the excess liquidity in the global system continues to rise, as forms of financial securities proliferate to attract that liquidity, as highly liquid financial markets multiply worldwide, and as the wealth of the new global finance capital elite accelerates.

3. Apart from estimating the growth of financial securities or the magnitude of total assets or transactions by shadow banking, a third way to measure the growth of the shift to financial investing is to track the growth of wealth and assets owned by and associated with the new financial capital elite itself, on whose behalf the shadow banks invest and who themselves are owners and shareholders in the shadow banks.[4]

The growth of the professional investor elites is reflected in the growing wealth and investable assets held by 'very high net worth' (VHNWIs) and 'ultra high net worth' (UHNWIs) individual investors. Both groups may include in their ranks senior level corporate managers and bankers—i.e. that segment which still engages in directly managing capital through their corporations. But the largest segment is composed of individuals who are professional investors (directly or indirectly associated with their shadow banks or just independent investors, who may invest in financial assets through the shadow banks or even directly in financial markets without the intermediary of the shadow bankers).

The explosive growth of shadow banks, and the rising numbers and asset wealth growth of the new finance capital elite (VHNWIs and UHNWIs), represent a major structural change in the nature of global finance capital in the 21st century. This change did not occur overnight. It is the consequence of decades of increments of quantitative structural change in the structure of global finance in the 21st century.

The Unstable Financial Asset Markets

The shift to financial asset investing leads to price bubbles, subsequent financial asset deflation when the bubbles burst, and in turn to instability, first financial and then transmitted to the real economy. As the total changes in asset values for the selected markets below suggest, the growth in financial investing could not have been possible without the massive increase in liquidity, credit, and leveraged debt that enabled it. Behind the asset inflation lies the debt—and therefore growing fragility—that has made it possible. Should asset prices and income for servicing the debt subsequently decline—a process that has already begun in a number of the markets—then the debt enabled fragility will be intensified by the negative income effects as well.

The following is a short list of select financial asset markets that now exhibit elements of a bubble or, because of their strategic position in the overall credit system and potential for contagion to other credit markets, pose a growing risk capable of precipitating, or serving as a contagion-transmission source, for another major financial instability event before the current decade ends:

At-Risk Unstable Financial Asset Markets

Financial Asset	$ Asset Value 2007	$ Asset Value 2014
STOCK MARKETS		
Equity Markets (US)	$14.4 trillion	$26.1 trillion
Equity Markets (Global)	$32 trillion	$64 trillion
BOND MARKETS		
Corporate Bonds (global)	$5.4 trillion	$7.8 trillion
Hi Yield Junk Bonds (US)	$1.0 trillion	$1.3 trillion
Hi Yield Junk Bonds (Europe)	$20 billion	$600 billion
US Treasury Bonds	$4.5 trillion	$12.8 trillion
Municipal Bonds (US)	$2.6 trillion	$3.7 trillion
EMERGING MARKETS		
Emerging Markets Corporate Debt	$5.5 trillion	$18 trillion
Emerging Markets $ Dollar Bond Debt	$135 billion	$1.0 trillion

Financial Asset	$ Asset Value 2007	$ Asset Value 2014
Emerging Markets Total $ Dollar Debt	$900 billion	$2.6 trillion
CHINA MARKETS		
Local Govt. Finance Vehicles (China)	$550 billion	$3.8 trillion
Private Corporate Debt (China)	$2 trillion	$11.8 trillion
Wealth Management Products (China)	$350 billion	$2.9 trillion
Entrusted Loans (China)	$272 billion	$2.9 trillion
China Corporate $ Dollar Debt	$45 billion	$367 billion
US & EUROPE MARKETS		
Defined Benefit Pension Funds (US)	$9.1 trillion	$11.1 trillion
Municipal Bonds (US)	$2.6 trillion	$3.7 trillion
Student Loans (US)	$548 billion	$1.3 trillion
Repurchase Agreements (US)	$3.1 trillion	$3.7 trillion
Mutual Funds (US)	$6.9 trillion	$12.6 trillion
Exchange Traded Funds (US)	$700 billion	$2 trillion
Leveraged Loans (US)	$100 billion	$628 billion
CoCo Bonds (Europe)	$0	$288 billion
Government Debt (Europe)	$7.4 trillion	$12.3 trillion
SELECT GLOBAL MARKETS		
Forex Trading (total)	$3.2 trillion/day	$5.3 trillion/day
Forex Trading (Retail)	$45 billion/day	$400 billion/day
Pension Funds (global)	$20 trillion	$36 trillion
OTC Derivatives (global-gross value)	$15 trillion	$21 trillion
CDS Indices Options ('swaptions')	$40 billion	$3.1 trillion
Repurchase Agreements (global)	$7 trillion	$4.3 trillion
Securitized Assets (US & Europe)	$1.45 trillion	$1.85 trillion
Securitization New Issues (US)	$1.0 trillion	$1.2 trillion
Securitization New Issues (Europe)	$912 billion	$243 billion

Where Is the Next Financial Fault Line?

Global Equity Markets

In the past year the stock markets in China erupted, contracting by nearly 50% in just three months, after having risen in the preceding year by 130%—truly a 'bubble event'. That collapse, commencing in June 2015, continues despite efforts to stabilize it. Chinese bankers then injected directly $400 billion to stem the decline. Including other government and private sources, estimates are that no less than $1.3 trillion was committed to prop up stock values. So far it has produced little success, with more than $4 trillion in equity values having been wiped out in less than four months.

Another $500 billion in foreign currency reserves were committed by China to prop up the currency, the Yuan, which has declined in tandem with its stock markets. To finance its efforts to support its currency, China then began to sell its large pile of US Treasury bonds. Nevertheless, capital continues in 2015 to flee China in large volumes in the wake of the stock contraction, expectations of more currency disinflation, an initial devaluation by China of the Yuan, and a general expectation of more of the same.

Both Chinese stocks and foreign exchange effects spilled over to other equity and currency markets throughout Asia, as well to stock markets in the US, Europe and other EMEs. In the case of the US and Europe markets, the contagion effect has not been that severe. Other countervailing forces, estimated around $150 billion, also exist in US-Europe-Japan—i.e. the potential of more QE and suspension of US interest rate hikes—that have offset the initial China contagion effects. Not so, however, in the EMEs where financial assets in stocks and currencies followed the Chinese trajectory more closely.

The stock and currency declines in China and the accelerating pace of capital flight from China will likely more than negate any future efforts by China to stimulate its real economy, already slowing noticeably. Money capital flows out of China perhaps faster than China's central bank and state banks will try to pump it in. Should China's stock markets decline another 10% to 20%, the financial markets in and out of China will experience even greater contagion effects and become potentially severely unstable.

Meanwhile, European, Japanese and US stock markets remain largely driven by the prospect of continuing QE, delays in US interest rate hikes, historic levels of corporate buybacks of stock, and record merger and acquisition activity—all of which provided a floor under artificially maintained stock levels. However, these forces may eventually be overwhelmed by China-EME market contractions. Contagion effects from the latter may eventually play a larger role in the 2015 US-European-Japanese stock financial asset deflation.

Except in the case of China, however, instability in global equity markets is not the potentially most severe source of financial instability in today's global economy. That dubious distinction will likely reside with the bond markets. Globally stock markets represent about $40 trillion in value. Global bond markets, in contrast, equal at least two and a half times that with more than $100 trillion in assets. A bond market crash, even in one of its segments, could easily spread quickly to other bond segments and in turn other financial assets quickly as well, resulting in a crisis far worse than 2008-09.

Global Bond Markets

Several segments of global bond markets are prime candidates for precipitating a financial instability event of major dimensions. One is the high yield or 'junk' bond market in the US and Europe. Another is the excessive corporate bond debt escalation in Emerging Markets, especially that increasingly growing sub-segment of EME bonds issued in dollars. Massive issuance of corporate bond debt in China and what are called 'CoCo' bonds in Europe should be added to the list. Sovereign bonds is another area of bond instability, especially in Latin America, Africa, and in the Eurozone southern periphery (especially Greece, Italy, Portugal-Spain) and even in that region of the Eurozone referred to as 'Emerging East Europe', including Ukraine. Longer term, the US Treasury bonds market might be added to the bond list of prime candidates for instability, given the emerging issues of growing Treasury bond volatility and concern over liquidity should T-bond transactions accelerate in a crisis.

Hi Yield junk bonds in the US, and to a lesser extent Europe where they are growing especially fast, are perhaps the most unstable—along with EME and China corporate bonds. The junk bond segment represents bonds issued at high interest rates by the more financially strapped companies who cannot raise money through investment grade bonds or obtain bank loans. The bonds are typically short term borrowing earmarked for long term investing, a dangerous combination should bond prices begin to fall rapidly in a crisis.

Within the junk sector in the US, a large proportion of the bonds have been issued to fund expansion of the shale-gas fracking industry which is now in severe contraction. Junk defaults have doubled in the US compared with the past year, and the default rate is forecast to double in 2015, according to bank research projections. As companies default and go bankrupt in oil and energy, the instability will result in price instability transmitted to other US junk bond segments. And as the US junk bond market contracts in general, it can easily spill over to Europe and to EME markets that have a similar 'high cost, short term' bond composition. While Europe has previously not been a big market for issuing high yield corporate bonds in the past, the market has there has accelerated especially fast since 2008 in terms of growth, from a mere $20 billion that year to $600 billion in the past year, as the traditional bank lending has declined and weak companies desperate for financing have turned to junk bond issues.

The escalation of corporate bond debt in EMEs has been even more unprecedented. In the case of Latin American EMEs in particular, a large (and growing) proportion of that debt is also issued in US dollars (unlike in China, where the majority of corporate bond debt is in its local currency). The special problem this presents is, since the debt is in dollars, that debt must be repaid in dollars to investors. But if EME economies are in recession or slowing rapidly and global trade is stagnating—both of which are now the case—it means EMEs can't earn from increasing export sales to the US or other countries requiring payment in dollars, the necessary income with which to make the dollar denominated payments on their bonds as they come due.

Government bond debt in the EMEs is yet another potential severe point of instability. This is true in particular of those EMEs that have been heavily dependent on 'servicing' or paying their sovereign debt from income earned from oil and other commodity sales. As prices for both have deflated dangerously and as demand for their oil and commodities have collapsed simultaneously, many of the EMEs are now approaching default conditions. Latin American EMEs— Venezuela, Brazil, Argentina, Ecuador—and African EMEs like Nigeria and others in Asia have will soon experience growing instability in their sovereign bond markets.

As for European sovereign bonds, especially in the Euro periphery, their level of debt has not been significantly reduced since 2009, while in Greece, Italy, and elsewhere Eurozone government bond debt still continues to rise. Ukraine government bonds represent a special 'black hole' for Europe, with thus far no end in sight of the need for financial support to keep Ukraine's bond markets, government and private, from further collapse near term.

In the case of US Treasury bonds, it may seem counter-intuitive that this traditional safest haven for bond investing is a candidate for instability, even longer term. But it is. It is not just that the US Treasury market has exploded from $4.5 to nearly $13 trillion in assets since the 2008 crisis. The problem is that structural changes in the US financial system in recent years have created increasingly volatile liquid markets for US government bonds, often marketed by high risk-taking shadow bankers. A potential crisis point is reflected in the increasing use of these bonds by corporations to borrow short term in US repurchase agreements, or Repos, market to fund longer term investments.

With Repos, a company puts up its government bonds as collateral to borrow cash short term from investors, often shadow bankers. Should short term investments collapse in price, liquidity for selling the bonds could prove significantly insufficient, thereby driving down the price of Treasuries to excess levels and causing bond rates to rise. The Repo market (see below) is thus a serious weak point in the US financial system and US bonds. US Treasury markets are thus subject to potential instability should the Repo market crack—as it did in 2008 in the case of Bear Stearns and Lehman Brothers investment banks, which had borrowed heavily and become dependent on Repo financing. They went under when the Repo market shut down for them. The vast increase in the Treasury markets of nearly $9 trillion, much at low interest rates, will pose a related problem as the US government needs to refinance them in coming years, almost certainly at much higher rates of interest. Short period, massive escalations of multi-trillion dollars in asset values almost never end well—as China's stock market crash, the subprime housing bond market before 2007 and the tech dot.com bust of 2001 all have illustrated.

As will be noted in more detail below, corporate bond debt has exploded to unsustainable levels in China as well—just as China's stock markets had. While not yet dollar denominated to a great extent, the rise in volumes of Chinese corporate bond debt since 2008 is so huge that the money capital that will be needed to refinance it all in the near term raises serious questions whether Chinese private corporate debt can ever be successfully refinanced. In 2018 alone, 5 trillion Yuan (about $800 billion) will need to be refinanced, or rolled over, according to Chinese government banking reports; hundreds of billions of dollars more as well, before and after 2018.

Given the especially large volumes involved and questionable repayment problems on the horizon—EME corporate bonds, Chinese corporate debt, bonds associated with Repo markets, government bonds in commodity-dependent EMEs, and Euro periphery government bonds all reflect serious and growing 'cracks' in global bond markets that are expanding.

Emerging Markets Corporate Debt

EME corporate debt represents a problem not only of excessive issuance of corporate bond debt, both in domestic currencies as well as in dollars, but non-bond debt—i.e. corporate loans—as well. In Latin America, dollar debt composition is especially a problem. In some countries, like Mexico, the majority of the debt is issued in dollars. Even after subtracting China from the escalation of corporate debt from $5.5 to $18 trillion in EMEs since 2007, EME debt issued in dollars has risen by almost $2 trillion in the non-China EME sector. In China, corporate debt in general has risen from $2 trillion to about $12 trillion. So non-China EME corporate debt has nearly doubled, from $3.5 to $6 trillion while China's has risen six-fold. Such magnitudes of corporate debt escalation cannot but end poorly.

The same risks apply with regard to making payments on this debt for EMEs, whether involving bond debt or loan debt. Loan debt is of even greater volume and thus a problem and potential source of financial instability, as repayments become more difficult as EME economies falter and slip into recessions.

Chinese Financial Markets

Compared to other EME financial markets, China's financial markets are potentially even more unstable, and because of the sheer size of China's economy and markets, are even more capable of precipitating a generalized global financial crisis. China's equity and corporate bond markets have been noted above, but there are additionally three big financial markets that are particularly unstable in China today—Local Government Financial Vehicles (LGFVs), Wealth Management Products (WMPs), and debt associated with what are called 'Entrusted Loans'. In all three markets, Chinese shadow banks are deeply involved in providing the credit and therefore excessively leveraged debt that makes these three especially unstable.

LGFVs are the way in which local governments in China have financed infrastructure and commercial and residential construction spending beyond the financing provided by Chinese government-operated banks. Much of the LGFV financing has been arranged through shadow banks. Local governments have then sold real estate thus obtained through forced sales from private owners to make payments on the debt. The problem is that land sales have been largely used up but the debt remains. In the process of debt escalation, real estate prices became a bubble. Now they are deflating, raising the real debt previously incurred while reducing the income source (real estate land acquisitions) for making debt payments. The LGFV debt was roughly 20% of China GDP in 2007, or $550 billion; it rose to 40% and $3.8 trillion by 2014.

It is estimated that 30% of the more than $3 trillion in all 'nonperforming' debt in China today from all sources is non-performing LGFV debt. That means debt payments are not being made and more than $1 trillion in LGFV debt is in technical default. The government solution has been to rollover the debt at lower interest rates. Whether it can continue to do so, as more than $7 trillion in such debt must be refinanced during 2016-2018, remains to be seen. The potential contagion effects of LGFV defaults starting in 2016 may prove significant, both within China and throughout the rest of the global economy.

A second major financial asset of great potential instability are the Wealth Asset Products or WMPs. These are also provided in significant degree through shadow banks. They represent bundled asset products sold to wealthy investors—comprised of roughly one third stocks, one third local government debt, and one third industrial loans of small and medium businesses and state enterprises that are financially in need of private funding. The debt is opaque and held 'off balance sheet', not on the books of banks or other institutions. Like LGFVs, the escalation in such financial assets has been from just several hundred billion in 2007 to $2.9 trillion in 2014. Tied to stocks and local real estate which have deflated in 2015, the WMPs have no doubt lost massive valuation as well, making them highly unstable.

A third severe problem area in Chinese financial markets involved 'Entrusted Loans', or ELs. These are associated with the major shadow bank sector in China called 'Trusts', as well as the Chinese banking system. Entrusted loans provide a kind of 'junk loan' to industrial companies in particular, especially government enterprises in coal, steel, and other commodities production, that have been in severe distress as Chinese growth has slowed and global demand for Chinese steel, etc., has declined sharply. These loans are highly leveraged and thus subject to great volatility should financial asset deflation spread between markets in China as stock markets implode, real estate values continue to decline, and LGFV and WMPs values fall further. Like LGFVs and WMPs, Entrusted Loans have surged from $272 billion in 2007 to nearly $3 trillion.

The three financial asset markets—LGFVs, WMPs, and ELs—combined represent more than $10 trillion private sector debt that is potentially highly unstable. When considered in relation to Chinese equity and general corporate debt instability, the potential for a general financial crisis in China is not insignificant. Granted, China's economy has great reserves in terms of foreign currency and assets available, and its government is capable of rapid response to major crises. However, the combined effects of all of the above may prove overwhelming in the short term, and government responses may not be able to offset the panic by investors in the short term that could lead to a major financial contraction, followed quickly by a subsequent real economic contraction by an economy already slowing in those terms.

US Financial Markets

US financial markets today are not the primary locus of instability. The massive injections by the Federal Reserve has offset the financial asset losses of most large banks and shadow banks, as well as big private investors, that occurred in 2008-09—in the process taking the losses onto its own Fed balance sheet. That private debt was not eliminated; it was only moved. Notwithstanding, there are several financial markets in the US that are candidates for financial instability.

The junk bond market was previously noted, as was the Repo market and its strategic relationship to US Treasuries and the issue of bond liquidity. Mutual funds' total assets have accelerated tremendously since the crisis as well, reflecting the extraordinary growth of financial wealth in the wake of the Fed liquidity injections and subsequent exploding values in US stocks and bonds. Mutual funds are also connected to the Repo situation, however. And should the Repo market experience significant liquidity problems, mutual funds will be exposed as well as bonds. The US government and Fed therefore are desperately trying to reform and shield the Repo and Mutual Funds markets from future instability, although they have succeeded poorly thus far in doing so.

Other growing unstable markets include those for Leveraged Loans and Exchange Traded Funds, or ETFs. The former have surged again as banks and shadow banks have been providing highly leveraged debt to companies and investors involved in historic high merger and acquisition (M&A) activity (up 179%)—which, along with corporate stock buybacks (up 287%), has been driving much of US speculative stock gains in the past year. One shadow bank alone, Blackrock, controls more than a third, over $1 trillion, of the assets in this market. Since 2013 global M&A investing has risen to $4.6 trillion in 2015, compared to $2.2 trillion in 2009, according to the global research firm, Dealogic. These loans represent short term borrowing to finance long term investing, a classic condition for financial instability. ETFs are a new financial innovation that allow investors to bundle stocks, bonds, mutual funds, and other assets and 'trade' them instantaneously as if they were stocks. Because they 'link' market securities for stocks, bonds, etc. into one financial asset, they represent a kind of securitized asset product. And because their price can change by the minute and second, ETF asset values are highly volatile and can collapse precipitously as any of the bundled asset market securities in them collapses, as they did by 30%, for example, on August 24, 2015 in the case of Blackrock.

US defined benefit pension funds and municipal, state and local bonds are also potentially unstable. Neither have fully recovered from the last crisis. Pension funds depend upon general interest rates remaining sufficiently high to ensure returns on investment to pay for retirement benefits. But a decade of central bank zero interest rates has played havoc with pension fund returns, forcing them to search desperately for more 'yield' (returns) by undertaking risky asset investments. Public sector pension funds are further at risk due to the still largely unrecovered financial losses experienced by many states, and especially cities, school districts, and other local government entities since the 2008 crash. Some states and many cities still today remain in the red financially from financial investment losses associated with the 2008-2009 crash. The picture remains highly uneven throughout the US for US defined benefit pension funds. Some states and cities are recovering, but many still are not. Should another financial crisis erupt, municipal bond rates will no doubt rise even further, resulting in a state and local government fiscal crisis far worse than in 2008-09.

Another area of consumer finance and debt in the US is the student loan market. In recent years it has escalated from several hundred billion to more than $1.3 trillion. While not a source of major financial instability, student debt functions already as a major drag on the real economy, and consumption in particular. In a strange arrangement, the federal government profits significantly from this asset, much but not all of which it has legislatively redirected away from the private banks.

European Financial Markets

Government sovereign loans and debt remain a major problem in the Eurozone in particular. The debt is unevenly distributed, making it politically explosive, moreover, where it is focused in particular in the Euro periphery. Eurozone monetary and fiscal policies continue to exacerbate the debt, causing government bond rates to remain excessively high in the affected economies and, conversely, driving bond rates in Germany and elsewhere into negative territory with further as yet unknown consequences for instability.

One proposed solution has been the issuance of a new security called a Convertible Bond, or CoCo bond. This new bond is designed to convert from a bond to equity in the event of a financial crisis. Because it may convert, and result in almost a near total loss as is potentially the case of equities compared to bonds, the CoCo bond pays a higher interest rate to investors. It is riskier in other words. It is a kind of government analog to junk bonds. In the desperate search for yield by many investors, they have piled into the security. However, should a severe instability event erupt in Europe, CoCos could quickly lose much of their value.

The general government debt problem, which now after 8 years in Europe has not abated but actually continued, combined with Europe's stagnant economic real growth, has resulted in a high level of non-performing debt remaining on Euro bank balance sheets. Non-performing loan and bond debt in the Eurozone is estimated by some to be as high as $1 trillion. As in China's case, and increasingly for EMEs in general, companies with a high level of current non-performing corporate debt typically become companies that default in a subsequent crisis.

Other Global Financial Markets

Two remaining financial markets of general global relevance are foreign exchange currency trading (FX) and derivatives speculation.

As the data table above illustrates, FX has exploded in terms of its size since 2009, which reveals the contribution of the massive liquidity injections by central banks, a good part of which has found its way to global currency trades and speculation. The daily trading volumes have almost doubled to $5.3 trillion in purchases of currencies daily. Much of that is done by central banks, banks, and global corporations, but a significant segment, 10% of the trading, is now 'retail'; that is, done by speculators large and small, hedge funds and even small investors who, until recently, had been financing this trade by use of credit cards. As governments continue to inject liquidity via QE they in effect create excess liquidity that fuels currency wars and volatility. And as countries attempt to devalue their currencies to gain a temporary advantage for exports, the volatility increases, drawing in more shadow bankers and speculators who feed off the volatility, making currency markets more subject to financial speculation and causing havoc to economies and economic policies.

Not least, another problem globally is the role played by derivatives— interest rate swaps, credit default swaps, and other innovative financial products— that continue to proliferate and grow and, in the process, add to potential contagion effects and further asset price volatility. Sometimes reference is made to what is called the notional value of derivatives, now in excess of $700 trillion. The more important figure, however, is not the notational but the potential loss values measured in what is called the 'gross value' of derivatives. While not $700 trillion, gross value and potential loss represents a massive $21 trillion, up from $15 trillion in 2008. In other words, derivatives and their potentially extreme financial destabilizing effects—which were clearly revealed in the 2008-09 crisis, have not been reduced. In fact, they have grown continually. And new forms of financial speculation involving derivatives have been created as well. An example is the 'swaptions' market for credit default swaps, or CDSs. It represents betting on the movements of CDS. The latter are a kind of 'bet' that financial assets will deflate significantly, in which case a 'payoff' for the CDS is made. But swaptions take it one step further: betting on the broad index of CDSs as a financial security itself.

Derivatives trading is growing rapidly, having reached record levels in 2014. Previously largely concentrated in the USA and UK, it has begun to grow as well in Southern Asia—in particular in Thailand, Singapore, Malaysia. Japan has begun significant volumes of derivatives trading. Europe is attempting to promote it. And China will open a trading section in Shanghai in 2015.

Securitized Financial Asset Markets

Derivatives are a form of securitization of assets, where securitization means bundling other discrete assets into a new financial asset that is then 'marked up' and resold independently as its own financial security. Securitized financial assets were central to the financial crash of 2008. However, as the data in the table above reveal, despite their key role in the last financial crisis and their contribution to risk and cross-market contagion, securitized financial assets have been staging a comeback, both in the USA and Europe in the past couple of years. This is especially the case for what are called 'Collateralized Loan Obligations', or CLOs, now the second largest segment of the syndicated corporate loan market and central to the unstable role involved with leveraged loans. In addition, 'subprime-like' securitization has returned to the consumer market—not in the form of subprime residential mortgages but in the fast growing subprime auto loan market in the USA. Meanwhile, in Europe a major effort is underway, under the direction of a cross-country 'Capital Markets Project,' to resurrect and expand securitized loans and debt markets in the Eurozone. A major securitization market program was launched in China in 2012 as well. While securitized assets, excluding derivatives, do not pose the same potential for instability as they did in 2008, nevertheless today they have been allowed to assume an increasing role once again in financial markets.

The Shift, Financial Fragility, and Instability

The preceding data show that financial asset markets have expanded rapidly, from less than $100 trillion in 2007 to more than $200 trillion in just the past 8 years. That expansion could not have been possible without the explosion in liquidity, credit and the extreme leveraging of debt over the course of preceding decades that has enabled financial asset price values to escalate to such phenomenal levels. That liquidity and credit-debt eventually translated into a shift to financial investing on the historic scale we are witnessing today, with all the fragility and financial instability that has accompanied it. The crash of 2008-09 has not slowed or tamed the shift and the speculation in financial asset prices that has accompanied the liquidity-debt explosion. If anything, the aftermath of conditions and policies since 2008 has in fact accelerated it.

But all the enablers of the shift and instability is only part of the story. Liquidity, credit, debt, leveraging, speculation and the super profits they have produced for the very few did not happen in a vacuum. There is a social context, an institutional framework, and profound shifts in social and class structure that have accompanied it. The liquidity had to be managed, the credit extended by some source, and the debt incurred by some borrowers for the shift to occur. A financial structure had to enable it all. The creation and proliferation of countless new highly liquid financial asset markets globally, as well the transformation and expansion of financial institutions already on hand, has created that structure. The shift additionally required the creation of divers new financial securities, with the buying and selling managed by these new institutions in these liquid markets. And, even more fundamentally, it has meant the ascendance of a new strata of finance capital elite to purchase and sell these new financial securities through that restructured global financial institutional network.

The chapter that follows addresses the restructuring of global finance in the decades since the 1970s that has created those markets, institutions, financial products, and new human agents—all of which together have enabled the shift to financial asset investing and all its consequences.

Endnotes

1 As will be addressed in detail in Chapters 16-18 subsequently, there is great confusion as to the relationships between real and financial asset investing among mainstream economists, which explains in large part their inability to understand how financial and real cycles interact. Mechanical Marxist economists, on the other hand, maintain that the causal determinations between the two forms of investment are from real investment to financial, with the latter caused by the former.

2 As explained in the following Chapter 12, 'shadow banks' are not discrete entities. They are composed of unregulated financial institutions, internal divisions of regulated commercial banks dedicated to selling speculative financial securities, and are also 'shadow-shadow' institutions embedded in non-financial corporations. A better term might therefore be 'shadow banking' as an activity rather than 'banks' inferring a discrete institution.

3 See Chapter 12 for definitions and examples of 'shadow banks'.

4 See following Chapter 12 for this as well.

12

STRUCTURAL CHANGE IN FINANCIAL MARKETS

Chapter 11 described the financial asset markets and the financial securities associated with those markets. Those markets, assets, and the shift to financial speculation as a critical subset of financial asset investment, are fundamentally made possible by the explosion of liquidity provided by central banks worldwide since the end of World War II, followed by the further acceleration of that liquidity in the 1970s with the collapse of the Bretton Woods agreement, the geographic spread of liquidity in the 1980s with global financial deregulation and the elimination of controls on global capital flows, and its accelerated velocity in the 1990s as internet technology enabled an even faster global cross-country flow of financial capital.

By the late 1990s, all the key elements for an even greater rate of global liquidity acceleration were thus in place. It was not by accident that what were previously geographically contained financial crises—in Japan, in northern European banks, and in the housing and junk bond markets in the USA in the late 1980s and early 1990s—began to 'globalize' beyond regions by the late 1990s. The Asian Meltdown circa 1997-1998 was just one prominent example; multiple sovereign debt crises in Mexico, Russia, Argentina and elsewhere in the 1990s were others.

From Liquidity & Debt to a New Financial Structure

The liquidity explosion by 2000 assumed not only the form of central bank-government 'fiat' money expansion, but increasingly of proliferating forms of 'inside credit' made possible by financial engineering. These took the form of various kinds of derivatives and other new forms of financial securities. The collateral values on which these securities were based were rising rapidly as financial asset securities prices also rose, and those values provided the basis for still further borrowing and debt which was then used to make other financial asset investments. And so it went.

Excess available central bank fiat money necessitated that private banks lend that money to investors. Liquid financial markets' expansion worldwide provided investors with the opportunity to exploit that lending by borrowing from the private banks and in turn investing in any of countless global liquid financial markets they chose. The extent of leverage (proportion of borrowed funds to investors' own funds invested) in the system grew accordingly. As derivatives (a form of financial security) expanded, so too did securitized financial assets (derivatives bundled together to form a new financial offering)—making possible 'super-leveraged' debt; that is, debt incurred by borrowing in order to purchase the new financial assets that were created out of the earlier financial assets. Securitization + leverage + inside credit (debt based on the rising prices of financial assets already created and bought) meant still more demand for financial assets and the growth of financial asset bubbles.

But all this still represents only the 'markets and securities' side of the shift to financial asset investing. Who was doing the financial investing in this rapidly expanding structure of highly liquid financial asset securities markets worldwide? What were the primary institutional elements of that structure? And who were the individuals? An explanation of the shift to financial asset investing—and its consequences for the real economy in terms of decreasing real investment, deflation in real goods and services, financial instability, and so on—requires that we address all three key elements: the changing structure of market and securities, the new financial institutional structure, and the new class structure of the new finance capitalists themselves.

Expanding global liquid financial markets, proliferating new financial instruments sold in those markets, and the financial institutions selling and buying those instruments on behalf of the new finance capital investor elite together constitute the broader 'structure' of fundamental financial change in 21st century capitalism—without which the financial fragility and instability in recent decades cannot be properly understood nor its future trajectory predicted.

The shift to financial asset investing requires all three elements. The explosion of liquidity and debt could find no outlet without this structural change that enables the shift—or perhaps alternatively, one would say, 'provides the outlet' that makes it possible. The causal direction, moreover, is mutual. The shift encourages the global expansion of the new "open" financial structure as well. The general set of causal relationships involving liquidity-debt escalation, structural change, liquid financial markets expansion, etc., in turn drives the development of financial fragility in the system that erupts periodically, precipitating and exacerbating financial instability events.

The greater the fragility, the more frequent and severe the eruptions and, in turn, the deeper and more protracted the real economic contractions that follow. When financial bubbles of deep and broad enough significance burst, the corresponding inverted asset pyramid 'cracks'. The extent and degree of fragility in the system on the eve of the financial eruption renders traditional fiscal-monetary solutions less effective to various degrees in generating a recovery, in part because it is not an entity that is impacted, but an entire web. If there is no policy response for an extended period, then the financial instability events continue to repeat and drive the real economy down to ever greater depths. That was the experience of 1929-1934 during the Great Depression in the USA. If the fiscal-monetary solutions appear, but are too weakly or slowly applied, then stagnation in the real economy may occur for a relatively long duration. Lingering fragility effects result in repeated short, shallow further contractions followed by weak and unsustained recoveries. That's what happened in the USA between 1907-1913—as well as during 2009-14.

Chapter 11 provided a brief overview of the highly liquid financial markets and multiplying financial securities most associated with the recent phase of the financial asset shift. This chapter describes the institutional framework of global 'shadow banks' that enables that shift and takes, as well, a first look at the human agents—i.e., the new global finance capital elite—who are equally important elements behind the financial shift. It is typical in the media and press to refer to 'the markets' as unhappy, exuberant, or over- or under-reacting to real conditions. But there is no such thing as 'the markets' as agency any more than corporations are 'persons'. It is people, in this case professional or near-professional investors, institutional and individuals, who are the agents. They are the 'markets'. And they are the starting point to identifying the new finance capital elite who are the ultimate drivers of the entire process and of the shift to financial asset investing in particular.

What Is a Shadow Bank?

It is important to note that there are several definitions of what constitutes a shadow bank, some narrow and others more broad and inclusive. The distinction is important.

At one end of the official spectrum of definitions is the US Federal Reserve's *Flow of Funds* report.[1] At the other end of the official view is the IMF's *Global Financial Instability Report*.[2] Note the reference is to 'official' definitions, since in this writer's opinion neither of the two sources captures the full extent, size and significance of the shadow banking sector of global finance today.

In fact, the shadow banking sector is composed of several segments. The first is what might be called the **Basic Shadow** banking sector. Another part is best referred to as **Hybrid Shadow** banking, where the lines blur fundamentally between the commercial banks and the shadow banks. A third is what this writer calls the **Embedded Shadow** sector. And a fourth, the **Emergent Shadow** sector.

The Fed's *Flow of Funds* (FOF) approach leaves out not only a good part of even the **Basic Shadow** banking sector, but almost all of the other sectors. For example, with regard to just the Basic Shadow segment, while the FOF view acknowledges that shadow banking grew sharply after 2000 and exceeded the traditional banking system by 2005, it argues shadow banking declined sharply after 2008 while traditional, commerce banks in the USA continued to grow in terms of assets, albeit more slowly than before 2008. Whereas traditional banks accounted for approximately $10 trillion in assets by 2007, shadow banks had $13 trillion. This ratio then reversed after 2008, to the extent that traditional banking had $13 trillion by 2011 while shadow banks' assets had fallen to $8.5 trillion. The problem is that this FOF view identifies shadow banks as limited to those financial institutions trading commercial paper, Repos, asset backed securities, and money market mutual funds.[3] It specifically excludes from its definition pension funds, insurance companies, hedge funds, other kinds of investment funds, finance companies, and a host of other institutions that clearly participate in the financial asset markets, either directly or on behalf of their member (and public) investor clients, or both, indirectly and directly. Adding these latter would expand the definition of shadow banks, adding tens of trillions of dollars of assets to their holdings, even in the USA. The FOF perspective, insofar as it is domestic, also excludes the global character of shadow banking in its official estimates and is therefore additionally underestimating the sector outside the USA.

The narrow FOF view also totally ignores **Hybrid Shadow** banks, i.e. the traditional/shadow bank relationships, and the shadow bank-like changes within, and behavior by, traditional banks. Traditional banks—sometimes referred to as commercial banks—often lend to the shadow banking sector, since the latter does not have direct access to the virtually interest-free money provided by the US central bank to the commercial banks, although that too has changed a little since 2008. They borrow at virtually zero interest and then lend to the shadow banks who in turn speculate in the high risk, highly liquid financial securities markets worldwide. Shadow banks may, on occasion, also lend to the traditional banks. Commercial banks also may speculate in the same markets, but their participation in such is limited by rules and regulations to which they, but not the shadow banks, are bound by law. So they participate by lending to the shadow banks that do high risk financial investing and 'kick back' their high returns in part to the commercial banks. Because shadow banks are not limited by regulations or minimum reserve requirements, they typically invest most of their capital in high risk financial markets, borrowing (leveraging) from the commercial banks to do so. When the latter, or other shadow banks, refuse to lend to another shadow bank that has become fragile by over-leveraging debt and then experiencing decline in income to service that debt—as in the case of the investment banks Bear Sterns and Lehman Brothers in 2008—then these banks crash, unless the government bails them out in some fashion. Bailouts can take the form of direct liquidity infusions by the central bank, guarantees of loans (as was the case for the technically bankrupt Citigroup and Bank of America in the US in 2008), forced consolidations of their operations, government purchases of their bad debt in exchange for payment to the government in the form of preferred stock, transfer of the bad debts to a national 'bad bank', and so on.

The traditional banks before 2008 participated widely and deeply in the shadow banking sector, often setting up their own 'off balance sheet' hedge funds and other investment vehicles. And still today, they have not been prevented from participating directly in the shadow sector by speculating in derivatives securities, selling high risk junk bonds, playing the role of 'financial intermediaries' in the Repo market, and so on.   Notwithstanding efforts by governments at financial regulation after 2008, traditional banking and shadow banking are still connected by numerous tentacles of speculative financial asset investment. And that interconnection constitutes a major potential for contagion still today. The lines between shadow and traditional banking continue to be blurred. And since the current market focus is shifting to financial asset investing, and since both shadows and traditional participate in the speculative asset markets, a hard line definition separating shadow and traditional banking—if it is to adhere to actuality—is not possible.

The FOF narrow view also disregards the growth of speculative and general financial asset market investing by large multinational non-banking corporations, or what might be called the **Embedded Shadow** segment—i.e. the non-financial corporate segment that in fact functions in part as a shadow bank. Much of the global revenue from the Fortune 500 multinationals accrues from the financial investing divisions of these companies.   Pre-2008, for example, most of General Motors' profits accrued from its financial arm, the General Motors Acceptance Corp (GMAC). Similarly for General Electric Corp.'s credit arm, GE Credit. These financial extensions earned much of their revenues and profits from financial investing prior to 2008; but after 2008 accounted for much of their losses. Contrary to public perception, it was not the bad real investments in SUVs and other 'gas guzzlers' that accounted for GM's record losses and near collapse in 2008-09—were it not for the US government's $90 billion bailout of GM and the US auto industry. Most of GM's losses were due to GMAC, which had speculated in subprime mortgage bonds. Since the bailout, GM has had to spin off GMAC, which was then reorganized into a more or less traditional bank called Ally Financial. Similar, GE Credit divested itself of much of its GE credit business. Despite these changes, it still is a fact that on average, the financial arms of the Fortune 500 multinational corporations continue to invest heavily in financial assets of various kinds, including derivatives, and obtain about 25% of their revenues from these activities, according to some sources.[4] Not surprisingly, in the wake of the passage of the US Dodd-Frank financial regulation bill in 2010, non-bank multinational corporations lobbied heavily against their exclusion from investing in derivatives and other risky financial assets, and were quickly excluded from the bill's coverage by Obama and Congress. The growth of the shadow banking sector should therefore include this segment of 'Embedded Corporate Shadow Banking' in non-bank multinational corporations.

A fourth, more recent sector of shadow banking is what might be termed the '**Emergent Shadow Sector**'. Arising post-2009, and growing rapidly today not only in the USA but in Europe and worldwide are what are called 'crowdfunding' public direct, or alternative, lending companies, like 'Lending Club' and others. Here the Basic Shadow and the Hybrid Shadow often participate together, lending capital to the new 'alternative' online and crowdfunded financial entities that in turn lend it to investors. The flow of capital may also occur in alternative directions: individual investors pool their capital that is then loaned to hedge funds and private equity or asset management companies, which in turn speculate in various financial markets. Whichever the direction, the point is that a new, rapidly growing form of shadow bank has begun to emerge in recent years and it is a 'hot' focus of funding.

The problem with the Fed's FOF view is that it envisions and defines Shadow Banks as merely 'financial intermediaries'—i.e. providing bank capital from traditional banks to those investors that want to speculate in risky opportunities that traditional banks are prohibited from lending to directly. The argument then offered in favor of shadow banks as financial intermediaries is that they provide a valuable function of allocating capital to where it is in demand more efficiently than the traditional banks. But shadow banks are not mere 'intermediaries'. They invest their own capital directly and invest indirectly for investors to each other, soliciting capital from wealthy investors as well. Their role has nothing to do with serving as intermediaries between investors and traditional banks, and a lot to do with destabilizing debt and capital flows, feeding financial asset bubbles, and financial booms and busts that increasingly amount to 'inefficiency' in a macro economic sense. Nonetheless the fantasy and highly ideological argument prevails among a certain segment of mainstream economists and the business media that shadow banks are somehow efficient and therefore 'good' for the global financial system.

The IMF's *Global Financial Instability Report* suggests a definition of shadow banking broader than the FOF view. It captures more, albeit not all, of the growing shadow banking system that has become the dominant sector of the financial system in the USA and UK is growing in the European economy and now posing a major destabilizing effect even in China.

Until 2010 there was virtually no shadow banking in China's economy. In Europe, its influence was minimal. Both Europe and China up to recently reflected a financial system in which bank lending to non-financial businesses was paramount. That reflects a traditional view of the capitalist economy—i.e. where banks lend to businesses, where lower interest rates stimulate more bank loans, and where those lower rates are the consequence of the central banks providing additional liquidity that raises the money supply. The lower rates stimulate demand for loans by the non-bank business sector. That leads to more investment, jobs, income and recovery. But that scenario no longer exists in large part. Capitalism in the 21st century is driven increasingly not by traditional bank lending into the real economy but by what are called 'capital markets'—i.e. our highly liquid global financial asset markets where businesses and investors buy and sell debt to each other, rather than borrowing from banks in the form of loans. The main conduit of that debt issuance has become the shadow banking system.

Central banks in the advanced economies have kept interest rates at near zero for more than five years, providing tens of trillions of dollars to traditional banks almost cost-free, purportedly in an effort to stimulate bank lending into the real economy that hasn't occurred. In addition they have provided nearly ten trillion dollars more in the form of quantitative easing. Is this simply evidence of a broken traditional banking and monetary system that, per the definition of madness, keeps making the same mistakes to the same unintended negative consequences year after year? The tens of trillions bailed out the traditional banks within two years. Yet the free money has continued to be injected, in the false expectation it would lead banks to increase loans to non-bank businesses. A related question is why has that massive money supply injection that produced record low interest rates for more than five years, not resulted in private bank lending and real investment? The short answer is the tens of trillions of dollars have been funneled through the traditional banking system in the advanced economies directly to the shadow banking system that has in turn redirected it mostly to financial asset investing—in equity markets worldwide, bond markets (especially junk bonds and other high risk new forms of bonds), into derivatives trading, forex trading, and other financial asset investments—to their own creations, in short. Government regulators have attempted tepidly and futilely to bring that redirected flow under some control, with little result. They have focused on traditional banks when the problem is shadow banks. Central banks exert little, if any, influence over controlling credit—outside or inside—in the shadow banking system—notwithstanding planned efforts to raise capital requirements in the traditional banks to slow the redirected flows, to propose token regulations on the shadow banks or changes to money market funds, or to manipulate in the future what are called 'reverse Repos' aimed at reducing liquidity in the shadow banking system.

Central banks, in other words, have not only failed miserably to control the global money supply and credit, they have failed to effectively supervise a global monetary system increasingly dominated by shadow banks. All they've done is pump unlimited money into the system, first to bail out the traditional banks and then under the deceptive theoretical assumption that more money supply and lower rates will stimulate real investment and therefore growth.

The traditional scenario of central banks providing money supply that lowers interest rates, encouraging commercial private banks to make loans, that in turn results in real asset investment—that system is fundamentally broken in the 21st century. Shadow banks are increasingly displacing traditional banks. And no matter how much liquidity central banks pump into the traditional banking system—via QE, zero rates, or other desperate financial creations— the prospect of a return to bank lending in the form of traditional loans into the real economy, as in decades past, is becoming increasingly unlikely.

How Big Is Global Shadow Banking?

The increasing displacement of traditional banks by shadow banking has already largely happened in the US and UK. As the IMF Report recognizes, assets held by shadow banks in the USA now exceed those of the traditional, commercial, regulated US banking sector by more than $5 trillion and as much as $10 trillion. According to the global business daily, the *Financial Times*, "75% of US capital markets are in the hands of non-bank institutions."[5] Contrary to the FOF approach and data of the US Federal Reserve, shadow banking has shown continued growth in the USA since the 2008-09 crisis, not less growth compared to the traditional banks, and current economic conditions in the USA are "conducive to further growth in shadow banks". In the UK, shadow banking assets are the largest as a percent of GDP than in any other economy. As the former government minister and banker, Lord Davies, remarked last year: "There is a vast restructuring of the financial landscape under way. We're at a tipping point now where banks are shedding more and more assets ... Over the next 10 or 15 years, what was shadow banking will become mainstream."[6] Shadow banking is rapidly emerging in Europe and China as well, and "has been growing rapidly in the Emerging Market economies", according to the *Global Financial Stability Report*, where it is "strong, outpacing that of the traditional banking system".[7] In particular, in the emerging markets, "China stands out".

The alternative 'official' estimate of the *Global Financial Stability Report's* broader definition of shadow banking[8] estimates that global shadow banking controlled about $26 trillion in assets in 2002. This grew to $75.2 trillion by year end 2013. The growth trend is indicated by the following table:

Table .12.1
Global Shadow Bank Asset Growth ($trillions)[9]

2002	$26 trillion
2007	$62 trillion
2009	$59 trillion
2012	$71 trillion
2013	$75 trillion
2014	$81 trillion (est.)

US Shadow Banking

The estimated US shadow bank share of the $75 trillion was approximately $25.2 trillion, or about one third of the global total of $75 trillion.[10] Estimates in 2013 were for additional growth of around $4 trillion a year in the USA shadow banking sector alone, and thereafter by a similar amount each year until the end of the current decade.[11]

By end of 2015, given the $8 trillion more for the US, another $4 trillion for the rest of the global economy is not unreasonable. So the total globally by 2016 could be as much as $87 trillion—with the US share around 40% of that $87 trillion or about $35 trillion. That's a lot of liquidity, and potential leveraged debt, available to financial asset markets and speculative investing.

Compare the US $25 trillion in 2013 to the total assets in 2013 of the five of the 19 largest commercial banks in the USA of around $6.5 trillion.[12] The rest of the largest 19 likely held no more than $4 trillion at most. The remainder of the regulated banks in the USA, approximately 6,900 smaller and regional banks, reportedly had total assets of $8.15 trillion. That means the traditional sector's total assets amounted to no more than $19 trillion in 2013,[13] and therefore clearly less than the shadow banks' sector's $25 trillion that year. The total gap between shadow and commercial banking sectors by 2015 will have grown no doubt even greater. Shadow banks have clearly become the dominant financial sector in the US economy, and they continue to grow rapidly in Asia and in some economies in Europe as well.

In this writer's view, however, even the *Global Financial Instability Report's* broader definition and estimate of the size of the global shadow banking sector at $75 trillion is likely underestimated. While the GFSR's definition is broader than the *Flow of Funds* definition, it still focuses only on what is called 'credit intermediation'. The GFSR list of institutional types involved are broader than the FOF's. But a still broader list of institutions that qualify as shadow banks is necessary.

Chinese Shadow Banking

Take the case of China. Recent studies show the size of the Chinese shadow banking sector, more broadly defined, is significantly larger than the GFSR's 2013 estimate. And certainly more by 2015.

Chinese shadow banks have been growing at record rates, representing the "biggest credit boom in history".[14] Traditional banks' assets in China were estimated in 2013 at $26 trillion. Non-existent in China in 2008, shadow bank assets by 2013 were estimated at roughly one fourth of that: around $6.5 trillion. By 2013, fully one half of all credit issued in China that year is estimated to have come from the shadow banking sector. The cumulative debt of China's more than 8,000 Local Government Finance Vehicles (LGFVs), a form of shadow banking that hardly existed in 2008, was as much as 36% of China's GDP in 2013, according to some western financial research sources. LGFV debt has been projected to rise to 40% of China's GDP, around $4 trillion, by 2015, up from $2.9 trillion in 2014. Fully one half of LGFV debt consists today of new debt issued to 'roll over' (i.e. refinance) old debt.[15]

Trusts—a major form of shadow banks in China—have increased assets by at least a half trillion dollars in the past 12 months, while LGFVs may have doubled their issue of local bonds. Total assets growth in these two leading sectors of shadow banks in China grew by at least $400-$500 billion in 2014, after having grown by just under $1 trillion in 2013. Again, in 2008 there was no shadow bank sector of any consequence in China. In stock markets, speculative investing is growing as well. Margin buying tripled in 2014 and early 2015. And China's peer-to-peer, alternative lending institutions form of shadow banking, while still relatively small, are growing as rapidly as in the West.

In China, shadow banks are more 'home grown' than offshore. However, global shadow banks participate in the speculative financial investing in China through the medium of the 'carry trade', where they purchase copper and other commodities, sell them into China, convert to Yuan, and then reinvest in wealth management products, domestic stock and bond markets, loans to local government, and through China's major shadow banking sector, the Trusts. This indirect form of shadow bank investing by offshore shadow banks, manipulating the commodities 'carry trade' is not included in the size and growth estimates of China's shadow banks.

Europe's Lagging Shadow Bank Sector

Except for the UK, in Europe shadow banking is relatively less developed in its newer forms. In older forms, like investment banks and investing banking departments of larger commercial banks, shadow banks continue to play a more limited role, not growing as rapidly as in the US, China and Asia.

A Short List of Major Shadow Banking Categories

The following short list of major shadow banking institutions presents a picture of the sector that is broader than both the FOF and the GFSR definitions of what represents shadow banking:

Basic Shadow
Hedge Funds
Private Equity Firms
Investment Banks
Broker-Dealers
Finance Companies
Pension Funds
Life Insurance Companies
Venture Capitalists
Business Development Companies
Asset Management Companies
Real Estate Investment Trusts (REITs)
Local Government Investment Vehicles
Mutual Funds
Money Market Funds
Trust Funds
Structured Investment Vehicles
Sovereign Wealth Funds

Hybrid Shadow
Boutique Banks
Private Banks
Bank Holding Companies
Bank Off Balance Sheet Trading

Emergent Shadows
Crowdfunding
Lending Clubs, Direct Lending
Peer-to-peer Lending Groups
Alternative Online Lending Sites

Embedded Shadow
Financial Departments and Investing Operations
of Non-Financial Multinational Corporations

When shadow banks are conceived as institutions that engage in independent, non-traditional financial activity, then the scope of the definition of what is shadow banking enlarges significantly. For example, certainly all forms of securitized asset investing belong in the realm of shadow banking activity. That should be true whether it occurs in the basic shadow segment, whether on-balance sheet by traditional banks, off-balance sheet by special purpose vehicles (e.g. SIVs) set up by banks or other institutions, or by finance departments of large multinational corporations, etc. That means the 'basic' shadow segment and traditional banking have become 'blended'. Shadow banking is thus in this sense defined by certain kind of financial activity, and any institution in turn that engages in that activity may be considered to be involved in shadow banking. In other words, traditional banks may act like shadow banks when participating in crowdfunding, when investing in derivatives on behalf of non-bank multinational companies, or when borrowing from mutual funds in order to speculate in foreign exchange, and so on. The institution is defined by the activity.

That activity is typically investing in very high risk financial assets and securities that represent a high yield return on investment potential, usually obtained by volatile price movements. It is that search for excessive yield that leads to financial fragility that, in turn, eventually results in financial bubbles and financial instability.

Shadow banks can be defined by other activities as well:

1.   Investing in securities in financial markets that are opaque, where there is little disclosure of the underlying assets or their true values, where there is little government supervision or oversight, or where there is weak or no 'clearing house' support associated with the trading of those securities. The 'architecture' of the financial markets that shadow banks invest in is typically highly interconnected with other such markets, as well as with more stable markets, and thus prone to contagion. When one goes bust, it often quickly drags down the connected others.

2.   Utilizing high leverage—i.e. a ratio of borrowed funds to investor funds often 10 to 1 or higher.

3.   Obtaining short term funds to invest in long term assets or using cash and near cash assets to buy harder to sell illiquid assets, like loans.

4.   Transferring the risk of default from the originator of the loan to another party.

Money market funds that, for example, pool securitized mortgages, peer-to-peer lending, and high risk 'convertible bonds', broaden the definition of shadow banks and shadow investing. To limit the definitions to 'intermediation'— as do the conventional FOF and GFSR approaches—is a mistake. What matters is the activities in which the institution subsequently engages. To identify only one of these activities—intermediation (i.e. connecting bank lending to end user customers)—obfuscates the extent to which their shadow banking activities could destabilize the financial system.

What we need to understand is what activities, carried on by what institutions, on behalf of whose investments, lead to high risk, highly liquid, debt-leverage driven, short term price appreciation financial returns. It is these kinds of activities that lead to financial fragility that amplifies financial instability when it erupts.

The GFSR definition expands upon the FOF definition but remains within its focus on conceiving of shadow banking as credit intermediation only. On the other hand, the GFSR recognizes this may not suffice as a definition. It leaves the back door open to a broader interpretation based on activity but does not go there itself. It acknowledges the full extent of shadow banking activities is unknown "largely because of a lack of details". Credit intermediation, it recognizes, is not necessarily limited to a role between traditional banks and investors, but may occur between shadow banks themselves, between investor and investor with the shadow bank the intermediator, or involve multiple elements of shadow, investor, and traditional banks.

Shadow banks have clearly become the dominant financial sector in the US economy, as they continue to grow rapidly in Asia and Europe as well.

The New Finance Capital Elite

But systems, like 'markets', are not independent living entities. They are but the conscious production of real people. They are created by and run by decisions that are made by real people. Not all people, of course, but a segment of the total populace. In the case of the financial system, a relatively small segment. And a relatively small proportion of what might be called the capitalist system and capitalists themselves—of which there are many millions in the USA and globally, both large capitalists and small. In fact, a workable, starting benchmark for estimating or measuring the finance capitalist elite who make the decisions behind the shadow and traditional banking systems is a contemporary assessment of the ranks of those who are called 'High Net Worth Individuals' in general; and in particular those categorized as 'Very High Net Worth' or 'Ultra High Net Worth Individuals'. Let's call them NWIs, or V-HNWI or U-HNWIs, or just HNWIs, for lack of better terms for the moment. Whatever the term, they represent the 'New Finance Capital Elite' that has grown rapidly in numbers, wealth, and political-economic influence during the most recent rise of the financial cycle that began in the late 1960s-early 1970s. They are the key decision makers in the shadow banking system. They often run that system and manage those shadow banks, as well as the senior levels of the traditional banking system. Occasionally the public gets to identify the tip of that iceberg— the Warren Buffets, Carl Icahns, the heads of large hedge funds and private equity firms, like Pete Peterson, the Jamie Dimons of JP Morgan. Offshore, the Carlos Slims in Latin America, the Ping Ans in Asia, and their counterparts in the UK and Eurozone.

In recent years several global research consultancies and bank research departments have been estimating the total investible assets of the new Finance Capital Elite. Most notable are annual reports by the Boston Consulting Group; the Singapore consultancy, 'Wealth-X', in joint projects with the Swiss bank, UBS, called the 'World Ultra Wealth Report'; Capgemini and RBC Wealth Management's

'World Wealth Report'; and others. Typical is the Boston Consulting Group's report, which is based on data obtained from a sample of 130 banks, wealth management companies, and government accounts.

These reports segment the investible assets according to categories of 'Very High Net Worth' Individuals' and 'Ultra High Net Worth Individuals'. The 'Very Highs' have annual liquid net assets available for investing of $1 million at minimum. Again, that's 'investible' assets, and not fixed assets like homes or other property that is not liquid and therefore not available for a quick investment. The 'Ultras' have a cut off of a minimum of $30 million annually available for reinvestment. The Capgemini-RBC report estimates there are about 13.7 million 'Verys' worldwide in 2013.[16]

The Wealth-X/UBS study estimates there were about 211,000 of the 13.7 million who are UHIs, with a minimum of investible assets of $30 million annually. By year end 2014, those numbers must be around 15 million and 240,000. The U-HNWIs growth since 2008, during the slow recovery in the USA and repeated recessions in Europe and Japan, has been spectacular nonetheless. UHI's numbers rose from 137,000 in 2008 to 211,000 in 2012.[17]

A further subset of the U-HNWIs that segment individual households with more than $100 million a year in investible assets, or what might be called 'Megas' or M-HNWIs, numbered no fewer than 12,000 two years ago in 2012. Today their numbers must be also significantly higher.[18]

As the Boston Consulting Group reported in 2013, global private asset wealth totaled no less than $152 trillion, which is about double that of global GDP for that year at $76 trillion. That $152 trillion is likely conservative, even in 2013. Total private asset wealth is probably in excess of $200 trillion today. The trend from the financial crash year of 2008 through 2013 is as follows:

Table 12.2
Global Private Investable Asset Growth[19]

2008	$92 trillion
2009	$111 trillion
2010	$121 trillion
2011	$125 trillion
2012	$135 trillion
2013	$152 trillion
(2014)	tbd

Both the bottom (minimum $1 million assets), as well as the very top of the 'mega' segment (billionaires), of this global asset distribution show record gains since the crisis in 2008. The 'bottom' millionaires in 2002 numbered 7.7 million. This grew to 10.6 million in 2007, on the eve of the 2008 crash, which reduced the number of millionaires to 8.8 million at the end of 2008 as both stock and bond markets plummeted that year. But millionaires recovered quickly and nicely in the wake of the crash. By 2012 their numbers worldwide were back up to 13.8 million and in 2013 to 16.3 million—a 60% rise over the previous peak of 2007.[20]

At the very top the same trend is evident. The numbers of billionaires worldwide grew from 1,360 in 2009 to 2,325 in 2014—a 70% increase. The USA led with 571 billionaires, with China second with 190, the UK with 130, Germany 123, Russia 114, and India 100.[21]

It is perhaps interesting to note, while the average annual growth rate of assets of the U-HNWIs in the boom period of 2002-2007 was approximately 4.8%, in the period of so-called recovery, from 2008 through 2013 when the global economy was considered sluggish, the growth rate for U-HNWIs was 13% annually on average.

The Wealth-X/UBS Bank study provides a breakdown of the geographic areas of the relative concentration of the UHIs total number of 211,000 in 2012.

Table 12.3
Ultra High Net Worth Individuals by Region[22]

North America	70,485
Europe	58,065
Asia	44,505
Latin America	14,150
Middle East	5,300
Oceania/Australia	3,955
Africa	2,775

The Futility of Shadow Bank Regulation

Finance capital is like water running down hill; it always finds a way around attempts to regulate it. This has been the case not just for recent years, or even recent decades. This has been its history for at least two centuries, when early proto-forms of shadow banking began to emerge in the early 19th century.

The futility of effectively regulating shadow banks is even more the case in the 21st century, given the truly global nature of the institutions, and the markets and securities in which they trade. To effectively regulate the activities of the institutions and the financial elite behind them, it would take a near-herculean cross-country cooperative effort among nations and their regulatory agencies that is extremely remote, at best. The sheer size, rate of growth, and complexity of inter-shadow bank capital flows makes this cross-country regulation all the more difficult.

In addition to 'between country' regulatory coordination, each country has its own labyrinthine institutional arrangement of shared regulatory responsibilities. For example, in the USA regulatory authority is shared by the SEC, the CFTC, OCC, and other federal agencies, not to mention state level analog regulatory bureaucracies. In Europe the problem is multiplied by dozens of countries, each with the same bureaucratic problem.

The opacity of the shadow banking activities is another issue making any success at regulation highly unlikely. There are always small country tax havens available somewhere. Efforts by government regulators to locate and get data on their activities and securities can be easily blocked by uncooperative local governments. During the 2008-09 crash, for example, the US Senate Finance Committee attempted to identify the assets of the financial elite that were stuffed away in the Cayman Islands. What they found was a 4-storey building there that harbored more than 10,000 corporate headquarters and their data. Attempts to identify which shadow banks and elites were shielding their records there came to naught. When the Senate Committee in hearings asked the IRS why it had not produced more detailed evidence, they were told the IRS rules prohibited them from continuing inquiries for more than two years. After that delay, they had to close the case. The opacity of shadow bank operations offshore make it additionally difficult to identify the details of their speculative investing, let alone the global, cross country capital flows of that activity.

Apart from the now global scope of shadow banking, its size, opacity, rate of growth and complexity, and the accompanying mountain of bureaucratic obstacles, the technological nature of global finance capital flows is another major reason why regulation is next to impossible. Most of the values of financial assets are electronic entries, the contents of which can be successfully hidden by countless means, if necessary, and quickly moved around the globe in order to stuff the evidence in some remote server elsewhere, when regulators come inquiring.

Then there's the added problem of political influence. Financial institutions are among the two or three most powerful and politically influential lobbying groups in the USA and elsewhere globally. Despite nearly having precipitated a global depression in 2008-09, they have successfully blocked any meaningful financial reform by the Dodd-Frank Act passed in 2010—a legislative effort that in 2010 was replete with generalities and left the all-important details for concluding anything effective to government agency bureaucrats and the financial lobbyists to work out. Five years after its initial passage, the Act is so full of exemptions, exceptions, and vague generalities that it is virtually worthless so far as regulating shadow banks is concerned.

In fact, a reasonable argument can be made that the Act has actually stimulated the growth of shadow banking in recent years. Its provisions are relatively more effective in regulating the traditional commercial banks.

Requirements that the traditional banks maintain higher levels and better quality of money capital as a cushion for the next financial crisis or that they separate out speculative trading activities from their traditional business has had at least one perverse effect: to push even more of this speculative business into the shadow banking sector. So even token further regulation of traditional banks is causing a further shift of investible assets to shadow banks. As just one example, limits on traditional banks' lending to junk-rated business in the new regulatory rules has meant a shift of that business to shadow sector private equity firms and business development companies. This loss of business for traditional banks is estimated by some to place at risk "at least $11 bn of the $150 bn annual profits made by US banks".[23] Even in the strategic Repo market, shadow banks are displacing commercial banks.

New technologies and chronic low interest rates engineered by central banks worldwide since 2009 have had the effect of further shifting assets in the direction of shadow banking. Chronic low rates by the Federal Reserve have pushed investors toward an even more desperate 'search for yield', forcing them to undertake increasingly risky speculative investments, driving them into the hands of the shadow banking sector. Technologies are also playing a role in the shift to shadow banks, spurring the rapid expansion of high risk investing in direct lending and online peer-to-peer lending, for example, the latest hot spot of shadow banking expansion.

Apart from traditional government agencies' roles in attempting to regulate banking and shadow banking, the US central bank, the Federal Reserve, has had since its inception in 1913, the task of regulating banks. Up to the 2008 crisis, however, that 'supervision' was limited to the regulated, commercial banks and specifically excluded shadow banks. Since the 2008-09 crash, however, the Fed has been considering how to regulate the shadow banks. Given that the Fed also 'bailed out' the shadow banks in the 2008-09 crash, it followed that if it was going to bail them out, it should and would be in a strong position to also somehow regulate them as well.

One new initiative by the Fed has been to try to retract excess liquidity in the shadow banking system by means of what is called 'reverse Repos' (repurchase agreements), where the Fed enters the Repo market to sell bonds into the repurchase market as a way to extract liquidity from the banking system. Less liquidity means less available for speculative excesses that lead to financial instability. But the Fed's recent efforts with 'reverse Repos' is just wishful thinking so far as regulation is concerned.

The Fed's extremely poor track record of supervision of the traditional banking system in the past—both recent and from its formation in 1913—is an indication of how likely it will be to succeed in its present attempts to regulate shadow banks.   If the Fed can't effectively regulate the in-country operations of US traditional banks, to what degree can one expect it to effectively regulate the global, fluid, and opaque nature and operations of shadow banks? As one business press commentator has recently remarked, shadow banking "has created a kind of money that is beyond reach of central banks' traditional instruments of oversight and control."[24]

Some who believe shadow banking can be regulated long term point to the option of legislation to keep shadow banks and shadow banking activity separated from commercial banking. They point to the Glass-Steagall Act passed in the 1930s and repealed in 1999. But Glass-Stegall by 1999 was a shell of its original provisions, having been picked apart piecemeal since the early 1980s. The problem with such legislation is twofold: first, it only applies domestically while shadow banking is global today. Second, all forms of private banking (including non-financial corporations) have to a degree become 'shadow' banks. The metaphor of a single wall between two types of institutions is false. Third, legislation identifies the institution type covered. The history of shadow banking since the 19th century shows once a particular form of shadow bank is brought under a regulatory umbrella, finance capitalists simply create another outside the regulated form and continue speculating in financial assets beyond the reach of regulation.

Technology, geographic coordination requirements, opacity, bureaucracy, the massive money corruption of lobbying and elections by financial institutions, fragmented regulatory responsibilities, the sorry track record to date of Fed and other agencies' regulatory efforts, and the multiple interlocking ties involving credit and debt between private banking forms—all point to the futility of regulating shadow banks in the reasonably near future.

If regulation of traditional banks has itself failed in the wake of the 2008-09 crash in the recent past, there is even less reason to expect regulation of shadow banks can succeed in the future—immediate or even longer term. The only solution to shadow banking is to ban all their speculative investing activities and to levy severe fines and criminal penalties on those institutions and their investors who operate outside the country and otherwise do business within it.

Why Shadow Banking Is Fundamentally Unstable

A tendency toward greater leverage and therefore debt as the means of financing securities and assets is in the nature of financial asset investing in general, and in particular in its speculative variant. The preconditions of greater liquidity and inside credit are enablers of this tendency. The ultimate expression of leverage is securitization—i.e. where debt is used to purchase financial securities based upon other financial securities where each credit (debt) extension to purchase is based on leveraging. The so-called derivatives revolution is the concrete representation of this process.

Because the debt is borrowed from many directions and sources, the debt becomes a kind of web of integration binding together the obligations of the financial securities and the institutions that issue them. What might be called an 'architecture of contagion' is the consequence.

The debt structure is unstable for other reasons as well. A condition of what is called 'maturity transformation' builds over time, as greater levels of debt are issued and increasing leverage occurs. Maturity transformation refers to the practice of borrowing short term funds to invest in longer term assets. In an immediate financial crisis situation (where financial fragility peaks, as will be explained in subsequent chapters in more detail), when payments for short term debt come due, longer term assets must be sold in order to cover payments on the short term coming due. But when financial asset prices are falling rapidly, as in a crisis, there are few, if any, buyers for the declining asset values. No one wants to purchase an asset in decline. So funding to roll over the short term debt coming due is lacking. That may force the holder of the asset to offer to sell it at firesale prices and, if it can't be sold, the result is default and potential bankruptcy. Maturity transformation builds over the course of the financial bubble, making the asset and the institution potentially unstable and, when the crisis breaks, de facto unstable.

Another source of instability in shadow banking and financial asset speculative investing is what is called 'liquidity transformation'. It involves using cash and near cash assets to purchase harder to sell assets, like corporate loans or corporate junk debt. It's even more difficult if they are about to default. Like maturity transformation, liquidity transformation also tends to build over time and as financial bubbles build in this or that risky market or financial security.

And in a world of zero, and even negative, interest rates investors are inclined to assume more risk due to their need for yield. Hence, the redirection of investment into high risk assets which typically share these 'unstable' characteristics. Shadow banks are the primary providers of such high risk assets, and their role grows as investors are forced in their direction. The longer the central banks hold interest rates at zero or less, the greater the tendency, indeed in many instances the need, to pursue risky yields—and the greater the financial instability in the system. Shadow banks capitalize on the 'chasing yield psychology'.

Finally, the markets and securities in which shadow banks focus their investment activity tend to represent financial assets that are typically highly volatile. Prices may rise far more rapidly than prices for real goods or services; they also decline more rapidly. In fact, the price deflation is typically even more rapid than the price inflation. It is perhaps somewhat of a stretch to call betting on price changes of financial assets investment per se. It is in ways more similar to rolling dice in a financial casino, except that some players in the global financial crap game get to use their own dice which is often loaded. That is, the markets are rigged or fixed beforehand—as has been revealed in recent years with regard to Libor (London interbank) interest rates, insider trading in equity markets, currency exchange rate manipulation, and countless other forms where the players play with loaded financial dice that give them an advantage.

Changing Financial Structure as Source of Financial Instability

Quantitative changes over time, beginning perhaps in the late 1960s but certainly in the 1970s-1980s, have led to a fundamental change in the structure of global finance capital in the 21st century due to:

- the size, relative role, and complexity of the shadow banking system;

- the growth of liquidity, debt and leverage;

- proliferating liquid financial asset markets and forms of securities;

- the shift to inside credit and to financial asset investing at the expense of real asset investing;

- the global integration of financial markets;

- the loss of control over domestic national money supply by central banks, and the corresponding decline of central bank policies and tools to generate economic growth by means of interest rate manipulation;

- the relative decline in the role of traditional, regulated commercial banks as shadow banking has steadily expanded;

- and the growing share of income, asset wealth, and political-economic influence of the new finance capital elite that have arisen in conjunction with the rise of shadow banks and the financial asset investing share of total global investment.

What the totality of these trends in effect represents is what might be called this writer's expanded definition of financialization. Unlike others who have been content to define financialization as the growing share of profits by financial institutions in general, or their employment share, or as the 'FIRE' sector (Finance, Insurance, Real Estate), or by reference to some other solitary indicator or two, our definition is one that describes a vast global network of institutions and human agents. It is not a static but a dynamic definition that addresses investment processes, that integrates institution-market-product and social class. Financialization is a process that results not only in growing global income inequality, as the global finance capital elite accrue for themselves an ever-growing share of income, but also in a growing endogenous instability within the global capitalist system itself.

Endnotes

1   US Federal Reserve Bank, *Flow of Funds*, Historical Annuals, December 11, 2014

2   See 'Shadow Banking Around the Globe: How Large and How Risky', International Monetary Fund, *Global Financial Stability Report: Risk Taking, Liquidity and Shadow Banking*, October 2014.

3   *Financial Crisis Inquiry Commission Report*, Figure 2.1, p. 32 (which is based on Federal Reserve FOF Report).

4   See Greta Krippner, *Capitalizing on Crisis: The Political Origins of the Rise of Finance'*, Harvard University Press, 2011, and data showing the ratio of portfolio income to profits.

5   *Financial Times*, June 17, 2014, p. 7.

6   Patrick Jennings and Sam Fleming, "Alternative Finance Steps Out of the Shadows", *Financial Times*, December 10, 2014, p. 4.

7   IMF, *Global Financial Stability Report*, October 2014, p. 66.

8   Based on the inclusion of obvious institutions like hedge funds, Reits, trusts, financial corporations, and other institutions left out in the FOF view.

9   *Global Financial Stability Report*, October 2014

10   *Wall St. Journal*, December 22, 2014, p. 2.

11   IMF, *Global Financial Stability Report*, and *Financial Times*, June 17, 2014, p. 7.

12   The total assets of the four largest banks—JP Morgan, Bank of America, Citigroup, Wells Fargo and US Bancorp., *Wall St. Journal*, March 10, 2014, p. C6.

13   Shayandi Raice, "Biggest Lenders Keep Growing", *Wall St. Journal*, January 4, 2014, p. B2, for the 44.2% estimate.

14   *Financial Times*, June 16, 2014, p. 5.

15   *Wall St. Journal*, January 28, 2015, p. 1.

16   Capgemini/RBC Wealth Management, *World Wealth Report*, 2012

17   Wealth-X/UBS, *World Ultra Wealth Report*, September 2013

18   Boston Consulting Group, 2012. For a summary, see *Financial Times*, November 29, 2013, p. 3.

19   Boston Consulting Group, 2012.

20   *Financial Times*, June 20, 2014, p. 16.

21   Bay Area News Group, February 15, 2014, p. 2.

22   Wealth-X/UBS Report.

23   Tracy Alloway, "Shadow Financing is 'threat to bank profits'", *Financial Times*, March 5, 2015, p. 22.

24   Paul McCully, "Make Shadow Banks Safe and Private Money Sound", *Financial Times*, June 17, 2014, p. 9.

13

STRUCTURAL CHANGE IN LABOR MARKETS

A major theme of this book is that as financial fragility rises over the long run, household consumption fragility and government fragility also expand. Like the other two forms, consumption fragility develops both secularly and cyclically, with cyclical forces like financial instability events and recessions intensifying the longer term secular trends.

Whatever the form of fragility—financial, consumption or government—the general causation is the same. Each form of fragility rises as a consequence of three forces: rising debt levels, deteriorating terms and conditions under which debt is repaid, and declining incomes from which to make debt payments. For consumption fragility, declining income from wages is a particularly strong determining factor.[1]

Financial and Consumption Fragility Compared

Fragility has roots in structural changes both in labor markets as well as in financial markets.[2] Preceding chapters 11-12 discussed financial fragility's origins, arguing they are ultimately rooted in changes in the structure of financial markets in recent decades. But just as structural change in financial markets plays a major role in the deepening of financial fragility over time—so too have structural changes in labor markets similarly led to growing household consumption fragility.

Financial fragility is associated with structural changes like the developments in shadow banking, exploding availability of liquidity from central banks, availability of inside credit, proliferation of liquid financial asset markets and forms of new financial securities, and rise of the new finance capital elite. These changes in financial structure have led to debt acceleration, but also to significant financial income growth during the boom phase. That financial income growth offsets the negative financial fragility effects from rising debt during that phase. However, the boom also leads to financial asset bubbles and crashes that wipe out the financial income gains as financial asset prices eventually collapse. Favorable terms under which debt repayments were possible during the boom phase also deteriorate during the bust phase. Terms and conditions for repaying debt become restrictive and have a negative effect on financial fragility as well. So all three key variables that contribute to financial fragility—debt, income for servicing debt, and terms of debt payment—all turn negative in the wake of a financial crash.

Something similar happens to household consumption fragility as well. Household debt rises during the pre-recession period and terms and conditions of borrowing are generally liberal. However, in recent decades at least, it does not appear that household incomes (wages) play as favorable a role in offsetting the negative effects of rising household debt during the 'boom' period, unlike in the case of financial incomes. That is, unlike financial fragility, household debt rises but wage incomes to repay debt rise far more slowly (or not at all). Wage income growth continues to significantly lag the expansion of debt. Taking the US as example, in the six decade period from 1947 to 2007, US household debt rose at an average annual rate of 9%, whereas household wage incomes rose at a far slower rate. This difference in the relation between household debt and wage incomes is an important contrast to financial debt and income. It has major consequences for household consumption fragility in a recession, and for the subsequent weaker recovery of consumption in the post-recession recovery period. Financial institutions are able to 'deleverage' their debt easier and faster than households in the wake of a recession compared to households. This has much to do with the slower growth of wage incomes, both before and after recession compared to financial incomes.

During a recession precipitated by a financial crash, household incomes decline rapidly as job losses mount and compensation (wages and benefits) are reduced. Simultaneously, terms of debt payment become more onerous and credit less available to households that might otherwise have been used to refinance debt payments. Meanwhile, debt itself rises in real terms, as prices for labor (i.e. wages) deflate.

Thus, an important distinction between financial and consumption fragility is that wage income growth does not offset debt as well in the pre-crisis phase. During the pre-crash and pre-recession phase, business income improves—due to rising prices for both goods and financial assets. But it is different for households. While debt rises, wages incomes have tended not to rise as rapidly as household debt accumulation. So when the crash and recession occur, working class households are already more fragile.

Why household wage incomes do not grow as fast as financial incomes during the boom phase—and then recover more slowly, if at all, compared to financial incomes in the post-recession recovery period—has even more fundamentally to do with the restructuring of labor markets in recent decades, especially in the advanced economies. It is those labor market changes that are responsible for slowing the growth of wage incomes, exacerbating the decline in wage incomes in the aftermath of the financial crash and the recession that follows.

It is therefore necessary to consider the major labor market changes that have occurred and how those changes contribute to weakening the growth of wage incomes before the recession and limit recovery of wage incomes during the recovery from recession. Both contribute to rising household consumption fragility long term.

Forms of Labor Market Structural Change

The major forms of labor market change in recent decades that serve to slow or reduce wage incomes, and consequently contribute to household consumption fragility, include:

- Changes in job structure

- De-unionization and restrictions on scope of collective bargaining

- Changes in the wage structure

- Reductions in 'deferred' and 'social' wages

- Changes in hours of work arrangements

- Emergence of the 'sharing' or 'gig' economy

These changes in labor markets, especially in the USA-UK, but increasingly in Japan and Europe and other advanced economies as well, have been evolving now for several decades—at least since the late 1970s. As they have deepened and expanded, the changes have been contributing significantly to the shift in income from working class households to corporations and investors.[3] During a financial crashes and subsequent economic recessions, moreover, that income shift typically intensifies and accelerates. The negative effects on wage incomes due to the labor market changes in turn amplify the depth and duration of the recessions and serve thereafter as a drag on the post-recession recovery period. Rising household consumption fragility from stagnating and falling wage incomes amplifies the recession and prevents a normal, sustained recovery post-recession.

The following labor market changes that are depressing wage income are most advanced in the USA and UK, but are growing as well in Europe, Japan and other advanced economies. In the latter cases of Japan and Europe, the changes are being promoted under the policy initiatives of business and politicians sometimes referred to as 'labor market reform' that represent changes already implemented in the US and to some extent the UK.[4]

Changes in Job Structure

Growth of Contingent Employment

Nearly everywhere, and in the advanced economies in particular, a major structural change in labor markets has been underway since the 1980s with companies increasingly hiring part time and temp workers while also converting formerly full time workers to part time and temporary work. The outcome is a growing category of jobs called 'contingent' employment.

Both involuntary and voluntary part time employment, as well as temporary employment (which may be either full time or part time temp) are part of this new, fast growing category of contingent workers. In the US case, part time contingent workers of course get less pay—on average 60% of full time—and often no benefits whatsoever. Temp workers are paid less as well, on average 75%, whether full or part time and receive minimal benefits. A two-tier workforce has thus arisen and has been expanding rapidly since the 1980s in the US case, saving employers tens of billions of dollars every year.

US estimates of contingent work are grossly underestimated. Officially more than 30 million out of a total labor force of 157 million are considered contingent.   However, temp category estimates are based only on official reporting by temp hiring agencies, and exclude direct temp hires by companies themselves. Also not included in temp numbers are the millions of workers who call themselves 'independent contractors', a group which has also risen rapidly by millions in the US alone. Many professionals and semi-professionals laid off by companies become 'unincorporated' contractors, subsequently returning to work on a temporary contract basis, often for the same companies where they were previously employed. In the process they earn less income overall and no benefits. Also not included in official government estimates of contingent labor are millions of workers recently swelling the ranks of what is called the 'shadow economy', where they work 'off the books' getting paid in cash that is not reported by them or their employers in order to avoid taxes. Most employed in the shadow economy are no doubt temp and part time, working occasionally in construction or other occupations. A third major group who are contingent and not officially included in estimates are the millions of US workers who have left the labor force in recently years, whose ranks are generally indicated in the declining official 'labor force participation rate' in the US. Many millions likely have left the official labor force but are working contingently in some capacity. In addition, a fourth category not adequately accounted for are many of the 11 million undocumented workers in the US who work in a contingent arrangement.

Whatever the category of contingent, incomes are far less than traditional wage income and benefits virtually non-existent. The result is a decline in overall wage income as the ranks of contingent labor have accelerated in recent decades and especially since 2000. This writer estimates that, for the US alone, total contingent labor is approximately 50 to 52 million, almost a third of the workforce of 157 million in the US.

A quick calculation shows how much income is being transferred in just the US case, from worker households and consumers to corporations as a consequence of the labor market shift to contingent work annually—i.e. a transfer in income from wages to business (and therefore to capital incomes eventually) that amounts to a reduction in wage income: If the average wage for full time, non-contingent labor in the US economy is $24 an hour, for example, and if the average wage for the 50 million contingent workers is assumed to be 65% of the full time average wage, or $15.50 an hour, that means a saving of $8.50 an hour for employers. Add another conservative 10% of the base pay of $15.50 an hour to cover the minimal benefits some contingents receive. That results in a combined wage and benefit savings of $10 an hour for employers of the estimated 50 million contingent workers in the US. Multiply that $10 an hour for 50 million by 1500 hrs. work per year (3/4 full time average of 2080), and the result is a massive transfer to business annually of $75 billion a year and every year thereafter—for just the US case. That $75 billion represents an annual compression of wage income for wage earning households in the US, and thus a contribution of that amount to household consumption fragility. If growing income is central to containing the growth of fragility—which rises when either debt rises, debt payment terms become more onerous, or income declines (or all the above)—then the structural shift underway to contingent labor represents a decline in income growth and a consequent rise in fragility.

The household wage income reduction from the rapid expansion of contingent labor has not been limited to the US. Although 'pioneered' since the 1980s by the Reagan and Thatcher governments in the US and UK by means of legislation and regulations providing incentives to US and UK employers, employers in other advanced economies in Europe and Japan have more recently been shifting to contingent work too, with the encouragement and assistance of their governments as well.

Estimates for the Eurozone—in countries like Italy, Spain and others in its periphery—show no less than 70% of all new hires since the 2008-09 crisis have been contingent. Even in the low unemployment economy of Germany, the estimate is that 55% of new hires have been contingent for the same period.[5] Japan's Labor Ministry has recently estimated that as many as 38% of workers now hold contingent jobs.[6]

In both Europe and Japan, business and politicians have launched new policy offensives of so-called 'labor market and structural reforms'. The reforms propose to allow more hiring of contingent workers, and allow businesses to convert more full time to contingent.

Japanese Prime Minister Abe's proposed structural reforms to get a stalling Japan economy going include a 'third arrow', at the heart of which is to change labor markets to make rules of hiring 'more flexible'. A recent business press article has correctly described Abe's plans: "He has sought to make it easier for firms to dismiss permanent workers and let them put temporary workers in positions restricted to permanent ones, arguing that will make businesses more willing to hire".[7] The same policy developments to expand and convert to contingent work are underway as well in Europe. Spain has already launched such reforms, with the result of driving down wages. Italy is in the process and France has announced 'labor market reforms' for the near future as well.[8]

Decline of Manufacturing-Construction Employment

A second area of wage income decline due to changes in the job structure has to do with the shift from relative employment in manufacturing, construction, and even transport work—where higher wages are typically paid—to lower paid service employment.

The decline of high pay manufacturing and construction employment ranks high in the structural change impacting labor markets as well. As recently as 2000 there were approximately 18.3 million workers in manufacturing in the US. Today that number is 12.3, or six million less, even after a so-called 6.5 year 'recovery' since the end of the last recession in 2009.[9] That job restructuring is not reflected in a decline in US manufacturing output, however. The USA has maintained its share of global manufacturing output share at around 23%-25%. Manufacturing has not disappeared in the USA; manufacturing *jobs* have.

Relatively high pay construction industry jobs have also disappeared by the millions and are not likely to ever return. Construction jobs collapsed to pre-2000 levels after 2007, from 7.3 million to as low as 5.3 million. Those numbers have 'recovered' to only 6.3 million.   Government and business policy makers have decided henceforth not to allow construction to absorb as large a share of capital as it did before 2007. The construction sector's decline represents another permanent structural change in US labor markets.

The manufacturing job decline is due to four main causes: free trade, offshoring and encouraging financial and tax incentives by governments to offshore, technology changes and government incentives to replace workers with new machinery and equipment, and the relatively low employment requirements of the new emerging industries and companies in social media, biotech, and communications.

For advanced economies (AEs), free trade agreements mean more jobs are lost to imports than created by exports. Net jobs are exported to emerging markets initially, albeit temporarily, resulting in wage income loss in the AEs.

Jobs created from gains in exports from the advanced economies, moreover, pay on average 20% less, according to various studies, compared to income from jobs lost to imports. So wage incomes received a double negative effect from free trade.

Free trade is associated with offshoring of jobs, as companies and industries affected, or to be affected, from cheaper imports relocated offshore. But not all offshoring is free trade related. Government tax and other incentives encouraging corporations to offshore create a further stimulus to offshore. Global competition in general adds further incentive to offshore. Jobs lost to offshoring mean reductions in income, offset only in part as workers shift to lower paying service employment.

At least as great a factor in manufacturing job decline in the AEs, and especially the US, has been the displacing of labor with new generation of capital, machinery and equipment. This trend has been accelerating due to AE governments' business tax cutting to encourage such displacement: accelerated depreciation, R&D credits, investment tax credits, and numerous industry-specific measures have all encouraged a more rapid displacement of labor. In the US, at least one third of the manufacturing job loss is attributable to this effect.

As employment and related wage income have declined in manufacturing due to effects of free trade, offshoring, technology displacement, and government policies encouraging all of the same, the creation of new jobs from emerging new technologies, industries and products has not offset the employment and wage income losses. New growth industries have simply not been job creation engines, as others once were in the past.

The fast growth industries in 21st century capitalism create few jobs per dollar of investment capital. They are not labor intensive. They do not create physical products that require the acquisition and production of materials from suppliers that create semi-finished or intermediate goods production jobs. Their finished products also do not require assembly or manufacture. Direct sales forces to explain the features and functions of the products are unnecessary. The buyer comes to the seller over the network. The new industries are more services oriented and are delivered to customers by means of networks, not by sales persons, so distribution as well as production jobs are minimal.

Social networking companies like Facebook, Google, and others are typical of these new fast growth-low employment industries. They are companies with high market valuations but relatively small work forces. These industries may pay relatively high wages but to a relative few. From a general macroeconomic standpoint, therefore, they do not create a large volume of total wage income for the general economy. They represent income gains for the few, and income atrophy for the many left outside their job orbit.

What the foregoing means is that a major characteristic of labor markets today, especially in the AEs, is that more jobs are lost—especially in higher paying manufacturing—than are created. A long term structural decline in decent paying employment has been underway for some time and apparently will accelerate. To the extent jobs are created in parallel to this trend, they are typically lower paying service jobs, which means more contingent jobs. But many workers, unable to financially survive on the lower pay service jobs, leave the labor force in various ways to work 'off the books', to make up for the wage income reduction by not paying taxes and foregoing health, retirement and other benefits which the 'shadow', 'undocumented' and disability conditions do not provide.

The displacement of labor with capital has another negative wage income effect for those still employed in manufacturing and construction: significant productivity gains for business and therefore cost savings and a greater share of income accruing to business. Another key characteristic of labor markets therefore is the reversal of sharing of productivity gains with workers by business. Income gains from productivity have accrued almost totally to corporations and their shareholders for the past four decades. That is unlike the period from 1947 to 1973, at least in the US, when gains from productivity were passed on in part to workers in manufacturing and construction. Productivity has continued historical trends since 2000; it's just that nothing of it has been shared with workers who are still employed.

Changing Structure of Unemployment

A third area of job restructuring resulting in reduced wage incomes is associated with the changing composition of unemployment.

The composition of unemployed in the past consisted largely of workers laid off due to cyclical economic events called recessions. Recessions were brief in duration, lasting typically 6-9 months on average. Most unemployed were recalled to work in reverse order of layoff as business picked up again. There was also what was called structural unemployment, where older industries and jobs were replaced by new products and companies. Government or company-provided job retraining and financial support was available to ease the transition. There were other jobs that required new skills that were learnable in reasonably short time. And there was what was called frictional unemployment, a small part of total unemployment, as workers moved in and out of the workforce due to education or other temporary personal reasons. But the workforce structure facing the unemployed is quite different in the 21st century.

Structural unemployment from technological change and global competition is upending old business models with a frightening rapidity. And business cycles are occurring more frequently, are more severe, and more protracted. As a result, unemployment is becoming more chronic and a growing 'base' of unemployed is slowly rising, from which recurrent recessions cyclically add to further.

A greater percent of the total unemployed are also only part time employed, or underemployed. Half of their employment is thus 'jobless' and should be considered as part of the total unemployed. Closely associated with the contingent labor market trend, the rise in the underemployed is thus another characteristic of the job structure in recent decades.

Another notable characteristic of the 'unemployment structure' is the trend of the long term decline in the labor force participation rate (LFPR). That concept measures the percentage of those who are eligible to work but drop out of the labor force. Sometimes called the 'discouraged' or the 'missing labor force' they represent another significant part of the unemployed. In 2000, the US participation rate was 67.3% of the labor force. By February 2015 it had declined to 62.8%. That's a 4.5% decline in a labor force of 157 million, or 7 million potential workers. These 7 million are potentially among the unemployed but are not counted as such due to technicalities as to how the unemployed are defined. But common sense suggests that if these former workers are not looking for jobs and have dropped out, they most likely don't have jobs, i.e. are unemployed.

Another change in the structure of unemployment, again in the US as example, is the more than 2 million increase in people on social security disability benefits just since 2008, a rise from 10 to 12 million. If they are disabled, they are not employed and are thus part of the unemployment structure. However, they are officially not considered unemployed. This 1 million amounts to what is called 'hidden unemployment', along with those who have left the labor force

Another element of the 'hidden unemployed' is reflected in the surge in the ranks of workers in the underground economy—a development that is occurring globally. Still another change in the unemployment structure is that those *officially* unemployed are remaining jobless for a longer duration than ever before. For most of the last half century the average duration of unemployment in the US has been around 20 weeks. Since the 2008 recession, however, this duration has doubled and remains steady in the 35-40 week range.

The long term trend called the 'jobless recovery' represents a further major structural change in unemployment. It refers to the months it takes to recover to the level of employed in the economy that existed just prior to the start of the recession. Since the 1950s, the duration of jobless recoveries has grown in the US, from less than 12 months to more than 48 months, or four years, after the 2001 recession. Since the start of the most recent recession, which began in October 2007, it took a total of 74 months, more than six years, to recover jobs lost. The duration of 'jobless recoveries' is thus extending significantly, and that expansion has occurred in a relatively short time from one recession to the other. Re-employing the unemployed after recessions is becoming increasingly difficult in today's labor markets. This too has resulted in downward compression on wage income growth over the longer term, as recovery of income is slower and more tenuous due to the greater frequency, severity (in terms of job loss), and longer duration of recessions.

When government bureaucracies calculate wage decline they do so based on wages of those still working, often only for those with full time jobs. But loss in wage income must consider those who lose all their wages, who experience a 100% wage cut (not counting subsidies as unemployment insurance) and a total wage income decline due to unemployment. A kind of a 'wage bill' for all wage earners should be the basis of calculating loss of wage income. When this approach is adopted, then wage income compression in the advanced economies is much greater than official figures showing wage change only for those still employed. And as structural causes due to technology and globalization of markets result in a steady rise in the unemployed over time in recent decades, combined with more frequent and more severe cyclical recession unemployment, the changing unemployment structure represents a major reduction in wage income that appears to be worsening consistently.

De-Unionization and Decline of Collective Bargaining

A second major development in labor markets that has also eventually led to a decline in income growth (or outright income decline) is the de-unionization of the work force. This has been occurring not only in the US but throughout the European Union and to a lesser extent in north Asia (Japan, Korea).

Again taking the US as a case example, in 1980 unions represented approximately 22% of the work force of 107 million at that time, or about 23.5 million.[10] By 2014 the percentage had fallen to 6.6% in the private sector and 11.1% overall, including public sector workers, for a total unionization of only 14.5 million.[11] Nine million union jobs had thus been lost by 2015. Had the 22% unionization rate been retained by 2014, 34 million of the 156 million total work force in 2014 would be unionized. That's 20 million more.

The most recent year for estimates, 2014, indicates how the overall labor force has grown but unionization has been continuing to decline in both absolute and relative terms. In 2014 the government estimated 2.6 million jobs were created. Only 41,000 of the net job gains in 2014 were union jobs.

The causes of the de-unionization of the work force in the USA are many. But among the most notable are the effects of expanding free trade agreements and the offshoring of jobs by US multinational corporations since 1980, encouraged and subsidized by government tax policies encouraging offshore foreign direct investment.[12] Another major determinant of de-unionization has been the incentives to displace labor with capital and the technological changes in the real economy that have encouraged the same. Political developments have also contributed, as governments have become more dominated by business interests (for various reasons) and politicians have aligned themselves more with business interests, especially those of large multinational corporations. The combination of globalization of markets, accelerating technology changes, and government support shifting more to business and investors has been devastating for unions worldwide. And as unions have declined, so too has workers' ability to maintain wage income growth, during both normal growth periods and especially during recovery from recessions.

The decline of unions is reflected as well in the narrowing scope of collective bargaining between unions and employers. Areas in contracts typically negotiated in the past are disappearing as subjects of bargaining, including annual cost of living adjustments, wage raises based on sharing of productivity gains, and maintenance of employer provided health and retirement benefits— to name the more notable. Conversely, more rights for management are being negotiated, including right to hire contingents, subcontract jobs, move jobs offshore, fire workers more easily, change hours of work and work schedules at will, and so on. The two thus go hand in hand—the destruction of unions and narrowing scope of collective bargaining.

With the decline in unions comes the decline in what is called the union vs. non-union wage differential. Union workers typically earn 20% more in wages and 40% more in benefits compared to non-union labor for the same occupations. Once at 20%, the differential has declined to 10% or less in many industries in the US and has declined even more for benefits. That's 10% less in wages, and even more in benefits, for 20 million workers, occurring every year, in the US alone. De-unionization compresses wages in additional ways for millions more workers, not just for union or formerly unionized workers. The negative wage income effects extend beyond the union ranks themselves. The slower wage growth has a 'spillover' effect to non-union workforces. As union wage incomes compress, wages for companies that are non-union that historically follow union wage trends, compress as well.

Similar declines in unionization and limitations on negotiating pay have been occurring throughout Europe as well. Policy initiatives in progress, from Greece to France and Germany, to establish new labor market reforms also have as a main objective the further limitation on union and worker rights and the expansion of management rights. These 'reforms' target in part allowing management to fire and lay off workers, further restrict what may be collectively bargained by unions, and institute new limits on the right to strike.

Twenty million fewer union workers in the US alone, no longer earning higher union wages and benefits, plus a narrowing of the wage differential for the 14 million who remain union, amounts to tens of billions of dollars in reduced wage incomes every year. At least the same amount likely occurs in Europe, Japan and other advanced economies—perhaps as much as $100 billion annually, which is in addition to the previously noted $75 billion annual wage income reductions from the shift to contingent labor employment. Those totals are easily doubled if the rest of the advanced economies are included.

Changes in the Wage Structure

The 'wage structure' generally refers to the distribution of wages between different occupations and/or industries within an economy. Wage can mean hourly pay, salary pay, pay in lump sum or bonuses, pay by commission or 'piece work', etc.

Hollowing Out the Middle Tier

In most AEs, up to recent decades there was a 'bell curve' in the wage structure. That is, the bulk of wages paid were in the 'middle', or median, households. Below were the working poor, and below them former workers receiving primarily transfer payments. Above the median grouping are the smallest number receiving the highest pay. The wage structure has changed dramatically, however, in recent decades. It is becoming more 'bimodal', with more of total wage income in the wage structure concentrated in the top and bottom tiers of wage earners. As the top 20% tier's wages rise and as more of the remaining 80% experience wage stagnation or wage declines, total wage income growth shifts to the top 20%. Total wage income also rises at the low end 20% of the labor force, not from wage increases but as more workers enter at low paid employment. The combined effects of relative wage gains in the top 20% and the employment level increases at the bottom 20% results in wage growth in the middle of the overall wage structure 'sagging' or 'hollowing out'. The net effect for the entire working class and the wage structure reflecting the class is an overall net slowing and declining of total wage income. Public complaints that wages aren't growing to sustain consumption really reflect this development that 'middle' wage incomes are declining and more than offsetting the wage gains elsewhere.

While total wage income may be growing in the bottom 20% tier, it is because more are entering that segment. But as they do, average wage income growth is slowing, or even declining. That is due to the atrophying of the minimum wage, impacting those eligible as well as those earning just above the minimum whose wage changes follow changes in the minimum wage.

Shrinking the Minimum Wage

The minimum wage shrinks when inflation is allowed to rise faster than wages mandated by government as minimums. The trend since the 1980s in the US has been for legislatures to wait longer periods before adjusting and to make only smaller and smaller, partial adjustments for inflation when they do adjust. The result is that employers save billions, and conversely, workers and consumer households lose billions.

Just the failure to keep the minimum wage rising to prevent its reduction in real terms amounted to $22.8 billion a year in employer 'savings'.[13] This loss to household income is undoubtedly much higher in absolute terms in 2015, even with the token increases in the federal and states' minimum wage levels that took place after 2006. At least $25 to $30 billion a year in income loss results from failing to adjust the minimum wage to keep up with inflation.

Overtime Pay Exemptions

Overtime pay has been progressively reduced not only as a result of wage theft for low wage workers. Higher paid workers have had their overtime pay reduced as well, all quite legally, as a result of government decisions to 'exempt', or reclassify, workers from hourly wage payment to salary pay which is not eligible for overtime, according to the law.

A favorite tactic of some businesses is to simply reclassify a worker as an 'independent contractor', and thereby remove that worker from mandated overtime pay. During the George W. Bush years, 2001-08, a major offensive was launched successfully by the US Department of Labor to reclassify 8 million US workers, who were then receiving hourly wages and thus eligible for overtime pay, as salaried and exempt from overtime pay premiums. It should be further noted that as employers shift to more part time and temp workers they in effect are able to manipulate their work force schedules more flexibly. That enables them to legally avoid having to pay overtime for millions, saving them additional billions of dollars a year, and costing workers billions in lost income. Estimates are that failure to pay overtime in the US alone adds up to $19 billion a year.[14]

General Wage Theft

Low wage workers alone in the US experience further wage income reduction as a result of the growing trend of 'wage theft'. Wage theft—i.e. the outright nonpayment of minimum wage and overtime pay to low wage workers— is estimated at between $8.6 and $13.8 billion a year in the US.[15]

While wage theft is especially rampant among low wage workers, it is an increasing trend across the wage structure. Illegal deductions from pay is a typical method, especially widespread for undocumented workers and others in the 'underground' economy, who are 'working off the books'. Illegal deductions typically accompany underpayment of minimum wages or overtime.

Another practice is to threaten workers indirectly with loss of their jobs if they file for workers compensation injury benefits, for which they are otherwise fully eligible. Not filing not only reduces legitimate income for the worker, but reduces the workers compensation contribution the employer would pay. Having workers work through breaks and lunch period constitutes a de facto nonpayment of wages and thus also another form of wage theft. Employers and supervisors outright stealing of tips for restaurant and other service workers is yet another direct, blatant form of wage theft. Still another involves having workers 'pre-sign' their time sheets and then the supervisor fills it in, reducing the actual number of hours worked.[16]

As a recent report by the Economic Policy Institute in 2014 concluded, "The total annual wage theft from front-line workers in low-wage industries in the three cities approached $3 billion. If these findings in New York, Chicago, and Los Angeles are generalizable to the rest of the U.S. low-wage workforce of about 30 million, wage theft is costing workers more than $50 billion a year."[17]

Reductions in wage income in the US from wage theft, failure to pay overtime pay, and allowing the minimum wage to lag adjusting for inflation amount to more than $100 billion a year. As previously noted, the 'hollowing out' of wage incomes in the middle range contributes still more to wage income 'compression', as they say. But so too does the general shift by employers from giving raises based on a percentage increase in an established 'wage schedule' in the companies. Percent raises to a schedule result in a kind of compounding of wage increases, as a percent change occurs on top of a previous percent change. Instead, the trend in the wage structure is increasingly toward providing raises, when they do occur, in 'lump sum' forms or bonuses. That eliminates compounding over time and thus slows wage gains as well over time.

Cost Shifting Health Care

Thus far reference has been made to what are called 'nominal wages'. But nominal wage incomes have been reduced as well by workers having to assume a greater share of escalating health insurance and health services costs. Having to pay higher monthly insurance premiums, more deductibles, more copays, and for coverage that is often reduced, results in a deduction from wages paid and thus lower wage incomes. This amounts to tens and perhaps hundreds of billions of dollars in real disposable wage income, and represents yet another major reason why household consumption continues to grow historically slowly, or stagnate in recent years.

Reductions in 'Deferred' and 'Social' Wages

Deferred wages refer to wages paid into private funds by employers, to be distributed to households at some future date as nominal (wage) income. Typical are private, defined benefit pension funds. Social wages are also deferred wage payments, deposited by employers into a government trust fund, to be distributed at some future date of age eligibility or disability as nominal income payments. A typical example of a social wage is that provided by a government program like social security in the US and similar national pensions in other countries.

Decline of Deferred Wage Income

When workers forego a normal wage increase and instead have their employer contribution directed to funding a retirement pension, or health insurance fund, or an education or other form of benefits fund, then this constitutes a 'deferred wage'. What would have been a nominal wage payment in the present is redirected to the fund. The expectation is that, in some future period, the worker will then reclaim that deferment as wage income—either receiving a monthly retirement payment (pension), or a claim to pay a health care provider for services, or tuition payment for a higher education tuition expense, etc.

Until recent decades, the primary form of deferred wage payment was called the 'defined benefit pension plan' (DBP). A DBP is a collective pension, provided for a work group (union negotiated or not) that guarantees workers in retirement a payment of so much per month based on their wages earned times their years of service with the company and paid monthly for life. If for some reason the employer and pension fund managers made bad investments, the pension still had to be paid out of the employer's other profits or operating funds. Over time, pension funds became very large depositories of finance capital, especially after government entities like cities, states, school districts, special departments, etc., introduced their DBPs as well. Pension funds became an important 'shadow bank' in the system, lending to other banks and, in the US, to other shadow banks like hedge funds after 2006.

One way to reclaim deferred wages paid into a DBP was to establish what have been called 401k plans in the USA, and their counterparts in the UK. Unlike DBPs, 401ks are personal pension plans. They allow the company to continue to claim the pension as an asset on its books and to continue as well to deduct company contributions to the 401k from its taxes, even though the company no longer has any liability to ensure any level of retirement wage payment or any payment at all—unlike in the case of DBPs.

401ks also cost employers less to fund than DBPs. In fact, companies need not make contributions to a 401k at all; it is strictly voluntary. And if they do, they may reduce or suspend them any time. By paying into 401ks companies thus reduce their equivalent wage pension contributions—and future wage income retirement payouts to workers are consequently also less. But there are other ways 401ks represent a 'reclaim' of wages. Employers may also direct workers' wage contributions toward buying the company's stock, which constitutes an indirect wage repayment back to the company. Investment by workers of their 401k balances into other companies' stock purchases reflect repayment of wages back, only in this case to other employers.

401ks grew rapidly in the 1980s and beyond, and their assets soon exceeded the assets in the DBPs. DBPs were increasingly discontinued and converted to 401ks, especially by non-unionized companies. In the early 1980s, before 401k conversions began, workers covered by DBPs in the private sector totaled 30 million in a workforce of 106 million. By the end of 2012 the number of workers covered by DBPs had declined to 15.7 million, out of a workforce of more than 150 million in the USA. By 2014 41% of employees at companies with 500 or more employees were covered with some kind of 401k, while the number for DBPs had declined to 16%.[18]

As the growth of 401ks accelerated in the mid-1980s, yet another form of pension (wage) reclaim by employers grew rapidly. Courts ruled that the defined benefit pension fund belongs to the companies. They could therefore legally 'skim' the profits from fund investments and use them for other company purposes—which they increasingly did. Often companies were acquired by other companies just to get the pension fund cash. The acquiring company kept the pension cash and rest of the cashless company was then sold off. The liability for the pension obligation was then passed off to a government agency, the PBGC in the case of the US, which made only partial retirement payments to workers, typically no more than half of their original monthly payments called for under the original pension fund.

Still another way pension wages were reclaimed by employers arose in the 1990s. The Clinton administration allowed companies to divert money from the DBP in order to cover their share of company cost for health insurance coverage—which was now rising at double digit rates for premiums in the 1990s. In other words, management used workers' deferred wages (in DBPs) to pay its share of rising health care costs. Workers would have to pay their own share of rising health care premiums, of course. Relative cost sharing began to shift from employers to workers as a result and that shift has continued ever since.

A net result of the reclaiming of wages by employers from DBPs and substituting 401ks for DBPs has been a decline in total available deferred wage retirement income. DBPs that guaranteed income have been disappearing while 401ks have not provided a corresponding retirement income substitution. The net change is the reduction of deferred wage income, with the benefits of that net reduction accruing to employers.

By 2014, in the USA all pension funds—DBPs (public and private) and private pension funds (401ks, IRAs, etc.)—combined were worth $22.1 trillion dollars. In the USA, 401ks constituted 58% of the total, or about $12.8 trillion.[19] But much of that $12.8 trillion is held by the wealthiest 10% of households. What remains therefore, for the rest, the bottom 80% US households in particular, is a fraction of that $12.8 trillion in the form of 401ks. On the other hand, it was among the median income households that DBPs were concentrated. So as DBPs have been destroyed, median family 'deferred wage' incomes have been reduced while they are not benefiting from 401k personal pensions much. As was recently revealed by US Senator, Sherrod Brown, three fourths of US workers aged 45-64 "have less than $27,000 in their (401k) retirement accounts and one-third do not have any sort of retirement account at all."[20]

The Decline in Social Wage Income

The social wage is comprised of contributions made by workers and employers, from what would have been nominal real time wage increases, to a social fund—like a government trust account—that distributes the income in a future period. The obvious example is the Social Security System in the USA and other national retirement funds in other advanced economies. Workers and their employers both jointly defer wage increases to the fund that they might have received in the present, in order receive a payment at a later date.

Since the late 1980s, every year the ceiling limit on the payroll tax, which is indexed to inflation, rises even though retirement benefit payments do not. That amounts to a diversion of wage income otherwise available in the present, but without any improvement in eventual benefits in exchange for the higher wage income contribution. At best, therefore, workers are paying more for the same level of benefits to be paid out in the future. At the same time, every year efforts are initiated by business and politicians to try to reduce the benefits as well. Alternative schemes regularly floated include proposals to allow households to withdraw their contributions, to invest social security trust fund surpluses in the stock markets, to raise the minimum retirement age, and so on. Should they succeed, it will mean workers will continue to pay more in deferred wages for even less benefit (wage payment) in the future.

The social security 'social wage' is composed not only of retirement benefits, but also medical benefits and benefits provided in the event of disability. In these elements, reductions in benefits have regularly occurred. In the case of Medicare, the health benefits program element of social security, coverage is consistently being reduced as monthly out of pocket costs also periodically rise.

Meanwhile, major benefit cuts in the social security disability program are already in motion. As two million workers have gone on social security disability benefits in the US since 2009, the SSDI disability benefits program has fallen deeply in the red. This has provided a prime opportunity for opponents of social security in general. SSDI benefits are therefore in the process of being reduced, which will mean less social wage income in another form for millions of households.

Whichever the program, the point is that workers' payments into social security, in the form of the payroll tax, represent a reduction in wage income in the present, in exchange for benefits (wage payouts) in the future that may be reduced, and often are.

In the UK, the focus of attack on the social wage in recent years is to undermine government public pensions by allowing withdrawals at age 55 before retirement. Another is to allow a cash-out at retirement and allow the funds withdrawn to be invested with insurance companies in the form of an annuity. Or allow the cash-out to be invested in sovereign wealth funds, another form of shadow banking.[21] That means bankers and insurance companies get the money to invest, similar to a 401k arrangement, and extract outrageous fees for managing the investment.

Whether diverting more wage income due to indexing of the payroll tax, paying more out of pocket for Medicare, or having major cuts in benefit levels, as in SSDI, the effect is a diversion of the social wage in the present, in order to receive fewer benefits or wage payouts in the future.

Changes in Hours of Work Arrangements

New concepts of work time are rapidly permeating the 21st century capitalist economy. They amount to working more—i.e. longer and faster—but with less pay, and even with no pay! To an extent, the shift to contingent labor is an expression of this trend. The traditional hours of work model in place until the 1990s or so, where workers were paid on an hourly basis, with legal limits, and a premium differential of time and a half as overtime pay, is a model that is in rapid decline. Traditional work time is melding with what was traditional non-work or leisure time.

One such new dimension might be called 'Tech Time', in which home is brought to work. Another might be called 'Home Time', where work is brought to home. Then there's 'Travel Time' and 'Double Time'. None of these traditionally non-work periods, during which the employee is now engaged in activities related to or required by the corporation, are compensated. They are all gratis time for the company and unpaid time for the worker.

Tech Time

Tech Time is the trend in the tech industry to facilitate workers spending more of their non-work time at work. The work environment takes on many of the features and functions of private life, in order to keep the worker engaged with the tasks of work. Leading edge tech companies in Silicon Valley, California, for example, provide free cafeterias with full course 'food court' meals at no charge. Why work late, then spend hours commuting home, to make the evening meal, go to bed, get up early enough to make breakfast, and then commute two hours again to work? Cut out the meals at home, and time, effort, and cost preparing them, and just eat for free at work. Better yet, why go home at all? There are recreational facilities on site, sports courts, workout gyms, swimming pools, free video game facilities, quiet areas for sitting and socializing. There are even facilities for sleeping and showering. Why go home and try to engage in such facilities, when they are not as conveniently located and provided at a cost? Just stay at the company for 12, 15 hours or more. In fact, why go home at all.

This is a harbinger of work life and center of the future—where what was traditional non-work time and activities are provided at work—providing employees more free time (to create for the company) and at less cost. Wages increasingly become 'payments in kind'.

Companies that hope to attract intellectual and professional labor—the growth industries of the future for the few—will have to compete increasingly on these terms. No longer just a wage and decent insurance benefits and a couple weeks' vacation a year will do. Companies will engage in a kind of environmental competition to attract the best—much like universities in the USA now compete for students with ever bigger swimming pools, gyms, recreation facilities, larger and fancier housing, and so on.

In the new industries there is a price for this, however. That price is the free, unpaid labor beyond the 8 hour day that is provided to the company—to say nothing of the clear loss of family life, which is too costly for the company and to productivity to tolerate. What better way to reduce productivity costs than to keep salaried workers engaged 24-7 in the company work environment. Leisure facilities and free food is far less costly than the extra hours of a de facto work day and the productivity it brings. In the end, though, it is just unpaid labor, and a corporate claim over non-work dimensions of life.

Home Time

Home Time is a related concept. Here, instead of the worker being in the workplace for longer hours, the work is brought to the traditional home environment, thereby extending work hours further. Today in more and more industries, workers are connected 24-7 by means of electronic media. Yesterday it was Blackberry email devices. Today it is iphones and ipads. Tomorrow it is Apple iwatches and constant real time videoconferencing on screens throughout the house or on one's person. The company work environment penetrates the traditional home environment, just as in Tech Time, the company work environment absorbs the home environment. But in both cases it is work for 'free', without any nominal wage income increase.

Travel Time

More traditional is the *Travel Time* concept of unpaid labor. With new jobs located away from city centers, where increasingly the younger labor force chooses to live, more time to commute to the work location in highly congested cities is becoming the norm. None of this time is compensated either. To accommodate the millenial labor force's dislike of long commutes, some companies are choosing to relocate to city centers. Others are choosing to bring workers to outside the city center work locations by providing private transport services, i.e. dedicated luxury buses that pickup workers in the city centers and deliver them to work. Technology allows them to participate in work activities during the travel time. Something similar occurs with air travel.

Double Time

Another more traditional concept, but perhaps the most widespread so far is what might be called *Double Time*. As companies pursue profits increasingly not by maximizing profit rates or profit levels but by profit margins—i.e. by reducing costs of operations to boost productivity—the model is to cut labor costs with layoffs and have remaining workers 'double up' by adding responsibilities of the laid off to those remaining employed. An example, affecting millions today, is K-12 teaching. Increasingly, teachers put in their normal 7.5 hour work day and then are required to tutor slow learners and those with disabilities after class. Or are required to counsel students, go to administration meetings, chaperone events, and countless other post-workday activities for which they aren't paid. Nor are they paid for assuming what were formerly assistant administrator functions. A similar example is Registered Nurses in hospitals who are increasingly required to assume tasks for which doctors doing their rounds were previously responsible. In retail stores, floor 'supervisors' are low paid sales workers who are required to undertake the task of managing other members of the floor team.

Unpaid Internships

Another unpaid work time trend is the rapidly developing 'free labor unpaid internships'. More workers seeking to establish themselves in the labor market are willing to work as interns without pay, just for the opportunity to 'try out' for the job. Companies are more than willing to accommodate them, with no commitment to actually hire them. In fact, many just recycle the unpaid interns, replacing last year's crop with the new unpaid every season.

While it is difficult to estimate the hours of unpaid work time from these changes, it is probably safe to assume the wage income lost amounts to at least tens of billions of dollars in the USA alone. This is really wage income that is 'claimed' by employers since they no longer are required to actually pay the wage itself.

The Emerging 'Sharing' Economy

Wage income reduction is taking on yet another form, emerging in the last few years in the phenomenon called the 'sharing', or sometimes the 'gig', economy. 'Gig' is slang referring to a short, impermanent job assignment. 'Sharing', another way to refer to the same phenomenon, refers to consumers sharing the work with those for whom the work in question was a permanent form of employment. Leading new companies driving the trend include 'taxi service' companies like Uber and Lyft, hospitality service companies like Airbnb, butler and personal services like Hello Albert, home cleaning services like Homejoy, and general services companies like Taskrabbit. The list is long and growing rapidly.[22]

In the sharing economy the lines between work and non-work blur significantly. Non-taxi drivers are enabled by software and communications controlled by a company (Uber) to pick up and drive those needing local transport. Uber shares the payment for the service with the nonprofessional drivers. Uber saves costs of operations significantly in the process. It doesn't have to provide vehicles or costs of their operation. It only pays the non-professional drivers for the time during which they actually earn revenues for it. It doesn't have to pay benefits to the drivers. And so on. It is only 'sharing' in a euphemistic and highly unequal sense. Drivers receive far less than a traditional taxi company would pay its drivers. The difference between the normal wage income and the wage income paid to the Uber driver represents a major reduction in overall wage income. Uber feeds off of the rise in the contingent trend, the low paid service job trend, and the chronic rise in unemployment trend that also characterizes changes in the structure of jobs.

Airbnb has copied the 'sharing' revolution pioneered by Uber. What Uber does for local transport, Airbnb does for local lodging and hospitality, getting consumers and households otherwise not working formally in the hotel industry to rent out their homes. It provides no hotel, but absorbs the majority of the revenue created. Taskrabbit is a further expansion of the 'sharing' concept into various new services. The sharing economy will drive down wage incomes significantly in coming years, as traditional employment and wage income forms are replaced by short term, gig forms where the consumer provides the equipment and assumes much of the traditional costs of doing business offloaded by the employer.

Debt as a Reduction of Future Wage Income

Real time, or nominal, wages paid in the present are also reduced as a consequence of households having to pay larger principal and interest charges on debt accumulated in the past. As household debt levels have risen dramatically in recent decades, debt itself becomes a factor that reduces disposable wage incomes—already being compressed and declining for all the reasons noted above. The irony is that, as wage incomes stagnate and decline for such causes, households turn increasingly to credit and therefore debt to supplement the decline in wage incomes. But that debt accumulation results in still further reduction in future wage income.

Once again using the US economy as case example, household debt in the US escalated from $4.6 trillion in 1999 to $12.68 trillion in 2008, according to the Federal Reserve of New York.[23] That is more than an $8 trillion increase, which represents principal and interest payments incurred that now must be deducted from current wage incomes.

Total US household debt declined modestly from 2008 to 2012, to $11.3 trillion. That reduction was not due, however, to rising household incomes paying down the debt but rather mostly due to banks 'charging off'—i.e. writing off—the debt, or from debt consolidations, or due to household bankruptcies. Most of the bank write-offs involve mortgage and credit card debt, as much as $1.3 trillion for mortgages alone, according to the Federal Reserve of New York.[24] Since 2012, however, US household debt has begun to rise once again, to $11.85 trillion as of the end of the second quarter of 2015, per the NY Fed's latest report

Whereas US household mortgage and credit card debt has been reduced due to charge-offs and other means, new forms of troubling debt increase have been accelerating—in particular for student, auto, and payday loans—the latter of which is now $46 billion and covers 15 million people, 70% of whom reportedly borrow month to month in order to cover basic needs.

The terms and conditions have also deteriorated for these fast rising forms of debt. Payday loans charge up to 400% interest; students typically pay interest of 7% to 8% to banks and the US government (when banks get to borrow from the government at 0.1%); and the average auto loan now is 84 months.

It is therefore a myth, promoted by public media sources, that a significant 'deleveraging' (reduction) of debt has occurred since 2008 in US households as wage growth has recovered. Household paydown of debt from incomes may have occurred for the wealthiest 10% who have experienced wage gains, but not for most of the remaining 90% of US households, whose debt reduction has occurred primarily in the form of charge-offs, consolidations or bankruptcies.

The charge-offs, plus the 10% paydowns, have had a modest effect on total household debt reduction in the US, but no more than 6% according to the New York Federal Reserve—i.e. from the peak of $12.68 trillion in 2008 to $11.85 trillion in 2015. That is not a picture of debt deleveraging from rising wage income. Household debt levels in the US have remained chronically high, plateauing if not escalating as rapidly as before.

Moreover, the household debt picture and trends are worse for many of the rest of the AEs and emerging markets. There, household debt levels have continued to grow after 2008 and in some cases significantly—as in Europe, Japan, especially China where the ratio of household debt to income has risen by 400%, and even in countries like Canada.[25] According to the McKinsey Global Institute, "Household debt continues to grow rapidly, and deleveraging is rare".[26] Total household debt increase since 2008 now exceeds $2 trillion in additional debt.

Wage Income, Debt, and Consumption Fragility

All the foregoing illustrate how compression, stagnation, and decline in wage incomes have been significant in recent decades, and derive to a large extent from structural changes in labor markets in the AEs, and especially the US economy, which tends to pioneer and lead in these changes.

An ironic consequence of the decline in wage incomes—critically necessary to pay for debt principal and interest as they come due—is the growth of debt itself. Declining wages due to structural change translates into insufficient income to cover basic necessities and standards of living for wage income households. So households increase their resort to credit, and debt levels rise further in turn. Wage income insufficiency leads to more debt which leads to yet more wage income weakening, as more wage income must be redirected to pay principal and interest which rises with the debt increase. It is a secular, and vicious, trend over the longer term, gradually suffocating wage earning households financially.

If declining ability to pay debt, and rising debt as a consequence, are important elements of growing household consumption fragility, then the spiral-like growth of both in tandem during so-called 'good' times of economic growth, results in growing consumption fragility even when it appears consumption is rising. The problem is more and more debt is required to enable the consumption. Thus a 9% average rise in household debt in the 'boom' years of 1947 to 2007 was required to produce a 3.6% growth in average annual consumption: about 3 to 1 in ratio terms. Today, however, it is estimated that consumption since 2008 is growing only 1.5% per year, and it takes a 1% increase in debt to generate a mere 0.2% increase in consumption.

The scenario turns worse once a financial crash and subsequent recession occurs. Now the previous debt levels remain and principal and interest must still be paid. But the wage income available for doing so collapses—as massive job losses occur, reductions in wage income for those still with jobs occur in various forms, and as the ability of households to borrow still more to make debt payments or maintain living standards is removed by lenders. Those who can refinance old debt, must now do it on extremely onerous 'terms and conditions': interest rates escalate, qualifications for loans become exceedingly tight and difficult, terms of debt payment extend for more years, repossession rights of lenders are more aggressively enforced, and so on.

The three determinants of household consumption fragility (as for all forms of fragility) begin to exacerbate each other: declining wage income leads to seeking more debt and under worse terms and conditions. Inability to repay debt leads to worse terms and conditions, which results in more interest deduction from wage incomes, and so on. The feedback effects between the three sources of fragility—income, debt, and terms and conditions—intensify in the wake of a financial crisis and consequent recession. Wage earning households come out of the recession in worse shape in terms of fragility than they went in. Cyclical events intensify the continued secular drift toward fragility.

How governments respond to this condition of household consumption fragility, as well as the development of financial fragility, both before and after a financial crash and recession, leads to the question of how government fragility is determined by financial and household consumption fragility—as well as how government fragility affects those other forms as well. That is the focus of Chapters 14 and 15.

Endnotes

1   This chapter focuses especially on the wage income factor in the determination of fragility, while also considering the role of household debt, terms & conditions of debt repayment and the interaction of debt and terms with income.

2   As subsequent chapters 14 and 15 will argue, government balance sheet fragility is determined largely in turn by the course of development of financial and consumption fragility and their interactions. However, government fragility may feed back upon financial and consumption fragility, further exacerbating these in turn.

3   For a detailed analysis of how and where this long term income shift has occurred in the USA between 1980 and 2005, see this writer's *The War at Home: The Corporate Offensive from Ronald Reagan to George W. Bush*, Kyklosproductions, 2006.

4   Labor market reform initiatives and policies are especially the focus today in Europe and in Japan. Both are essential to driving down wage costs in order to make export costs more competitive from these regions to the rest of the world markets. In significant ways, however, the changes proposed under 'labor market reform' mimic changes in labor markets already implemented in the US and, to a lesser extent the UK, economies.

5   Sarah O'Connor, "Recovery Prompts Rise in Precarious Job Contracts", *Financial Times*, August 5, 2014, p. 3.

6   Mitsuru Obe, "Japanese Jobs Are Plentiful but Often Temporary", *Wall St. Journal*, March 13, 2015, p.7 (based on data by Japan Labor Ministry, showing the doubling of the number of contingent jobs since 2000, to more than 20 million today, while the number of full time permanent jobs has been declining over the same period, from about 38 million to 33 million).

7   Mitsuru Obe, p. 7.

8   For a review of recent European 'labor market reform' initiatives, see Jack Rasmus, 'The Eurozone's New Austerity Model', *teleSURtv, English Edition*, October 19, 2014.

9   See the 'B' Tables in the US Labor Department's monthly *Employment Situation* reports, B-1 Tables, for these industries, comparing December 2000 with the latest full year, 2014.

10   Howard Fullerton, "How Accurate Were Projections of the Labor Force in 1980?", *Monthly Labor Review*, July 1982, p. 16.

11   For the union numbers, see Cherrie Bucknor and John Schmitt, "Union Membership 2015", *Union Membership Byte*, Center for Economic and Policy Research, January 23,2015, p. 1.

12   For an analysis of the various causes of de-unionization in the USA since the late 1970s to 2005, see Jack Rasmus, Chapter 3, "Corporate Wage Strategies: The Thirty Year Pay Freeze", in *The War at Home: The Corporate Offensive from Ronald Reagan to George W. Bush*, Kyklosproductions, 2006.

13   Jack Rasmus, *The War at Home: The Corporate Offensive from Ronald Reagan to George W. Bush*, Kyklosproductions, 2006, p. 164.

14   Kim Bobo, *Wage Theft in America*, New Press, 2011 expanded edition.

15   Ross Eisenbrey, "Wage Theft by US Employers are costing US Workers Billions of Dollars a Year", *Economic Policy Institute Blog*, February 3, 2015.

16   Steve Greenhouse, "More Workers Are Claiming 'Wage Theft'", *The New York Times*, August 31, 2104. For a more comprehensive discussion of forms of wage theft, Kimberly Bobo, *Wage Theft in America*, New Press, 2011, pp. 1-55.

17   Brady Meixell and Ross Isenbrey, '"An Epidemic of Wage Theft", *Economic Policy Institute Report*, September 11, 2014.

18   Michael Rapoport, "Longer Lives Hit Pension Plans Hard", *Wall Street Journal*, February 24, 2015, p. B1.

19   That $12.8 includes 401ks of about $7.8 trillion, and the remainder in Individual Retirement Accounts, or IRAs, another form of privatized pension. The other roughly $10 trillion is DBPs, with roughly $6 trillion in private corporate DBPs (single and multiemployer plans) that remain and the approximate $4 trillion in public sector DBPs.

20   Sherrod Brown, 'Letters to the Editor', *Wall St. Journal*, January 30, 2014, p. 12.

21   Editorial, "More Haste, Less Speed on UK Pension Reform", *Financial Times*, March 13, 2015, p. 10

22   For a more thorough overview and sanguine view of the 'Gig' economy that sees a potential 540 million employed worldwide in such forms of work, see Mckinsey Consulting, 'A Labor Market that Works: Connecting Talent with Opportunity in the Digital Age,' June 2015.

23   Federal Reserve Bank of New York, *Quarterly Report on Household Debt and Credit*, May 2015. See also, Ben Mclannahan, "Eager to Lend Banks Welcome New Ways to Filter Creditworthy Clients", *Financial Times,* October 16, 2015, p,. 14.

24   *Current Issues*, Federal Reserve Bank of New York, v. 19, n. 2, 2013, p. 6.

25   McKinsey Global Institute, *Debt and (NotMuch) Deleveraging*, February 2015.

26   McKinsey, p. 6.

14

CENTRAL BANKS & STRUCTURAL FRAGILITY

Monetary policy is managed by the central bank. In the USA, the Federal Reserve (FED) is the central bank. In the other major, advanced economies, it's done by the Bank of England (BOE) in the UK, the Bank of Japan (BOJ) in Japan, the European Central Bank (ECB) in the Eurozone (whose governing committee is composed of the central banks of the 17 associated continental economies which decide on its policies), and the People's Bank of China (PBOC) in China. Virtually every country has its own central bank.

Monetary Policy Tools—Old & New

Before discussing how and why central banks and their policies contribute to systemic fragility and therefore financial instability, it is perhaps useful to provide some background.

Mainstream economists typically refer to the three primary objectives, or mission, of central banks as: to influence the money supply in the economy to get private banks either to lend more or to lend less; to supervise the private banking system to prevent high risk behavior that might endanger the entire system; and to act as lender of last resort to bail out the private banks when supervision fails and they do get into trouble. To carry out these objectives, central banks traditionally have employed three *basic* monetary tools: setting reserve requirements, changing the central bank's discount interest rate, and buying or selling US bonds from or to private banks, sometimes called 'open market operations'.

Reserve Requirement refers to the amount private banks must keep on hand and not lend out to other businesses or consumers. If the central bank raises the reserve requirement, private banks will have less to lend out. All things equal, that means less borrowing for investment by non-bank businesses and for big ticket items (cars, houses, education loans, etc.) by households. That means less investment and consumption and therefore less economic growth. Should the central bank lower the reserve requirement, it means more to lend, more borrowing, and more investment and consumption. But the reserve requirement has been hardly used as a primary tool by the FED and other central banks for decades.

The Discount Rate is the interest rate at which the FED loans money directly to private banks. That too is seldom used as a general rule.

Open Market Operations (OMOs) has been the most frequently used FED tool to influence the money supply and lending by private banks—that is, until the recent crash. With OMOs the central bank buys US Treasury bonds from the private banks, exchanging money for US Treasuries the FED previously sold the banks. Buying bonds back from the private banks results in banks having more money to lend. But, as will be explained shortly, simply having more money on hand to lend to businesses and households doesn't necessarily mean the private banks will lend it out.

In 2008, the three traditional monetary tools (reserve requirement, discount rate, open market operations) were quickly understood as insufficient. They could not inject money and liquidity into the economy fast enough, or in sufficient volume, in order to offset the massive losses being incurred on private banks' balance sheets, which were caused by their collapsing financial asset prices and escalating defaults. The losses in the private banking system from collapsing financial assets held by the private banks had led to a freeze on their lending. Without access to credit from the banking system, non-bank businesses were in turn shutting down, laying off millions a month between 2008 and leading to a virtual shutdown of investment and household consumption. So the FED decided to deploy new experimental tools in order to inject even more massive amounts of money/liquidity than it had been even before the crash, in order to stop the collapse of the banking system and stave off another great depression like that of the 1930s.

There were basically four new, experimental tools:

1.   *Special Auctions:* Private financial institutions in greatest threat of collapse, shadow bank and commercial-traditional banks alike, were able now to bid ('auction') on what interest rates they were willing to borrow from the FED.

2.   *ZIRP or zero bound interest rates*: The FED lowered the Federal Funds Interest Rate—i.e. the key rate at which private banks could borrow from each other, from a normal 2%-5% rate to 0.15%. It would keep it there for the next six and a half years.

3.   *0.25% Interest paid* to the banks: The FED also instituted a program whereby the FED paid private banks interest of 0.25% for the

money they borrowed if the banks redeposited the money back in the FED.

4. *Quantitative Easing*: In 2009 through 2014, the FED also introduced a program called quantitative easing or QE. With QE the FED did not wait for banks to come to it to borrow, it went to the banks (commercial and shadow), as well as to wealthy individual investors, to buy back the bad, toxic bonds and securities held by these institutional and individual investors, as well as US Treasury bonds held by investors.

The $25 Trillion Global Bank Bailout

The US QE added just short of $4 trillion in bad assets and other bonds to the FED's balance sheet—i.e. debt purchased from private banks and investors.[1] The money it raised to make the purchases was essentially 'printed' by the FED, not obtained from taxing the public.[2] It is unknown, and still unreported to this date, what price the FED actually paid for the individual purchases of the bad assets. Most of the assets had already collapsed in price, in many cases to 20% of their original value. So if the FED paid more than 20%—a very likely fact—it then effectively subsidized banks and private investors for their losses; that is, it bought the bad assets above prevailing market prices.

The FED's $4 trillion QE was introduced in three separate QE programs from 2009 through October 2014. Simultaneously, as QE was providing trillions of dollars to the private banks, the ZIRP and special auctions programs probably injected another $10 trillion more into the US private banking system. There was also a fifth initiative or program, by which the FED 'swapped' (exchanged) more than a trillion dollars of foreign currencies (mostly Euros and other European currencies) with foreign banks to prop them up as well—i.e. giving them US dollars in exchange for their currencies. No specific figures are available for the money injection associated with the 0.25% interest paid to banks that borrowed free money. But when all sources are added up, around perhaps $15 trillion in liquidity was injected by the US FED to bail out the banks in 2009 and after.[3] That's just the US central bank. Other central banks—in Europe, Japan, China and other leading AEs and EMEs—also contributed liquidity, both by traditional monetary means and by similar new tools.

The Bank of England injected a minimum of 650 billion pounds into its QE program, or just about $1 trillion, plus additional amounts from its own ZIRP zero interest rate program. Prior to 2015, the European Central Bank, had injected about $1.5 trillion in dollar equivalent Euros by means of what it called its LTRO (long term refinancing option) liquidity program. In 2014 it introduced another program, an ABS (asset backed security) bond buying program, worth several hundred billion more. Another $1.1 trillion followed in early 2015 with the ECB's $65 billion a month, 18 month-long QE program. That's at least $2.5 trillion in liquidity injection by the ECB, not counting at least an equivalent amount in UK QE and ZIRP. The ECB also has had a ZIRP program for much of the period since 2009. Finally, other Euro area central banks' not in the ECB introduced their own versions of ZIRP and QE since 2009. Conservatively, the European experience has easily added another equivalent $5 trillion in liquidity injections to date since 2009.

Japan has had a near zero ZIRP policy for years, and by means of ZIRP and other policy tools has been injecting free money into its banks and economy for at least a decade. The Bank of Japan then introduced its own version of QE in spring 2013, at first buying securities from private investors at a rate of $44 billion per month or $530 billion a year. The BOJ subsequently accelerated its QE bond buying program in October 2014. The bond buying was raised to $60 billion, in dollar terms equivalent to $682 billion a year. So after two and a half years of QE, Japan has injected at least another $1.5 trillion, not counting ZIRP before 2013. The Bank of Japan is reportedly considering, as is the Eurozone, yet another iteration of QE later in 2015 or early 2016.

The People's Bank of China (PBOC) has not introduced a QE. It has relied on more traditional tools to inject liquidity since 2009, like lowering reserve requirements, reducing interest rates, lowering other costs of borrowing, and so forth. It also turned increasingly to encouraging capital in-flows from global shadow banks, thus adding further liquidity to its economy in addition to its central bank's traditional injections. Estimates vary of how much liquidity China has injected into its economy since 2009 by these various means. Estimates range from $1 to $4 trillion, depending on definitions.

Assuming the low end figure for China at $1 trillion, that brings the total global liquidity injected by the FED, BOE (Bank of England), BOJ (Bank of Japan), ECB (European Central Bank) and PBOC (People's Bank of China) to at least $25 trillion minimum.[4]

To summarize, of the total liquidity injected by just the major central banks worldwide since 2009, QE alone is responsible for more than *$9 trillion*— an amount that is still rising. In terms of all forms of liquidity injections—i.e. QE, ZIRP, auctions, traditional monetary measures, etc.—the total is at least *$25 trillion* since 2009.

This massive money injection has not resulted in strong, sustained real investment or global economic recovery apart from a brief recovery in China and emerging markets circa 2010-2012, which earlier chapters have called the global 'dead cat bounce'. Since 2013 that global recovery has continued to slow everywhere, at times recovering short term but slowing over the longer run. Nor has it resulted in normal recovery of wages, or stopped the slide toward deflation. Neither has the $25 trillion resulted in runaway goods inflation against which some economists have repeatedly warned.

What the $25 trillion has accomplished is continued massive debt accumulation by businesses, households, and governments alike worldwide, as the Bank of International Settlements and other studies noted in prior chapters have documented. By injecting liquidity central banks have enabled historic accumulation of private sector debt. By bailouts via QE and other measures, central banks have taken some of that bad private debt onto their own balance sheets. While the central banks transfer some of the private debt onto their own balance sheets, the means by which they do so—i.e. massive liquidity injections—eventually generates more debt and leverage by the private banking system. Thus, over the longer term, both private sector and central banks' debt levels grow. The monetary solution to the excess liquidity and debt problem becomes in turn a cause of more debt. The cause becomes simultaneously the effect, and the effect the cause once again.

Why Free Money Continued After the Bailouts

An important further question that follows is: If private banks' balance sheets were restored by central banks' massive liquidity injections in 2009, why did the FED and the other central banks continue to inject trillions more free money over the next five years by providing near zero interest rates and still more QEs?

The Lehman Brothers investment bank was not bailed out in September 2008, but allowed to fail. The government mortgage companies, Fannie Mae and Freddie Mac, were bailed out in early September 2008. AIG, the colossal insurance company, was bailed out with $85 billion in October 2008. A series of special auctions held by the FED rescued other major financial sectors, including shadow banks like GMAC, GE Credit, mutual funds, and others, with liquidity injections in 2008-2009. The technically bankrupt Citigroup and Bank of America were bailed out by various means, including being provided with guaranteed loans of $300 billion (Citigroup) and a nearly equal sum (Bank of America). If the banking system in the US was essentially stabilized by the second half of 2009, why did the FED continue to pump tens of trillions of dollars more into them from 2009 through 2015, with second and third versions of QE and with more than six years of further zero interest rates? What was all that continuing free money injection for, if not bank bailout?

It was about bailing out investors and restoring capital incomes for the entire class of financial investors. By funneling money and liquidity through the private banks, into the hands of investors and speculators, the objective was to boost stock, bond, derivatives and other speculative investment markets. Central banks, especially the FED and the BOE, kept pumping free money into the system to boost financial asset market prices and thus the capital gains profits and asset wealth of the financial elite. It was about restoring their wealth and assets, not just rescuing their banks.

It's not as if the US and UK banks still needed more liquidity by 2011-2012. The trillions injected in the years immediately following the 2008-09 recession more than filled the black holes on their balance sheets caused by the financial asset losses that occurred in 2008-09. Nor was it about the private banks being short of funds to lend to non-bank businesses and consumer households after 2009, or surely not so after 2010. They had reserves aplenty. They just didn't lend them to normal non-financial businesses or households.

In the USA alone, US banks today still continue to sit on a cash hoard of excess profits and reserves of more than $2 trillion. Given the rapid recovery of bank profits and stock prices by 2010, in the US and UK especially, the question is why did the free money continue to flow from the FED and other central banks to the private banking system with QE and ZIRP policies continuing for another five years in the US? And why do ZIRPs still continue today in all the AEs? And why does QE continue to expand in Europe and Japan? Why does the 'free money' continue to gush from central banks seven years after the official end of the prior global recession in June 2009?

ZIRP has injected even more liquidity than QE since 2009. And Japan and Europe are adding to the ZIRP with more QE. Meanwhile, China's PBOC continues to lower interest rates, to reduce private banks' reserve requirements, and to encourage private banks to loan out more of the $20 trillion of deposits they currently have on hand—all liquidity boosting operations. Simultaneously, China continues to encourage more offshore money capital inflow into its private banks as its economy continues to slow. Many emerging market economies already in recession are desperately trying to do the same.

The central banks' cheap money spigot thus remains fully open globally—a gift of free money from central banks to private banks, commercial and shadow alike, and to their wealthy finance capital elite of preferred investors—and all this at least five years after banks have been effectively bailed out. How does one explain this apparent anomaly of continued massive liquidity injections, even after the bank bailouts?

One possible answer to why the money injections have continued well past bailout is that banks and investors have simply become addicted to the free money.[5] And since the banking industry continues to dominate the political systems in the AEs with ever more generous campaign contributions, lobbying, and other largesse to politicians, governments today encourage their central banks to keep feeding the 'golden money goose' of central bank liquidity and free money. It is not coincidental that all the presidents and prime ministers of the advanced economies that came to power after 2008, or have continued in office after 2009, have all been very closely connected to their private banks: Cameron in the UK, Abe in Japan, Merkle in Germany, and not least Obama himself – whose largest campaign contributors in 2008 were hedge funds, bankers, and real estate interests.[6]

Another possible explanation why the liquidity injections have kept coming is that the FED and central banks believe their own ideology, i.e. that if more money and liquidity were provided, at least some of it would 'trickle down' in the form of more bank lending. But after six years of sub-average, stop-go real economic growth in the US, and repeated recessions in Europe and Japan, and now dramatic slowing in China and emerging markets, lending by banks to non-bank and household customers is still not back to pre-2008 levels. Moreover, the sub-par lending that is occurring is not having much of an effect on real investment and real economic growth.

Even favorable studies of FED policy show that at best no more than one-third of monetary injection results in real economic stimulus. And those are the most optimistic assessments of effect of central bank liquidity injections on the real economy. Thus, a mountain of money injection by the AE central banks has produced a mole hill of real economic growth, declining rates of real investment, employment in mostly low pay-contingent jobs, and continuing stagnating incomes and consumption by consumer households.

Yet another explanation for why the free money gusher has continued unchecked for seven years now is that monetary policy was viewed as the 'only game in town' after 2010. Fiscal policies were either token or negative (i.e. austerity) and governments had to show they were trying to do something. The alternative was more monetary policy. And when it didn't work, they just 'doubled down' on the same failed policy and programs.

After the November 2010 midterm elections in the USA, for example, the modest fiscal policies of the Obama administration of 2009-10 were suspended. From 2011 on, the policy focus was to withdraw the token fiscal stimulus of 2009-10 and then some. Nearly $1.5 trillion in deficit reductions occurred after August 2011, which was about twice the initial 2009-10 fiscal stimulus. With fiscal policies in reverse, only monetary policy remained even though it was proving increasingly over time, year after year, to have little positive effect on the real economy. Not coincidentally with the withdrawal of fiscal stimulus in the US in 2011, FED monetary policy and specifically QE was expanded with QE2 and then QE3. After having bailed out the banks and big corporations to the tune of trillions of dollars by 2011 but providing virtually no stimulus to the rest of the general economy, governments and the central banks felt they had to show they were doing something to try to bail out Main Street. Central banks began changing their justification arguments for more QE and liquidity. Instead of generating a 2% level in general prices, QE and liquidity were now supposed to lower the unemployment level. A new target for existing policies was offered that was more acceptable to the public. Later, an even more appealing target replaced the unemployment rate—QE and ZIRP were necessary to get wage increases going again. But all this was mere pretext. QE and liquidity is always about restoring asset prices and investor and wealthy households' asset wealth.

Apart from reasons of providing cover for intensifying fiscal austerity, ideological conviction, and growing addiction of investors in general to free money, another explanation for why the liquidity spigot has been kept open by central banks is that the massive liquidity injections will produce a rise in goods and services inflation that will lead to a restoration of business confidence. That will lead to more real investment, and consequently to more jobs, incomes, consumption and thus economic recovery, thereafter.

But this too is just another variant of ideology at work. Excess liquidity not only does not lead to more investment by reducing interest rates to zero, it does not lead to more investment just because goods prices rise, either. All the versions of the view that money injection will lead to more investment hinge on the assumption that increasing banks' cash on hand will lead to more bank lending; and that non-bank businesses will also want to borrow that further lending. However, both notions don't necessarily follow simply because there's more money in the economy. And who, after all, should know better that this is not the case than the bankers themselves, who know they are not lending into the real economy? Banks may hoard the cash, or lend it to non-job creating, financial asset investing. Either way, real investment doesn't occur and real goods prices don't necessarily rise.

So long as the banks redirect money injections (i.e. money supply) to financial asset investing, it will result in less, not more, real investment. And only real investment can result in a rise in real goods and services inflation, job creation, and therefore potential wage increases. So when banks don't lend where it is really needed, real investment drifts lower, low quality, low wage service jobs are created at best, real goods prices drift toward deflation, and business confidence—contrary to the justifications and theory—does not return. What central bankers today don't understand is that the relationships between money, interest rates, and real investment have broken down in the 21st century global economy. The old relationships have given way to new relationships between financial asset investing, real assets, and inflation (both goods and assets).

In Europe and Japan the ideological notion that central bank liquidity injections leads to real investment has been given yet another twist in interpretation: QEs and excessive money injection serve to drive down the exchange value of a country's currency. That targets stimulating exports rather than business confidence. More export growth in turn stimulates domestic investment in real goods needed for export. If the country's GDP is heavily dependent on exports—as for example is Japan's or Germany's or other smaller European countries—then 'devaluation by QE' is the way to stimulate domestic exports, according to European Central Bank thinking. More liquidity, via more QE, will lower the Euro's value, make European businesses more competitive, increase export demand, and in turn generate more investment that will reduce unemployment, raise goods prices and investment, and, in turn, economic recovery. However, it hasn't worked quite this way. $5 trillion in equivalent dollar liquidity, and the recent QE, has not reduced unemployment, increased bank lending, stopped the drift to goods deflation, or generated more sustainable real economic recovery.

The problem with this policy of 'devaluation by QE', and its ideological justification, is that all countries can play the 'devaluation by QE' game. One country's economic advantage in stimulating exports by implementing QE is soon offset by another's doing the same. Japan's 2013 QE and currency-export gains thereafter proved temporary, as did the Eurozone's in response to Japan's. Dueling QEs leads nowhere except to deflating goods prices everywhere. As the dueling QEs continue, financial asset prices remain the primary gainers from the process. Real investment gains a little from the devaluation-export surge, but soon dissipates. However, financial assets boom as most of the liquidity from the QEs flows into financial asset markets.

The foregoing discussion about why the free money injections continue leads to yet another set of related, even more fundamental questions. Not only is it important to ask why the free money injections continued well after the banks were effectively bailed out. It is also important to ask: If the $25 trillion was more than needed to actually bail out the banks, and if the excess trillions over bailout did not go into generating real investment, employment, household incomes and therefore economic growth—where then did the unnecessary extra trillions of excess liquidity injection go? If bank bailout costs, direct bank profits subsidization, and bank excess reserves still on hand of $2 trillion fall far short of the $25 trillion, what happened to the remaining residual worth trillions?

This writer's explanation is that the $25 trillion went from the central banks to the private banks. After restoring their balance sheet losses and after continuing to hoard another $2 trillion (and more in Japan and Europe) in excess reserves on their books—they then diverted and redirected the remaining residual trillions as follows:

- into loans to US and other multinational corporations that were heavily investing in both financial and real sectors of emerging market economies between 2010-13 (including to China);

- into loans to shadow banks and wealthy investors who thereafter invested in liquid financial assets and securities worldwide—including in equity (stock) markets, bond markets (corporate and sovereign), derivatives markets of all kinds, select hot property markets, speculation in foreign currencies and money markets, and in other financial assets;

- into money injections redistributed to their own investors by initiating buybacks of their own stocks and paying out dividends to their own investors as well as bonuses to themselves;

- into various direct investments in financial securities, commodities, and financial markets worldwide, seeking higher yields (rates of return) on financial assets, instead of lending to small and medium enterprises or consumers and thereby relying on lesser returns from traditional bank 'interest rate spreads' from loans to companies in the real economy;

- into financing rising volumes of leveraged loans, mergers & acquisitions activity, etc., in partnership with shadow banks.

The above list suggests much of the massive injection of liquidity by central banks had been significantly diverted from normal real asset investment in their respective domestic markets to financial asset markets (at home and abroad) since 2009, and/or to real asset investing into China and emerging market economies from 2009 through 2013. Given that the latter diversion is now slowing—as China and emerging markets' economic growth slows and money capital has begun to flow back out of EMEs—the lion's share of the continuing liquidity injections occurs in the form of ZIRP, as well as from recent Japanese and Eurozone QEs.

Between 2010-2013, some of the prior liquidity injections of that period diverted to Chinese and emerging markets did result in real growth in those sectors of the global economy. Money capital flowed out of the US, Europe and even from Japan into the emerging markets during that period—explaining a good deal as to why the US recovery was so 'stop-go' and why Europe and Japan repeatedly fell into multiple recessions. As real investment was diverted from their own economies, investment in EMEs and financial markets escalated. China and commodity producing EMEs benefited most. The rest was either hoarded by the banks, or paid out in stock buybacks and dividends to their individual investors in the US, Europe or Japan. But even a good part of that paid out to banks' investors also probably flowed out. Some of the payouts to wealthy investors may no doubt have found their way into various offshore tax shelters, as wealthy finance capital elite increasingly parked their capital gains in such shelters in order to avoid paying domestic personal income taxes.

What is ultimately important is that the $25 trillion did not flow, as in previous decades, into domestic investment in real assets, into creating a reasonable number of decent paying jobs, or into providing an impetus to domestic wage increases and income gains that, in turn, could fuel consumption and a normal recovery. The normal recovery did not occur—either in the US, Europe or Japan. How could it, when it mostly flowed into emerging markets, financial assets speculation, was hoarded, or distributed to bank managers and investors?

Central Bank Liquidity Feeds Financial Asset Inflation

As Chapter 11 showed, total investment in financial assets has boomed since 2009. All manner of such markets have accelerated in terms of total asset values. The money capital, i.e. liquidity, had to come from somewhere. Some no doubt came from the expansion of forms of 'inside credit'. But much more almost certainly derived from the excess liquidity created by central banks, especially the FED. The FED lends to banks which in turn lend to shadow banks and professional investors, who then speculate in financial markets. Banks get the free money from the central bank and then re-lend at higher rates, which are still attractive to shadow bank and other professional borrowers since their eventual returns are even greater as financial asset price inflation occurs as the excess demand for assets escalates, surging on the foundation of debt, leverage and ultimately liquidity injections. The shadow bankers and professionals invest at higher rates in markets for corporate junk bonds, volatile foreign exchange, and derivatives of all kinds, borrowing to finance mergers and acquisitions, and so on. Banks do some of the same directly, as well as lend to the shadow banks and speculators. Non-financial corporations borrow in order to buy back stock and payout more dividends, instead of using internal profits or cash flow to reward shareholders, who demand ever more distribution of returns as financial asset values rise. Rising financial asset values and distributions reward individual investors, who then plough further gains back into the markets. The process feeds on itself; financial capital gains follow capital gains. Financial asset values escalate, in some cases to asset bubble levels.

Just one notable example of the relationship between excess liquidity and debt-fueled financial asset investing, is the particularly strong correlation between QE liquidity injections and financial asset bubbles in equity (stock) markets.

The following graph illustrates that every time one of the eventual three QE programs in the USA was announced between 2009 and 2014, US stocks accelerated to new record levels. When the preceding QE injection was coming to an end, the stock market retreated sharply, until a new QE was rumored to be forthcoming. That happened twice with QE1 and QE2 in the US. With the most recent QE3 program, the FED got smart and did not indicate an 'end date' or total amount for the program, but rather an $85 billion a month injection that would continue as long as necessary. When QE3 began to wind down in 2013-14 and US stocks leveled off, new liquidity began to flow back into the US from offshore emerging markets (where a lot of it originally went in the first place)—in effect substituting for the FED-induced QE.[7] The strong correlations between QEs and the US S&P 500 Stock index are reflected as follows:

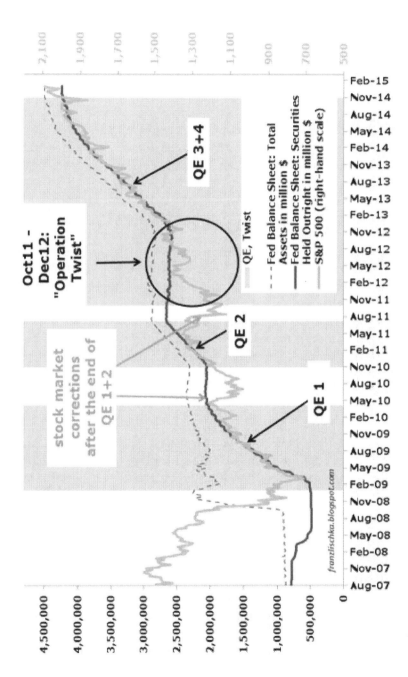

source: franzlischka blog

A very similar pattern is evident with Japan's QE program launched in 2013, which was further boosted in 2014, and now is being rumored for yet a third escalation in 2016. When first announced, Japanese stock markets boomed in 2013 by more than 70%. Japanese stocks then flattened when it appeared the money injection would come to an end. Another injection by the Bank of Japan in 2014 resulted in yet another stock surge, which again flattened. When Japan's third QE version is eventually introduced or even just announced, which most likely will happen in 2016, no doubt Japanese stocks will once again surge equity values in Japan.

The very same pattern initially occurred in the Eurozone when its QE was first launched in early 2015, a $1.1 trillion equivalent injection, at the rate of $65 billion a month for the 18 months to follow through late 2016. After an initial surge, however, Eurozone equity values relapsed due to broader developments in 2015 in Euro sovereign debt negotiations with Greece, slowing Chinese and EME demand for Eurozone exports, and other events. The Eurozone in late 2015, like Japan, is debating again whether to introduce still more QE in 2016. But just in the first three months following its first $1.1 trillion QE, stock market indices throughout the Eurozone's main economies surged.

Similar scenarios are possible concerning other financial asset markets, QEs, and other liquidity injection programs. Data tracking correlations between QEs, liquidity, and corporate junk bond markets would show the same. So would Foreign Exchange (forex) currency trading, Merger & Acquisition activity, Leveraged Loans, and other financial asset markets. Financial asset markets boom whenever central bank QE (and other non-QE) liquidity injections occur. In short, QEs and liquidity injections by central banks in general are the 'stuff' of which financial asset bubbles are made. Even before the QE money actually flows into the economy, the mere expectation of it is sufficient to set off the financial speculation in anticipation.

The massive money volumes from QEs and other liquidity injection tools are redirected quickly into financial asset investing, and diverted from what might otherwise have been investments in real assets that produce jobs, income, and recovery. Only wealthy speculators and investors, individual and institutional, benefit. Capital gains returns rise dramatically for those with capital incomes, as jobs income and wages income stagnate for the rest and income inequality worsens.

What all this suggests is either that monetary policy tools (both traditional and experimental) are broken or that the economic theories and analyses of both wings of mainstream economics (Hybrid Keynesian and Retro-Classicalist) are broken—or that perhaps all are broken! Monetary policy in the form of massive money supply (liquidity) injections, zero interest rates and QEs doesn't result in sustained real economic recovery; it results in financial asset price inflation. Real goods and services prices slow and eventually deflate, as real investment growth slows and declines.

Monetary policy and central banks therefore no longer serve the general economy, but today are organized first and foremost in the service of finance capital. They have evolved from an institution proclaimed to have the official mission and objective of ensuring economic growth and price and currency stability to become increasingly evident as an institutional mechanism for ensuring capital gains from investments in financial securities across numerous global, highly liquid financial asset markets for the benefit of the global finance capital elite.

The Contradictions of Central Banking

Over time, greater and greater amounts of central bank liquidity injections have been generating less and less real investment and economic growth.[8] Nor have goods and services prices risen or even remained stable; instead, they have been disinflating everywhere, and in a growing number of economies sliding slowly into deflation. In contrast, financial asset prices from 2009 to 2014 were almost everywhere inflating rapidly and in many instances to bubble dimensions. However, some of these bubbles have since burst, and the excessively high values are deflating as well. The latter include global oil and other commodity futures prices, stocks in China and other emerging markets, foreign exchange values across the world, and, increasingly, bond prices—both sovereign and corporate. In prior decades the FED and central banks were able to employ monetary tools to trade off inflation for investment, employment and economic growth. By engineering higher interest rates, the FED could cool down an overheated economy and reduce excess inflation in goods and services by reducing investment, employment and consumption. However, today that trade off relationship has broken down. FED monetary tools have little (and declining) effect on either inflation or real investment and employment, and therefore on wage incomes and consumption. Despite more than six years of massive money injection and zero rates, as previous chapters have documented, real investment continues to slow, employment barely grows if at all (and then in low paid service jobs), economic growth stagnates, and prices continue to drift toward deflation.

Today central bank monetary policies primarily generate financial asset price inflation, financial asset bubbles, while they divert investment into speculative forms of investing in financial securities. Financial asset inflation is thus 'traded' for a drift toward real goods deflation; real investment at home is traded for speculation in financial securities worldwide; and real jobs, wages and income growth for most households is traded for accelerating capital gains income for investors and their financial institutions.

The major contradiction today, therefore, is that central bank monetary policies do not work well any longer with regard to stimulating the real economy by means of low interest rates—while high interest rates are not introduced to discourage the over-stimulated financial sector of the economy.

While the global economy is growing increasingly insensitive and unresponsive to low interest rates as a tool to stimulate recovery from recessions, it has grown highly sensitive, and responsive, when it comes to raising interest rates to slow the economy. For more than five years, near zero rates in the US hardly generated any real investment, jobs, and real growth; but as soon as the US central bank and its UK economic echo, the Bank of England, raise interest rates, there will follow a very quick, negative response by the real economy.

Stated alternatively, interest rates reduction has minimal impact on generating real investment and growth, while interest rate hikes likely have growing impact on reducing real investment and growth.

These preceding contradictions have their source, their origins and cause, in the deepening of systemic fragility in the system. It is systemic fragility to a large extent that is rendering monetary policy increasingly ineffective in getting the economy to respond positively to lower interest rates, while it is that same systemic fragility that is causing monetary policies to exacerbate financial instability and over-sensitivity to interest rate hikes.

Central bank excess liquidity has become a contradiction not only in terms of failing to stimulate growth in the real economy. It has also become contradictory so far as the other major mission of central banks is concerned— i.e. providing stability in currency exchange rates. Highly unstable and volatile currency exchange rates have the effect of discouraging trade in real goods and services and thus slowing real growth. However, excess liquidity encourages financial asset volatility and therefore redirects money capital into global financial speculation in currency markets. That creates more exchange rate volatility and instability. Central bank policies thus eventually lead to more instability in financial markets such as currency exchange.

As the recovery from 2008-09 began to falter globally in recent years, currency instability and volatility has correspondingly risen, along with other forms of financial asset investing and speculation. As Chapter 11 has shown, the amount of money flowing into global currency markets has surged tremendously since 2009. Shadow banks and professional investors have committed increasing volumes of capital to speculating in currencies. Even so–called 'retail' investors have entered the market in larger numbers, some speculating in currency volatility by using their credit cards. The excess liquidity has fed the debt-driven speculation and increased the volatility from the 'demand' side. Governments and central banks have simultaneously increased the supply side of money available for foreign exchange speculation, as currency wars have intensified.

An initial bout of currency wars erupted in 2011-12, as both Japan and Europe descended into another recession at the time and as US recovery slipped to zero growth in early 2011 and again in late 2012. In mid-2013 as the

US announced plans to start phasing down its QE3 program, emerging market economies' currencies plummeted. In 2014 the collapse of global oil prices began, and EME currencies fell still further, as the US dollar began to rise. By 2015 a full currency war was in progress, as both Europe and Japan attempted to stimulate their exports by means of 'devaluation by QE'. Japan in 2013 gained a temporary advantage in the QE-currency-export war. Europe announced its plan, and Japan's advantage disappeared. Japan introduced a boost and its currency again temporarily recovered. The mutual 'competitive devaluations' by monetary policy now underway in Japan and Europe have led US policy makers to hold back on their announced plans to have the FED start raising US interest rates. China entered the currency war and lowered its Yuan in August 2015 in order to compete with the rest for a total global export pie that is shrinking as global trade and the global economy steadily slows. Although China's initial foray was minimal, it is highly likely it will eventually have to devalue further again—especially if Japan and Europe engage in another bout of QE to depress their currencies and if the US does not raise its interest rate soon. In short, central bank monetary tools and policy today have failed to provide currency stability, just as they have failed to ensure sustained economic growth and recovery, or to ensure price stability and prevent economies from disinflating and eventually deflating.

Central banks' massive liquidity injection policies have thus created a number of contradictions. They have not stabilized prices—preventing neither financial asset inflation nor goods disinflation/deflation. They have fed financial inflation, and thus engineered indirectly the inevitable financial asset deflation that follows. Central banks have not stimulated real investment, jobs, and wages much either. Liquidity has flowed instead to financial markets and consequently destabilized prices. They haven't ensured currency stability, but have instead promoted currency instability. All these three major missions and objectives of central banks today have failed: domestic price stability, currency stability, and economic growth (as real investment, jobs, and wage growth).

The remaining mission and objective associated with central banks, according to proponents of central bank monetary policies and supporters, is as 'lender of last resort', that is, bailing out private banks that have, or are about to fail. That of course has always been the primary function of and real reason for creating a central bank. Regulating the money supply, stabilizing prices, providing a central 'clearing house' for payments between banks, promoting employment and growth—all have always been of secondary importance as central bank objectives.

Lender of last resort—i.e. bailing out the private banks by providing whatever liquidity is necessary whenever they periodically create financial bubbles that burst and wipe out financial assets—is the fundamental function of central banking. In this regard central banks, the FED included, have been successful. They have fulfilled their primary function in the recent global crash. However, in so doing, they have established the basis for the next crisis by providing more liquidity than was necessary to bail out the private banking systems worldwide. Excess liquidity to bail out the banks would have been serious over-injection. But the liquidity has just kept on coming, well after the initial bailout, feeding financial assets growth, prices, and creating bubbles that will deflate even more dramatically than in 2008-09.

With the 2008-09 crisis, central banks faced the fundamental contradiction: they were 'damned if they did and damned if they didn't' bail out the banking systems with historic liquidity injections. It is true, as central bankers claim, including US Fed chairman Ben Bernanke, that if they didn't bail out the system in 2008-09 another great depression would have resulted. But it is not true that the bailouts had to continue well beyond 2010 and in some cases (i.e. in Europe, Japan and now China) continue to escalate to this day. The private banking systems in the US and UK were bailed out long ago, but the monetary injections continued unabated thereafter and have continued now for seven years. The liquidity was far more than needed. But it was 'oh, so profitable' for investors and financial institutions, so the central banks and politicians made sure it would keep coming. Just as in 2005-07 when the subprime mortgage speculation continued, even though many knew better and knew what the eventual consequences would be, no one wanted to kill the golden goose.

As Charlie Prince, CEO of one of the large US banks at the time, replied when asked if he saw the crash coming and, if so, why didn't he stop investing in subprimes: 'When you come to the party, you have to dance'. More knowledgeable sources thus knew the crash was inevitable.

And so it is once again, today. Snce 2010, the excess liquidity has continued to flow, enabling excessive debt and leverage, over-expansion of financial markets. The fundamental cause—i.e. excess liquidity, consequent excess leveraging of debt, and financial asset investing—has not changed. Only where the liquidity and debt has been directed has changed. Not at housing and subprimes and derivatives associated with them, but at other financial asset markets and derivatives today. The central banks were hand-maidens to the prior excessive risky financial investment behavior, and so they have been again since 2009. Only this time on an even greater scale than before.

While the central banks' policies of liquidity injection have proved contradictory with regard to price stability, currency volatility, and real investment, jobs, wages and growth, their fundamental contradiction was bailing out the private banking system and in the process creating the liquidity conditions for yet another financial instability in the future—an event that appears to be drawing closer. On the other hand, the central banks did have a choice whether to continue excessive liquidity injections via QE, ZIRP, etc. well beyond that which was needed to bail out the banks. They didn't stop, as the historic record shows.

That suggests the source of their 'decision' to continue injecting free money lies elsewhere as well. It is the decision of the ruling elites, especially in the AEs, to accommodate the demands of financial capital and require their central banks to continue providing the free money policies nonetheless. That in turn suggests that perhaps the even more fundamental contradiction lies in a political system dominated as never before by the finance capital elite.

The short term financial gains are so lucrative that they and their political representatives cannot reach a consensus as yet to halt the excess liquidity and bring debt under some semblance of control. The benefits to them are historic— in the short term. The costs in the longer term may be so as well. But it won't be the first time consensus among bankers, investors and politicians has favored the short run over the longer run negative consequences. It of course happened in 2005-2008, as it did in the 1930s on a grander scale.

Why Central Banks Don't Stop Financial Bubbles

Given the extreme negative economic consequences of an asset price bubble collapse, one would think the central bank would consider it a priority to prevent the bubble before it reached a point of collapse. But that's not the case. Central banks, including the FED, have been reluctant to intervene to prevent asset price bubbles. They prefer to let it burst, and then clean up the mess—either at public expense or by printing money. After all, that's what the 'lender of last resort' on an aggregate macroeconomic scale is all about—the most fundamental reason for their creation and existence. That's specifically why the US Federal Reserve was created in 1913, in response to the financial crash of 1907 and subsequent recession that continued, on and off, until 1913. Private banks could no longer bail each other out. Allowing crashes to turn into decade long depressions, as in the 1800s, was no longer politically feasible. And elected politicians did not want to be seen as bailing out the banks. The alternative was to create a central bank, the Federal Reserve in the US case, to take the heat off of politicians and other bankers for bailing out the banking system.[9]

Financial bubbles come in various forms. Most frequently they have involved:

- stock market bubbles and collapse, as occurred in the US in 1987 and in NASDAQ tech stocks in 2000;

- housing price bubbles, as in the 1980s and again in 2006-07;

- US Junk bonds in 1986; stocks and real estate in Japan in 1988-1990;

- currency exchange rate bubbles, as in the Asian crisis of 1997-98;

- global oil and commodities 2008-2013 and deflation, 2014-15;

- China's stock market bubble 2014-2015 and crash of 2015.

In the US in the 1920s, it was bubbles in stocks and housing and commercial property. In 1907 it was copper and other commodities. And in the 19th century railroad and canal bonds.

One reason central banks don't intervene before the bubble crashes is, they say, that it is difficult to determine when a surge in financial asset prices represents a true bubble, as opposed to just a temporary mispricing of assets.

A likely more fundamental reason why central banks don't intervene, however, is that private bankers, investors, and a lot of other moneyed interests make big speculative profits when asset prices run up. It would thus be a high political risk for a central bank to try to stop the run-up. Or for private bank CEOs not to participate and ride the asset price wave. Recall the previous quote of bank CEO, Charlie Prince: 'when you come to the party, you have to dance'. Keynes recognized this phenomenon of professional investors being pulled along by the 'herd' of general investors even when they know that a financial day of reckoning is coming.[10] Like Prince and Keynes' professional investors, central bankers—unable or unwilling to intervene—are dragged along by conditions and events.

Just as major investors and shareholders of a private bank would have made life miserable for, or even removed, any major bank CEO who refused to participate in the 'golden speculation goose' that was subprime lending in 2005-2007 while it was in full swing, so too would powerful financial interests have done whatever necessary to unseat a chair of a central bank that attempted to 'stop the show' in the middle of so much profit making opportunity. Big investors would almost certainly have called on their substantial political support to rein in a central bank that attempted to restrain a bubble prematurely when billions are being made from asset speculation.

It is something of a myth, therefore, that central banks are independent. They never were and are not now. The question is 'independent from whom'? Banking interests and professional finance elite don't want the central bank policies dictated by government officials when times are good; in that sense the central bank is quasi-independent, perhaps. Bankers and investors only want the central bank to bail them out when times turn bad—i.e. when they have serious systemic asset losses. Otherwise, it's hands off, i.e. independence from politicians.

But central banks are never independent from the bankers, wealthy investors and the finance capital elite. To this day, it is generally understood that the US government always allows the bankers to privately vet and choose who will serve as the district director of the strategically important New York Fed. And in previous decades, only bankers sat on the governing board of the 12 Fed districts. Today a mix of academics and banker-friendly representatives, with a few government bureaucrats at their side, constitute the governing boards of the US FED. But private meetings with heads of major banks and financial institutions occur all the time, especially in New York. A kind of collusion on policy between FED officials and bankers is the quiet but constant norm. And to this day as well, the operating costs of the US central bank are still paid by the banks themselves. Diverge too far from the banking system consensus and central bank chairs might very well find themselves without a job soon, or certainly not reappointed when their term came up for possible renewal. Nor could they expect to receive the rich compensation that typically follows after they complete their term in office should they propose policies that diverge too far from basic bank interests.[11]

Nevertheless, while central bank officials are no doubt influenced not to interfere with asset price bubbles due to pragmatic, 'realpolitik' reasons, the argument is still raised that intervention to stop bubbles is not possible because it is difficult to define a bubble and therefore at what point intervention should occur. An asset bubble might occur when "the asset price exceeds fundamentals by a significant amount and this persists for some time".[12] But what's 'fundamental', how much is 'significant', and how long is 'some time', all become debatable.

Billionaire financial speculator, George Soros, suggested something like this. In his view, escalating financial asset prices cause a corresponding upward adjustment in the 'fundamentals' as the asset inflation takes place, so that it becomes difficult to determine if an asset bubble is actually occurring. It appears to investors as if the fundamentals and the asset inflation are not inconsistent.

This was also the basic position of US Federal Chair, Alan Greenspan, for decades. Throughout his entire 20 year term, from 1986 to 2006, Greenspan's view was the FED couldn't properly or accurate determine what was a bubble. So the proper focus of the central bank was not to prevent a bubble but to "mitigate the fallout when it occurs and, ease the transition to the next expansion".[13] This basic US central bank view of 'let the asset bubble grow and go bust, and then clean up the mess' came to be known as the 'Jackson Hole Consensus', taken from the location in Jackson Hole, Wyoming, where US central bankers, global central bankers, private bankers, and academics meet annually to assess monetary policies.

Greenspan's successor, Ben Bernanke, meanwhile supported his predecessor all the way on this subject of intervention while he was positioning himself to take over from Greenspan while Bernanke was just a member of the FED governing board. In 2001 Bernanke argued there was no need to target asset prices or bubbles; just target the inflation of real goods prices with traditional monetary tools.[14] Targeting goods inflation—not financial assets inflation—was sufficient.

In a 2005 paper Bernanke suggested no central bank intervention to stop the housing-real estate bubble about to peak could prove successful. A central bank intervention to stop the subprime bubble would create financial instability and a recession would occur that would be worse than allowing the bubble to continue. All that was needed, Bernanke added, was for the central bank to 'drop money from a helicopter', if necessary in unlimited amounts to bail out banks in the event of a massive asset bubble collapse. He would thereafter be known as 'helicopter Ben'. From 2009 through 2013 Bernanke continued to adhere to the 'Jackson Hole' consensus and pump trillions into the US economy, ignoring the contribution of such to new, emerging asset bubbles.

Europe's central bankers have adopted more or less a similar 'Jackson Hole' view: target 2% in goods prices and don't intervene to stop asset price bubbles. Just bail out the banks afterward. However, Europe's central bankers face a more difficult problem than the US FED. Europe has no bona fide central bank. Its European Central Bank was a mere 'proto-central bank' at best. Its governing committee was composed of the 19 countries' central banks in the Eurozone. Europe, and Japan today continue to target goods inflation by injecting massive QE liquidity into their economies with the objective of raising goods inflation to a 2% target rate. But both the Japan and Eurozone QEs are failing miserably in attempts to achieve the 2%. Deflation and price stagnation continues in both economies. Europe and Japan are thus following the 'Jackson Hole Consensus'. The question there is not pricking price bubbles. It's about generating them. From mid-2014 until June 2015 China wasn't concerned much about asset bubbles—at least not in stock markets. Then came the crash of its Shanghai and Shenzhen equity markets in June 2015 that still continues. Now, of course, they are concerned—but after the fact—as the PBOC and China struggle to clean up the mess of a financial asset deflation event of major proportions, the contagion effects of which are still to be determined.

The refusal by central banks worldwide to intervene to prevent or stop financial asset bubbles is the norm and always has been. Various arguments justifying the non-intervention have been raised—i.e. concerning identifying bubbles, at what point to intervene, the effects of intervention, or the relative costs of intervening vs. doing nothing and just cleaning up post-crash.

But of course central banks are 'intervening' all the time, just on the side of contributing to the creation of financial bubbles through liquidity injection policies, weak supervision of private banks and virtual non-supervision of shadow banks. The consequence is growing financial instability in the global economy.

Central Banking and Systemic Fragility

The FED and other central banks' basic dilemma and contradiction—i.e. bail out the banks to prevent a more serious financial and economic crisis vs. contribute to the next financial crisis by injecting liquidity to bail out the banks—has its own origins in forces more fundamental than central bankers' policy choices. Those more fundamental forces are to be found in the restructuring of the global financial system itself that has been occurring for decades, which Chapters 11 and 12 have previously addressed.

The central banks are poorly structured to confront these 21st century forces and the on-going systemic structural changes. For one thing, they have been losing control over the basic global money supply as business and investor access to financial markets is now available globally in an instant due to technology. Today there's a vast excess of available credit beyond the national limits of a central bank's jurisdiction. A large borrower may find the domestic policies and interest rates irrelevant since it is possible to go anywhere globally to borrow, though a small player is largely confined to the domestic market.

Supervising the banking system to prevent excessively risky behavior is increasingly difficult, as the financial system is global and transactions inside it occur at the speed of light and can be 'secured' to not leave a 'paper trail'. Hundreds of thousands, perhaps millions, of financially astute and clever professionals work within the global financial system, many whose task is to figure out new ways to make money from money and stay ahead of the regulators. In contrast, central bank and regulatory agency bureaucrats are few in relative number in relation to the massive human forces on the side of the banks trying, and succeeding, in 'gaming' that system every day.

Another problem is that while central banks can influence short term interest rates, their control of long term interest rates is basically nil on a global scale. They may influence short term supply of money capital, but not long term and have essentially no way to influence money demand. They can provide incentives to private banks to lend, but cannot in the final analysis force them to do so. And they have no way to incentivize borrowers to borrow. That is, they have limited influence over money supply and short term rates, and very little, if any, over money demand and long term rates.

They are responsible in large part for their massive liquidity injections of recent years, but that response and liquidity injection is mostly reactive to a global financial system that is accelerating beyond their control and to global financial instability events their policies may enable but which they, the central banks, themselves do not initiate. The problems and crises within the global financial system are 'endogenous' and structural; the central banks are external or 'exogenous' to that system and try to influence it from afar—not a very effective position from which to supervise.

Central banks can't or won't stop the financial asset bubbles, as was noted, and their response to bubbles in the short run tends to contribute further to them in the long run. They only intervene 'after the fact' to try to clean up the messes made by excessive profit and capital gains-seeking financial institutions and finance capital elites willing to take ever-greater risks in order to continue to achieve greater profits from financial asset speculation and investing.

The basic banking system supervision role of central banks has fallen way behind the curve and continues to fall further with time. They have little influence over the behavior of the shadow banking system, which is growing rapidly as the traditional banking system is in long term decline. Capital markets, dominated by shadow banks, are far more influential in the 21st century than traditional bank lending when it comes to providing credit and that trend too is accelerating. But central banks have yet to figure out how to tame these new, high risk, speculative institutional engines of the global financial system. They continue to morph too quickly and move geographically and develop new forms of securities and ways of exploiting markets instantaneously. And they're good at covering their tracks.

Then there's the matter of central banks and credit itself. Central banks have no tools with which to tame the growing shift toward 'inside credit' creation by financial institutions, especially the shadow banks.

So central banks are limited to actions that are largely reactive to crises in the global financial system when they occur, even as they contribute to those crises by employing the very same measures to resolve the crises that produce them—i.e. excess liquidity injections that spur further debt and leverage that lead to still more and greater financial instability. It is a vicious, destabilizing circle and central banks have not yet figured how to get out of it.

Central banks therefore contribute to systemic fragility—i.e. a concept that is designed to estimate and measure the potential for financial instability events within the system—in a number of ways. They contribute first and foremost to systemic fragility by providing the excess liquidity to financial institutions that is the basis for the accelerating of leveraged debt, one of the three major elements that define fragility. Their most direct contribution to systemic fragility is thus to financial fragility. Without the extraordinary liquidity injections of recent decades, financial fragility—and the debt on which it is based—would not have occurred. On the other hand, there is the question whether, with the collapse of the Bretton Woods international monetary system in 1971-1973, central banks could have avoided the extraordinary liquidity injections they provided. The collapse of Bretton Woods left a vacuum into which the central banks had no alternative but to step. But that new role—combined with the advent of new technologies, elimination of controls on global capital flows, and other developments—led to the excess liquidity injection out of necessity as much as out of policy error.

Central banks have contributed to systemic fragility in other indirect ways as well, by exacerbating household consumption fragility as well as government balance sheet fragility.

By holding interest rates near zero (ZIRP) for nearly seven years now, the result is stagnant income growth for tens of millions of households who are retired and on fixed incomes. Zero rates also play havoc with pension funds which, if they fail in another crisis, will mean even more household fragility. That lack of household income growth from ZIRP also has a negative feedback effect on consumption fragility. It means households must resort to more borrowing, and thus more debt, in order to even maintain consumption. But debt means more household fragility. Consumption fragility thus takes a double hit: from stagnating fixed incomes, on the one hand, and from subsequent further debt accumulation as households struggle to retain their consumption levels amidst less income growth.

As quasi-government institutions themselves, central banks also contribute to government balance sheet fragility. This occurs in several ways. First, by directly purchasing bad assets from institutional and individual wealthy investors by means of QE, the central bank essentially transfers the debt from private banks' balance sheets onto its own central bank balance sheet—in the process adding to government debt and therefore balance sheet fragility.

But monetary policies of central banks further contribute to the growth of government balance sheet debt and therefore fragility by the failure of their monetary policy to generate a robust, sustained recovery from recession in the real economy. That lack of sustained recovery results in the continuation of government fiscal deficits. The government deficits result in the need for governments to borrow more and thus a rise in government (sovereign) debt over time.

The following chapter addresses the various *fiscal* forms of government balance sheet fragility. But to the extent central banks transfer existing debt from financial institutions to their own central bank balance sheet—as occurs in the case of QEs—then central banks should be considered as contributing to government fragility as well, since they themselves are a quasi-government institution.

Add to this their obvious contribution to financial fragility due to their historic liquidity injections of recent decades, plus the consequences for household consumption fragility that are the consequence of central bank ZIRP policies—and it is clear central banks are a major institutional factor contributing to all three forms of fragility—financial, household, and government balance sheet fragility.

It follows that any meaningful reduction in systemic fragility that hopes to contain the further drift toward financial instability must fundamentally address the shortcomings and failures of central banks as institutions today, how they function, and the policies they opt for. The institution that purports to serve as a containment of financial instability is in fact a major cause of that instability.

Endnotes

1   Part of the $4 trillion was also long term US treasury bonds.
2   Technically, it is electronically created, or 'printed', but the idea of created from nowhere holds in both cases.

3   Note that no mention is made of the $750 billion Troubled Asset Relief Program (TARP) passed by Congress and given to the US Treasury to use to bail out the banks. TARP was never used for the purpose of bank bailouts. Banks were bailed out by the FED, not Congress. For more on TARP, see this writer's 2012 book, *Obama's Economy: Recovery for the Few*, Pluto Press, Chapter 8. Briefly, about half of TARP was given to the 9 large banks and the next tier of smaller banks. Some was redirected to the auto company bailouts. Hundreds of billions were never distributed, but given back to the US Treasury. None was used to bail out homeowners, which Congress indicated should occur in providing the funds. Banks providing and servicing home loans opposed the intended use. The banks were bailed out by FED auctions, ZIRP, QE, and Congress in the interim allowing banks to lie about their balance sheet conditions by suspending what was called 'mark to market accounting'. The FED conducted phony 'stress tests' of the banks in the meantime to encourage investors to buy bank stocks, which also helped to 'recapitalize' the banks. Rising bank profits and stock prices thereafter continued the banks' recovery.

4   This does not count, of course, the hundreds of billions, perhaps trillions more injected by other major developing countries' central banks—i.e. Indonesia, South Korea, Brazil, Turkey, Mexico, and scores of others.

5   See this writer's article, 'Are Banks Becoming Addicted to 'Free Money'?',

6   For an analysis of Obama's 2008 campaign positions on banking and real estate, and his association with financial interests, see this writer's *Obama's Economy: Recovery for the Few*, Pluto Press, 2012, Chapter 1.

7   One may argue then that QE and other liquidity injections flowed into four targets: first, into real asset investment in China and emerging markets in 2010-2013; second, into financial asset markets globally from the beginning and continuing; third, into real investment to a limited extent within the respective domestic economies, and, fourthly, was simply hoarded by banks as unnecessarily high excess reserves—in the US alone more than $2 trillion.

8   Even in China, it is estimated that in 2010 every $1 of money injected resulted in $1 of GDP increase. But by end of 2014, after trillions of dollars more in liquidity injection, that ratio had declined to $4 of money injection to generate a $1 increase in GDP.

9   See Jack Rasmus, *Epic Recession: Prelude to Global Depression*, Pluto Books, 2010, Chapter 5, which specifically addresses the financial panic of 1907, the epic recession that followed, and the origins of the Federal Reserve.

10   See J.M. Keynes, Chapter 12, *The General Theory*, 1935. (see also Chapter 16 in this book that follows).

11   For example, US FED former chairman, Ben Bernanke, in office received only a government officer's salary of several hundred thousand dollars a year. When he retired, however, he went on the 'speakers circuit', giving speeches at the invitation of bankers and other corporations, for which he was nicely paid a sum of around $250,000 per speech. That's how government officials in high places, who serve corporate interests well during their term in office, are nicely compensated after leaving office. That way no apparent conflict of interest while in office occurs. Perhaps the most egregious example of such was the $3 million dollar single speech that President Reagan gave after leaving office. It was arranged by various corporate benefactors, conveniently outside the country, in Tokyo, Japan in order to minimize US media reporting.

12   A.G. Malliaris, "Asset Price Bubbles and Central Bank Policies: The Crash of the

Jackson Hole Consensus", in *New Perspectives on Asset Price Bubbles*, edited by Douglas Evanoff, George Kaufman and A.G. Malliaris, Oxford University Press, 2012, p. 412.

13 Quoted from Malliaris, "Asset Price Bubbles and Central Bank Policies: The Crash of the Jackson Hole Consensus", in *New Perspectives on Asset Price Bubbles*, edited by Douglas Evanoff, George Kaufman and A.G. Malliaris, Oxford University Press, 2012, p. 423.

14 Ben Bernanke, "Should Central Banks Respond to Movements in Asset Prices?"*American Economic Review*, v. 91, 2001, pp. 253-57. Bernanke thus showed his misunderstanding of the relationship between goods and financial asset prices during a bubble buildup.

15

GOVERNMENT DEBT AND SYSTEMIC FRAGILITY

If fragility, in its simplest form, is the result of insufficient income with which to pay for principal and interest on debt, then not only financial institutions, non-financial businesses, and households may become fragile but government institutions as well.[1]

To thoroughly consider the relationship between government debt and government income it is first necessary to define further what is meant by government 'income' and government 'debt'.

Defining Government Debt and Income

The best, most accurate estimation of government debt includes not only debt of *formal national structures of government*—like legislatures and executive branches—but also regional mid-level and local forms of governing bodies. Government debt should also include balance sheet debt of central banks, which are *quasi government* entities—as well as of other government agencies, national or local, that are in fact *hybrid government* institutions.[2] By hybrid is meant they share characteristics of public administration but also raise cash in financial markets through equity (stock) offerings and that otherwise operate much like private corporations.

Central bank debt is held on central banks' own balance sheets, separate from general government debt totals, which represent the multi-year accumulation of annual legislative-executive budget deficits. *General government debt* is defined hereafter as debt of central government institutions (legislatures, executives, etc.), as well as most (but not all) state-provincial-local government.[3] Select government agencies, of both central and local governments, may also be included in general government debt totals, although what is included varies widely country by country.[4]

Two other important definitions, when addressing government debt, are 'gross' debt and 'net' debt. *Gross* general government debt is the more accurate than *net* government debt. Net debt refers to gross debt, minus whatever assets the government may have to offset that gross debt—such as gold stock, IMF special drawing rights (SDRs), and other sources of assets and receivables with which theoretically debt payments may be made.

In summary, when used in this chapter, *General Government Gross Debt* is what we are referring to when addressing government, or sovereign, debt. Were central bank and other agency debt included with general government debt, the combined amounts would constitute what might be called *Total Gross Government Debt*. Unless otherwise noted to include central bank and other agency debt, data representing general government gross debt, as defined by the IMF, BIS and other global research sources, will be used in the Tables and discussion to follow.

For purposes of defining government 'income', the most obvious form is from tax revenues. But governments may also earn income from interest on their issuance of securities (government or sovereign bonds) or loans. Other forms of 'fees' may exist as revenue and income sources. In many countries there are government owned and run enterprises that generate a form of income from the operations of those enterprises. Perhaps the most notable case is China, where many strategic enterprises, and military goods production in particular, are directly owned by the national government or by its military forces. Total government income can be even more difficult to estimate than total debt—not only because reporting of government enterprise income is often not transparent, but because the prices of the goods and services produced by government enterprises may be fixed by the government and kept artificially low as a result of internal transfer pricing, instead of at market prices. Profits and income are consequently minimized. Countries manipulating their currency exchange rates to keep them artificially low in order to be more competitive in exports may also by such policy in effect alter government income levels, either positively or negatively, through reduced tariffs and excise fees and other ways. Total government income would be much higher, were other forms of national income, as well as state-local government tax and other income, included. However, due to collection and aggregation of data issues, the convention in this chapter will be to limit the definition of income to tax revenue income at the national or central government level. Doing so, however, significantly underestimates the degree of government fragility.

Estimating Government Debt

There are two ways in which government debt is generally stated, and the difference is important. First is representing Government Debt as a percent of the country's GDP.   In contrast to 'General Government Debt' as debt accumulated in the sense of a 'level' or magnitude of debt of a country's currency, 'Government Debt as a percent of the country's GDP' is a ratio. As a ratio, the trend in debt may appear less serious than it is if there's a robust, or even normal, growth in GDP levels. The debt accumulation problem may not appear as serious as it is, if GDP continues to rise robustly. The assumption is that if GDP is growing, the government is more able to service the debt (pay principal and interest when due). But this is not necessarily true. GDP growth will have a potentially positive effect on debt servicing only if it translates into growing government tax revenues with which to service the debt. And GDP may grow but government may reduce tax revenues at the same time. So the ability to service the debt may not in fact improve, and could even worsen as GDP rises.

There is a similar contradiction in the case of many Emerging Market Economies (EMEs). The government's debt may have been incurred in the currency of a lending country (e.g. US dollars). That debt is repayable only in that currency of that lending country. Dollars (in this case) are earned from exports. But if export income is declining (due to falling prices or demand by other economies), then it matters little what that country's domestic GDP level is. It won't be able to pay principal and interest on its debt as it comes due. In other words, the ratio of debt to GDP as an indicator may make it appear the EME government is better able to handle a growing debt load in an absolute sense, while in fact its ability to do so is deteriorating.

Both approaches to measuring government debt are provided in Tables 14.1 and 14.2 that follow.[5] Table 14.1 does not suggest that government debt is especially severe, and that debt has reasonably stabilized since 2012. In contrast, Table 14.2 clearly indicates otherwise.

TABLE 14.1[6]
GENERAL GOVERNMENT GROSS DEBT
As Percent of GDP
G7 Economies & China

	2001	2007	2010	2012	2014
USA	53	83	94	102	104
UK	37	43	78	89	91
Japan	153	183	216	237	246
Germany	59	65	82	81	73
France	56	63	80	88	95
Italy	108	103	119	127	136
Canada	82	66	84	88	88
China	17	19	33	37	41

Per Table 14.1, government debt rose somewhat significantly in the US and Japan between 2001 and 2007, but hardly at all in the other G7 economies or China during that same period. When viewed in 'percent of GDP' terms, it would appear government debt increase was not a particularly serious problem in the other G7s or China. In the US and Japan, the government debt rise was more pronounced, 2001-07, but still not in the extreme when viewed as percent of GDP. The relatively worse US and Japan contrary experience was due to weak economic recovery from the 2001 recessions, and therefore slower than normal government income (tax revenue) growth in both countries, as well as rising government spending in the case of the US. In contrast to US and Japan, Europe and China experienced relatively strong economic growth in 2001-07, which minimized the growth of government deficits and therefore debt. But together, the period 2001-07 in percent terms suggests a steady secular growth in government debt.

Between 2007-2010 all G-7s, including China, experienced significant increases in debt as a percent of GDP, as the global recession of 2008-09 reduced government tax income and raised spending simultaneously.

After 2010 the rate of growth of debt slowed, and in some cases like Germany's, actually declined as a percent of GDP. It would thus appear that the government debt surge problem had been stabilized after 2010. However stabilization was only an appearance, made possible by viewing debt as a ratio to GDP. The ratio measurement hides the true scope of the government debt problem and can be misleading when GDP rises, even if that rise is not particularly robust.

Because Debt to GDP ratios can be misleading, estimating government debt as a ratio is not a preferred indicator. Government Gross Debt is the better indicator with which to estimate Government Debt trends and, in turn, the impact of government debt on Government Balance Sheet fragility.

TABLE 14.2 [7]
GENERAL GOVERNMENT GROSS DEBT
in National Currency (trillions)
G7 Economies & China

	2001	2007	2010	2012	2014	
USA	5.6	7.0	14.7	19.8	26.2	(US dollars)
UK	.38	.62	1.1	1.4	1.5	(UK pounds)
Japan	776	938	1,041	1,124	1,197	(Yen)
Germany	1.2	1.5	2.0	2.1	2.1	(Euros)
France	.87	1.2	1.6	1.8	2.0	(Euros)
Italy	1.3	1.6	1.8	1.9	2.1	(Euros)
Canada	.93	1.0	1.4	1.6	1.7	(Can. Dollars)
China	2.7	7.2	12.6	18.6	25.8	(Yuan)

Table 14.2 shows that an especially intense escalation in government debt occurred after 2007. The rise was most rapid during the recession period of 2008-09. Thereafter, however, the rise of government debt levels did not moderate for the US, China, Japan, and the UK. US government debt continued and nearly doubled after 2010, as did China's. Japan and the UK also continued to increase government debt levels well above their GDP growth rates after 2010.

The Eurozone government debt levels did not continue to grow as rapidly after 2010, most likely attributable to the introduction of severe fiscal austerity measures in Europe. Compare this with the US and especially China where policy makers did not initially opt for fiscal austerity. The US introduced a modest fiscal stimulus package in 2009, in the amount of about $800 billion (about 5% of US GDP). China introduced a massive fiscal stimulus package in 2009, amounting to between 12.5% and 15.6% of its GDP depending on measurements. The US would opt for a mild form of austerity, beginning only in 2011. China would continue with fiscal stimulus.

The more moderate Eurozone government debt rise after 2010 is misleading in yet another way. The escalation of European government debt did not occur in northern Europe countries, like Germany, France and others. Europe debt escalation was concentrated in its periphery—i.e. in Spain, Portugal, Greece, Italy, Ireland, UK, and to a lesser extent in other eastern European economies. This means Germany and northern Europe effectively 'exported' their share of debt increase to the Euro periphery. That export of debt was made possible by the introduction of a common currency, the Euro, as well as policies of northern Europe bankers and governments.

When measured in terms of government debt levels, therefore, and not in terms of percent of GDP, all the G-7 and China economies continued to experience a significant government debt buildup after 2007, especially during the 2008-10 recession years, but also during the 'recovery' period after 2010. That continued growth of government debt in the Advanced Economies (AEs) and China post-2010 suggests that government debt is driven by longer term secular forces apart from, and in addition to, the financial crash and recession of 2008-09. Both secular and cyclical causes clearly overlap.

This scenario of rising gross government debt in the G-7 and China contrasts sharply with the experience of the major Emerging Market Economies (EMEs) in all three periods: 2001-07, during the 2008-10 crash, as well 2010-2014.

Using the measure 'debt as a percent of GDP' obscures, once again, what was really going on with government debt in the EMEs. When measured in percent of GDP terms, EME debt growth 2001-2007 was not particularly significant. Nor did EME debt appear to rise significantly after 2010. Debt as a percent of GDP actually declined for a number of key EMEs before 2008 because EMEs were growing robustly in GDP terms. The same can be said for EME economic growth after 2010. EME growth would not begin to slow noticeably until 2013-14.

EMEs benefited from the big fiscal stimulus packages introduced by both China and, to a lesser extent, the US in 2009-10. The EMEs also benefited greatly from massive capital inflows from the AEs, especially the US and UK and their quantitative easing (QE) central bank money injection policies. As their exports and economies grew rapidly beginning in 2010, once again due to the fiscal and monetary effects in the US, UK and China, EME economic growth served to moderate and obscure absolute levels of government debt buildup due to economic growth.

That EME recovery started to slow, however, by 2013, especially for those EMEs which were dependent on commodities and semi-finished goods exports and in particular on oil exports. By late 2014 many key EMEs would find themselves in recession as well. Commencing circa 2013, the fiscal and monetary investment and money flows that were being diverted from the AEs and China to the EMEs began to reverse. Chinese demand for EME exports slowed. And the global oil price deflation that began mid-2014 depressed EME currencies and stimulated capital outflows from the EMEs. To stimulate their economies and now slowing GDP, and to finance the cost of rising import prices and to attract more funds for investment, EMEs turned to more debt—especially in the private sector and among businesses. A rise in absolute levels of both corporate debt and government debt began in 2013 and thereafter, just as the obscuring effect of a rising GDP began to disappear as well. While fundamental EME debt trends and debt deterioration were obscured 2010-2012 when measuring debt as a percent of GDP, they become more evident when absolute levels of debt are considered, especially after 2012, as indicated in Table 14.3 that follows.

TABLE 14.3[8]
GENERAL GOVERNMENT GROSS DEBT
in National Currency (trillions)
Emerging Market Economies

	2001	2007	2013	2014	
Argentina	144	546	1,369	2,158	(pesos)
Brazil	921	1,733	3,209	3,372	(reals)
India	18,547	36,916	67,373	77,858	(rupees)
Indonesia	1,319,703	1,384,791	1,977,702	2,635,830	(rupiahs)
Mexico	2,783	4,280	6,746	8,226	(pesos)
Russia	4,258	2,861	7,871	11,406	(rubles)
Venezuela	28	152	751	1,499	(bolivars)

To take a few examples: Brazil's debt levels doubled in 2007-2014 and Argentina's nearly quadrupled. India's debt levels more than doubled, as did those of Mexico and Indonesia. Oil commodity exporters did even worse in terms of government debt rise, as collapsing crude oil prices globally led to more borrowing to offset the loss of oil sales revenue and income. Russia's debt quadrupled by 2013-14, while Venezuela's rose more than 10 times 2007 levels by 2014.

Behind the preceding quantitative data lay fundamental qualitative trends and causes that together explain why government debt levels have been rising and will continue to rise—in the AEs, then in China commencing around 2009-10, and now beginning as well in the EMEs in 2014 and after. Understanding these trends and why government debt will continue to rise—both longer term and cyclically short term—is important for understanding the role of government debt in determining government balance sheet fragility; and for understanding ultimately how government balance sheet fragility interacts with other forms of fragility (financial and consumption) to generate growing systemic fragility in the global economy.

Key Trends: Government Debt, Income & Fragility

Trend #1: Secular Trends and the Rise in Government Debt

In 21st century capitalism, the lines between government-public and corporate-private continue to blur to an extent never before in history. Rising secular government debt is the consequence of the growing integration of government with the corporate sector that has been developing and deepening at least since the 1970s, although it can be shown that the process goes back even further.

Subcontracting Government Services

What were once exclusive public, or government, functions, previously conducted by formal government structures, executive agencies, the military, the bureaucracy, public education institutions, local police functions, and even direct legislative activity have in recent decades been 'outsourced'.

Increasingly, education services are privatized at both pre-college and college levels. A growing list of police and military services, and even entire functions, are contracted out. Hired mercenaries from private companies now fight side by side with military personnel and provide nearly all the logistical military support. Previous publicly owned local utilities are sold off to private bidders. Public roads, built at taxpayer expense, are sold to private interests to manage and maintain, in exchange for charging tolls. Private insurance companies are given the right to participate within formerly public-only national health services, picking off the healthiest and best paying customers. Public hospitals are acquired by 'for profit' chains. Public national pension funds are opened to banks to manage, to skim off fat fees, and eventually plunder. The examples are many, and multiply by the year.

Nonetheless, all these government contracted services must be paid for by government. The payments for the contracted services in turn contribute to deficits. The deficits are then largely financed by borrowing funds (i.e. incurring debt) from private investors and from other government trust and pension funds [9]

The contracting out of government and public services over time results in a form of subsidization of business income and debt, raising income and reducing the need for borrowing and debt in the corporate sector, while reducing income for the government sector and requiring government to borrow more (i.e. add debt) to cover the government income loss.

Privatizing Government Production, Assets, and Services

A similar process of shifting of income and debt between government and the private sector occurs when governments engage in selling off publicly owned and operated enterprises and functions. In the US, government ownership and management of production has not been a tradition. But on occasion this has taken place: the Tennessee Valley Authority (TVA) created by the federal government in the 1930s to bring electrification to rural areas; the US government built and owned factories during World War II; city-owned public utilities; etc. All have been sold off or are in the process in recent decades. When sold off, i.e 'privatized', the result is that a former source of government income is 'transferred' to the private sector that buys the once public assets. The private sector now benefits from the income stream. Government in turn must therefore borrow more debt to offset loss of income generated formerly from government enterprises and public assets.

The privatization of public goods and services trend continues in the US today, with rising sale of public goods like roads and freeways, public parks, and other sources of government income now being increasingly 'privatized'. At the other end of the government-owned enterprise spectrum, where income from enterprise goods production exists, is China. Many factories in key strategic industries are still government owned. China's army owns and operates its own military hardware companies. In between are emerging market countries which still own 'nationalized' industries and companies. And in Europe there remain publicly owned and operated enterprises.

But the trend everywhere globally, even in China, has been the 'privatization'—i.e. selling off—of such government owned enterprises. Where-ver, the effect is the same: First, it results in the loss of an income stream from such operations with which to service existing debt. Second, government must then often purchase those services from their private owners. That adds to government spending and contributes to deficits and need to borrow more and increase debt.[10]

Another secular trend contributing to government debt flows from the growing direct, and indirect, subsidization of private corporate income by government. This includes forms of both cost and price subsidization by government.

Direct subsidies means making actual payments to private corporations out of government tax revenues. Companies are in effect being reimbursed with a government check for a growing list of their costs. Indirect subsidization means the government assumes partial cost of production of the companies and/or pays them artificially above market prices when it purchases the goods or services from the corporation.

Central government tax laws are especially structured to allow national governments to write checks to companies when those companies experience losses, and even when not. Banks, Pharmaceutical, Tech, Oil and Energy, and Military production companies are the prime beneficiaries of such practices in the USA. Many companies in these industries pay virtually no taxes whatsoever to the US federal government, especially in recession years, and receive direct payments from the government.

There are many 'indirect' forms of government subsidization as well, either offsetting costs or providing excess income to the corporation. When the government 'underwrites' or insures private loans to a company, it agrees to pay for those loans should the company go bankrupt eventually, thereby removing risk for the lending banks and reducing it for the borrowers. Other indirect subsidization occurs, for example, with government funding basic research and development costs of a growing list of industries and businesses.

Still another form of indirect subsidization at government expense relates to the elevated prices government pays for purchases of goods or services from private corporations. A best case example is spending on defense products. Since defense goods are produced essentially by corporations with a de facto monopoly, governments end up paying monopoly excess prices for the defense goods. Then there's US government purchasing of police and other special military support services from private companies, where the cost of such services paid are typically higher than if they were provided, as in the past, by US military personnel themselves.[11] For decades governments have been paying agricultural producers above market prices for products they grow, or paying them not to grow. This was originally designed to keep smaller family farms in business during the depression of the 1930s. Today those producers are multi-billion dollar agribusiness corporations but they still receive the subsidies.

Another big recipient of government subsidies is the health care and the pharmaceutical industries in the US. In the case of the latter, government at both federal and state levels subsidizes the cost of prescription drugs for retirees at whatever the price the companies may choose to offer. And the government is prevented by its own laws from negotiating lower prices with the drug companies.

Another more recent example in the general health services industry in the US is the Affordable Care Act (ACA), aka 'Obamacare'. Like prescription drugs for retirees, ACA is in effect a program that ultimately subsidizes health insurance companies—i.e. raising their income at the expense of increasing government expenditures, deficits and debt and diverting incomes from other households and private sources to subsidize health insurance companies.

The major, long run secular trends of recent decades—i.e. subcontracting out more and more government services, selling off of remaining government owned and operated enterprises and public assets, and providing an ever-growing list and volume of direct and indirect, cost and price, subsidization programs to private corporations—altogether mean less income and more cost to government while increasing income and reducing costs for private corporations. These secular effects contribute to government deficits—as income streams from public goods and services are lost and government spending for subcontracting services rises. That adds to deficits that require government to finance with still more debt.

Shifting Debt: From Corporations to Government to Households

As an alternative to adding more debt, government has the option of reducing spending on social programs and/or raising taxes—sometimes called austerity. While austerity policies may reduce the amount of additional debt needed by government, austerity programs reduce consumer households' disposable income, especially at the median income levels and below, and thus encourages households to take on more debt to maintain levels of consumption. So debt is not really reduced, it is just shifted from corporations-investors to government balance sheets and thereafter in part on to households.

To summarize, much of the rise in long term, i.e. secular, government debt thus reflects a growing trend of subsidizing incomes of corporations and/or transferring debt from the latter to the government sector. An important debt transfer occurs in the opposite direction, however, from government to households. Some of the government debt is offloaded to households due to austerity fiscal policies or higher consumer taxation. As government deficits and debt rise due to the subsidization and debt shifting benefiting corporations, government income transfers to households slow, taxation on consumers rise, and government spending programs benefiting median household wage incomes decline. In a sense, therefore, private corporation and investor debt is ultimately transferred to households as well as to government.

Trend #2: Business Cycles and Short Term Government Debt

The rise in government debt is short term cyclical as well as longer term secular. The secular trends noted previously are exacerbated periodically on a regular basis by cyclical events that cause a further acceleration in general government gross debt.

These cyclical overlays are associated with financial system crashes requiring government action to bail out the financial system, as well as additional government action and spending to bail out non-financial corporations, as the financial crash-induced credit crunch that inevitably follows a financial crisis drives the economy into increasingly frequent, deeper, and longer duration recessions, as well as sub-normal, slower and more protracted recoveries.

Government Debt from Central Bank Bailouts

With a banking crisis, the central bank bails out the banks and the financial system with both direct and indirect subsidies. The central bank does this in a number of ways, as were discussed in detail in the preceding chapter 14, including but not limited to 'special auctions', zero interest rate loans (ZIRP) from the central bank to financial institutions, quantitative easing (QE) programs, and other measures—all of which serve to provide forms of 'income' to the financial institutions. As the prior chapter noted, this has amounted to approximately $25 trillion since 2008. Some of this assumes the form of new debt assumed by central banks, which was estimated at $9 trillion as of 2015 for AE economies alone, not counting EMEs.

That $9 trillion represents a debt transfer from banks and financial institutions to central banks, which are quasi-government entities. Monetary policies represent a kind of corporation 'cost subsidization' and thus add significantly to government debt.

Government Debt from Government Bank Bailouts

After 2008 banks and financial institutions in the US were bailed out not only by the central bank, the Federal Reserve, but also by the general government.

For example, bank mortgage servicing operations were bailed out by general government in the US in 2009-10 by means of Obama's $50 billion housing and real estate subsidization programs. Originally intended to bail out homeowners whose home values had collapsed below the value of the original mortgage, the $50 billion program ended up mostly providing various indirect subsidies to the big five US bank mortgage servicers primarily implicated in the crash, while providing minimal assistance, for a temporary period only, to a mere several hundred thousand of the 14 million homeowners in the US who lost their homes after 2007.

Another way banks were indirectly subsidized by general government during the recent crisis was by the US government providing loan guarantees to the banks, as it did in the case of Citigroup in an amount of $300 billion. Smaller regional banks were provided with hundreds of billions from the US government's $750 billion TARP (Troubled Asset Relief Program) funds authorized by Congress in October 2008.[12]

Government Debt from Special Agency Bailouts

Special government mortgage agencies—like Fannie Mae, Freddie Mac, and the Federal Housing agency in the US—further subsidize bank losses during a cyclical crisis by purchasing mortgages securities issued by the banks at their original price, even when a financial crisis has sharply reduced the market value of those mortgages. Agencies must make the purchases by law. The mortgages that get 'dumped' on these agencies by private sector financial corporations thus represent a transfer of losses and debt to these government agencies.

Government Debt from Non-Financial Corporate Bailouts

As a financial crash typically leads to a general credit crunch, and the non-banking sector remainder of the economy slides into recession, the general government institutions—legislatures and executive—also provide direct and indirect subsidies to the non-bank companies in trouble that are in addition to longer term subsidies provided by general government to the non-bank sector, including but not limited to the following:

Government purchases of the preferred stock of the company. This is precisely what the US Congress did in 2008 with US auto industry. The bailout amounted to a direct cost of $90 billion. The government did the same with the insurance company giant, AIG, which cost the government $180 billion.

In Europe and elsewhere, such non-financial corporate direct bailouts are sometimes accompanied by a partial 'nationalization' of the companies involved. But it is nationalization in name only. The same management continues to run the company. Government inspectors merely review their operations. And when the company is profitable once again, the government sells its shares in the company it purchased in the 'nationalization' (often before the share price rises too far), thus allowing private investors to buy back in and to benefit from the bailout the government financed with taxpayer money. This was the case as well with the AIG corporation in the US and the recent rescue in 2008.

There are many additional ways by which general government indirectly subsidizes non-bank businesses in the wake of a cyclical economic crisis event. Taking the US example again, the general government in 2009 paid for continuing unemployed workers' health insurance coverage provided by their previous employer, through a program called COBRA. COBRA benefits are provided at a much higher cost to the individual employee, than the original insurance cost to the employer for the employee. By paying this higher insurance premium the government in effect subsidized the health insurance companies. The employee may have been able to continue benefits, but the insurance company received the money payments. The costs amounted to tens of billions of dollars, pocketed by the insurance companies.

In 2010 the US government began subsidizing the wages companies paid to workers whom they might newly hire. Another program similarly paid in part for the hiring of military veterans.

Using the US as an example, what the experience of the 2008-09 financial crash and the subsequent deep contraction of the general US economy reveal is that the central bank bails out the banks and the general government mostly bails out the non-banking business sector. Some token bail out programs are offered for the general consumer and worker, but even those amount to 'trickle down' benefits that first pass through the balance sheets of private companies, bank and non-bank alike.

Government Debt from Transfers and Subsidies to Households

While over the longer term the secular trend has been the reduction of transfer payments and direct government assistance to households, during shorter term business cycle events in which recessions occur governments tend to provide an increase in transfer payments—such as unemployment benefits, welfare income assistance, food assistance and other subsidies to households. These non-wage forms of income do have the effect of offsetting wage income losses for many households below the highest levels. The income gains are financed in large part by government deficits and therefore contribute to government debt increases.

Two trends accompany this 'transfer and subsidies' during recessions, however. The first is that, in the past decade the transfers and subsidies have been sharply reduced compared to past decades. Austerity policies have replaced in many instances what in the past would have been a distinct and notable increase in transfers and subsidies to households. The other observable trend is that when transfers and subsidies have increased, that increase has been short lived, for an identifiable period only, after which the transfers and subsidies are again withdrawn. The continuation of austerity programs, for example, has been the case with the Eurozone and, to a somewhat lesser extent, with Japan; the US and UK examples reflect an initial increase in transfers and subsidies to households as the recession deepens, but then a subsequent withdrawal of much, if not all, of the transfers-subsidies once initial signs of recovery from recession begin to appear.

This unequal treatment of assistance to households contrasts with government assistance to financial and investors and non-financial corporations, for whom government assistance continues without little abatement for years after the end of the recession. Government subcontracting of services, sale of public goods and public infrastructure, and direct and indirect cost subsidization often not only continue, but grow in magnitude. Central banks in particular continue their extraordinary assistance to and subsidization of financial institutions, in contrast to the lack of such similar assistance by central banks to households even during the depths of the recession.[13]

Trend #3: Government Income & Government Debt

General government spending provides but half of the explanation of rising government deficits and debt. Slowing growth of government tax revenue is the largest determinant of growing government deficits and debt. And like government outsourcing of services, selling of public assets, increasing subsidies to corporations and investors, spending on bailouts and all the rest of the policies underlying the rise in government spending, deficits and debt—the decline in the relative growth of general government tax revenue contributes as well to government deficits and debt. It too has both long term secular as well as shorter term cyclical origins. In fact, both the long term trend and short term business cycle effects on declining government tax income contributes to government deficits and debt even more than spending on transfers, subsidies, bailouts, and other government expenditures does.

Secular Corporate Tax Reduction

Since the 1980s there has been a secular 'race to the bottom' in corporate and investor taxation between the Advanced Economies (AEs). A similar race to the bottom has been occurring 'within' the AEs; that is, between their regional (state, province, district) government structures. The two trends even overlap: states may provide deep tax cuts to lure foreign corporations to their region, as well as compete with other states within their own country and economy to provide tax incentives for corporations to relocate to their region. The corporate-investor tax cut 'race to the bottom' is everywhere and is intensifying since 2000.

The 'financialization' of the global economy, and the shift to financial asset investing and speculation in financial securities discussed in preceding chapters, are also associated with the relative decline in corporate-investor taxation and government income from such taxation. Financial transaction taxes are opposed fiercely by financial interests and thus far have been prevented in nearly all AE and EME governments. Financial assets and securities transactions are barely taxed anywhere, in contrast to production of goods and services. Thus, too, the extent that the shift to financial assets and securities sales has occurred and diverted investment and production of goods, it has resulted in a slowing of government taxation income.

Another development reducing government income has been the increase in government tax cuts for research and development, and from investment tax cuts, faster depreciation, and expansion of corporate tax loopholes for multinational corporations. These forms of corporate-investor tax cuts have grown, as competition between economies globally has intensified and governments seek increasingly to provide a technology stimulus through taxes for their respective private corporate sectors.

The expansion of free trade agreements also has the effect of reducing income from tariffs and excise taxes at the national government level. Government's loss of income is corporate sector's income gain.

As far back as the 1970s and especially since the 1980s, nominal corporate tax rates have been on a long run downward trend. The outcome has been a decline in corporate-investor taxes as a share of total government tax revenue. Specific measures by which nominal corporate taxes in the US, for example, are dramatically reduced in terms of effective rates, or what is actually paid in taxes to government, include making Investment tax credits that were once only available for investment in the US applicable to multinational US corporations' investments abroad. The requirement that corporate tax credits produce some proof of job creation before claimed was discontinued. Depreciation allowances (a kind of tax cut) were accelerated and expanded. The gap between corporate income and taxable corporate income was widened from 5% to 32%; that is, more and more forms of corporate income were simply declared non-taxable. Corporate profits were taxed at the lower 15% capital gains rate, instead of 35% rate, by redefining profits for certain financial institutions as 'carried interest'. Foreign profits taxation (on profits from foreign based subsidiaries of national corporations) was left mostly unenforced by governments. Multinational corporations and wealthy investors were allowed to shelter income in various offshore havens by the government. Taxes on foreign operations of US multinationals were left unenforced, and companies were allowed to shift profits income between countries at will to offshore holding companies or subsidiaries[14] and by manipulating internal pricing and therefore profits between subsidiaries.

Cyclical Corporate Tax Reduction

Crashes and recessions also lead to a sharp decline in corporate tax income payments to government, which also raises deficits and requires more debt. Government corporate tax refund checks balloon during recession periods. Special tax cuts are introduced by legislatures. Depreciation is accelerated even faster. Corporate layoffs during a recession are allowed by law to be charged as expenses, which are then used to reduce corporate taxation. The consequence of these and other secular and cyclical reductions in government income from taxation of corporations is that, while the nominal US corporate tax rate in the past quarter century has not changed much, the effective tax rate—i.e. the rate at which taxes are actually paid—has declined significantly.

A 2013 study by the US Government Accounting Office, found that US corporations paid a global effective tax rate of only 12.6%--not the official 35% rate.[15] This compares to 1990, when the nominal tax rate was 34% and the effective tax rate not much different at 33%. When US states' corporate taxes are added to the effective federal rate of 12.6%, the total effective tax rate—federal and state combined—on US corporations amounted to about 17%--i.e. less than half the official nominal rate of 35%.

The declining effective tax rate for corporations translates into corporate tax revenue declining as a share of total government tax revenues.   And as effective taxes on corporations have declined, taxes on working class households' earned income have risen in parallel.

Table 14.4[16]
U.S. CORPORATE TAXES AS SHARE OF TOTAL FEDERAL REVENUES

Year	Revenue Share
1954	32%
1964	21%
1986	12.2%
2009	6.5%
2010	8.8%
2011	7.8%
2012	9.8%
2013	9.0%

Investor Incomes Tax Reduction

Government tax income has not only been reduced as a consequence of corporate effective tax reduction in recent decades, but as a consequence of similar effective tax reduction for wealthy investors as individuals. In the US, the reduction in the former, at both federal and state levels, shows up in the Corporate Income Tax effective rate and share of total government revenues. But the concomitant reduction in wealthy investors' taxation shows up in the Personal Income Tax calculations. Whereas the shift to lower corporate and higher worker payroll tax shares of total government tax income is readily apparent, the data showing a shift in lower taxes for wealthy investors (benefiting from capital gains, dividends, and other investor tax changes) does not show as readily. Along with earned income (wages and salaries), investors' income in the form of capital gains, etc., is also included in the share of Personal Income Taxes of total government tax income. Personal Income Tax revenue as a share of total government revenue has remained steady at around 44%-45% or so. But that is only because taxes on capital incomes for wealthy investors have declined while taxes on earned income for the rest have risen relative to that decline.

Governments have been reducing long term taxes on wealthy investors since the early 1980s, led by the US and the UK initially in the 1980s. Here the focus has been on reducing taxes on investors' capital gains, dividends, and inheritance taxes. Prior to 1980, both capital gains and dividends were taxed at rates higher than earned income. A reversal has occurred along the way, however, and capital gains and dividends are now taxed at much lower rates than earned income. While the top nominal rate of taxation on personal incomes (i.e. the investor class) is officially 39.5%, the wealthiest investors (whose total incomes are virtually all capital incomes) pay a nominal tax rate as low as 15% for capital gains in the US and 20% for dividends income. And that is still not the effective rate they pay. Their many and clever tax lawyers then reduce the 15% and 20% rate still further by taking advantage of the many tax loopholes. Or they arrange ways to move their income offshore to avoid US taxation altogether. Or they shelter their income from taxes in ways that border on fraud, or actually do engage in fraudulent tax avoidance.

The long term, secular decline in taxes on capital incomes of wealthy investors, which began around 1980 as well, accelerated significantly in the early 2000s in the US under the George W. Bush regime. Nominal tax rates on personal income from capital gains and dividends, as well as other taxes on inheritance of wealthy estates, were reduced to historic lows of 15%. Meanwhile taxes on earned income, both nominal and effective, remained unchanged—especially for those earning incomes of less than $100k. When ever-rising payroll taxes, which were indexed to inflation and therefore rose every year since 1986 when indexing was introduced, are thrown in—the result has been, in the US, an 'internal' shift in the Personal Income Tax: wealthy investors paid relatively less as capital income taxes were reduced to 15% or less, while average workers paid 25% and more when payroll tax hikes are included.

The trend of government allowing investors to keep an ever greater share of capital incomes from corporations—the ultimate source of those capital incomes—intensified as a consequence of the cyclical event of the 2008-09 financial crash and recession and the chronic slow economic recovery in the US since 2009. The secular trend since the 1980s of reducing tax income from wealthy investors escalated with George W. Bush's investor tax cuts of 2001-2003, and then accelerated even more rapidly after 2010.

Something similar happens with regard to capital incomes of wealthy investors during a cyclical event like a recession or a financial crash. The collapse of financial asset prices in stock or equity markets, or bond or other markets, allows wealthy investor individuals to record a capital loss and reduce their taxes by the value of the loss. Investor income from capital gains is also relatively easily diverted to offshore tax shelters to avoid taxation when returns in the US are high. Like corporations, wealthy investors (financial capital elite of very and ultra high net worth individuals) electronically move their capital gains around globally to minimize tax burdens.

Addendum: Corporate Cash Piles and Distributions

Over both the long and the short term, the reduction in corporate incomes taxes allows corporations to pass on more of the profits and income of the corporation to shareholders and investors. Due to the reduction of capital gains and dividends taxation, investors are allowed to keep an ever larger share of the income distributed to them by their corporations. Corporate and investor tax cutting trends thus go hand in hand.

As to how much gets distributed from the corporate sector to that sector's shareholders, in the US the distribution has reached historic proportions. As US corporations registered record profits after 2010, they passed through to their wealthy investors and shareholders more than $5 trillion. And that's only for the US, and the very largest 500 US corporations. S&P 500 corporations alone are expected to provide more than $1 trillion in dividends-buybacks in 2015.

Table 14.5
US CORPORATE BUYBACKS AND DIVIDEND PAYOUTS ($BILLIONS)

	US Dividend Payouts[17]	US S&P 500 Stock Buybacks[18]
1990	$236	NA
2000	$576	NA
2004	$809	$197
2007	$1,093	$589
2008	$1,075	$339
2009	$871	$137
2010	$885	$299
2011	$963	$405
2012	$1,146	$398
2013	$1,303	$475
2014	$1,308	$553
2015	NA	$604 (est.)

The US typically represents 80% of global share buybacks, so the global total of buybacks roughly amounts to $725 billion. Share buybacks in Japan and Europe have been rising, as corporations in these two economies in recent years have begun to mimic the US practice. In Japan, share buybacks have roughly doubled since 2012 and dividend payouts have risen even faster, for a combined payout of nearly 15 trillion Yen—i.e. more than $100 billion.[19] While Europe has lagged both the US and Japan in payouts and buybacks, with EU corporations sitting on more than $1 trillion in cash, pressures are building there to raise buybacks as well.[20]

The opposite is true for corporate dividend payouts—i.e. larger in Europe and Japan compared to the US as a share of total, dividends plus stock buybacks.

The historic corporate buybacks and dividend payouts are not the entire story, however. Even after the combined buybacks and dividends, globally corporations are sitting, as of 2015, on trillions more in retained cash. Europe's largest non-financial corporations are estimated to hoard $1.1 trillion in cash and corporate cash hoarding in Japan, after dividends and buybacks, is estimated today at $2.4 trillion, according to a June 2015 report by the Bank of Japan. In the US, Moody's Analytics Research estimates non-financial corporations continue to hoard $1.7 trillion, with another $1.1 trillion in offshore subsidiaries. Excess reserves at US banks are additional. And none of the US estimates include share distributions by shadow banks like hedge funds, private equity firms, and such, or unreported hoarding of cash and liquid assets in tax havens globally by wealthy investors and corporations.

The point is that this record distribution of corporate profits and cash in the form of payouts and buybacks would not have been possible without the unprecedented accumulation of corporate and investor tax cuts that have occurred since 1980 and especially since 2000 and have continued in the aftermath of 2008-09. The global finance capital elite have been getting richer at an accelerating pace because AE governments especially have continued to subsidize their corporations ever more generously—boosting corporate income and transferring corporate debt—to government balance sheets. The consequence is rising government debt and less government income with which to service debt.

Government Income and Failing Economic Recovery

Declining government tax income from corporations and investors has not been the only cause of declining government income.   The other major determinant of the slowing government tax income problem is the lack of a robust economic recovery since 2009 throughout the major AE economies. Lower economic growth means less government income from taxation, not counting tax cuts for corporations and investors.

In Japan and Europe, slower rates of economic growth have meant much lower tax revenue. Japan has slipped in and out of four recessions since 2009, entering its fifth in late 2015. Similarly, Europe has experienced at least two recessions, and arguably a third, while its southern periphery has been locked in deep stagnation. In the US, the stagnation has occurred at a slightly higher level. Economic growth has relapsed no less than four times since 2009, resulting in no growth or negative growth in GDP terms each time. US growth for the past six years has been only half to two-thirds of what has been normal historically in the wake of recessions in the post-1945 period.   The UK has followed a somewhat similar trajectory—not as strong as the US but not as weak as the Eurozone economies within Europe as a group.

The lack of sustained economic recovery from recession contributes to government tax income decline, just as does tax cutting for corporations and investors. Combined, sources of tax income decline contribute more to the growth of government deficits and debt than does government spending on corporate subsidies, outsourcing, for bailouts, and so on—by some estimates approximately 60% more.

Spending and income causes of rising government deficits and debt are most clearly evident in the case of the US. US federal government debt (excluding State & Local government, special agency, and central bank debt), rose by more than $12 trillion between 2000 and 2014, from $5.6 trillion to $17.8 trillion, according to the St. Louis Federal Reserve Bank.[21] Add another $3 trillion for US central bank debt. And another $3 to $4 trillion for various US federal agency debt for Government Sponsored Enterprises (GSEs), as they are called: Fannie Mae, Freddie Mack, and Federal Home Loan Banks for mortgages, loans to agriculture under the Farm Credit agency, and more than $1 trillion in student debt held by the government. That's an increase in total US government debt just short of $20 trillion since 2000. And it doesn't include several trillions more for state and local US government borrowing of municipal bonds and therefore debt.

With rising government debt, and slowing government tax income, the key question is how has the US financed this historic run-up in debt? How are other economies doing the same, especially China and EMEs, both of which have experienced extraordinary debt increases since 2008? And there's Japan as well, with the largest government debt load as percent of GDP in the world, around 240%. And Europe, with historic levels of debt as well and the double problem of interest rates on government bonds in negative territory, with investors having to pay the governments in order to buy their bonds.

In the case of the US, the method by which such government debt escalation has been sustained has been the establishment of the neoliberal policy this writer refers to as the 'twin deficits'. A weak version of the same has been established in the Eurozone as well. How the rest of the global economy—specifically China, EMEs, and Japan—will attempt to sustain their government debt levels has yet to be determined. However, the prognosis is not good for the latter and not long term sustainable either for the US and Europe.

Trend #4: Neoliberalism Solutions to Government Debt: the 'Twin Deficits'

The foregoing trends reveal how government policies function to transfer private sector debt to government balance sheets, both secularly as well as cyclically, as well as how government tax cutting, largely on behalf of corporations and investors, functions to restore income for corporations and investors while reducing income for government.

The inevitable consequence of both debt transfer and income subsidization is rising government debt. This has been the scenario for more than three decades, especially within the AE economies.

How is it then the government can continue to borrow (incur debt) in order to pay for the accumulation of record levels of debt, while simultaneously reducing private sector taxes that adds to deficits and more debt? What enables that process to continue? The means by which this has been enabled since the early 1980s in the US case is what has been sometimes called the 'Twin Deficits'. To use a metaphor, government spending and tax policies may represent the gasoline and oil that enables the vehicle of debt to 'run'. But fuel is nothing without an engine—and the engine of government debt is the 'twin deficits'—a trade deficit and a budget deficit. Without the former—the trade deficit—there can be no budget deficit of any significant dimension for an extended period, such as has occurred for nearly four decades. A global trading currency is also needed to make the debt engine—i.e. the twin deficits— really work.

Emerging from the global capitalist economic crisis of the 1970s— in which the global economy was experiencing declining investment, falling productivity, global oil instability, collapse of the Bretton Woods international monetary system and currency volatility, inflation and unemployment (stagflation), rising union and worker militancy—a new restructuring of key economies (especially the leading economies of the US and UK at the time) was undertaken by AE economic and political elites. This combination of new policies and restructuring is sometimes called 'neoliberalism'.[22]

The twin deficits were an essential element of Neoliberal policies when introduced in the late 1970s-early 1980s, a fact which most critics of Neoliberalism often overlook. Without the twin deficits, many of other Neoliberal policies that have evolved since the 1980s would not have been possible.

The twin deficits arrangement comes in two variants. The first, developed in the 1980s, with the US hegemonic in relation to the global economy at large. The second developed after 1999 after the launching of the Euro currency union, intra-Europe, with the core Eurozone economies hegemonic and the Eurozone's periphery, especially its southern edge, dependent. A third form may arise in Asia, as China challenges the US with its Yuan as a world trading currency and forms a greater Asia free trade zone. But this has not happened yet. The Yuan is not yet a global currency, although in the process of becoming such. A global trading currency is thus necessary for the twin deficits to function. The US has it with the dollar. The Euro, created in 1999, also satisfies the EU's requirement. Within the next five years, so too will China's Yuan.

US Twin Deficits

In the US case, prior to the late 1970s-early 1980s, AE economies competed with the objective of gaining exports at the expense of global competitors. Those economies without trading and reserve currencies like the dollar and the Euro (and to a lesser extent the British pound and Swiss franc) still today follow the export competition path.

In the early 1980s, however, the US economic elites shifted strategies, from maximizing domestic exports at competitors' expense to maximizing US corporations' foreign direct investment (FDI). Neither China nor the Soviet Union were yet included within the global monetary system. The US would also address and resolve its economic crisis and problems of the 1970s not by reinvesting in manufacturing and productive activity within the US to the extent as it had done before, but by encouraging and promoting US corporations to increase investment offshore, and subsequently import products back to the US from a lower cost (and more profitable) base offshore.

In order to facilitate the re-import of US multinational corporations' products produced abroad back to the US, two developments would have to take place. First, a freer flow of money capital would have to occur without governments' interference or controls. Controls on international money flows would have to be reduced and eliminated. Second, restrictions on the re-importation of goods produced abroad back to the US would also have to be reduced. During the 1980s, along with other major trading economies in Europe and Japan the US engineered the elimination of controls on international capital flows. Within a decade, most were eliminated. It also embarked upon reducing restrictions on goods flows. That was to be achieved in stages, in the form of promotion and expansion of free trade treaties. But that would not come until the 1990s and after. In the interim, special trade relations restructuring was undertaken in the 1980s by the US with its major trading partners in Japan and Europe.

With the elimination of controls on international money flows, the way would open to promote US corporate foreign direct investment. As part of its new neoliberal policies, as money flow controls were eliminated the US government simultaneously increased its incentives to US corporations to expand foreign direct investment by providing US multinational corporations generous new tax incentives to invest offshore and more generous export-import bank subsidies as well. By the mid-1980s the third neoliberal trade element was also introduced—the restructuring of trade with Japan and Europe.

Under the new restructured arrangement, the US would purchase more imports from these countries than the US would sell exports to them, thus resulting in a trade deficit. Not a trade surplus or even a trade balance, as was the US trade strategy in the pre-1973 Bretton Woods period. Now the emphasis was on foreign direct investment and expansion of US corporations abroad as the means by which to more effectively compete with Japan and European corporate rivals. But to get the competitor countries to allow more US FDI into their economies, a quid pro quo would permit them to export more to the US in exchange. A US trade deficit was thus necessary to make the new system work.

The second crucial element was also necessary to make the new 'more US FDI for more imports', neoliberal arrangement work. In addition to the US running a trade deficit, Japan, Europe, plus the petro dollar economies of the Middle East, would be required to recycle their dollars obtained from a trade surplus with the US back to the US. That recycling of dollars would take the form of buying US Treasury bonds. The trade deficit would provide the excess dollars to recycle. Their own domestic capitalist elites would get rich from the profits from unimpeded exports to the US market. The US would also open its financial markets to foreign money capital inflows to the US, from which offshore elites could profit as well. US multinational corporations would get to invest (FDI) directly into their economies, and thus also participate in the 'export back to US' from a lower cost production base even more profitable than if they were producing in the US. US corporations would not also no longer have to compete with a higher cost structure, as they did in the 1960s and early 1970s, losing ground to global competitors.   Local economic elites and US multinationals would together both benefit tremendously.

Free trade treaties that would eventually follow would accelerate this arrangement: the US would obtain a lowering of barriers to its FDI into world markets, which was its main free trade objective, along with eliminating US barriers to re-importing US goods to the US. And trading partners would also enjoy the more profitable lowering of US import barriers.

This restructuring was concluded with Japan and Europe in the mid-1980s, with minimal resistance on their part, with the US 'Plaza Accord' agreement with Japan in 1985-6 and the subsequent 'Louvre' agreement that followed almost immediately thereafter with Europe. American consumers would buy cheaper Japanese and European imports, and in turn Japan, Europe and OPEC would recycle the dollars they accumulated from US consumers back to the US. Government treasury bonds and bills were the favorite purchase, but US policy progressively allowed purchase of other private assets in the US by Japan and Europe to rise as well.

The massive flows of US dollars, as money capital (FDI), by US corporations and investors 'out' of the US into those sectors was matched by recycling of dollars accumulated as a result of the rising, chronic trade deficit back to the US. The general recycling of dollars was now enabled by the elimination of controls on money capital flows. The elimination of money capital flows would also serve to accelerate the process of global 'financialization' and the penetration of US banks and shadow banks globally. It would also provide further impetus to domestic banking deregulation in the US and elsewhere.

The US would remain economically hegemonic by means of this system of arrangements, replacing the prior terms and structure of its global economic hegemony represented by the Bretton Woods international monetary system in effect from 1944-1973.

To make the new system work, an agreed new central trading and reserve currency was necessary. That of course was the dollar. Under the old Bretton Woods, the US was required to sell its gold to buyers on demand. It also could not devalue its currency. Now all such limitations were removed under the new 1980s neoliberal system.

Under the new system the Japanese Yen would also become a global trading currency, along with the US dollar, British pound, and later the Euro. Japan would eventually develop the lucrative 'Yen carrying trade', which gave Japanese financial investors their own special 'cut' of global financial speculative profits.

The losers in this game were workers, especially in the US. American workers lost higher paying union jobs, as cheap manufacturing imports to the US devastated employment, entire occupations, and reduced wages. But workers in Japan, Europe and elsewhere also lost, as the cost of US goods imported into their economies rose significantly and reduced their real disposable incomes. US capital moved in larger volume into those countries' economies, while foreign (Japan, Europe, etc.) manufactured goods moved to the US economy. The FDI and money flows (from US) were offset by goods imports and reverse money flows (back to US).

The trade deficits and the recycling of dollars back to the US in turn made it possible for the US government to run chronic and rising budget deficits—i.e. deficits that would translate into escalating national government debt and the $18 trillion plus federal government debt today. The money to fund the deficits would now come from recycled dollars from offshore—from Europe, Japan, OPEC, indeed from almost everywhere else in the global economy. The rest of the world economy would become dependent upon US consumers purchasing their exports; And US consumers would become dependent on debt—their own and the US government's from its borrowing of the recycled dollars.

In time, the trade deficits that recycled dollars to the US and other US policy measures created an ever growing fund of dollar inflows for financing deficits and debt. The flow of money capital back to the US to purchase US government debt grew larger and larger. The growth accelerated especially after China trade was opened and China began recycling hundreds of billions of dollars every year back to the US. The expansion of free trade treaties in the 1990s and consistently after further accelerated the process after 2000. The growing dollar recycling, ultimately a product of US trade deficits and FDI, made possible the escalation of US federal government debt. Because trillions were being recycled it permitted the US to undertake an historic $10 trillion cumulative reduction in government taxes on corporations and investors between 2002-2014, while simultaneously enabling US government spending on wars and military goods and services to rise another $5 trillion as well. For the first time in its history, after 2001 the US did not raise taxes in order to pay for wars, as it spent at minimum that amount in the wars in the middle east after 2001. For the first time it accelerated war spending as it cut taxes—and it did so, moreover, as it developed even new forms of multi-billion dollar mega-subsidies to corporations at the same time and spent trillions more in financial and non-financial corporate bailouts after 2008.[23]

The twin deficits—a trade deficit necessary to ultimately finance and enable a US government budget deficit of historic dimensions—were perhaps the most important neoliberal policy arrangement to come out of the 1980s. It was the fundamental core and means by which the US restored its global economic and financial hegemony after the crises of the 1970s that challenged that hegemony. But the policy also meant an historic escalation of US national and gross general government debt—from less than $2 trillion in 1980 to $5.6 trillion in 2001 to more than $26 trillion by 2015.

The Eurozone's Failed 'Twin Deficits' Strategy

The Eurozone experiment with twin deficits is a variation on a theme represented by the US twin deficits, an attempt to replicate after 1999 within the Eurozone's 18 countries and economies what the US had achieved in the 1980s and expanded successfully thereafter. Like the US experiment, it required a trading and reserve currency. That was enabled by the creation of the Euro currency and Euro currency union after 1999. The Eurozone twin deficits differs in that it operates only within the smaller global sector of the Eurozone economies where the Euro is the trading currency. Thus, only 18 of the European Union (customs free trade zone) 28 economies are part of the Eurozone, so the twin deficits apply only to that subset of the European AE sector.

The twin deficits arrangement within the Eurozone also operates via an exports surplus and a recycling of Euros arrangement. But it operates backwards, inversely, and represents an intractable imbalance. It therefore has failed and continues to fail. And as it fails, it raises continually the idea that the Euro currency system itself may not prove stable and thus durable over the longer run.

With the introduction of the Euro in 1999 and its implementation soon after, the northern European manufacturing centers, especially Germany, enjoyed a special advantage vis a vis global competitors elsewhere (Europe, US) in exporting manufactured goods to the Eurozone periphery economies, especially the southern periphery of Portugal, Spain, Greece, and even Italy. But the periphery economies, which could not export much in the way of goods and services back to Germany and the north for competitive reasons, did not have sufficient Euro capital with which to purchase the German-Northern Europe goods. So the more powerful northern Europe bankers loaned them the Euros to purchase the goods. Periphery economies were also loaned funds to build up their national infrastructures, as northern Europe corporations relocated and invested in the periphery as well. More Euro money capital flowed to periphery banks, periphery governments, and a rising middle class with incomes with which to buy more northern European goods and services. Both private corporate, household, and government debt built up within the Eurozone periphery.

German and northern European manufacturers and bankers benefited greatly by the credit and debt extended to the periphery. The money they loaned came back to capitalists and even their workers in part as purchases for their internal exports by the periphery. Northern bankers earned interest on loans extended to periphery banks and governments. Periphery businesses and middle classes often sent their share of the production and income boom in their economies back to northern-German banks for safety and interest. The new periphery businessmen and middle classes gamed the corrupt political systems in the periphery to avoid paying taxes. The periphery elites did quite well. The northern Europe capitalists and bankers did even better. The credit they extended to the periphery came back several fold. In the meantime, debt built up in periphery governments, central banks, banks, private periphery businesses and households. Then came the 2008-09 global recession.

By 2010 debt payments after seven years of buildup could not be covered. By 2010 the weakest of the periphery economies—where the housing and financial speculation was the most intense—were in especially deep trouble. Because they were unable to make payments, the northern bankers and politicians extended them yet more credit, to make payments on the prior credit and debt. In exchange, the periphery economies were required to introduce severe fiscal austerity programs in order to ensure tax surpluses with which to make payments in the future on the old and new debt. But austerity reduced economic output and made it even more difficult to obtain taxes to make the payments. Without a true central bank in the Eurozone, private bank bailouts in the periphery were not possible. Northern governments loaned money to periphery governments in the hope some of the credit would trickle down to bail out the periphery private banking system. But that didn't happen. Periphery governments became even more indebted.

Then the second European recession hit in 2011-12. More periphery government bailouts were needed. This time, another round of bailouts by the northern bankers and governments in effect paid off the private investors who had also extended credit to the periphery governments and banks. The private shadow bankers exited, and northern governments were left to collect the massive debt burden that had accumulated in the 2000-07 boom, the bust of 2008-09, and the austerity, which induced further contraction and the second Europe recession of 2011-12.

The problem with the Euro 'twin deficits' problem is that it is a caricature of the US global twin deficits. There was no central mechanism established for enabling the return flow of a share of profits from sale of goods flows, a role that might have been played by the European Central Bank. Germany and the north were the origins of both the money recycling and the exports surplus. If the Eurozone periphery economies were to run a trade deficit with Germany and the north, then a corresponding arrangement was necessary for Germany *et. al.* to recycle the gains from its trade surplus back to the south. What was created, however, was more loans and credit extended to the south, to be recycled back to the north. Germany and the north were, in effect, enjoying their trade exports surplus and demanding a recycling of euros from the south that they themselves, Germany and the north, had to provide as loans to the south. It was an arrangement that reflected more a classical colonial exploitation scheme, albeit within a modern economic zone like Europe. A special form of economic colonialism, in other words.

Debt, Income and Government Fragility

If rising debt and slowing (tax) income are determinants of fragility, then the global trend is growing government balance sheet fragility. The problem, however, is not so much a rise in national government debt per se. The problem is more a matter of gross general government debt driven by one of its key elements—local government debt. It is also a problem of how national government debt results in policies that exacerbate private sector debt, both business and households.

National governments have in the final analysis solutions available with which to address excessive debt accumulation. The solutions are not unlimited, but they do provide national governments the ability to tolerate excessive debt levels that local governments cannot. For one thing, national governments can borrow more easily to refinance existing debt in a crisis than can state and local governments. The latter can, and often do, default and even go bankrupt. National governments seldom default, although the economically weaker may on occasion. However, no major government or economy globally has done so. National governments can deal with excessive debt and/or declining income to service that debt by simply 'creating their own income' in the form of printing money. Local governments are more like corporations, and cannot do so. Terms and conditions of debt financing and repayments—i.e. the third key variable of fragility—are generally also more stringent with regard to local government debt. National governments can also generate income more easily in other forms. Their tax systems are generally more robust compared to local governments and they therefore may be able to raise new taxes to generate income in emergencies with which to pay down debt. They can also, as has been shown, create arrangements to make refinancing almost automatic, like the twin deficits to encourage buyers of their bonds. National governments may consequently grow more fragile as debt continues to grow and income growth slows without becoming correspondingly more financially unstable.

In contrast, state, provincial, and local governments are limited more in ways to generate new income in emergencies. They must either raise tax income or borrow more in private bond markets—in effect adding debt in order to pay for debt. However, raising new forms of taxes and fees may prove politically difficult under crisis conditions, and the credit markets may even deny access to state and local governments when seeking to refinance. Local governments must thereafter rely on 'bailouts' from the national government in such cases.

The data show that the two areas of general government debt that have been contributing the most to that debt have been debt of local governments and central bank debt.

Chapter six described in detail how China's total debt escalation, both government and private, is significantly comprised of local government debt. Of China's more than $20 trillion additional total debt, government and private, since 2007, one half is associated with real estate property, where local governments have been deeply involved. In the US, a number of US states, and more numerous local governments, are still financially fragile today, eight years after the 2008 crash. Another crisis will produce far more serious local government financial defaults.

Central bank debt may prove a more serious problem in another financial crisis as well, notwithstanding the ability of central banks to simply create money income by printing it. The problem with central bank balance sheet debt (transferred from the private sector) is its impact on policy tools for addressing another crisis. It is clear even today that ZIRP policies have driven interest rates to zero and even negative levels and it does not appear after eight years that key central banks, like the US Federal Reserve, or the European Central bank or banks of Japan and England, can raise those rates once again. And if they cannot, then interest rate policy is an ineffective monetary tool for the next crisis. All that remains is quantitative easing—the effects of which on the real economy may have fallen so low that even it may prove almost totally ineffective in stimulating a real economy mired in another serious recession. In bailing out the private banking system in the wake of 2008-09, the central banks may have neutralized their ability to do so again in a subsequent crisis and recession.

Yet another, third indirect way that national government debt escalation poses an important dilemma is the feedback effects excessive national government debt escalation can have on business financial and household debt—and therefore on financial and consumption fragility.

While national government debt is not a source of instability in itself—i.e. national governments seldom default and thereby set off a chain effect of financial instability—national debt tends to exacerbate financial fragility and household consumption fragility. Its contribution to systemic fragility is therefore more than the sum of its own debt accumulation and fragility.

This occurs in several ways: when central banks and national governments bail out banks and non-financial corporations from a financial crash and recession, they accelerate the injection of liquidity into the banking system and economy. This offsets the banking system losses. Those losses are in effect transferred to central bank and government balance sheets. In net terms, debt is not eliminated, only transferred to government. The liquidity injected then fuels further debt leveraged financial investing and minimal real investment. Financial asset prices once again surge and debt accumulation returns to the private sector. The debt transfer to government thus leads to more private debt accumulation. Total debt—government and financial—rises further. This time with government debt higher and financial debt returning to prior levels or higher.

Government debt accumulation has another fragility-inducing effect. This time associated with household consumption fragility. Because government debt rises as spending on bailouts occurs, so too do government deficits. To slow the rate of increase of deficits, government reduces spending elsewhere. The collapse of the real economy also produces less government revenues, leading to still further government spending reduction. The rising deficits from both these sources results in fiscal austerity policies as governments attempt to slow the rise of deficits and need for more debt financing. If austerity is not the initial response—as was the case in the US and UK in 2008-09—it soon becomes so. In Europe and Japan the response was to move directly to austerity; in the US and UK, to introduce token government spending and tax cuts (i.e. anti-austerity) but soon to shift to austerity as well. Austerity targets households, rather than businesses. Its effect is to reduce household incomes, which contributes to rising household consumption fragility. A secondary effect is for households to then add more debt to offset the income loss. That leads to yet more household consumption fragility.

In this manner, government debt transfer and income subsidization of banks and non-bank businesses leads to government shifting some of the debt and income loss it experiences in the process, to the household sector and consumption. Thus government not only stimulates more debt longer term to the financial sector, but shifts debt short term as well to households. Rising debt for financial corporations, and rising debt and declining incomes for households, leads to more financial and consumption fragility. Together, with rising national government debt, all three sectors add to total systemic debt increase and systemic fragility.[24]

The preceding chapters 7 through 15 considered how real variables— like investment, debt, income, structural changes in financial and labor markets, etc.—and government policy variables together interact to add to the fundamental forces responsible for the three forms of fragility and the aggregate of systemic fragility in turn. What the analyses suggest is that the ways in which debt, income, and other determinants related to both, mutually interact to create financial instability is not well understood by mainstream and other economic schools of thought in the 21st century. Mainstream economics tends to view these variables more independently, rather than in terms of their mutual determinations—which are expressed in the concept of systemic fragility. Nor do the various schools of thought understand well how fragility and financial instability are inter-related. The following chapters therefore address why this is so, and what are the gaps of understanding in contemporary economic theory responsible for this lack of understanding. For without a better theoretical understanding, no amount of empirical narrative or description can explain the current state of the global economy and where it might be headed.

Endnotes

1   Chapter 19 provides a more developed theory of 'fragility', including determinants in addition to income and debt.

2   An interesting dilemma is how to categorize debt of state owned enterprises (SOE). Is such debt a form of corporate, private debt? Or should it be considered government debt? In this book, it is considered the former.

3   See the definitions of 'general government' in Tables 14.1 and 14.2 that follow, which are based on IMF definitions and conventions.

4   For example, in the US, quasi-government institutions like Fannie Mae, Freddie Mac, and others hold mortgage debt from private financial institutions that originate mortgages and then sell it to Fannie and Freddie. One might also include loan guarantees by the US government to businesses, ongoing subsidies to business, business loans from the government, etc.

5   Definitions of what constitutes 'General' government, Gross Government Debt, and 'Debt as Percent of GDP' are the typical definitions, as used by Eurostat, the Europe Union statistical agency. Per Eurostat, 'General' government refers to central governments, state, regional and local governments, as well as special agencies and funds, such as 'social security' funds that exist outside the preceding forms of government in the UK, Norway, and elsewhere. Governments are defined as "non-market producers financed by taxes, compulsory payments by private sector to the sector that principally redistributes national income and wealth". 'Gross Government Debt' means "all liabilities requiring payment of principal and interest, including debt securities, loans, insurances, Pensions and other accounts payable".

6   Source: *IMF World Outlook Database*, April 2015

7   Source: *IMF World Outlook Database*, April 2015, measured in trillions of national currencies. Data for China estimated based on $1 = 6 Yuan rounded.

8   Source: *IMF World Outlook Database*, April 2015, measured in trillions of national currencies.

9   In the US, approximately half of the US federal government's deficits and $18 trillion plus federal debt is money borrowed from private investors and corporations worldwide; and another third is money borrowed from the surpluses created annually by the Social Security Retirement System and government worker pensions.

10   A counter argument is that the government enterprises and services were losing money in the first place, and thus contributing to deficits and debt. But this argument ignores the important fact that the prices charged for the products or services by government were often subsidized for the public—i.e. not set at market prices to generate a profit but artificially low, sometimes below cost of production, in order to prove to the public a lowest possible cost good or service.

11   One of the more visible private firms assuming US military operations once performed by US military personnel is the notorious and multiply rebranded

'Blackwater' corporation used by the US military in the middle east and elsewhere globally.

12   Approximately $125 billion of TARP was authorized for this group. The auto industry bailout, AIG bailout, and additional funds allocated for GE's credit arm and other miscellaneous institutions accounted for about $450 billion of the $750 billion. The rest was never spent and, after wrangling between Congress and the Obama administration whether to use the remaining funds to bail out individual homeowners (a decision that was called for by the legislation authorizing TARP but was rejected by Congressional Republicans who would not support the spending of the remaining funds on homeowners, as the legislation originally intended). The remaining funds were eventually returned to the US Treasury. TARP was thus never used to bail out the banks. That was done by the US central bank, the Federal Reserve and its policies of ZIRP and QE. Congress provided support by agreeing to suspend the requirement that banks report their true losses, called 'mark to market accounting'. The central bank conducted phony bank 'stress tests' to convince stock buyers the banks were now recovered, and their stocks were a good buy. Suspension of market to market accounting assisted the misrepresentation that banks were recovered by 2009.

13   The excuse given for central banks not assisting households is that it is not their legal mission to do so. That mission is limited to financial institutions, the argument goes. But this argument is specious, since assistance could easily be provided by central banks to bailing out pension funds, a form of shadow bank, to protect and restore the loss of households' asset wealth in pension funds; or assistance by central banks to purchase household mortgages for homes in negative equity, to allow households to refinance. The latter is really no different than central banks buying bad mortgage bond assets from wealthy investors.

14   A typical example was the 'corporate inversions' initiatives of tech and pharmaceutical companies in 2013-14.

15   US Government Accounting Office, 'Corporate Income Tax: Effective Tax Rates Can Differ Significantly from the Statutory Rate', May 2013.

16   Historical Tables, US Budget, Fiscal Year 2014 and prior years, Tables s.1.a.

17   For all US corporations, *Financial Accounts of the United States*, Federal Reserve Board, Z.1 Historical Tables, Table S.1.a, March 12, 2015.

18   For largest Standard & Poor's 500 Corporations only. Dividend payouts for all corporations per 'Flow of Funds' tables of Federal Reserve Table S.1.a.

19   Kosaku Narioka, "In Japan, More Doors Crack Open to Activists', *Wall St. Journal,* January 20, 2015, p. B1. Data from Bank of Japan and Nomura Securities.

20   Ralph Atkins, "A US-Style Trend for Buybacks is Starting to Make Sense for Europe", *Financial Times*, May 29, 2015, p. 20.

21   *Historical Tables of the Budget of the United States*, St. Louis Federal Reserve Bank, FRASER database, Table 7.1, Federal Debt at Year End. See budget revenues and outlays, and income sources, as corroboration of the preceding of cyclical-secular spending and income contributions to federal US deficits and debt.

22   The preceding global capitalist restructuring occurred at the end of the Second World War and was reflected in a number of new institutions and inter-capitalist power relationships based on the Bretton Woods international monetary system. Before that, a failed attempt to fully restructure occurred in the wake of World War I. While the US succeeded in its own version at the time, Europe

and Japan failed to do so, leading to partial military approaches to restructuring in Germany, Japan, and elsewhere. Today, post-2008, global capitalism is attempting to implement another restructuring but thus far has succeeded in doing so only in part and incompletely. Continuing economic and financial instability is the continuing consequence.

23 One example of the latter mega-subsidy programs was the 2005 introduction of the Medicare Prescription Drug Plan (Part D) for US seniors. Costing $50 billion a year and rising, not one tax was levied to cover the cost. Portrayed as a benefit to retirees, which in part it was, it was more so a massive subsidy to the pharmaceutical corporations who were permitted by the law to raise whatever prices they wanted on drugs with governments in the US prevented by law from challenging or even negotiating discounts. A similar mass subsidy would following in 2010 with the introduction of the 'Affordable Care Act' (aka Obamacare) which is in essence a $1 trillion dollar decade subsidy to health insurance companies, providing some benefits to users but eventually allowing similar unchecked price gouging by the companies.

24 Second and third derivative feedback effects—i.e. from households to government debt and households to non-financial business income and debt thereafter occur in the longer run as well.

16

HYBRID KEYNESIANS & RETRO-CLASSICALISTS

The conceptual apparatus of mainstream economics has failed. That is true of both its major wings, which here are called 'Hybrid Keynesianism' and 'Retro-Classicalism'.[1] Neither adequately explains the new anomalies created by the financialization and globalization of the world economy and the greater role financial variables play in the 21st century in destabilizing that global economy. Neither wing understands, except at a superficial level, how financial asset investment and real asset investment mutually determine each other, producing a condition of systemic fragility and a growing tendency toward financial instability events that bring down the real, non-financial economy in the wake of financial crises, and thereafter operate as a major drag on real economic recovery. The failure of mainstream economics is rooted in its inability to explain how debt and income mutually determine each other—more specifically, in its inability to adequately explain how financial cycles and real cycles interact and lead to more frequent and serious financial crises and economic contractions, and thereafter to a historically slower than normal economic recovery.

In terms of recent historical events, mainstream economists have failed to adequately explain how the financial-banking crash of 2008-09 occurred, how that crash produced an exceptionally severe real contraction that was qualitatively and quantitatively different from preceding 'normal' recessions, how the recovery from that 2008-09 contraction has been well below historical averages, or how the global system is drifting once again toward a subsequent—perhaps even more severe—financial and economic crisis that most probably will occur within the next two to five years.

Global capitalism is not static. It is constantly changing. Periodically throughout history the agents of capitalism—i.e. their elite decision makers, the leaders of their political parties, and representatives in their governments and state institutions—recognize the need to undertake a major restructuring of their institutions and mutual relationships in order to address the periodic crises that inevitably occur. Major wars, depressions, financial crises, technology revolutions, and the rapid expansion of capitalism itself precipitate the periodic major restructurings. Mainstream economic analysis always lags behind these restructurings and changes. Its major concepts, propositions, theories and models do not change as quickly or in parallel in order to explain the new conditions.

Ideas are conservative, especially those that are heavily laden with justifications of the old order prior to restructuring. The ideas of the prior order focus primarily on explaining conditions and structures which precede the appearance and emergence of the new anomalies. The old conceptual framework and analyses become less able to explain the new conditions as these change over time. They therefore become less predictive. As the decline in their explanatory relevance and predictive inefficiency grows, new ideological arguments and analyses are increasingly overlaid on the old analyses. An ideological edifice of misrepresentations thus builds over time, rendering the old views even more ineffective in explaining the changed reality. The old conceptual apparatus thus becomes even less adequate in explaining the new conditions. A fundamental conceptual breakthrough becomes necessary.

Within the two wings of mainstream economics, many attempt to update and make the old approaches more relevant. However, insofar as they are fundamentally continuing to adhere to, and unable to break thoroughly from the old conceptual framework, their efforts appear, then quickly dissipate and disappear, like cheap fireworks spinning off into the night sky. What remains is a kind of eclectic empiricism with theories that are unable to explain the new conditions and models with little predictive power.

Conceptual Limits of Classical Economics

The roots of contemporary mainstream economics' failure to understand financial variables, financial investment, and the financial instability today go back to classical economics of the 18th and 19th century. Mainstream economics has yet to fully break with the limited conceptual framework established by classical economics; even though over the past century it has attempted to do so, it has succeeded only in part.

Long Run Growth Focus

Classical economic analysis, from the mid-18th to mid-19th century, was preoccupied with long run economic growth—i.e. with real variables like capital accumulation, productive labor, productivity, and the contribution of land and natural resources to growth. Capital accumulation was the key to growth. How capital was accumulated in the long term was the focus. The role of productivity (viewed as division of labor) was central, as was the creativity of productive workers who made things. Those who did not make things did not contribute to economic growth. Urbanization and trade broadened the market for goods and thus more production.   Production generated profits that financed more investment. It was considered important that wages, rents, and bank interest did not absorb the additional profits and that capitalists themselves remained 'parsimonious'—i.e. did not consume their profits but ploughed them back into real investment. Competition among capitalists also played a role, stimulating cost cutting and the introduction of new technology that reduced costs and raised labor productivity.

At the top of the classical economics agenda, therefore, was the quest to understand what determined real investment and productivity change, what distinguished productive labor from non-productive labor, and what was the role in the process played by land and resources since much of growth was still agriculture related and agricultural production was viewed as essential for expanding industrial production.

Income as 'Zero Sum' Game

In this long run growth scenario, profits were thus the most important form of income. Other forms—wages, rents, interest—were derivative and considered deductions from profit. Wage income was required to keep labor producing. Rents were a necessary evil, paid to parasitical landowners who produced nothing.   Interest was also regarded as a residual from profits, and only as necessary when capitalists needed to borrow from banks to finance investment when their retained profits were insufficient to finance the next round of investment. In classical economics income analysis was therefore weak. Income from profits was key to growth. Its reduction resulted in less growth or disruptions to growth. Income in other forms played a less essential role in long run economic growth determination, and almost none in explaining short run disruptions to growth that today would be described as recessions, great recessions, or depressions. Disruptions would always self-correct and lead back to long run growth, so why bother trying to understand them or correct them?[2] The focus was on long run growth determinants, on how to create more surplus product output, and thus in turn more profits to finance more real investment.

Good Debt vs. Bad Debt

In this long run growth scenario debt was viewed positively, so long as bank credit (lending) was used to finance real investment. This was good debt, which helped expand investment when internal profits to finance investment was lacking. Debt that financed non-productive investment was not viewed as positive. It was a diversion from what otherwise might have been bank lending to real investment. Credit and debt thus were represented as the borrowing of some other capitalists' excess profits that weren't being immediately used to finance investment, but were instead deposited as savings in banks for purposes of investment by others. There was no concern that excess credit and debt might lead to just the opposite—a deep and extended contraction of investment down the road. Private business investment was thus viewed positively, so long as it was issued by banks to industrial capitalists who needed loans beyond their available retained profits in order to finance real investment.

Consumer debt was not an issue. Consumer household debt had not yet been 'invented' as a variable for analysis. No bank would lend money to working class households where wages could hardly provide for family essentials, let alone wage income left to pay interest on a debt. Working classes, moreover, had no collateral with which to secure loans. Governments incurred debt, but mostly only in wartime. Raising debt for other government purposes was undesirable.

Financing Real Investment & the Savings=Investment Identity

There was little attention given in classical economics to investing in financial assets or securities. That was considered non-productive investment. Investing in financial securities added nothing to economic growth. Insofar as investment was always real and financed from profits, or from bank borrowing, how financial assets investing interacted with real investment was not an issue or a concern.

What the industrial capitalist did not re-invest from profits or spend on himself in the form of consumption, he 'saved' by depositing in the bank.[3] That savings was the pool for future borrowing-lending by other capitalists. Thus investment financed directly from profits plus investment financed indirectly from profits as savings were the two means by which investment was financed. Other forms of financing investment by selling stock or issuing bonds or other means were not matters for economic analysis. The area of finance now called 'capital markets' simply did not exist or was as yet in infancy.

In this view banks were receptacles or conduits for the unspent profits (e.g. savings) of non-bank capitalists. What industrial capitalists did not spend on current production, or reinvest in capital for future production, they either spent on themselves as a kind of capitalist consumption, or else 'saved' and deposited in banks. Thus profits determined savings which determined future investment. A kind of identity between savings and investment was assumed. And since it was further assumed that all savings were loaned out by banks there was no 'hoarding' of savings by banks. Banks were never reluctant to lend—in the long run. Of course, they often were in the short run, but the short run was not of major theoretical concern.

Thus for classical economics, profits alone determined investment, directly from internal profits and/or indirectly from profits 'saved' in the banks that subsequently re-loaned the savings out for investment by other industrial capitalists. From this flowed the identity in classical economics that profits leads to savings that equals investment. The view that savings equals investment, is still widely held by many mainstream economists. But this view is, at best, only partially accurate. Profits are not the sole, or even primary, source for financing investment; savings does not necessarily lead to investment; nor is the causal relationship from savings to investment. In fact, one might convincingly argue, as others have done, that it is investment that determines savings, not vice versa.

Money, Banking and Credit

Classical economics was similarly weak on understanding the role of money and banking in growth or in causing periodic severe disruptions to that growth. Banking theory was poorly developed.[4] The classical quantity theory of money was especially crude and undeveloped. Classical economics especially misunderstood how credit and debt interacted with price to create financial asset bubbles, speculative investing, and financial crises that led to periodic disruptions to long run economic growth. Preoccupied with how long run factors—land, labor, capital—determined long run economic growth, classical economics did not focus much on the short run and therefore on business cycles and real investment.

Even less so did classical economics address financial cycles or causes of banking crashes. Explanations of banking crises were minimalist. After all, they were short run and tended to be ignored. Failure to address short run cycles was due to several causes. First, data for short run analysis, real or financial, just didn't exist at the time, and would not become available until well into the 20th century. Short run contractions—recessions and depressions—did occur and classical economists like Smith and others were aware of them. But given the insufficient data, and the absence of methods of quantitative analysis associated with data, business cycle analysis was just not as high on the agenda as understanding what made capitalist economies grow.

Money, and the institutions that provided a good deal of it (banks), were allotted a secondary role in the overall process of growth. Money enabled capital accumulation and growth, but only if its amount (i.e. money supply) was provided in quantities in proportion to that growth. It was a 'goldilocks' theory of money: there was a quantity of money (supply) that was not too much and not too little, but was 'just right' to enable economic growth. Growth was determined by real factors (land, labor , capital) of production. Money per se was 'neutral' in terms of creating economic growth and therefore in terms of disrupting that growth. It could not cause real economic growth even though it was necessary to enable it. If too much money was made available, then the excess would only lead to inflation; if too little, to deflation. There was thus an ideal supply of money at any one given time that would enable real growth but not lead to inflation or deflation.

In this limited view of money, the possibility that credit may assume forms other than money was not even considered. Money may be used to provide credit (and thus a debt to the borrower). But the idea that credit might originate somehow without money was an unknown notion.

Money assumed the form of precious metals—i.e. was a commodity itself, mined with its own cost of production. From the mid-18th century onward, money also increasingly assumed the form of currency or paper, or what was called 'fiat' money, or sometimes 'bills of credit'. This form of money was not mined, was not a commodity, but was created by the banking system itself. Unlike commodity money, it had virtually no cost of production. However, this important distinction was not explored for its possible consequences for stability, when paper-fiat money increasing displaced commodity money in the 19th and 20th centuries. While classical economics recognized that somehow banking crises occurred with the over-issuance of paper money, it was nonetheless weak on understanding the differences between these two forms of money and how they interacted. Debates occurred as to how much paper currency (bills of credit) should be issued in relation to gold money. Was the proper ratio 1 to 1, or something higher, and how high? But apart from that, which was used as money made little difference for the economy.

Classical economics was also notoriously weak on understanding money beyond just a stock or supply. Moreover, it believed that that stock, or supply, of money determined interest rates, whereas the demand for money, also a determinant of interest rates in fact, was considered irrelevant because it was assumed to be a constant variable. Not least, investment was always considered 'real investment'; that is, investment in buildings, machinery, tools and the like, i.e. in producer goods in contemporary terminology, or in real goods produced by those producer goods.

Banks loaned out money for real investment purposes based on the rate of interest. But there was no analysis of interest rates as determined by money demand as well as money supply. Nor any analysis of what is called 'money velocity', which is how fast that money supply 'turns over' in a given period. It was just money supply that was important for interest rate determination and therefore for investment.

From this crude classical view of money and credit flowed a number of important errors, which still to this day persist in much of mainstream economics. First, interest rates are only one of many determinants of investment. Second, interest rates themselves are a function of money demand and money velocity, not just money supply. Third, interest rates are only a cost of investment and, like other 'costs' of investment—like wages, raw materials, etc.—do not alone determine investment. In fact, costs of production, whether in the form of interest rates or other, may at times prove irrelevant to the decision to invest. The supply of money or interest rates are often negated by volatile subjective psychological expectations by investors as to where interest rates may be headed (up or down); how fast they have already or will have risen; or by expectations of the profitability of the investment project in question in comparison to other investment opportunities— including financial asset as well as real asset investments.

Investment is not just about interest rates, interest rates are not just about money supply, expectations are always relative, and profits are not the only source of finance for real investment. However, classical economics generally misunderstood much of the above.

When classical economics discussed money it was either commodity money (gold etc.) or currency-fiat money issued by banks. Money could be used for credit, but credit was inconceivable without money. There was no such thing as the 21st century notion of 'inside credit' that was independent of traditional money forms.

Classical economics did acknowledge that banks might over-lend, creating inflation, as too much money chased too few goods. Adam Smith and his contemporaries recognized that banks may be pressured by customers, become undisciplined, and lend too much to merchants and industrial capitalist customers who were always pressing to use bank money (debt) instead of their own to finance investment—especially after extended periods of growth and good times. Bankers were thus the unfortunate, albeit undisciplined, victims from time to time of their customers. There is no notion of bankers as the perpetrators and cause of the over-lending. Finally, bank lending and debt was discussed in the context of lending for real asset investment, never lending for financial assets or for speculation in financial securities. Nor was there any notion that banks might hoard money and credit. How could this occur, if it was assumed they will lend all that is 'saved'?

Steady State, Stationary State & Perpetual Equilibrium

Classical economics did discuss problems of stagnating economic growth, where growth slowed to a virtual standstill. But this was not in the context of short run crises or business cycles. It was, again, in the context of long run economic growth and its determinants. The causes for such a slowdown, or 'breakdown' of growth, it was believed, must lie in what caused real investment or capital accumulation to slow. Thus growth of the capital stock, and/or slowing of the productivity growth associated with that capital stock, must therefore lie at the root of the slowing of the long run growth rate. What was it that disrupted investment and capital accumulation? Was it profits growth slowing (since profits were the source of real investment and accumulation)? Was it the slowing of productivity growth (as land become less fertile and agricultural productivity spilled over to industrial)? Or other causes that otherwise interfered with the long run growth process? But these questions were largely ignored by classical economics, or else briefly or inadequately addressed.[5]

Another wing of classical economics argued short run contractions or stagnation were irrelevant, since in the long run the economy would naturally self-correct and return to an equilibrium.

Price System as Re-Stabilization Mechanism

How the overall economy 'self-corrects' and thereby restores itself to a condition of equilibrium is through the movement of prices, according to classical economics. Prices for products as well as for factors (land, labor, capital) adjust to market forces, move up and/or down, and in the process (once again over the long run) return to a balance where aggregate supply and demand are equal. The aggregate re-balancing, i.e. return to equilibrium, is the outcome of countless 'micro-level' product and factor decisions and movements. The actual perfect balance point, the perfect equilibrium, may never be attained in fact. But the price equilibrating process continually moves it toward that condition. The price system is the equilibrating mechanism that restores the economy to perfect stability, called equilibrium. But equilibrium is just a logical assumption of some fictional point of stasis or stability. It is never observable. One might just as convincingly define equilibrium not as some actual point of stability that is attainable, but rather as just some kind of moving average of a series of disruptions and disequilibrium conditions.

An important point concerning the role of the price system as the mechanism by which the economy self-corrects is that the price here functions as 'one price system fits all'. That is, all prices move the same: supply and demand market forces move prices toward equilibrium, which in turn moves the real economy toward the same. What happens at the micro level with supply and demand for individual products is somehow 'rolled up' or 'writ large' to add up to an economy-wide equilibrium state created by the general price level. This scenario qualifies for what is sometimes called the 'post hoc fallacy'. Moreover, it is assumed—in the 'one price system fits all' of classical economics—that prices for goods and services behave that way. So too do prices for factors, like land, labor and capital. Interest rates, which are just the 'price' of money, move the same: supply and demand for money adjust interest rates (the price of money) that in turn adjust investment and capital accumulation that in turn move the economy toward restoring equilibrium. Goods prices behave the same way as factor prices and money prices. One price system fits all.

Absent from this classical perspective is any discussion about financial securities or financial asset prices. Or how financial asset prices might impact goods and/or factor price or money price movements. Nor was it considered that financial securities might not respond to supply and demand market forces the way goods or factor price or interest rates might respond. Or that financial asset prices could drive volatile changes in goods, factors, or money prices under certain conditions.

The prospect that the price system, especially financial asset prices, could function as a fundamental destabilizing mechanism—not as a stabilizing force—was not considered by classical economists. In their world, all prices always functioned to restore equilibrium and system stability.

There was no financial asset price theory or theory of how the different price systems interacted with each other, exacerbating and feeding off each other especially in conditions of economic instability. The price systems operated similarly in response to supply and demand, but they did so within their respective spheres, with little interaction or mutual determination.

A corollary notion in classical economics to the idea of the single price system as a stabilizing mechanism is that prices play a key role in shaking out less efficient and less profitable enterprises, i.e. a positive factor assuring a self-correcting return to equilibrium and stability. However, there is much evidence to the contrary. Price changes in an industry or economy in general may 'shake out', that is destroy, very efficiently operated and profitable enterprises as well as the inefficient and unprofitable.

Another major failure of price as the classicalists understood it was the idea that inflation (price level) is always and everywhere the result of too much money chasing too few goods. Inflation was thus always fundamentally a monetary phenomenon. This misconception flowed from the 'quantity theory of money' view of classical economics, where the supply of money, M, times the velocity of money, V (which was assumed constant in the long run) was equal to all the goods produced, Q, times their price, P. So, MV=PQ. But V, velocity, as a constant drops out, leaving M=PQ. Dividing both sides of this simple equal by Q leaves M = P, in other words, the amount of money in the economy determines the price level and inflation. It was that simple, and that simply incorrect.

Of course, in reality, prices are not always a function of money alone. If that were true, the $20 trillion in money liquidity pumped into the US economy just since 2008 should have produced runaway goods and services inflation, but it didn't. Prices for goods—both for producer and consumer goods—have instead slowed (i.e. disinflated) and trended toward deflation. Nevertheless, as will be discussed below, the Retro Classicalist wing of contemporary mainstream economics still holds to this false notion, originating in classical economics' quantity theory of money's incorrect assumption that increases in price levels (inflation) are always a result of excess money supply.

To summarize briefly with regard to classical economics: its views on income, debt, investment, money, banking and credit, the price system, equilibrium as inherent stability, and bias against the short run together represent a conceptual framework that ignored financial variables and cycles.

A Postscript on Marx's Economics

While Marx attempted, and to some degree succeeded, in breaking from the conceptual limitations of classical economics, it is generally not well understood or appreciated—especially by those of his adherents who argue there is nothing more to be said beyond what was said by Marx himself—how much Marx remained within the classical economic conceptual framework. That framework held back the development of his work during his early and middle period of economic analyses, including that contained in Vol. 1 of his work, *Capital: A Critique of Political Economy*, published in the 1860s. Perhaps because Vol. 1 was focused on critiquing political economists before him, it was difficult for Marx to completely break from the conceptual framework of that which he was critiquing. It was not until Marx's later notes, especially in Vol. 3 of *Capital* that the possibilities and the implications for such a more thorough break begin to appear. But Vol. 3 was just notes, observations, and insights and was not published as a finished work. It remained a work in progress at best, even though interesting reflections on banking and credit, financial speculation and investing, and related themes are discernible in that later work.[6] Chapter 17 that follows will consider and address Marx's later views and what they may suggest for purposes of understanding the role financial cycles may play in disrupting economic growth of the capitalist economy, both short and long run.

The Neoclassical Detour: 1870s to 1920s

Despite massive decade-long depressions in the 1870s, 1880s, and 1890s in the US and Europe, precipitated by bond market and stock market implosions and associated banking crashes that preceded the deep real economic contractions, what was then mainstream economics virtually ignored these events. Instead, it immersed itself in newly found adaptations of crude calculus math (marginal analysis) to provide explanations of how consumers and businesses made decisions under ridiculous assumptions unrelated to the real world. Concepts from classical economics that preceded the mid-century shift were borrowed and adapted to the new tasks: supply and demand, equilibrium, quantity of money theory, savings and interest rates determining investment, banks as neutral intermediate agents, debt as determined by interest rates, profits as the primary income variable and other income forms as derivative, and all the assumptions of a self-correcting economy including the view of the price system as the mechanism for restoration of stability.

What passed for 'macro' analysis at the time was a futile attempt to 'roll up' the analyses of how consumers made purchases and businesses produced goods to an aggregate level. The conceptual apparatus at the micro level—itself overweight with grossly unrealistic assumptions and ideological notions—was considered the foundation for explaining the aggregate economy. Adjustments to equilibrium at the macroeconomics level were simply aggregated replications of processes at the micro level. Macro was buried and disappeared into Micro, to be resurrected thereafter in zombie form. Analysis of the economy had become simply 'micro writ large'.[7]

This was sometimes later referred to as the period of 'neoclassical economics'. But there was little 'neo' about it. It was mostly old classical wine in new bottles, and the bottles leaked. The new economics after 1870s lacked even the empirical observations that were the foundation of Adam Smith's approach. Steady states and stationary states, or recognition of demand side 'gluts', were now shelved away. Productive labor as the core of price was replaced with the idea that price was whatever the market said it was, whatever supply and demand determined it was. Economic analysis was buried under a heap of super-abstract, deductive, first principles reasoning that purported to reflect reality.

By the early 20th century cracks in the edifice began to appear. Some mainstream mavericks began to question the extreme assumptions of then mainstream economics about the quantity theory of money, about interest rates as the prime or even sole determinant of investment, about the preoccupation with long run, about short run as just increments of the long run, and about income as a zero sum game.[8] Growing volatility in the real economy before and after World War I demanded a more serious analysis of the short run, of income, and of investment in a deeper sense. The explosion of banking and finance in the early 20th century also demanded a more accurate analysis of the role of banks (and the new shadow banks) in the periodic instability that was now wracking the global capitalist economic system.

More data availability during and after World War I made possible for the first time some degree of consideration of short run business cycles. Explorations in business cycles and short run contractions began to appear. Banking crises and financial markets, and even crude explorations of how financial cycles interacted with the real economy, were now topics of analysis.[9] A fresh look at monetary theory emerged.[10] Most of the mainstream economics profession remained deeply committed to the old 'static' equilibrium analysis and all the associated misconceptions. They continued to try to explain the growing volatility and the obviously growing importance and role of banking, shadow banking, and financial securities markets in the 1920s within the old conceptual framework—even as it was becoming increasingly obvious that framework was deficient. Their outmoded views continued to hold sway even as the Great Depression of the 1930s set in, first in Britain in the latter half of the 1920s and then virtually everywhere after 1929.

Then the economist J. M. Keynes rolled his economic grenade under their tent, with the publication of his *General Theory of Money, Interest and Employment* which appeared in 1935.[11] But Keynes' *General Theory* (GT) did not blow up neoclassical economics. In fact, it adopted some of it into its own conceptual toolbox, for example, adapting marginal analysis to investment decision making. The GT never totally broke from the conceptual framework it attacked in neoclassical economic analysis. But it did inject new concepts that challenged neoclassical economics fundamentally on a number of fronts. That partial challenge made it possible for the more clever neoclassical adherents to regroup. By the late 1930s they had rejected the most absurd of neoclassical assumptions and had absorbed the more useful of Keynes' new contributions. The process then began by which the less challenging and more useful elements of Keynes' GT were adapted to the remaining elements of neoclassical economics. Out of this merger was born what was to be called the 'neoclassical synthesis' in the post-World War II period. That synthesis of pre-Keynes plus selected useful elements of Keynes evolved thereafter in the post war period into the 1970s to become what is called here 'Hybrid Keynesianism'. The crisis of the 1970s was reflected in a crisis of this then-dominant wing of mainstream economics at the time, leading to a reorganization of neoclassical and classical monetarist views that this chapter calls 'Retro-Classicalists'.

A restructuring of the real economy, US and global, emerged in the 1970s as well, sometimes referred to 'Neoliberalism'. Much of mainstream economics since 1980 has sought to provide ideological cover for the then and ongoing Neoliberal transformation of the global economy, led by changes in the USA and Britain.[12]

It is useful at this point to look at what Keynes introduced that challenged and changed mainstream economics in the 1930s. Keynes' contributions—both what was subsequently absorbed of his original views (and altered at times) by his Hybrid Keynesian epigones, as well as then challenged and rejected by the epigones' Retro Classicalist opponents—is important for understanding why both wings of mainstream economics today (Hybrids and Retros) fail repeatedly to explain and predict the trajectory of the global economy in this century.

The Hybrids are not really Keynesians, but the Retros are intellectual reactionaries attempting to adapt and restore economics to its neoclassical perspective. Nonetheless, their views today remain the mainstream contenders in contemporary economic analysis.

Keynes' Original Contributions

Keynes' contributions are many. Some are explicit; some are only suggested or implied. Some constitute conceptual breaks from the preceding dominant neoclassical perspective; some only break partially with that perspective; and some attempt to critique neoclassical economics while retaining its limited conceptual framework.

Keynes' partial conceptual challenge allowed both subsequent critics and adherents to lay claim to his views. That led in the post-1945 period to fundamentally different approaches borrowing this or that idea or concept, proposition, argument, etc., from Keynes when it was useful and injecting it into their own perspective—a view that was often contradictory to Keynes' own perspective.[13] In short, Keynes' own mixed conceptual ambiguities made Hybrid Keynesianism of the postwar period possible. It also made it possible for Retro Classicalists to attack the Hybrid version of Keynesianism, which was temporarily the dominant of the two wings from 1945-1970s, with convincing effect once the general real economic crisis of the 1970s deepened and undermined the Hybrid wing's influence. If Hybrid Keynesianism is a product of Keynes' views, integrated with the views of Keynes' neoclassical predecessors, then Retro Classicalism is a product of Hybrid Keynesianism integrated with the neoclassical views that Keynes criticized.

Short Run over Long Run

One of the more fundamental notions emphasized by Keynes in his original work was that the short run is more important than the long run, or as he put it in his famous, oft-quoted phrase: 'in the long run we're all dead'. The short run was not simply increments of long run equilibrium. Conversely, the long run was basically a series of adjusting short run disequilibria. To hold this view meant that the economy was not essentially self-correcting, even in the longer run. In an economic world turned 'upside down', as in the case of a depression or severe economic contraction, economic variables did not necessarily behave in the same relationship to each other that they might in a more stable growth situation.

Income is not Zero Sum

Income is not a zero-sum game, as the original classical economists believed. Nor are profits the pre-eminent, most important form of income that drives all other forms of income. Wage incomes are just as critical to economic growth as income from profits. Raising wages does not necessarily reduce profits, per the classicalist' view of the relationship as a 'zero sum' game. Nor does reducing wages necessarily lead to more profits. The two forms of income, profits and wages, mutually determine each other in a much more complex way than classical economics assumed.

In the classical view, profits drive capital accumulation. Wage incomes are a residual consequence—as are rental and interest income. Rising wages (and other costs) might cut into profits somewhat if wages rose over the capital accumulation cycle, which classical economics assumed. But if costs (wages or other) were prevented from rising too much or too fast, it was also assumed that profits restoration and growth would be maintained. Profits therefore largely determined wages and were certainly considered relatively more important for economic growth.

How Keynes differed on this point—and how he rejected the zero sum view—was revealed in his historic debate at the time with one of neoclassical economics' better known apologists, economist Cecil Pigou. According to Pigou, when in a depression, with falling prices, slowing investment, and consequent declining employment the solution to recovery was to reduce wages further. This would lower business costs, release more income for investment and eventually lead to rising employment, consumer incomes, and rising investment and consumption to restore economic recovery. Whatever reduced business costs in the short run would lead to recovery in the longer run. Just 'take the medicine' today to help business investment to ensure recovery for all tomorrow. The reason that recovery did not occur in a depression, according to Pigou, was that institutional constraints prevented business from cutting wages enough. If only wages—in effect the 'price' for labor'—were reduced, the price system would restabilize the economy by leading to more disposable business income and thereafter more investment and consequent employment. The great stabilizer, the price system (in this case factor prices like wages), was prevented from doing its 'invisible hand' magic to restore the economy to equilibrium.[14]

But this 'Pigou Effect' had the opposite of its logically argued prediction, according to Keynes. Reducing wages further in a depression or great recession resulted in a further decline in household income and therefore in consumption. That reduction in consumer spending translated into less demand for business products. Recognizing this lack of demand, business would not expand investment even though it had more income (profits from wage reduction) with which to do so. It would simply hoard the extra income from wage (and other cost) reductions. Thus cost reduction as a means to induce investment fails in a situation of economic contraction.[15]

Meanwhile, because of no recovery of consumption and continued stagnation of investment, real prices in the economy would continue to decline in the depression. That deflation raised the real debt that business had accumulated in the boom period before the depression. Rising real debt meant rising real costs for business and thus a further drag on investment. This logic occurred whether wage cutting assumed the form of laying off more workers to cut wage costs or reducing wages of those who still retained their jobs

In short, cutting wages and thus household income had the exact opposite of intended effects argued by Pigou and neoclassical analysis: it led not to more investment but to less, and drove the economy into a progressively lower level of economic activity. As real debt rose, deflation—i.e. the price system—did not lead to restoration of equilibrium, but instead to a further disequilibrium condition.

The Achilles Heel of Capitalist Economy

Keynes' *General Theory* is fundamentally about investment or, as the classicalists would say, capital accumulation. But unlike the neoclassicals and original classicalists before them, in Keynes' view investment depended on a certain balance in the distribution of income across social classes. As Keynes' himself recognized, a capitalist economy had two economic Achilles heels: an endogenous trend toward income inequality and the inability to ensure full employment. As Keynes remarked in concluding Chapter 24 of his *General Theory* entitled 'On the Social Philosophy Towards Which the General Theory Might Lead', a capitalist economy fails to provide for full employment and generates "an arbitrary and inequitable distribution of wealth and incomes".[16]

Keynes framed this statement in such a way as to suggest that, since income inequality is a fundamental characteristic of capitalist economy, inequality was endogenous to the system. Both inequality and a level of unemployment are necessary for the system to function. More importantly, income inequality tends to grow over time and creates serious imbalances in the system. Capitalism's systemic imbalances tend to create what Keynes calls the 'rentier class' of capitalists who exacerbate the basic inequality trend and general imbalances. The example to which Keynes refers specifically was "the functionless investor", whom he declared needed to be slowly "euthanased".[17] This functionless investor class, discussed at length in Chapter 12, represents one of his more important contributions to understanding the role of finance capital in distorting real investment and economic growth.

Real Asset Investment, Interest Rates, and Money

For Keynes, real investment was essential to economic growth. However, in a major break with his predecessors, investment was not the key target variable in restoring economic growth in conditions of depression or severe economic contraction. Attempts to generate investment directly, through reducing interest rates (and increasing the money supply to lower rates) would fail. That is, lowering the cost of investment by interest rate cuts would not stimulate investment any more than reducing costs of production by lowering wages would induce investment. Nor would, for that matter, cutting business taxes.

Of course all these 'business cost reduction' measures to stimulate investment and growth are mainstays of contemporary mainstream economics policy measures, and have been for decades. Monetary and central bank policies to lower interest rates, budget deficit cutting that reduces social benefits compensation (wage) income, and massive business tax cutting are not Keynesian. They are, however, major Hybrid Keynesian propositions—and are shared by Retro Classicalists in part as well.

Price Mechanisms as De-Stabilizing

Keynes in the *General Theory* period (1935-36) did not believe that interest rates per se determined investment. Nor did he believe, in turn, that increasing the money supply was the sole determinant of interest rates. Nor do prices necessarily stabilize the system. Keynes saw income as the key determinant for stabilization, where classical and neoclassical economics sees the price system as the key to stabilization.

Just as wages represent a price system—i.e. the price of labor—so do interest rates represent a price system—i.e. the price of money capital. However, in Keynes' view, just as driving down labor prices (wages) does not restore equilibrium, so too driving down money prices (interest rates) doesn't lead to a restoration of equilibrium. Given their negative effect on income and consumption, reducing wages (the price of labor) only further destabilizes the economy, while lowering the price of money (interest rates) fails to re-stabilize the economy due to what Keynes calls the 'liquidity trap'. In yet a third indictment of prices as a stabilizing mechanism, as both labor and money prices fall and the economy continues to contract, asset prices continue to deflate with virtually no effect on stimulating asset investment demand. Asset deflation and consequent real investment stagnation leads to reduced production, employment and wage income. That eventually translates into disinflation and deflation in prices of goods. All four elements of price—wages, money, assets and goods—fail to resurrect the economy. Classical and neoclassical assumptions about the stabilizing role of price are therefore in error, in Keynes' view. Income is the key determinant and not just profits income viewed independently or primarily. Price movements are a consequence of failing income and investment, not vice versa, and therefore price per se cannot generate a return to growth and economic recovery. There is no such thing as 'the' price system. How the different price systems interact, feedback and inter-determine each other is important—as is how that interaction is a consequence in the final analysis of changes in income. Income change trumps price change in Keynes' analysis, and that is a major shift in economic thought introduced by Keynes.

Keynes' Break with Classical Monetarism

If interest rates (reduction) did not drive investment, according to Keynes, then what did? And how was classical-neoclassical economic theory wrong with regard to money supply, rates and investment?

It is important to understand that Keynes was considered the pre-eminent monetary theorist in the 1920s. His 1930 two volume tome, *A Treatise on Money*, was the definitive statement on monetary theory at the time.[18] Where Keynes differed fundamentally from his neoclassical predecessors, as well as Hybrids and Retros today, was his emphasis on money demand and money velocity as the determinants of interest rates—not just money supply. Classical economics' adherence to the quantity theory of money ignored money demand and viewed money velocity (how often money was spent or 'turned over' in a given period) as constant and therefore irrelevant, making money supply the determinant of interest rates, or the price of money, as well as of inflation (price) in general. So inflation was viewed as always a product of excess money supply. Keynes rejected that basic argument. In a time of depression or crisis, the demand to hold money—i.e. investors holding on to cash instead of investing it in some non-cash asset—easily offset any increase in money supply. In addition, money velocity would slow significantly. Central banks could pump all the money they wanted into the economy and it would simply be hoarded— by banks, by investors, and by the general public to some extent as well. Interest rates may fall, even to zero, but not stimulate investment. The desire to hold money as a safety precaution, plus the need to sell off assets to hold as cash as asset prices and values were collapsing due to depression, plus the slowing demand for money for purchasing goods—all lead to hoarding and not to investing or consuming. Holding cash, i.e. liquidity, was a better investment than other assets. The latter were falling in price and value, whereas cash was rising in real value as deflation continued. More liquidity—i.e. the central bank injecting money—leads to agents in the economy (banks, corporations, investors, etc.) withdrawing liquidity from circulation and hoarding it. That is the liquidity trap. This was a central conceptual advance by Keynes. It meant that central bank and monetary policy—whether in the form of QE, zero rates, or other monetary measures as has been the case in recent years—was a dead end in terms of resurrecting economic recovery when a severe contraction of the real economy was the case.[19]

Expectations and the Psychology of Investment

If central banks increasing money supply and declining interest rates led to the liquidity trap, what generated investment? In another key conceptual advance, Keynes argued it was 'expectations'—as to the direction of change of future profits, rates of change, of replacement cost of capital goods, and even future interest rates, as well as a host of other 'psychological' and not easily quantified variables. Investment was not tied to a simple idea of reducing interest rates by increasing the supply of money, or reducing wages, or any other cost reduction of investment; it was not just about profits either. Unlike the classicalists' view, it was about risk taking by capitalists and perceptions of the future, near and longer term. That was sometimes summed up by Keynes in the phrase, 'animal spirits', of investors—i.e. another not so easily quantified concept.

For Keynes, investment is the consequence of what he called the 'Marginal Efficiency of Capital' (MEK), which is a combination of variables that interacted with each other and are heavily influenced by expectations. MEK represents a schedule of investment projects ranked by expected profitability, along with the projects' respective cost of replacing the old capital plus the cost of money (interest rate) borrowed to finance the projects. The problem in a deep economic crisis, according to Keynes, is that expectations of profitability collapse faster and deeper than reductions in the price of capital replacement or the price of money in response to the expectations collapse. The costs always lag the (lower) expectations in a severe economic contraction. And if profitability expectations fell faster, investment would not take place regardless of how much the costs of the investing fell. Once again, the price mechanisms (price of the capital replacement and price of money or interest rates) do not restore equilibrium despite their decline. Both expressions of the price mechanism fail, contrary to classical 'invisible hand' theory where supply and demand adjusts in some magical way to move the economy back to equilibrium. And contrary to neoclassical theory where supply and demand always adjust to return to equilibrium, regardless of the form price takes—whether price of money, price of labor, or price of goods.

Yet another way in which price fails to restore equilibrium can be traced to investors and businesses hoarding money—i.e. cash, which is perfectly liquid. Keynes viewed cash as an asset as perfectly substitutable for other forms of assets, both financial and real. If an investment in a real asset (property, buildings, inventories, equipment) was falling in price (deflating) due to the economic crisis, then investors would sell off those assets to avoid further losses in value and hold onto the cash from the sale instead. In deflation, the value of cash rises in real terms, as the value of other assets decline. So the best investment was to hold cash, thus causing the demand for money to rise. The same applies when financial asset prices (stocks, bonds, etc.) deflate. Investors dump financial assets falling in value in order to obtain and hold cash that is rising in value as deflation continues. But if falling asset prices, real or financial, mean more hoarding of cash, and therefore less investing, then falling asset prices (real or financial) are in effect contributing to further real economic contraction. They are not working to restore equilibrium; they actually contribute to further disequilibrium. Again, the price mechanism in such cases further destabilizes the real economy—rather than restoring it to growth.

Keynes' *General Theory* is not about explaining what caused the Great Depression. It is instead an attempt to explain the economics and policies needed to recover from depression. It is also fundamentally a critique of preceding neoclassical economic arguments that, if applied in policy form, not only fail to generate a recovery but actually make recovery even less likely to occur. In a number of ways, neoclassical economic policy is thus worse than doing nothing. Keynes' debate with Pigou brought out that point, as Pigou erroneously argued for reduction of wages as a precondition for recovery.[20]

Keynes' focus on real variables—like real investment, wages, employment, money, etc. in the *General Theory*—contrasts somewhat with his 1930's *Treatise on Money*. The *General Theory* is about the 'recovery second half' of the short run business cycle and how to generate a recovery from the trough of a deep economic contraction; the *Treatise* focuses more on the first half of the business cycle, i.e. prior to a bust and the sharp contraction. Neoclassical economics viewed equilibrium as the natural state of the capitalist economy. Observable disruptions to that equilibrium—i.e. recessions or depressions—were aberrations to equilibrium that were overcome just as naturally by the magic of the price system and the always successful adjustments of supply and demand. Not so for Keynes. Severe disequilibrium instances, like depressions, could continue for some time. Return to equilibrium might occur but at a lower level of production and economic growth where investment, employment and income were less than before. This lower level of equilibrium state could continue for a long time, moreover. [21]

In Keynes' 1930 *Treatise on Money* there is a consideration of financial variables and financial speculation that is absent in the *General Theory*, where the analysis is almost totally focused on real investment and real cycles.[22] The key word here is 'almost', since in Chapter 12 in the *General Theory* Keynes does address the topic of financial cycles—albeit in a limited and general way, representing something of an aberration to the general flow of the entire book that focuses on real variables. To understand Keynes' contributions to financial speculation, financial cycles, and financial instability, it is important to consider some of Keynes' key notions in that chapter.

On Financial Speculation & Instability

In Chapter 12 Keynes distinguishes between 'enterprise investment', or investment in real assets like buildings, equipment, etc., and speculative investing that occurs largely in the form of investing in financial assets. The latter, financial securities investing, has tended to grow over time, and accelerate in boom periods. Keynes sees this long term growth as driven by the separation of ownership and investing, due to the rise of the professional investor as a 'class'. The professional investor is driven by short term expectations of profit gains. Short term profits gains are found in financial asset markets, especially those that are highly liquid, like stocks and tradeable bonds. Investors can jump in and out of these markets and record capital gains based on short term price movements of the securities. Professional investors are therefore focused on expectations of profitability in the near future. What drives price for financial securities in financial markets is therefore demand—and demand based on expected future demand. Supply forces play little role in determining price. Securities prices, based thus primarily on demand forces, escalate faster and rise higher than prices of goods and services; and conversely may fall faster and farther than goods prices. Financial securities are thus potentially more profitable. Financial assets are thus more prone to financial speculation—i.e. betting on price appreciation (or depreciation), from which greater capital gains may be obtained in the short run than profits from real asset investment over a longer run. The professional investor has therefore what Keynes called "a fetish for liquidity". What Keynes refers to as the 'professional investor' is financial speculation by a new, and rising, finance capital elite class. Apart from their focus on the short run price appreciation of financial securities, the professional investor's "peculiar zest is making money quickly", relying more on borrowing and debt with which to invest. Enterprise investing is long term and in real assets; speculative financial asset investing is short term, price driven investing. The two forms of investing contend with each other, according to Keynes. But speculative investing achieves an upper hand when highly liquid financial asset markets proliferate and expand. Then speculative financial asset investing may predominate. Even in Keynes' time, he acknowledged the growing "predominance of speculation over enterprise in the United States".[23]

Keynes concludes chapter 12 and his analysis of the rise of the professional investor to eventual predominance—focusing on financial asset speculation, debt based, and price-driven, short term capital gain profits—by noting that 'animal spirits' that once applied to enterprise investing may shift to more profitable financial speculative investing. The shift in 'animal spirits' and liquid capital to financial investing could in turn lead to an exaggeration in slumps and depressions. Finally, Keynes's very last paragraph in the chapter concludes that these trends toward financial investing at the expense of enterprise (real asset) investing could not be checked or controlled by monetary policy and interest rate manipulation, but would require the State "taking an ever greater responsibility for directly organizing investment".[24]

While these ideas were presented in general terms they nonetheless contain much food for thought, and represent a major break from neoclassical economics. They raise the possibility of a central role for financial asset investing and speculation; suggest that financial variables and markets may seriously disrupt real asset investing both in short and long runs; raise the idea of financial cycles interacting with real cycles, and non-rational and even irrational behavior determining the direction of overall investment; and note the rise of a new class of capitalists or at least a section of the class. None of these ideas are remotely considered in neoclassical analysis. However, the ideas in chapter 12 were not very well integrated into the rest of the *General Theory* chapters and were subsequently generally overlooked and disregarded in the debates that followed Keynes' book and virtually disregarded as Keynes' ideas were later transformed into 'hybrid' Keynesianism.

On Credit & Debt

Keynes' contrarian views on debt are not directly stated but must be inferred throughout his later work. Discussion about the limits of interest rate policy are indirectly related to the role of debt, since rates are associated with the borrowing of money capital for purposes of investment in general. On the one hand, Keynes does not see business debt as key to investment and recovery. As noted previously, favorable interest rates and therefore debt are insufficient to generate real asset investment in a severe economic contraction. Business also avoids borrowing for purposes of real asset investing in such conditions where its expectations of profitability are otherwise low. This moderately 'negative' view of the role of debt in relation to interest rates and real investment contrasts sharply with classical and neoclassical views that always saw debt as a source of finance for real investment and always contributing in a positive way to investment.

Furthermore, Keynes saw debt as not going to general real investment, but rather enabling excess financial investing, given that the professional investor-speculator tended to borrow (incur debt) as much as possible to finance short term financial speculative investing. In the 1930 *Treatise*, debt contributes to the rise of the 'bull speculator' who invests increasingly excessively over the boom cycle in riskier and riskier projects.

One may further indirectly presume that, for Keynes, consumer household debt was a double-edged sword. Initially, consumer debt increased disposable income for households and thus stimulated consumption. But in the longer term, this short run debt had the effect of reducing longer run disposable income. Interest on debt incurred in the present (time t) must be paid in the future (time t + 1) thus reducing real wages and real disposable income in the future.

Keynes' view of government debt was contrary to his view that 'business debt is ineffective and potentially destabilizing in the future' and 'consumer debt simply shifts income over time'. Raising government debt was preferable during economic contractions. Government budget deficits (the accumulation of which equal government debt) were desirable and even necessary so long as full employment had not yet been achieved. Deficits wouldn't lead to inflation, so long as full potential output had not been reached. Moreover, increasing deficits and debt as a result of government spending was preferable to raising deficits and debt due to tax cuts. This is because government spending income multipliers had a greater effect on income and output because the spending multiplier was larger than the tax multiplier.

For Keynes then, business debt was ineffective in stimulating real investment given prevailing conditions of economic contraction, while business use of debt for financial asset speculation was potentially destabilizing whenever the boom phase of a business cycle ended. Household debt stimulated consumption in the present but depressed it in the future, so was neutral at best. Conversely, government debt due to deficit spending was preferable, since budget deficits that created the debt had a positive multiplier effect on income and the economy. In contrast to business and household debt that potentially might be hoarded or redirected outside the economy or into financial speculation, government debt had the additional advantage of not being hoarded.

For Keynes, some debt was ineffective, some neutral, and some effective. It depended on the impact it had on actual incomes and spending. This view contrasts sharply with that of classical and neoclassical economics, in which debt is primarily viewed as business debt that nearly always helps stimulate investment in real assets.

The Limitations of Keynes

Despite his numerous innovative contributions, some involving conceptual breakthroughs, Keynes more often than not attempted to critique his neoclassical predecessors from within their old conceptual framework. For example, 'marginal analysis' and rational decision making were still employed by Keynes.

Retaining Marginal Analysis

Notwithstanding his proposing new roles for expectations and psychological factors in decision making, Keynes' 'marginal efficiency of capital' (MEK) concept was central to his investment theory. Household consumption also contained a marginal element. Keynes' multiplier effect depended on the consumer's 'marginal propensity to consume' (MPC). MEK meant investors would choose that investment project that had an incrementally higher expectation of greater rate of return compared to other projects. Expectations of profitability was the key, with costs of capital and borrowing secondary. MPC meant that consumers would spend a proportion of an incremental increase in their income, and a lesser proportion of the increase as income levels rose. Whether related to investment or consumption, however, marginal implies rational decision making, occurring at the increment. But investors were both rational and irrational. So which was more dominant and determining, rational and marginal or non-rational or even irrational? Certainly financial speculation contained a highly irrational element. If both rational decision making at the margin and non-rational coexisted side by side, what was the process and how did they interact? All this was not developed in Keynes, who raised the new ideas but often did not follow up.

Savings = Investment

Keynes also accepted the classical-neoclassical notion that total Savings and Investment were one and the same. That is, income that was generated by production, and distributed to households and consumers, was either spent (consumed) or saved. If saved, it went through the banking system and was borrowed by business to use to invest, along with business's share of the original income from production. Classical economics assumed all that was not consumed was ipso facto saved and reinvested. Savings thus determined investment. While Keynes accepted the basic S=I identity, he viewed the causal relationship inversely: it was investment that created the income that was then saved, so Investment determined Savings. The correct direction of causality is important for a host of policy choices. But it seems by remaining within the

Savings=Investment conceptual framework, Keynes remained immersed within the broader concept of Equilibrium. He consequently did not totally reject the notion of equilibrium but merely amended it: equilibrium was still possible, but not in the sense of a return to prior levels of output. Equilibrium could occur, albeit at a much lower level of production and output. And it could stagnate there for some time, perhaps a very long time if the correct recovery policies were not introduced. Thus the options were either recession or depression, on the one hand, or economic growth on the other. But the third option of a continuing stagnation condition was left undeveloped.

Mutual Causality of Two Forms of Investment

Keynes' investment theory represented yet another limitation. If two kinds of investment were increasingly competing for liquidity and money capital—real asset investing and financial asset speculative investing—what was the relationship between the two? Why was one becoming more dominant over the long run? And what were the processes by which financial speculation fueled by excess credit and debt creation destabilized the economy?

If MEK is key to understanding investment, does financial asset investing occur based on the same MEK formula Keynes proposed for real asset investing? Do real and financial asset investing occupy the same ranked schedule of investment projects indicated by a MEK? If so, does financial speculation crowd out real asset projects in the MEK schedule? What's the consequence for long run investment, employment, and producer and consumer goods deflation if that's the case? On all such points the *General Theory* is silent.

The Missing Institutional Framework

The rise of the professional investor-speculator represents the over-development of the capitalist economy in a certain direction. Keynes attributes the origins and perhaps growth of this agent to the growing separation of ownership and investing in the 20th century capitalist economy. But is it that simple a cause? While Keynes mentions 'institutions' associated with this development, he does not describe or explain the institutions, how they function, and what is their relationship to the new professional investor-speculator. What is the institutional framework and how has it evolved over time; how is it different today than decades ago? Various kinds of 'shadow banks' were operative in the 1920s and 1930s—investment banks, insurance companies, broker-dealers, financial Trusts, etc. It would not have been too difficult to integrate agents (professional speculators) with institutions with financial markets.

The Class Neutral Capitalist State

Nor is there any discussion of the role of the State in this professional investor-finance institution development. But to Keynes the shift to professional investing appears purely market driven. But it is hard to believe the State has played no role in enabling and assisting the ascendancy of the professional speculator. The State in Keynes is envisioned as a kind of Deus Ex Machina, that will tame the worst attributes and behavior of individual capitalists, investors and businesses and set the economy again on a path to recovery. Thus the State is class-neutral. History shows its role as quite the contrary.

Credit, Debt & Multipliers

While Keynes' focus on income instead of price is a major advance and enabled the development of the concept of the multiplier, Keynes did not consider further how credit and therefore debt might distort the multiplier. How do debt levels, rate of debt change, and other elements affecting how and when debt is paid all affect the marginal propensity to consume and thus the multiplier? In an economy like today's, where forms of earned income like wages are increasingly substituted by credit/debt as income, what does that portend for consumption over the longer term? Does the expansion of consumer credit enable the slower growth, or even reduction, of wage incomes? And if so, what does that mean for multipliers? As noted above, the income side of economic analysis was advanced significantly by Keynes. But no equivalent advance was made by understanding the role of credit and debt—or how debt interacted with different forms of income. Consumer credit was viewed as just another form of income in the short run that thereafter contributed to more consumption—much like debt was just another source of finance for businesses to invest beyond what internal earnings or profits might finance.

Money vs. Inside Credit

Like his predecessors, Keynes did not distinguish between money and credit. Money was credit when loaned out to investors, businesses, or households. But the idea that credit might operate without the necessity of money—thus expanding available liquidity even more—was not addressed or even envisioned by Keynes. Is money a sub-category of credit, or is credit a sub-category of money? There was no distinction between inside credit and outside credit, although Keynes' distinction between real asset, or enterprise investing, and financial asset, speculative investing would logically lead one in that direction. Whether inside credit impacts financial speculation more than real asset investing seems also like a proposition worth investigating. Keynes' theory of money demand requires further development in the direction of integrating inside credit with money demand and the idea of liquidity preference.

Expectations and Financial MEK

Keynes' expectations theory impacts the MEK in various ways. Expectations of profitability affect the MEK, and so do expectations of the direction and rate of change of interest rates. If expectations affect these two variables, they must also affect the prices of the two variables, profitability and interest rates. So expectations influence producer and consumer (i.e. goods) prices as well as the price of money (interest rates). Apart from the MEK, expectations also have a major impact on financial asset prices. In Chapter 12 much was said about how the professional investor-speculator anticipates the future movement of financial asset prices in the process of deciding to invest in financial securities, be they stocks, bonds, or whatever. But Keynes never considered how expectations that affect producer goods prices, by influencing the MEK, might also interact with expectations that affect financial asset prices. The latter occurred outside the MEK, which was about real asset investment. But should there not be another 'financial MEK'? And how then would the two MEKs mutually determine each other? How would financial asset prices affect producer goods prices, and vice-versa? Keynes distinguished between the two forms of investment—enterprise and financial speculation. He acknowledged that they can have an important effect on each other. As he noted in Chapter 12, the condition of the economy became "serious when enterprise becomes the bubble on a whirlpool of speculation". Nevertheless, he did not integrate their two MEKs, or ask if that integration might lead to a rise in the one (financial) MEK at the expense of the other (real) MEK. Nor did he consider how prices for producer or real asset capital goods and prices for financial securities assets interacted in a boom stage of a business cycle immediately leading to a bust and depression, and thereafter in that subsequent depression stage as well.

This relative disregard for financial asset price instability was understandable perhaps, since Keynes purposely sought to de-emphasize neoclassical economics' over-estimation of the role of price. That de-emphasis was done in order for him to give greater emphasis on the role of income in determining stabilization (which neoclassical economics largely disregarded).

The Two-Price Theory Potential

Keynes indirectly laid the groundwork for establishing the idea of a two-price theory: one for financial asset prices and another for goods prices, and explaining how the two do not necessarily behave the same way in relation to supply and demand. The neoclassical notion of 'one price system' and one price fits all was implicitly rejected by Keynes. But he didn't take that analysis further to the next step and ask: in what ways precisely does deflation or collapse of financial asset prices impact other price systems (labor or factor, money, and goods)? Finally, if financial asset prices and other prices drive the real economy away from equilibrium, not towards it, how do the separate price systems function as transmission mechanisms to the real economy, causing it to become more unstable as well?

The Austrian Credit Cycle

When a general perspective for explaining economic reality begins to collapse in the face of an anomaly it cannot account for—like a financial crash or a rapid, deep and protracted contraction of the real economy—that perspective fails on a number of fronts. Neoclassical economics could not explain the Depression—neither its origins, its trajectory, nor how to exit the crisis. It fractured along a number of fronts or directions. Keynes' work represents one alternative direction taken in response to the neoclassical collapse. Another at the time was the offshoot of neoclassical economics sometimes referred to as 'Austrian economics'. Its key proponent in the 1930s was the economist, Friedrich Hayek.

Austrian economics correctly focused on the destabilizing role of credit and the contribution of excess debt to financial crises and economic instability. However, its solution to the destabilizing role of credit and debt was fundamentally 'reactionary'. That is, to explain how to confront the crisis it collapsed back into advocating the self-correcting economy that would successfully restore equilibrium. Unable to forge a new conceptual framework, Austrian economics from Hayek onward simply adopted the 19th century classical and neoclassical view that the economic system could, and would, self correct on its own, provided the government did not interfere with the self adjusting market mechanism. Whereas Keynes made a partial conceptual break in the face of the anomaly of the depression, Hayek and other Austrians offered a conceptual capitulation to the economic ideology of J.B. Say and the self-correcting market economy worldview that prevailed more than a century earlier.

For the Austrian view, the government was ultimately the cause of the credit-driven crisis and therefore the solution to that crisis must include the government not interfering with the recovery. The origin of the crisis was the excess liquidity and credit that was created by central banks—in their view, the government—by over-expanding the money supply. The excess money supply resulted in unnaturally low interest rates that led to excessive bank borrowing, a credit boom, over-borrowing at the expense of saving. The result was 'mal-investment', or bad investments. Excess debt-based borrowing created 'bad' investment whereas savings created 'good' investment. Natural interest rates were associated with savings, driving good investment; unnatural interest rates were associated with debt, driving bad investment. Both co-exist, but the central bank created an imbalance that led to excess credit, speculation, bad investment and eventual crisis. Government—in the form of central banks—was thus the root cause of the crisis. It therefore could not be part of the solution to the crisis by definition.

Excess 'bad' investment led to rising capital and consumer goods prices and wages. This meant that the transmission of instability was transmitted via money prices (interest rates) to financial asset, goods and labor prices. Central bank monetary policies aimed at bailing out the banks and propping up asset prices only led to more bad investment. And government spending aimed at propping up wage incomes only led to bad consumption. Preventing the central bank from interfering in the recovery would eliminate the artificial low interest rates, returning rates to their natural state, and thereafter restoring balances between investment and consumption. Absent central bank interference, the economy would naturally 'self correct'. Excess debt would naturally liquidate itself if left alone. One sees a similar antipathy toward central banks and their interest rate policies today among US libertarian and US Tea Party circles, many of whom, unknowingly, are inheritors of the Austrian-Hayekian view.

Whereas one might say Keynes did not address the credit-debt and therefore financial contributions to the origins of the Depression of the 1930s but focused instead on what real economic measures might end the Depression, the Austrians did focus on credit-debt but simply abdicated proposing any real solutions. They simply concluded: let the banks fail, let the bad assets 'liquidate', and the market will adjust back to equilibrium based on the price mechanism of money (interest rates) stabilizing the other price systems, and all price systems thereafter restoring equilibrium to the rest of the real economy. Credit-debt may cause the problem, but price (interest rates) would restore balance once again—providing the government stayed out of the picture.

From the foregoing, it is clear that the Austrian business cycle view sees excess credit and debt as important factors in creating a crisis. However, it excludes the market from responsibility for endogenous excess 'inside credit' creation by the private banking system and speculators. Rather, it avers: remove the central bank root cause, and the economy will correct based on adjustments in prices—not the adjustment in goods prices, as in classical economics, but adjustment driven by money prices (interest rates). Government can't eliminate excess debt once it's created. Only the market can, by means of asset liquidation. In its essence, therefore, Austrian economics is a money supply explanation of the origins of a depression, wedded to a "the market will engineer a return to equilibrium" solution.

Later, in the post-World War period, the Austrian view had significant influence on the 'Retro' wing of mainstream economics. Both view money supply imbalances as the main cause of crises, and therefore the route to the solution to the crisis. To avoid an excess credit and debt driven financial crash that precipitates a general economic contraction, just prevent excess money injection into the economy. If that fails, and the financial crisis and contraction occurs, then just do the same (i.e. nothing) to enable the market to do its magic and return the economy to equilibrium and growth.

Austrians were correct to emphasize the role of liquidity and excess credit and debt creation as playing key roles in creating a financial crisis, but they had no solution to the crisis apart from letting the market naturally liquidate the excess debt that was created in the boom phase and ensuring that the government stays out of the recovery effort as the market makes its adjustments. Let the banks and other businesses fail, and let defaults and liquidation of assets follow their 'natural' course. That will create the preconditions for a new recovery. Keynes was wrong, in this view. The real economy would not settle into a well below average new equilibrium, with less real investment, more unemployment, and reduced production. It would fully recover eventually to pre-financial collapse and contraction levels.

The Hybrids

The development of Hybrid Keynesianism began almost immediately following the publication of Keynes' *General Theory* in 1936, as a certain grouping of economists in the UK and the US around Oxford-Cambridge in the UK and Harvard University critiqued Keynes for ignoring neoclassical propositions that were still relevant in their view. A running debate between Keynes and these critics occurred immediately after 1936 focused on the topic of the continuing relevance of interest rates. Another topic of their critique was that the *General Theory* was not 'general', but instead specific only to economic depression conditions. Yet another was that Keynes' arguments did not apply to conditions of economic stability and growth periods, during which goods inflation might occur. Keynes lacked a theory of inflation, critics argued. Keynes did not fully appreciate the advances of classical and neoclassical economics which were still highly relevant.[25] The neoclassical old guard simply could not let go of their broken paradigm in the face of Keynes' challenge. So they decided to absorb the elements of Keynes' analysis that did not fundamentally overthrow their old conceptual framework. They modified their old framework to incorporate part of Keynes, while rejecting outright elements of Keynes' *General Theory* that logically led to the need to throw out neoclassical analysis in toto.

Hybrid Keynesianism became entrenched soon after World War II in academic circles in the US and UK. It adapted elements of Keynes and refined its new 'integrated model' that became institutionalized in what became known as IS-LM macroeconomics, where 'IS' represented Investment-Savings on the real side and 'LM' represented money demand and money supply on the money side of economic analysis. Money demand and money supply became the basis for interest rate determination, and rates then mediated the Savings to Investment relationship. Fundamentally, therefore, it was the old 'interest rates determine real investment' idea of classical economics. Interest rate levels and changes, determined primarily by money supply, in effect 'lured' savings from households to businesses, which borrowed the households' bank deposits to invest in and produce real producer and consumer goods. Keynes' challenge to this assumption—based on the argument that investment determines interest rates and not vice-versa—was reversed once again by early Hybrid economics. And if interest rates play the key mediating role in driving investment, that assumption amounts to arguing that price (interest rates as price of money) once again is the key to restoring equilibrium in the real economy. Income was not the primary determinant, as Keynes originally suggested. It was price (interest rates). This early Hybrid view of interest rates and investment was not only congruent with pre-Keynes neoclassical thought but, as noted above, with Austrian economic analysis as well.

This primacy of interest rates in the hybrid view leads to the consequent view that central bank monetary policy is the more important policy tool for stabilizing the economy, especially in periods of economic growth and inflation, but also in periods of economic recession and depression. This is where the Hybrids depart from the Austrians. Hybrids see central bank determined interest rates as central to economic recovery, whereas Austrians viewed central bank rates as destabilizing and preventing recovery. In contrast, Keynes discounted interest rates as a means to re-stabilize an economy in depression.[26]

While acknowledging Keynes' contributions in the area of money demand analysis, Hybrids nonetheless emphasized money supply and central bank action as the more flexible monetary option with which to influence interest rates. They did not deny a role to money demand—over which the central bank had little influence in any event—but money supply was still dominant so far as the determination of interest rates was concerned. That attribution of primacy to money supply and interest rates was a very 'classical' view.

Had Hybrids emphasized money demand over money supply, that would have led Hybrids back to Keynes' original notion that demand for money can offset central bank money supply and interest rate manipulation. And that view that money demand may at times trump, or negate, money supply would mean that interest rates might not have much positive effect on the real economy no matter how low rates were driven by central bank money supply operations. The 'LM' side of the hybrid IS-LM model would have collapsed. In short, while Hybrids gave lip service to Keynes' contributions on money demand, money supply and interest rates were still considered dominant.

Expunged from all this as well was any reference to any role played by 'expectations' in determining interest rates and/or investment. But referencing Keynes without 'expectations' is like deleting all reference to 'labor exploitation' in Marx's *Capital, to* 'equilibrium' in neoclassical economics works. Expectations were fundamental to Keynes. Delete this aspect and it's no longer Keynes. But with the ascent of Hybrid Keynesianism in academia in the post World War II period, expectations analysis virtually disappeared altogether from Hybrid Keynesianism.

Eliminate expectations, and there is no Keynes investment theory. The marginal efficiency of capital (MEK) does not exist. Businesses invest only based on what their past profits may have been, not what they think future profits might be. Consumers spend only based on the current level of income, not also on what they expect their future income tomorrow, or later, may be. There is no time dimension, either for investment or consumption. Even interest rate determination becomes absurd, by assuming that businesses and consumers borrow based only on current rates and not where they 'expect' future rates to be.

Classical and neoclassical economics maintained that profits were the primary determinant of investment. Borrowed funds—i.e. credit—also supplemented financing of investment when profits were insufficient or when capitalists wished to use other people's money instead of their own. But Keynes' investment theory added a more fundamental dimension with its proposition that expectations of future profits were more important than the level of recent profits. Expectations of profits was the foundation of Keynes' MEK concept, and played a greater role in determining investment than did the cost of replacing capital or the cost of borrowing funds (i.e. interest rates) with which to finance investment.

But expectations are highly psychological and therefore qualitative and difficult to quantify. Hybrid Keynesians for decades therefore chose to ignore what was not easily quantifiable and increasingly turned in the postwar period to more mathematical methods of analysis, employing such methods often as a substitute for developing better economic concepts that might have advanced economic analysis. The turn toward more mathematical analysis may in fact have set back conceptual development in other ways. While it is a more efficient language with which to translate a more general language, it is also more prone to ideological manipulation.

While rejecting Keynes' contributions in terms of 'expectations', Hybrids embraced Keynes' contributions with regard to income, the marginal propensity to consume, and the multiplier with little adjustment. Income as well as price (interest rates) were therefore both together important for economic recovery. Government spending and government tax measures—i.e. fiscal policy—were essential to income analysis just as central bank monetary policies were to money supply and interest rates. So, one might argue that Hybrids are neoclassical on the monetary side while Keynesian on the income side of analysis.[27]

However, while accepting Keynes' contributions in terms of income analysis, and the important conceptual contribution based on income called the 'multiplier effect', Hybrids fail to explain adequately why the 'multiplier' is steadily having 'less effect' over time. This is due to several reasons, associated with changing labor market and financial market structures in recent decades for which Hybrids fail to account.[28]

First, Hybrids fail to adequately account for the negative impact of debt on both consumer and business spending. Second, they consider all income injections by government (spending or tax related) as having the same multiplier.

Income is income, it is assumed, and the main determinant of the multiplier is the level of disposable income for the household or business at the time of the income injection. Third, the composition and timing of the income injection is disregarded as well.

Concerning the first point, Hybrids do acknowledge what is called the 'debt overhang' for households. But the analysis of the 'overhang' is weak, limited to the argument that a large household debt means a government income injection is partly diverted by households to pay down debt instead of being spent; thus the multiplier effect is less because the amount used to pay down excessive debt is not spent on consumption. While this is true, there is no consideration of the magnitude or type of debt that is overhanging; nor the terms and conditions of the debt payment; the term structure of the debt; the recent changes in the household's disposable income; and other factors. These are all parameters that define 'fragility' as used in this book. For Hybrids, however, debt is just a level that somehow diverts income injection and thus reduces the multiplier effect by some amount.

Second, Hybrid economics assumes the magnitude of income injected by the government will produce the same multiplier effect, subject only to the level of disposable income which is normal for multiplier analysis. It doesn't matter if the income injection occurs in the form of a subsidy payment, a transfer payment, or a job. But these do matter. In recent years income injections have increasingly assumed the former rather than job creation. Households likely spend less of the former, saving more of it, than in the case of income from job creation.

Third, Hybrid theories make no distinction as to the composition or timing of the income injection. Government spending that goes mostly to states to spend in turn does not result in as large a multiplier. That's because a good part of it is hoarded by the state, or else paid in the form of a one-time subsidy for a social service instead of a state or local government job created.

What happened in the US economy in 2009-10 is a good example. Approximately $300 billion was injected by the US federal government and given to the States to spend in turn. It was heralded as going to create 6 million jobs. Most was hoarded by the states or dribbled out in small doses. Little resulted in actual job creation. The federal government, when criticized, had to respond with the 'spin' message that the billions of dollars at least resulted in fewer jobs lost. But even that did not occur, as state and local governments for years thereafter continued to cut government jobs. On the business side, government business tax cuts in 2009-10 of more than a trillion dollars between 2009-2011, was also largely hoarded. Or invested offshore. Or diverted to financial securities investment that created no real asset investment, jobs and income.

The problem with Hybrid multiplier theory is that it functions like a 'black box'. The main DSGE models, for example, simply assume an 'X' amount of government income injected into the economy will produce a 'Y' amount of jobs created and therefore income spent and a given multiplier. The US DSGE model assumed in 2009 that $787 billion of federal government fiscal stimulus— composed mostly of tax cuts, subsidies to states, and long term, capital (not labor) intensive investment projects, would result in a 'Z' multiplier effect and the creation of 6 million jobs within 18 months, including a million manufacturing jobs and half a million construction jobs. But both the latter continued to shed jobs, as did the rest of the economy in the 18 months. Not surprisingly, the multipliers were far lower than the models predicted.

An even more glaring shortcoming of Hybrid Keynesian analysis is its consistent failure to distinguish between real asset investment (equipment, buildings, etc.) and financial securities investments, as well as how the two forms of investment mutually determine and impact each other. At a more general level, Hybrids also have no explanation for how financial cycles (booms, busts, banking crashes, liquidity crunches, etc.) affect real business cycles (recessions, great recessions, depressions), as well as how the latter feed back into and affect financial instability in turn. The rise of the professional speculator-investor that Keynes discussed in Chapter 12 of his *General Theory* never appears in Hybrid analyses. And the growth of shadow banks and the effects of shadow banking on the economy constitute a massive black hole at the center of Hybrid Keynesian analysis in recent years. The financial playground of the finance capital elite— what's sometimes called the 'capital markets' where highly liquid financial asset speculation takes place—is progressively replacing traditional bank lending and rendering central bank money supply operations increasingly irrelevant. But little attention is given in Hybrid analysis to these highly significant trends and developments.

A bifurcation exists in the analysis of Hybrids, with business finance academics adhering to the 'efficient markets hypothesis' (EMH) that maintains, in total conformity with classical economics, that markets are always more efficient than government and markets will always return to equilibrium if left alone. That is, nothing different here since J.B. Say in 1800. Meanwhile, Hybrid academic economists have even less of a notion of how financial variables impact the real side of the economy. Part of the reason for this general disregard for financial forces and how they impact the real economy is that Hybrid economists have been trained for the past 70 years to look almost exclusively at real variables provided by the National Income and Product Accounts (NIPA) database that was created in the 1930s. The NIPAs don't include financial market data. From the beginning, Gross Domestic Product (GDP), which the NIPA summarize, excluded financial variables from GDP analysis. Trained in quantitative analyses that apply NIPA and related real variables, Hybrid economic analysis disregards most financial variables. There is no thought that perhaps the rise of highly liquid global financial markets, countless new forms of financial securities, and even the evolution of non-financial multinational corporations into 'shadow-shadow' banks might have something to do with the progressive decline in the growth of real investment, and therefore economic growth, and employment. Or the rise in business debt. Or the growing instability in the global economy in recent decades.

Classical and neoclassical (as well as Marxist) economics viewed investment in real assets as financed either from internal profits or from bank borrowing. There was little attention paid to forms of financing, like equity (stock), bond, or other forms. There was just the dictum: profits determined investment, supplemented by bank loans. This was not surprising, since stock and bond markets were undeveloped in the 19th century. And capital markets and derivatives funded largely by shadow bank financial institutions were non-existent. Hybrid economics in the post-1945 period acknowledged the rise of equity and bond markets as key sources of financing of investment. But still, in the 21st century, it does not adequately account for capital market-shadow bank financing—whether for real asset or financial securities asset investing.

The explosion in financial engineering and new forms of securities creation is directly related to the rise and growing influence of 'inside credit' financing, especially for financial asset markets. However, Hybrid economists pay little attention to this development, and remain wedded to the traditional view of relationships between the central bank and private banking system process of money creation. The notion that credit need not involve money creation and lending in this traditional sense is not considered. The excess liquidity that has been made available by central banks since the collapse of the global Bretton Woods system in the early 1970s—i.e. 'outside credit'—has been exacerbated by the corresponding rise of inside credit made possible by the historic restructuring of the global financial system itself since the 1980s to the present. Both globalization and financialization have reduced the effectiveness of traditional central bank-commercial bank money creation effects on the real economy, while simultaneously the rapid growth of non-money 'inside credit' has added to the excess liquidity that has driven debt at all levels (business, household, government) to historic heights. Central banks have been steadily losing control of the money supply for decades. But one would not know it from contemporary mainstream Hybrid economists.

The Hybrid wing of mainstream economists is particularly confused on the role of price. One might almost say it is 'schizophrenic' on the subject. Price is viewed as a stabilizing mechanism, but only if assisted by government policy intervention. For decades after Keynes himself viewed the price mechanism as not necessarily capable of re-stabilizing the economy, and even capable of destabilizing it, Hybrid Keynesians were at a loss to provide a consistent, integrated theory of price and inflation. Moreover, the Hybrid analysis of inflation referred to different adjustment processes associated with real goods, for labor prices (wages) or for money prices (interest rates). And there was no analysis whatsoever of financial asset prices or how the latter interacted with the former three price mechanisms for goods, money, or wages.

Money price (interest rate) inflation was due to changes in money supply and/or money demand, with a strong bias toward money supply, which reflected the influence of neoclassical, wedded to token acknowledgement of Keynes' money demand function. The central bank determined rates, at least short term interest rates. Money prices returned to equilibrium as money supply and money demand adjusted with the assistance of the government's central bank.

With regard to labor prices (wages), prices were determined by relative oligopoly bargaining power between big corporations and big unions, in what was called 'administered' price theory. Economic growth shifted bargaining power in favor of unions and thus of wage gains somewhat, while slower growth or recessions shifted the power to determine wages more to corporations. The government regulated business and unions to ensure neither gained excess bargaining power at the expense of the other, so the Hybrids claimed.

Goods inflation was demand driven, on the one hand—either the consequence of 'too much money chasing goods' (the classical-neoclassical main argument) or the result of excess production above full employment in the economy. Conversely, because wage increases were also viewed as a prime determinant of price inflation, goods prices were simultaneously also the consequence of supply side forces. Government fiscal and monetary policies again regulated supply and demand forces, ensuring they did not depart too far or too long from equilibrium.

In all three cases, prices eventually returned to equilibrium—even if market forces were aided by government intervention to restore equilibrium. Government was now a player in the 'return to equilibrium' assumption. Whereas equilibrium could be achieved only if the government did not interfere, according to the neoclassical view, now equilibrium was possible so long as government (central bank or government fiscal policy) carefully 'nudged' the economy to return to equilibrium perhaps a little faster than otherwise might have been the case with no government involvement.

The Hybrid view of equilibrium was even stronger than Keynes' version. Gone was Keynes' less sanguine view about equilibrium—that equilibrium might be re-established, but at a stagnant, below normal growth level of production and employment. In short, like neoclassicals, for Hybrids full return to prior equilibrium was achievable. The only difference from neoclassical analysis was restoration that was brought about by government assisting the market. Price at all three levels—money, wage, and goods—worked as a stabilizing force, albeit aided in the adjustment to equilibrium by government 'fine tuning' of central bank and legislative action.

This diverse, disjointed Hybrid view of price and inflation was reflected in the development of what was called the 'Phillips Curve' analysis in the late 1950s and 1960s. Finally, Hybrid Keynesianism had its heretofore missing inflation theory. Wages largely determined price levels for goods on the vertical axis of a famous simple graphical representation of a downward sloping curve, while changes in output determined employment levels and thus the unemployment rate on the horizontal axis.   As production and the economy slowed and unemployment consequently rose, union wage bargaining power declined and so did wages. And since wages were considered the major determinant of 'administered' prices, the price level fell as production and employment declined. This was both 'demand' driven price change, as the economy slowed, as well as 'supply' side price change, as wage cost decline also reduced prices.   Both supply and demand determined inflation.   The idea that financial asset price deflation in a financial crash might drive a decline in wage, goods, and interest rate prices was beyond this scenario.

The Phillips Curve also provided a nice 'trade off' between expansionary fiscal and monetary policies that stimulated production and GDP, and contrary fiscal-monetary policies designed to slow the economy. Slowing reduced output but also wages and prices; a rise in GDP conversely resulted in a rise in wages and prices.   The problem with the Phillips Curve, however, was that its key relationship between price and employment/real output changes disappeared in the 1970s. With that disappearance, both the price mechanism system of Hybrid Keynesianism as well as its policy justification collapsed. Hybrid economics could not even explain the real side of the economy any longer, let alone the financial side or how the two interacted. Into the vacuum left in economic analysis in the 1970s entered the new monetarists, who thereafter evolved to what today might be called the 'Retro Classicalists'.

On the matter of debt, Hybrid Keynesians offer no analysis for how business and corporate debt can lead to financial instability. Business debt is viewed similar to classical economics—i.e. bank loans provide an alternative source of financing for real investment purposes. Business debt is thus viewed positively. How excess liquidity and debt might lead to future inability to make payments on the debt and therefore lead to economically destabilizing business defaults is not addressed; nor how defaults may accelerate financial asset deflation. How debt, deflation, and defaults contribute to greater financial and real economic instability is further ignored.

Consumer, or household, debt is viewed similarly positively, as a source of additional income for households with which to stimulate consumption. How and at which point household debt becomes a drag on disposable income and therefore consumption is not given sufficient attention in comparison. Acknowledgement that debt overhang may restrict consumption is considered only in the sense that it may lead to more pay down of debt in lieu of consumption. Debt overhang and multiplier effects are not adequately analysed.

On the other hand, Hybrid Keynesians are even greater advocates of government debt and the deficits that create debt. They see no problem with central banks adding trillions of debt to their balance sheets as they bail out banks, shadow banks, and investors with quantitative easing programs. The same applies to general government deficits and debt. So long as the economy is performing below full employment and potential GDP, the government may incur further deficits and debt to stimulate economic recovery by means of fiscal policies. Demand side inflation due to such policies is assumed to be and remain negligible. Hybrids like Paul Krugman, for example, continually advocate greater government deficits as a means to generate recovery, pointing to the lack of goods inflation as indication there are no consequences for further deficits and debt accumulation. Moreover, it doesn't matter how the deficits and debt are increased, just so long as they are. How government deficits and debt enable business and corporate debt to continue to rise, with all the eventual implications for future instability, is viewed as unimportant. How government debt excess leads to austerity fiscal policies that reduce household incomes and lead in turn to more household debt is also ignored.

All three forms of debt do not interact significantly or determine each other in Hybrid Keynesian analysis, making it largely static by failing to consider the dynamic interactions between the various forms of debt. Or the interactions and feedback effects between debt and price instability (deflation).[29] Or how debt and deflation feed off of defaults (failure to make debt payments), and vice versa. Or how the debt-deflation-default processes may accelerate the contraction of the real economy following a financial crash event.

For Hybrid Keynesians, disruptions to equilibrium—as in the case of depressions, great recessions, and normal recessions—are the consequence of 'external shocks' to the economic system. The economic system is fundamentally in equilibrium. The shocks knock it off its equilibrium pedestal. For neoclassicals (and Retros), no government assistance should be provided to help restore equilibrium; for Hybrids, assistance expedites the return to equilibrium. But both support the notion that equilibrium is the natural state and that the system is basically stable, only to be periodically shocked by external events from that equilibrium natural state. This view means that a capitalist economy has no internal, or endogenous, characteristics that drive it regularly and periodically from stable growth and equilibrium. Equilibrium and 'external shock' recessions thus go hand in hand, as a joint ideological notion.

Hybrids argue that external shocks may be supply oriented (such as oil price shocks) or demand oriented (government policy over stimulating the economy). No matter which kind of shock, however, government fiscal-monetary policy can successfully engineer a return to stability, it is assumed.

A related problem with Hybrid analyses is that the differences between normal recessions, so-called great recessions like 2008-09, and bona fide depressions, is purely quantitative. The relatively more severe 'great' recessions, and even depressions, are just normal recessions 'writ large'. The assumption is that the causes of 'normal' recessions are similarly operative for 'great' and greatest (depressions). There are no significant qualitative differences at work that cause a depression that are not also present, albeit in weaker form, in a normal recession.[30] In fact, one of the most amazing shortcomings of Hybrid analysis has to do with the many contradictory explanations of the causes, trajectory and end of the Great Depression of the 1930s. To this day, there is no unanimity among Hybrids (or Retros for that matter) as to what caused the 1930s depression, why it continued for so long, or even why it ended. There are virtually dozens of single issue explanations: some monetary, some fiscal; some supply side, some demand side; some domestic, some international. Perhaps the single most important economic event of the 20th century has no definitive explanation after more than 75 years of endless commentary by professional Hybrid economists.

This confusion as to the differences between the different economic contractions, and confusion over the 1930 depression's causes itself, has important implications. If the same qualitative forces are at work across all three forms of contraction, then if traditional fiscal-monetary policies are able to successfully end normal recessions it should follow that just more of the same in greater magnitude would end the relatively more severe great recessions and depressions.[31]

Clearly, however, that is not the case historically. Normal recessions may be precipitated by external shock events. But depressions, and even great recessions—a kind of potential prelude to depression conditions—are not set off by supply or demand policy shocks. They are precipitated by financial instability events and financial crashes, following years of buildup of excess liquidity, debt, and financial asset speculation. Even the most recent 'great' recession experienced since 2008 confirms that traditional policies have clearly failed to restore growth back to pre-crisis levels or to equilibrium in any sense. Despite unprecedented money injection in the tens of trillions of dollars by US and other central banks, real asset investment and growth continue to slow, as financial bubbles proliferate and accelerate, and total debt steadily grows. Traditional fiscal-monetary policies are declining in terms of their positive effects on the real economy, while intensifying the negative effects on the financial system.[32]

The problem with Hybrid Keynesians is that they are statically historical. They see all real contractions through the lens of the dozens of normal recessions that occurred from 1947 through the 1990s, which were 'external shock' driven. They fail to see a new and more severe form of contraction driven by financial forces arising, beginning in the 1970s, initially in muted form and not yet generalized across markets or geography but thereafter expanding and occurring in parallel with 'shock' recessions. Finally in the 21st century, these take precedence over forces generating normal recessions, giving rise to the new, parallel, financial-crises-precipitated contractions outlined in earlier chapters in Part Two of this book.

Because Hybrid Keynesians mostly disregard the causative role of financial forces and financial instability in generating real economic contractions of a particularly severe nature, which appears to be the new norm in the 21st century, they are unable to adequately understand the nature of the global crisis that emerged in 2008 (with roots going back decades)—a crisis that still exists, has only been morphing in form and location worldwide ever since, and remains irresoluble. They continue to insist to view all contractions through the lens of normal recessions, as if there were no fundamental qualitative differences. How could they admit there are? To do so would mean traditional policies would not work. That would require recognizing that not all contractions are the product of 'external shocks'. And that would mean admitting that periodic instability in the system has internal, endogenous causes—and that these causes are financial as well as real.

To summarize briefly the more important shortcomings and limits of Hybrid Keynesianism, this wing of mainstream economic analysis represents a conceptual and theoretical dead end because it:

- has no theory of financial cycles and how they interact with real business cycles;

- makes no analytical distinction between real asset investment and financial asset investment;

- does not integrate or account for fundamental changes in both financial and labor markets in its analysis;

- rarely and if so, poorly, considers the role of business and household debt and the impact of both on real investment and household consumption, generally regarding debt as a more positive force than a destabilizing one;

- regards government debt as acceptable so long as the economy is at less than full capacity and full employment, regardless of its levels or its impact on household and business debt;

- has no convincing explanation why multiplier effects have declined in recent decades;

- views all forms of income injection as having the same magnitude effect on multipliers and GDP;

- refuses to consider Keynes' expectations analysis in its theory of interest rates and investment;

- still basically adheres to the false neoclassical notion that interest rates determine real investment, and that money supply is the more important determinant of rates;

- cannot distinguish between money and credit, or accommodate the historic challenge of shadow banks and capital markets to traditional bank lending and central bank policies;

- continues to view the price mechanism as a stabilizing force, returning the economy to equilibrium, albeit with government assistance;

- lacks a theory of financial asset prices or how they impact other price systems and cause disequilibrium;

- views the economy as ultimately self-correcting, given government assistance; and

- considers all contractions of the real economy as the same, with no qualitative differences between normal recessions, great recessions, or bona fide depressions.

Hybrid Keynesianism is especially deficient, therefore, when it comes to analyzing excessive debt and its financial instability implications. And it has equally failed to update its analysis of income in light of the unprecedented run-up in debt of all kinds since the 1980s and the deepening tendency of the global capitalist system toward financial instability and crises. Hybrids have failed to understand the character and importance of systemic fragility growing within the global economic system.

The Retros

The 'Retro-Classicalists', like the Hybrids, also originate in the pre-Keynes neoclassical school of economic analysis. But just as the Hybrids represent a response to Keynes himself, the Retros represent another wing of neoclassicalists who rejected the Hybrids' attempt to integrate part of Keynes with neoclassicalism economic analysis. The two wings—Hybrids and Retros—thus represent a return to restore neoclassicalism, albeit the Retros more directly. However, neither major wing of mainstream economic analysis today represents anything that might accurately be called 'Keynesian' in any original sense.[33]

Retros in the form of more or less pure monetarists believe in a kind of 21st century quantity theory of money. Complex, sophisticated equations boil down to the same fundamental argument as put forward by classical quantity theory of money: namely, money supply is the primary, even sole, variable to explain financial and economic instability. For some, even the mediation of interest rates is unimportant. The central bank should simply grow the money supply steadily and all will be as well as can be expected. Any further interference will generate a degree of less well than can be expected.

Recessions and depressions are always due to monetary policy errors by the central bank or other market causes. Inflation and deflation are thus always and everywhere a monetary phenomenon, caused by injecting too much or too little money into the economy. Retros are first and foremost supply side monetarists of one ilk or another. Even the cause of the Great Depression of the 1930s is reduced to a central bank policy error of not providing sufficient money supply in 1931 and thus allowing a recession to transition to a depression and erring again in 1937 by withdrawing money from the economy and causing a second relapse. Conversely, the Depression only began to end in 1939-40 as the central bank finally began to inject money into the US economy and gold from Europe flowed into the US in anticipation of war.[34] In short, business cycle fluctuations large and small always occur as a consequence of central bank 'on again, off again' policies with regard to money injection. Fast forward to the October 2008 crash in the US and the argument is the same: the US central bank's uncertain policies at that time "were a likely cause of the panic, or at least made the panic worse", to quote a leading Retro-monetarist theorist in the US in 2012.[35]

This view assigns no causation to the private banking system, especially the shadow banking sector, in precipitating the 2008 crash. The crash was a rolling event, beginning at least in late 2007 and reaching a peak in September-October 2008. The role of derivatives and financial speculation in stocks of banks, mortgage companies, and other related securities apparently had nothing to do with the crash in the Retro view. It was the central bank that was responsible, even though the process was building for at least 18 months prior to late 2008. The central bank's failure to prevent the crash is somehow repositioned in order for Retros to maintain its failure to stop the crash in effect caused it. There is no doubt that the role of central banks in the long run played a big role in providing the excess liquidity that led to excess debt and high risk speculation in financial asset products. But one cannot simply let the shadow banking system off the hook and focus all blame on the central banks when analyzing what caused the crash of October 2008.

Retros reject the idea of government injecting income into the economy through fiscal spending and tax cutting as well. Through a convoluted redefinition of the government spending multiplier, they insert new variables into the multiplier equation in the form of wealth assets (stocks, bonds, etc.) and future income that effectively reduces the amount of the income injection actually spent by households. They point to the disappearance of the Phillips curve and redefine the relationship between economic production and employment, on the one hand, and its effect on wages and prices on the other. Introducing the notion of a 'natural rate of unemployment' (NRU), they argue there is only a rare and occasional tradeoff between unemployment and inflation, so fiscal stimulus is ineffective. [36] The NRU notion means even when the Phillips Curve relationship occasional reappears, it is truncated by occurring only when the NRU (around 5%) is achieved. So fiscal policy up to that point is ineffective.

For Retros, discretionary government policies in all forms, whether monetary or fiscal, not only fail to correct the crisis but make matters worse. This message is a virtual verbatim repeat of the classical economic views of J. B. Say and the neoclassical inheritors of Say in the 1920s and 1930s: the only solution is a steady growth of the money supply and, when severe contractions of the economy occur, to let the market liquidate bad assets, permit banks and businesses to fail, and allow the price system to restore equilibrium.

Retros as monetarists constantly warn that government deficits, leading to debt accumulation, will inevitably lead to excess inflation. The massive central bank injections since 2008 involving tens of trillions of dollars of money injection will inevitably lead, they warn, to runaway inflation in goods prices. Hybrids, like Paul Krugman, in turn constantly challenge them to show where the inflation is, since goods prices are slowly receding almost everywhere in the advanced economies. Financial securities and asset prices are excluded from both the Retros' claim and Krugman and the Hybrids' challenge. But excess liquidity injection by central banks plus the continued growth of inside credit by the private financial system *is* driving inflation—just not in goods prices. It is manifested in financial asset price bubbles. In parallel, goods prices and labor prices (wages) continue to disinflate and stagnate, and even now decline in the weakest links of the global capitalist economy: Japan and Europe. The escalation of liquidity diverted to financial asset prices drives the asset price bubbles, while the redirection of money capital from real investment to financial asset investing and from the advanced economies to offshore emerging markets serves to reduce wages, incomes, and the demand for real goods and services. The Hybrid-Krugmans and the Retro-Taylors are both wrong and in a sense both right. The policies of the US and other advanced economies' central banks are generating inflation— in financial assets, while simultaneously slowing investment in real assets and reducing job income and consumer demand in the advanced economies.

This Krugman-Taylor debate reveals more about the lack of understanding by both wings of mainstream economics when it comes to the financialization of the global and US economy and its contribution to financial instability. Like the Hybrid Keynesians, the Retro Classicalists provide no explanation of how financial cycles interact with real cycles. Investment is still expressed only in real terms, no differently than nearly a century ago. Contrary to what many are by this time finding glaringly obvious, financial asset investment is viewed as unimportant to economic stability and the business cycle. How financial investment may distort and divert real asset investment is not a subject of inquiry among mainstream economists.

Retros explain the financial crisis of 2008 from the perspective of classical economics. The crisis was the product of individual action, not of institutions or of processes endogenous to 21st century global capitalism. The causes of the crisis are attributed to 'moral hazard' actions of rogue individuals, who departed from the otherwise stable investment norms of other capitalist investors, managers, and entrepreneurs. Moral hazard is a term coined to describe excessive risk taking, undertaken with the belief that such risks, if they result in a crisis, will be compensated for by the market or government. In other words, bailed out. Investors engage in high risk, moral hazard behavior with the understanding they will not in the end have to pay for it. Someone else will. The public and other stable behaving investors and producers allow the moral hazard to occur because they lack the information about it at the time. Information exchange is 'asymmetrical'. The excessive risk takers know what is going on but the rest or producers and consumers, i.e. the public, do not. Once again, the concept of asymmetrical information is focused on the individual in content and meaning. There is no institutional analysis of the crisis. It is about individual decision making. Those causing the crisis are rogue traders at the French bank, Société Générale, not the bank itself or its practices, or the 'London Whale' JPMorgan Chase's derivatives trader. Or the CEO of Lehman Brothers, Richard S. Fuld. The rogues leave the capitalist 'reservation', so to speak. Regulators are duped because the information is asymmetrical, not because they know and are complicit. It's not about institutionalized shadow banks operating outside all regulatory influence, whose hedge fund and private equity owners, the new finance capital elite, speculate in newly created financial instruments that link together all financial institutions, so when one crashes it brings down a major segment of the financial edifice. While Retros address the subject of financial excess and speculative investing, they purge it of all institutional or systemic characteristics. It becomes an individualist problem. It is reduced to ideological notions of individual behavior. Indeed, speculation is 'good' since all it does is make businesses more efficient by providing simple arbitrage opportunities.

Another element of Retro analysis is the return to business costs as the key to understanding the determinants of real investment. This is a return to classical supply side analysis as the key to investment. Not only should government not intervene to inject income into households and consumers as a means to generate consumer spending and recovery, it should repeal as well all prior costs levied on business in the past to ensure that recovery. That is, it should eliminate all economic regulation since this imposes a cost on business. It should repeal all taxation on business and investors. It should eliminate legal requirements on business concerning wage costs—i.e. minimum wages, unions and bargaining, retirement and health care benefits costs sharing by business, and so on.

To summarize the Retro Classicalist view,

- It assumes a money supply fetish, where real growth and stability is achievable simply by the central bank ensuring a proper supply of money. Even interest rates are of secondary importance to money supply.

- There is no distinction between financial asset investment and real investment or how they interact; nor in a larger sense how financial cycles and real cycles mutually determine each other.

- Financial instability is the result of individual rogue behavior, moral hazard and asymmetrical access to information, and has nothing to do with banking or shadow banking practices or the financial elite that run them.

- The central bank causes financial crises, not bankers and investors, and allows, through bad policy, for recessions to become great recessions or depressions. All forms of government intervention are counter-productive and lead to more instability, not less.

- Keynesian and Hybrid Keynesian income analysis is over-rated and proper theory reveals multipliers are ineffective in generating recovery. There is no tradeoff between production and unemployment on the one hand and wages-price levels on the other, except sporadically in history and at a very narrow range after unemployment is reduced to its natural rate.

- Discretionary fiscal policy and discretionary central bank monetary policy are ineffective and counter-productive. The economy is self-correcting. When caused by central bank policies, financial crises, recessions and depressions should be allowed to run their course by means of liquidation.

- Inflation is always a monetary phenomenon, which means goods inflation. Money, labor and financial asset prices are irrelevant, regulated by market forces. Therefore their interactions and determinations are not significant as a subject of analysis.

From the preceding it is clear that both Hybrid Keynesians and Retro-Classicalists together share a relative disregard for financial forces and variables. Financial asset bubbles are controllable either by central bank and government fiscal-monetary policy response, or better, by the market itself. There are no theories of how financial asset and real asset investment impact each other. The price mechanism will return instability back to equilibrium, with or without government 'nudging' or assistance. Debt is only a danger on the government side, and only given narrow, specific conditions. Debt is a positive contribution to real investment and consumption. The forms of debt do not have mutual effects on each other. Recessions and depressions are due to external shocks, due to supply side or policy based demand side errors. The fundamental structural changes in global capitalism in recent decades require no revisions to basic neoclassical theory or policies. The propositions introduced by Keynes himself decades ago are only selectively relevant (and decreasingly so) or largely irrelevant. Neoclassical economics and its policy consequences are more appropriate today than ever before.

The preceding paragraph is but a short, incomplete summary of the very many reasons why mainstream economics, in both its wings and their various offshoots, basically fails to describe the capitalist global economy in the 21st century. That failure to describe leads to policies doomed to fail. And it leads to a fundamental inability to predict the future trajectory of that economy as well.

Endnotes

1   The term, 'Hybrid Keynesians', refers to those views generally, although incorrectly, described as 'Keynesian' today. Their views borrow some of the original elements of Keynes' theory, reject others, and add to the remaining mix views and propositions that preceded Keynes and which the latter adamantly rejected. The 'Retro-Classicalist' wing represents most of the remaining mainstream economics profession that is critical from one perspective or another of the views of the 'Hybrid Keynesian' wing. A good number of the 'Retros' assume a position of criticism that would be called a variant of monetarism; that is, a view that money supply is the key, primary determining variable for explaining business cycles, including recessions and inflation. They are designated here as 'Retros' since this perspective is fundamentally similar to classical economics' 'quantity theory of money'. Similar but not exactly the same.

2   There was therefore not much of what would later be called 'demand' analysis. It was almost all 'supply' side. Whatever was good for profits and real investment was good for economic growth. Whatever reduced production costs increased profits, investment and more growth. One exception to this supply side, long run view was Thomas Malthus. Malthus raised the question of the periodic appearance of short run 'gluts' of overproduction, which were caused by insufficient non-profit forms of income with which to purchase the rising production of goods. Gluts of produced goods occurred because production rose faster than wage-rent-interest incomes.

3   Workers in contrast did not contribute to aggregate savings, since their wage income was inadequate. They spent all their share of the income from production and did not save. Landowners did have excess income over expenditures, due to their ownership claim to land that earned them 'rents'. But rents, like interest income obtained by bankers, were considered as deductions from profits, i.e. residuals from profits income. Rental income was typically wasted on conspicuous consumption by landlords. Classical economics therefore

viewed landowners (rent) as parasitical, deducting rents from capitalist profits, and thereby reducing investment. Bankers too were sometimes viewed as a necessary evil, financing productive investment when profits were insufficient.

4   One exception perhaps was the British banker and economist, Henry Thornton, who wrote from personal empirical observation about how excess credit issued by banks could lead to financial instability and banking crises. See his, 'An Enquiry into the Nature and Effects of the paper Credit of Great Britain', 1802. But Thornton was an exception to the rule within classical economics at the time and his views were disregarded.

5   Adam Smith, for example, suggested that somehow productivity slowed despite real investment growth and that the economy slipped into a 'steady state', which he explained in some detail. David Ricardo adapted Smith's notion, called it a 'stationary state', and argued it was driven by declining productivity in agriculture over an expansion phase. Neither suggested the stagnation or contraction might have something to do with financial cycles.

6   And perhaps as well in the significant volume of his work still not published or translated; the work of such is reportedly being undertaken in Germany today but not yet available in English.

7   The 'economic bible' that summarized 19th century economic analysis was Alfred Marshall's 1890 *Principles of Economics*. (Note that reference to 'political' economy, that all works from Smith to Marx used, was now expunged from the lexicon of economics.)

8   Pre- World War I, the American, Irving Fisher, and the Swedish economist, Wicksell, began to challenge these prevailing views and their assumptions, cracking the door open to further questioning.

9   Joseph Schumpeter, Fisher, and even the late Marshall took a new look at finance, investment and debt, as did a number of newcomers.

10   The leading money theorist in the 1920s was J. M. Keynes himself. The most advanced consideration of the role of money, banking, and financial analysis at the time was Keynes' 1930 tome, *A Treatise on Money*.

11   Keynes' *General Theory* was preceded by several of his shorter articles and public essays in the interim between 1930, and his *Treatise on Money,* and 1935.

12   Which have been referred to, respectively, at times as 'Reaganomics' (US) and 'Thatcherism' (UK).

13   That is one of several ways or techniques by which ideology works at the level of language, as noted in this writer's previously referenced article, 'Applications of Ideology in Economic Policy', CRITIQUE, , Routledge, Glasgow, v. 37, no. 14, December 2009, pp. 1-14.

14   This was pure economic ideology, not economic science. Observation of reality produced the opposite of Pigou's argument. The class basis of Pigou's argument is simply profits income creates economic growth and a 'good' economy, whereas wages income prevents a recovery to that good economy, and is therefore 'bad'. As will be shown subsequently, mainstream economics debated for decades the alleged 'sticky (downward) wages' as a cause of insufficient recovery from recessions and the idea is still presented in introductory economics texts.

15   This is true whether cost reduction occurs as wage cuts, or interest rate or business tax cuts.

16   J.M. Keynes, "*The General Theory of Employment, Interest and Money*", MacMillan, London, 1936, Chapter 24, p. 372 of the 1967 edition.

17   Keynes, *General Theory*, p. 376. This 'rentier' who should be slowly 'euthanized' refers to the 'functionless investor' in Keynes' Chapter 12. 'Rentier' refers to a business or investor who obtains excess profits at the expense of profits of others, i.e. a transfer of profits by means of legal or other power, but not 'earned' in the market place.

18   J. M. Keynes, 'The Pure Theory of Money' and 'The Applied Theory of Money', *Collected Works*, Vol. V, St. Martins Press, London, 1971

19   Chapter 16 will show how much of mainstream economics, the 'Retro' wing in particular, not only adheres to the monetary policy solution today, but even argues that the recovery from the depression of the 1930s was made possible primarily by central bank money supply and liquidity injections in the second half of that decade. Retros maintained the 1930s depression would have been only a recession, were it not for Federal Reserve errors in 1930-1932 that resulted in a reduction in the money supply. The Fed thus turned the recession into a depression, according to their view. Conversely, they maintain the depression 'ended' as a result of the Fed finally pumping up the money supply in 1939-1940. Thus, depressions are always a consequence of bad monetary policy. As for fiscal policy, Retros maintain it is always disruptive and never a solution to a crisis, so they are systematically opposed to fiscal intervention while agreeing to a 'qualified' government intervention on the monetary side, provided that intervention increases the money supply according to a fixed 'monetary growth rule'.

20   Today we see much of mainstream economics repeating Pigou's error by advocating 'austerity' policies, albeit by proposing to reduce 'social wages and social benefits', instead of direct wage cuts at the point of production as proposed by Pigou.

21   This idea of a lower, stagnant level of equilibrium has similarities, however, with Smith's 'Steady State' or Ricardo's 'Stationary State'.

22   In the *Treatise*, Keynes discusses in depth what he refers to as 'bull market financial speculation' and 'bear market financial speculation' in the run-up of financial and other assets prior to an eventual financial bust and deep contraction of the real economy.

23   Keynes, *General Theory*, Ch. 12, p. 158, MacMillan, London, 1967.

24   Keynes, p. 164.

25   The work that set the process of forging 'hybrid Keynesianism' in motion was the monograph by UK economist, John Hicks, 'Keynes and the Classics'. Decades later Hicks would reject his own analysis as incorrect.

26   Keynes was, however, more ambiguous as to the role of interest rates in an economy not in depression or producing well below its full output potential.

27   That is why the Hybrid version of Keynesianism is sometimes referred to as the 'Neoclassical Synthesis' to distinguish it from basic 'neoclassicalism'. Synthesis here refers to integrating neoclassical propositions, concepts and key arguments with a selection of Keynes' own original propositions and arguments.

28   The reader is referred back to chapters 11 and 12 of this book which specifically address the various financial market and labor market restructuring of recent decades that are responsible for declining multiplier effects in the 21st century.

29   The possible relationships between debt and deflation were discussed in detail in the 1930s by the economist, Irving Fisher, in his 'Debt-Deflation Theory of Depression', *Econometrica*, v.1, n.1, 1933 , and in further detail in his book,

Booms and Depressions, Adelphi, New York, 1932. Although formerly a main advocate of neoclassical analysis, like Keynes, facing the reality of the Great Depression at the time, Fisher attempted to break new ground by trying to link financial cycles with real cycles at the time. Whereas Keynes' *General Theory* focused on the economics of recovery from depression, Fisher's analysis focused more on the origins of the Great Depression, including its financial origins in the decade of the 1920s. Mainstream Hybrid Keynesians ignored Fisher's contributions even more than they did those of Keynes.

30   For this writer's rejection of these assumptions and why the three forms of economic contraction are different, see Jack Rasmus, *Epic Recession: Prelude to Global Depression*, Pluto Press, 2010, chapters 1-3.

31   A constant Hybrid advocate of just 'more of the same' fiscal-monetary stimulus has been Paul Krugman, in his weekly columns for *The New York Times*.

32   For this writer's predictions back in late 2011 that traditional fiscal monetary policies would fail to engineer a full recovery in the US, and would perform even worse in other advanced economies, see Jack Rasmus, '*Obama's Economy: Recovery for the Few*', Pluto Press, 2012.

33   Spinoffs from both major wings have of course occurred on various occasions over the past seven decades. A variant of Hybrids much closer to Keynes himself is sometimes called 'Post- or Left Keynesianism', which differentiates itself from mainstream Hybrids by insisting on a return to Keynes' views concerning expectations analysis. A more recent variant, more distant from Keynes, is called 'New Keynesian' economics. On the Retro side, Austrian economics represents another spin off from neoclassical, closer to Retros than Hybrids. More recent variations on the Retro theme include 'New Classical school', 'Real Business Cycle school', the 'Chicago school' and, most recently, even some of the advocates of what is called 'balance sheet recessions'.

34   The classic Retro-Classicalist accounts of how the US central bank was responsible for the depression were provided by Milton Friedman and Anna Schwartz, *Monetary History of the United States*, University of Chicago Press, 1962, and Allan Meltzer's more recent *History of the Federal Reserve, vol. 1*, University of Chicago Press, 2003, see Chapter 5.

35   John B. Taylor, *First Principles*, W.W. Norton, 2012, p. 45.

36   These two propositions thus negate in large part Hybrid Keynesians advocacy of income's positive effect on stimulating the economy. The Retro view is that government income injections won't result in much actual stimulus to the economy.

17

MECHANICAL MARXISM

Like contemporary mainstream economics, Marxist economists today have been unable to effectively address the structural changes in 21st century global capitalism—in particular the structural changes in finance capital and the new forms of labor exploitation that have arisen in today's global economy.

Like mainstream economics, contemporary Marxist Economic Analysis (MEA) has especially failed to explain the continuing financial instability in the global economy and the consequent impact of that financial instability on the real economy—i.e. how that financial instability has been transmitted to real economic contractions (recessions, great recessions and depressions in select countries), to declining real asset investment and the global drift toward deflation, and to the steady long run slowdown in the growth of global trade and GDP.

This failure to explain the fundamental changes that have occurred in financial and labor markets and their real and financial consequences—which is true for all schools of contemporary MEA—applies especially to that wing of contemporary Marxist economics referred to as hereafter as 'Mechanical Marxism' (MM).

This failure of MM, to which this chapter is largely dedicated, is in part due to the refusal of its advocates to integrate the fundamental changes in the financial and labor markets in capitalism over the past four decades into a new conceptual framework that expands Marxist economic analysis beyond its traditional preoccupation with production of value and the falling rate of profit (FROP) thesis as the key to understanding capitalist economic instability.

Having changed little from Marx's original analysis a century and a half ago on production, exploitation and the role of profits, MM continues to attempt to explain today's global economic crisis in both its financial and real dimensions by employing Marx's original triad of ratios: the rate of surplus value (RSV), the organic composition of capital (OCC), and the falling rate of profit (FROP), which is derived from the former two. Together, the triad of ratios encompass processes that focus on the production of real goods (producer or consumer) that are created solely by that subset of labor that Marxists (as well as classical economists before them) call 'productive labor'. These production processes and the limited view of labor as productive labor are in turn associated with traditional forms of primary labor exploitation that determine FROP.[1] In turn, the FROP drives the (reduced) extent of real investment and determines economic crisis. That crisis, moreover, propagates from the real production side to the financial side and not vice versa. Little is said about how the financial may determine the real or how the two, real asset investment and financial asset investment, may feed back upon each other and mutually cause, and exacerbate, both real business cycles and financial cycles.

In the MM view, changes in profits determine real investment and changes in investment determine economic growth or its disruption in the form of business cycle contractions (recessions) or collapse (depression)—all in a very linear, direct, single direction causative relationship. Financial variables and forces are secondary, derivative, and 'financialization' (which is narrowly defined) is a consequence of the slowing or decline of profits from the production of real goods involving the subset of the total labor force called 'productive labor'.

MM is not the only perspective in contemporary MEA, however. An alternative wing, just emerging in recent years, might be called 'Methodological Marxist Analysis' (MMA). Unlike MM, it is not necessarily wedded to any particular formula or concept that Marx may have developed associated with productive labor or the three ratios associated with FROP. MMA views the Marxist method of analysis as the key link to understanding the current crisis. Originating in new thinking in Europe about Marx and finance capital in recent years, MMA is more open-minded toward analysis that is not strategically dependent upon the FROP concept. MMA also attempts to understand the direction that Marx himself was suggesting in his notes on banking and credit in his incomplete, unpublished notes on the subject in Vol. 3 of *Capital*, one of Marx's last works on economics.[2] However, this wing has not yet established a comprehensive theoretical basis for doing so. The two wings thus have distinct, different orientations toward the role of Marx's FROP, and toward understanding the role of finance capital, credit and debt, and changes in financial structure in general capitalist instability in the 21st century.

Like the 'Hybrid Keynesian' (Hybrids) and 'Retro-Classicalist' (Retros) wings of mainstream economics addressed in the preceding chapter, contemporary MEA is fundamentally bifurcated and thus also divided along at least two lines, Mechanical Marxists (MM) and Methodological Marxist Analysis (MMA).[3] What follows is a critique of MM, from the perspective of its inability to effectively address two important trends in the global economy—the restructuring of finance capital and financial markets and the emergence of new forms of secondary and tertiary exploitation of labor that are expanding rapidly—outside, and in addition to, the traditional Marxist analysis of primary exploitation in the production process, upon which Marx's famous triad of ratios, including the FROP, is based.[4]

Critiquing the Propositions of Mechanical Marxism and the Falling Rate of Profit (FROP)

FROP Explains Short Run Business Cycles

The adherents of the MM wing of contemporary MEA are found mostly in the US and UK. They give central importance to the tendency of the rate of profit to fall as the key explanatory variable for understanding global capitalist economic instability. FROP serves as the central organizing concept around which MM explains business cycles and crises, both real and financial, long term and short, even though there is evidence that Marx himself viewed FROP more as a way to explain a longer run 'breakdown' crisis of capitalism, and not as a theory of short run business cycle disruptions.[5]

In the preceding chapter on mainstream economics, it was explained how the 'Retros' wing also attempts to adapt from neoclassical economics what is basically a long term, supply side analysis to explain short run business cycle contractions. The neoclassical approach, dominant before Keynes, proved a total failure at explaining business cycles. Its long run, supply side approach failed miserably on the eve of the Great Depression of the 1930s at explaining the causes of the depression or at providing workable solutions to end it. Nonetheless, MM attempts it as well. Both illustrate that conceptual frameworks designed to explain long run capitalist growth, or its reversals, do not work well in explaining financial instability events like banking crashes, system-wide fragility development, or the causal relationships between financial and real cycle contractions.

Negative Productivity, Supply Side, and Collapsing Long Run into Short Run

MM analysis parallels classical economics in yet another way. Classical economists (i.e. Smith, Ricardo, and others) tried to explain how slowing productivity over the long run somehow leads to a 'steady state' (Smith) or a 'stationary state' (Ricardo) in capitalist economies. In other words, productivity is somehow associated with capitalism's tendency to economically stagnate in the longer run.

Marx's own 'Organic Composition of Capital' concept, and its central role in determining FROP, may be considered a similar attempt to understand how productivity has negative effects over the longer run, albeit OCC represents a more sophisticated and developed approach than Smith's 'steady' or Ricardo's 'stationary' state explanations.

How productivity contributes to growth has been a primary focus of attention in economics ever since Adam Smith more than two centuries ago. However, the analysis of the negative impact of productivity on economic growth has not been given nearly as much attention as how productivity contributes to growth. Smith, Ricardo and others sensed there was something endogenous to the capitalist economy, and somehow related to productivity in capitalist production, that disrupted capitalism's economic growth cycle. But this suspicion was grounded in a long run view for Smith, as well as for Ricardo and others. It was not a way to explain short run business cycles, recessions or depressions. Capitalism did not 'break down' in the long run, according to Smith-Ricardo, but it certainly slowed to a halt and stagnated (i.e. their respective 'steady state' and/ or 'stationary state' hypotheses). While identifying this possibility, neither Smith nor Ricardo went on to develop it in their analysis. Both were more concerned by far with explaining long run capitalist economic growth rather than its disruptions. It was left to Marx to try to do so.

Marx took up where Smith, Ricardo and others gave up on this question of productivity and slowing long run growth. But instead of proposing a simple steady or stationary state, Marx employed a much more sophisticated analysis of productivity's potentially negative effects. That analysis was embodied in his theory of exploitation in general, and specifically in his new concepts of the Rate of Surplus Value (RSV) and the Organic Composition of Capital (OCC), and in the relationship between these two important ratios. In other words, by introducing RSV and OCC Marx began to break from the conceptual constraints of classical economics on this question of long run stagnation. But Marx's conceptual break from classical economics was incomplete, remaining within the context of a production process-oriented analysis employing classical economic concepts like fixed and variable capital (comprising the OCC) and surplus value extracted by capitalists from labor (RSV) in a production process that was based on productive labor only. While he was light years ahead of Smith-Ricardo, Marx's effort was still framed within a focus on long run, supply side involving the production of real goods, and on how value was distributed in that production process (i.e. exploitation) when production was based on the subset of the labor force called productive labor.

While this was all revolutionary in the sense of new concepts and ideas creation, it was also conservative in that the conceptual categories associated with Marx's new concepts were still very much derived from the classical economics lexicon—i.e. productive labor, surplus, value, fixed and variable capital, perfect competition and all its highly restrictive assumptions, etc. This conceptual baggage would prove inhibitive to better understanding the role of finance capital in enabling and precipitating capitalist crises.

However, one cannot fault Marx too much because of that. One of the hallmarks of classical economics was its major inability to understand money, banking and finance; and Marx, remember, was critiquing still very much from within the conceptual framework of classical economics even as he was breaking from it.

The point is that Marx, like Smith and Ricardo before, sought to understand how and why capitalist production 'tended' to slow over the long term while a primary proposition of MM is that FROP determines short run business cycle disruptions. MM thus attempts to 'fit' Marx's FROP hypothesis into an explanation of short run—i.e. as a way to explain recessions and depressions—which it was never meant to do even by Marx who, it might be argued, viewed the idea of FROP more as a factor in the long run 'breakdown' of capitalism.

It is not that MM and FROP is totally in error. It is just that what may be significantly true in the long run is not necessarily true in the short run in macroeconomics. The neoclassicalists of the 1920s-early 1930s, today's Retros, and the MM all make this error.

Only Productive Labor in Goods Production Creates Surplus and Profits

For Marx, and the classicalists, only productive labor created wealth and therefore economic growth. Productive labor was labor used to create goods. It also imparted 'value' to the goods since all value originated with labor—a view held by Smith, Ricardo and others before them, as well as by Marx. In contrast, labor that did not produce goods—most services, or commercial activity that was not necessary for the transport or sale of goods produced by productive labor— did not impart value. The classicalists and Marx were in complete agreement on how productive labor was defined and how it alone imparted value to the good that was produced. It followed that, if only productive labor imparted value to goods, then only the surplus value extracted by capitalists from workers in the production process was convertible to profits. Surplus value becomes profits, when the products created were eventually sold.

It is obvious that profits are also created by capitalists that sell services or sell goods that were not created by productive labor. But the point is that only profits from the sale of goods that involved productive labor were, and are, central to the FROP hypothesis, both in Marx and MM.

It is change in this specific subset of general profits that determines whether the rate of profit falls or not. And it is the rate of surplus value—i.e. rate of exploitation which is the same thing—along with the change in the organic composition of capital—i.e. the ratio of fixed to variable capital in production of goods—that together determine whether the rate of profit falls or not. But it is still all limited to profits from value extraction based on goods production by productive labor. There is no FROP where labor is involved in services creation, or in the narrow case where goods are not produced by productive labor.

What this means further is that profits from the sale of financial assets and securities does not affect the FROP. Financial assets are not created by productive labor. They are not created by labor at all. Labor selling the assets adds no value to the assets either. It logically follows that financial assets and prices do not drive profits from FROP. And since only FROP profits determine real investment and business cycles, financial assets have no effect on real investment (i.e. capital accumulation) or business cycles. Financial variables and financial assets don't determine real business cycles.

This purely deductive proposition flowing from the idea of productive labor, value extraction from labor, surplus value creation, and profits as surplus value only is of course nonsense. Simple observation of the economy shows that financial assets and financial investment do have a major impact on business cycles. Financial crashes do propagate to the real economy, causing and accelerating real contractions. Not all profits are derived from value extraction from productive labor. And the FROP applies to a specific subset of the economy, not the general economy. Nevertheless, MM advocates argue that profits and FROP are the primary determinants of real investment and thus growth, or the disruption of growth.

Only Primary Exploitation of Productive Labor Determines Changes in Profits

If profits are the outcome of labor value extraction from workers by capitalists, the question then becomes how that extraction occurs. In Marx, the primary methods of labor exploitation are the lengthening of the work day and the intensification of output from workers within a given day. These are called 'absolute' and 'relative' surplus value, respectively. Together they constitute the 'Rate of Exploitation' or 'Rate of Surplus Value (RSV)', according to Marx; that is the first ratio of the ratio triad of RSV, OCC, and FROP which is derived from RSV and OCC.

Absolute and relative surplus value both occur in the immediate production process involving productive labor. That is how exploitation itself occurs. MM adheres to the 'letter of the text' in Marx where Marx discusses how surplus value is extracted by industrial capitalists by means of work day extension and by increasing worker productivity by adding more fixed capital to labor or variable capital.

But MM stops there at primary exploitation. Exploitation occurs only in the process of production, not outside it. When capitalists pay workers their wage, that wage is always less (except in special, temporary circumstances) than the value they created for the capitalist and which the capitalist extracted. If profits as surplus value kept by the capitalist were less than what the capitalist paid the worker in wages—i.e. the worker's share of value created—then the capitalist would experience a net loss and would not continue production. But exploitation may occur not only in the process of producing goods—i.e. it is not limited to primary exploitation. Exploitation may also occur after wages are paid. This was a concept Marx briefly referred to in his late notes as 'secondary exploitation'.

Just as forms of capital—and finance capital in particular—have evolved by the 21st century, so too have forms of labor exploitation evolved by the 21st century. Marx also raised the idea of forms of secondary exploitation in his late unpublished notes but never fully developed the idea as well. Primary exploitation continues, but added to it are expanding forms of secondary exploitation and even the emergence of tertiary forms.[6]

In Marx's earlier analysis, primary exploitation forms were the focus. However, today secondary forms of exploitation are becoming central to the capitalist process of surplus extraction from labor. In general terms, secondary refers to the reclaiming of wages previously paid to workers, whereas primary exploitation involves reducing the initial payment of the wage below value created.

So what are 'secondary' forms of labor exploitation? In primary exploitation, the idea is for the capitalists to keep for themselves as much value created as possible and pay workers a residual, called their wage. But exploitation doesn't stop there. Secondary exploitation assumes forms in which capitalists re-claim, i.e. take back, some of the wages that were originally paid in the first place; or, what is the same, taking back some of the share of the total value workers created that was paid to them as nominal wages by the capitalist. It takes place outside and after the production of goods with productive labor—that is, outside the FROP process.

Reclaiming of wages today takes various forms. Wages include total compensation, not just the hourly nominal wage or weekly salary. Wages as compensation includes payments by capitalists to workers' pension funds, both private and public (social security, medicare), unemployment insurance fund contributions, disability insurance funds, health insurance plan contributions by employers, other fringe benefits contributions, and so on.

In recent decades, under neoliberal capitalist policies, the reclaiming of these forms of total compensation by capitalists, either directly or through government action on their behalf, has intensified. With the help of the capitalist state, secondary exploitation has expanded. Previous employer-provided, defined benefit pension plan funds have been reduced by corporations, used to reinvest in projects benefiting corporation stockholders, spent by managements on speculative investment projects, converted to individual market-based 401k plans (which capitalists then exploit by charging fees), or abandoned by corporations and then dumped on government agencies, after which workers get a mere partial pension payment, if that.

A similar process occurs with government retirement plans like social security, as States globally have reduced retirement payments by raising retirement age, reducing early retirement, or reducing disability benefits for early retirees. Government aided schemes to reduce national health care services, or to come up with new ways to privatize public health care systems as the State simultaneously penalizes employer-provided health insurance plans with a view to shutting them down, also constitute secondary exploitation in the form of reclaiming of social and deferred benefit forms of wages.

Secondary exploitation is also intensifying in the proliferating forms of outright wage theft and in the massive expansion of contingent labor ranks. The expanding availability of credit to workers is in actuality another disguised form of secondary exploitation. As nominal wages are frozen or reduced, credit and consumer debt in lieu of wage increases are made available. But credit and debt requires interest to be paid out of future nominal wages. So credit is a form of secondary exploitation, i.e. reduction, of nominal wages not yet paid. In exchange for credit, workers in effect are required to take a future real wage cut. All the above represent forms of secondary exploitation that are proliferating today.[7]

Tertiary exploitation is even newer, even more recent, but promises to become an increasingly effective form of exploitation in the 21st century as labor markets and capitalist production continue to morph and rapidly change. Overlaid on continuing primary and secondary exploitation, tertiary exploitation involves converting leisure or nonwork time to work time, but paying a lower wage, an 'in kind' wage, or no wage at all for the former nonwork time claimed. Tertiary is thus a blending of work and non-work time in countless new ways that are now occurring in the 21st century. This trend is reflected in what is euphemistically, and ideologically, referred to as the 'sharing economy'.[8] For example, when the company, Uber, hires a worker to drive on his free time, it in effect takes the wage from a former traditional taxi driver, who is now unemployed and without a wage, gives a fraction of that traditional driver's wage and benefits back to Uber's driver to whom it also pays no benefits, and keeps the difference as profit. Or, as another example, when a tech worker stays at the company 24 hrs for days, working on some team project, sleeping at facilities provided by the company, and eating the free cafeteria meals provided, that worker is being paid 'in kind' via the meals, but far less than if he had received a wage for the extra hours given the company.[9]

Secondary and tertiary exploitation do not occur in the traditional Marxist analysis of the production process. Exploitation may not occur in time, t, but wages once paid in time t are reclaimed in time, t + 1, 2, and after. Or wages are paid in kind for hours worked. Or even not at all, as in the case of proliferating unpaid internships for entry level workers. But these new forms of exploitation are not addressed in the FROP process that MM considers the central organizing concept for explaining the capitalist economy and the major business cycle disruptions. Nevertheless, they represent value extracted after the production process.

Furthermore, if other forms of labor exploitation, secondary and tertiary, are occurring—even if outside the production process—then shouldn't capitalist profits be even greater than that reported just from profits from primary exploitation of productive labor? Secondary and tertiary exploitation represent value, and thus profits, not captured by FROP analysis. FROP therefore underestimates profits, and by so doing over-estimates the rate of profit decline as well.

Redefining Profits to Fit the Theory

MM employs a narrow definition of profits. Profits are created from the production of real goods only. Profits from financial investment, trading financial securities, or financial speculation are excluded. So too are services not necessary for the production of goods employing productive labor to reach markets and be sold. None of the preceding have any effect on a falling rate of profit.

But there are even more serious problems with profit estimation by MM. Even FROP-related profit estimation is a problem for MM. MM uses government data on profits to make its point that a falling rate of profits sets in motion forces that lead to a business cycle downturn or collapse. But government databases include profits from services and other economic activities that by definition should be excluded from FROP analysis. Here, the concept of profits is not limited to production, but FROP is a concept limited to profits from production only. There is thus a major incongruence between the concept of FROP used by MM to predict and explain business cycle contractions, and the data used by MM as evidence for its case.

The gathering of data on profits is yet another problem. MM acknowledges that multinational corporations do business and earn profits in many countries. However, those different countries have different degrees of accuracy in their data collection processes. Some emerging market economies gather data on profits poorly, or virtually not at all. Corruption in reporting, in order to avoid local taxes, is also extensive in almost every economy. Profits are redirected within corporations to special funds, like depreciation allowances. Or into financial investments called portfolio funds, a category which contradicts the idea of FROP from production-only profits. Profits get grossly under-reported for various reasons. To further complicate the matter, some economies employ different accounting practices that define profits differently. And in economies like China, where a significant amount of production occurs in government enterprises, the practice is to reduce market prices to subsidize certain goods for political reasons (e.g. defense spending and food or transport subsidies). In such cases it appears there are no profits, while of course there in fact are.

How then to aggregate globally the different quality of data, the different statistical and accounting practices, the redirection of profits, avoidance of profit reporting and different definitions in order to prove the FROP argument of a decline in the rate of profits change? Data collection and reporting, data definition, and profits reporting avoidance to minimize taxes are thus all major problems for estimating profits globally. And if the data aren't accurate, how accurate can the argument be that depends on the data? All this means is that it is extremely difficult to argue and show quantitatively there is in fact a FROP prior to a business cycle contraction. What's left is a largely qualitative, deductive assertion that profit rates decline to precipitate a business cycle.

MM advocates consistently argue, referring to limited, insufficient government data, that the crisis of 2008 was brought on by a falling rate of profit that immediately preceded it. However, even highly limited and inconsistent (with FROP) US data show corporate profits were in fact escalating rapidly on the eve of the crisis, albeit all profits, including from services and other non-productive labor. So to show that profits were falling, MM strip out various categories, making numerous questionable assumptions, in order to get to a reduced data subset that show profit rates declining. It is all very much an exercise of smoothing the data to make it fit the theory.

The data assumptions are quite arbitrary. For example, US data for profits distinguishes corporate profits from non-corporate 'business income'. For non-corporate forms of business, 'profits' are called 'business income'. But the latter are still a form of profit, nonetheless. Capitalists are capitalists, whether incorporated or not. But MM reference data for corporate profits and therefore exclude 'business income' profits earned by proprietorships, partnerships, etc. This exclusion reduces profit totals and makes it easier to show a declining rate of profits on the eve of a business cycle downturn. 'Business income' tends to reflect profits from services, since far fewer corporations are services. And we know, per MM, services don't represent productive labor and therefore qualify as a source of profits. MM does the same for rental and interest income.

So profits from non-productive labor, from the trading and creating of financial assets, from most of all services, and from unincorporated businesses even if they used productive labor to create their products. This all nicely 'pares down' the indication of total profits on the eve of the business cycle shift.

Even having done this, all MM show is a correlation between profits and the business cycle, not a causative relationship. To show a causation, MM would have to provide a convincing 'transmission mechanism' by which profit rate slowdown translates in steps to a decline in real investment and therefore GDP and growth. But they don't. The correlation is thus assumed to represent causation. But over the past decade and a half at least, total profits have accelerated while real investment growth rates have slowed.

Problems with definition, data access, profits underreporting, assumptions, logical inconsistencies, and all the other above problems make it extremely difficult to employ profits in any quantitative sense as it occurs over the entire range of investments in a 21st century economy to prove a FROP is associated with causing a business cycle shift.

And there are other issues associated as well with the term, FROP, itself. For example, MM proponents note that it is not the level of profits but its 'rate of change' that has the important tendency to fall, which precipitates business cycles. But what exactly is meant by 'rate'? Is it just the addition or subtraction from the level of profits from the previous period, divided by that previous period, to get a percentage change or 'rate'? Or does 'rate' refer to a change over time in the 'rate' itself? A rate of change of the rate? Rate can also refer to some kind of ratio, where profits (however defined) are divided by some other variable to get a ratio. What is meant by rate is as important as what is meant by 'profits' itself.

There are other definitional issues with MM use of FROP analysis as well. FROP includes reference to a 'tendency' of the rate of profit to 'fall'. What is meant by 'fall'? Does it mean a rate that is still rising but simply not rising as fast? Or does it mean a rate of profits that is actually negative and less than before? Do profit gains at a slowing rate of increase trigger the business cycle contraction, or does it require an absolute decline in profits and a negative rate to precipitate a contraction? And at what point does the rate change—either slowing or negative—have to occur in order to precipitate a contraction? What is the threshold of the rate change required? None of this is clarified or even discussed by MM. The same line of questioning may be raised with regard to the notion of 'tendency'. How does one measure or estimate the magnitude of the tendency at any given time? Is the tendency always operative, or only under certain conditions? What changes explain how the tendency becomes operative at some point? These points may seem semantic, but they are not. They are central to the argument that the FROP leads to a decline in real asset investment (i.e. capital accumulation) that in turn sets in motion a business cycle contraction. MM never addresses such points, or adequately defines the terms it uses.

Profits Determine Real Asset Investment

For the rate of change of profits to determine business cycles, profits realized from a prior round of production must first re-enter the economy some way, and for MM, that way is through the financing of business real investment. Therefore, another key proposition in the MM view is that profits drive real investment. That assertion is not only shared with Marx but is very much a classical economics notion, one might add. Capitalist industrialists may reinvest their own retained profits. Or they may borrow funds from banks with which to invest when profits are insufficient. However the latter are just recycled profits that other capitalists decided not to immediately reinvest in production but deposit in the bank to earn interest in the interim. But retained profits reinvested and bank loans are both profits, just in different form.

In this view other forms of investment—i.e. in equity (stocks), corporate debt (bonds, paper, etc.), and other sources of finance from what today are called 'capital markets', today dominated by shadow banks, are not considered as sources for financing real investment. Neither is credit provided by the State through tax refunds and subsidies, which capitalists may use for financing investment. Nor by central banks through quantitative easing money injection. Nor are various forms of inside credit provided today by the shadow banking system, investor-to-investors (crowdfunding,) sources of financing, or even new forms of digital money, like Bitcoins, regarded as a source of finance. All this does not exist in the conceptual framework of the MM as sources of finance, apart from profits, for real investment purposes. It is simply retained earnings, i.e. profits from production, plus traditional bank lending, that drives investment. Clearly this is an extremely narrow view of how investment is financed. It's not just about, or even mostly about, profits as the source of investment finance.

In the world of MM, profits from production are the primary determinant of real investment—i.e. profits either as retained earnings or as bank loans from recycled savings of earnings of other capitalists. Investment for MM thus carries a strong bias to consider investing as only real asset investment, and not financial asset investment. Or, at most, to consider financial asset investing as secondary and less important as profits driven real investment.

One must really turn a 'blind eye' to the many forms of finance that have arisen, and continue to arise, as the structure of finance capital has revolutionized in recent decades, and certainly since the mid-19th century. But if other sources of financing investment are assuming a greater relative role in the 21st century, then what does that mean for FROP analysis?

Real Investment Drives Financial Asset Investment

For MMs, real investment eventually determines financial investment in a linear cause and effect process. In fact, the slowing of real asset investment gives impetus to rising financial asset investment (or 'financialization'). The latter is thus a consequence of the former. The solution to global economic instability, whatever its form, therefore originates with the former—i. e. with restoring production profits and financing real asset investment from profits; and not the latter—i.e. not with preventing financial asset price bubbles or reducing the shift to financial asset speculation that is being fueled by runaway liquidity creation by central banks and expanding forms of inside credit.

Mainstream Retro-Classical economists argue that business tax cuts, deregulation, limitations on unions, limiting minimum wage adjustments, allowing business to abandon employer provided benefits, and scores more measures designed to reduce labor costs and provide more disposable income to businesses, are the way to raise 'business confidence' and thus encourage more real asset investment. Retros argue the shift to financial investing and speculation in financial assets is the consequence of government not sufficiently enacting the above measures. MM argues that declining rate of profits in real production occurs first and that leads capitalists to turn to financial investment for the search for profits they could not achieve by means of real investment and production. But the perspectives are fundamentally the same, whether Retro or MM: declining real profits is the fundamental development that leads to 'financialization'.

What is meant by 'financialization' is defined narrowly by MM. At times financialization is typically measured as profits accruing to banks as financial institutions, assuming that the more profits rise for the banking sector the more 'financialization' has occurred. At other times the indicator of financialization is the share of total capitalist profits accrued by the FIRE sector of the economy, which represents finance, insurance, and real estate. When not using financial profits as the definition of financialization, the share of banks or FIRE of total GDP is used as the indicator. Another approach is to argue the rise of financialization is reflected in the growth of employment in that sector, compared to the non-financial economy. Still another has been to define financialization in terms of the growing political influence of banks and financial institutions on government policies.

Financialization cannot be measured or defined by a particular number—profits, GDP, jobs, or any other. FIRE company profits tell us little about the nature of financialization today, or the transmission mechanisms by which finance capital is creating disproportionalities and instability within 21st century global capitalism. Corporations defined as 'banks' or 'insurance' or 'real estate' in US government national accounts are but a segment of the total institutions that could qualify as 'financial' insofar as, for example, what are typically defined as industrial or commercial corporations generate on average around one fourth of their total revenue from financial operations. Should they be considered part of finance capital? One of the world's largest manufacturing conglomerates, General Electric, prior to 2008 generated most of its revenue from its financial arm, GE Credit Corp. And it is unknown to this day what are all the institutions involved in the majority of global financial derivatives trading since such trades are virtually opaque and not traded on a public exchange. Banks, hedge funds, and manufacturing companies engage in massive derivatives trading on a daily basis—and so too do other less formal non-incorporated groups of wealthy capitalists and investors who daily pool, exchange, and bet their financial assets in markets about which little is recorded or known.

Financialization is therefore not a number, in the sense of profits or any other single quantitative indicator. Financialization is a complex global process that involves very high net worth investors; their formal and informal 'shadow' institutions and trading arrangements; the highly liquid markets for financial securities in which they buy, sell, and deal globally; and the constant development of forms of financial securities that they buy and sell in these highly liquid global financial securities markets.

MM provides no convincing explanation of a transmission mechanism even for its presumed impact of real investment on financial investment. Notwithstanding that, the process of how real investment slowing leads to financial investment rising is very linear, unidirectional, and thus 'mechanical'. Nor does MM raise the question whether financial asset investment is driving the slowing of real asset investment. Nor consider that the two forms of investment, real asset and financial asset, interact with each other—i.e. that there exist important feedback effects between real investment and financial asset investment. There is no consideration of financial asset and financial speculative investing, nor of course how those two forms of investing interact with each other. Financial investing is relegated to the 'nether world' of what is called 'fetish' forms of capital. Financial investment and financial asset speculation do not drive real asset investment; rather they are determined by it.

Financial Assets are 'Fictitious' Capital & Independent of Real Investment & Cycles

The MM idea that financial assets and securities represent 'fictitious' forms of capital is derived from Marx. As explained further below, in his notes in Vol. 3 Marx expressed conflicting views on the role of such forms of financial capital. On the one hand they were considered irrelevant, since the source of fictitious capital was that part of the 'credit system' that Marx indicated "lies beyond our plan". That plan focused on traditional commercial and bank credit[10] and therefore "Special credit institutions, like special forms of banks, need no further consideration for our purpose".[11] Marx's apparent disregard of shadow banking and financial speculation in these passages were contradicted, however, by his own comments elsewhere in Vol. 3 of Capital. That kind of contradiction is of course understandable in one's 'work in progress' in the form of notes. But MM takes the former comments as Marx's last word, and ignores the other comments by Marx which strongly suggest there exists something significant in terms of alternative financial institutions, financial speculation, fictitious capital, etc. so far as it concerns the potential for destabilizing the capitalist economy. What MM ignores is Marx's comments that 'fetish forms of capital', which is 'money creating money', is a form of independent exchange value that has the capacity of expanding its own value independently of production. It is "capital yielding a definite surplus value ... unassisted by the process of production and circulation".[12]

MM's one-sided consideration of Marx's notes means that for MM financial securities do not represent real value. They are not produced by labor, the source of all value creation and where labor transfers its value to products. Fetish or fictitious capital represents only a legal claim. It has no use value.

Nevertheless, it does have a price. Its price is bid up by supply and demand competition for the legal claim to the financial asset. A good example is stock prices, which reflect fictitious capital. However, buying and selling equities is not like buying and selling a product. It is about buying and selling a legal claim. The market price of such claims, MM recognizes, fluctuates according to market supply and demand. Nonetheless, that fluctuation is a consequence of forces and developments occurring in the real economy, where FROP ultimately drives the process, in the view of MM. So production processes ultimately determine financial asset prices.

Fetish forms of capital are created outside the production process. And because fetish capital does not create value, it is not critical to the production process of real goods. That is, it has nothing to do with FROP from which capitalist instability and business cycles derive. It follows for MM that if fetish capital doesn't create value and does not influence FROP, then it is not relevant and is not a cause of business cycle contractions. Only real production, real value, and FROP can explain recessions and depressions. For MM the unidirectional, linear correlation is interpreted as causation: financial instability is a consequence of real economic instability, not a cause of real economic instability. Conversely, real economic instability (recessions, depressions, great recessions, etc.) are the ultimate source of financial instability.

Financial Asset Prices Are Not Responsible for Economic Instability

A corollary proposition of MM, which it also shares with classical-neoclassical as well as with contemporary Retro economists today, is a 19th century view of the role of the price system in destabilizing the economy. As noted in the preceding chapter, Classical, Neoclassical, and their 'Retro' inheritors today, all view the price system as a stabilizing factor and equilibrium as the natural state to which the economy returns—with the help of the price system—providing that government interference is kept minimal or not involved at all in any attempt to restore equilibrium. MM does not go quite as far in that absurd assumption. What matters is real investment, which is a function of profits and not so much the price or costs of capital. Prices for labor (wages) and prices for goods sold after production may influence consumption. Products must be sold, i.e. 'realized' as Marxists say, in order for profits to occur and return back to the investment and production process next round. But all this is still about prices for real products. Financial asset prices are assumed not to have any effect on prices for real products or the price of real capital replacement or expansion. Financial asset price bubbles are not central to the basic process. And prices of goods and capital are secondary to the process. For MM, it's not that the price system destabilizes. It is that the price system is a secondary element in the production of real goods and the FROP process. For the classicalists like Smith the neoclassicalists that followed him, and the Retros today, prices restore equilibrium. For MM, the price system and price movement is a consequence of disequilibrium occurring in the real side of the economy. But financial asset price changes are still outside the real production process and do not determine that process.

To sum up, market prices are just distortions of value and therefore not critical (in the long run for Marx, but for MMs in the short run as well). Mechanical Marxists either have no explanation or do not address how financial asset price bubbles contribute to financial instability, crashes, and consequently how financial asset price deflation and collapse contributes in turn to deep and protracted real contractions in the economy called great recessions and depressions. Financial asset and securities prices are forms of 'fictitious capital' that are determined by, not determining of, real production and the FROP.

Banks Are Intermediaries Redistributing Profits as Credit

This in turn leads to another narrow view with regard to banks and banking crises shared by MM. Banks are considered to be financial intermediaries that recycle profits of some capitalists who decide not to re-employ their past profits and money capital immediately back into real investment. Bank lending is just a form of delayed profits re-investment. In exchange for this service, banks charge industrial capitalists an 'interest'. That is why Marx himself viewed interest as a deduction from profits, along with land rents. The money banks hold is recycled back into investment and production—in the long run. In the short run, of course, banks may hoard the profits they hold, or loan it offshore, or reinvest it themselves into financial securities and assets. All that represents a major 'leakage' from the circulation of money capital back to real investment and therefore production. That hoarding often contributes to a decline in real investment at times. And if enough of the profits to be re-loaned by the banks is delayed, diverted (offshore) or disrupted (cycled into financial asset investment), then real investment may decline. But these processes represent how financial assets may negatively impact real asset investment over time. And that would violate the MM idea of the primacy of real investment and production driving the business cycle.

On the other hand, some MM note that this is still profits driving real investment, albeit with a delay. But what they don't acknowledge is that the diversion of real profits, via the banking system into financial asset investment may have the effect of accelerating more financial speculation and investing— that financial investing determines financial investing, and not just that real investment decline drives the shift to financial speculation.

To express it in Marx's own terminology, money capital, M, realized from the sale of real products, may not return to the production process via financing another round of real investment, but may lead to money being created from money, or M creating M', instead of M eventually leading back to produce real commodities, C. Marx's classic M-C-M schema representing the full circulation of capital process, may lead instead to M-C-M-M', at least in part. That M' in turn may mean less M available for the next round of C and commodities production.

Banks then are not neutral intermediaries simply shuffling around profits from capitalist to capitalist for a fee. That was a classical economics view. Smith in particular poorly understood the nature of banking in his own period.[13] Banks are potentially a great source for disruption and instability. And 'banks' in this sense does not mean traditional commercial banks, but the accelerating proliferation of what are referred to as 'shadow banks', as described and discussed in depth in the preceding chapter in Part Two of this book on Changing Financial Structure in the global capitalist economy today.

Today it makes little sense to even talk about industrial capitalists vs. finance capitalists—which was Marx's focus, to a large extent, in the early 19th century. Marxists like Hilferding and Lenin took up that dichotomy, as do the Mechanical Marxists today, who largely continue to see the economic world in terms of industrial capitalists vs. banks or even finance capitalists. While their preoccupation with production and FROP conditions their views in this direction, the reality is that industrial and finance capitalism are blending. The lines between the two increasingly blur.

Multinational industrial corporations in particular have assumed a 'finance' as well as a 'production' of commodities character. As others have pointed out, on average multinational corporations generate at least one fourth of their 'profits' from financial investing and speculating. They often loan to financial institutions, not borrow from them. Shadow banking continues to morph into many new forms, including 'deep shadow' (or shadow-shadow) banking, where industrial and financial corporation definitions become meaningless distinctions.

These non-traditional banking forms are the institutional locus where much of global financial asset investing and speculation take place, although they are also increasingly integrated with traditional commercial banking as well. Thus the MM approach to distinguish, in the classical Marxist sense, simply between banks vs. industrial capitalists or finance capital vs. industrial increasingly fails to conform to global reality in the 21st century. Where MM errs is in assuming finance capitalists, as bankers, are a distinct strata of capitalists separate from industrial capitalists and/or are the latter's commercial capitalist cousins (who transport, store and sell the products created by the industrial capitalists). Some of this stems from Marx's own political writings on class political alignments and revolutions in Europe, where finance capitalists as a strata battled it out with industrial capitalists for political influence in the 1830s, late 1840s, early 1850s and even after. In these political struggles, banking capitalists often allied themselves with remnants of the old landowning aristocracy—both sharing power for a period at the expense of rising industrial capital. The latter prevailed eventually, however, and the finance capitalists abandoned their erstwhile landed allies by the second half of the 19th century, at least in Europe. The competition and contention then became one between finance capitalism and industrial capitalism.[14] But today that dichotomy has no meaning. Nonetheless MM adhere to it in indirect form, as they maintain that real asset investment by 'industrial capitalists' ultimately determines the level of activity of financial asset investing and that, conversely, the latter does not significantly determine the outcome of real asset investing which is the domain of production and FROP.

Money, Credit and Debt

Just as 18th-19th century classical and neoclassical economics employed a simplistic view of the role of banking, and thus a crude view of what caused banking crises, so too does MM err in that direction. That error also flows from a selected reading and interpretation of Marx on the subject, which again was often contradictory. In Vol. I of *Capital*, money is basically commodity money— i.e. gold, silver, etc. Paper money and currency also play a role, of course. But the bias in early Marx was toward commodity money, gold. That bias fit well with the idea that commodities had value from labor used to create them, since gold—like any other commodity—required labor. But Marx's view of commodity money—as are all such views—is almost totally irrelevant for understanding global finance capital today. It is similar to the views of some Retro-classicalists today who believe the way to stabilize the global economy is to return to a gold standard. Gold is just another speculative investment play, no different in essence from oil futures, or soybeans, bitcoins or other forms of 'digital money' that are created primarily for speculative purposes. Bitcoins are the 'digital tulips' of the 21st century.[15]

MM does not appreciate the necessary distinction between money and credit. The banking system may create money, but the primary source of its power is its *ability to create credit*. Money is only one form that credit may assume. The expansion of money by banks, or by central banks when they print it as part of quantitative easing programs, of course enables credit. But the private banking system, especially shadow banks, need not advance money in order to advance credit. Credit may be extended without the involvement of money. With the developments in electronic communications, the internet, and other technologies it is increasingly possible for financial institutions to extend credit to investors. Central banks are thus losing control of the credit system, since they are limited to issuing money, even if doing so occurs in the form of electronic entries to a private bank's reserves at the central bank. Attempts by central banks to withdraw that 'fiat' money from the markets and the private banking system by means of central bank operations, like central bank bond sales via open market operations, is thwarted by banks, shadow banks, and even online investors now creating 'inside credit'. As the shadow banking system expands, and central bank influence over regulated, commercial banks declines relatively, the central banks lose more control over the financial system than even before. Financial practices like margin buying, using collateral based on prices of prior investments, electronic fast trading, derivatives hedging, and countless other financial processes today add to the rapid expansion of inside credit. As inside credit practices grow, central banks' ability to determine the direction of the economy declines.

Because of their bias against the financial side of capitalist instability, MM proponents have not integrated these developments into their analysis of production and FROP. Indeed, so long as FROP remains in its present 'production of value from labor only' form, it cannot accommodate the realities of 21st century finance capital.

The other side of credit of course is 'debt'. The lender extends credit, the borrower establishes a debt. Debt is viewed by MM as mostly positive. Bank lending for purposes of real investment is a good thing. Even bank lending to households helps enable the purchase of the goods produced in greater volume by the increase in real investment. The disruptive, destabilizing forces represented by excessive debt are not addressed adequately by MM, however.

Too much household or consumer debt is viewed as the consequence of insufficient wage income growth and occurs as labor exploitation by capitalists increases in production. Household debt is 'positive' in that it reduces the downward pressure on wages that results from the overproduction of goods. But the positive effect of debt as a substitute for falling wages is only temporary. Consumer debt is not a long run solution enabling capitalists to 'realize' profits from the sale of their goods when wage incomes are falling or inadequate. Consumer debt represents yet another secondary form of labor exploitation itself. Consumer debt means households—mostly workers—must commit less of their future wages not yet paid in order to 'finance' consumption in the present. Household debt represents a way for capitalists to continue 'realizing' sales and profits in the short run as they reduce wages, at the expense of realization in the future. Thus household debt must always lead to even more debt in order to keep the 'realization of value' process, that occurs in the post-production of value process, going.

But who is charging the 'interest' on the debt to be repaid in the future? None other than finance capitalists themselves! So finance capitalism is engaging in a form of exploitation that was previously considered the domain of industrial capitalists alone. If finance capitalists are engaging in exploitation, it then follows they are not outside the production of value and FROP process. They are indirectly (and increasingly) part of it. But MM theory has not explained how this is so, or integrated it into an advancement of the FROP hypothesis.

Nor is the rise of government debt levels globally in recent decades adequately integrated into MM and FROP theory. At the national level, total government debt consists of federal debt and central bank (a quasi-government agency) debt.   As noted in previous chapters, central bank debt just from quantitative easing programs today approaches $10 trillion. Other central bank debt reflects lending to banks. Other government agencies' debt is also financial related. In the US, for example, the debt of government housing agencies (Fannie Mae, Feddie Mac, FHA, etc.) now is several trillions of dollars. Student debt is also mostly held by government agencies. This is overwhelmingly debt that has been run up to bail out or prop up financial institutions, directly or indirectly. As in the case of consumer debt—i.e. mortgage, installment, credit cards—it is debt owed to financial institutions.   Both consumer and government debt levels are significantly mitigating the effects of traditional fiscal and monetary policies, as Chapters 13 and 14, of this book specifically addressed. However, MM and FROP theory have no analytic basis to acknowledge the role of excessive debt in preventing a robust sustained economic recovery from recessions. Nor do MM and FROP explain how excessive household debt contributes to a faster, deeper, and more protracted collapse of the real economy once the recession begins.

In short, whether the subject is money, credit, or debt, MM employs a highly limited and simplistic understanding of how these institutions really function in the 21st century.

Summary

Mechanical Marxists do not understand, or refuse to admit, that capitalist economy has changed in the past 150-200 years and that the forces that determine the 'motion' of Capital (development, evolution, change) are no longer the same as they once were, even just decades ago.

The global capitalist economy has fundamentally changed, and that change has been most profound in the financial sector as well as in the relationships between capital and labor in the production process involving both 'productive' and non-productive labor. MM addresses neither sufficiently, if at all. New forms of capital have arisen within finance capital and the latter's impact on the overall economy is far greater than ever before. So too have the inter-relations between these forms and the ways in which they feed back on each other, including shifts in their various causal relationships.

Mechanical Marxists continue to attempt to explain instability in the global capitalist economy based primarily on the concept of the FROP and what goes on in the narrow segment of the real economy where profits only occur as value creation from production. Profits alone drive real investment and the rise of financial asset investment is the consequence of the fall in the rate of profits in real goods production. Anything that has to do with capitalist business cycles, is reduced to an explanation based on the falling rate of profit tendency: that FROP drives the instability in the real side of the economy (production of goods) and that in turn determines developments on the financial or exchange side of the economy. Rejected is the idea that the evolution of finance capital in the past half century may itself be responsible for the growing financial instability and growing frequency and severity of financial crises in recent decades, and that those financial instability events may in turn be largely responsible for the decline in real investment, growth rates, and the deep recessions, great recessions, and depressions that have also been occurring of late. For Mechanical Marxists, the causal relationship is that real investment and growth slow or decline due to the falling rate of profit for real goods production—and that in turn determines the rise of finance capital, instability and crises.

But this is not at all how the real world works.

A Note on Marx on Finance in Vol. 3 of *Capital*

It is interesting that Marx—the source for MM and FROP theory—was himself far more open minded about the potential destabilizing role of finance in the capitalist economy. That was especially so during his last years of writing on what he considered his primary subject of inquiry—understanding the motion of Capital. Motion here refers to its evolution, its changing forms, how those forms developed, how they interacted and, in turn, how Labor was affected by the change and responded to it. Capitalist economy was acknowledged as ever-changing in content and form. Thus Marx recognized that no theoretical concept necessarily must remain unchanged.

To cite just a few interesting passages in Vol. 3, in Chapter 24, where he discusses the form(s) of capital he calls 'interest-bearing capital', Marx refers to its "self-expanding value" capabilities. This is where "money creating more money" occurs.[16] These are fetish forms of capital "yielding a definite surplus-value". That is, "its own value independently of reproduction". This is where M'-M", not M-C-M' occurs, where M" are these fictitious forms of finance capital, i.e. proliferating forms of 'interest bearing capital'.

What's interesting is that Marx further suggests this may disrupt the circulation of capital in general. Or, as he says, "In interest-bearing capital the movement of capital is contracted". Does 'contracted' here mean that the turnover of fetish and financial forms of capital is faster? Or is he referring to capital from the sale of real products being somehow disrupted in its circulation by forms of fictitious capital?

Marx also interestingly notes that the production of real value has its limits. The workday is only 24 hours, thus there are obvious upper limits of value creation from lengthening the workday, a form of primary exploitation. It is limited by time. Relative surplus value also has its limits, determined by the level of population and prevailing productive forces, according to Marx. Not so, however, with interest-bearing forms of fetish (financial asset) capital. Here "the limit is merely quantitative and defies all fantasy".[17]

Elsewhere, Marx focuses on 'money dealing capital'. Money dealing in its 'pure form' occurs when money lending happens "set apart from the credit system". Marx acknowledged that industrial capitalists also engaged in 'money dealing capital' transactions. Does this mean that industrial capitalists also share 'shadow banking' characteristics, earning profits from money dealing as well as production of goods? Apparently Marx recognizes that money as a source of credit may occur separately from other sources of credit and the 'credit system' itself.

Credit used by bankers may assume various forms. In chapter 25 addressing credit and fictitious capital, Marx notes how bank credit and trade finance lead almost naturally to speculative investing, trade and speculation being "so nearly allied, that it is impossible to say at what precise point trade ends and speculation begins".[18] So Marx acknowledges the existence of financial asset speculative investing that is facilitated and enabled by credit—whether in 'pure' form or other speculative forms.

When credit is applied to industrial capital, however, Marx considers it a positive force. It reduces the cost of circulation, equalizes profit rates across industries, accelerates the production of commodities and the 'metamorphosis' of commodities into money forms. On a broader, macro scale credit "accelerates the material development of the productive forces and the establishment of the world market".[19]

But then, recognizing contrary, negative consequences of credit, Marx states, "on the other hand, credit helps to keep the actual buying and selling longer apart and serves thereby as a basis for speculation".[20] It not only accelerates the expansion of capital, it also accelerates the contradictions, leading to "the purest and most colossal form of gambling and swindling" as well.[21]

In a passage remarkably similar to Chapter 12 of Keynes' *General Theory*, where Keynes speaks of the rise of the professional investor where investing and ownership by entrepreneur industrial capitalists becomes separated, Marx declares that credit and financial speculation "reproduces a new financial aristocracy, a new variety of parasites in the shape of promoters, speculators, and simply nominal directors; a whole system of swindling and cheating by means of corporate promotion, stock issuance, and stock speculation".[22]

This passage is immediately preceded and connected by Marx's statement that fictitious forms of capital (like stocks) represent "the abolition of the capitalist mode of production within the capitalist mode of production itself, and hence a self-dissolving contraction, which prima facie represents a mere phase of transition to a new form of production".[23] While Marx here speaks of joint stock companies, clearly he sees financial investment and manipulation of equity markets as a case example of a broader phenomenon of financial investing and speculation that reflects the rise of a "new financial aristocracy" that "destroys private industry as it expands and invades new spheres of production".

In his last writings Marx obviously sees finance capital, financial asset investing and speculation, as no mere consequence of industrial production nor mere enabler of that production. This was something new, arising out of the bowels of industrial capitalism, a new kind of even more voracious surplus-seeking beast, capable of even devouring its own originators.

The point here is that Marx recognized that both positive and negative consequences of credit (and therefore debt) were possible. But it appears MM focuses primarily on the positive effects of credit-debt, and does not bother to develop an analysis of the negative side in relation to its primary preoccupation with FROP.

Like the classical economists before him, Marx considered interest as a deduction from production profits. Interest was therefore a form of profits. How then, if interest is a form of profits, are interest profits not integrated into a general theory of FROP? Should it be? And if so, are all forms of 'interest bearing capital'—i.e. financial asset investing—candidates for inclusion?

To understand why these issues do not appear until Vol. 3 of *Capital*, it is necessary to bear in mind that Marx wrote in the German tradition, proceeding from the general to the particular, from the more abstract to the more concrete, and from the long run to the short run. Vol. 1 of *Capital* reflects the former in all these approaches—i.e. general, abstract, long run. The focus on value was thus the core. But capitalism is more than its core. It is also the rest of movement and change surrounding the core. Marx planned to move on to consider all the phenomena 'fluctuating around the core', which included considering more the effects of price. Profits, wages, market prices are all 'exchange variables'—or what was referred to as the sphere of the circulation of capital, after products were created and before the money and other forms of capital that appear after production are 'returned' to production. Exchange value and circulation of capital was just as important as the production of capital (as surplus value) from labor. For Marx, what matters is understanding the entire 'reproduction of capital' cycle, from initial processes of labor exploitation, creation of surplus value, to realization of surplus value in the sphere of circulation where price and exchange dominate, to the re-introduction of money forms of capital back into the production process. And the latter is the domain where finance capital exerts its major destabilizing influence and potentially disrupts the full circulation of capital that can result in the decline of real asset investment, capital accumulation, and contribute thereby to a FROP and capitalist cycles.

It is in this 'domain of circulation' as well that forms of exploitation were possible, beyond just that of primary exploitation in the production process. Marx discusses, for example, how workers get swindled by 'lending houses', in what could be a preview of subprime mortgage scandals in the US in the early 21st century, or 'payday finance' lending exploitation and wage theft today, or excessive interest rate and fees charges by credit card companies. "This is secondary exploitation, which runs parallel to the production process itself", according to Marx.[24] In other words, for Marx, exploitation is not just primary, not just limited to extracting value from labor in the production of goods by means of lengthening the workday or intensifying production (productivity) by getting workers to produce more in a given work day. Exploitation can occur by capitalists taking back part of the partial wage share paid to workers in production. It is about reclaiming the workers wage share of the value they produced. Does this also suggest, one might ask, that the price system in the exchange-circulation of capital sphere becomes a way of extracting surplus value initially paid as wages? If so, then does that limit the price system to prices for goods only? How about financial asset prices as well? When homeowners lost trillions of dollars of their 401k pension plans in the financial crashes of the dotcom tech bubble in 2000-2002, would that collapse of financial assets qualify as secondary exploitation? Or when the market value of their homes crashed in 2007-14? Capitalist speculators got rich, but workers as consumers (the sphere of exchange) lost the value of their wages that they paid into their pensions and their homes. Is this not secondary exploitation from financial asset price bubbles and eventual collapse? MM economists may acknowledge these undeniable historical events. But nowhere do they integrate them directly into their theories of exploitation and the FROP analysis based on that primary exploitation only perspective.

Marx was interested not just in the production of value but in the reproduction of value—not just half of the total circuit of capital, but its entire circuit from commodity production through the various money forms capital assumed post-production and how those money forms were recommitted to investment and the next round of production of value that followed. In this later phase of that full circuit, much could occur to disrupt the process. But Marxist theory—from Marx himself through to today's MM—has not done much to develop its analysis of the post-production of value movement of capital and what happens in the sphere of exchange.

This excludes almost half of the circulation of capital sphere. The possibility that financialization of the economy may result in the slowing of the rate of circulation of capital back, preventing its return to real asset investment, or that financialization may permanently divert capital from returning to real investment, are propositions MM does not consider. To the extent contemporary Marxist economics addresses the sphere of circulation—where finance capital increasingly dominates—it does so in a very undeveloped way that hasn't changed much for at least three quarters of a century.

One may therefore conclude that MM and FROP theory are perhaps not necessarily wrong. It's just that they are at best only 'half right'.

The idea of 'Systemic Fragility' is proposed as an answer to the failures of contemporary mainstream economics, in both its 'Hybrid Keynesian' and 'Retro-Classicalist' variants, as well as the 'mechanical' wing of Marxist economic analysis, to adequately integrate the growing importance of endogenous sources of financial instability into their explanations and predictions of the recent past and future direction of the global capitalist economy.

Capitalism is a force that is ever-changing, ever evolving, in both its forms and relationships. Hybrid Keynesian, Retro-Classicalist Mainstream Economic and Mechanical Marxist analyses all look backwards today in an attempt to understand the changes. All apparently believe there is some kind of theoretical 'lodestone' they can rediscover from their past analyses of capitalism in a prior period—whether the money supply, or aggregate demand, or falling rate of profit—that serves as the conceptual basis for understanding 21st century global capitalism. But analyses based on these concepts are deficient today. The task is to develop a new conceptual framework that better explains the new realities of financial instability and the new forms of labor exploitation that together better describe the evolved, and ever-evolving, character of global capitalism in the 21st century.

Endnotes

1   For those unacquainted with traditional Marxist analysis based on the FROP, the latter is a ratio derived from two other key ratios in Marx: the rate of surplus value (sometimes called the rate of exploitation) and a ratio of two forms of capital—fixed and variable—which Marx termed the 'Organic Composition of Capital'(OCC). The two ratios in turn determine the third ratio called the 'Falling Rate of Profit' (FROP). Briefly, the key relationships between the ratios work like this: as fixed capital rises in relation to variable in the OCC, the rate of profit falls. That ratio shift occurs naturally and inevitably over time due to capitalist competition and related forces. That rise in OCC incentivizes the capitalist to increase the rate of exploitation, or surplus value extraction from labor, in order to maintain the rate of profit. In primary exploitation, that intensification of exploitation is achieved by either lengthening the work day or by intensifying output from workers given a defined work day, or both. But if workers organize and resist the increase in the rate of exploitation, then the downward pressure on profit from a rising OCC will not be offset by rising exploitation. Profits will tend to fall. And since profits (aka capital accumulation) are the primary determinant of investment in real assets in Marx (as well as for classical economics in general), then investment will decline and capitalist growth will slow, or even decline, as a consequence. If the twin forces depressing profits occur rapidly, it will provoke an economic contraction. However, as will be explained shortly, Marx never envisioned this process of FROP to provoke business cycles. For Marx, the process represented a long term tendency. Nevertheless, MM advocates interpret the process and FROP to explain short run business cycle contractions as well as a long run tendency, contrary to Marx's own analysis.

2   Michael Heinrich, '*An Introduction to the Three Volumes of Marx's Capital*', Monthly Review Press, 2004. See also Costas Lapavistsas, *Profiting Without*

Production, Verso Books, 2013; John Bellamy Foster and Robert McChesney, *The Endless Crisis*, Monthly Review Press, 2012, and even David Harvey's more balanced view of Marx on finance in his latest, *A Companion to Marx's Capital, Vol. 2*.

3   For more on this 'bifurcation' theme, see Jack Rasmus, 'The Bifurcation of Marxist Economic Analysis', *World Review of Political Economy*', Winter 2012, v. 3, n. 4, pp. 410-443.

4   While MMA adopts a more open position toward the changes in financial structure that have occurred in recent decades, in contrast to the MM wing, neither wing of contemporary Marxist economic analysis adequately considers, in this writer's view, the equally fundamental changes that have occurred in labor markets—specifically the growing impact and import of secondary and tertiary forms of labor exploitation which this writer has raised. For this writer's perspective on the structural changes in both financial and labor markets, see Chapters 10-12 of this book.

5   See the recent works Kliman, Roberts, Brenner, and other US Marxists.

6   Tertiary is a form of exploitation coined by this writer. It is associated with the rise of what's called the 'sharing economy' and in the blurring of work and non-work time, where the latter is being claimed by the capitalist economy without a wage being paid. Or a payment 'in kind' is made in lieu of wages paid. See more below.

7   Readers should refer back to Chapter 13, and the discussion of how labor markets are being restructured in the 21st century. Here the point is that this is directly related to the further exploitation of labor, secondary exploitation, in the Marxist sense.

8   Discussed as well in Chapter 13, and raised again here in brief to show the relationships between capitalism's fundamental restructuring of labor markets and the increased total exploitation rate, where exploitation is not limited just to the formal process of production or to FROP consideration.

9   A practice common at companies like Facebook or Google.

10   Marx, *Capital,* Vol. 3, International Publishers, p. 400.

11   Marx, *Capital*, Vol. 3, p. 404.

12   Marx, *Capital*, vol. 3, p. 391-2.

13   Others like the real banker, Henry Thornton, understood it better. However his views did not get included in the 'canon' of classical economics. See Henry Thornton, *An Inquiry Into the Nature and Effects of the Paper Credit of Great Britain,* London, 1802. Reprinted by Nabu Public Domain Reprints, 2014.

14   A famous turn of the 20th century analysis along these lines was Rudolf Hilferding's *Finance Capital*. Even Vladimir Lenin made a similar contrast in order to make a point about the new stage of global Imperialism that capitalist economy was entering at the start of the 20th century. But this dichotomy has little relevance today, in the 21st century, where large multinational corporations are increasingly financial institutions as well as non-financial in their operations.

15   'Digital tulips' refers to the speculative bubble in the 1600s in Holland when excess liquidity from Netherlands' colonial trade led to speculation in tulip

bulbs. As the price of bulbs rose, as a money hedge, more investment flowed into tulips. The price of tulips became a great play in financial capital gains speculation. It lasted until someone decided to take their money and run. The price of tulips then collapsed and everyone left holding the bulbs lost their capital in the financial asset price crash that followed. Bitcoins are a similar financial play.

16   Marx, *Capital*, by capitalists Vol. 3, pp. 391.

17   Marx, *Capital,* Vol. 3, p. 398.

18   Marx, *Capital,* Vol. 3, p. 405.

19   Marx, *Capital,* Vol. 3, p. 441.

20   Marx, *Capital,* Vol. 3, p. 436.

21   Marx, *Capital*, Vol. 3, p. 441.

22   Marx, *Capital*, Vol. 3, p. 448.

23   Marx, *Capital*, Vol. 3, p. 438.

24   Marx, *Capital*, Vol. 3, p. 609.

CONTRIBUTIONS & LIMITS OF MINSKY'S 'FINANCIAL INSTABILITY HYPOTHESIS'

A notable exception to the general underestimation of financial variables by mainstream economists and Mechanical Marxists was the economist, Hyman Minsky. Writing from the 1970s through 1995, Minsky's views represent an attempt to resurrect and extend the insights on financial instability raised by Keynes and others in the 1930s, which were ignored by both wings of mainstream economists after 1945. Minsky thus represents an important link in the transition of economic analysis of crises from a preoccupation with real side forces and variables to a more balanced consideration of the interaction of financial and real cycles. Minsky also introduced the idea of 'fragility' in the analysis of financial cycles. For both reasons a consideration of his views in relation to this writer's central notion of Systemic Fragility is appropriate at this point before proceeding to this writer's own summary views in the concluding chapter that follows.

Drawing from ideas of Keynes that were conveniently ignored by the mainstream after 1945, Minsky attempted to restore financial forces to economic analysis, in effect picking up where Keynes left off. As he liked to say, while Keynes developed an investment theory of the business cycle he, Minsky, built upon Keynes by introducing a financial theory of the investment cycle. For Minsky, Keynes' 1935 *General Theory* represented an 'aborted revolution'.[1] During the period he himself wrote, from 1970-1995, mainstream economics, Minsky argued, had ignored just those ideas of Keynes that were now the most relevant, as declining real investment and rising financial instability in the 1970s, 80s and early 90s were once again becoming apparent. Minsky maintained that mainstream economics largely ignored "the financial mechanism, which is central to Keynes's interests", which it "treated in a most truncated fashion", if at all. He therefore called for a 'second revolution' in economics, reinterpreting Keynes and focusing on "financial relations, disturbances, and instability" that by the 1970s had begun to play a major role once again in the evolution of the economy.[2]

But whereas Keynes had focused on the professional speculator as an individual agent driving financial speculation and financial asset investment, Minsky sought to develop a more institutional analysis of financial instability. In the process, he also drew heavily on other economists contemporary to Keynes, such as Irving Fisher's early 1930s view of how debt accumulated in the period prior to a financial crash, which then exacerbated both financial instability and the real contraction as excess debt drove deflation. Minsky also embraced the notion that profits determine investment, which was proposed by the Marxist economist, Michael Kalecki, from whom Minsky admittedly derived his own particular emphasis on the analysis of 'cash flow' necessary for the servicing of debt. Cash flow was a key variable for Minsky, but it derived largely from profit streams from prior real asset investment. Drawing from others, like the economist, Henry Simon, who was his mentor early in his career, Minsky also introduced an institutional focus to the problem of financial instability.

Minsky's theory might be summarized in what he called the 'Financial Instability Hypothesis' (FIH), a key element of which was his concept of financial 'fragility'. There are obviously a number of similarities between this writer's concept of 'Systemic Fragility' and Minsky's financial fragility. But there are notable and critical differences as well. Just as Minsky embraced ideas of Keynes, Fisher, Kalecki and others, and then went beyond their contributions, this writer's notion of Systemic Fragility expands upon and extends well beyond Minsky's.

Minsky's contributions were significant. But his FIH and related ideas were also limited in a number of ways, as subsequent discussion will explain. Nevertheless, just as Minsky extended and developed further the ideas of Keynes, Fisher and others, so too is it necessary today to take the best of Minsky's insights on the nature of finance capital and develop them further—as well as those of Keynes, Fisher and others who have contributed to the understanding of the relationship between financial cycles and real cycles and why the former are becoming more critical in the 21st century to the instability of global capitalist economy.

While Minsky, Keynes, Fisher and others made significant contributions to understanding the nature of financial-real economic interactions, as did Marx and others before them, in the view of this writer none have adequately developed a theory of financial-real cycle interactions or explained how financial forces destabilize the capitalist financial system and in turn the real side of the economy, nor how mutual feedback effects may occur under certain conditions causing a further deterioration of both the financial and real economy. Minsky,

Keynes, Fisher and others added important pieces to the financial instability puzzle, but not a thorough theoretical framework with which to predict the evolution and trajectory of financial instability in 21st century global capitalism. One cannot fault them for not having done so, however.

Marx and Keynes Were Before Their Time

In Marx's time, the new forms of finance capital were just beginning to emerge. After focusing on the fundamentals of the production of value as the driving force in the real economy, Marx had planned to address more thoroughly how value from production morphed into its various exchange value and money forms, as capital moved in the circuit from production through money forms back to production. This was the sphere of 'circulation of value' for Marx, where banking and finance appeared by the late 19th century to become more disruptive of the flow of value in the circulation of capital.[3] However, Marx only began to comment on this in his preliminary observations in his last writings and notes. He did not finish his work. Nor, had he 'finished', is it likely Marx could have provided a thorough analysis of finance capital since that form of capital was only beginning its ascendance. He was simply too early.

Nor can one fault Keynes in his *General Theory* for not developing his analysis of finance and 'speculative investing' (and how it differed from his contrary example of 'enterprise investing') beyond the brief treatment Keynes gave it in chapter 12 of his *General Theory*, which was full of financial investing insights. But those insights were not effectively integrated with the rest of the chapters in the *General Theory* that addressed in large part the real investment function and how that function related to business cycles and monetary and fiscal policy. Keynes could have said much more in the *General Theory* about how financial speculation affects real investment and vice versa. Indeed, much more could have been said concerning relationships between investment and consumption in general, but it wasn't. Keynes' exploration of financial cycles in his earlier 1930 work, *A Treatise on Money*, was left out of his 1935 *General Theory*.

The *General Theory* was very much oriented toward real variables, which Keynes saw as the solution to the recovery from the Depression at the time. The *Treatise on Money* suggested that financial variables may have been important in causing the financial crash of 1929, and banking crashes that at the time were central to trajectory of the Depression, but in the *General Theory* financial variables were not central to ending it. In fact, much of the *General Theory* argued that monetary policy solutions (money supply, interest rates, etc.) were irrelevant to ending the Depression. The General Theory was not a theory about how the Depression originated; it was about how to end it once it had occurred. Keynes was thus certainly aware of financial forces. He just chose to de-emphasize them since they were not central or the solution to recovery.[4]

With the birth and development of Hybrid Keynesianism starting in the late 1930s, financial forces, variables and causes of cyclical instability in the capitalist economy were virtually ignored. Hybrid Keynesian economic analysis would come to focus almost exclusively on what were called 'General Equilibrium Models' built upon real variables, and a simplistic notion of money and credit. Money was simply M1, M2, etc., and the sole source of credit. No distinction was made between money and credit, which would have led necessarily to the consideration of financial forces and variables, had it been. Nor was any distinction made between financial asset prices and goods prices, or how they interacted. There was only one price system of any importance, goods prices, and prices were stabilizing not destabilizing forces. The only important difference between Hybrids and Retros on the topic of price stability was that Hybrids believed nominal government action was necessary to assist the stabilizing character of prices, whereas Retros held that such action did not assist but interfered with the otherwise natural stabilizing effects of the price system.

With the advent of another global crisis of the capitalist economy in the 1970s characterized by a collapse of the global Bretton Woods monetary system early in the decade, followed by slowing and stagnating real investment in the advanced economies amidst growing price instability, mainstream economic analysis was thrown into turmoil. Unable to predict or explain the crisis, Hybrids were thrust aside and Retros returned in force. With the collapse of Bretton Woods the vacuum was filled by central banks globally, who were now responsible for stabilizing the global system by means of money injection and retraction. However, while injection was easy, retraction proved extremely difficult from the beginning, and virtually impossible by the 21st century. However, central bank policy, now ascendant as the key institutional stabilizing force, buttressed the Retro-classicalist economic focus on money as the key economic variable.

This elevated importance given to money and central bank policy would become a key element of the general 'Neoliberal' policy revolution that began to emerge in the late 1970s—a theory and policy expression of the more fundamental real economic crisis of that decade. Neoliberalism would add other policy (and theory) elements to fiscal policy: tax cuts for investors and businesses, deregulation, privatization of public goods and services, free trade and offshoring of jobs, destruction of unions and collective bargaining, compression of wage gains, privatization of retirement and health care benefits, rise of contingent (part time, temp, contract) labor, and other 'domestic' policy measures. But most critics of neoliberalism fail to see beyond the obvious domestic policies and understand the even more central elements associated with a restructuring of the international monetary system—the now central role given to central banks worldwide, and the consequent global financialization of the economy beginning in the 1980s and intensifying ever since. Writing in the 1980s and 1990s, Minsky picked up on these latter developments as the neoliberal policies, especially as they related to financialization, began to lead to conditions of growing financial 'fragility', instability, and more frequent financial crises.

Like Marx and Keynes, Minsky too was 'before his time', although he was much closer temporally and geographically since the core of the new changes in financial structure and institutions was the US economy and not Europe. He developed his views as the inherent financial instability within capitalist economy, suppressed in the 1945-1965 period, began to re-emerge once again by the late 1960s. For reasons that will not be addressed here, the postwar capitalist economy from 1945 through the mid-1960s was basically stable financially and relatively so in real terms as well. By the late 1960s, however, early signs of a changing financial structure began to appear. Minsky began writing in the mid-1970s about this re-emergence, and continued to do so until 1995 when it became abundantly clear a qualitative shift in financial instability had emerged, which was increasingly indicated by financial instability events in the US in the 1980s, and in Europe, and especially Japan's historic financial crash, in the early 1990s. So Minsky could perhaps see the outlines of what might come but not the fuller picture—because it had not yet fully developed. He was not 'before his time', but was definitely too early. It would take another two decades of rapid financial system evolution and the advent of the generalized global financial crisis that erupted in 2007-09 for conditions to fully mature.

Minsky on Financial Instability

In a major break from mainstream economic theory, beginning in the 1970s and through his latest published articles in 1992-95, Minsky wrote that capitalist economies were endogenously unstable over the longer term. The origins of this instability lay, moreover, on the financial side. Minsky argued the financial system evolves over the longer term from 'robust' to 'fragile' and thus toward instability. Fragility was a term that implied a potential for instability.[5] The endogenous drift toward instability was not always apparent, given that it occurred over prolonged periods of prosperity. The global economy was more or less financially stable over the period 1945-1965. Recessions in the real economy were relatively mild and short-lived, easily corrected by traditional fiscal and monetary policies. Financial cycles were not precipitating and exacerbating real cycles, which thus remained mild in comparison to the repeated banking crashes in the 19th and early 20th centuries and the periodic great depressions that occurred every couple of decades or so. Signs of new instability began to emerge once again, Minsky noted, in the late 1960s, intensified in the 1970s, and accelerated further in the 1980s. The financial instability events of the late 1980s-early 1990s—the US savings and loan and junk bond crises, the stock market crash of 1987, Japan's financial implosion that followed, regional banking crises, repeated international sovereign debt and currency crises in emerging markets were his main empirical observations from which he developed his own financial crisis theory, which he called the 'Financial Instability Hypothesis', or FIH.[6]

For Minsky, the capitalist economy was a complex structure of institutions, financial relations, and agents' behaviors that evolved over time toward a more fragile and thus unstable condition. Real investment in capital stock was at the heart of the process, much as for Keynes. The growing financial complexity, fragility and instability disrupted that real investment process. His theory of profits drew from Keynes, but was more similar, with a financial twist, to the views of the 1930s Marxist economist, Michael Kalecki, who argued that profits from the production and sale of real goods (producer and consumer) were the primary determinant of real investment. Minsky too argued that profits were the key determinant of real investment but that rising business debt over time significantly affected profits as the main determinant of real investment, as well as decisions by investor-agents about whether to invest in real assets. In other words, profits determined real investment (as Kalecki argued) but debt and financial instability disrupted the process as the financial structure of capitalism evolved endogenously over time from robust to fragile:[7] profits from real investment determined future investment, but debt and fragility could interrupt that causative link.[8]

When relatively robust, the financial structure and regime were stable. The financing of real capital assets was described as a 'hedge' and a hedge capital financing regime.[9] When a firm, and the system itself, was 'hedge financed', repayment of debt was possible from cash flow generated by past investments. Hedged firms also relied more heavily on equity (stock) financing over borrowing, issuance of corporate bonds, and other forms of business debt. When debt was used to finance investment to some degree, it was long term debt not short term. In a hedged firm and regime, cash flow was sufficient to cover both debt interest and principal payments. However, over time, as investor agents (business or professional) became more optimistic, as typically occurred in good economic times, and their expectations of future profits rose, they began to finance real investment increasingly from debt. The ratio of debt to equity and to cash thus rose, and so too did the need to repay the growing principal and interest levels out of cash flow. Since cash flow derived primarily from profits created by previously owned real assets, more and more cash flow was needed to finance debt as debt rose steadily over time. As a result less cash was available for reinvestment in real assets. Profits from real investment consequently slowed over time. And the longer the period of 'good times', the more the shift to debt financing to take advantage of same, and thus the greater the eventual drain on cash flow and profits from which cash flow itself derived.

As this process evolved, firms became less robust and evolved from 'hedge' conditions to what Minsky called 'speculative' capital asset financing units, where cash flow was sufficient only to cover interest due but not sufficient to cover principal payments. Speculative units thus repeatedly have to 'rollover' (refinance) maturing debt, often at a higher rate of interest and on less favorable terms and conditions for repayment. In 'poor' times, especially recessions and periods of slow or stagnant economic growth, rollover was more frequent and occurred on worse terms as well (i.e. higher interest rates, shorter terms, affording more opportunities for the lender to seize the firm's assets in the event of nonpayment, etc.). Refinancing terms worsened similarly for firms that were repeatedly having to rollover and refinance for reasons other than general economic slowdown. Speculative units (firms) were highly dependent on a normal, stable economy and financial system, without which they became highly prone to defaulting on payments. Before defaulting—i.e. failing to repay either principal or interest—speculative units deteriorated into what Minsky called 'Ponzi' units.[10]

Ponzi units and firms had to borrow additional debt in order to pay principal and interest on old debt, not just 'rollover' or refinance the old debt. Cash flow was insufficient to repay either principal or interest. The firms debt-equity ratio worsened dramatically. No investors ordinarily were interested in purchasing stock of a company in severe debt, unable to repay its debts and moving toward a bankruptcy and possible seizure of its remaining assets. In the case of a financial crisis erupting, Ponzi firms are highly likely to default if new debt is not made available. But new debt, if provided, is frequently so costly that it hastens, not prevents, the eventual bankruptcy.

When a large percentage of firms have moved from hedge to speculative and then to Ponzi, along a continuum of robust to fragile, the system itself becomes more fragile in the business sector of the economy. When financial crises—stock market crashes, banking crashes, etc.—occurred, the financial regime that was more fragile—i.e. weighted or more populated with 'ponzi' units—tended to amplify the financial crisis and more rapidly propagate the financial instability throughout the system. Extreme fragility among banking and financial institutions might also actually trigger a financial instability event, according to Minsky. This was especially true if firms and banks were deeply involved in issuing short term debt to purchase long term assets, which often occurred in latter stages of a long run growth period.

This general scenario of evolving toward more financial fragility typically occurred as debt levels rose and composition of debt deteriorated (i.e. shifting from long term to short term debt, from lower to higher interest rates, and toward more onerous repayment terms and conditions imposed on borrowing firms). When the rate of real investment rose as real economic growth (GDP) rose, profits and cash flow in turn were created to support the rise in debt. But after a point, business indebtedness outpaced profits and cash flow available to support debt payments. This condition accelerated when a recession occurred or economic growth stagnated, making debt rollover or debt addition increasingly difficult. That pushed hedge units into speculative, speculative into Ponzi, and Ponzi into defaults. To avoid default, previously accumulated real assets had to be sold, often at fire sale prices. When widespread, this amplified and propagated the fragility condition still further.

In other words, fragility was an endogenous condition that grew steadily as a secular trend over time, but was also a condition that accelerated during economic stagnation or recession. On the other hand, while Minsky postulated the secular evolution toward financial fragility over an extended period, he did not clarify the transmission mechanisms by which this occurred in any detail except to suggest, along with Fisher, that financial asset deflation was associated with the process of deteriorating fragility. Furthermore, financial asset prices served not only as a transmission mechanism but as a system destabilizing force.

Neither Fisher nor Minsky explained how financial asset prices function as a transmission mechanism on the 'upside' before a crash, promoting the endogenous shift from hedge to Ponzi. How financial asset inflation is associated with debt accumulation during a 'boom' phase is thus as important to understand as how deflating financial asset prices affect debt during a 'bust' period. In other words, financial fragility is a condition that can build secularly preceding a financial instability event as well as accelerate after an event. This dual pro-cyclical characteristic of fragility—i.e. rising in both boom and bust periods—makes it particularly perverse once it begins to evolve endogenously.

To fully appreciate the problem of fragility in the modern capitalist economy it is important therefore to understand how fragility's main determining variables dynamically interact; how the relationships between the three variables may change over time; and how various transmission mechanisms participate in these changing relationships between variables.

Minsky posited three main variables as determining fragility. They were debt, cash flow, and other 'terms and conditions' that influenced the ability to repay debt from cash flow. Debt was expressed in terms of levels or magnitudes, but implicitly in terms of composition as well. The 'terms and conditions' third variable was really a group of potential variables. Long term vs. short term was important, as well as how much short term debt was used to finance long term real asset investment. Cash flow was a form of income, which Minsky viewed as derived from profits, and thus from the real side of the economy. Financial fragility was thus in part determined by the real investment, at least in so far as cash flow from profits was necessary for repayment of debt. The third variable included not only the long vs. short term mix condition, but the uses to which short term debt was applied. The level and rate of change of interest rates was an important 'terms and conditions' factor as well.

Minsky's linear shift from hedge to speculative to Ponzi represents a de facto income-debt relationship. If debt rises, then so does fragility. And if income (cash flow from profits) growth slows or declines, so too does fragility. In the boom period before a financial crisis, income (cash flow) rises faster than debt. Eventually, however, income growth begins to slow while debt accumulation continues, even accelerates. Debt eventually exceeds the ability of available income streams of the business to finance existing debt. Furthermore, when financial instability and recession occurs, real debt rises more rapidly as prices deflate and real income falls. In this manner, both income and debt accelerate the rise of financial fragility.

This leads directly to a question of how Minsky viewed the price system in general and in particular how he viewed prices in relation to his idea of financial fragility. Here he drew heavily on Keynes' 1930s Two-Price systems theory, a radical idea at the time. The two price systems were prices for goods and outputs, on the one hand, and prices for capital assets on the other. The neoclassical (pre-Keynes) idea that 'one price system fits all' and that all prices returned to equilibrium by means of an equilibrating supply and demand process, and that therefore the price system stabilized markets (financial and other), was rejected by Keynes and Minsky in turn.

By capital assets Minsky clearly meant physical assets from real investment—i.e. buildings, structures, equipment, and such. But at other times he referred to capital assets not only as physical assets but as financial securities and financial assets as well. The distinction was not always clear. His apparent assumption was there was no essential difference between real capital assets and financial assets and securities. However, as the concluding chapter to this book will explain, distinguishing between how prices behave for real capital assets and financial assets is as important as distinguishing between capital asset prices and goods-outputs prices.[11]

The function of the price system was not simply to allocate resources and distribute income, as assumed by neoclassical economics. According to Minsky, capital asset prices had to be sufficiently high to justify real investment that, in turn, produced the profits from which cash flow was created. And cash flow was necessary to finance debt payments. As Minsky noted, "The cash flows that prices carry enable debts to be paid, induce and partially finance investment, and enable new financial obligations". It therefore followed, he added, that "there are really two systems of price in a capitalist economy—one for current output (goods) and the other for capital assets. When the price level of capital assets is high relative to the price level of current output, conditions are favorable for investment; when the price level of capital assets is low relative to the price level of current output, then conditions are not favorable for investment, and a recession—or a depression—is indicated ... One key problem of economic policy is to fix the economy so that the two price levels are such that there is an appropriate amount of investment."[12]

This view implies that capital asset deflation will have the effect of discouraging real asset investment. Declining real asset investment lowers profits from real investment. Prices for capital assets were therefore an important determinant of profits, which produces the cash flow necessary to finance (i.e. pay for) debt. In the two-price theory, therefore, capital asset prices are even more fundamental than goods-outputs prices since, without adequate price for the capital assets, the investment that produces the goods would not even occur and thus there would be no goods to sell at any price. The former (real capital assets) creates the latter (goods or outputs). Capital asset prices ultimately determine goods prices, so they are primary.

Of course, goods prices also have an impact on capital asset prices. If the goods aren't sold, profits are also affected.[13] But Minsky viewed capital assets and their prices as initiating the relationship between capital asset investment and goods output. So the former remained primary.

But the more important missing point in Minsky's two price theory is that he makes no distinction between real capital assets and financial capital assets. Just as real capital assets may determine and drive goods prices, so too might financial asset prices drive and determine real capital asset prices. Capital asset prices had to exceed goods prices to induce real investment, according to Minsky. But what if financial asset prices (and therefore profitability from such) exceed real capital asset prices? Would that not divert investment from real capital asset investment to financial asset investment? And would that diversion not slow real capital asset investment, as demand for real investment assets declined and therefore depressed the price (and profitability in turn) of real capital assets?

Moreover, what would financial asset prices exceeding real capital asset prices mean for the real capital asset prices-goods prices relationship? Would lower real capital asset prices relative to goods prices depress real investment still further? That would represent a double negative on real investment: higher financial asset prices diverting investment from real capital assets to financial securities, and the consequent lower real capital asset prices relative to goods prices discouraging real investment still further. Or what would be the parallel impact of financial asset price increases on goods prices indirectly, instead of through the effect of lower capital asset prices? What this suggests is that escalating financial asset prices could seriously destabilize real investment, reducing the demand for real capital investment in various ways. But these questions were not explored by Minsky.

In a very Kaleckian fashion, Minsky simply concluded that "'What determines profits?' is a key question for understanding how our economy works."[14] Yes, but profits from what: real capital asset investment? Financial asset investment? Or goods production and sale? Profits just from real capital assets is not the whole 'profits picture' in 21st century global capitalism. This very Kaleckian assumption is only in part correct. Profits from financial asset investment simply cannot be ignored as a determining force. But that's exactly what both mainstream and Mechanical Marxist analyses today, with their fixation on real production, effectively assume. It seems as if Minsky also has at least one foot in that camp.

If prices are a key element in all three cases—real capital assets, goods and outputs, and financial capital assets—for determining profits, then which price system is the primary driver and determinant of the other two? Under what conditions, or phase of the business cycle, is which price system primary? And is the determining relationship always the same regardless of the phase of the business cycle? Is it always a linear determination? If not the same or always linear, how do the three price systems interact and mutually determine the other?

These were critical questions Minsky did not address. The Hybrid Keynesian view has always been notoriously deficient in terms of its theory of price. Beginning within this wing, and attempting to break from it, he nevertheless continues some of its errors of analysis. He correctly argued the neoclassical 'one price fits all price system that always returns to equilibrium and stabilize markets' was nonsense. He acknowledged that capital asset prices were different, and that the interaction of capital asset prices with goods prices was important to understand as a determinant of real investment. But he erred in not going a step further and recognizing that financial asset and financial securities prices behave differently from real capital asset prices, just as capital asset prices behaved differently from goods prices.[15]

Minsky's failure to sufficiently distinguish real from financial price behavior derived from distinguishing insufficiently between financial asset investing and real asset investing. He still viewed financial instability as ultimately originating in the real side of the economy, in real side profits production. It was there that insufficient real investment lowered profits, which reduced the cash flow necessary to service the debt that accelerated during the boom period. It was insufficient real investment that eventually reduced the ability of firms of make payments on accumulated debt, which led in turn to the shift of 'units' from robust to more fragile, from hedge to Ponzi, that could trigger financial instability events. The conditions for financial instability originated on the real side of the economy, not within the financial system itself.

Minsky's apparent preoccupation with real asset profits may have flowed from his more or less total agreement with Kalecki's limited view of profits. Profits came from real investment and real production. Profits from financial asset speculation were not in Kalecki's equation.[16] Sources of external finance—i.e. equity and corporate bond issuance, bank lending, and other financial instruments—were of secondary import to Kalecki. Investment depended primarily on internal profits, and profits derived in turn from real investment. It was a very much 19th century view of finance. But in the 21st century investment, whether real or financial securities, is financed far more than ever before from external sources of credit than from internal profits. Today firms mostly borrow from external sources in order to distribute their 'internal' profits to shareholders or to hoard the cash on their balance sheets.

This view that investment is financed basically from internal profits leads to a view that sees the real side of the economy as the origin of instability on the financial side—instead of seeing the two sides, financial and real, interacting in a dynamic way or admitting that the financial side is playing an increasingly important role in that interaction in the 21st century, as the true origin of instability. Minsky of course recognized the role of debt and debt sources of external finance, as well as equity finance and internal profits, nevertheless saying that while debt may impact system behavior, "the key determinant of system behavior remains the level of profits".[17]

Minsky's view on debt itself was that it was as central to fragility as income (as cash flow). The hedge to Ponzi continuum was determined by the two variables, income (cash flow from profits) and debt. Both were key to the growth of fragility and therefore instability. Fragility was an income-debt relationship that could deteriorate from either a slowing or decline of income to pay debt or a rise in that debt. Minsky further observed that financial innovations seemed to escalate along with a rise in the level of debt. They enabled new forms of credit that accelerated debt that in turn raised fragility. As he put it, "financial innovations and changes in financial practices are part of the process that increases the fragility of financial structures over the run of good times."[18] But a deeper exploration of the development and role of 'inside credit' was left unaddressed except for commentary on mortgage securitization and the rise of credit card receivables.

Another area of Minsky's FIH requiring comment is the role of government policy—fiscal and monetary—in re-stabilizing the financial system and real economy following a financial crisis and subsequent deep real economic contraction. Here the period in which Minsky wrote, as well as his close ties to Keynes, led him to optimistic conclusions about how government action—both central bank and federal budget—could successfully 'constrain' fragility, as he put it. Unconstrained fragility development led to wide asset price volatility, and to liquidity (cash) and/or solvency (bankruptcy) crises at banks and other corporations. But central bank 'lender of last resort' liquidity injections could halt the increase of fragility and financial instability on the financial institution side, according to Minsky, while federal budget deficit spending could provide a similar rescue on the non-banking side by subsidizing profits.

This essentially optimistic view was no doubt a product, in part, of his observations of the 1988-1992 financial crises in the US, which involved the collapse of the savings and loan sector, a crisis in junk bond financing of leveraged buyouts, and the brief but deep stock market crash of 1987. What he observed was that government intervention at the time headed off a potential 1929-33 type of debt-deflation cycle during 1988-1992. The US Treasury intervened, Savings & Loans were taken over, and the fragility and asset deflation on the financial side were not allowed to pass through to households as a result of deposit insurance and other government actions.[19] At the same time, a collapse of non-bank corporate profits was prevented by the Federal Reserve pumping more liquidity into the banking system. A floor was thus placed by coordinated government institutional action that reduced the need for corporate and bank asset 'firesales' that would have exacerbated asset deflation and debt further—leading to a Fisher-like 'debt-deflation depression'. This was enabled by increased budget deficits.

Minsky's solution to a financial crisis therefore was for 'big government' to subsidize profits by deficit spending and for the 'big bank' (central bank) to bail out the banking system. He thought this could happen because he observed it. He also historically observed that something similar had happened in 1934-36 with the Roosevelt administration/US Treasury creation of various New Deal government institutions that bailed out homeowners and households as well as farmers and small businesses. This solution perspective places Minsky very much in the Keynesian camp (although not the Hybrid Keynesian). Minsky also called for discontinuing social welfare and transfer programs and replacing them with employment programs. He also proposed breaking up the big banks and general financial reform.

Government consequently was an important variable in the Minsky view, but more as a re-stabilizer of the financial instability and crisis than as a contributor to systemic fragility. Whereas Minsky discussed fragility in depth in terms of its application to the business sector, bank and non-bank, and whereas he recognized fragility was a factor as well for households, he did not apply fragility analysis to the government, seeing it rather as a force that potentially was able to 'constrain' fragility with the correct policies and institutional reform, as he put it. It was not a source of fragility itself. He did not raise the idea that government action did not really resolve or reduce fragility in the system, but merely shifted it from the private sector to itself. Or that there were no limits to central bank or government deficit spending in the attempt to 'constrain', to check, to suspend the development of fragility and to halt the self-sustaining downward spiral of debt-deflation-default that emerged in the wake of a financial crash and major financial instability event.

Minsky's Contributions

Minsky's contributions to understanding the nature of finance capital today were many. And so were the limits to his theory. No one economist has provided the full analysis. Not Keynes, not Fisher, not Marx, not Hayek, not those with lesser contributions along the way, and, not Minsky either. To maintain that Minsky's theory is 'the' analysis of finance capital and financial instability in modern capitalist economy, as some of Minsky's adherents today do, is to think that capitalism is static and never changing. That, of course, is incorrect.

Minsky's major contributions begin with his argument that capitalist economy is endogenously unstable, and that much of the origins of that instability is located on the financial side and in investor psychology. A kind of corollary of this is his point that even in good times instability is developing endogenously within the system. Financial instability—as indicated by financial fragility of both bank and nonbank firms—is a secular phenomenon of capitalism, in other words. By locating fragility and instability in the period preceding a financial crash or other financial instability event, Minsky thus went beyond Fisher and Keynes, who either focused on the immediate post-crash period (Fisher) or on how to recover from the nadir of the combined financial and real economic contraction that followed (Keynes).

Minsky's conceptual innovation of 'fragility' was able for the first time to describe how financial instability was the consequence of a dynamic relationship between debt and income, as well as other grouped variables that exacerbated the liability structures created by the debt and income buildup over time. Prior to Minsky's unification of the three variables under the umbrella and more operative concept of fragility, mainstream economists emphasized either one or the other variable and de-emphasized the others. The problem was either excess debt or insufficient demand, or too high short term interest rates engineered by the central bank—or all the above. Adjust either one or the other and the outcome would be a return to general equilibrium. But for Minsky, the natural state was a continual drift toward disequilibrium driven by financial liability structures along with insufficient income streams to pay for debt.

Although not always clear on the point, Minsky viewed financial instability as the primary determinant of real side economic contraction. But as he also argued real asset investment is what created the profits, and thus the cash flow income, from which to service debt, his view was ultimately that it was financial and real investment interacting upon each other that explained crises. Declining real investment, profits and cash flow exacerbated fragility and therefore instability; and so did the debt-driven evolution of units from 'robust' to 'fragile' debt-intensive financial regimes. The causal relationships cut both ways—a stark contrast to those today who argue either the real economy determines the financial or vice-versa.

That fragility also had something to do with deflation was another contribution—with both financial asset and goods deflation. In turn price had a lot to do with the decline of real investment that yielded slower profits, cash flow, and fragility. Minsky's resurrection of Keynes' two-price theory—for capital assets and for goods-outputs—was a direct challenge to and refutation of the neoclassical and today's mainstream economics view that all prices behave the same and all allocate resources more or less efficiently and restore the system eventually to equilibrium.

Another important contribution was to provide an institutional context for the explanation of fragility and instability. Heretofore, the focus was on individual agents, as professional investors or corporate CEOs, making investment decisions without an institutional framework.[20]

Banks and financial institutions were not neutral 'intermediaries', according to Minsky, simply allocating credit where needed and thus not causal agents in a financial crisis, as much of mainstream economics views them. Banks and financial institutions were 'profit seeking' institutions no different from non-banks in that regard. Their history was one of financial innovation in order to develop ways to manipulate debt in order to make as much financial profit as possible.

Minsky held that financial fragility was paramount. Since it was at the heart of the debt financing drift from hedge to Ponzi, while simultaneously also a product of real investment-profits-cash flow, financial fragility was the 'form' of fragility that was most important. However, he also acknowledged that financial fragility could spill over to households and thereby exacerbate household (consumption) fragility as well. So Minsky indirectly raised the very real likelihood of causal interactions between forms of fragility.

He also contributed by addressing how government policy interacted with fragility. Like firms and households, governments were 'units' as well. But in his view, government units, by means of traditional fiscal-monetary policy actions, were key to checking and reducing fragility, as well as mitigating the feedback effects between the forms of fragility (firms-households) that might worsen fragility and instability. Here Minsky went beyond both Fisher and Keynes once again. Fisher had no solution except either price inflation by means of central bank liquidity injections, or letting the system self-liquidate the bad financial and other assets. Minsky rejected liquidation and also, like Fisher, advocated for 'big bank' measures. But he preferred solutions implemented by the US Treasury instead of the central bank. Breaking up the big banks was also high on his proposals for recovery. In a number of ways his views were thus very much 'New Deal' Keynesian, except that he argued against the ineffectiveness of certain kinds of government income assistance, rejecting welfare or transfer payments, but approving government deficit spending that focused on employment and real job creation. Big government assistance meant federal government jobs income, not just any form of income injection by government. He expressed other somewhat anti-Keynesian views on perhaps abolishing the income tax, privatizing pensions, ending cost of living indexing, and even balancing the federal budget under normal conditions.[21] The main goal, as he put it, was "to promote conditions that sustain profit flows".[22] These latter views to some extent place him more in the Retro-Classical wing of today's mainstream economics, than as a traditional New Deal original Keynesian.

The preceding does not exhaust Minsky's various contributions and unique insights into the relationship between finance and real determinants of instability and financial and real crises. But it summarizes the more important, perhaps. However, in making these contributions Minsky's view reveals a number of important limits and even errors—of both omission and commission. The limits show the importance and necessity of expanding analysis beyond his contributions, building upon his insights where relevant and accurate, while rejecting or amending those when inaccurate, and disregarding the irrelevant.

The Limits of Minskyan Analysis

Minsky refers most often to 'capital assets' in general. And then the relationship between capital assets, on the one hand, and real investment assets (structures, equipment, etc. on the other). The more interesting contrast and dynamic, however, is between financial assets in the form of financial securities (equities, bonds, foreign currencies, proliferating derivatives of all kinds, etc.) and real asset investment. A major shortcoming of contemporary economic analysis is the failure to address the mutual causal interactions between financial asset and real asset investment investing.

The Missing Dichotomy of Investment

There is no such thing as 'investments'; there is the critical dichotomy of 'financial' vs. 'real' investment. There is real gross domestic investment, or I^g, and there is financial asset investment, I^f. And there is the important question whether factors are driving investors increasingly toward I^f with the result of 'crowding out' I^g, or whether, as Minsky argues, it is declining I^g that is leading to more I^f. Or, perhaps even more so, there is a mutual, dynamic relationship between the two forms of investment, I^f and I^g.

Whatever the preferred interpretation, one's preference requires the explanation of a transmission mechanism as evidence of one's preferred causal direction. Simply declaring a correlation between the two and assuming a particular causal direction is not acceptable. Minsky does not provide a convincing transmission mechanism as evidence for his assumption that it is the decline of profits from real investment that is responsible for slowing cash flow that in turn adds to financial fragility and therefore financial instability. Though he does imply that rising debt by firms—also a contributing factor to fragility— may originate from financial asset investment, he never spells out in detail how it occurs. The possibility that there is a relationship between financial asset investing generating excess debt, and real asset investing producing fewer profits, is left unclarified. His adherence to a Kaleckian theory of profit-real investment determination prevents a more fundamental explanation of how profits-cash flow-real investment is negatively impacted by debt driven financial asset investing, and vice-versa perhaps.

The Burden of Kalecki's Theory of Profits

Profits from real investment and real production is only part of the picture. Profits from 'exchange', from money creating money (in the Marxist sense), not just profits from production of goods, should be included. Failing to do so reflects the bias against financial variables that characterizes much of mainstream economics and Mechanical Marxism. The question that follows is whether profit opportunities in the late 20th-early 21st century from exchange and speculating in financial assets are greater than from real asset investing? And if so, why so? And do those greater relative profit opportunities from financial investing emerge as a result of declining profit opportunities from real investment (for whatever reasons), or are the latter the result of the rising profit opportunities from financial speculation and investing? Again, what's the causal relationship and mechanism for evidence of the causal relation? Minsky's theory of profits is undeveloped.[23]

Two vs. Three-Price Theory

From the above derives yet another limitation of Minsky's view, correctly acknowledging the important distinction between goods prices and capital asset prices, but requiring a further breakdown of asset prices between real capital assets and financial capital assets. How and why do prices for financial assets and securities behave differently than for physical capital assets and, still further, for goods and services prices? Minsky correctly explains why the two-price theory refutes the notion of neoclassical and contemporary economics that prices are stabilizing and key to restoring equilibrium. But he does not develop in detail how asset prices destabilize and cause disequilibrium. What are the important relationships between debt, prices (both financial asset inflation and deflation), and goods prices? Are financial asset price fluctuations an important 'transmission mechanism' toward creating fragility? What about the impact of financial asset prices not only on goods prices but on money prices (interest rates) and labor prices (wages)? Like his theory of profits, Minsky's theory of price is undeveloped as well. His analysis points logically to further development, but he doesn't follow it to conclusion.

Cash Flow vs. Income Analysis

Cash flow analysis is a central focus of Minsky. It is equally important as debt to the determination of financial fragility. Fragility is a function of both variables. But cash flow is itself too narrow a concept. Forms of income in general should be the focus, not just a particular form. Cash flow represents income (though not all sources of such) for firms. But if the concept of fragility is to extend beyond just that of firms, and include households and government units as well, which should be the case, then other forms of income are necessary for analysis of fragility in a systemic sense. As the concluding chapter will discuss in detail, financial fragility of firms is only part of the picture. Consumption fragility of households is another, as is government balance sheet fragility. What are the appropriate income forms for the latter two forms of fragility, then? Is it real disposable income for households? Personal income? Earned wages? And for government, are tax revenues the appropriate income form? Or should sale of government bonds be included in government revenue? In the case of systemic fragility that considers the three forms of fragility—financial, consumption, and government balance sheet—how do the accompanying forms of income (cash flow, real disposable income, tax revenues, or other)—interact and determine the levels of each other? Cash flow as income is only relevant if fragility is limited to the notion of firms.

Fragility's Undeveloped 3rd Key Variable

Minsky clearly acknowledges that a third variable, in addition to debt and cash flow, is appropriate for the development of fragility. That variable is the terms and conditions upon which principal and interest payments on debt are made. This 'terms and conditions' (T&C) variable is really a group variable, composed of different factors. Minsky notes that the term structure of interest rates is part of the group T&C variable—i.e. the 'mix' of short term vs. long term debt a firm may have undertaken. But certainly other T&Cs are important potentially as well. What about 'covenants', payments in kind provisions (PIKs), default trigger definitions, etc. that are included in credit (debt) provisions by financial institutions to firms? The third variable is left largely undefined by Minsky.

Government as Solution vs. Source of Fragility

While Minsky recognizes government as a 'unit' of analysis, along with firms and households, the government unit is not sufficiently differentiated. He implies government as federal or national legislative-executive branch. But provincial-regional-state & local government units are just as, perhaps even more, critical to government balance sheet fragility evolution, if for no reason than their income source for financing debt is even more limited. Federal-national government units can print fiat money as income in an emergency; units below that level cannot. That raises in turn the role of the central bank as a government unit, since the printing of money (called 'quantitative easing') originates with the central bank which is technically at least only a quasi-government agency. Another problem in Minsky's treatment of government is that he also sees it as an 'external' factor that successfully mitigates fragility. It is internal, but at the same time 'exogenous' to the fragility process.

Government (federal-national) is viewed optimistically as capable of checking and reversing fragility, instability, and its negative real economic consequences by means of appropriate fiscal-monetary policies. The idea that such policies may not successfully mitigate fragility is not considered. As he put it in one of his last writings, the policy tools available to government (circa 1994) meant that "the much greater relative size of government in the post war period than in earlier times makes it impossible for profits to collapse as completely now as in the past".[24] His optimistic view of government policy action at the time— perhaps more true then but far less so today—assumed that such government spending and tax measures necessary for bailout would raise government debt no more than 25%-50% of annual GDP. This sanguine assumption clashes with today's approximate 100% US federal debt to GDP ratio, and similar ratios in Europe, more than 200% in Japan, and China's *total* debt to GDP ratio of nearly 250%.

With government and total debt levels well above 50% in 2015, the potential effects on spending and investment multipliers, and on central bank efforts to generate real investment amidst the effect of such debt on money multipliers and short term interest rate elasticities, were never considered by Minsky.

Nor did he consider that government debt may negatively exacerbate private sector (firm and household) debt, or income availability to service debt. There is no consideration of the effects of government debt and government fragility on government policy effectiveness to reduce private sector debt and fragility. Current global examples of excessive government debt consequences on policy and private fragility in Greece, Japan, and even China—in all cases nearly at or exceeding 200% of GDP—may represent a refutation of Minsky's overly optimistic evaluation of government as a fragility negating force.

Thus one of the greatest limitations of Minsky's analysis was his assessment of government's positive effects on financial fragility, as well as his underestimation of its contribution to systemic fragility. What he couldn't see in 1994 was that the financial instability he observed in the real world in the 1980s and 1990s—which government policy was able to successfully check temporarily—was a far more moderate instability that would give way by 2007-08 to a more virulent form.

Dynamic & Systemic vs. Financial Fragility

Minsky's primary focus on financial (business) fragility leads him to fail to develop in equal detail the dynamics of fragility in the other 'units' of households and government. It is really a view of fragility centered on the investment function rather than on systemic fragility. This leads to the failure to analyze the various dynamic and 'feedback' effects between the three major forms of fragility—i.e. financial, consumption, government balance sheet—that is necessary for a systemic analysis. With the primacy given to financial fragility, and only occasional acknowledgement of spillover effects to households (since it was assumed government policy would successfully mitigate household fragility), a more comprehensive view of fragility at a systemic level was not developed by Minsky.

Transmission Mechanisms

Correlations passed off as causations is a chronic problem in mainstream (and Mechanical Marxist) economic analyses. A correlation is often identified and then a certain direction of causation is proposed, or not even explicitly argued but quietly assumed. But transmission mechanisms are key. This includes explanations with reasonable evidence of how one variable determines the other at several levels. First, within the three variables that define fragility in all forms: that is, between debt, income, and T&Cs. Second, transmission mechanisms that operate to mutually determine between the three basic forms of fragility themselves—financial, consumption, and government balance sheet. And thirdly, how the combined forms of fragility, i.e. systemic fragility, impact the real economy and vice versa in turn. Minsky proposed a 'continuum from robust to fragile' for financial fragility, but nothing similar for consumption fragility or government fragility—let alone their combined systemic fragility. Transmissions between variables are never linear, moreover. The feedback effects are always dynamic and multi-directional. In one of his last publications, Minsky proposed two 'submodels'—a 'financial structure submodel' and a 'cash flow submodel'. However, his explanation of how the two submodels interacted to produce a 'formal model', which he summarized in less than two pages, was merely an outline—much too simple, and ultimately therefore unconvincing.

Institutional Framework

There's simply no way to understand financial fragility in the 21st century without considering the revolution in financial institutions and structure that has been developing since at least the 1970s and especially since the 1990s. This structure includes the simultaneous bifurcation and merging of commercial banks and shadow banks. Bank lending by commercial banks has been giving way to the rise of capital markets and shadow banks, with major consequences for fragility and instability. Shadow banks remain largely unregulated, global, and focused primarily on financial asset markets; they are major sources of credit for speculative investing, originators of much of financial engineering and innovation in general and derivatives in particular, and increasingly the preferred investment vehicles of the rising and rapidly expanding—in number, wealth and assets—new finance capital elite. The elite and these institutions create the expanding liquid financial asset markets in which much of the financial asset investing takes place. Together, the new markets, new proliferating forms of financial securities, the innovation in credit that has accelerated debt, and the shadow banking institutions themselves constitute a 'global money parade' of more than a hundred trillion dollars of investible short term assets that ensures 21st century capitalism remains on a trajectory of ever-increasing financial fragility and instability. But Minsky's analysis does not consider these elements. Individuals are the agent-investors, presumably the financial decision makers in the banks and firms that are evolving from robust to fragile. He assumes most financing of capital assets is done via internal profits, even though recognizing external forms of finance. Bank loans are the next most important. And equity financing thereafter. But debt from expanding liquid capital markets provided by various forms of shadow banks does not loom especially large in Minsky's pantheon of financing institutions. It is there. But way back and, ironically, in the shadows of his analysis. It is simply not possible, however, to understand 21st century finance capital without including this broader institutional, non-governmental framework.

Origins of Debt

Minsky's analysis gives central importance to the role of debt and cash flow, as previously noted. However, while debt is recognized as one of the key variables, where debt comes from and why it has been accelerating is not addressed in sufficient detail. Debt is at the same time credit. Credit is not issued to borrowers unless either of two things happen: money is provided by banks in the form of loans or by investors in the form of corporate bonds, commercial paper, or other financial instruments. Money is liquid—i.e. easily convertible in one or another form of non-money, less liquid asset. But the extent of existing liquidity must have come from somewhere. That origin lies with central banks and the subsequent issuing of credit (debt). There would be no sizeable debt without the expansion of the money supply or of non-money forms of credit. The analysis should therefore begin with how and why so much liquidity-money has been injected into the global economy over the recent decades. Why have central banks pumped so much liquidity, so much money, into the global economy is the fundamental question. As previous chapters have argued, it begins in earnest with the collapse of the 1944 Bretton Woods international monetary system in the early 1970s. It is exacerbated by the removal of controls on global capital flows in the 1980s. Technology and globalization also play key roles ever since the digital and internet revolutions of the 1990s. But there is almost no analysis by Minsky of the origins of the debt that he argues grows ever larger, riskier in composition, and thus raises fragility over time. Excess liquidity precedes, and subsequently enables, excess debt accumulation. And though one presumes government policies are capable of reversing fragility, it is difficult to explain how government institutions and liquidity generation are also a source of fragility and instability as well.

Money v. Inside Credit

The problem of excess liquidity enabling excess debt is that debt from liquidity is not the only source of credit in the 21st century. Credit is issued when money is made available by financial institutions to investors in the form of bank loans, or other money providing instruments. But credit may also be issued by private financial institutions by allowing investors to purchase additional financial assets based on the market value of their previously purchased financial instruments. In other words, no new bank loans or bonds are issued. 'Credit' to purchase additional financial instruments is made possible based on the price change and value of previously purchased instruments. No money is actually changing hands.[25] Forms of such 'inside credit' have been proliferating in the 21st century, enabling the accumulation of more and more debt. For mainstream economics, debt is always the consequence of a private bank actually providing money to the investor. But where debt originates—i.e. from money-credit or from 'inside' or collateral value sources—is an important distinction that Minsky does not address.

Business Cycles & Phases of Profits-Debt

If Minsky's view of profits is overly influenced by Kalecki, then his explanation of the late 20th century capitalist business cycle may be said to be unduly influenced by Fisher. In fact, it is a melded Kalecki-Fisher view of the business cycle driven by the interaction of profits and debt. In the early phase, profits begin to rise and business debt declines as business deleverages its previous debt accumulation. In a second phase, a robust expansion occurs in the real economy. Profits rise and business debt once again accumulates. This is followed by a third 'boom' phase, where debt continues to rise but profits growth toward the end of the boom period slows. A fourth phase follows, in which debt declines as defaults and write-offs occur and profit decline accelerates.

Since the profits side represents a slowing of real asset investment that translates into profits slowing and, in turn, less available cash flow with which to service debt, Minsky's business cycle theory is in first appearance a 'real side to financial side' causal explanation of business cycles. On the other hand, since not all business debt accumulation is obviously a response to slowing real investment and profits, there remains room for a financial investing and debt accumulation element in the analysis. The missing explanation is, if so, how do the two explanations—real investment and financial investment—mutually determine each other? What are the processes and mechanisms? Minsky is silent on this.

This is very much a business investment financed primarily by the profits theory of business cycles, which leaves out a host of other real and financial variables of obvious import to business cycle determination. Moreover, what exactly does Minsky mean by profits? How are profits defined? Is it by profits levels? By rate of change (and if so what is meant by 'rate')? Since Minsky's view of profits is derived primarily from Kalecki, the problems are similar to those associated with a Mechanical Marxist 'falling rate of profit' theory noted in a previous chapter—but also relevant to the mainstream economics practice of excluding financial asset investment, speculation, and capital gains from profits in business cycle analysis.

Another problem with Minsky's 4-Phase business cycle theory is his acknowledgement that at some point excess fragility can 'trigger' a financial crash, setting in motion a subsequent deep real cycle contraction like a depression or 'great' recession. This is a 'financial side to real side' proposition concerning how business cycles move. But the 'trigger mechanism' is never spelled out specifically. One is left to assume it is perhaps Fisherian. But how precisely does the financial cycle transmit to the real cycle? And do financial factors accelerate the propagation of the real side decline as it apparently deteriorates following a precipitating financial instability event.

So while there is room in Minsky to develop some kind of a 'real side to financial and financial side to real' joint theory of business cycles, how the real cycle and financial cycle mutually determine each other is left undefined and at a high level of abstraction.

Minsky's business cycle theory would have to at least begin to explain how his profits-debt theory precipitates a financial crash that sets in motion a real cycle contraction that is not a 'normal' recession. That would require clarifying how quantitatively and qualitatively a 'great recession' and/or depression differs from a 'normal' recession. The latter are not simply 'normal recessions writ large', as a number of mainstream economists assume. His theory would require further explaining how fragility not only causes an initial deeper real contraction but also a more durable, long term economic slowdown and related protracted period of recovery. Business cycles do have phases, but the phases of a financial crash-induced real cycle are not identical to 'normal' cycle phases. It is not clear how focusing on profits-business debt alone explains all this. His theory of business cycle is more a high level empirical observation of correlations between profits, debt and recessions than it is an explanation of how financial and real cycles mutually determine each other when fragility reaches a level that triggers a deep real cycle contraction.

The preceding critique of the limits of Minsky's analysis should be weighed against his many contributions toward understanding how financial instability originates, develops, leads to financial instability events (stock market crashes, banking crashes, severe credit crunches, widespread liquidity and solvency crises, etc.) and how those instability events are related to the real economy (and vice-versa). The preceding critique seeks to provide a useful introduction to some of the key issues still unanswered by Minsky—and not even addressed by both mainstream economics and Mechanical Marxist analysis. They have been raised as a segue and introduction to this writer's view of systemic fragility in the concluding chapter that follows.

Endnotes

1   For his analysis of Keynes, see Hyman Minsky, *John Maynard Keynes*, Columbia University Press, 1975.

2   Minsky, Introduction to *John Maynard Keynes,* pp. vii-xi.

3   Marx's focus on the production side of the economy in his Vol. 1 of *Capital* was the outcome of his observations on European capitalism in the period 1840-1860. In the decades that followed the financial side of capitalist economy had begun to change rapidly. His Vol. 3 notes reflect his attempt to come to terms with these changes.

4   A dramatic contrast to the focus of policy globally since 2008, where the solution to recovery has been primarily central bank monetary policies of liquidity injection and interest rate reduction—i.e. a further indication of how recent policies are not really Keynesian but rather a combination of mostly Retro-classicalist, with some Hybrid Keynesian, proposals.

5   Minsky's two seminal works published in the early 1980s were *"Can 'IT' Happen Again? Essays on Instability and Finance"*, M.E. Sharpe, 1982, and *"Stabilizing An Unstable Economy"*, Yale University Press, 1986, reissued in 2008 by McGraw-Hill. But it would not be until the financial instability events in the US, Japan, and Northern Europe in the late 1980s and early 1990s (i.e. US Savings & Loan crisis, Northern Europe banks, and Japan's financial implosion in 1990-92) that Minsky's more complete view was developed in a series of key articles.

6   See Chapters 3 and 5 in his *Can 'IT' Happen Again?* 1982 publication, and further refinements in his later 1991-95 articles noted below.

7   'Robust' meant 'not susceptible' to financial instability events. Shocks to the system were relatively quickly absorbed. 'Fragile' meant 'not able to quickly recover from' and respond positively to volatility and severe disruptions to the financial system.

8   The question is, what was more important and when—i.e. profits from real investment for further investment, or debt disrupting the real investment-profits-real investment relationship? Even more fundamental, however, is debt from what—financial speculation or real investment? And profits from what—real investment or financial asset investment? But Minsky never raised such questions.

9   This reference to 'hedge' was, in this writer's opinion, an unfortunate choice of terms, leading readers to assume it has something to do with hedge funds, a form of shadow bank, but in fact has little to do with such institutions.

10   Again, perhaps another poor choice of terms, implying some sort of illegal financial scam instead of a condition of severe financial stress and imminent bankruptcy that the concept was meant to describe.

11   One might therefore argue there are not two distinct price systems but three. Each 'behaving'—i.e. determined by and determining—different sets of key variables, all three price systems interacting in important ways that influence the development of various forms of fragility.

12   Hyman Minsky, *Stabilizing An Unstable Economy*, McGraw-Hill, 2008, p. 159-60.

13   In Marxist terminology, profits are not 'realized' and capital cannot fully circulate or reproduce itself.

14   Minsky, *Stabilizing An Unstable Economy*, p. 160.

15   More on this difference of behavior in the concluding chapter.

16   Kalecki, a Marxist economist, was hampered by the typical mechanical Marxist view described in the preceding chapter: namely, profits from production of real surplus value was primary, not profits from exchange values created by capitalist financial institutions 'creating money from money' instead of from real goods produced by productive labor. The financial side of the full circuit of capitalist reproduction was thus undeveloped by Marxist economists—in the 1930s and still today. For Kalecki's theory of profits, see M. Kalecki, 'Theory of Profits', *Economic Journal*, June-September 1942, pp. 258-267. Minsky's very similar view is presented in his Chapter 7, 'Prices and Profits in a Capitalist Economy', in his *Stabilizing An Unstable Economy*, McGraw-Hill, 2008, pp. 157-190.

17   Hyman Minsky, 'The Financial Instability Hypothesis", Working Papers No. 74, Bard College, May 1992.

18   Hyman Minsky, 'Sources of Financial Fragility: Financial Factors in the Economics of Capitalism', March 21, 1995, Hyman Minsky archive, paper 69, Bard College.

19   It is interesting to note how, in 2007-09, the fragility and instability was allowed to 'pass through' to households. Government intervention was left primarily to central bank liquidity injections supplemented by token deficit spending. Not surprisingly, the economy did not respond as well after 2009 as it did back in the early 1990s.

20   This 'individualist' approach is still dominant in mainstream circles today, which see financial instability as the consequence of 'asymmetrical information' and 'moral hazard' decisions by individual investor decision makers. If it's an individual problem, then there is not endogeneity within the system that drives financial instability.

21   For his further discussion on "a quick and dirty list of some policies" needed at the time of the US financial crisis and recession of 1990-91, see Minsky, *'Financial Crises: Systemic or idiosyncratic'*, Working paper No. 51, Bard College, April 1991, pp. 28-29.

22   Minsky, *'Financial Crises: Systemic or Idiosyncratic'*, p. 29.

23   As is, for that matter, profits theory of both mainstream and Marxist economic analyses.

24   Hyman Minsky, *'Sources of Financial Fragility: Financial Factors in the Economics of Capitalism'*, paper 69, Bard College, Hyman P. Minsky archive, March 21, 1995, p. 21.

25   An extreme example is perhaps what is called 'naked short selling' by speculators. Here an investor commits to sell a stock or other instrument at its current price, and then buy that instrument or stock when its price has fallen. It thus buys at a low price what he previously sold at a higher prices. But no money actually changes hands. It's all an electronic transaction. No central bank. No private bank provides a loan or sells corporate bonds. These kinds of transactions involving debt are examples of 'inside credit'. Money may be used as credit, but not all credit may have to be associated with money.

19

A THEORY OF SYSTEMIC FRAGILITY

One of the central themes of this book is that the global economic crisis that erupted in 2007-08 did not end in 2009. It simply shifted in 2010, both in geographic location and form: from the USA and UK to the Eurozone and its periphery and to Japan. The crisis began to shift again, a second time, in late 2013, to Emerging Market Economies and then China. That most recent phase continues to unfold and intensify in mid-2015. In terms of 'form', the shift has been from mortgage bonds, derivatives, and equity markets in 2007-09, to sovereign debt markets in 2010-12, and, since 2014, increasingly to forms of private corporate debt, commodities and oil futures, Chinese and emerging markets equities, and currency exchange markets.

The Historical Context

In 2007-09 virtually the entire global economy was affected by the financial crash and then experienced a subsequent deep contraction of the real economy on a global scale as well. Certainly the financial crash of 2007-09 at minimum precipitated the deep real economic contraction that followed, sometimes known as the 'Great Recession'.[1] It obviously enabled that contraction in a host of ways. And it was most likely also fundamental to the contraction in important ways as well. This generalized financial and real crisis of 2007-09 was clearly the first such event since the late 1920s-early 1930s in which financial cycles and real cycles clearly converged and then mutually amplified each other in various negative ways. It will not be the last.

Financial crises and recessions from the 1960s up to 2007 have been localized geographically and/or limited to specific financial asset markets. There was little convergence and amplification. During that period real economic contractions—i.e. recessions—were localized and were the outcome in most cases of supply or demand 'shocks', or else were conscious government policy-induced recessions, rather than financial crisis precipitated contractions.[2] They were what might be called 'normal' recessions. They were therefore relatively short and shallow in terms of their contraction, and were thus relatively responsive to traditional fiscal-monetary recovery policies introduced by governments and central banks. Such normal recessions are almost never precipitated by major financial instability events, although moderate financial instability may have followed the real contractions. But financial instability was almost always limited and contained to a particular financial market, type of financial security, or an occasional financial institution default.

This localized financial instability and short and shallow recessions began to change in the 1990s, however. The first notable case was Japan's financial crash and subsequent 'epic' real recession that followed, a combined financial-real event from which its economy still has not fully recovered a quarter century later.

However, even Japan's recession in the early 1990s was not yet a generalized global financial crash or a consequent global real contraction event. That kind of generalized, combined financial and real crisis would not come until 2007-09. The 2007-09 event would prove not only quantitatively more severe than prior financial and real crises, but qualitatively different as well. So too would the trajectory of the global economy post-2009—i.e. a faltering global recovery that proved both quantitatively and qualitatively different from prior recoveries from normal recessions.

Like the 2007-09 crash and the 'great' (epic) recession itself, the post-2009 period thus represents something quite new. If the 2007-09 crash and deep contraction was an event diverting the global economy in a new direction, then the 2010-13 period represents the initial stage or phase—itself giving way to a subsequent second phase that has been emerging since late 2013.

In the 2010-13 first phase of global 'recovery' following the crash of 2007-09, the core Advanced Economies (AEs)—the USA and United Kingdom—were able to stabilize their banking systems with massive liquidity injections by their central banks. This achieved, however, only a partial and a historically weak recovery of their real economies. The other two major sectors of the AEs—Europe and Japan—neither restored financial stability quickly nor were able to achieve sustainable real economic growth. The Japanese and European real economies stagnated at best and fell into double-dip recessions once again while experiencing renewed financial instability in certain sectors and/or regions of their financial systems. In sharp contrast to the AE experience, during the same 2010-13 period China and the Emerging Market Economies (EMEs) experienced a rapid recovery in both financial and real economic terms. Both Chinese and EME economies boomed during this initial 2010-13 phase, China's growing at a rate of 10%-12% and other key EMEs nearly as fast. Money capital from the AEs flowed in at record rates and financial and commodity markets rose to record levels.

What then explains this dramatic difference between the AEs and China-EMEs during the first recovery phase of 2010-13? Real economic conditions? Financial conditions? Major differences in policy choices compared to the AEs? Indeed, what explains the notable differences within the AE regions during this period—US and UK stabilizing (albeit partially and incompletely) while Europe-Japan regressed economically and financially again? Was it just a matter of policy responses or something more fundamental?

This unbalanced global scenario of AEs compared to China-EMEs, during the first 2010-13 recovery phase, began to change by late 2013. The uneven and unbalanced conditions between AEs vs. China-EMEs did not correct; they simply shifted: The rapid real growth in China and the EMEs, which characterized the 2010-13 period, began to slow significantly starting 2013. By late 2015 China's real growth rate was reduced by half, and a growing number of key EME economies had slipped into recession by 2014. Global oil and other commodity markets began to deflate rapidly beginning mid-2014. Financial bubbles and instability began to emerge, especially in China. The global money capital flows into China-EMEs began to reverse, this time away from China-EMEs toward the AEs. Currency volatility rose worldwide. To forestall renewed financial market instability, both Japan and Europe introduced quantitative easing (QE) policies and accelerated their central bank money-liquidity injections—while the US and UK discontinued theirs. Both central bank and fiscal austerity policies became more congruent across all the AE regions, as the US and UK followed Europe and Japan in the direction of fiscal austerity starting 2011 and as Japan and Europe followed US and UK central bank quantitative easing policies, starting in 2013 in Japan and 2015 in Europe. What were thus previously divergences in monetary and fiscal policies between the AE core regions and the Europe-Japan regions now began to converge by 2013-14.

AEs as a group thus settled into slow to stagnant real growth by 2015, just as both real growth slowed rapidly and financial instability rose in China-EMEs. The US economy experienced repeated, single quarter negative GDP relapses in 2014 and 2015 and the UK's induced property investment brief recovery of 2013-14 came to an end by 2015 and it stagnated once again. Japanese and European growth stagnated as well, in the 0%-1% annual range.

Although the second phase of 2013-2015 is still evolving, a comparison of it and the preceding first phase, 2010-13, shows the following main characteristics:

The AEs stabilized their banking systems in the first phase but failed to generate sustained recovery in their real economies during that period. Never having really recovered in real terms since 2009, both Japan and Europe continue to stagnate by mid-2015, as the US and UK economies also show growing signs of renewed weakness in their real economies as well. More than six years after the officially declared end of the recession in mid-2009, the AE economies appear weaker in real terms today despite having stabilized their banking systems. China and the EMEs, moreover, appear decidedly weaker in 2015 than in 2010—both in terms of financial instability and real economic performance. In both AEs and China-EMEs, total debt—business, financial, household, government, central bank—has continued to rise as real income sources are undergoing growing pressure. Should financial and real economic events occur that produce a significant contraction of real incomes in one or several of these sectors—even if temporary—systemic fragility could easily and quickly deteriorate further as the feedback effects between financial, consumption, and government balance sheet fragility exacerbate each other. Coming off a much weaker economy today compared to 2007, another financial instability event and a potentially worse 'great recession', will find both central bank and government policymakers even less prepared or able to confront the next crisis. All sectors—households, corporate-financial, and government are more fragile—except for the big banks and big multinational corporations, and the top 10% wealthiest consumer households, who have been able to reduce their fragility as a consequence of record recent income gains. But the vast majority of businesses, households, and local and regional governments have not been able to build a liquid income cushion. And even for those narrow sectors with sufficient income cushion, in the event of another financial implosion, and subsequent real economic contraction, those income gains will be quickly offset by the collapse of financial asset wealth—thus leaving the excessive debt levels to be serviced from insufficient income and on unattractive debt refinancing terms.

In other words, systemic fragility on a global scale is worse, not better, after more than six years of so-called 'recovery' from the official ending of the previous financial crash and severe economic contraction in mid-2009.

Some Queries from History

The preceding short scenario raises important theoretical questions: why was the crisis that erupted in 2007-08 on a global scale a generalized event? Why was it clearly precipitated by a financial crash? How did the financial crisis enable the extraordinary deep and rapid contraction of the real economy, and prevent a normal recovery of it for more than six years? How are financial conditions and variables 'fundamental' to the general crisis? In other words, how does one distinguish causes that were merely precipitating and enabling from causes more fundamental— both real and financial? Were the financial forces and conditions that have been responsible for growing fragility fundamental to the 'great recession' and weak global recovery that followed—or just precipitating and perhaps enabling? How do financial conditions and events drive real economic contractions—i.e. 'great recessions' or worse, depressions? Why are financial instability events over the last four decades apparently becoming more frequent and severe, and what is happening in the real economy that may be making it more sensitive to the growing frequency and severity of financial instability events in recent decades?

These queries lead to another set of related critical questions: why have government policies since 2009—i.e. more than $20 trillion in central bank liquidity injections, trillions more in business-investor tax cuts, and still hundreds of billions more in direct and indirect non-bank business subsidies and bailouts—proven largely ineffective in generating a sustained global recovery and been unable to prevent a return of financial asset bubbles that continue to grow and expand and have now begun to unravel again?

Not least, what are the fundamental changes in the 21st century global capitalist economy that are responsible for the new, more intense interactions between the financial and real sectors of the economy? Or, put another way, how and why are financial cycles exerting a relatively greater effect on real cycles today than in the past? And why will they continue to do so?

Thus far, contemporary mainstream economic analysis has been unable to convincingly answer these questions. As a major theme of this book argues, that inability is due in large part to its outmoded conceptual framework.

The material origins of systemic fragility were addressed in the 9 major trends addressed in Chapters 7 to 15 of this book. They represent the historical markers or forces, i.e. the fundamental determinants that are developing, evolving, and in the process raising global systemic fragility and leading to a generalized financial instability once again, as in 2007-09. The 9 trends were described separately in chapters 7-15. But what's needed for analysis is an explanation of their interactions and how they combine to contribute to the development of systemic fragility.

What follows in the remainder of this chapter is a literary summary of the main ideas associated with systemic fragility. For data and evidence in support of the ideas, the reader is encouraged to refer back to Chapters 7-15.

Excess Liquidity at the Root of Debt Accumulation

Systemic fragility is rooted first and foremost in the historically unprecedented explosion of liquidity on a global scale that has occurred since the 1970s. That liquidity has taken two basic forms: First, money provided by central banks to the private banking sector—i.e. 'money liquidity' as it will be called. Second, a corresponding explosion of forms of 'inside credit' by banks and shadow banks that allow these unregulated financial institutions to expand credit independent of, and beyond, the money credit provided by central banks—i.e. referred hereafter as '(inside) credit liquidity' or just 'credit liquidity'.

Centuries ago, when gold and other metals were the primary form of money, the problem was the actual and potential production of goods was greater than the availability of money (as gold, etc.) to finance the production and enable the circulation of those goods. Today, however, in the 21st century, the growing problem is the opposite: money and credit are being created far more easily and rapidly and in greater volume than is necessary to finance the production and circulation of real goods and services. Just as the development and expansion of currency and bank bills of credit forms of paper liquidity eventually rendered gold and metal forms of money less important in terms of total money creation, so too will new forms of money liquidity creation eventually surpass older forms of money creation now provided by institutions of central banks and the commercial banking system. Liquidity expansion will accelerate even faster.

Excess liquidity has therefore been a major and growing problem within the global capitalist economy and this will continue and grow as a problem in the foreseeable future. The problem, however, is not liquidity per se or even its excess; the problem is the transformation of that excess liquidity into debt, and the consequences of that debt for fragility and financial instability.

Money Liquidity

As earlier chapters noted, the collapse of the Bretton Woods system gave central banks the green light to embark upon generating their own particular form of excess 'money liquidity' creation. The decision by US and other advanced economy economic and political elites in the late 1970s and early 1980s to eliminate controls on global money capital flows enabled the liquidity explosion, engineered by the central banks, to disseminate globally. With the collapse of Bretton Woods in 1971-73, central banks were now responsible for 'regulating' and stabilizing currency exchange rate fluctuations in order to facilitate world trade and capital flows. That required injections of liquidity periodically to maintain stability for the world's various currencies within an acceptable range of fluctuation against the US dollar and a few other key currencies. That currency stabilization task used to be done by the gold standard, and then the dollar-gold standard that was Bretton Woods system from 1944 to 1973. But all that changed with the 1971-73 collapse of the Bretton Woods system. Thereafter, currencies were free to fluctuate widely and volatilely, unless central banks intervened to maintain relative stability, which they began to do in the late 1970s.

The growing frequency of recessions and financial instability events in the 1980s and 1990s continued to destabilize economies, currencies, and banking systems, and in turn threaten world trade and economic growth for the many countries highly dependent on trade. That called for more liquidity injections to check the periodic recessions and financial instability events.   So growth and severe disruptions to growth both called for and received more central bank liquidity injections, in addition to that needed for currency stabilization.

There was another factor. In response to the crisis of the 1970s, the US capitalist elite in the early 1980s decided to focus on expanding US capital more globally instead of focusing primarily on internal growth. This also called for the provision of more money capital, as US businesses accelerated their global expansion in that decade.   With the collapse of the Soviet Union the opportunities for still more global expansion arose in the 1990s. More liquidity was necessary. With the integration of China into the global economy in the early 2000s, even more liquidity was necessary. With new digital technology and networking in the 1990, new industries and products appeared, requiring still more liquidity. Expanding free trade beginning in Europe and the US in the late 1980s, which accelerated throughout the 1990s and has done so ever since, demanded still more liquidity.

In short, the end of Bretton Woods, the globalization of money capital flows, the expansion of capitalist trade and economy both externally and internally, the growing frequency and magnitude of financial instability events and recessions, etc.,—i.e. all called for more money, more liquidity. And the central banks and private banking system provided it for more than a quarter century from the mid-1970s into the 21st century. Massive amounts more would be needed, however, to bail out the financial system when the general global financial crash occurred in 2007-09.

Central banks have been pumping increasing amounts of money liquidity into the economy through commercial banks since the 1970s and the collapse of the Bretton Woods system. However, central banks do not actually create money. They *indirectly* enable private banks to do so, by providing private banks excess reserves on hand that the banks can then lend, which does increase money liquidity in the economy when lending occurs.

But this too has been changing, resulting in even more liquidity injection into the system, as central banks' recent revolutionary policy innovations like 'quantitative easing'(QE) have been introduced since 2008. QE represents central bank *direct* money creation, not just the indirect liquidity injections through the commercial banking system. With QE, central banks print money (electronically) and use it to purchase back financial assets from private investors. The assets purchased are then registered on central banks' balance sheets as debt (in effect transferring the debt from private banks and investors to the central banks' balance sheets), and the printed money used to buy the assets from investors is injected into the economy, adding to the general liquidity.

As previously noted, since 2008 more than $9 trillion in QE liquidity has been injected into the global economy and more is likely to follow soon from Japan and the Eurozone. In addition, indirect central bank policies over the past quarter century have injected tens of trillions more, of which only a small proportion has been retracted. Traditional central bank policies since 2008, which have reduced bank interest rates to virtually zero in the advanced economies for seven years now, have injected an additional ten to fifteen trillion dollars as well.

While central banks have been responsible for the growth of both indirect and direct (QE) liquidity expansion, other new forms of money and credit were, and are, being created as well. For example, 'digital currencies' like bitcoins and other forms of digital money are proliferating within the private economy. These forms are created neither by central banks, private commercial banks, or shadow banks. The new money forms remain outside the control of central banks and even the commercial banking system. Changes in technology under capitalism will almost certainly enable the expansion of additional new forms of money liquidity in years to come in increasing volume. All foregoing examples represent the creation of excess money liquidity that is likely to escalate from all the above sources. Central banks today have little control over the parallel trend of expanding non-money forms of inside credit liquidity. And credit liquidity generation is where the shadow banking system in particular has been playing a major role.

Inside Credit Liquidity

While shadow banks also extend credit in the form of money to their wealthy investor clients, the unregulated shadow banking sector also extends credit to investors where no money is involved, thus enabling their investor clients to purchase more financial assets and securities. This 'credit liquidity' is based simply on the price and value of previously purchased products. If the price of previous purchased securities rises, so does its value as collateral, on the basis of which further credit is extended to investors. No money in the traditional sense is necessary or provided. The credit is based on exchange values of existing securities, not on new money loaned to purchase more securities.

While credit liquidity may not expand in this way as frequently where real assets are concerned, it works especially well with financial securities and other financial assets. Credit is extended, and more financial assets are purchased, simply based on the rising price and market value of previously purchased securities. Margin buying of stocks is one such example of inside credit creation. Many forms of derivatives securities are purchased in this way. Corporations also obtain credit based on the value of their retained assets. And banks are extended credit in the form of 'repurchase agreements', or repos, for the short term based on the value of banks' assets put up as collateral. It all works, until the value of the assets used as collateral for the additional credit begins to collapse. Then the inside credit extended has to be paid with real money. In the meantime, however, in periods of economic expansion and thus rising financial asset prices, technology and financial innovation continues to expand forms of (inside) credit liquidity which finances investment— especially in financial securities.

From Excess Liquidity to Excess Debt

Whether commercial, shadow, or deep shadow, banks provide credit to other businesses. By far the largest segment of debt growth in the US economy since 1980 has been business debt. According to the Bank of International Settlements, the fastest growing debt sector by far since 2008 globally has been the business sector—not government or households. This is in part due to the fact that business is able to 'leverage' investments with debt more easily and to a greater extent than households or government units. By leverage here is meant the ability to obtain credit from financial institutions and reinvest it, matching it with only a small fraction of their own money capital. For example, borrowing $9 of money and adding only $1 of their own capital, for a $10 total investment.

Leveraging is also more conducive to financial asset investing than physical or real asset investing. Since financial asset prices tend to rise more rapidly and higher compared to prices of goods and services, credit is more available for further purchases of financial assets. For example, an initial stock offering price per share may average $20-$30 on initial offering, but if successful may rise into the hundreds of dollars per share within a year. That is not how goods prices behave. A successful real product when introduced, like a smartphone for example, will almost never rise in price, but instead begin to decline within a year. That means the market value of financial assets may rise as rapidly as the price of the asset rises. That market value increase in turn enables more leveraging of debt in order to purchase more of the financial asset.

Excess liquidity not only translates into more debt for financial investing. It also means more credit is available for household consumption based on borrowing. The availability of cheap credit to households plays a role in wage income growth slowdown. Employers can afford not to raise wages as frequently, or not at all, since wage income households address their income shortfalls by accessing credit to offset the lack of wage growth. Standards of living are defended not by demanding higher wages, or organizing into unions to get wage increases, or demanding minimum wage increases. Debt instead is the vehicle for maintaining living standards that previously were supported by wage gains that reflected annual productivity.

The excess liquidity also contributes to rising total government debt, both federal and local, as well as agency and central bank. The excess liquidity means interest rates have been kept low. That provides an incentive for government to issue more debt. In the US, for example, that means at the state and local government level more issuance of municipal bond debt. At the agency level, the lower rates are reflected in more mortgage debt that is guaranteed and purchased by federal housing agencies like Fannie Mae and others. And by buying up mortgage bonds by means of its QE policies, the central bank in effect transfers private sector bad debt to its own central bank balance sheet.

The lion's share of government debt occurs at the federal or national level, however. The US federal debt has now exceeded $18 trillion, most of which has been accumulated since 2000. Federal government debt accumulates in several ways. Deficit spending increases and tax cutting raises debt. That spending increase may be attributed either to social programs or defense spending. In the US example once again, defense spending has accelerated as the US has conducted wars in the 21st century for which it has not only not raised taxes, for the first time in its history, but actually cut them. Estimates of the cost of wars thus far since 2000 for the US range from $3 to $7 trillion. And the 21st century wars are continuous, without end. Tax cuts amounted to nearly $4 trillion under George W. Bush, more than $2 trillion more under Obama's first term, 2009-12, and another $4 trillion over the following decade, 2012-2022, as part of the 'fiscal cliff' legislation of January 2013.

On the social spending side, government spending on healthcare related programs has also soared, as the health insurance, private hospital chains, pharmaceutical companies, and health services sector has concentrated, established deep financing from Wall Street for acquisitions. This has raised prices at double digit annual levels for years since the mid-1990s. The consequence has been escalating costs in Medicare, Medicaid, and most recently the Affordable Care Act (Obamacare) programs. The passage in 2005 of Part D, the prescription drugs program, alone has added more than $500 billion to the US deficit and debt in the last decade, in part due to skyrocketing drug prices and also as a consequence of the US government refusing to pass a tax to pay for it, preferring to fund it totally out of deficits.

Government deficits and debt accumulation has also been due to cyclical causes, and not just the secular trends just noted. The growing frequency of financially induced real contractions of the economy has led to government bailout costs. While the federal reserve has been the source for bank bailouts that have raised its share of total government debt to approximately $4 trillion, parallel bailouts of non-bank companies impacted by the financial crashes since the 1980s have also raised government non-bank debt. This source of debt especially escalated after 2008.

All this increase in government debt could not have been possible, however, without the development of what is termed the 'twin deficits' solution, which has been described in more detail in chapter 15. Briefly once again, the 'twin deficits' is the neoliberal solution created in the 1980s in which the US allowed a trade deficit to develop so long as trading partners (Europe, Japan, petrodollar economies, and then China after 2000) agreed to recycle the dollars they accumulated from the trade deficit back to the US by buying US Treasury bonds in the trillions of dollars. That recycling allowed the US in turn to run a budget deficit of ever growing dimensions—resulting in the $18 trillion plus debt.

Much of the total government debt—both central bank, national government, and even local government—represents the transfer by various means of private sector debt onto government agency balance sheets. Thus, as private debt—primarily bank, corporate, and investor— has risen since the 1970s for reasons explained, government debt has followed. Without the State having thus absorbed the private debt, and continuing to do so, the financial instability and crashes to date would have been significantly more frequent and more serious. Action by the State has thus kept the global capitalist system afloat, and ensured the patient remains on 'life support' even as its condition continues to fundamentally deteriorate.

So in a host of ways, the excessive liquidity creation leads to more debt creation at all levels—i.e. financial institutional, households, and government debt in various forms. And excessive debt creation is an important component of fragility at all levels—business financial fragility, household consumption fragility, and government balance sheet fragility. Debt is just the mirrored reflection of excess liquidity, and together excessive debt/liquidity drive the system toward systemic fragility and instability. The vehicle is escalating the trend toward financial asset investing, and its corresponding negative influence on real asset investment.

Debt and the Shift to Financial Asset Investing

Financial Asset v. Real Asset

Financial asset prices are far more volatile to the upside than goods prices, especially in a boom phase of a business cycle. With financial assets, 'demand creates its own demand', one might say, driving up prices while supply factors play a lesser role in dampening price swings. The more the price of the financial asset rises, the more buyers will enter the market to make further purchases of the financial asset, thereby driving its price still higher. Conversely, since the 'cost of goods' for making financial asset products is extremely small, rising supply costs do not discourage or lower the demand for the asset.

The opposite behavior occurs with goods prices, where demand plays a less volatile role and supply a more dampening role. Should the price rise, fewer buyers will purchase the product, unlike financial securities where rising prices attracts more buyers. That's because goods themselves are not as highly liquid as financial securities. Goods cannot as easily or quickly be resold and, if they are, are almost never resold at a higher price but instead at a lower one. In other words, there is no profit from price appreciation with goods prices whereas for financial assets profits are mostly determined by price appreciation. That means there is significant potential for profit from price appreciation for financial assets, which is another feature attracting buyers.

There is also more profit potential related to production costs, since there is virtually no 'cost of goods' involved in producing financial securities—little raw materials required, no intermediate goods, very little in the way of labor costs, no transport costs since nothing is physically delivered to the buyer, no inventory carrying costs, and so on. Financial assets are electronic or paper entries created originally with a small team of 'financial engineering' experts. This lack of production and therefore supply costs makes financial assets more profitable to produce.

There is a third factor that also makes financial asset prices more profitable. Because they are sold online, by phone, or by some other communications media, a large and costly sales force is not needed. Distribution costs are negligible. Moreover, the potential market reach—i.e. what is called the addressable market in business jargon—is the worldwide network of financial investors who are generally 'savvy' enough to seek out the sellers, rather than having sellers 'go to the buyers'. At most, minimal advertising costs are involved for the sellers of financial assets and securities.

In the simplest terms, then, financial assets have an advantage over the production of real goods—whether autos, clothing, food, machinery, or whatever—in all three categories of profit origination: price appreciation, cost minimization, and volume sales potential. They are simply more profitable—providing that prices are rising. In a contraction phase, the potential losses from falling financial asset prices are correspondingly greater compared to goods prices. But while the contraction may be steep in the short run, financial asset prices typically recover the losses much faster than goods prices in the recovery phase.

Another reason that financial assets are more attractive than real assets is that financial assets are traded (bought and sold) in highly liquid markets. That means an investment may be made and then quickly withdrawn (sold) if the asset price is not rising sufficiently or begins to fall. This is not possible with real investment and real goods. The real asset or company invested in must produce the good, and then sell it, over a longer cycle and time period. If costs rise and market prices fall in the meantime, the investor cannot withdraw to reduce losses as quickly. There is thus greater risk in real asset investing and goods production and sales. On the other hand, with financial assets, losses can be minimized faster as well as profit opportunities taken advantage of more quickly.

The ability of investors to purchase financial securities by leveraging purchase with debt, the various ways financial assets are potentially more profitable, plus the greater flexibility in quickly moving investment around as new opportunities emerge, all together provide a significant incentive for investors to direct their money capital and available credit toward investment in financial assets.

Conversely, investing in real assets means less profitability potential, given that price appreciation is negligible and that costs of production tend to rise significantly over the boom phase of the cycle. It means an additional costly distribution channel where the seller of goods must 'go to or seek out' the buyer. And it means less flexibility to move one's money capital around, to minimize losses and maximize gains. Why then would not the professional investor—i.e. the new finance capital elite—who cares only for short term, maximized capital gains not redirect his money capital from real asset into financial asset investing? He is not interested in building a company, becoming the biggest, gaining market share, acquiring and thus eliminating competitors. He is interested in short term, price appreciating capital gains. And for that financial asset investing is by far more attractive.

In short, because financial asset investing is typically more debt leverageable, because it is potentially more profitable in the shorter run, and because it is more liquid, flexible, and therefore less uncertain—investors can and do move in and out of financial markets more easily and quickly. They take price appreciated capital gains profits in a short period, and then move on to other short term, liquid, financial asset market opportunities. Or, if prices fail to appreciate, move just as quickly out of the liquid markets and minimize losses. Within a given year, for example, an investor may move a given amount of money capital from stock investing in Asia, to shale gas junk bond debt in the US, to derivatives in the UK, to speculating in Euros and Swiss francs, and so on. Money capital is not tied up long term as in the case of real asset investment, nor with as great uncertainty of outcomes.

Financial Asset Investing Shift

To sum up: the greater opportunity to leverage with debt, the greater relatively profitability, the shorter investment cycle and therefore the less uncertainty that is associated with investing in highly liquid markets—all provide investors a much greater relative incentive to invest in financial assets and securities instead of real assets. Given all these advantages, it is not surprising that a relative shift toward financial asset investing has been taking place for decades now. The relative profitability potential is simply greater. And in a world economy in which professional investors have grown in number and now control an unprecedented volume of investible money capital, that shift to financial assets investing is not surprising. Keynes' warning eighty years ago about the rise of the professional investor who prefers financial assets and securities, compared to the enterprise owner-investor who prefers real asset investing, has become the rule, not the exception.

The shift to financial assets does not mean that real asset investment disappears. Some of the explosion in excess liquidity and debt is directed to real asset investment and the production of real goods. And periodically major opportunities for real investment arise internally with the coming of new technologies like the internet, wireless communications, social networking, etc. Other external opportunities for real asset investing also emerge from time to time: the opening up of investment in Russia and east Europe in the 1990s; the significant real investment opportunities in China and emerging market commodities production that arose after 2000; or the North American shale gas and oil boom after 2008. But the time frame for profit generation from real asset investment is typically relatively short. Real asset investment becomes saturated after a few years, or after a half decade or so at most. Overproduction occurs. Costs rise and price increases are difficult to sustain. Competition provides more supply and dilutes demand. Sales peak and then decline. The boom is relatively short and the downside that follows is generally protracted.

In contrast, with financial asset investment the boom may extend and prices continue to rise over the longer term. So long as prices rise steadily and don't over-accelerate, financial asset investing grows. There is no 'overproduction'. As for the downside, while it may be deep on occasion, it is relatively short term. In 2008-09, for example, financial assets like stocks and bonds contracted sharply but then 'snapped back' quickly and attained new record levels in just months following the crisis. In contrast, prices and sales of real assets like homes and other goods contracted less initially, but have yet to attain prior levels of price and sales volumes six years after the recession ended. Prices for equities, bonds, and other financial securities have risen steadily since 2009, whereas prices for goods have been disinflating and even deflating throughout the advanced economies—and now in China and emerging markets—since 2009.

Despite the growing importance of financial compared to real asset investing, mainstream economic theory still does not recognize or give appropriate weight to this financial asset investing shift. Investment is measured in real terms, based on real data obtained from national income accounts. There's little place for financial variables in their General Equilibrium Models. How financial variables impact and determine the trajectory of the real economy is not explained in sufficient detail. At the same time, Marxist economists also continue to dismiss financial assets, referring to them as merely 'fictitious' capital and considering their role even more irrelevant.

Both mainstream and Marxist make little distinction between financial asset investing and real asset investing, or how they mutually determine each other. Investment is investment, as indicated in the Gross or Net Private Domestic Investment category of the National Income Accounts. If GDP is a measure of the performance of the real economy, financial investment variables have no effect on GDP level outcomes. It is the real side that drives the economy, and financial instability in turn.

The view from both the mainstream and Marxist analysis is that other non-financial forces are responsible for the slowing of real asset investment. And because of that slowing, investors are turning more toward financial asset investing. The real side is what is driving the 'financialization' of the economy (which is usually defined narrowly, and incorrectly, as a rising share of total profits going to banking and finance). Mainstreamers argue what is causing the slowdown of real investment is slowing productivity, excessive benefits compensation, too high federal taxation, and other costs. Marxists argue it is the falling rate of profit due to a rising ratio of fixed to variable capital, workers resisting employer exploitation, or growing capitalist competition that is responsible.

Neither acknowledge that the shift to financial investing may be due to the easier and higher profits from such investing—an outcome of the financial sector restructuring that has occurred the past four decades. Neither accept the notion that perhaps the higher and more certain profitability from financial investing is what is driving available money and credit more toward the financial side of the global economy, reducing money and credit that otherwise would have gone to real asset investment.

While it is apparent that money and credit is flowing increasingly into financial assets and financial securities investing, their argument is that the decline in real investment is causing the rise in financial. But the observable correlation—with real investment slowing and financial investment accelerating—may have an alternative causal explanation. It may be that financial asset investing is 'crowding out' real asset investing simply because the former is more profitable than the latter. It may not be only an excess of liquidity that is driving financial investment; it may be that the financial side is not simply getting the excess available liquidity and debt left over after real investment occurs. It may be that the greater attractiveness of financial investing is diverting money and credit from real investment to financial investment. It may be real investment is slowing—not because of slowing productivity, or rising compensation costs, or too high government taxes, but because financial side and financial investing is just more attractive and potentially profitable in 21st century global capitalism.

As a final comment on the financial investing shift, it should be noted that as the shift grows over a longer period following a crash of financial assets, financial investing tends to assume more of a speculative character. By 'speculative' here is meant investing in highly price volatile financial asset classes and for an even shorter term duration than average for financial asset investing in general. Speculative investing focuses on quick 'in and out' purchases of assets in highly liquid markets, in expectation of a fast price appreciation (or depreciation) and consequent capital gain profit. It may also employ a greater amount of debt leverage in the investing. Speculative investing appears as chasing 'yield'—i.e. seeking higher returns than average by investing in more risky asset classes like corporate junk bond and leveraged loan debt, distressed sovereign debt, more 'naked' short selling of stocks where bets are placed on stock price declines and no actual purchases are made, or on the most unstable currencies in expectation of currency exchange swings.

Speculative investing not only tends to rely relatively more on debt leverage but is more likely to be incurred via inside credit. A good example in 2015 has been the growing reliance on margin buying of stocks in the China equity bubble of 2014-15. That was followed by shadow bank investors then taking advantage of the significant stock financial asset deflation by engaging in short selling of Chinese equities. In the case of margin buying, the heavy debt inflow drove up China equity prices faster and higher than could be sustained for long, while the short selling had the effect of driving those same asset prices down faster than otherwise would have occurred.

In summary, couched within the shift to financial asset investing is the more unstable element of financial speculation. This tendency toward the more speculative forms of financial asset investing is generally an indication of growing financial fragility within financial asset markets in general. However, in the Chinese example, neither the uncontrolled margin buying nor the subsequent short selling of equities could have been possible without the extraordinary run-up in liquidity and debt in China since 2008 that made the shift to financial asset investing possible, leading to the escalation of financial fragility within China to dangerous levels.

The New 'Spread': Financial vs. Real Investment

Business economists and media commentators like to reference the 'spread' between long term and short term interest rates as indicative of the aging business cycle and equity market expansion. The 'spread' between financial asset and real asset investing may represent a more important long run indicator of the economy's trajectory.

The excess liquidity that leads to greater usage and leveraging of debt results in a convergence and subsequently a growing gap between financial and real asset investing over time. Liquidity, debt and leverage may expand real asset investment, when the periodic 'fits and starts' of such investment opportunities arise internally or externally. But the shift to financial asset forms of investing has proved to be more sustained over the last quarter century. Since 2000, financial asset investing has continued to accelerate, notwithstanding the abrupt 'correction' that occurred in 2008-09.

In contrast, real asset investing has continued to drift lower steadily since 2000, except for relatively brief surges related to oil-related capital spending, the opening of China to western investment capital inflows after 2000, and the emerging markets investment boom that followed. However, all these examples of real investment cycles have proved short-lived. The real asset investment that occurred after 2000 has been largely concentrated in these three areas—oil and energy, China, and emerging markets infrastructure and commodity development. By 2014-15, however, all three have clearly reversed and either slowed or contracted. Real asset investment is likely to slow even more over the coming decade.

In contrast, financial asset investment accelerated steadily and rapidly until 2008, only briefly contracted 2008-09, and then surged to further record levels since 2010 to the present. Should another financial crisis occur in the next five years, it may be deep but will likely be short again, as it was in 2008-09. Further liquidity injections by central banks and governments will no doubt occur in order to bail out the financial system, temporarily stabilizing it but in the process of bailing it out creating the conditions for another financial crisis later. But bailing out and jump-starting real investment and the real economy will not be as easy, even in the short run.[3]

The 'external' or geographic expansion opportunities for restoring even the modest real asset investment growth rates of the past decade do not appear as likely as in previous decades. The former Soviet bloc, Chinese, and emerging markets opportunities for real investment are not repeatable. Perhaps Africa's resources and the development of its infrastructure will fill that role, but the African potential is nowhere near as large as the others have been. As for 'internal' expansion opportunities, the physical assets needed for the new industries do not appear as great in terms of structures, equipment, inventories and other assets that will be required. The digital technology-internet-communications investment revolution that began in the mid-late 1990s was far more real physical asset intensive compared to the social networking, bio technology, and other candidates for real asset investment. Nor will the alternative energy investment opportunities result in a real investment surge similar to the tech surge. Alternative energy will have to be financed in large part by the government sector, as part of the predicted growth of government as share of GDP from around 20%-22% (in the US) to the 30%-35%. That will take longer and occur more slowly.

In contrast to this modest scenario for real asset investing, financial asset investment will continue to grow relatively, and in some cases absolutely, in size and total assets compared to real asset investing.

Facilitating that faster financial asset growth will be the new financial structures of institutions, liquid markets, and new financial securities, continuing financial product innovation, and the global network of the incredibly wealthy new finance capital elite that are now globally widespread and entrenched. It is estimated more than $100 trillion in investible assets are available in this global structure of institutions-markets-investor agents. Much of this wealth has been created from financial investing and speculation in the past. And it is not about to disappear or remain idle.

At the same time, central banks and governments have little alternative to continuing to pump more liquidity into the system in order to prevent the global banking system from collapsing. The system is now addicted to more or less free money. It cannot function if central banks raise interest rates to 4% or more. It remains simply too fragile.

Once envisioned as a brake on the shift to financial investing, the financial sector re-regulation that was launched in the wake of the 2007-09 global crash has been a dismal failure. What remains of token banking regulation in what were formerly, but no longer, the weakest sectors of global banking—the US and UK—have been and will continue to be dismantled piecemeal over time. It is a myth therefore that global finance capital can be regulated by any one country or government. Finance capital is like water running down hill; it eventually finds a way around government regulators.

Financial regulation is futile for another reason: the political changes in the advanced economy countries in particular have reduced general democratic influence while the influence of corporations, including bankers and investors, has continued to rise. That makes it even less likely that regulation of financial institutions will prove significant enough to check the next financial crisis, let alone slow the continued expansion of financial investing in the interim.

Liquidity injections by central banks will continue, as will more inside credit through the shadow bank system. Both will ensure the continued expansion of debt, and that means continuing debt will raise fragility in the system for years to come.

Given the almost certain long term continuing expansion of financial asset investing, and the corresponding continued slowing of real asset investing in the 21st century, the question arises: what are the consequences of this dual trend—for theory, for policy, and the trajectory of the global economy?

For theory, the dichotomy of investment raises the question: what is the causal relationship between financial asset and real asset investing? Is the slowing of real asset investing due to causes other than financial? Is the slowing driving the shift to financial asset investing; or is the rise of financial investing resulting in a slowing of real asset investing? Is it causality in both directions? If so, is it equal in determination? What is the process by which financial determines real, and real the financial? And what are the identifiable transmission mechanisms or variables? Transmission variables and processes are critical. Otherwise there is only a correlation between slowing real asset investment and rising financial asset investment, and correlations are too often misrepresented as causation.

The dichotomy of investment has significant implications for economic policy. If there is a shift from real investment toward financial assets that means less employment as well as employment at lower wage incomes. Real asset investment is more heavily weighted toward construction, manufacturing of producer and consumer goods, mining, industrial production, transport equipment and services, the inventorying and warehousing of goods, and research & development related services.

Financial investing involves more professional services. The number of employed per dollar of investment is far less in financial than in real asset investing. Consequently, the total income created is less as well. This means less household consumption as the household sector receives less of the total income created from financial asset investing—so insofar as the 'bottom 90%' receive little or no income from financial capital gains. Since financial transactions are hardly taxed, the slowing of real investment and subsequent decline of wage income and consumption translates into less tax revenue for government units as well. In other words, the shift to financial investing means a shift in income—from wage earning households and government units to financial institutions and wealthy investors.

Both households and government become more 'fragile', since fragility is a function of slowing or declining income from which to make payments on principal and interest from debt. This has a negative feedback effect. The slowing wage income gains for households means households often end up taking on more debt in order to maintain standards of living that otherwise fall from less earned income. Thus, consumption fragility rises for double reasons—slowing income and rising household debt. The same process takes place for government units, especially on the local level. Lower tax revenue collected leads to government units having to assume more debt (selling muni bonds by local government and Treasury bonds by national government).

These examples show that fragility can breed fragility *within* a sector (households or government) as declining income results in rising debt; and that the opposite may also occur—i.e. rising debt leading to declining income as future debt payments reduce future income streams. Whether due to rising debt loads, declining incomes, or both, fragility may also breed fragility *between* sectors. Should declining incomes lead to less consumption, it means less tax revenue income for government units and therefore an increase in that sector's fragility factor as well. And if tax income slows, government units face a deficit and may have to borrow more to maintain spending levels. That means more debt and thus even more fragility.

One can immediately see the implications of all this slowing income growth and rising debt for government policy. Does the government raise taxes to restore income loss and avoid having to raise debt? If so, it may reduce its fragility factor, but only at the expense of raising fragility in the sector where taxes are raised (i.e. households or businesses).

More on these, and other, examples of feedback effects in policy and transmission mechanisms within and between fragility categories shortly. For the moment, it is evident that the growing dichotomy between real and financial asset investing that occurs as financial asset investing rises relative to real assets, has major policy implications.

Inflation-Deflation and the Two Price Theory

As for the implications of the financial shift for the trajectory of the global economy over time, the financial investing shift means not only important income inequality trends develop--with implications in turn for future economic growth that income inequality brings—but also important price trends result from the financing shift.

Slowing real investment means slowing productivity in goods production, cost cutting, further job cuts, slower wage gains, and less income. Less income suggests less consumption demand. At the end of this string of effects is goods deflation, which eventually emerges as consumption demand declines due to lower wages and income.

In contrast, the financial shift means more demand for financial asset products and therefore more asset price inflation. The demand-driven character of pricing for financial assets tends to feed on itself. Demand leads to price increases resulting in still further demand and price increases. In the case of financial securities, unlike goods prices, there are few offsetting supply and cost restraints to slow or dampen the inflationary tendency. Therefore, while goods prices tend to dis-inflate, and then eventually deflate, as a consequence of the financial shift, conversely financial assets tend to inflate and accelerate as financial bubbles emerge.

There is the added element, moreover, that financial asset price behavior appears more prone to inflationary expectations, compared to goods prices and expectations. Inflationary expectations appear to accelerate faster in the case of financial assets. The converse is also true, deflationary expectations play a larger role with financial assets.

The even more important question is how do changes in financial asset prices affect goods prices? And do changes in goods prices affect financial asset prices similarly?

So far as equity asset prices are concerned, it does appear that a rise in the price of a product for a particular goods producing company may be reflected in a rise in that company's stock price, at least to the extent the goods price rise results in greater profit. But we are talking here about aggregates, not individual prices for this or that product or even company. The question is whether the general price level for goods rises when financial asset prices rise. Since 2009, at least in the advanced economies, this does not appear to be the case. Goods prices have been disinflating and drifting toward deflation, while financial asset prices have been accelerating in stocks, bonds, and other financial securities. Nor do there appear to be strong correlations showing financial asset inflation driving up the general price level for goods.

So during the boom phase, neither price system seems to determine the other very much. Financial asset prices may rise as the availability of credit in general expands. But after a point financial asset prices develop a dynamic of their own, rising as demand drives further demand, even as goods inflation slows. On the downside, in the case of deflation, however, financial asset deflation and goods deflation do appear to have a stronger mutual effect on each other.

For example, in the event of a financial or banking crash, as occurred in 2007-09, financial asset prices across the board—i.e. mortgage bonds, stock prices, municipal bonds, derivatives securities, etc.—declined rapidly. Liquidity froze up. Financial institutions withheld loans and corporate debt issuance dried up. With collapsed asset values on their balance sheets, banks and financial institutions refused to lend to non-banks and hoarded available cash and liquid assets, which were still insufficient to cover their deep financial asset price deflation and accounting losses. With no sources of lending for even their every-day operational loans, non-bank businesses cut costs—mostly wage costs via mass layoffs and other compensation freezes and reductions—aggressively and immediately. Suppliers were also cut off from payment, and had to follow with the same. At the same time as the severe cost cutting, non-bank companies attempted to generate more short term income by dumping their inventories and trying to undersell competitors by lowering their product prices. Just as the financial asset price collapse became a generalized phenomenon at the time, so too did the mass layoffs, cost cutting, and goods price cutting. The financial crash thus set in motion the process of real economic contraction that led to goods price deflation as well.

The opposite deflation effect—from goods to financial assets—is also more likely in the wake of a financial crash and consequent steep contraction of the real economy. This may occur directly and indirectly. In direct terms, declines in goods prices may reduce profits or other key business indicators, which may result in a decline in stock prices;

or, reduced cash flow may raise concern by investors as to whether the company can make its debt payments. That causes the company's bond prices to fall in turn, as its interest rate for obtaining new debt rises.

The process of goods deflation provoking financial asset deflation may occur more indirectly as well. For example, non-bank companies' access to borrowing with which to finance operations declines rapidly during the initial recession contraction. Their available 'income stream' from sale of products serves as the main source from which to make continued debt payments, since further borrowing and debt is not available in this phase. But the mass layoffs that accompany the recession downturn sharply and quickly reduce household wage income and consumption. To entice demand from households, and ensure the necessary continued income-cash flow stream with which to pay debt, price reductions for goods becomes the remaining primary source of cash flow for continuing debt payments. And when many companies are attempting to do the same, goods price decline leads to more good price declines—i.e. to goods deflation. In this indirect manner, financial asset deflation can ultimately translate into goods deflation as well.

What's further important to note is that these two processes— i.e. of financial asset price deflation eventually provoking goods price deflation and goods price deflation ultimately causing further financial asset deflation—is a mutual interaction. Both processes feed back on the other in a contractionary phase. There are two price systems and the two intensify their mutual reaction under certain conditions.

In other words, there is a dynamic and even dialectical process by which deflation in the one price system drives deflation in the other. This mutual deflationary process occurs primarily in the post-financial crash real economic contraction phase. The greater the mutual effect, the more the two price systems together intensify the contraction, each feeding off the other. When the deflation in financial assets becomes especially severe, it results in defaults. Financial asset prices may then virtually collapse, as courts and bankruptcy proceedings sell off the remaining assets by auction. Should enough defaults simultaneously occur, or defaults for highly visible companies occur, the psychological effect of fear of asset price collapse and contagion spreads to other companies causing other financial assets to decline more rapidly as well.

Understanding these mutual feedback processes is possible, however, only if one recognizes the fact of a 'two price theory' where financial asset price behavior is different than goods price behavior. Not all prices behave the same in relation to supply and demand. Not all price movements restore equilibrium, which requires the 'supply and demand' equilibrating assumptions based on pure competitive markets which do not exist. Mainstream economic theory, which does not recognize the 'two price system' idea, fails to explain how financial asset and goods prices interact, especially in the contraction phase. Nor does it address why, in the boom phase, financial asset inflation develops an independent dynamic of its own from goods price movements. But this is not the only error that mainstream economic analysis makes with regard to the role of price in financial instability and in precipitating great recessions and depressions in turn.

From Stagflation to 'Definflation'

Economics has a term for declining real growth amidst rising inflation: it's 'stagflation'. It became common during the crisis of the 1970s. The term refers to 'real' variables—both GDP and goods prices. 'Stagflation' occurred when GDP slowed and declined while price inflation accelerated. That inverse relationship between GDP and inflation has reappeared, although this time the variables are not GDP and goods prices but goods deflation, on the one hand, and financial asset price inflation and aggregate valuation on the other. Perhaps another new term is necessary to represent the new 'inverted relationships', where financial asset prices inflate while goods prices disinflate and deflate. For lack of a better suggestion, perhaps 'Definflation' might be appropriate.

The emergence of stagflation in the 1970s posed a serious policy dilemma for economists. Prior to stagflation, if fiscal-monetary policy focused on economic stimulus and growth, then GDP could be expected to rise and unemployment decline. The trade-off was that goods inflation would also rise. If the policy focus was on reducing inflation, then fiscal-monetary policy would aim to contract the economy, reducing income and therefore demand for goods and lowering goods prices. The trade-off was more unemployment. But 1970s stagflation discredited that theory. Fiscal-monetary stimulus would not reduce unemployment but would increase inflation further, and fiscal-monetary policies seeking to slow the economy, made unemployment worse without reducing prices. Policy was stymied. Something similar is the problem today. Monetary policy is attempting but failing to prevent the slowing of real investment and the drift to deflation in goods prices, while simultaneously boosting financial asset investment and inflation.

The consequences for the long term trajectory of the global economy are serious. How can we halt the drift toward goods deflation if monetary policy primarily boosts financial asset investment and inflation and not only does little to halt goods deflation, but may actually contribute to it? How can we restore real asset investment to prior growth rates when increasing liquidity leads to financial investing since it is potentially more profitable and holds other advantages as well? Can the growing problem of income inequality be resolved by token adjustments to wage incomes, even as real investment is slowing and financial capital gains and capital incomes from financial profits are accelerating? How is it possible to slow and reverse the shift to financial asset investing, inflation, and redistribution of national income to capital incomes at the expense of wage incomes, without a fundamental change in the size and class policy orientation of government? And without major damage to financial sectors?

Economists are at a loss to explain how to get out of the policy dilemma of deflation amidst inflation today in 2015, just as they were in the prior crisis in the 1970s as to how to get out the 'stagflation' policy contradiction.[4] That leads to a related subject and debate that is also associated with the shift from real to financial asset investing worth briefly commenting upon.

The Irrelevant 'Money Causes Inflation' Debate

Just as in the 1970s when they debated somewhat futilely whether there was in fact a policy tradeoff between inflation and employment, since 2008 mainstream economists have been continuing to debate whether the excess money supply (i.e. liquidity) injections by central banks will lead to excessive inflationary pressures at some point.

The one wing of mainstream—who are called in chapter 16 'Retro-Classicalists'—argue that Federal Reserve policy will eventually result in runaway inflation. The other wing—the 'Hybrid Keynesians'—argue there is no evidence this is occurring or will occur. Both are wrong, and both are right. Which means both are confused. The 'Hybrids' (liberals like Paul Krugman) are correct that the massive money injections have not led to goods inflation. In fact, goods prices continue to drift lower in the US, are still lower in Europe and Japan, and are even slowing in China. Krugman of course refers to goods inflation. But Krugman's error lies in not addressing financial asset inflation, which has accelerated rapidly due to the record liquidity injections. The 'Retros,' (conservative Monetarists like John Taylor), insist on goods inflation coming around the corner (or the next, or next). But Taylor is also ignoring financial asset inflation. In other words, both Hybrids and Retros are fixated on goods prices and ignore financial asset prices, when it is the shift to financial investing that is ultimately responsible for both financial asset inflation and goods disinflation-deflation. Both continue to debate the effects rather than the causes, in other words.

Neither wing of mainstream economics—Hybrids or Retros— understands that the explosion of liquidity and debt that is driving mostly financial investing, and less so real asset investing, is leading to a drift toward deflation in goods prices, while stoking inflation on the financial side. The goods deflation trend suggests not only that most of the central bank-provided liquidity in recent years is flowing to financial investing, but that it is also likely redirecting a certain amount of central bank liquidity away from real investment to financial, for reasons previously explained.[5]

Liquidity As Brake on Real Growth

The excess liquidity created since the 1970s—over and above what real investment has been able to absorb—has been flowing into financial asset investment. It has become far easier to create additional liquidity than it has been to find real investment outlets for it. The amount of liquidity has been so massive, and the growth of related debt levels so rapid, that governments and their central banks have been losing control of both—excess liquidity and incessant debt creation. Not surprisingly, the shift to financial investing has followed.

After having unleashed finance capital in the 1970s and 1980s to address the crisis of the 1970s, to expand capital globally to open new markets, to establish the unstable alternative to the Bretton Woods international monetary currency and trading regime, the system has not been capable of containing, managing or regulating the excess liquidity nor the excessive debt creation that has erupted in turn.

The historic contradiction is that the liquidity explosion set in motion in the 1970s is becoming a brake on economic growth it is supposed to generate. The massive liquidity and the ever-rising debt it has created have become a destabilizing force for the system, as financial asset investing crowds out real asset investment, and in turn is generating a host of related problems like chronic low job creation, stagnant wage income growth, weak consumption trends, slowing productivity, drift toward goods deflation, rising income inequality, and constantly emerging financial asset bubbles worldwide.

Restructuring Financial and Labor Markets

The trends associated with liquidity, debt, the shift toward financial asset investment and speculation, the slowing of real asset investment, the growing spread between the two forms of investment, the consequences for income growth to pay debt, the drift toward goods deflation amidst proliferating financial asset price bubbles—all together contribute toward fragility in the system. But this fragility does not occur in a vacuum. There is an institutional framework that is both the product of these trends and simultaneously a determinative factor of the trends themselves. Minsky referenced the institutional factor as relevant to financial fragility. Keynes spoke of the professional investor as responsible in part for instability in enterprise (real asset) investment. Both left room for further development of these contributions to understanding financial instability.[6]

Financial Market Structural Change

The financial structure of global capitalism has changed tremendously and fundamentally since the 1970s. There has been an explosion of financial institutions that have played a key role in channeling the massive liquidity and credit injected into the global economy over the past four decades into investment projects—most of which have been financial asset in nature. New financial securities and products have been created for this excess liquidity to purchase. That means new, liquid financial markets have been created in which to buy and sell these financial securities. But investment is made by investors, i.e. by agents, who are both collective and individual. Financial institutions, old and new, buy and sell the new securities in the new markets. So do super wealthy individuals, who do so directly or else place their money capital in the hands of these institutions to invest on their behalf. They constitute the new 'finance capital elite' in the global economy—i.e. the inheritors of Keynes' notion of the 'professional speculator' and of Minsky's notion of the institutional framework behind financial fragility.

By new financial structure we mean this network of financial institutions sometimes called shadow banks, the liquid financial asset markets in which they speculate worldwide, and the new finance capital elite composed of the management of these shadow institutions and the 200,000 or so global very high and ultra high net worth individuals who invest either through the institutions or directly themselves in the financial markets.[7] Conservative estimates indicate this network of global shadow banks and high net worth investors today control approximately $100 trillion in investible liquid and near liquid assets.

It is this new financial structure of institutions, markets, asset products, and agent investor-elites that together constitute the definition and meaning of 'financialization'. Other narrow definitions based on share of total profits or employment, or the 'FIRE' (Finance, Insurance, Real Estate) sector, or influence in government quarters, or other variables are but 'symptoms' of financialization further defining the term.

Shadow banking expansion is a concomitant institutional expression of the key trends and growth of systemic fragility. The shadow sector continues to grow, evolve in form, and deepen within the global capitalist economy. Commercial, regulated banks have become integrated with the shadow sector in various ways, including institutionally. That was one of the problems that led to the generalized credit and banking collapse in 2007-09. It was the investment banks (Bear Stearns, Lehman Brothers), the dealer-brokers (Merrill Lynch), insurance companies (AIG), mortgage companies (Countrywide), GE Credit, GMAC, Fannie Mae-Freddie Mac, and others—all shadow banks—that first collapsed. Because of their integration with the commercial banks, these too were dragged down. Major banks like Citigroup, Bank of America, WaMu, RBS and others in the UK, and Eurozone banks in Belgium, Ireland, Iceland and elsewhere went 'bankrupt' or were put on life support by governments even though technically insolvent (e.g. Citigroup and Bank of America).

Shadow banking has also spread into non-bank multinational corporations. GE, Ford, GM, and others have themselves long operated 'finance company' shadow banks. And today a growing percentage of multinational companies are de facto, in house, shadow banks as well— what might be called 'Deep Shadow' banks. Shadow banking is spilling out into new corners of the economy all the time, pioneering new ground in online finance and what's called 'crowd funding'. All these institutions would not exist, however, were it not for the excess liquidity available for them, and their elite investors, to invest and for the proliferating liquid markets in which they invest. Nor would they exist without the financial innovation that has created the financial products which they buy and sell in those markets.

Considering just the history of the US economy, every serious 'great' recession and depression since the early 19th century has been associated with some form of shadow banking engaging in speculative financial asset investing. Excess liquidity and debt have always been a prelude to a financial banking crash that then dragged down the real economy.[8] In the wake of each crisis, banks and shadow banks were regulated. However, after a period new forms of shadow banking arose again and the shift toward financial speculation and instability resumed.

The restructuring of the financial sector in the US and UK economies did not just happen. It was the outcome of conscious policy initiatives that began in the late 1970s and early 1980s, and continued to evolve thereafter. Changes came slower and later in Europe and Japan. And the penetration of shadow banking and financial speculation in China only dates from the end of the 2009 global crash, but has accelerated there the fastest to date. Policies included not only pushing financial deregulation but enacting special tax privileges, ease of institution start up, permitting opaque trading of securities (especially derivatives), and other measures.

Although a number of 'official' reports on shadow banking have appeared in recent years, most have defined it narrowly by focusing on a few selective characteristics. Some associate the institutions with certain financial markets and instruments. But none tie the institutions, instruments and markets involved with the 'agents' element—i.e. the finance capital elite of professional investors and speculators worldwide.

Creating and expanding the 'markets' and financial instruments traded was even easier. With the exception of equity, commodities, and bond 'exchanges' most markets are virtual and electronic. And even those are increasingly redirected in part to what are called 'dark pools', where only the financial elite and institutions get to trade stock and other securities, in total secret, invisible to the rest of the John Doe trading public. As for financial engineering of new securities, hire a couple of 'whiz kids' from the Wharton School of Finance and they develop the new 'games'. It all begins to resemble less a form of investment per se, and more a form of financial 'consumption' by the very high net worth financial elite.

As the financial sector restructuring continued to evolve through the 1980s and 1990s, the number and size of shadow banks, of liquid markets, and of securities increased several fold—as did their profits and the total investible assets under their control. As the structure developed so too did the scope of the financial investing. Innovations like 'securitization' of various financial asset classes and the rapid expansion of derivatives accelerated the investing in financial assets. The great returns fed the continuing structural change, which encouraged even greater returns. By the 2000s, financial assets were being created out of anything that might have some kind of income stream—like bonds issued based on a rock star's concert tour or from a UK pub chain's beer sales. And securities were merged with other securities to create a third security, which was then 'marked up' and resold. For example, mortgages on homes were merged into mortgage bonds, marked up and sold. The mortgage bonds were then 'securitized' by being merged with, say, Asset Backed Securities (ABS), marked up and resold again as a 'collateralized debt obligation' (CDO). CDOs were combined with other CDOs to create a synthetic CDO and resold. And credit default swaps (CDS) were then issued as insurance contracts sold on the CDOs in the event this shaky edifice of securities might somehow tumble.

All along the way, debt was increasingly leveraged in the purchases of the various tiers of products. Financial returns rose so long as asset prices did, and more debt and leverage occurred. Escalating debt meant rising financial fragility. But the fragility from debt was offset, shielded and obscured by rising income streams from the price appreciation—so long as prices continued to rise. Once the price of financial assets began to slow, the income stream vanished. But the debt remained. And as asset prices turned down, the offset to fragility from rising price and profit income evaporated. Now financial fragility was driven not only by high debt levels but by the second variable, income, rapidly falling as asset prices collapsed. All that was 2007-09.

Today the financial structure continues to evolve. New online forms of shadow banks are rapidly evolving. New derivatives are being created. Asset management products are the hot item in China, for example. And the financial elite continue to move their money around the numerous global liquid financial markets. Out of Euros, pesos, and Canadian and Australian dollars into US dollars. Out of commodity futures into US and Euro junk bond debt. Out of China stocks into high end US and UK real estate property. Out of emerging market stocks into Exchange Traded Funds (ETFs). Out of betting on Chinese stock price rises into betting on a Chinese stock price collapse.

What the preceding describes is how financial fragility, to use Minsky's term, has continued to rise since 2009. The private business debt levels have escalated, as perhaps five trillions of dollars in junk bonds and corporate investment grade debt, leveraged loans, and other securities have been issued since 2009. That debt will remain unless defaulted or written off. But the income or cash flow (to use Minsky again) can easily evaporate should asset prices fall—i.e. should a major China-precipitated global stock market correction occur, or bond prices rise too rapidly once the US and UK start raising interest rates, or oil prices fall below $40 a barrel and commodity prices continue to tumble further. Then both debt and income decline begin to reinforce each other. Then fragility accelerates, perhaps to a point that may 'trigger' a financial instability event of global proportions.

Minsky, Keynes and others focused on the financial side of fragility, i.e. on bank and non-bank business fragility driven by the debt-income relationship just noted. Minsky mentions household fragility, but sees it occurring as a consequence of spillover effect from deteriorating financial fragility. But this is incorrect. Spillover may occur. But there is a separate dynamic of structural change—in labor markets and impacting wage incomes—that has been developing in parallel to financial structure change. Labor market change also began in the late 1970s and has continued to develop ever since.

Labor Market Structural Change

Similar to financial sector structural change, labor market change has not occurred by accident or by some natural process. It too has been the consequence of conscious policy decisions made by politicians, government, and industry business leaders since the late 1970s. And since 2000 those changes have been further intensified.

The rise of wage incomes has slowed significantly throughout the advanced economies due to the general shift from hiring full time, permanent workers to hiring part time and temporary workers—the latter at lower rates of pay and weekly total earnings due to shorter hours. Everywhere in the advanced economies this has been a major trend. It is a practice that dates from the 1980s but has accelerated after 2000. Additional wage compression has occurred as these workers are denied normal retirement eligibility or have their retirement benefits reduced and, in the US, are forced to pay more for less healthcare benefit coverage. Workers either must pay out of pocket for the loss, or do without retirement income, thus lowering their real wage income further.

The more frequent and deeper recession cycles and the slower job recoveries that have typically followed have also reduced wage incomes. Secularly for decades now, tax incentives for moving companies and jobs offshore have gutted formerly higher paying jobs and thereby also reduced incomes in the United States.

Minimum wage and overtime pay laws have atrophied over the period with the same effect. Forms of wage theft by service sector employers have also increased. More young workers are desperately undertaking 'wage-less' internships with employers in the false hope of someday being hired to a real job. Meanwhile, employers turn over and 'churn' them in order to continue to get others to work without having to pay them. The so-called 'sharing' economy (Uber, Lift and other transport companies) is destroying jobs and income for taxi drivers and public transport workers, and this trend threatens to break out into other industries enticing more employees to work part time for less and with no benefits. The net income declines, as those who gain income realize less additional income than is lost by others losing their jobs.

Unions have been increasingly decimated or destroyed since the 1980s, thus eliminating union wage differentials that provided more income for unionized workers. The institutional vehicle for unions achieving wage differentials—i.e. collective bargaining—has been chipped away for decades. The main tactical weapon, the right to strike freely, has been circumscribed and all but effectively prohibited. Laws and agency rules have wrapped a legal web around union organizations and their activities, funneling unions and their members into an ever narrowing field of permissible activity.

The reduction of what were once 'export-import' wage differentials has been added to the elimination of union wage differentials with the same effect. Free trade has replaced the export-import wage differentials in advanced economies, with new jobs with lower wages. Meanwhile, no firm evidence is provided that shows net wage incomes from free trade has risen to equal or offset the net wage income loss in advanced economies.

All these developments reflect major changes in labor markets, especially in the advanced economies. Many of the above labor market changes originate in the production process, introduced by employers as cost saving initiatives to offset declining productivity and profits. But governments have been totally complicit in the process, passing legislation and rules that encourage employers to introduce the labor market changes. Governments then subsidize those changes with tax incentives, and eliminate previous legal limits and restraints on the practices that previously existed.

Occurring first most intensively in the 'core' of the advanced economies, US, North America, and the UK, similar changes in labor market conditions that reduce wage incomes have since been introduced or proposed in Europe and Japan under the cover of what's called 'structural reforms' or, more explicitly, labor market reforms. These structural reforms are designed to compress wage incomes in order to make exports more competitive to steal growth from competitors. Japan and Europe are today particularly engaged in introducing and expanding labor market reforms—aka wage and benefit compression—to boost exports and domestic production at the expense of other competitors. Labor market change along the lines introduced by the core advanced economies, in effect now for decades and intensifying, are therefore also spreading geographically. They are becoming one of the several defining characteristics of 21st century global capitalist economy.

Labor market structural changes thus have the consequence of reducing real wage incomes for the majority of households and consumers. Stagnant or declining real wages means a rise in consumption fragility, all things being equal. But wage stagnation also results in a rise in consumer household debt, as households attempt to maintain living standards under pressure from stagnating and falling wage incomes by taking on more consumer debt. Fragility grows more or less simultaneously from two directions—from slowing consumer incomes and rising consumer debt. The result is reflected in the growing share of debt financed consumption, compared to consumption growth reflecting income gains, in total household consumption.

The growing share of debt-induced consumption by households in recent years not only raises consumption fragility. Household debt also has the effect of dampening government fiscal multipliers, making traditional fiscal policies less effective. It is one reason why economic recovery since 2009 has been so anemic. In that sense, residual household debt after 2009 is similar to business and bank debt, which dampens the effect of money multipliers on non-bank borrowing, and in turn lowers actual and potential real investment.

Structural Change and Fragility

Both financial restructuring and labor market restructuring have steadily raised fragility over time. Both lead to excessive debt. Financial restructuring has enabled and assisted the shift to financial asset investing, facilitating the leveraging of increasing amounts of debt. Independently, labor market restructuring has resulted in stagnating and declining wage incomes, requiring households to turn to more debt in order to maintain living standards and consumption. While both financial restructuring and labor market restructuring have their own independent dynamic contributing toward fragility, the fragility they create in their respective sectors—financial and households—also feedback on each other and thus intensify the fragility of each.

A final observation is that financial sector debt has played a larger role in generating financial fragility than household debt has toward consumption fragility. For example, in the US data shows that escalation of total debt—business, banking, consumer and government—has been mostly business debt and most of business debt has been financial institutional debt. Data by the Bank of International Settlements corroborates this trend worldwide. It is private sector debt that has accelerated fastest since 2009 and that has been mostly corporate debt, not consumer debt. Since 2000, and 2009 in particular, government policies have restored income to business and financial sectors. So declining income has not been a major contributing factor to financial fragility.

However, this has not been similarly true for households and consumption fragility, where governments have not restored incomes to the majority of households. Consequently, declining income has been a contributing factor, along with rising debt, to households. Non-government policy forces also contribute to this decline. Financial asset prices recover and accelerate after a financial crash much faster than labor prices (i.e. wages). Financial institutions recover more quickly than households after a crash and recession. Unlike the business and financial sector, households cannot raise their prices—i.e. wage—incomes. Continued labor market restructuring holds down wages even in the recovery from recession phase, whereas continued financial market restructuring serves to raise financial asset prices and therefore incomes during the recovery phase. That is a fundamental difference between financial restructuring and labor market restructuring.

A consequence is that households remain more consumption fragile in recovery due to the dual effect of stagnating wage incomes and rising household debt than financial institutions, banks, shadow banks, etc., that experience debt escalation in recovery but also income (cash flow) recovery as well that serves to postpone financial fragility. That is, until financial asset prices (and incomes) collapse in another crisis. Then financial fragility accelerates for financial institutions as well. It is only then—in the immediate crash and contraction phase—that the two forms of fragility—financial and consumption—begin to feed off of each other and each causes the fragility of the other to worsen in tandem.

Fiscal-Monetary Policy: From Stabilizing to Destabilizing

Both fiscal and monetary policy must be considered among the nine key trends that are associated with rising systemic fragility and therefore instability.

Mainstream economic theory views fiscal and monetary policies as serving to restore stability in the system once a financial crisis and/ or recession occurs. Fiscal policy—i.e. government spending and tax measures—are viewed as providing a necessary stimulus when either a financial crash or real contraction occurs. Taxes are cut. Spending is increased. GDP recovers. For monetary policy, the central bank increases the money supply through what are called 'open market operations', or by reducing reserves private banks must keep on hand and not lend, or lowering the central bank's interest rate at which private banks may borrow from it. Mainstream theory explains that this leads to lower interest rates that stimulates borrowing from banks. This all seems logical, but it's not how the system works—not since 2009 or even 2000 in the advanced economies especially.[9] The question at this point is how and why do traditional forms of fiscal and monetary policies today, especially in the advanced economies, contribute to systemic fragility.

The tendency of monetary policy to lead to more fragility, not less, is the most obvious. Take central banks' pumping excess liquidity into the global economy ever since the end of Bretton Woods in 1973, followed by the elimination of controls on global capital flows in the 1980s, and the technology revolution in the 1990s that accelerated money flows electronically by manyfold. The massive liquidity injections have contributed significantly to debt, financial asset speculation, and other structural factors that have resulted in escalating fragility. Central bank supervision of the private banking (and shadow banking) sector has proved a colossal failure. That too has allowed, even encouraged, the almost unaltered rise of financial asset investing and speculation. Bank policy of more than seven years of near zero, and real zero or lower, interest rates has contributed mightily to household consumption fragility as tens of millions of households dependent on fixed interest income have witness their income streams from interest virtually disappear. Zero interest rates policy amounts indirectly to a transfer of income from retirees and others on fixed incomes to banks, shadow banks, and speculators.

Monetary policies, both traditional (open market operations, etc.) and emergency (special auctions, quantitative easing, QE, and zero-bound rates) have bailed out the private banks since 2009, at least in the US and the UK, but have done little or nothing for stimulating the real economy. Estimates are that it now takes four dollars of central bank money injection to get one dollar of real GDP growth, compared to two dollars for every dollar in previous decades. That's a 'multiplier effect' of only 0.25. That's true not only in the advanced economies, like the US, but apparently, by latest estimates, in China as well. Central bank policies of massive liquidity injection as the primary policy response to a crisis may bail out the banking system, but only temporarily. That same liquidity that bails out the banks in the short run, also adds to the excess liquidity that simply leads in the long run to more debt and more financial speculation that ends up creating another crisis again. So monetary policy has been, and remains, only a temporary palliative to the fundamental causes of the crisis and, in fact, actually exacerbates those same causes over the longer term. Such monetary policy is like giving a terminal cancer patient a massive dose of chemotherapy, which only buys time for the patient, makes him sicker, destroys his immune system, and weakens him for when the patient's condition worsens once again.

Fiscal policy fares no better so far as reducing fragility is concerned. In theory, government spending targeting consumer households should raise household income and thus reduce consumption fragility. But the composition and timing of the spending is what counts, not just the magnitude of government income support. If the spending is in the form of subsidies it only provides a temporary stimulus that disappears as soon as the subsidies run out. If spending is on long term infrastructure projects, especially if capital intensive instead of labor intensive, then such spending also has little effect for the same reason. And if the stimulus is in the form of tax cuts, in a high debt and fragile household scenario most of the tax cuts will be hoarded or used to pay down past debt—thus adding little to the economic recovery.

What Can Be Done

What is needed is government spending or programs that eliminate household debt directly, and also result in creation of (non-terminating) jobs directly by the government. Only job creation produces an income stream that doesn't dissipate, but continues after the initial spending occurs. But recent economic history shows that, in the advanced economies at least, even poorly composed and timed fiscal policies were only dabbled with in the immediate post-2008 crisis period. Thereafter, actual policies with regard to government spending were just the opposite. What happened, and continues to happen, was not fiscal stimulus but fiscal austerity.

Fiscal austerity policies result in a significant reduction in household wage incomes and therefore a rise in consumption fragility. So where austerity policies have been most pronounced—i.e. in Europe and Japan—consumer spending has not recovered. Policy makers and press pundits then wonder, amazingly, why that is the case. However, the explanation is simple and evident: as household income stagnates or declines, consumers turn toward more debt. Together the declining wage incomes—caused in part by fiscal austerity policies—and rising debt loads add doubly to consumption fragility.

Even when occurring in the form of fiscal spending designed to stimulate the economy, government spending effectiveness has declined. Government consumer spending and tax multipliers have had a declining influence. High levels of household debt have the effect of blunting and reducing government spending multipliers, as consumer households use government spending injections to pay down past debt instead of finance new current consumption. And stagnating wage incomes have the effect of blunting multipliers as well, as government spending results in more hoarding of the spending for 'rainy days' they expect are more likely to occur again instead of spending the added in come on new consumption.

Government spending and tax cutting that target corporations (bank and non-bank) also get 'bottled up' instead of resulting in more real asset investment. Much of the business tax cuts in particular are redirected to offshore investment projects, if they exist; to more profitable financial asset investing; to stock buyback and dividend payouts; to purchasing, merging and acquiring competitors; or are just hoarded on company balance sheets.

Whether targeting consumer households or business, traditional fiscal policy has a declining effect on generating incomes—and that means more fragility. But in any event, traditional fiscal policy has hardly even been used since 2000 and especially since 2009 in the US, UK and other advanced economies. What's been employed is fiscal austerity—and that definitely has exacerbated consumption fragility, while encouraging more financial asset investing and therefore business debt and more fragility on the financial side.

Evidence is therefore abundant, and increasingly so, that monetary policy definitely causes an acceleration in financial fragility by encouraging bank and non-bank debt build up, while chronic low interest rate consequences of monetary policy reduce household income and raise debt that exacerbates consumption fragility as well. Simultaneously, fiscal austerity policies negatively impact household income and debt even more strongly, while fiscal stimulus policies targeting bank and business tax cuts encourage still more financial asset investing, stock and dividend buybacks, mergers & acquisitions, etc., all of which encourage more business debt.

Actual fiscal-monetary policy thus has become a cause of financial, consumption, and therefore systemic fragility in the system over time, rather than serving to reduce that fragility. Policy is an important contributing cause of systemic fragility.

A Brief Recapitulation of Key Trends & Systemic Fragility

To understand how the nine trends contribute to, or are associated with, systemic fragility it is necessary to define further what is meant by contribution. How do the nine trends differently cause fragility and therefore financial instability? What are the qualitative differences among the trends in the determination of systemic fragility? To begin with, some causal factors are *precipitating* a crisis. Other causal factors are best understood as *enabling*, both in the build up to the financial crash and in the immediate post-crash contraction. Still other causes are *fundamental* and originating in nature. And not only the nine trends but fragility itself becomes a cause of fragility, as the development of systemic fragility results in feedback effects described in more detail shortly.

Of the nine trends, those that qualify as 'fundamental' are the explosion of liquidity within the global economy since the 1970s, the accompanying escalation of debt, the relative shift to financial asset investing that follows as real investment slows and financial asset investing and speculation in financial securities rises, and the accelerating disparity between incomes of the several hundred thousand new finance capital elite and those of the hundreds of millions of wage earners.

The important 'enabling' trends and factors would include the restructuring of both financial and labor markets globally and the contribution of government policy (fiscal, monetary, and other)—as both restructuring and policy enable, encourage and assist the expansion of debt and stagnation of incomes.[10]

'Precipitating' causes of financial instability events (market crashes, banking system crashes, severe credit crunches, major financial institution insolvency and bankruptcy events, wars, natural crises, etc.) are not among the nine trends. What precipitates, or sets in motion, a major financial crisis is typically associated with a major shift in investor-agents' psychological mindset and expectations. Here the price system, especially the acceleration of financial asset price deflation, plays a close supporting role in that expectations shift by investors.

To briefly recapitulate the nine trends and their relationship to fragility and financial instability: the explosion of liquidity since the 1970s, attributable to central banks creation of 'money credit' plus internal changes in the financial structure that has increased 'inside credit' liquidity, has led to a corresponding excess growth of debt, especially private sector debt. The availability of debt has led to its general leveraging in the purchase of financial assets. Financial asset investment profitability has diverted money capital from real asset investment alternative opportunities. Excess liquidity has become far greater in any event that might be employed in real asset investment. Fragility is a basic function of rising debt and slowing or declining growth of incomes required to pay for debt, plus a set of group variables that affect payment capabilities as well. Financial restructuring has produced a corresponding new structure comprised of shadow banks, deep shadow banks, and integration of commercial and shadow banks, an expanded global network of highly liquid markets for transacting financial assets, and proliferating forms of financial securities traded in these markets. This new structure and the unprecedented financial incomes it has generated for professional investors has created a new finance capital elite of no more than 200,000 very high net worth individuals. This new structure, the new elite, and the development of systemic fragility are components which must be included in the proper definition of 'financialization'. Concurrent with the financial restructuring has been a fundamental restructuring of labor markets on the real side of the economy. Labor market restructuring has produced a stagnation and decline of real wages and therefore household consumption fragility from falling incomes and related rising household debt. This occurs simultaneously as financial restructuring has raised debt and financial fragility. These are long term secular trends. However, financial crises and consequent real economy contractions intensify the mutual effects of financial and consumption fragility on each other in the post-crash period and deep contraction period. Government fragility also rises long term secularly due to policies that reduce government income sources even as government subsidizes the private sector and government debt rises. Government debt accelerates with cyclical crises, financial instability and real contractions, as government transfers private debt to its own balance sheets as well. Systemic fragility renders government fiscal-monetary policies less effective as it negates multipliers and reduces elasticities of interest rates on consumption and investment. In crises and post crises periods, the mutual feedback effects between three forms of fragility intensify as well. Financial asset price volatility plays a key role in the growth of systemic fragility, in intensifying the financial and real crises when they erupt, and in reducing the effectiveness of traditional government fiscal-monetary policies from stabilizing the crises.

Measuring the Three Forms of Systemic Fragility

As already noted, the three forms of fragility are financial fragility that affects private sector investment, consumption fragility that impacts households, and government balance sheet fragility that has consequences for government policy effectiveness and government ability to prevent deeper than normal real economic contractions and to generate a sustained recovery from those deeper contractions.

The three forms of fragility may be aggregated to estimate systemic fragility. Since debt levels and liquidity are potentially measurable, each of the three forms of fragility should in theory be capable of producing a fragility index. Systemic fragility in turn should be capable of representation by means of an aggregated index based on the three indices. However, the aggregation of the three forms of fragility cannot be created by a simple addition of each of the three fragility forms. Systemic fragility is more than just the 'sum of the parts'. The magnitude of systemic fragility is the product of the many, complex interactions and feedback effects that occur between the three forms of fragility. This feedback contribution makes the creation of a systemic fragility index more problematic.

Within each of the three forms of fragility the major determining variables are debt, income available for debt payments, and a group variable of elements that affect payment of debt from available incomes.

The debt and income variables include not only levels or magnitude of debt but the rate of change in levels and magnitudes. How thoroughly debt and income is defined is also important.

For example, forms of basic income with which to pay debt may include cash flow for financial institutions and businesses and wage income for households. While these are the basic definitions as per Minsky's analysis of fragility, they are not sufficient.

For determining financial fragility, Minsky's cash flow variable is too narrow a concept. The income variable influencing financial fragility should be defined as cash flow plus other forms of near liquid assets held by businesses that may in a crisis be relatively quickly converted to cash in order to make debt payments. Moreover, the rate of change in this broader income variable, and not just its level, should also be considered.

For households and consumption fragility, the proper income variable should be wage earning households' real disposable income plus income in the form of transfer payments to these households. Both levels and rates of change of income are important. Since the vast majority (90% or more) of households' income is from wages and transfer sources, adopting the real disposable income as the wage income variable is acceptable. However, insofar as the wealthiest households (especially the top 1% and the even more especial 0.1%) constitute a share of overall investor households whose income derives in part (rising with income level) from financial investment and capital gains incomes, a distinction might also be made between the two when assessing the development of consumption fragility.[11]

And for government units, it is not just tax revenues that constitute 'income' but the ability to quickly sell bonds in markets as well. Another major factor related to government fragility is the ability of the national or federal government to essentially create substitute income quickly and when necessary in the form of printing of money that it can then 'lend' to itself when income from tax revenue and bond sales to private investors (and other governments) is insufficient. Since only national governments are legally allowed to 'create income' for themselves, it is probably important to distinguish between national government fragility and state-province-local government unit fragility, where in the case of the latter direct income creation is not an option.

Minsky's approach is also undeveloped in assuming that financial fragility's internal variables of debt and income operate for financial institutions (banks, shadow banks, etc.) in the same way as for other non-bank businesses. Insufficient distinction is made between the two, given that financial asset deflation impacts banks more severely and rapidly in a crash than it does non-bank business. Financial asset price collapse causes a collapse of bank cash flow + near liquid assets, and thus raises bank real debt much faster than for non-banks whose cash flow is affected negatively by falling real goods prices which decline much slower. This is a critical distinction. Minsky's failure to account for it reflects his general underdevelopment of the two-price theory factor, as he himself acknowledges. Also undeveloped is the intermediate form of bank-nonbank business institution—i.e. the multinational corporation that today is a hybrid of bank and nonbank, or what we've called 'deep shadow' bank, where its business model is based on both real asset and significant financial asset investing activity. And then there is the related question of whether, and if so how, shadow banks in general are potentially more fragile than commercial banks and how that is explained by the basic variable duality of debt and income.

On the debt side of the fragility definition, the sources and kinds of debt incurred are probably important as well, not just the total debt levels or rates of change. For example, there are a number of different kinds of business debt (corporate bonds, paper, bank loans, etc.) that are important due to the terms and conditions associated with payments in the different instances. In the case of banks and financial institutions, bank fragility may be higher when there is a greater weight of repurchase agreements or repos in their total debt portfolio while the proportion of junk bond debt to total debt impacts non-bank fragility. Similarly, composition of debt is important for consumer households (mortgage, credit card, student loan, payday loans, etc.). And even government debt, especially at the local government level where debt composed of derivatives like interest rate swaps is involved.

Here is where the third key variable defining fragility becomes important—i.e. what might be called the 'terms and conditions' of debt servicing (T&C variable) that interacts in important ways with both debt and income to jointly determine fragility.

Minsky's view is undeveloped with regard to the T&C variable. T&C is a group variable that is composed of various elements that may exist in different combinations and 'weights' associated with a particular debt. T&C as a group variable may include elements such as the level of interest charged on the debt; the term structure of the debt (short term v. longer term debt); whether the debt interest payment is fixed or variable and thus subject to volatility in interest amount; penalties, fees and other charges on missed payments; provisions of the debt that define under what conditions default may occur when principal and/or interest is not paid on time; post-default obligations; time limits for defining default (30, 60, 90 days?); powers of the lender of the debt when default is declared; bankruptcy processing, and other provisions that are called 'covenants' that define payment options for the borrower; alternatives to payment (e.g. option to pay 'in kind'), refinancing conditions, and so on.

The T&C variable is thus complex, and its composition and effects may vary considerably between different forms of debt (e.g. investment grade vs. high yield 'junk' corporate bond debt, corporate commercial paper debt, securitized debt, national government sovereign (T-bond) debt, local government municipal debt, household installment, credit card, or student loans, leverage loans made by private equity shadow banks to businesses, and so on). The difficult-to-quantify character of the T&C variable makes estimating a fragility index for each of the three constituent forms of fragility especially difficult. But the T&C variable's important and influence on fragility nonetheless increases greatly when a financial instability event is precipitated and a rapid change in financial asset price deflation occurs.

Thus within the three forms of fragility—financial, consumption, and government—that determine systemic fragility are three critical variables—debt, income, and terms and conditions of debt servicing.[12] The interaction between debt, income and T&C variables determine what might be called a first approximation of the level of each form of (financial, consumption, government) fragility. But this would be a first approximation only, since the levels of fragility—and their aggregate summation as systemic fragility—are the consequence as well of the various feedback effects between the three fragility forms. And those feedback effects are enabled, in turn, by transmission mechanisms or processes that also constitute the equation of systemic fragility.

Fragility Feedback Effects

A major differentiation between the theory of systemic fragility introduced here, compared to other theories based on fragility as a determinant of financial instability, is the acknowledgement of what might be called 'feedback effects'. The term is shorthand for the recognition that fragility is a dynamic and not a static concept. And that its development does not occur in a linear manner.

By 'feedback' and dynamic is meant that there exists a complex web of mutual determinants involved in the development of the aggregate condition called Systemic Fragility. Mutual causations between variables are at work, occurring at various levels.

As several examples have already indicated, there are mutual determinations between the three forms of fragility—financial, consumption, and government balance sheet. The internal variables of debt, income, and T&C also mutually impact each other—in some cases offsetting and reducing fragility and in other cases exacerbating it within each of the fragility forms. And there is a third, still more general level of interaction and determination—between financial asset and real asset investment as a consequence of growing fragility in general.

Within each form of fragility, the three variables involved—debt, income, and T&C—interact in various ways. For example, slowing or declining income with which to pay debt may result in higher debt, as a nonbank business resorts to borrowing more in order to service the debt. Or, its T&C may worsen as it rolls over the debt at a higher interest rate and/or shorter payback term, or with a loss of previously favorable 'covenants'. Rising debt in turn reduces available income for investment, as more of future income must be assigned to paying the higher debt. When debt term expires, lower income flow and higher debt levels may result in debt refinancing on worse terms than previously, which reduces the ability to make future payments. There are various combinations of mutual interactions between debt, income, and T&C over time.

A similar scenario applies to consumption fragility. Declining consumer real disposable income and/or reduction in transfer payments may force households to take on more debt to maintain living standards. Debt levels rise, and in turn higher total interest and principal must be paid on the debt. That means less future real disposable income after the higher payments are made. The higher a consumer's debt load and debt payments as a percent of disposable income, the worse the credit terms that consumer receives when borrowing. Higher indebtedness and lower income results in having to pay a higher interest rate for a home mortgage or auto loan. The quality of that indebtedness also affects payment terms. Excess credit card debt, for example, may force a household to resort to payday loans, obtainable only at excessive interest rates.

And within government units, especially local government, a fall-off in tax revenue affects a credit rating so that the municipality, school district, or other government agency is forced to pay higher interest rates on bond issues it offers. Higher interest payments due to more debt and higher rates means a reduction in future income. Income and debt mutually exacerbate each other, and government fragility rises.

Even national level governments may face similar difficulties. A good example is Greece. In the Greek case, like many Euro periphery governments after 1999 and after the creation of the Euro currency, Greece borrowed heavily from northern European banks. Its sovereign debt levels rose steadily from 2000 to 2008.[13] When the great recession in 2008-09 depressed Greece's real economy, its tax revenue income declined. Its ability to finance past debt therefore was not possible. Northern European governments, and cross-government institutions, thereafter restructured and refinanced (rolled over and added to) Greek debt in 2010. That added further to the total debt levels to be paid. T&C were made more unattractive as well. As part of restructuring, Greece was forced to divert its tax income to pay for the higher debt. So its debt rose and its income available for the higher debt payments simultaneously declined. Debt and income decline were exacerbating each other and fragility growing for all three reasons, including deteriorating T&Cs. Government income diverted for debt payments, as a consequence of austerity policies, had the further effect of reducing Greek GDP, which further lowered tax income, and made Greece even more fragile. A second European recession in 2011-12 repeated the process, and debt was restructured a second time in 2012 with the same general effects. A third debt restructuring in 2015 is in progress. It too will raise debt levels, total debt payments due, and reduce Greece's income from tax sources still further as Greek GDP collapses once again.

The possible feedback effects between the three key variables within each of the forms of fragility are numerous. The intensity of these interactions serves to raise the level of fragility within each form. Moreover, that intensity rises during and immediately after a financial instability event, which accelerates the development of fragility within each form.

Increasingly fragility *within* each form leads in turn to greater feedback effects *between* the three forms of fragility as well.

Several examples have been shown previously of how financial fragility may interact and intensify household consumption fragility—and vice-versa. When a financially precipitated recession occurs, interactions between forms of fragility intensify and the processes become generalized. A 'race to the bottom' then ensues, leading to generalized price reduction (goods deflation), labor cost cutting and more household consumption fragility.

In the case of the financial fragility of banks and financial institutions, this feeds back on both nonbank businesses and households, raising the fragility of both. This typically occurs as collapsing financial asset prices for banks results in a freezing up of bank lending, both to nonbank businesses and to consumer households. With new loans frozen, banks' new income generation does not occur. They cannot sell financial securities, since no one wants to buy securities when financial asset prices are collapsing.[14] Bank fragility then translates into nonbank fragility, as nonbank businesses, unable to obtain day to day business operating loans from banks, must resort to the cost cutting with the effects previously noted. In this way a nonbank business, that is not necessarily fragile to begin with, may be quickly forced into a fragility condition by the banking system and have to cut costs and/or take on more debt from other sources at less attractive rates and terms. The freezing up of bank lending has a similar effect on households. Bank layoffs mean declining income and rising fragility for employees associated with the banks. Nonbank cost cutting due to lack of bank loans produces the same effect for households. Bank financial asset price collapse may mean loss or reduction of pension retirement income to households. It also typically results in a decline in interest income earned by households. Mortgage refinancing as a means of increasing household income also dries up as banks freeze lending. There are various conduits by which bank fragility translates directly or indirectly (via nonbank fragility) to household income stagnation, decline, and therefore rising consumption fragility. Bank lending freeze up may also force households, like nonbank businesses, to seek credit elsewhere on worse T&C arrangements, also contributing to household consumption fragility.

Bank fragility also feeds back, directly and indirectly, on government balance sheet fragility. The freezing up of bank lending results in a decline in real investment and household consumption that slows economic growth and thus government tax revenue. Government also ends up spending more in recession situations (discretionary and non-discretionary spending typically rise). The combination of more spending and less tax income means rising budget deficits which must be 'financed' by raising more government debt. Thus government fragility rises due to both declining income and rising debt.

Government also transfers debt from the private sector—especially from banks and strategic nonbank businesses it bails out—following financial crashes and deep recessions. Government may buy the bad assets on bank balance sheets and transfer them to its own—either its central bank or to what is called a nationalized 'bad bank' which holds the various toxic assets until the government can resell them. Massive government direct loans, subsidies, and loan guarantees to strategic nonbank businesses may also occur. Banks' ability to sell bad mortgage debt to government agencies also amounts to an offloading and transfer of debt, and fragility to an extent, to government.[15] By enacting deep bank and business tax cuts, government indirectly also transfers private sector debt and fragility to itself. Banks and business income is raised as a consequence of less taxes to pay, while government income declines and thus its own fragility is raised.

Government units may also absorb debt from households in a similar fashion, in effect subsidizing mortgage refinancing for homeowners facing foreclosure or experiencing 'negative equity' value in the homes. However, this occurs far less than the much more numerous and generous debt transfer programs provided to banks, financial institutions and investors. More typical is government subsidizing household income, in effect reducing its own income, transferring debt and fragility to its own balance sheet. Secularly over the long term, but especially in post-financial crash crises, government may fund an increase in its transfer payments to households bolstering household income at the expense of its own deficits and debt. The rise in household consumption fragility is to an extent thus offset, while government's own fragility from more spending, deficits and debt is in turn raised.

Thus far the examples of 'feedback' direction have been from financial fragility, and especially bank fragility, to household consumption fragility and even government balance sheet fragility. But consumption fragility may also 'feedback' on both financial and government fragility.

As household income stagnates or declines due to many of the labor market structural changes noted, there is less consumption and therefore less household demand for nonbank business goods and services. That may result in less business revenue and therefore less business income. This feedback effect may be reduced to the extent that households, despite declining income, do not reduce their consumption but instead take on more consumer debt to maintain consumption levels. However, there is a limit to how much extra debt households are able, or may want, to take on to maintain consumption. Household debt accumulation has upper limits. Consumer debt reduces future disposable income, as more interest on the debt must be paid.[16] Stagnating-declining household incomes (and fragility) feed back to both further nonbank financial fragility as well as more future household consumption fragility.

Consumption fragility also feeds government balance sheet fragility. Reductions in household income and/or rising debt have the consequence of less consumer spending. Less household spending means less sales tax revenue; that especially impacts local governments highly dependent on this particular form of tax revenue income.[17] In the US economy, deep recession conditions are associated with significant loss of household incomes due to layoffs, wage cuts, etc., which may translate into mortgage failures, foreclosures, and falling local property values. That results in less property tax revenue income for local governments, raising their fragility. Dependent on local government and property tax revenues, Public Education services are then cut unless national governments spend more in order to maintain such services. In this manner, rising consumption fragility indirectly forces an increase in local government fragility via tax revenue income decline as well as national government fragility via more spending, deficits, debt and national government balance sheet fragility. Less household consumption impacts income tax—as well as local sales and property tax—revenues similarly. Less consumption means less business production and less hiring, both of which reduce taxable income that would otherwise accrue to governments. And there is a secondary, derivative effect on government fragility. Not only may government debt levels rise, as government has to borrow more in order to offset tax income loss, but the terms on which the additional debt is borrowed may raise debt costs as well. State and local governments running large budget deficits pay higher rates of interest for the municipal bond debt they sell in order to finance their high deficits due to tax income decline.

Financial fragility feeds into consumption fragility, and vice-versa. Financial and consumption fragility feed government balance sheet fragility in various ways. But the feedback direction may also occur from government balance sheet fragility to financial and household consumption fragility. This is where fiscal austerity policies play a particularly significant role. Austerity is about offloading actual, and/or potential, government debt onto households. Government balance sheet fragility is reduced at the expense of rising consumption fragility. Austerity means a deep reduction in government spending. That means more retained government income. But cutting spending in the form of household transfer payments means less household disposable income. Less government spending means lower deficits and less debt to finance as well. Austerity also means government selling off public assets, which raises temporarily government income levels. But it forces households to turn to private, higher priced, alternatives to the once government provided services and programs. What were once perhaps free public services and goods must now be paid for by households, reducing their disposable income and raising household fragility. Austerity also means raising taxes and reducing government pensions and retirement payments, or national healthcare services or payments. All that raises government income or reduces government costs, while lowering household disposable income and raising household costs. In austerity, most of the tax increases are local government fee increases, sales taxes, and other 'regressive' taxation impacting median and below households the most. Occasionally, the tax hikes also affect investors and businesses. And the pension, retirement, and health care cuts are significantly directed at middle income households.

What the foregoing reflects is that there are numerous ways and 'paths' by which fragility in each of the three forms in turn 'feeds back' upon one or more of the other forms. Sometimes the feedback is direct—i.e. from government to households, or banks to nonbank businesses and households, or households to government or nonbank businesses. Sometimes it is transmitted via income declines, sometimes debt, or other times both simultaneously more or less. The feedbacks may also occur indirectly: i.e. rising financial fragility leading to consumption fragility and thereafter to government fragility as the latter responds. Or financial to government to households. Or many of the other possible combinations involving two or more.

But the major point is that feedback effects do occur. Fragility does not develop within each of the three forms independently of the other. It 'accelerates' overall as the intensity of the feedback effects grows during periods of financial instability events and subsequent deep and rapid decline in the real economy. There are not only 'accelerator' effects, but also what might be called 'elasticities of response' between the different forms of fragility feedbacks.[18] Perhaps a minor change in financial fragility generates a significant feedback effect on consumption fragility—i.e. a big further rise in consumption fragility. But a rise in consumption fragility produces less of a significant change on financial fragility.[19]

Transmission Mechanisms of Systemic Fragility

A final, but very important, topic to consider is the importance of 'Transmission Mechanisms' (TXMs) or processes with regard to fragility. This is an area that has been left particularly undeveloped in other analyses that attempt to explain the relationship between fragility, financial instability, and economic cycles.

Transmission mechanisms operate at several levels in the process of determination of systemic fragility. Feedback effects—i.e. mutual determinations—occur between the three internal variables— debt, income, T&Cs. At a higher level, between the three forms of fragility—financial, consumption, government balance sheet. And at the most general level between financial asset investment and real asset investment. All the mutual determinations require some kind of transmission mechanism between them.

At least three key transmission mechanisms appear essential to Systemic Fragility. They are: 1) the price system, 2) government policy, and 3) investor agents' psychological expectations.

Price Systems as TXM

The neoclassical view is that there is only one price system and all prices behave the same—that is, all prices respond in the same way to supply and demand forces. Whether financial asset prices, goods & services prices (output prices), input prices (wages as price for labor, real capital goods, land), or money prices (interest rates) are involved, the response to supply and demand is similar. Supply interacting with demand adjusts prices to return the economy back to equilibrium. In other words, one price system fits all and the price system is the key to economic system stabilization.

This neoclassical view does not conform to reality, however. In the case of financial assets, demand plays a much greater role; the role of supply is almost negligible. With financial asset price inflation, demand induces still more demand, driving prices ever higher so long as prices continue to rise. Supply does not moderate asset price inflation. And financial asset prices 'adjust' rapidly and abruptly downward (i.e. deflate) only when investors conclude that further price appreciation is not possible and price stagnation or decline is imminent. It is thus a psychological perception or expectation of imminent price shifting that precipitates the reversal and price deflation, not supply side forces. The shift to deflation is unrelated to extra supply or rising costs, as in goods prices, since 'cost of goods' for producing financial securities is virtually negligible.

Financial asset price deflation is a mechanism *within* a form of fragility that intensifies and exacerbates the effect of one fragility variable upon another—i.e. debt on income, income on debt, T&C on debt, and so on. Take the example of growing financial fragility among banks. Financial asset deflation reduces bank income available to make bank debt payments to another bank from which it may have borrowed. When asset deflation begins, investors do not buy new assets from the bank. Bank revenue falls. Income from the sale of bank equity declines as well. This general income decline occurs, moreover, at a time when banks actually need to increase their income in order to cover the asset losses from falling asset prices as well as make payment on their own debt. Less income plus falling asset values plus rising real debt translate into an increase in bank financial fragility.

How then does this greater bank fragility transmit to another form of fragility, i.e. from financial to consumption and/or government fragility? Here again the price system serves as transmission mechanism, as financial asset deflation spills over into goods deflation and even to wage deflation thereafter. Here's one scenario of bank to nonbank to household fragility transmission enabled by price systems:

Banks are capitalist businesses like any other, but they are also different in that they are the capitalist institutions that provide credit to the rest of the system. They function based on a 'fractional reserve' basis. When bank asset prices deflate and bank losses grow, banks stop lending to ensure they retain sufficient reserves. They hoard available income (cash assets) as much as possible in an asset deflation situation in order to offset losses. When financial asset deflation is moderate, banks respond with what's called a moderate 'credit crunch' (lending interest rates escalate); when asset deflation is more serious, a 'liquidity crunch' occurs (bank lending dries up temporarily as banks impose administrative obstacles to prevent lending as well as raise lending rates); when banks default on a debt payment due it's an even more serious scenario, a 'solvency crisis'. An insolvent bank is a candidate for bankruptcy and court distribution of its remaining assets at auction.

The degree of bank financial asset collapse thus corresponds roughly to the degree of bank lending contraction. And as bank lending contracts, so too does the real economy. Nonbank businesses cannot obtain operating loans to keep their businesses going. Banks just won't lend. Nonbanks are then forced to raise more revenue income by lowering their product prices and/or by reducing their labor prices (wages) to cut costs, or both. In this scenario, what starts as financial asset deflation for banks 'transmits' to the rest of the economy as nonbank businesses institute goods and/or wage deflation. That goods and wage deflation reduces income for nonbanks and for households, in turn raising their fragility. The transmission is from asset prices to goods prices to wage prices. But the process starts with financial assets.

An alternative to nonbanks lowering their goods and/or labor prices is to cut production and/or layoff workers. The production cuts and layoffs result in less government tax revenue and thus raises government fragility. The layoffs amount to an aggregate wage reduction, with the same effect on consumption fragility.

Transmission by price system can also occur in the opposite causal direction. Forces behind declining goods or labor prices unrelated to financial asset deflation can transmit nonbank or household fragility to banks and financial asset deflation. However, that reverse direction of causation does not typically precipitate financial asset deflation as often or as dramatically as the latter precipitates goods and wage deflation. That's because financial asset prices are, by their nature, far more volatile for reasons stated. So what is more often observed is financial asset deflation transmitting financial fragility to nonbanks and consumption fragility to households.

Just as there are multiple 'feedback' effects between forms of fragility, so too are there multiple ways price systems can transmit income decline and debt rise, and thus fragility, between the three different forms of fragility. The steeper the asset price deflation that occurs after a financial crisis erupts, the more intense the transmission from one form of fragility to another. Also, the more fragile the other forms are when the crisis and asset deflation begins, the stronger the transmission from one fragility form to another. For fragility grows secularly and steadily over the long term, and then accelerates when a financial crisis erupts and the real economy contracts sharply in response to the crisis.

Government policy changes also function as transmission mechanisms, causing fragility to intensify among variables within a form of fragility as well as between forms of fragility. Here one might argue that government 'prices' serve as a transmission mechanism.[20]

In the wake of a major financial instability event like a stock market crash or banking insolvency crisis, for example, the government central bank takes monetary action to pump massive liquidity into the banks to offset their financial asset collapse and losses. To do this the central bank drives down its lending rate to banks and bank-to-bank lending rates to zero, as has happened throughout the advanced economies since 2008 and continues now for the seventh year. Lowering the 'price' of money (i.e. interest rates) by government action lowers costs for banks and raises bank incomes by means of cost cutting. Banks can also rollover and refinance their previous debt by borrowing new debt at virtually no cost. That income support and debt interest (T&C) reduction together reduces banks' fragility. However, it also reduces income for households and raises therefore consumption fragility. Interest income previously earned by households from higher interest savings rates disappears. Households' fixed income is reduced and consumption fragility thus rises due to the lower income. In effect, central bank zero interest monetary policy results in a de facto transfer of income from households to the banking sector. Households subsidize the banks. From a fragility analysis standpoint, it means fragility is transmitted from banks to households.

The lower interest rates also reduce central banks-government fragility by lowering the government's debt financing costs. So both banks and governments like a zero interest policy. That's one key reason why it has continued for so long and is favored over fiscal policy throughout the advanced economies still, after seven years. Greater reason, no doubt, is that keeping rates low for a long duration simply provides low-to-no cost liquidity with which to invest in accelerating financial asset prices or to use to leverage to finance expanding offshore real investments by multinational corporations. The purely economic reasons also provide geopolitical advantages as well. Low rates in order to stimulate the real economy are more a justification, and certainly a secondary objective.

The shift in government monetary and interest rate policy is a fragility transmission mechanism enabling feedback from one form (bank financial) to another form (household consumption). Or, it might be argued that the price for money is the transmission mechanism.

Another government price mechanism by which fragility is transmitted from one fragility form to another is government taxation—i.e. taxes as the 'price' for government services. By reducing taxes on banks or nonbank businesses, the government in effect frees up more income for business (reducing its fragility) while lowering its own tax revenue income and raising its own fragility. Lower tax revenue and income may have a 'knock-on' effect requiring the government to take on more debt to offset the business tax cut and government revenue income loss. So government debt rises, income declines, and its fragility rises as that of business falls. This amounts to a transfer of fragility from the business-bank side (i.e. financial fragility) to government balance sheet fragility. Government might do the same for households. However, such parallel fragility transfer is often only token in magnitude and effect. More often since 2008, governments have responded with austerity, shifting its greater debt and lower income (fragility) due to bank and nonbank bailouts to households. In other words, austerity tax policy amounts to a transfer of debt/income and fragility from banks and nonbanks to households and consumers, through the medium of the government.

Other types of government policy may also serve as transmission mechanisms bringing about a shift of fragility from one of the three forms to the other by lowering debt/raising income in one form and lowering income/raising debt in another. For example, free trade policies raise business revenue income at the expense of households' wage income. That means a shift of fragility from business to households, all things being equal.

Government policies that aim at privatizing pensions and retirement systems, or privatizing and de-collectivizing (Obamacare in the US) health insurance systems, result in major cost savings for business that reduces their fragility, but also results in lower deferred wage incomes and benefits compensation for wage earning households.

The trend throughout the advanced economies in recent years is to implement what is called 'labor market reforms,' policy that aims at reducing unions, collective bargaining, and employment rights to help business cut costs and raise income. It also results in lower wage income. Fragility is offloaded from business and on-loaded to wage earning households.

A third transmission mechanism that increases fragility *within* a particular form, as well as *between* the three forms, is Investor-Agents Expectations.

Expectations among the global finance capital elite as to where financial asset prices are going in given markets are critical to the direct transmission of fragility between financial and consumption, and indirectly to government fragility as well. Consensus expectations among the elite as to whether financial asset prices in a given market are about to peak typically set in motion the selling of assets in that market. The selling then accelerates as second tier investors follow suit. Asset price deflation may thereafter turn into a rout, as 'retail' investors then provide further momentum and financial asset deflation accelerates. Members of the finance capital elite thus precipitate a reversal of asset price inflation.

This may occur by collusion between major shadow bank institutions or even commercial banking institutions. In recent years evidence of such collusion has repeatedly appeared—as in the case of fixing of Libor interest rates and derivatives trading on London exchanges. Or it may occur as the result of more tacit signals by major buying or selling by well known traders of the big institutions, shadow or commercial. A pattern appears to repeat, where money capital and credit flows from shadow banks and big investors into a particular market, where the asset prices rise appreciably, then assets are sold in growing volume, financial profits are taken, and the global money parade moves on to another financial securities market.

One day it's Asian stock and equity markets, then it's corporate junk bonds, then Exchange Traded Funds, then oil commodity futures price changes, then it's Japanese or Euro currency speculation as QE programs are about to be introduced. The sea of liquid capital awash in the global economy sloshes around from one highly liquid financial market to another, driving up asset prices as a tsunami of investor demand rushes in, taking profits as the price surge is about to ebb, leaving a field of economic destruction of the real economy in its wake. Financial asset bubbles build and then collapse, accelerating financial fragility. When the pullout occurs, financial losses negatively impact the availability of money capital and credit for nonbank businesses, raising fragility among nonbank enterprises and the households dependent on them for wage income. Investor-agents' expectations alternately drive financial asset prices to bubble ranges, and then cause them to collapse as money is moved out again and sent elsewhere, almost instantaneously and electronically to other liquid markets which now have more asset price appreciation potential.

What results is stock markets appreciating to levels that have nothing to do with fundamental earnings of the companies in them, an unrelenting chasing of yield by investors in ever riskier markets, and a growing volatility of currency exchange rates—to name but a few of the more recent negative effects. What moves the markets in terms of major shifts and swings are not the common investor, but the major 'institutional' (read: shadow bank) investors who buy and sell in large blocks of securities.

Decisions of the big investors, the finance capital elite, are at the center of these major shifts in direction (up or down) involving financial securities prices. And their decisions are heavily influenced by their expectations as to where a given financial market's price level is reaching a top or approaching a nadir. Investors outside this elite may trade once a shift in direction has occurred (thus making few profits or taking major losses for 'getting in late' and 'getting out late'). But it is this global elite that drives the major shifts in asset prices, which is where the real money is made.

Their expectations and decisions have implications for financial fragility and its transmission to nonbanks, households and even government balance sheets.

Preliminary Equations for a Theory of Systemic Fragility

The theory of systemic fragility as stated above is not a finished product. It is still very much a work in progress—both in terms of the development of a more comprehensive conceptual framework and as a set of equations that might measure quantitatively the development of Systemic Fragility. That measure could potentially produce an Index of Systemic Fragility that might help determine at what point, historically and empirically, Systemic Fragility erupts into a major financial instability event severe enough to produce a sustained and deep contraction in the real economy—i.e. a 'Great' or 'Epic' Recession or worse. The first step in development of such a measure of Systemic Fragility requires a set of simultaneous equations that describes the interactions between the three forms of fragility, as well as the three key variables within each form of fragility. A preliminary effort at that expression of Systemic Fragility in equation form is offered in the Appendix that follows, to allow the idea of Systemic Fragility to be measured.

And to begin it, the theory is restated in the Appendix to follow, in preliminary form at this point, via notations and equations.

Endnotes

1   This writer has criticized the term, 'Great Recession', elsewhere as inadequate

    and misleading for several reasons. For explanation, see Jack Rasmus, *Epic Recession: Prelude to Global Depression*, Pluto books, 2010. And for an explanation why and prediction that traditional fiscal-monetary policies would fail to restore advanced economies to their historical growth averages, and financial instability will inevitably return, see Jack Rasmus, *Obama's Economy: Recovery for the Few*, Pluto Press, 2012.

2   In the US, for example, the recessions of, 1970, 1973-75, 1980, and 1981-82 especially, were the consequence of external supply shocks and/or government monetary and fiscal policy-induced causes of recession. These external origin recessions might therefore be called 'normal', in contrast to endogenous financial crises-induced recessions that are not 'normal', to which therefore this writer has given the term, 'epic' recessions.

3   It will require widespread nationalizations of key industries and companies by government in order to stabilize the economy, a direct government job creation program, and a rise of government share of GDP in the case of the US economy to between 30%-35%.

4   That is in part because mainstream economics still does not acknowledge what Keynes and Minsky after him identified as the 'two price theory', where financial asset prices do not 'behave' as goods prices do. The two price systems are distinct, although they do mutually determine each other. The notion that the price system stabilizes the economy (real or financial) by returning prices to equilibrium as a result of the interaction of supply and demand is fundamentally challenged by the 'two price theory'. See preceding chapters 15 and 17 for more discussion on this. The solution to the stagflation dilemma that found traction in the 1970s was called 'monetarism'. But it too proved ineffective as a policy solution to the 1970s crisis.

5   The US central bank's massive money injection policies since 2008 have not all gone to financial investing and speculation. A good amount of it flowed out of the country to China and emerging markets where it likely fueled more real investment than financial, at least until 2013. Another amount contributed to the historic stock buybacks and dividend payouts since 2010, in the US alone calculated at more than $5 trillion for just the largest 500 US corporations, as US businesses borrowed trillions of dollars by issuing corporate debt with which paid for a good part of the buybacks and dividends. Still another amount remains hoarded on corporate and bank balance sheets.

6   See chapters 16 and 18, respectively, in this book.

7   Readers may want to revisit chapter 12 for more specific details.

8   See Jack Rasmus, chapter 4, *Epic Recession: Prelude to Global Depression*, Pluto Press, 2010 for finance's role in depressions in 19th century in 1830s, 1870s and 1890s, and the 1907 crash and 'epic' recession that followed.

9   Why this is no longer so was addressed in detail in chapters 14 and 15 on monetary and fiscal policy.

10   'Incomes' in this case will be defined as cash flow for financial fragility, wages for household consumption fragility, and tax revenues and borrowing associated with 'twin deficits' for government fragility. 'Debt' as defined in its various forms of business, consumer, and government previously. A third group variable, 'terms and conditions' of debt repayment is yet to be discussed, but it too is a consequence of restructuring and policy enabling factors.

11   The top 1% income households are not necessarily congruent with the 200,000 global finance capital elite and truly professional investors. Their income

levels place them in the highest 0.01 and even 0.001% of household income distribution.

12   Moreover, segmenting within each of the three fragility forms—i.e. bank vs. non-bank, wage earning vs. high end, national vs. local government—is probably called for, as is distinguishing between types of debt and types of income.

13   A parallel process was also occurring after 1999 in the case of Greece and other Euro periphery economies, in which private Greek-periphery nonbank companies borrowed from both Greek and northern European banks. Private debt escalated even faster than government debt until the first and second debt restructuring agreements in 2010 and 2012, in the course of which private lender debt was exchanged for northern Europe government debt in Greece and elsewhere. Private investors were 'paid off' and their debt was assumed by northern European government, and Euro government agency (European central bank, IMF, European Commission), institutions.

14   An exception may be high risk taking investors and shadow banks that specialize in 'shorting selling' of stocks and other financial assets—i.e. 'betting' that prices will fall and reaping a capital gain when they do.

15   A good example is the arrangement in the US where government agencies, Fannie Mae, Freddie Mac, and FHA, must buy mortgages sold to them by private sector mortgage companies and banks. That includes mortgage debt that is falling in market price.

16   Perhaps a good example, again in the US, is the impact of excessive student loan debt on the consumption capability of the 21-29 age group and the stagnation of the housing sector in entry new home construction as a result of this group's inability to afford home purchases, due in large part to excessive student loan debt loads. Much of the current US $1.2 trillion in student debt might have otherwise resulted in home purchases. Big ticket future consumption is thus reduced by current debt levels.

17   The same effect occurs for those national governments that raise much of their revenue from what are called 'Value Added Taxes' (VAT), such as in Europe.

18   Elasticity is a term here borrowed from economics that simply means a change in one variable is affected to a certain degree by a change in another variable. A variable is 'elastic' if the change in the one variable produces a greater degree of change in the other variable. It is 'inelastic' if it produces only a minor change in the other variable that is less than the change in the first variable. There are in other words different elasticities between the three forms of fragility effects on each other.

19   Estimating the intensity (acceleration) of the feedback effects of a change in one form of fragility on another, as well as the sensitivity (elasticity) of the change of one form on another, are thus important factors to consider in an advanced quantitative estimation of Systemic Fragility.

20   One might therefore argue there are not just two price systems, but three at work in the transmission processes.

APPENDIX: PRELIMINARY EQUATIONS

The ultimate objective of establishing an alternative conceptual framework to the various schools of contemporary economic analyses, based on the concept of systemic fragility, is to develop a quantitative index that measures the degree of system fragility in today's global economy.

In some cases, the new concepts associated with systemic fragility are readily quantitative; in others, they are qualitative and thus require conversion to quantities. The objective is to quantify the interactions between the key forces that determine systemic fragility, in order to reflect numerically the development of the degree of fragility in the system. A kind of volatility index is therefore envisioned. That quantitative index is not unlike, for example, the 'Vix' index that represents stock market volatility. In the present case, however, the goal is an index that represents the development of financial instability in a major economy, region, or the global economy itself, and indicates the point at which financial instability events may erupt that lead to a generalized crisis in the real economy as well.

The equations that follow are preliminary to that goal of developing a Systemic Fragility Index and consequently represent a work in progress requiring significant further development.

As described in the preceding Chapter 19, *A Theory of Systemic Fragility*, the key variables within each of the three fragility forms—financial, consumption, government balance sheet—are: debt, income with which to service principal and interest on debt, and other terms and conditions that may affect debt and income. How the three forms themselves interact to mutually determine each other, and how the transmission mechanisms between the forms transmit the mutual determinations, are not addressed in the preliminary equations that follow. That task requires the further development and restatement of the three basic equations that follow, with their own set of transmission mechanisms, expressed as a set of simultaneous equations. That task is left to future work in progress.

EQUATION #1: FINANCIAL FRAGILITY

Note: Financial fragility applies to both financial institutions and non-financial institutions. The weights given to the different variables in the equation will necessarily differ depending on whether the institution is financial or non-financial. The same qualification applies to financial institutions that are 'shadow' banks or commercial banks. So too does it apply to whether the corporation is a hybrid shadow bank, such as typical of multinational corporation with a high degree of 'portfolio', or financial, investment mix to their total investment activity. Financial fragility is a concept that should also apply to individual agents, like professional investors acting as financial speculators, who are not directly employed by a shadow bank, bank, or hybrid corporation—i.e. the majority of the global 'finance capital elite' of very and ultra-high net worth individuals.

The **basic equation** for financial fragility is represented as:

$$FF = I'_{f} + \frac{(rl_{f} + icrl_{f} + liql_{f})}{D} \frac{(P_{f}^{e} - P_{f})}{d^{t+1} - d^{t}} + (X) + (Z)$$

where,

I'_{f} plus I_{f} represent total financial asset investment,

I'_{f} represents the level of *autonomous* financial asset investment, and

I_{f} represents the level of *non-autonomous* financial asset investment composed of rl_{f}, $icrl_{f}$, and $liql_{f}$;

where,

rl_{f} is an appropriate basket of short term and long term central bank interest rates, key private bank rates (e.g. federal funds rate), corporate bond and loan rates, and sensitivity of I_{f} to changes in those rates,

$icrl_{f}$, is the sensitivity of I_{f} to change in 'inside credit' provided by shadow and other banks,

$liql_{f}$, is available income for potential financial asset investment in the form of cash-flow, near-cash liquid assets, and available open lines of credit to investors,

D, the level of total debt to be serviced—financial and, if applicable, real asset; and

where financial asset investment responds to financial asset inflation and changes in debt generating that investment and inflation when:

P_{f} represents financial asset prices in Time, t, and

P_{f}^{e} is the expected rate of *future* financial asset price appreciation from Time t to Time, **t + 1**,

$d^{t+1} - d^t$, the percentage change in debt—from the level of debt, **d**, at time **t**, to the level of debt, **d'**, at future time **t + 1**.

The two previous elements of the **FF** equation, the one representing current income levels and accumulated prior debt levels and the second representing future changes in income from financial asset inflation (or deflation) and changes in debt levels, are further determined by the variable, **X**—Terms & Conditions—representing factors potentially further affecting debt variables and the variable, **Z**—Government Policy—further affecting debt and/or income,

where **X** is composed of the following sub-elements:

X_1 covenants, PIKs, debt moratoria, default trigger suspensions,

X_2 debt refinancing, ease of debt roll-overs, debt-equity swaps, default period extensions,

X_3 ratio of short to long term debt, variable to fixed debt, and term payment structure; and

where **Z** is composed of the following sub-elements:

Z_1 government bad debt purchases (via QE, GSEs,'bad bank', etc.) and direct bailouts (TARP),

Z_2 government increase in corporate subsidies and tax reduction during crises,

Z_3 government accounting rule suspensions (e.g. 'mark to market') during crises.

EQUATION #2: CONSUMPTION (Household) FRAGILITY

Consumption Fragility applies to households whose income is composed more than 90% of wage, salary, and transfer forms of income. It excludes households whose income is more than 10% composed of forms of capital incomes, including capital gains, interest, dividends, rents, royalties, and inheritance income.

The **basic equation** for consumption fragility is represented as:

$$CF = C'_f + \frac{y(wC_f + tC_f + rC_f)}{D} \cdot \frac{1}{d^t - d^{t-1}} + (X) + (Z)$$

where,

C'_f plus C_f represent total household consumption by the bottom 90% households,

C'_f represents the level of *autonomous* household consumption, and

C_f represents the level of *non-autonomous* household consumption, composed of wC_f, tC_f, and rC_f, where

wC$_f$ is consumption from wage income, where wage income is determined by net job creation, nominal wage changes, and changes in earnings due to hours of work,

tC$_f$ is consumption from transfer income, including 'in kind' payments such as food stamps, and tax refund income,

rC$_f$ is consumption from additional credit income extended, in Time t, to households for purchases, in Time t, of mortgages, autos, credit cards, personal installment loans, and student loans and the responsiveness of household debt addition to interest rates,

D is the level of total debt to be serviced; and

where household consumption is influenced both by real goods and services as well as changes in debt:

y is an adjustment for inflation in *consumer goods and services*, and

d^t – d^{t-1}, is the response of household consumption to *the most recent period* change in households' debt levels—from the level of debt, d, at time t-1, to the level of debt, d, at time t.

The two previous elements of the **CF** equation, the one representing current income levels and accumulated prior debt levels, and the second representing future changes in income from goods & services inflation (or deflation) and changes in debt levels, are both further determined by the variable, **X**—Terms & Conditions—representing factors potentially further affecting debt variables and the variable, **Z**—Government Policy—further affecting debt and/or income;

Where **X** is composed of the following sub-elements:

X$_1$ deferment of debt principal payments, debt interest reductions, debt payment moratoria

X$_2$ debt refinancing, debt consolidation, debt write offs, debt term structure extensions

X$_3$ changes in composition of short-long term interest and/or fixed-variable interest payments

And where **Z** is composed of the following sub-elements:

Z$_1$ reduction in household taxes (sales, payroll, tax refunds or one time rebates)

Z$_2$ government increase in subsidies or direct hiring of unemployed

Z$_3$ mortgage or other debt assistance (HAMP, HARP-like programs).

EQUATION #3: GOVERNMENT (Balance Sheet) FRAGILITY

The **basic equation** for government balance sheet fragility is represented as:

$$GF = \frac{(T - G - tlg + I + E)}{Dg} + \frac{(Tlg + tlg - Glg)}{Dlg} + \frac{r(B-iB)}{Dcb} + M_{yz}$$

where,

GF represents general government fragility, including federal-central government and state and local government, affiliated government agencies with revenue raising and spending functions, and central banks of federal-central governments with bond issuance and direct money creating capabilities;

where,

(T-G-tlg+I+E) is federal-central government revenues from taxes **(T)**—excluding revenues from government bond issuance; government spending **(G)** represents spending on goods and services—but excluding transfers to local governments **(tlg)** and revenues from government bond issuance; Interest income **(I)** from sources other than bonds; and **(E)** revenues from sales of government production, sales and auctions of public goods and assets, and all other non-tax, non-interest income;

where,

(Tlg + tlg −Glg) is state, provincial, and local government revenues from taxes **(Tlg)**, and receipt of transfers from central government **(tlg)** minus local government spending; and

where,

Dg and **Dlg** represent accumulated debt at, respectively, the federal-central government and state-provincial-local government levels.

Central bank income is represented by the remaining elements of the equation, where

r(B-iB) is debt raised on central bank balance sheets from traditional central bank bond and shorter term bills sales (e.g. US Treasury bond-bills from 'open market operations' and other special auctions. The 'r' factor represents interest rate level incentives to bond offerings, **B** represents net income raised from sales/purchases of bonds, and **i** represents interest income received from bond transactions;

M$_{yz}$ is money created by central banks by non-traditional 'quantitative easing' (QE) programs, funding of government 'bad banks' to offload bad assets from commercial financial institutions, and other bond buying from liquid assets not obtained from tax revenues or other government sources of income or borrowing;

Y represents the amount of **M** created to achieve a targeted natural rate of unemployment,

Z represents the amount of **M** created to achieve a targeted annual 2% general price level,

Dcb is the total accumulated debt on the central bank's balance sheet.

NOTE: Government debt, and therefore Government Balance Sheet Fragility, is primarily derived debt, a consequence of dynamics associated with both Financial and Consumption Fragility. Government fragility is thus a consequence of, and in turn a cause of, the former.

INDEX